About the Author

Bob was born in Bristol. His career was in the marketing, retailing and distribution of a broad range of technologies, and latterly the event management of technology exhibitions. More recently he has been providing event research for the launches of a number of overseas exhibitions for others.

He has been writing for the last seven years, both fiction and non-fiction.

Bob is married, with two children and five grandchildren,
living in rural Oxfordshire.

For more information visit
www.thePCpioneers.com www.wikiPCpedia.com
www.thePCstory.com and www.thePCtimeline.com

The cover image

Did you identify the individuals featured in our PC pioneer
A-to-Z montage on the front cover? They are:
John Atanasoff, Tim Berners-Lee, Vint Cerf, Michael Dell, Doug Engelbart,
Jay Forrester, Bill Gates, Ted Hoff, Jonathan Ive, Steve Jobs, Leonard Kleinrock,
Butler Lampson, Bob Metcalfe, Bob Noyce, Ken Olsen, Seymour Papert,
Safi Qureshey, Ed Roberts, Clive Sinclair, Linus Torvalds, Masayuki Uemura,
Don Valentine, Steve Wozniak, Eric Xu, Yang Yuanging, Konrad Zuse

Don't miss Bob's novels

Two thrillers for you to read 'Still Water' and 'Gene Genie'
see www.BobDenton.co.uk

Bob Denton

The PC Pioneers
www.thePCpioneers.com

© Copyright 2014
Published by Bob Denton

The right of Bob Denton to be identified as author of
this work has been asserted by him in accordance with the
Copyright, Designs and Patents Act 1988.

All Rights Reserved

No reproduction, copy or transmission of this publication
may be made without written permission.
No paragraph of this publication may be reproduced, copied or transmitted save with
the written permission of the publisher, or in accordance with the provisions
of the Copyright Act 1956 (as amended).

Any person who commits any unauthorised act in relation to
this publication may be liable to criminal
prosecution and civil claims for damages.

A CIP catalogue record for this title is available from the British Library.

ISBN 978-0-9569643-7-3

Second Edition 2014
First Published in 2011

Dedication

To Jane, my wife, friend and tireless editor!

Acknowledgements

To Matt Denton for the cover design.

As Isaac Newton wrote in a letter in 1676,
'If I have seen a little further it is by standing on the shoulders of giants.'

In 1828 Samuel Taylor Coleridge modified this notion,
'The dwarf sees farther than the giant, when he has the giant's shoulder to mount on.'

The PC pioneers is my opportunity to acknowledge my personal 'giants' who were only too happy to provide their shoulders for me to gain perspective, to catch glimpses of distant horizons, and even occasionally to cry upon,

This work is therefore in thanks to Ken Turner, to David Pope and to Richard Hease.
Thanks for the ride guys!

Introduction

1 - PC dreaming – putting PC development into context

    The PC was not evolutionary

    The PC was certainly a product of its time

    PCs to serve the community

    PCs and train-spotting

    The PC movement gathers momentum

    Stirrings in a Menlo Park garage, Homebrew Computer Club

2 – Numbering systems

    Keeping tally

    Counting on it

    Look ten fingers

    Something for nothing

3 - Creative friction – those that defined computing

    Charles Babbage and the hurdy-gurdy men

    The Mob – eugenics or augmentation?

    Trauma with tables

    Babbage siphons off all the funding

    Analysing the differences

    Fascinating Ada

    The thoughts of Vannevar Bush

    Ciphers and fish - Bletchley Park and Alan Turing

    Heath Robinson and Colossus

    Carrot or stick – the development of radar

    Ted Nelson hyperthought

    Ride that wave – LINC and HP

    The 'Mother of all demos - Augmentation Research Center

    Towards a joined-up thinking

    MIT points the way – Kleinrock and Roberts

4 - It was rocket science – the PC catalyst

Convict No N1442

Object PS-1

Playing catch-up

IPTO facto – time share

All in a whirl

Establishing wisdom - SAGE

Switching from valves to transistors

Minicomputers

Olsen and the Family

Space men

5 - PARC and ride – Xerox designs the PC

Xerox to rival IBM

Gaggle of gurus

Small thinking – Alan Kay

To the max – Lampson and Thacker

Émigrés Collaborate – English and Duvall

Singing Alto – the first personal computer?

Bravo! - Simonyi's word processor

Gypsy Mott takes off – Mott and Tesler

Networking from out of the ether – Metcalfe and Ethernet

Dry copies

Optical Allusions – Starkweather and laser printing

A postscript coming first? – John Warnock

WIMPs – opening the windows

Taking note – Kay and NoteTaker

Let's talk of dolphins and dandelions – D*

Birth of a star

Geometrical progression

Patently unprotected

6 - In patents we trust

Keeping tabs

Power plays

Patronage and patents

Shift and shuffle

Till we meet again

Simple as ABC

EDVAC patent

Coining it in

Free sheets to the wind

7 - New components for a new market – electronic developments

Stepping stones to the PC

Tiny bells

IC IC IC

Moore's Law

I'll Hoff and I'll puff

Who was first?

8 - Kit and Caboodle - hobby computer kits

PC Genesis

Build your own computer

Scoping the d-i-y business

Open the show Hal

Not a recipe for success

Meanwhile out West

Adding fizz to the proceedings

Correspondence coarse

Served up with chips

British kits

Second-rate star goes nova – the Altair

9 - Worshipping at the Altair

Establishing fundamentals - BASIC

Opportunity knocks at the gates

Software without charge

They also served - Altair boys

Box shifters – Byte shop

Filling the gap – Processor Technology

IMSAI and Computerland

Kits by catalogue - SwTPc

Homebrewing the SOL

Getting it taped – Kansas City and CUTS

Disk jockeying – Shugart and Ernest

10 - Wait for ages, then three come along – Apple I, PET and TRS-80

No longer just a hobby

Apple - Early Wozniak

Cream Soda computer

Phreaking out

Working for others

Own designs – Apple I

Selling fruit – Jobs and Wayne

Taking a byte – Paul Terrell and the PO

The end of the beginning – divest?

Ripening – Mike Markkula

Keeping up appearances – Apple II

Adding colour – Apple II

Going to market – Apple III and an IPO

The beat goes on – Apple Corps

Military titles – Commodore from typewriters to calculators

Acquiring a mascot. PET

A second victory – VIC-20

Further promotion – Commodore 64

Retailing computers - Tandy

Trash sells – TRS-80

Getting basic - TinyBASIC and Microsoft

Government interference – FCC regulations

Jet setting – PET Jet, berms and Flight 191

Slow penetration

Comparisons are studious

11 – Games people play

Belligerent games – early computer war gaming

Games with mainframes

Board games on a computer

Spacewar!

Gaming for money

Play with enthusiasm

12 - Video game consoles

Coming home

Intelligent television

He all, he all, he always told me that

For all the family – Nintendo NES

Megabucks – Sega Master System

Counter blow – Nintendo SNES

New horse in the race – PC Engine and TurboGrafx

Serious new player – Sony comes to play

Handing out more fun – handheld consoles

Five-a-side – 5th generation consoles

Six of one - 6th generation consoles

Lucky seven - 7th generation consoles

13 - The second wave – as PCs abound

Candy and Colleen

Bullish approach – Hi-Toro to Amiga

Comings and goings – Atari v Commodore v Amiga

In search of excellence – Atari XE and ST

Texas hold 'em - a case study of its time

The corgi that roared – Mettoy Dragon

Approaching the spectrum – Clive Sinclair

British apple? – NEB funding for a UK PC

Through a Prism – Sinclair distribution

Going global

Silicon Fen

Splitting the proton – the BBC Micro

Electron storm – Acorn Electron

Urbane spread

One giant leap – Sinclair QL

Portability - Psion

Sugar craft - Amstrad

14 - The East enters the fray

A light in the east - Toshiba

Elevating the argument - Hitachi

Building mountains - Fujitsu

Transistor radios to world domination - Sony

Self-propelled - Sharp

Coming down the line - NEC

Timing it right - Seiko/Epson

Other Japanese players – Canon, Matsushita, Mitsubishi, Oki…

Taiwan- Acer, ASUS, Quanta…

Korea – Daewoo, Goldstar, Samsung

China – Great Wall, Founder, Lenovo

Russian revolutions – MIPT, LEMZ, Elektronica, Pentagon, Kraftway

15 - Getting serious – IBM's entry

The seventy stone gorilla is roused - IBM

IBM Entry Level Systems

Software sourcing for the IBM PC

Operating systems

Applying BIOS

Selection process for the IBM PC

Launch of the IBM PC

Sending in the clones - copyrighting a ROM?

Reverse engineering - Compaq, Phoenix, Zenith

Action and reaction – the PC XT

A PC for peanuts – PCjr

Let's have another try – PC AT

It was all getting personal – PS/2

16 – Getting into Apple-pie order

Apple III problems

Apple visits PARC and designs the Lisa

Jef Raskin defines and names the Macintosh

Jobs takes the helm – redefining the Macintosh

Strength in depth – the Macintosh team

Not so much insanely great as insanely grating!

A new dimension in software - Mac software

The Apple Macintosh launch

Jobs' discomforter

Writing the next chapter – Geometry and 3D Silicon Graphics

3M computing - Sun Microsystems

More 3M - the NeXT big thing

17 - Clever GUIs – PCs get user friendly

Software driven – Microsoft evolves

Remorseless growth - DOS

Symbiotic relationships – Microsoft and GUIs

At the human interface – Interface Manager

Sand in your eyes – Microsoft and the Mac

Jockeying for position – GUIs, Microsoft and Apple

Steamy windows – Microsoft Windows at last

Fresh openings – UNIX to Linux

Copyleft and GNU

Tux the penguin - Linux

Putting a hat on it – Red Hat

Is it catching? Viruses and malware

Fact following fiction

Vermicelli

Immunisation

18 - Communicating by computer

Linking television and computers

Viewdata

Micronet 800

Minitel

Getting connected - modems

Towards the ARPANET

Making networks manageable

NPL names it – packet switching

Build it and they will come – bidding for the ARPANET work

ARPANET going international

An alternative French approach - Cyclades

Networking software - Vint Cerf and TCP/IP

Working with the network - FTP, Telnet, Mbone

A spammer in the works – eMail and spam

19 - Keeping connected

PC Interconnections – Xerox PARC networking

Squeezing messages down the phone line - ISDN

Hawaiian approach - ALOHAnet

Ethernet and 3Com

Thinking different – AppleTalk to Airport

Network operating system - Novell

Routers – Cisco and Telebit

Network Forums - Usenet

Bulletin boards

Fido

EUnet

Secret connections

No military purpose

BITNet

Janet

Disbursement

20 - Slavery without shame – Robotics and AI

The Ministry of Truth and Androbot

Robots in history

Industrial robots

Tortoises and Turtles

Fictional robots

Defining robots

Personal Robots

Artificial Intelligence and robots

Robotic pets and toys

21 - Number crunchers – spreadsheets, dbases and accounting

Forecasts and what-ifs - spreadsheets

Keep it in context – Context MBA

You've been framed - Framework

Lotus blossom – Lotus 1-2-3

Super-calci-fragilistic - SuperCalc

Getting it all under control - databasing

Close relations – relational databases

Expressing oneself – IRI and Express

Financial databasing – IMRS to Hyperion

Consulting the oracle – Ellison and Oracle

Developing SQL - Sybase

Running the marathon – ISAM to Informix

Vikings and foxes – PC databasing

Ratliff's Vulcan – the evolution of dBase

Omega to Access

That's it in a nutshell – the path to FileMaker

Bean counting – accounting by computer

Business accounting

Clouded thinking - SaaS

Home budgeting

22 - Publish and be damned – WP and DTP

Typewriting

Mightier than the sword - Remington

IBM typewriters

WP machines

Word Processing Software

WordPerfect

Graphics

Going in to print - TeX

Founding Adobe and developing Postscript

15th century printer to PageMaker - Aldus

Juggling the catalyst for Quark

Adobe's rapid progress

Make it snappy - Photoshop

Who says they're not out to get me? Geschke's kidnapping

Moving it around – Acrobat and PDF

Laying it out – Adobe InDesign

Corel

Macromedia coalesces

Multimedia waves

It came to me in a flash

Weaving dreams

Look out for the fireworks

23 - Read all about it – the PC and books

Early digitisation

Project Gutenburg

Floppy books

Books on CD-ROM

First digital book?

BiblioBytes

Downloading books

eBooks and ISBN

The ePub format

Early eReaders

Online eReading

Full text – Google Library Project

Open Content Alliance and MSN Book Search

Pulp fiction – backlash against Google plans

Bookselling – Google Editions

Digital rights – Adobe and Microsoft

Second generation eReaders

Amazon Kindle

Even more eBooks

Apple iPad

24 - Dub dub dub

Early search engines

CWIS and Gopher

CERN

World Wide Web

The web spreads

Early information providers

GEnie and Prodigy

Browsers

Music to our eyes – Viola, Cello and Opera

The next medley – Mosaic, Spyglass, Microsoft and Netscape

Colonisation – navigators, explorers and safaris

The return of Mozilla

Shiny new approach - Google Chrome

Web services

Architext to Excite

Filo and Yang's Yahoo!

DEC's AltaVista

Microsoft MSN

Hotmail

Messenger

Jeeves and Ask.com

25 - Creating Google

Attracting income - advertising on Google

Lift off – Google attracts investment

Foundation – Google's early commitment to philanthropy

Culture of non-compliance with the norms

Google growing up – attracting professional management

Google constant innovation

Google and AOL

Google Compute

Gmail

Picasa

Google v Overture

Planet Google

Google communication

China and Baidu

Freenet

Amazon – online bookseller

Napster – music sharing

Wikipedia reference source extraordinaire

26 - Online auctions - eBay

Early eBay progress

eBay management team

eBay Motors

Remarkable eBay transactions

eBay Traders

PayPal

Giving Works

eBay pushing the fabric

Half.com

Craigslist

Adding eBay categories

Drop shipping

Skype

Ranking sellers

27 - It's a date – social networking

Six Degrees of separation

Keeping in touch with old friends

Video file sharing - YouTube

Business Networking - LinkedIn

Give me a Hi5

I need my space

Survival of the fittest - Facemash

Rowing rows - Harvard Connection

Launching thefacebook

Further conflict - ConnectU

Under the influence - Sean Parker

Progress through new services

Happy Birthday Bebo

Russian socialising - Badoo

From despatches to Twitter

Evan Williams and Blogger.com

All of a twitter

750 tweets a second

28 - On the move – PC progress

A PC exit for IBM

PCs sold on-line – Dell and Gateway

Into the new millennium with Apple

Steve Jobs' four-cell plan

Jobs' Digital Hub

Revolutionising music - iPod

Acquisitive Microsoft

Acquiring strength - HP

PCs on the move

Wireless connectivity

Personal Digital Assistance

Phones get smarter

Keep taking the tablets

Apple updates the tablet

29 - Analysis - what has the PC done for us?

What happened to the paperless society?

Email challenges

The Net - a perfect market?

PC Productivity

Maintaining your identity

Artificial intelligence

Looking for a DETAILED INDEX?

Introduction

'Computers are useless. They can only give you answers.' Pablo Picasso

Just under forty-five years ago the term personal computer first appeared as a concept in print. Today over a billion personal computers are in use around the world. It is also forty-five years since the beginnings of the Internet emerged as the ARPANET. Today it has approaching two billion users - that's close to a third of the world's population all interconnected.

The PC and the Net have changed the way we communicate in business and how we keep in touch with family, old colleagues and school friends. This business and social networking has had a profound impact on how businesses promote their wares and services and how modern media interacts with us.

The PC and the Net have fundamentally changed the ways in which we capture, manipulate, and distribute our photographs and videos and they help us to catch up with the television shows that we have missed. They have changed our means of acquiring, buying and playing music.

Along the way they have altered how we buy books and software, how we swap and sell unwanted and used products, how we review, research and reserve our travel, accommodation and holidays. They provide the means for us to access news, financial markets, sports fixtures and results, weather reports...

They also provide us with an instant dictionary, an encyclopaedia, a wealth of trivia facts, a thesaurus, a huge library of eBooks, a translator, a calculator, an address book, an appointments calendar and they can arbitrate by providing answers to our many queries, idle thoughts and family 'disputes'.

As a tool for researching books such as this, the PC connected to the World Wide Web proves to be an absolutely indispensable source.

Its forerunner ARPANET was first mentioned at an Association for Computing Machinery Conference held from 1-4 October 1967 at Gatlinburg in the Smoky Mountains of Tennessee.

The ARPANET was born within the cloisters of academe and built with military funding and intent. However it was the introspection of pure science used by those designing particle accelerators to examine the tiniest parts of matter that brought us the World Wide Web. Today it really matters with some two billion regular users.

These users are able to access 185 million websites and review some 200 million blogs. They are sharing and downloading 10 billion images and over 12 billion videos. Between them they send over 200 billion emails each and every day. The remarkable nature of Internet growth means that the moment I typed those stats they were already out of date!

It is just over forty years since the first PCs were built, a little over twenty years since Tim Berners-Lee created the World Wide Web to popularise the Net.

This is all so very recent! While the many innovators are still alive and economically active, it seems appropriate to celebrate their contributions.

How did it all come about? Was it Bill Gates and Steve Jobs who created the personal computer industry? Certainly their PR machines would lead you to believe that this was the case. And most of the press and literature would suggest that this was solely an American evolution.

We shall see that the vital precursor to PCs was the microprocessor, first developed by Ray Holt. But the project was a military secret, so initially the MPU patent was granted to Gilbert Hyatt. The original designer of the mainframe computer was settled at law as being John Atanasoff and we shall see that so far as the French courts is concerned they ruled that the personal computer was developed by François Gernelle. Heard of any of them?

We will take a look at how progress was made right around the world. But relax; we will not set out to appraise the details of the technologies in detail. Instead we set out to celebrate the lives, ideas and careers of the people who made it happen.

For me things only really become interesting when considering developments from the viewpoint of the people who created them and the often erratic process of the PC evolution.

The very earliest PC pioneers seldom appear to have set out with a clear ambition, few set out to make a fortune from their ideas. Often they confronted a problem in their work and in seeking a solution came up with a development or a step along a path that assisted the personal computer market to evolve. On other occasions they were simply showing off their innovative ideas to their friends.

We shall see how often these developments came about from the work of driven individuals, pressing on against the beliefs of the established wisdom and committed to a dream or belief which they maintained the tenacity to see through.

These were also advanced by dynamic duos, where two individuals came together and sparked off each other's ideas to provide a synergy that moved the PC forward. Some of these might be considered as 'odd couples' often coming together quite serendipitously.

There were also a number of moments in time when a large group of individuals coalesced and triggered off, and scored from, each other's creativity. Perhaps it was just the competitive spirit that drove them to excel. The creative tension brought about by their proximity took on a life all its own. This was certainly true of many early macro turning points in the personal computer development process, places where quantum leaps were launched.

A work of history?
'When you take stuff from one writer it's plagiarism; but when you take it from many writers, it's research.' Wilson Mizner

Undeniably then, this in its scope is a work of history. The word 'history' derives from the Greek and means a 'systematic inquiry' and I trust readers will consider this to be just that. However the subject will be approached in a somewhat random way and not seek to be a simple timeline of chronological development. For this more tabular purpose we have provided our sister website www.thePCtimeline.com

In working through the progress of this market we will come across a whole series of individuals who have been awarded the sobriquet 'father' of this, that or the other. All of those who contributed, the people and the organisations, are listed on another of our websites www.thePCpioneers.com

A broader approach to the subject, given that it does not need to be crammed in to a book and can be readily updated, is evolving at yet another website www.wikiPCpedia.com, you can add your comments and thoughts.

The Ancient Greek, Herodotus, was heralded by the Roman philosopher and statesman, Cicero, as the 'father of history'. This was based on his seminal work of nine volumes that charted the Ancient World, its peoples, their communities and activities. It was written between 431 and 425 BCE. But he has also been called the 'father of lies', accused of plagiarism, bias and inaccuracies.

He and most other classic historians tend to share one huge benefit that I do not. This is that the vast majority of their subjects are usually long dead and turned to dust well before they sit down to prepare their opus. For this book many of the individuals are of course, thankfully, still alive and very active.

One of the strangest facts of the modern human condition is that everything we read about others we have a tendency to believe and yet everything ever written about ourselves appears to be malign and plain wrong. So I have to trust that my subjects will keep this in mind and see this material as an honest toil with the simple goal of showing the general thrusts of the market from the perspective of those who made them happen.

Further, the PC user is often clan-ish, and many of those who shared this journey will surely disagree with my expressed views and assumptions. They may very well feel that I have left out or misrepresented some key individual or organisation, or omitted what they believe was a significant step, process or widget along the way.

Of course www.wikiPCpedia.com is a wiki site and this allows all readers to propose changes or additions, remedy errors or misunderstandings and make everyone aware of their views so that the wrong may be righted, or at least a debate can be commenced.

Herodotus wrote his books from a strong moral stance, He believed that life was not stable, that Chance and Fate were always at work to seduce and steer us off course. He also believed that the moral decisions we make are key since hubris, or arrogance, will bring down Nemesis, the retribution of the gods.

Clearly Herodotus would have had a fine appreciation of the evolution of the personal computer.

1 - PC dreaming – putting PC development into context

'There are two major products that come out of Berkeley: LSD and UNIX. We don't believe this to be a coincidence.' Jeremy S. Anderson

The PC was not evolutionary
Personal computers did not emerge from a vacuum or in to one; they were a feature of their time and of the current social movements.

Many histories suggest a natural process from abacus to calculator, difference engine to tabulating machine, mainframe computer to minicomputer - then out pops the PC, mewling and puking as the natural successor.

But that was not how it developed. Intriguingly three of the early computer pioneers, each a guru of his time and organisations, had pretty limited expectations for their creations, and they made some poor forecasts.

In 1943 Thomas J Watson Sr of IBM gave an infamous quote, or 'misquote',
'I think there is a world market for maybe five computers.'

Howard Aiken, who built the Harvard Mark 1, said in 1947,
'Only six electronic digital computers would be required to satisfy the computing needs of the entire USA.'

Ken Olsen the founder of DEC and its range of minicomputers as late as 1977 said,
'There is no reason anyone would want a computer in their home.'

Huge mainframe computers emerged after WWII where they were designed for ballistics calculations and decryption. The IBM operation was derived from earlier tabulating machines which had been developed to manage the US Census and other number crunching data processing tasks.

Post-WWII, by working closely with the US government and a number of major universities, IBM made itself indispensible as cold war national security fears mounted and it garnered defence spending and took over academic projects to emerge as the mainframe superpower.

Those left in its wake were disparagingly termed the 'seven dwarfs', soon declining from seven main competitors to being just five, now dismissed as the 'BUNCH' - Burroughs, Univac, NCR, Control Data and Honeywell.

But all of them, and others that emerged around the world, had a sincere commercial self-interest in maintaining a mystique around their equipment, happy that this would assure them of huge price tags and margins. There was little early interest in developing standards that could be used between companies or even within a company's product range.

These operations had absolutely no interest in developing low cost PCs.

In academe, government offices and business most of those who served these early computing behemoths did little to simplify or explain how they worked. Their arcane secrets made them indispensible. This mystery allowed them to rise through management and to serve on boards.

There was little effort to distribute the capabilities of these computers. Any processes were usually originated and managed firmly within the high priesthood that grew around these expensive investments. If individuals outside this elite should need a task processed by the mainframe then the hoops they were made to jump through were often extreme and usually fruitless.

Even at IBM very few senior managers placed a terminal at their desks, believing this to be something for lower-level data processing staff members. In much the same way early word processors were seen as designed for mere typists and secretaries.

There was no desire here for distributed or personal computing.

The PC was certainly a product of its time

Of course it has become popular to suggest that,

'...if you can remember the 1960s then you weren't really there...'

But we need to recall the social fabric back then.

As we entered the 1960s, here in the UK we suddenly became a happening place, though the word was 'fab' or 'swinging' back then. We rebelled and railed against the 'establishment'; essentially by that we meant our parents and their existing institutions.

We were inspired by the music of the Beatles, the Stones and the Who. If you were a Mod you were fashioned by Mary Quant, Biba and Carnaby Street, otherwise you harked back to the 1950s as a Rocker.

Trendsetting pirate radio stations like Radio Caroline were launched and then banned; BBC's Radio One was the establishment's response. All this did make us feel much more connected with the rest of the world. Che Guevara and James Bond were cool.

The period brought us feminism and free love. The US civil rights movement inspired marching on the streets, sit-ins on campuses... San Francisco had its 'summer of love' and perhaps the Woodstock festival, best symbolised the message of celebrating the joy of life - and flowers.

There were Dubcek's Prague Spring, Bob Dylan's protest songs, the Maharishis' transcendental meditation, Bob Marley's reggae, Jimi Hendrix's Purple Haze, psychedelic drugs...

They were certainly heady times.

Aloft, the Apollo mission managed to reach the Moon in July 1969, before the end of the '60s, just as John F Kennedy had proposed. Clearly anything we set our minds to do, we could achieve!

Yet the establishment still bit back with its national conscription, nuclear angst, colonial remorse, the Bay of Pigs, the Cold War, the Berlin Wall, the Six Days' war, the assassinations of JFK, Martin Luther King, Robert Kennedy...

The Vietnam War saw the USA dealing with further unrest on its streets and on its campuses; in Washington DC 500,000 people marched against the war as US troop losses reached the 100,000 milestone. In Vietnam the US forces faced the Tet offensive and the shame back home as the My Lai massacre was exposed.

China was undergoing the Cultural Revolution and taking the first step of Mao's 1,000 mile journey, having a little earlier exploded its own atomic bomb.

A popular purchase of the time was a translation of Mao's little red book *Quotations from Chairman Mao Tse-Tung.* Quotes from this famous publication are intriguing:

'The history of mankind is one of continuous development from the realm of necessity to the realm of freedom.' 'Natural science is one of man's weapons in his fight for freedom.' 'Often, correct knowledge can be arrived at only after many repetitions of the process leading from matter to consciousness and then back to matter, that is, leading from practice to knowledge and then back to practice.'

They are intriguing because they serve to sum up the course not just of the Peoples' Republic of China but those of PC development as well.

PCs to serve the community

Lee Felsenstein reflected both strains of enthusiasm present in California of the 1960s and 1970s. He was a radical activist who worked with underground newspapers, earning kudos by being arrested at a Berkeley sit-in in 1964. He pursued the other theme of his time in seeking to find a way to reduce the cost of computing. He combined both activities by wanting to improve access to computing for everyone.

Transamerica Corporation had allowed the Community Memory operation, called Resource One, access to an old and unused SDS 940 computer utilising XDS-940, a time-share operating system developed at Berkeley.

RANDOM ACCESS MOMENT:
This particular SDS 940 computer had an amazing provenance. Of course Scientific Data Systems had originally designed it, with ARPA funding. SDS

had been acquired by Xerox to prompt its foundation of PARC. But stranger still, this was the actual unit that had been at the heart of University of California Berkeley's Project Genie. It was also later the very unit on which Engelbart and ARC's NLS On-line System was developed. It was therefore the recipient of ARPANET's 'LO', the first cross-network message. Spooky! A lot like Arthur C Clarke's sentinels, it seems this computer might be considered as some-other-worldly talisman of early PC progress!

The SDS 940 was managed by Felsenstein; its systems software for time-share and its community databases were written by Peter Deutsch who was also working at Xerox PARC.

Efrem Lipkin moved to the West Coast from Boston where he met Felsenstein and in the early 1970s, together with Mark Szpakowski, the three developed the Community Memory Project.

The Community Memory Project focused on experimenting and researching the general public's reaction to meeting and using computers; of course few had seen one prior to that time.

As part of this they located an ASR-33 Teletype terminal connected by modem to the SDS 940 from outside Leopold's Records in Berkeley. It ran at just 110 baud, 10 characters per second, and the terminal was very noisy. Users could post messages using keywords and others used the keywords to find relevant messages.

Leopold's was a store run by Berkeley students as a reaction to chain group record stores in the area that they thought were taking students' money and not recycling or keeping revenues within the area.

There was a traditional bulletin or notice board outside the store where the usual patchwork of notices could be posted. By placing the terminal beside it they directly hooked in to an existing marketplace.

A Community Memory helper would drum up interest and offer advice. The photocopied instructions described the service thus:

'COMMUNITY MEMORY is the name we give to this experimental information service. It is an attempt to harness the power of the computer in the service of the community. We hope to do this by providing a sort of super bulletin board where people can post notices of all sorts and can find the notices posted by others rapidly.

'We are Loving Grace Cybernetics, a group of Berkeley people operating out of Resource One Inc., a non-profit collective located in Project One in S.F. Resource One grew out of the San Francisco Switchboard and has managed to obtain control of a computer for use in communications.

'COMMUNITY MEMORY is a kind of electronic bulletin board, an information flea market. You can put your notices into the Community Memory, and you can look through the memory for the notice you want.'

It was available at no charge to access the material, but to add comments cost 25 cents and to have your own forum cost one US dollar. Understandably, because of its location outside Leopold's, musicians were significant among the early users, but perhaps the long-recognised link between musical and mathematical skills was operating here too?

One early user, Benway, became the very first Net personality. Mark Szpakowski adopted this moniker from Doc Benway a character in several William S Burroughs novels. Burroughs used to lampoon medicine and science. The Net character would post items that very much fit with the era and the location,

'Applies to: All Boogies, Beaners, Bolos & Bozos [keywords]
 'Doc Benway here ... Nurse, slip me another ampoule of laudanum... Use authorised data base access protocols only...   ... sensuous keystrokes forbidden... ...do not strum that 33 like a Hawaiian steel guitar...'

Szpakowski would be a regular contributor to the PC business. He later worked on the hardware of the Sol PC. He wrote a multi-user email system for a Datapoint mini-computer. Working in UNIX and dBase he helped develop an early international Bulletin Board and an email service called Dharmanet.

Lee Felsenstein summed up the goals of Community Memory as,

'The village square is a commons - it belongs to no one but is used by all. The agora is a commons of information - a way of interacting. It is not property.'

This thrust to democratise and distribute computing was central to the next steps that would create personal computing.

PCs and train-spotting

MIT, the Massachusetts Institute of Technology, had a good war. Vannevar Bush, an ex-faculty member, was appointed to the Office of Scientific Research and Development from where he arranged the flow of research funding to generate developments of use to the war effort. MIT became a notable recipient of these funds, growing to become the largest US R&D contractor during WWII.

Post-war, MIT's involvement in national security matters often involved computers and this meant it received many of the earliest computer installations - Whirlwind, TX-0, TX-2, IBM 7090, IBM 704, PDP-1 and many other early computers. It was the ready access to these that was to create a turning point along the route towards the personal computer.

A group of talented individuals came together, providing each other with a mix of support and challenge that advanced the understanding and development of how to get the most from these computers. They would point the way to the definition phase of personal computing.

Many of this group of MIT students mingled as members of the college's Tech Model Railroad Club (TMRC). The club operated a massive model railway set-up and used some impressive technology to manage it. With this technical awareness they eyed MIT's mainframes and wanted access but this was policed by its operators.

These very hands-on can-do individuals were confronted with computers that they had to queue to use, that were guarded by a 'priesthood' who did all that they could to ensure the students were kept away from them. If you were lucky enough to have an approved usage then you still had to wait your turn, prepare your program on punched cards and wait a day or two, usually only to be told that the program did not work.

The TMRC set about finding ways to improve this access, for example using obscure times, usually overnight, to gain access. It is intriguing that this 'midnight oil' approach started here, right at the very beginning of the business. It became a regular feature of the PC industry both for gaining low-traffic access and also to take advantage of off-peak lower-cost telecoms.

Through honing their skills in these snatched overnight moments the TMRC eventually earned more formal rights of access; their skills were required by the very people who had been standing in their way.

The TMRC members were not hackers in the sense we use the term today but used this term for themselves as those who developed technical skills to come up with innovative ideas. To hack a piece of hardware or software meant that you sought to get the absolute most from it. You hacked away at the rough edges like a sculptor to come up with your work of art.

An illustrative example of this is a simple utility subroutine called the decimal print routine. The TMRC hackers were very competitive, each seeking a different way to approach a problem, but just as importantly seeking ever more elegant solutions for their software. By elegance this often meant achieving the required outcome with the fewest instructions; particularly relevant in those days of extremely small memories and slow processing.

A decimal print routine was a handy routine used in many programs to convert binary numbers into their digital counterpart before printing. Many would be content taking a hundred and more instructions to achieve this operation. This would be perfectly adequate, but the MIT hackers disliked adequate and managed to 'bum' it down toward fifty instructions. Bumming was used as the term to describe the trimming of instructions from a routine by using new approaches and more elegant algorithms.

Eric Jensen finally won this competition when he found a way to reduce it to just forty-six instructions - a virtuoso hack. His peers showed him the ultimate accolade by then leaving this problem alone, accepting that it was now finally resolved and moving on to new challenges.

Another example was when the MIT PDP-1 was delivered. Alan Kotok, one of the TMRC members, was unimpressed by the assembler that Bolt, Beranek & Newman Inc (BBN) had written for it.

He and a small group of hackers dedicated some 250 man-hours across a real-time weekend to considerably improve upon the original. DEC or BBN would have taken longer than that just to define and scope the project!

The TMRC members worked to seek to make mainframe computers more available, more user-friendly and were to develop an array of innovative applications for them.

The PC movement gathers momentum

At around the same time as Felsenstein was making progress with Community Memory, Bob Albrecht who had been working at Control Data Corporation, decided that the activity of the early electronics and computing hobbyists in the area needed a publication to link, promote and feature their progress.

Initially he founded Dymax that would publish books on BASIC but he later launched the People's Computer Company as a regular magazine for enthusiasts.

'George Firedrake' was one of Albrecht's noms de plume as he set out his stall in the first newsletter thus,

'Computers are mostly used against people instead of for people; used to control people instead of to free them; Time to change all that - we need a... Peoples Computer Company.'

Peoples Computer Company was certainly not an academic journal. It was anarchic in appearance, mixing its fonts and its metaphors, using pretty loose layouts and interspersing listings in BASIC, handwritten notes, cartoons...

But it provided a whole group of enthusiasts with an organ for their notions and it drew together a community of what was otherwise a series of isolated individuals.

Peoples Computer Company also ran Wednesday night meetings where readers could get together and chew over ideas and issues. But over time the Peoples Computer Company tended to gravitate more towards software and programming; it was more about using the computers than building them.

Stirrings in a Menlo Park garage, Homebrew Computer Club

Gordon French and Fred Moore realised that they were much more interested in the hardware side. Gordon French had developed the 'Chicken Hawk' d-i-y computer around an 8008.

When both of them failed to become members of the Peoples Computer Company board, and seeing that its Wednesday night meetings were likely to stop, they acted. They invited those interested in hardware to a meeting in French's garage. What is it about West Coast garages?

The invitation read,

'Building your own computer? Terminal? TV Typewriter? I/O device? Or some other digital black-box? Or are you buying time on a time-sharing service? If so, you might like to come to a gathering or people with likeminded interests. Exchange information, swap ideas, talk shop, help work on a project, whatever...'

They first got together in March 1975 and went on to hold fortnightly meetings of what they called the Homebrew Computer Club (HCC).

The club became famous for its august membership. This included: Steve Jobs and Steve Wozniak, who formed Apple; Adam Osborne, the portable computer innovator; Bob Marsh and Gary Ingram, who founded Processor Technology and the SOL-20; Lee Felsenstein, later to design the SOL-20 and Osborne 1; Harry Garland and Roger Melen, who launched Cromemco; George Morrow, who built CP/M based computers; John Draper, a phone 'phreak' who went by the name of Cap'n Crunch and would later produce WP software; Marty Spergel, who became an electronic parts supplier; Allen Baum, friend to Wozniak and fellow HP employee.

We saw earlier how the coming together of a group of very bright individuals at MIT and the formation of the Tech Model Railroad Club had proven significant. It was their restricted access to early mainframes that transformed them into hackers and this kick-started so many PC careers and development paths.

The Homebrew Computer Club was another such group that prompted another leap forward in the development of personal computers.

Both groups wanted better access to computers for themselves and for others. Where the MIT TMRC team pursued rather academic goals, this second group was much more commercially focused, even though this was often not their original inspiration. Both groups achieved their advances by trying to impress their peers.

Silicon Valley had been established by Shockley and others and had drawn a technical population into the area. Homebrew was formed by the second generation of those working in the electronics industry.

At the first meeting of the HCC Bob Albrecht delightedly brought along one of the first Altair 8800s that had been sent to the PCC for review. It was this product and the subsequent actions of the Homebrew Computer Club that essentially ignited a whole business.

2 – Numbering systems

'Music is the pleasure the human mind experiences from counting without being aware that it is counting.' Gottfried Wilhelm Leibniz

Keeping tally

First and foremost computers were routinely applied to computations; it is all there in the name. Let's take a look at some of the history of this task.

The word 'computer' was first used in the early 17th century but it was applied to a function not a piece of equipment, it meant 'a person who performs calculations'. In fact right up to the middle of the 20th century the word computer, just like dishwasher, was used to describe a person's role and not a device.

This act of computing or calculating as a mental exercise rather than the application of calculating equipment has of course been around for a very long time.

The earliest find so far in the genre of counting devices is the 'Ishango' bone which has been dated to 20,000 BCE. It consists of a series of etchings made upon a baboon's fibula. It was discovered in 1960 in the Congo, quite close to what has been established as a ground zero for modern man, the place from where Homo sapiens migrated to populate the world some 70,000 years ago.

The bone's etched markings were quite sophisticated and are assumed to have been made with quartz. Some suggest that the bone was used to mark the passing of time, perhaps a six-month lunar calendar. Others suggest that the markings show a rather good appreciation of mathematics. The very sophistication suggests therefore that this type of device had been in use for some time prior to the Ishango bone dating.

But whatever its date and purpose most propose that it is some sort of counting device, a very early tally stick.

Tally sticks were used down the years in many countries. By medieval times debts were being recorded by a 'split tally'. This was an early form of double-entry accounting. Marks were made around a stick and then it was split down its length so that both lender and debtor could retain a clear record of the transaction.

They were also much in use as a proof of the payment of taxes. The UK's Exchequer for example used split tally sticks for its tax collections right up until 1826 when they were finally legally abolished.

In 1834 the then British prime minister, Charles Grey, was much better known for his aromatic blend of bergamot-flavoured tea, his other title being Earl Grey. Grey's government decided to ceremonially burn the amassed old tally sticks. They unwisely decided to use a stove within the House of Lords for the purpose.

Charles Dickens, no less, criticised the decision and talked of 'counting devices destroying the halls of government'. He went on to describe the event and its cost in some detail.

'In 1834 ... there was a considerable accumulation of them [tally sticks]. ... What was to be done with such worn-out worm-eaten, rotten old bits of wood? The sticks were housed in Westminster, and it would naturally occur to any intelligent person that nothing could be easier than to allow them to be carried away for firewood by the miserable people who lived in that neighbourhood.

However [the sticks were no longer] useful and official routine required that they never should be, and so the order went out that they should be privately and confidentially burned. It came to pass that they were burned in a stove in the House of Lords. The stove, over-gorged with these preposterous sticks, set fire to the panelling; the panelling set fire to the House of Commons; the two houses [of parliament] were reduced to ashes; architects were called in to build others; and we are now in the second million of the cost thereof.'

In 1835 JMW Turner, the landscape artist produced a famous painting of the houses well alight. Entitled *The Burning of the Houses of Lords and Commons*, it is today on show at the Philadelphia Museum of Art.

This tally stick fire burned down much of the Houses of Parliament, all apart from the Westminster Hall. It did significantly more damage than Guy Fawkes might ever have achieved and much more than the later WWII incendiary bomb attacks on the Houses.

Counting on it

However a vital precursor to any form of tallying, accounting, counting, calculating or computing is the creation of a system of numbers.

Numbers are said to be one of the key features that distinguish mankind from other animals although natural scientists do suggest that birds can actually discern numbers. Apparently they may be able to recognise one, two or three things but any larger group the bird-brain handles with the concept of 'many'.

We humans too were perfectly content with that simplistic numeric approach until civilisation found us living cheek-by-jowl. As we began to trade our labour and skills within an ever-expanding social community we needed a broader concept.

One of the earliest civilisations, the Mesopotamians, met these problems first and developed a proper system of numbers. Mesopotamia as a term literally means 'between the rivers', the two rivers in question being the Euphrates and the Tigris. It was where modern Iraq is today.

The richness of these two rivers' deposits fostered the development of agricultural techniques. The wealth of the crops became the basis of the local people's ability to combine and prosper as communities and to expand into cities; and cities certainly needed numbers.

By 4000 BCE the Mesopotamians had evolved a whole series of counting systems, used to count slaves or to tally containers. The agricultural produce needed the development of a system for quantities, weights, volumes and so on. Bizarrely at this stage there was a notation for one sheep or one day but there was no general symbol for the concept of 'one', each was distinct.

By around 3000 BCE this had evolved into a unification of the twelve or more separate systems that they had been using. This system was subsequently passed down to the Babylonians, the Assyrians and the Persians.

The system was based on the root of 60, or sexagesimal (meaning sixtieth), which proved to be a very useful base number as it is divisible by no fewer than twelve integers - 1, 2, 3, 4, 5, 6, 10, 12, 15, 20, 30 and 60 itself. Quite why they and other civilisations used 60 is unclear, except maybe for the wealth of divisors.

The basic unit of distance was a cable, with a league being the value of thirty cables and a rod defined as one sixtieth of a cable. The unit of area was a garden with 1,800 gardens being termed an estate. The unit of volume was a bowl, and sixty of these formed a bushel.

For the measurement of time they set the basic unit as a day. These were combined so that thirty days summed to a month, and 360 days to a year. It is of course from this era that we still express time and angles based upon the same root of 60.

The Babylonians were the first to introduce the notion of positional significance in arranging its cuneiform numerals. By 2700 BCE they had developed the abacus.

Look ten fingers

The Egyptians were the first to introduce the use of the base of 10 in around 3100 BCE. Perhaps this is why their vassals had Ten Commandments?

By 1000 BCE the Romans had a decimal system in use that derived from earlier Etruscan and Greek systems. They used a series of just seven simple symbols made from very basic strokes that could be scored or scribed. These could combine to express any number using I, V, X, L, C, D and M; some suggest these simple strokes derived from tally sticks. Roman numerals have a clear positional significance so that IX means 9 and XI means 11.

RANDOM ACCESS MOMENT:

I personally discovered something of a flaw in the Roman system when you try to apply it today to the very large numbers that back then were probably seldom contemplated. During 1990 we were preparing to launch the Property Business Show for 1991 and the creative team came up with a brochure featuring a Greco-Roman building with pillars that would show the roman numerals for 1991 across its frieze, but just how was 1991 written?

The natural approach would be to long-windedly come up with MDCCCCLXXXXI, but this was not particularly elegant. But MDCCCCIXC did not seem to be correct positional usage. Deducting the nine or IX from that final C felt wrong as would it be read as being attached to the C preceding it or to the final C?

It felt no better to take it away directly from 2000 or MM, thus MIXM or IXMM; though movies and TV program 'ident' pages did later adopt the MIXM approach for its useful brevity. At the time we contacted the British Museum for an authoritative view; they pondered it and confessed that they just did not know.

Abū Abdallāh Muhammad ibn Mūsā al-Khwārizmī was a Persian mathematician, geographer and astronomer. His 825 CE (note: we shall use CE rather than AD) publication of *On the Calculation with Hindu Numerals* was a major turning point in establishing a universal standard for numbers.

It was translated into Latin in the 12th century as *Algoritmi de numero Indorum* and championed by Fibonacci among the merchants in the trading city of Pisa. Algoritmi was the translator's attempt at a Latin version of al-Khwārizmī; it later became the origin of the term 'algorithm'. The system spread throughout Europe, Adelard of Bath first translating it into English in 1120.

In 1930 Tobias Dantzig, a Latvian-American immigrant, bemoaned the incredibly slow progress of change in numbering systems in his book *Number: The Language of Science,*

'This long period of nearly five thousand years saw the rise and fall of many a civilization, each leaving behind it a heritage of literature, art, philosophy and religion. But what was the net achievement in the field of reckoning, the earliest art practiced by man?

An inflexible numeration so crude as to make progress well nigh impossible, and a calculating device so limited in scope that even elementary calculations called for the services of an expert. And what is more, man used these devices for thousands of years without contributing a single important idea to the system! ,,,

...Yet, even when compared with the slow growth of ideas during the dark ages, the history of reckoning presents a peculiar picture of desolate stagnation. When viewed in this light, the achievements of the unknown

Hindu, who sometime in the first centuries of our era discovered the principle of position, assumes the importance of a world event. Not only did this principle constitute a radical departure in method, but we know now that without it no progress in arithmetic was possible. And yet the principle is so simple that today the dullest school boy has no difficulty in grasping it.'

In my youth we British still tortured our school children and those in parts of the residual Empire and Commonwealth with a panoply of base numbers. We had to learn to work with 16 ounces to each pound, 14 pounds to the stone, 8 stones to a hundredweight, and 2240 pounds in a ton.

We had 8 pints to a gallon, 8 quarts to a peck, 4 pecks in a bushel, 36 gallons to the barrel. Then there were four farthings to the penny, 12 pence to the shilling, 20 shillings to a pound, and 21 shillings in a guinea.

Plus, 12 inches to the foot, 3 feet to a yard, 6 feet to a fathom, 66 feet in a chain, 220 yards in a furlong, 1760 yards in a mile, 9 square feet in a square yard, 43,560 square feet in an acre, 640 acres in a square mile.

It is no wonder that we were much confused and that mathematics proved a pretty unpopular subject.

Something for nothing

The modern binary system, sitting at the heart of all PCs, uses a series of 1s and 0s as its basis; it is sobering to note that one half of this system, the digit 0, has an interesting history of its own.

The Babylonians had recognised the need for a zero and they routinely used a space to indicate it, but they never thought to develop a distinct character for the nought itself.

The Greeks on encountering the topic kicked off a long debate querying just how 'nothing' could ever be considered to be something. This led not only to a great deal of philosophic angst but also a heated religious dispute focusing on the subject of zeros and vacuums.

Apparently as a parallel development the Olmec people of Mexico in creating the Mayan calendar and the Mayan numerals are thought to have included a symbol for zero from as early as 400 BCE; definitely they were doing so from 40 BCE. However their numbers used either the base 4 or base 5 which never really caught on elsewhere.

It was left to India to introduce the world to the notion of positional numbers rather than stand-alone integers. India also gave the zero its proper status as a number in its own right.

The Indian sage Brahmagupta, a mathematician and astronomer, set out the rules that are still essentially how the zero is used today. He also introduced the concept of negative numbers in his book, *Brahmasputhasiddhanta*, or *The Opening of the Universe*, written in 628 CE. He used the book to introduce the use and rules for the zero which he called the dot or *bindu*. This was the first time the notion of the zero was in print and the first discussion of it as a number in its own right.

The system spread from India via Persia to the Arab countries. By the time the Muslim Moors moved across from north Africa to occupy Spain, from 700 to 1492 CE, they took with them their modern number system including the '0'. From these roots the system spread throughout Europe from around the 11th century onwards.

The system was to a large extent spread by virtue of the massive development of trade brought about by the Crusades and underwritten by the development of the trade guilds.

Pierre-Simon, Marquis de Laplace, an 18th century French mathematician and astronomer, is rather more famous for Laplace's equation but discussed the coming of the '0' thus:

'*...a profound and important idea which appears so simple to us now that we ignore its true merit. But its very simplicity and the great ease which it lent to all computations put our arithmetic in the first rank of useful inventions...*'

But the world had to wait until the French Revolution (1789 -99) for the introduction of the unified, logical, metric system that most countries use today.

Tim Glynne Jones in *The Book of Numbers* puts a slightly more modern spin on the matter,

'*Is zero a number? If you're one of those people who insist that white is not a colour, you probably think not. After all, it's neither positive nor negative. It is simply nothing, so how can it exist as a number? Well, as the saying goes, if you can put money on it in Vegas, it exists.*'

3 - Creative friction – those that defined computing

'The saddest aspect of life right now is that science gathers knowledge faster than society gathers wisdom.' Isaac Asimov

The word 'computer' was first used in the early 17th century but it was applied to a function and not to a piece of equipment.

It was used to mean 'a person who performs calculations'. In fact right up to the middle of the 20th century the word computer, just like dishwasher, was used to describe a person's role and not a device.

The computer as we mean it today did not start to show up until the 1940s, but devices used to calculate have a long history. It was the abacus and mechanical calculator that would lead to difference engines and tabulating machines – and these would lead to mainframe computing.

Charles Babbage and the hurdy-gurdy men
The man most often considered as the 'Patrician of Computing' is Charles Babbage.

Charles Babbage appears to have held strong views and to have expressed them forcefully from a very young age. He was apparently disappointed on going up to Trinity College Cambridge, and finding what he concluded to be a disappointing standard of mathematics tuition. Can you imagine many students having the audacity to query their instructors before they had even started?

He believed that the British establishment of the time unjustly favoured and pushed Newton's version of calculus for merely jingoistic and political reasons - Sir Isaac Newton was a national institution after all.

Babbage and several friends preferred the much more flexible Liebnizian calculus, and they formed the Analytical Society to argue for a change of approach to this and other matters. Such early activity highlights the character of a man who had a strong sense of his way being the right way - perhaps often seen by him as the only way!

Nonetheless Babbage was an extremely successful individual. A founder of the Astronomical Society in 1820, by 1828 he was the Lucasian Professor of Mathematics at Cambridge University; this was the Chair held by Sir Isaac Newton almost a hundred and fifty years earlier and in more recent times by cosmologist Stephen Hawking.

Babbage was certainly a patrician figure, involved with the launch of the British Association in 1831 and was the principal founder of the Statistical Society of London in 1834; the same year as the tally stick bonfire!

He also published some eighty books; equivalent to one per year of his life! With these various moves he managed to command a centre-stage position in the British establishment that he had in his early days so vociferously attacked.

Babbage was a visionary across many subjects. He was involved in specifying the signals to be used in lighthouses. He proposed a 'black box' recorder for monitoring the status that prevailed during a railway crash. He was also a believer in decimalising the UK currency. He posited that once coal reserves were exhausted then tidal power should be exploited. But he obviously felt that he was not appreciated enough by his peers, sounding something of a luvvy when he said,

'Another age must be the judge!' Charles Babbage

He was right at the centre of Society, regularly entertaining the celebs of the time, personages such as Charles Dickens, Lord Tennyson and Charles Darwin.

All these achievements lend him the attributes to be appropriately described as the 'Patriarch of Computing' and yet he was a very irascible character too.

He routinely railed against the masses, referring to them as 'the Mob' and complaining incessantly of the street nuisances of his time. He appeared to have an almost pathological distaste for the noise of the many organ-grinders.

He did not suffer fools gladly, complaining:

'On two occasions I have been asked, "Pray, Mr. Babbage, if you put into the machine wrong figures, will the right answers come out?... ...I am not able rightly to apprehend the kind of confusion of ideas that could provoke such a question.'

This of course was a rather early consideration of what we would now term the GIGO principle (garbage in, garbage out). His prickly personality, as exhibited in the comments above, was to prove a significant problem when his plans for computing unfolded and as a result the finance that he required would prove elusive.

He set out to find an elegant solution when he first announced his plans to design and build a calculating engine in 1822.

The Mob – eugenics or augmentation?

Babbage routinely railed against the masses, referring to them as 'the Mob' and complaining incessantly of the street nuisances of his time. He appeared to have an almost pathological distaste for the noise of the many organ-grinders.

William Shockley, the transistor and semiconductor innovator, also became beset by the same worries as Babbage about the masses.

Shockley developed strong views based upon his fears that the less intelligent were having far more children than those more intelligent. He believed this would lead to a decline in the gene pool and the general intelligence of mankind.

Very unpopularly, he also applied some of this thinking to race, concluding that eugenics was the only solution. These beliefs led him into much controversy; he took out a libel suit against a publication when a reporter suggested he was a Nazi. Though he did win his case his personal unpopularity is perhaps reflected in the fact that he was awarded just $1 in damages.

Doug Engelbart, an early PC innovator, began pursuing more esoteric goals for the development of mankind itself. There are distinct echoes of Babbage and Shockley in some of his statements, though he was very much in favour of the mass of humanity.

'Our world is a complex place with urgent problems of a global scale.'

'The grand challenge is to boost the collective IQ of organizations and of society. A successful effort brings about an improved capacity for addressing any other grand challenge.'

'The improvements gained and applied in their own pursuit will accelerate the improvement of collective IQ.'

It was perhaps this very dissatisfaction with the norms of their time that drove these individuals to develop their notions for change.

Trauma with tables

Back in Babbage's time actuaries, astronomers, engineers, navigators and surveyors each had to rely upon referring to a set of printed mathematical tables. But these tables had first to be manually calculated. Inherent errors were made in calculations, but the transcription and subsequent printing processes added ever more layers of human error.

In the 1830s one analysis of a random selection of forty volumes of numerical tables showed 3,700 identified errors and there was little confidence that all had yet been discovered.

Babbage was clearly fascinated with these tables; in his avid pursuit of the subject he amassed the largest collection of them, more than three hundred volumes. This was in part why, in an effort to eliminate these errors, he wished to develop a machine that would both calculate and then print the tables.

From a development of computing viewpoint he was of course a very significant contributor. He defined how to calculate numerical tables with machinery by using the method of differences. This iterative approach meant the elimination of the need for equipment to be able to multiply or divide; this was the basis of his Difference Engine.

The notion of a Difference Engine had in fact been conceived back in 1786 by Johann Helfrich von Müller, an engineer in the Hessian army. This was a German mercenary unit employed by the British Empire during what it called the American Revolution and what the USA called the War of Independence. A few years earlier von Müller had improved upon the Leibniz Stepped Reckoner and used the experience to surmise the next step, but he failed to get support or funding for his idea.

Unlike the calculators preceding Babbage's Difference Engine, the whole process was planned to be automatic rather than requiring regular and informed human intervention. Perhaps reflecting his doubts about humanity in the round?

The Difference Engine as designed by Babbage would have been huge. It required 25,000 precision parts, and if built it would have been eight foot tall (2.44m), seven foot wide (2.13m) and three feet deep (0.91m) with a weight of a massive fifteen tons (tonnes) – though in this it was clearly a sign of things to come!

But this concept was somewhat ahead of its time in that the design requirement stretched the then current manufacturing capabilities much too far. The search for a suitable maker in a broad survey of the UK and continental European manufacturing capabilities led directly to Babbage's book published in 1832, *On the Economy of Machinery and Manufactures*.

He presciently bemoaned the coming of the global village when he noted, *'The accumulation of skill and science which has been directed to diminish the difficulty of producing manufactured goods, has not been beneficial to that country alone in which it is concentrated; distant kingdoms have participated in its advantages.'*

Only a portion of his Difference Engine design was ever created and this necessitated the development of some of the most complex precision engineering of the time.

Babbage, because of his stature in the establishment, was successful in attracting all manner of attention to his projects and he received a good deal of government funding for his ideas; but this was often to the detriment of other inventors of his time.

Babbage siphons off all the funding
One such inventor was a west countryman, Thomas Fowler, hailing from Torrington in North Devon.

In 1828 Fowler patented his Thermo-siphon, a heating system based on convection that was a vital stepping stone towards modern central heating systems.

But patent law in the UK was very weak and his ideas were soon widely plagiarised. Others needed only to make minor changes to his design to be allowed to flaunt the patent. He wisely chose not to spend his life and a fortune trying to protect his invention and ended up making very little from that notion.

Yet Fowler was still a success, he ran a bank in his home town and became the treasurer of the local Poor Law Union. It was in this latter role that he had to perform complicated calculations to establish payments that were due to the various parishes within his remit.

This resulted in his producing some of the very mathematical tables that so engaged Babbage. It was while producing these that Fowler established that any number could be produced by combining the powers of 2 and 3 and using this fact he published his binary and ternary tables in 1838.

This work then prompted him to develop a 'calculating machine' that would operate using the ternary system, with only the digits 1, 2 and 3. Fowler was invited to present his machine to the Royal Society in 1840. At that meeting he described it thus,

'This Machine was constructed entirely with my own hands (principally in wood) with the utmost regard to economy and merely to put my Ideas of this mode of calculation into some form of action. It is about six feet long, one foot deep and three feet wide. In brass and iron it might be constructed so as not to occupy a space much larger than a good portable writing desk and with powers such as I have described.'

The Astronomer Royal, Professor George Airy, and leading mathematicians of the time including Augustus De Morgan and Charles Babbage, were among those who reviewed Fowler's ternary machine. But no support, investigation or sponsorship was subsequently offered.

Fowler's son The Reverend Hugh Fowler subsequently wrote,
'The government of the day refused even to look at my father's machine on the express ground that they had spent such large sums, with no satisfactory result, on Babbage's.'

Analysing the differences

Babbage appointed Joseph Clement, a master toolmaker, to build his first Difference Engine, but they all too soon fell out.

The engineer had been persuaded to move home to work nearer to Babbage but then the latter failed to come up with the promised compensation for the move. As a result Clement stopped work on the Difference Engine in 1833.

Far from showing any concern, Babbage concentrated on making constant changes to his plans and then completely shifted his attention to a more ambitious project, the Analytical Engine. His early work on the second system also allowed him to define a version of the original Difference Engine that would require only 4,000 parts, but no effort was ever applied to building this v2.0 difference engine.

Difference engines were not general-purpose devices in that they simply processed numbers entered into them and worked with them in set sequences. His subsequent and more ambitious Analytical Engine was conceived to be 'programmable' and thus to calculate any algebraic value; this represented the first true computer design.

Babbage's Analytical Engine too became something of a moveable feast with inadequate financing to complete the project. He responded to this by constantly refining and changing his ideas and designs until his end.

He died having never built one of his devices. It was left instead to his youngest son, Henry Prevost Babbage, to create six working engines using his father's designs.

One of these was sent to Harvard University as the college celebrated the 250th anniversary of its foundation during 1886. As we shall see it was later discovered by Howard H Aiken, the pioneer who went on to build the Harvard Mark I.

In 2002 London's Science Museum finally created each of the 8,000 components needed to build and operate Babbage's Difference Engine No 2.

While Babbage blustered a Swedish engineer, Per George Scheutz, developed a wooden difference engine in 1837 and by 1843 he and his son Edvard had also produced one with a printer too. By 1853 they had a full scale difference engine that they termed a 'tabulating machine'.

A Brit, Bryan Donkin, created a version of the Scheutz device in 1853 which enjoyed success when the British government purchased it.

Fascinating Ada

Ada Byron was the only legitimate child of Lord Byron, the result of an extremely short marriage between him and Anne Isabelle Milbanke. Formally she was Augusta Ada King, the Countess of Lovelace, but is more usually known simply as Ada Lovelace.

She was something of a sickly child and died at only thirty-six years of age. Headaches had affected her sight in childhood, and then measles caused paralysis in her teens, leaving her on crutches for many years. Perhaps to quell any poetic tendency, her mother saw to it that she was trained in mathematics and music. One of her teachers, a noted mathematician himself, concluded that she was,

'...an original mathematical investigator, perhaps of first-rate eminence.' Augustus de Morgan.

But that did not stop her having flights of fancy; she designed a flying machine in 1828.

Lovelace took up a regular correspondence with Babbage from 1833 when she was seventeen years old. He was not achieving any backing for his

Analytical Engine but in 1842 an Italian mathematician, Louis Menebrea, published a document in French on Babbage's planned device.

It was Ada who translated this for Babbage and she soon went on to develop algorithms for the Analytical Engine, despite it never being built. She is therefore heralded as the first computer programmer though she preferred the title Analyst and Metaphysician.

At one point she developed a program to calculate a sequence of Bernoulli numbers; these were useful in both number theory and trigonometry. Perhaps she showed that she was truly her father's daughter when she wrote,
'The Analytical Engine weaves algebraic patterns just as the Jacquard loom weaves flowers and leaves.'

Ada Lovelace is still much appreciated by the computer industry. Her image appears in the holographic seal on Microsoft products.

A real-time software language that became popular in avionics was developed in the late 1970s by CII and named Ada after her. It was designed to replace the many different languages used by the military; its version of the software is code-named 'MIL-STD-1815', the letters for Military Standard and the number commemorating the year of her birth.

The British Computer Society, albeit somewhat late to the bandwagon, has since 1998 awarded a medal in her name.

The thoughts of Vannevar Bush

It is worth just pausing and recalling something of the circumstances of the twenty years that were bracketed by the two world wars; they were very austere times.

The USA maintained its Prohibition Laws between 1919 and 1933, leading directly to the speak-easies, to Al Capone, John Dillinger, Bonnie and Clyde… There was the Great Depression at the end of 1929 that struck initially in the United States but then its effects spread across the world. It took until the mid '30s before economies began to stabilize - just in time to finance the next world war!

Perhaps this sounds an unlikely breeding ground for brilliant ideas – or maybe it was precisely what it took to drive the creative juices?

Vannevar Bush was one of the early influential thinkers in this period. He had operated within the US National Research Council during WWI when some 6,000 scientists were charged with using their sciences to aggressive intent; they worked to improve everything from laboratory equipment to submarines.

Following the war, in 1922 Bush helped to form a company that would sell the S-tube, a gaseous rectifier that advanced radio technology. This company became Raytheon that in the 1940s moved into radar and became a significant US defence contractor. Post-WWII it made the Patriot missile system and today is the third largest US defence contractor behind Boeing and Lockheed. Bush's equity in this organisation secured his long-term financial position which allowed him to pursue much broader and more significant ideas.

In 1927 Bush developed plans for a Differential Analyser that could solve differential equations with up to eighteen variables. The Bush analyser was completed in 1931 to become the most accurate calculator of its time.

But it did not inspire universal approval. John Mauchly (ENIAC to UNIVAC) used a Bush analyser at the Moore School of Electrical Engineering and said of it.

'When large and related problems, which could be set on the machine for weeks, were to be solved it was in constant use, but when small problems were being dealt with, engineers found it more expedient to solve then mathematically, without taking days to set up the machine.'

However it was to be Bush's management and administrative skills that took him much further. Having experienced the way in which scientists and the military had failed to gel during WWI he set about ensuring that this would change.

He became the president of the Carnegie Institute of Washington where he disbursed significant monies into scientific research. While chairman of the National Advisory Committee for Aeronautics he pressed the politicians to form the National Defense Research Committee (NDRC) in 1940.

Disappointed by slow progress he sought a direct audience with President F D Roosevelt where he outlined his objectives on a single page of paper. Roosevelt took just ten minutes to approve it; Bush was appointed NDRC chairman.

Bush set the NDRC four main thrusts: radar; chemistry and explosives; armour and ordnance; patents and inventions. The organisation later transmogrified into the Office of Scientific Research and Development (OSRD) with Bush still its director. OSRD ran a huge team that encouraged many significant developments in radar, sonar and weapons systems.

Perhaps most notably OSRD managed the A-bomb and H-bomb 'Manhattan Project' until 1943 when control was ceded to the US Army. But it was not all aggressive science. It also developed mass production techniques to ensure that supplies of vital penicillin and sulfonamide drugs were available.

Where Bush had direct impact upon our subject area was post-war. In July 1945 he published his thinking in two important and yet very different papers. Firstly, he laid out his thoughts in a report to the president, entitled *Science, The Endless Frontier*. This led directly to the creation of the National Science Foundation. Its motto is self-explanatory,

'Supporting Education and Research across all fields of Science and Technology. America's Investment in the Future Where Discoveries Begin.'

Secondly and in the same month, Bush wrote *As We May Think* in the *Atlantic Monthly* magazine expressing concern about the way technology had become increasingly destructive. His article considered more peaceful and constructive applications.

'Consider a future device for individual use, which is a sort of mechanized private file and library. It needs a name, and, to coin one at random, "memex" will do. A memex is a device in which an individual stores all his books, records, and communications, and which is mechanized so that it may be consulted with exceeding speed and flexibility. It is an enlarged intimate supplement to his memory.'

He later explained that Memex derived from Memory and index.

Bush proposed that the device would centrally store a massive number of books, reports and correspondence to disseminate knowledge more broadly. He saw this as a way of circumventing the degree of specialisation that was developing momentum to the detriment of any ready cross-fertilisation of ideas.

There was a need to provide a capable indexing system for rapid availability and cross-referencing. It would store and make available instantly, this collective memory to all and encourage new knowledge by stimulating innovative interconnections.

He compared his Memex notion to the way in which the brain operates but, perhaps disappointingly, he proposed using microfilm, with a series of screens and viewers - a technology that was the current vogue. However his proposal was spot on with regard to how one might file vast amounts of data, and then have the means to cooperatively update and access it.

Many who followed claim that this Vannevar Bush Memex article led directly to inspire them to subsequent developments; Ted Nelson to develop hypertext, Ivan Sutherland to design his Sketchpad program, Vint Cerf and Robert Kahn to evolve the ARPANET into the Internet and Tim Berners-Lee and Robert Cailliau to conceive the World Wide Web.

Ciphers and fish - Bletchley Park and Alan Turing

Alan Turing's influence on the theory and development of computing is significant. Yet in the 1920s when he attended Sherbourne School, Dorset in the UK the emphasis there had been on classics and his keen interest in the sciences was seriously questioned. Somewhat revealing of the era and the British public school system, his headmaster stuffily challenged Turing's commitment by saying,

'...he must aim at becoming educated. If he is to be solely a scientific specialist, [then] he is wasting his time at a Public School.'

Despite the attempt to push him towards focusing on the classics he was tenacious and prodigious, providing mathematical proofs and insights ahead of his time without receiving any appropriate formal training.

During the mid 1930s, while still in his early twenties, Turing defined many concepts in computing and specifically in algorithms that would prove to become fundamental in computer science theory.

In November 1936 he wrote *On Computable Numbers* and outlined his thoughts on a 'universal' computer which became the concept many would pursue, their goal thereafter defined as creating the 'Turing machine'.

No surprise then that during the war Turing became head of Hut 8 at the Government Code & Cipher School at Bletchley Park, where they were charged with putting Turing's theoretical thinking into practice on the decoding of German naval encrypted signals.

Before the war the Poles had captured a German Enigma machine and crypto-analysts had developed an electromechanical machine to decode the German field and theatre messages; it named it the Bomba.

The Enigma codes scrambled messages using a three or four stepping rotor system. Enigma sent its messages in Morse code which it could scramble in over 150,000,000,000,000,000,000 different ways!

In 1941 a somewhat more complex system was detected being used for high-level messages by the German High Command. Enigma interceptions identified that the Germans called these teleprinter system messages *Sägefisch* or sawfish. The messages were therefore codenamed by the Allies as 'Fish'. Material they had decoded from the Enigma also indicated the equipment used was called a *Geheimschreiber* or secret writer.

The task of designing the first of these systems for the Germans had been given to the Lorenz company that came up with the SZ 40/42 machine; called Tunny by the Allies. This system used teleprinters and their 32-character Baudot code; this was the code used by the telegraph system before ASCII was developed.

The starting point for the encoding rotors was changed three times each day based upon issued code books. Sadly there was no captured device to hand or any details of its structure to help give the Allied code-breakers a headstart; they had to wait for human error to come to the aid of the decrypters.

The first British intercepts identified that these were enciphered by a modified version of the Vernam System developed in the USA. The system added characters throughout the message to hide and confuse its original content. It was concluded that they needed two versions of the same message to have any chance of cracking it. And that is precisely what they got.

In August 1942 a German operator, finding a Lorenz message sent from Athens to Vienna had not been received, sent it again but vitally failed to reset the device between the two despatches. Better still he had used an abbreviation right at the beginning. This was enough to provide insight into not only decoding the message but also to using it to imply the machine's structure.

A 'Tunny' Machine was built to decipher the Lorenz messages but it often took six weeks to establish the settings so that the resulting decoded message was much too old to be helpful.

Other German systems existed, such as the Siemens and Halske T52 teleprinter, known as a *Geheimfernschreiber* or secret teleprinter; the Allies called this the Sturgeon. It had ten pinwheels to scramble the message and even if two similar messages were detected the deciphering was not going to be so easily achieved. The code was eventually broken by the Bletchley Park team but these decryptions did not happen as routinely or regularly.

A final device, the Siemens T43 one-time tape machine, arrived late in the war and was used in only a few locations. Its code was adjudged to be unbreakable.

Early on Turing's team developed a new decoding device that they named the Bombe in recognition of the earlier Polish Bomba. These Bombes were quite large, about 3 feet (1m) high, over 6 feet (2m) long and 3 feet (1m) wide and weighed around one ton (tonne).

They worked on the principle of iteration and elimination, disproving each incorrect setting rather than trying to forecast the correct one. The speed of applying this trial and error method was vital.

The British Tabulating Machine (BTM) company based in Letchworth had been formed at the beginning of the century to deal in Hollerith's and subsequently IBM's products. It was commissioned, by a Bletchley Park secret plan codenamed Cantab, to build over 210 of these Bombes.

BTM also linked four Bombes to create the Giant which proved too big to move to Bletchley. Whenever the Giant successfully completed a decoding exercise, a phone call to Bletchley would advise 'The Giant has caught a whale'.

Heath Robinson and Colossus

Max Newman was born in the UK; his anglicisation of Maxwell Neumann was understandable; his father, a German, had been interned in the UK during the first war. Perhaps due to his name change or perhaps his Jewish ethnology Newman did not face the same fate in WWII. As a mathematics lecturer at Cambridge he was one of Turing's inspirations.

When Newman arrived at Bletchley Park he was originally set to work on a German teleprinter cipher, a task that he found unchallenging. From late 1942 he was set the task of developing an automated system for decoding. He, together with Donald Michie, several engineers and a bevy of Wrens, worked in what was called the Newmanry.

The Newman device was jokingly named by the Wrens who operated it as 'Heath Robinson' after the cartoonist William Heath Robinson who specialised in drawings of fantastic and eccentrically complicated machines. The device itself proved none too elegant and none too accurate.

Turing worked with Max Newman to develop techniques and a device to decode the German's next generation, the Lorenz cipher. This used more complicated code and was used only for the key messages from the General High Command. Its early messages were able to be decrypted manually by the Bletchley Park team but subsequent upgrades made this impractical.

Newman was aware of the work Tommy Flowers had done with the telephone network and soon consulted with him.

Tommy Flowers, a London East-End son of a bricklayer, served his apprenticeship in mechanical engineering at the Royal Arsenal in Woolwich. He went on to earn a degree in electrical engineering at night school, later joining the communications side of the General Post Office where he moved to its Dollis Hill Research Station in north-west London.

In the 1930s Flowers worked on applying the potential of electronics to telephone networks, work that held him in good stead for the Bletchley Park code-breaking task.

Flowers went to Bletchley and examined the Heath Robinson; he proposed replacing its mechanical switches with thermionic valves. There was concern in that this plan entailed using over 1,500 valves and to date the most complicated device had used just 150; would it prove accurate?

In less than a year Flowers created what they called Colossus, named because it took up a whole room and weighed more than a ton. Their fears proved groundless; its accuracy was much greater than that of the Heath Robinson and it ran at five times the speed.

Colossus could run through millions of operations at a rate of 5,000 characters a second, though working at these speeds stretched the mechanical components which required regular repairs and replacements.

Colossus II, with 2,500 valves, followed in June 1944 and proved instantly invaluable when it revealed that Hitler had overruled his generals and chosen to believe the Allied misinformation regarding the timing and planning for the D-day landings. Montgomery and Eisenhower were thus reassured that they could proceed as originally planned.

In total ten Colossus IIs were commissioned; they went on to decrypt Italian and Japanese codes too.

Carrot or stick – the development of radar

It is remarkable the breadth of talent applied to the development of radar either side of, and during, WWII.

As children in Britain we were told that our WWII fighter pilots had proven so successful in intercepting German bombers because they ate a lot of carrots, and these helped them see better in the dark - go on children eat up all those vegetables!

The background to radar was first observed by a member of the Imperial Russian Navy in 1895 while using equipment to detect lightning. Using this between two ships he noticed the interference when a third ship passed, but he did not follow this through.

It was a German, Christian Hülsmeyer, who developed a device to help ships avoid each other in fog; he patented this as his 'telemobilscope'.

Nikola Tesla, a Serb who worked in both France and the USA, set out the theory of radio location in 1917. In 1934 the UK Air Ministry heard rumours of the Germans working in this scientific sector and there were suggestions it might be to produce some sort of 'death ray'. The Air Ministry therefore mounted research of its own to investigate the matter; it was concluded that the use as a death ray was impractical but the detection of aircraft was entirely viable.

A number of countries set out to create the required technology and WWII led to some rapid progress. The UK devices were called RDF (range and direction finding); it was the Americans who first called it radar (radio detection and ranging). By the end of the war its use was widespread, not just by the UK and USA, but also by Germany, Japan and the USSR.

Just prior to the war the Germans scheduled regular Graf Zeppelin II airship flights along the British coast to investigate its radio masts. These detected what the Germans assumed to be radar and in 1940 they took temporarily successful countermeasures.

The US Army had radar on Hawaii in December 1941 and it did detect a flight of aircraft but this was misinterpreted as an expected US bomber flight, so the warning centre did not provide an alert to the Pearl Harbor attack.

Subsequent allied technology proved to be simpler and more effective and its role in winning the Battle of Britain was to be significant.

Radar was later to become the inspiration for weather forecasting, international telephony, the mapping of planets and even microwave ovens!

Ted Nelson hyperthought

One of those inspired by Bush to emerge in the 1960s was Ted Nelson. Half Norwegian he grew up in Greenwich Village, New York's bohemian central that so inspired the writings of William Faulkner and Eugene O'Neill - the birthplace of the beatniks.

It is important to recall that the late 1950s and 1960s in California was the time when a whole counter-culture was evolving; this being the term used in an attempt to fit a whole series of movements into one pithy term. Name 'em and constrain 'em?

The period was politically confused; many who had leaned pre- and post-war towards Communism were offended by the invasion of Hungary by the Soviets in 1956. Some were moved to seek a safer haven in the New Left movement.

The notion of nuclear deterrence led to the UK's Campaign for Nuclear Disarmament (CND) in 1958; marches and sit-ins were organised leading to a broader and more voluble, and global, peace movement.

In the USA the civil rights movement had started passively in the South during the 1950s but by the '60s it had developed a momentum for mass and direct action campaigns of marches, sit-ins, boycotts...

Women's liberation and feminism also blossomed in the '60s, though I think many of us non-PC 1960s guys had a somewhat confused reaction to the burning of bras; in some aspects welcoming the act itself, if not entirely the sentiments.

From 1964 onwards the anti-Vietnam movement organised its own marches and protests. And in the mid-'60s the beatniks of Greenwich Village in NY and Haight-Ashbury in SF were 'relaunched' as hippies, taken from the '40s word 'hipster' applied to jazz fans. They had their summer of love and launched flower-power.

So the early development of personal computers was happening alongside this other activity. This was not something that was driven by nerds locked away in a social vacuum, but very much on the campuses where the counter-culture was alive and kicking.

Ted Nelson earned a master's in sociology from Harvard and probably helped by his background developed a clear view of the potential for human-augmentation by computers. He soon became something of an IT-philosopher.

He deliberately styled himself as something of an outsider, self-publicising his thoughts to the joy or irritation of others in the early PC business. He was keen to tell anyone who would listen that he was a genius and he readily summed up his rather pessimistic philosophy in a Greenwich Village-esque manner,

'Any fool can use a computer. Many do.' *'...most people are fools, most authority is malignant, God does not exist, and everything is wrong.'*

From as early as 1960 he set out to prompt the development of a computer network that would use a much simpler and user-friendly interface to broaden its appeal. In 1965 he founded what he called his Project Xanadu. He is said be the first person to coin the terms hypertext and hypermedia.

Hypertext means on-screen text that has instant links to other text, so that the material becomes more interactive and useful to the user; it allows branching through the text rather than following it serially. Hypermedia is where links are not just to other text but also to graphics, audio and video.

One might think therefore that Nelson would have been delighted by the Internet and the World Wide Web that we enjoy today. On the contrary, he says,

'HTML [Hyper-Text Mark-up Language] is precisely what we were trying to PREVENT – with ever-breaking links, links going outward only, quotes you can't follow to their origins, no version management, no rights management.'

Nelson's books have usually been insightful and timely. He published Computer Lib in 1974, The Home Computer *Revolution* in 1977 and *Literary Machines* in 1981. These were followed by *The Future of Information* in 1997 and *Geeks Bearing Gifts: How The Computer World Got This Way* in 2008. With each he set out to report on what he believed was happening and forecasting what might happen next; occasionally with some accuracy.

Back in 1965 Project Xanadu had taken on the look of a Utopian concept, more a dream than a reality - until a year later when Brown University in Rhode Island set out to pursue some of Nelson's thinking.

Andy van Dam, a Dutchman, was one of the co-founders of Brown University's Computer Science department in Rhode Island. He worked with Nelson and others developing the Hypertext Editing System (HES). This system comprised of both links and branching text, though the IBM System/360 that it was created upon proved none-too-helpful with these new approaches.

Later NASA implemented HES at the Houston Manned Spacecraft Center for the documentation of the Apollo space program (rocket science again!). Brown University was to discontinue HES in 1969 but van Dam helped produce an improved system; this he called File Retrieval and Editing SyStem (FRESS).

FRESS allowed the size of files to be completely arbitrary, its text arrayed in lines only when it needed to be displayed. The text had two types of marker, either tags to show footnotes and other comments, or jumps that linked to other documents. These markers were rather laboriously inserted via a special terminal and a light pen or via a keyboard. The system was used at Brown but made few converts elsewhere.

However both HES and FRESS would prove to be important steps in the general direction towards the World Wide Web.

In 1981 Nelson launched his Operation ZigZag and the ZigZag virtual machine to develop his concept. Having dedicated much of his life to these ideas he did fully appreciate the problems that his work faced,

'Paradigm confrontation is rarely fun for people; new ideas tend to be unpleasant and threatening.'

Ride that wave – LINC and HP

The first conversational use of the juxtaposed words 'personal computer' is usually attributed to MIT, specifically to its Laboratory Instrument Computer Lab (LINC).

The notion of a personal computer was indeed probably first outlined then - not as a development plan, but as an act of frustration. The MIT Labs faculty and students and TMRC members were among the first to be granted regular access to some of the very earliest mainframe computers.

But far from satisfying their needs they were among the first to experience the inflexibility of early computers - the difficulties in accessing and interacting with these monsters. Thus they were also early to realise the need for a computer that was more available, more approachable, more responsive, more personal.

The term was used to look to an enlightened future when there would be more ready access to computers rather than having to approach them via a 'high priesthood' of operators and their cumbersome processes. The term personal computer was therefore expressed verbally at MIT from as early as 1962, but was not directly disseminated in any printed form.

The first ever use of the term personal computer in print was something of a misnomer. It appeared in an advertisement in the October 1968 issue of *Science* magazine.

In looking at it I am reminded of old magazines where pages and pages of advertisements linked the latest buzz word to products and proclaimed the benefits for them being magnetic, or electrical, or plastic, or electronic, or green...

In fact the first product referred to as a personal computer in print was merely a calculator! Hewlett-Packard promoted its first programmable scientific desktop calculator as,

'The new Hewlett-Packard 911A personal computer.'

We marketeers do love to thrust our product out onto a new wave and grab some of its momentum for ourselves and our products.

Contrast this approach with the IBM 704 computer, the first mass-produced mainframe computer as it launched in 1954. It filled a room, had an upgraded high-speed magnetic core memory and was the first to have floating-point arithmetic. Yet IBM termed it merely as a 'calculator', its manual stated,

'The type 704 Electronic Data-Processing Machine is a large-scale, high-speed electronic calculator controlled by an internally stored program of the single address type.'

The January 1983 edition of *Time* magazine altered its regular Person of the Year feature to make way for the personal computer, proclaimed as 'Machine of the Year' with the headline *The Computer Moves In.*

This precedent for unseating a Person of the Year has happened very infrequently - again in 1989 when the endangered Earth was proclaimed 'Planet of the Year'. It was changed in 1999 to 'Person of the Century' to honour Albert Einstein's achievements.

The 'Mother of all demos - Augmentation Research Center

One of the key moments in the development of personal computers occurred just two months after the term was first used in print - in December 1968 at the Fall Joint Computer Conference held at the Brooks Hall within the 'Hippie HQ' of San Francisco.

A presentation was scheduled to be given at the event. The flyer promoting it was a classic piece of under-statement given the significance that it was to deliver,

'This session is entirely devoted to a presentation by Dr. Engelbart on a computer-based, interactive, multi-console display system which is being developed at Stanford Research Institute under the sponsorship of ARPA, NASA and RADC [the US Air Force Rome Air Development Center in New York]. The system is being used as an experimental laboratory for investigating principles by which interactive computer aids can augment intellectual capability. The techniques which are being described will, themselves, be used to augment the presentation.

The session will use an on-line, closed circuit television hook-up to the SRI [Stanford Research Institute] computing system in Menlo Park. Following the presentation remote terminals to the system, in operation, may be viewed during the remainder of the conference in a special room set aside for that purpose.'

Those who attended the presentation and those who wrote reports of it subsequently gave it the moniker 'The Mother of All Demos'. It certainly was a remarkable multimedia event.

The technology used to make the demonstration was as dramatic as the message it delivered. Video was displayed on a 20-foot (6.1m) screen using a new projector on loan from NASA. A home-made modem connected the presenter to colleagues who were sitting at remote computers based at Menlo Park in Stanford.

Doug Engelbart was presenting one of the very first on-screen teleconference and video conferences. He was assisted on the day by Don Andrews, Bill English, Bill Paxton and others.

Doug Engelbart was born in Oregon, USA with a mix of German, Swedish and Norwegian family origins. During WWII he was halfway through college when he was drafted into the US Navy and based in the Philippines.

Immediately following the war he came across Vannevar Bush's 1945 article in *The Atlantic Monthly* magazine. He was much motivated by Bush's notion of the Memex which influenced his aspirations for research once peacetime fully arrived.

He went on to earn his PhD at Berkeley and taught there, before joining the Stanford Research Institute where he was able to pursue his ideas. His notions had crystallised into seeking ways to augment human intellect. He wanted to establish how human capabilities could be assisted with complex problems in both the fact-gathering and solution-finding phases of tackling issues.

While a postgraduate at Berkeley from 1954-5 he had his first encounter with a computer when working on the development of a 1,300 vacuum tube mainframe, the California Digital Computer. As a radar technician he was already familiar with analysing information displayed on a screen and foresaw that computers might be the way forward for his chosen goal.

Engelbart had a rare vision that saw beyond the mere number crunching tasks that were then considered as the only fare for computers. He set about finding a symbiosis between this equipment and its operator that could bring dividends.

Engelbart envisaged bright individuals sitting at interactive workstations, pooling their collective capabilities and intellect to consider and resolve pressing issues. He followed many thinkers of the time in seeing technology as a two-way street; while humans conceived the technology, when used it would in turn shape human thinking and approaches.

He developed a term for this called 'bootstrapping' - the process of developing a technological tool or process on the hoof. Building it, testing it during real-time development and then the thinking process to modify it as you went along. This was the 'suck it and see' approach to development, learning by trial and error rather than waiting for full understanding before commencing a project. Government and military research funders rather liked this approach.

He produced a report entitled, *Augmenting Human Intellect: A Conceptual Framework*, which gained him ARPA funding to create what he called the Augmentation Research Center (ARC).

ARC was sited within the Stanford Research Institute (SRI). Engelbart established it as a research centre for augmenting human intellect, but it is best known for the technologies and techniques developed in pursuit of that goal.

Engelbart and the ARC team were the first to develop and demonstrate the notion of bit-mapped screens where individual pixels could be used instead of dull columns and rows of text. This bit-mapping permitted the integration of text and graphics creating a very user-friendly interaction or interface for the user.

They went on to develop a host of collaborative tools such as multiple on-screen windows. They developed presentation software that was a forerunner of the web browser. They developed hypermedia publishing, shared-screen teleconferencing, groupware which was the granddaddy to today's server software, and so on.

Perhaps the most lasting and impactful thing that the ARC team previewed in San Francisco was an 'X-Y position indicator for a display system'. From that description can you recognise it? They had hoped to give this device some serious and worthy name but someone on the team had called it a 'mouse' and the name stuck.

Through SRI Engelbart was granted the patent for the mouse in 1970 but he never received royalties for it. Though at some stage Apple did license the mouse from SRI for a payment of around $40,000, few followed its example.

RANDOM ACCESS MOMENT:
someone suggested that the mouse was not the first 'point and click' interface – this was produced in Connecticut in 1854 by Horace Smith and Daniel Wesson - they produced the first lever action pistol as Smith & Wesson.

Engelbart and his team had brought all these things together to create oN-Line System (NLS). This rather strange abbreviation came about as Engelbart had previously developed an Off-Line System that already used the acronym OLS.

This was the first collaborative system that used hypertext fully and practically. Initially the NLS development was based around a time-share SDS 940 system with sixteen user terminals.

It was his NLS, not yet fully implemented, still in the 'bootstrapping' phase, that formed the remotely-accessed centrepiece of the December 1968 demo. At the time ARC had achieved a very helpful workstation for just one individual; the multi-user collaborative elements were not yet realised.

The reception of Engelbart's presentation was spectacular and the team returned to ARC to press on taking NLS forward; though it was subsequently hi-jacked by the ARPANET.

A year earlier in April 1967 Engelbart had attended a contractors' meeting run by ARPA's IPTO. He volunteered for ARC to become the Network Information Centre for ARPANET which meant that it managed the directory of connections and the early RFCs (Requests for Comments).

Two of the early nodes were local to SRI at the UCLA labs and the University of California Santa Barbara, the third at some distance in the University of Utah. The very first message sent through the ARPANET was to later come from the UCLA to Engelbart's ARC lab at SRI.

Towards a joined-up thinking

By the late '50s and early '60s there was a proliferation of mainframe computers and increasingly a need evolved for users to be able to communicate with each other via these devices. Between users of the same mainframe the means to do this had been developed in an ad hoc way. Talking between computers proved initially rather elusive, as each monolithic system was so very different and there were no standards that enabled them to interact easily or to pass messages readily between them.

Travel around the various academic institutions and research agencies, and each would be found to have uniquely customised its hardware and software - a 'Tower of Babel' cacophony of different approaches. Something needed to be done.

It prompted a rush for greater cooperation between research teams, which in turn put pressure on finding a means of sharing material and notions within large local teams and particularly between often remote locations. The energy to find a real networking solution was to become part of ARPA's remit. At about this time another concept emerged, one that suggested they needed to plan for a network able to survive a nuclear attack.

Prior to his appointment with ARPA's IPTO Lick Licklider had followed a well-trodden route from both MIT and Harvard to become a vice president at Bolt, Beranek & Newman Inc (BBN), a high-tech R&D organisation. BBN was initially focused upon acoustics. Later and most famously it was the organisation that analysed the sound from films taken at the site where J F Kennedy was assassinated. Still later it investigated the deletions in the Nixon Watergate tapes.

BBN's detailed analysis techniques helped the company to become one of the most sophisticated early users of computers. As an example Licklider was loaned one of the very first production PDP-1s for use with this work.

He was lured from BBN to ARPA to run a behavioural science department as well as IPTO so both of his interests could be pursued. At IPTO, Licklider is credited with helping to bring about networking and the Internet but this in fact refers to his widely circulated ideas rather than any products actually created by him.

In 1960 his paper *Man-Computer Symbiosis* encapsulated his central idea that the human-machine interface needed to be improved.

'It seems reasonable to envision, for a time 10 or 15 years hence, a 'thinking center' that will incorporate the functions of present-day libraries together with anticipated advances in information storage and retrieval.

'The picture readily enlarges itself into a network of such centres, connected to one another by wide-band communication lines and to individual users by leased-wire services. In such a system, the speed of the computers

would be balanced, and the cost of the gigantic memories and the sophisticated programs would be divided by the number of users.'

Licklider had run a personal analysis that prompted his *Man-Computer Symbiosis*. He showed he used 85% of his time preparing to think, getting the facts and figures assembled and plotting analyses and making calculation and therefore only 15% of his time was actually available for thinking. He hoped that his symbiosis would improve the latter statistic.

At BBN in 1962 with a colleague Welden Clark, Licklider issued another paper entitled *On-line Man-Computer Communication*. In it they detailed that while humans were good at decision-making and analysis they were quite slow at it. They suggested that computers were best placed to store and retrieve data faithfully and run computations rapidly. They proposed the need for time-sharing on these expensive computers and looked forward to an era of computer-based learning and computer-aided design. In the paper they rounded up the current status,

'...*Although more interactive multi-access computer systems are being delivered now, and although more groups plan to be using these systems within the next year, there are at present perhaps only as few as half a dozen interactive multi-access computer communities.*'

'...*The commercially available time-sharing services ... ... of the System Development Corporation in Santa Monica, the University of California at Berkeley, Massachusetts Institute of Technology in Cambridge and Lexington, Mass. - which have been collectively serving about a thousand people for several years.*'

'...*twenty years from now some form of keyboard operation will be taught in kindergarten, and forty years from now keyboards may be as universal as pencils...*' '...*In a few years, men will be able to communicate more effectively through a machine than face to face.*'

These and a further paper issued in August 1962 entitled the *Intergalactic Computer Network* had caught the attention of ARPA.

In October 1962 he was appointed head of IPTO and in his two years there he achieved a great deal. He agreed the funding of Doug Engelbart's ARC, MIT's Project MAC and other network projects at Stanford, UCB, UCLA and SDC.

MIT points the way – Kleinrock and Roberts

Leonard Kleinrock gained his master's in electrical engineering and his PhD in computer science at MIT. For his doctorate in 1961 he looked at the subject of data networks. His influential findings were published in 1964 as *Information Flow in Large Communication Nets*.

He had drawn on past reviews of telephone networks and explored the nature of a computer data network, its requirements and how it might behave in busy conditions. He came up with a host of formulae and theorems to suggest when a network might reach its capacity and jam.

This early work by Kleinrock was highly theoretic without ambition to develop a product. It would lie dormant for some years only to re-emerge when he was a professor at UCLA.

Larry Roberts and Thomas Marill at MIT's Lincoln Laboratory in 1965 linked up its TX-2 on the east coast with an SDC Q-32 on the west coast across a standard telephone line. In this manner a time-share computer could then run a program remotely on another. This was a very early dial-up call and the first WAN (wide area network).

4 - It was rocket science – the PC catalyst

'Success consists of going from failure to failure without loss of enthusiasm.'
Winston Churchill

Convict No N1442

Of course personal computers came about because of an accumulation of ideas and incidents, innovations, individuals and institutions. But if you do try to seek out a single moment in history that ignited the development of the personal computer then implausibly you need to travel back to a gulag labour camp in eastern Siberia.

It was a Ukrainian referred to there as convict # N1442, who would provide the vital catalyst that would accelerate real progress towards personal computing.

He was a scientist arrested in Stalin's Great Purge of 1938. Hundreds of thousands were imprisoned and accused of Trotskyist leanings, espionage, sabotage or conspiracy against the Soviet Union.

N1442 was badly beaten during his interrogation at the KGB headquarters. His jaw was broken and he was convicted to serve a forced labour term in the Kolyma gold mines. This was considered to be a death camp as many died there, some of exposure or malnutrition. Many were simply overworked in the mines or became victims of accidents and beatings by guards and fellow inmates.

The harsh weather and poor diet contrived to give N1442 scurvy and he lost all his teeth. Yet he survived all of this to be transferred to a camp where scientists and engineers were set to work on a number of major Soviet projects; he would serve six years in total.

Sergey Korolyov, aka N1442, worked on the design of both the Tupolev bomber (Tupolev was a fellow inmate) and the Petlyakov dive bomber, but progressively he was able to move towards working on rocket science. This had been his interest in his pre-war career at the RNII, the Soviet Jet Propulsion Research Institute.

For the success of his work during WWII, Korolyov was given the rank of colonel in the Red Army and was well-decorated. He was a trusted member of the team despatched to Germany just before the end of the war seeking to recover V-2 rocket technology.

The German war effort of course is renowned as a key birthplace of rocketry. Russia and the USA, soon-to-become post-war superpowers, grabbed as many German rocket scientists as they could as a basis for their upcoming space race.

Heeresversuchsanstalt Peenemünde, or HVP, was one of five Third Reich military proving-grounds, each working under the guidance of the German Army Weapons Office. Directed by Dr Wernher von Braun its pinnacle was the development of the V-2 guided missile. It was there where anti-aircraft rockets were produced, a wind tunnel was built that could reach Mach 4.4 and the first closed-circuit television system was also created.

Once Peenemünde's significance became known to the Allies, they mounted a number of raids to level the site. As a result, the Germans had been in the process of relocating it as WWII drew towards its close.

The race to take Berlin was key to that WWII endgame, but there was another separate headlong rush and this was to acquire the Peenemünde scientists.

The American OSS (Office of Strategic Services) mounted Operation Paperclip pursuing German scientists to get them to agree to work for the USA. In total some 1,800 scientists and technicians were clipped off to the USA including a large number of rocket scientists.

Of course this was an extremely sensitive matter. Anyone with a clear Nazi Party membership or who had actively helped the Nazi war effort was not to be included. Though Von Braun obviously fell within this category the Joint Intelligence Objectives Agency circumvented this by creating false legends for him and for others. A whole raft of aerospace engineers was acquired in this manner; the USA and UK netted some $10bn of value in patents and processes by this effort.

The Russians had actually reached the Peenemünde site first, finding it heavily bomb-damaged. Their own operation *Osoaviakhim* (named after a 1930s Soviet group of aerospace and rocketry enthusiasts) 'imported' 2,200 specialists in the fields of aviation, nuclear technology, rocketry, electronics, radar technology and chemistry.

Object PS-1

Korolyov returned home accompanied by 150 German rocket scientists and helped to set up a new institute in the suburbs of Moscow. From there he took the German V-2 design forward to develop the Soviet R-2, R-3 and R-5 ballistic missiles. But his long-term interest was in using rockets for space travel and he proposed the creation of the R-7 for launching satellites from as early as 1954.

The years 1957 and 1958 were designated by the international scientific community to be the International Geophysical Year; the 'year' actually lasted for eighteen months. As part of this 'celebration', US President Dwight D Eisenhower proudly announced on 29 July 1955 that Americans would launch a satellite as part of this special year.

Ten days later the Political Bureau of the Central Committee of the Communist Party of the Soviet Union, aka its Presidium, gave Korolyov the go-ahead to launch a satellite in response to the American announcement.

In a little under a month Korolyov personally managed the assembly of a satellite he called Object PS-1. It was launched by a modified two-stage R-7 rocket which had a chequered history to say the least.

Of previous launches the first R-7 lasted just 98 seconds. The second failed to take off at all despite three attempts. The third R-7 developed a longitudinal rotation and had to be exploded 33 seconds into its flight. The fourth achieved take-off and flew for 6,000km (3,700 miles) but then had to be destroyed at an altitude of 10 km (6.2 miles) when its head separated on re-entry to the atmosphere. The fifth had a successful launch but again exhibited a head problem. Not terribly confidence inspiring.

So this latest modified R-7 was to be only the sixth attempt at launch, its payload was to be the Object PS-1. Helpfully there was some degree of slack as this satellite was a tad smaller than the R-7 had been designed to handle. This sixth R-7 was subsequently named the Sputnik Rocket and its payload became Sputnik 1, the Russian word meaning simply 'satellite'.

Sputnik 1 achieved an elliptical orbit on 4 October 1957, travelling at 29,000km/hour (18,000mph) and taking 96.2 minutes on each orbit of Earth. Its signal was listened to from all around the world for 22 days until its batteries died; it fell back to earth ninety days later on 4 January 1958.

The Sputnik launch threw the USA into complete disarray, initially not according to US leaders who dismissed it as merely a neat trick. It was the US citizenry that developed a collective hysteria - they still had fresh recollections of the country's unpreparedness for Pearl Harbour. It was not rocket science to realise that with this technology the Russians would soon be able to deliver a nuclear warhead to any point on the globe.

A leading political aide, trying to muster some government enthusiasm, pointed out that the Russians had taken a whole four years to catch up with the US atomic bomb technology, only nine months to catch up with the hydrogen bomb, but now it was the US that would need to catch up in the space race.

Lyndon B Johnson, Vice President to John F Kennedy, later summed up the feelings of the American public,

'In the eyes of the world, first in space means first, period; second in space is second in everything.'

The Russians compounded the injury when Sputnik 2 carried the first animal into orbit, a dog called Laika. For propaganda purposes this was launched less than a month later to coincide with the 40th anniversary of the October Revolution.

Playing catch-up

As a result of the Sputnik furore, just four months later in February 1958 President Eisenhower created the Advanced Research Projects Agency (ARPA). It later became DARPA; the added D for Defense. Even today the mission statement shown on its website has echoes of the paranoia engendered by the Russian satellite,

'...to maintain the technological superiority of the US military and prevent technological surprise from threatening our national security.'

President Eisenhower presided over the spend of more than a billion dollars on research and development in the aftermath of Sputnik. His Secretary of Defense, Neil H McElroy, suggested,

'...the Soviet Union is farther advanced scientifically than many had realised...', '...the weapons of the future may be a great deal closer upon us than we had thought, and therefore the ultimate survival of the Nation depends more than ever before on the speed and skill with which we can pursue the development of advanced weapons...'

As a result McElroy authorised the Air Force Thor and the Army Jupiter Intermediate-Range Ballistic Missiles (IRBMs) into production before tests had been completed. He also moved quickly to speed up the navy's Polaris IRBM and the Air Force's ICBM (InterContinental Ballistic Missile), namely the Atlas and the Titan. He also set about developing the Minuteman missile and its underground silos.

But more importantly, for our subject matter, in 1958 McElroy was appointed to manage ARPA, initially responsible for research and development into anti-missile weapons and satellites.

McElroy appointed Roy W Johnson to run ARPA. Johnson was a VP from General Electric Corp. who had been active in a recent decentralization exercise at that company; McElroy had met with him while at Proctor & Gamble. Johnson agreed to a two-year term and also accepted a drop in salary from $61,000pa to just $18,000pa to run ARPA - though he did get to keep his GE shares!

ARPA quickly set about advancing research and development across all scientific disciplines, though in 1960 it was instructed to hand all its civilian space programs back to NASA and the military programs back to the military services. NASA of course continued to fund a great deal of effort into miniaturisation and computer techniques. It also advanced research in many other areas including computer graphics, expert systems, database management, virtual reality...

Subsequently ARPA was charged with finding unique and innovative research in the private sector, in academe and other non-profit organisations, as well as within its own government and military laboratories.

ARPA, founded as a knee-jerk reaction to the fear of being surpassed by the Soviets, had early and significant success in identifying many of the most significant individuals and creative groups based around the USA. Having been identified they were encouraged and funded. It was ARPA's activity that led to the development of both the PC and the Internet.

So it was Korolyov's Sputnik that lit the blue touch paper that inspired the foundation of ARPA. This in turn ignited a whole generation of individuals and creative clusters.

IPTO facto – time share

In the 1960s ARPA's division the Information Processing Techniques Office (IPTO) set out to develop advanced computers and computing networks. It poured massive funds into some thirteen research groups, about thirty times the previous norm, and it also funded their access to the latest equipment.

IPTO provided funds to MIT and the University of California Berkeley to develop techniques for time-sharing; to Scientific Data Systems to develop the SDS 940 as part of Project Genie; to MIT and Stanford to set up Artificial Intelligence (AI) labs; to the University of Utah to create advances in computer graphics; to Doug Engelbart's Augmentation Research Center, for developments including On-line System (NLS); to the Xerox PARC team to advance its myriad of R&D activities; to create computer science graduate programs initially at Stanford and Purdue in Indiana and later at Berkeley, Carnegie Mellon and MIT; to create the ARPANET and subsequently the Internet.

The most significant advance that the US government and ARPA's IPTO achieved for computing was support for those showing interest in the development of computer time-share systems. Post-war computers were big and expensive and IPTO concluded was that the way forward was to allow users to share these scarce resources. It was acknowledged that users had bursts of data entry followed by quiet periods and so the notion of interlacing users or timeshare was born.

By helping to develop the techniques and technologies for time-sharing of mainframe computers it certainly gave more individuals access to the power of large computers. But perhaps inadvertently it sowed the seeds of discontent too. Many who became computer literate were soon frustrated by their limited access and this led to the conception of a more personal form of computing.

In 1957 John McCarthy at MIT developed the first time-share approach which resulted in its Compatible Time-Sharing System (CTSS). The word compatible referred to its being able to operate with the IBM 7094's FORTRAN Monitor System. It was demonstrated first in November 1961.

Fernando José, or Corby, Corbató joined the MIT Computation Center after graduating and spent the rest of his working life at MIT. When McCarthy left to join Project MAC it was Corbató who became the prime architect of CTSS which only ever operated in two locations.

During this period he originated what he called Corbató's Law which stated,

'The number of lines of code a programmer can write in a fixed period of time is the same regardless of the language used.'

CTSS did influence IBM to issue its time-share systems CP/CMS, Control Program/Cambridge Monitor System. This early IBM time-share system featured an inter-user messaging system, one of the earliest forms of electronic mail.

It was against this background that J C R Licklider as the head of IPTO provided $2 million to fund a large collaborative project at MIT known as Project MAC (project on mathematics and computation).

The word 'project' however is confusing as what was established was essentially a new laboratory that worked on many aspects of advanced computing. But Robert Fano, its first director, realised there were financial and political benefits within MIT if it remained Project MAC rather than be considered a competing lab.

As part of this effort the MIT team, which included McCarthy and Marvin Minsky, set about developing a time-share operating system based upon their experience. By 1964 Licklider had moved on and it was Ivan Sutherland who was to continue the funding.

The field was busy. Over 1963/4 Dartmouth developed the Dartmouth Time Sharing System, the first large-scale time-share service. Around this time MIT with GE and Bell had first used a DEC computer to manage a telephone switch, making the first connection between the networks of the past and of the future. By 1965 Western Electric had introduced the first public switched telephone network (PSTN) which had a computer at its heart so any user could call any other user directly.

MIT, again supported by GE and Bell within Project MAC, announced a new system in 1965 called MULTICS (multiplexed information and computing service). Corbató had also been the team leader for MULTICS.

The advances that Project MAC developed, not just in time-sharing operating systems but also in artificial intelligence and other areas, influenced IPTO to advance time-share technology further.

In 1965 it assisted DEC in providing the first commercially-available time-share system. Based upon one of its PDP-6s, as its time-share operating system it used a very early version of what would become TOPS-10.

The MIT Tech Model Railroad Club (TMRC) hackers took exception to the notion of having to continue to share their access. They believed the MULTICS system would prove to be too slow and too limiting and they also disliked the security system it had adopted.

As a result the hackers produced their own version using a PDP-6 to create what they called Incompatible Timesharing System (ITS). This preserved an open approach and brought a number of significant improvements to the art.

However in 1968 the ITS system was judged as too insecure when a meeting was convened to agree a standard time-share system for the new DEC

PDP-10. Academics and corporates instead chose a 'safe pair of hands' and opted for the Bolt Beranek & Newman system called TENEX, developed by Daniel Bobrow, Jerry D Burchfiel, Daniel Murphy and Ray Tomlinson.

ARPA's IPTO also assisted Max Palevsky and others at Scientific Data Systems (SDS); which was founded in September 1961.

SDS had worked closely with NASA to produce the first non-military silicon transistor computer - the SDS 910. The first installation of this computer was at the Goddard Space Flight Centre. NASA in fact routinely purchased 40% of the SDS production capacity for use with its telemetry, control and simulation requirements.

Receiving ARPA money for time-share development, SDS worked with the University of California to develop the second commercially available time-share product called Tymshare.

Bob Taylor had been working on flight simulation at Martin Marietta and from there moved to NASA in 1961. While at NASA he released another source of funds for SDS and others. He was recruited to ARPA's IPTO, initially to assist Sutherland and later taking over as IPTO director from 1966.

Licklider had returned to MIT by 1968 to become director of Project MAC while also remaining a professor in the Department of Electrical Engineering at MIT. By then IPTO's investment had created a very flexible operating system that was to become broadly adopted; MULTICS had some fifty time-share installations around the world.

Bell Labs had however concluded that MULTICS had grown too complex and withdrew its support from Project MAC. Instead Bell adopted GE's operating system GECOS for its internal use.

Ken Thompson, Dennis Ritchie, M D McIlroy, and J F Ossanna were among the last of the Bell team members who had worked on MULTICS and they were none too impressed by GECOS. They decided to design their own operating system that would retain the multi-user communal environment that MULTICS had created.

While working on the PDP-7, Thompson and Ritchie created an operating system during 1970 which addressed a single user approach. Another team member named it Uniplexed Information and Computing System (UNICS), but really of course it was a reference to MULTICS. But once the operating system became multi-user it was renamed as UNIX.

Part of the allure of UNIX was that it wrote the main items of the operating system in a kernel that was just 11,000 lines of code. In comparison, twenty or so years later Windows NT 3.1 had well over five million lines of code!

C Programming language emerged from the work on UNIX at Bell Labs. It was called C simply because it derived from an earlier version called B! In 1978 Brian Kernighan and Dennis Ritchie published a book to formalise C.

The language became so useful that in 1972/3 UNIX was rewritten in the C programming language. Some 10,000 of the lines of code were changed into the high-level language rather than machine code. This made it extremely portable, requiring just a little work to port it from platform to platform - and it took off.

In 1974 Bob Fabry at the University of California Berkeley acquired DARPA funding to look at improving UNIX. He already had an AT&T licence for UNIX and used the funding to create the Computer Systems Research Group. It issued Berkeley UNIX or BSD (Berkeley Software Distribution) from 1977.

These government investments were more than justified by the inspiration supplied to those who subsequently helped create the PC market.

For example in 1968 a certain Bill Gates, then just thirteen years old, had the good fortune that the mothers' club at his school used monies generated by a rummage sale to fund its time-share activity.

This was provided by a teletype terminal, rented at $89 per month, providing access to a local General Electric computer at $8 per hour. Gates used this to learn how to program in BASIC, his first effort in programming being a tic-tac-toe or noughts and crosses game. His software allowed the player to compete against the computer.

Later the school hired time on a DEC PDP-10 owned by a local organisation the Computer Center Corporation (CCC). Gates and Paul Allen spent so much time on it that they felt the need to hack into it. They exploited system weaknesses so their usage would not be logged and gave them free access.

When this breach was discovered the CCC initially banned them and two other fellow students for the intrusion. But with time they were able to demonstrate their skills and the CCC would hire them to help seek out the bugs inherent within the system.

All in a whirl

If the ignition sequence for PCs was the Sputnik and ARPA, then a separate strand that led towards the personal computer can be traced to MIT, the Massachusetts Institute of Technology. MIT was founded in 1861 to focus on science and technology. It took a more European approach to learning by including significant laboratory work.

Sadly its founding was somewhat upstaged bare weeks after gaining its charter by the outbreak of the American Civil War. Despite the inauspicious timing of its origins MIT grew to merit seventy-five Nobel Prizewinners and almost fifty National Medal of Science winners, so it has clearly proven to be a remarkable institution.

One of MIT's major figures would become a significant PC thinker and pioneer, Vannevar Bush. Bush was the MIT vice-president and Dean of Engineering throughout the 1930s.

In WWII Bush was appointed to the Office of Scientific Research and Development from where he arranged the flow of research funding to generate developments of use to the war effort. MIT was a notable recipient of these funds, growing to become the largest US R&D contractor of the war.

MIT's Radiation Laboratory worked extensively on radar during WWII. Its Instrumentation Laboratory concentrated on systems such as gyroscopes, bomb sights and post-war it contributed heavily to Polaris and the Apollo missions.

Pre-Sputnik fears already existed concerning the US readiness against air attacks. The Soviet development of an A-bomb in 1949 and its success with long-range bombers had triggered terrestrial concern. But it required Sputnik to expand its thinking to consider attacks from space.

In the post-war period MIT had taken another major step forward following a report in 1950 by the Air Defense Systems Engineering Committee that concluded the USA was not prepared for an air attack.

MIT's Radiation Laboratory had worked closely with the committee through the war and its proven skills in electronics led to the establishment by federal funding of the Lincoln Laboratory at MIT in 1951. Its charter was to investigate how to use advanced technology to handle the problems of national security; today its mission statement is still *Technical in Support of National Security*.

One of the Lincoln Laboratory's early roles was to take forward an earlier MIT project, the Whirlwind computer. Initially this was to be a replacement for the Link Trainer.

Edwin Link had been an organ and nickelodeon builder (just the sort of person Charles Babbage had despised and railed against!). Link was also a keen pilot but not being able to afford to log much flying time he used his past experience with bellows and valves to develop a flight simulator.

His progress with this technology was greatly assisted by what the newspapers came to call the Air Mail Fiasco of the 1930s. The Army Air Corps had been designated to fly the Air Mail service in the United States and in the first eleven weeks of their running the service twelve of their pilots had been killed.

To make his point about the value of his instrument training and simulators Link flew to a meeting with the Army Air Corps through a fog, a fog that the Corps itself would have considered to be far too dangerous for its pilots to take off.

Link went on to produce a whole series of these trainers that were used by all the Allied countries during the war. In total some 500,000 pilots were trained on them. Now MIT was being asked to seek to improve on that significant performance!

MIT's first attempt involved building a large analogue computer but this proved to be far too unreliable. One of the team attended a demonstration of the Electronic Numerical Integrator and Computer (ENIAC) and was inspired instead to create a computer. But it could not be a computer that would merely take a set of instructions and chunter away until it came to a conclusion; they clearly needed to innovate for this application.

Jay Wright Forrester had been developing feedback control systems and servo-mechanisms for radar and gun turrets during the war and proved to be the right person to take on this project. It was he who convinced the navy to go digital for a solution.

Forrester and Robert Everett came up with a design in 1947 but the project went through many twists and turns and its objectives were frequently modified along the way. The major innovation was to change the previous method of feeding information into computers bit by bit and instead to use a parallel 16-bit input.

Whirlwind went on line in April 1951. It was the first computer to operate in real-time as it responded directly to the pilot's actions. But Whirlwind was soon to have a second career to handle air defence applications.

J Halcombe Laning worked at MIT on the Whirlwind project and in 1958 he and Neal Zierler developed MAC (MIT Algebraic Compiler). This was the very first operating algebraic compiler that could directly accept standard algebraic formulae and convert them into useable machine code.

Forrester's team soon become frustrated with the unreliability of the British-designed Williams-Kilburn tubes that Whirlwind used as memory. One of Forrester's students, William Papian, developed an approach for core memory in his thesis entitled *A Coincident-Current Magnetic Memory Unit*. This allowed a relatively small number of wires to control a large number of toroidal cores.

For this development Forrester is usually credited with inventing the first magnetic core memory, a random access memory technology that so improved reliability that it rapidly spread throughout the early computer market. However it was Frederick Viehe, implausibly an inspector of streets for the Los Angeles Department of Public Works, who was granted the first patent back in 1947 for work he had done on core memory in his home laboratory.

Harvard-based An Wang, later of word-processing fame, co-developed a pulse transfer control device that took core memory to another level. He created a write-after-read cycle that overcame the problem of reading data.

The process usually erased the data when it was read but Wang's system would automatically restore the record after reading it.

Core memory was quickly adopted by the computer industry, and was the memory of choice for twenty years until semiconductor IC memories would take over.

Establishing wisdom - SAGE

MIT resources for the Whirlwind project had become extremely stretched and the US military was considering scrapping it when in August 1949 the Soviets detonated their first atom bomb. The ensuing concern resurrected interest in the project, and plans were advanced for a faster and larger Whirlwind II.

Lincoln Laboratory took the Whirlwind experiences forward to develop an approach for a new government requirement called Semi Automatic Ground Environment (SAGE). It was Whirlwind's real-time processing of data was seen as the basis for an air defence system for North America.

The SAGE application was designed to collect and analyse data from the US radar network which led directly to the development of what was then the world's largest computer. The MIT team reviewed IBM, Remington Rand and Raytheon as potential partners in the project. IBM was selected and the teams jointly developed what they called the IBM AN/FSQ-7. This computer drew upon the planning for Whirlwind II and is often confused as Whirlwind II itself- although it was not.

IBM AN/FSQ-7 took up a half-acre of floor space (2,000 sq m), it weighed in at over 275 tons (tonnes) and it used 3 megawatts of power to run its 55,000 vacuum tubes, hundreds of which would burn out and be replaced every single day. Each SAGE installation used two of these monsters for 'built-in redundancy' and the arrangement did achieve a high degree of reliability.

Fifty-two of these were built and linked together to manage three combat centres, twenty-four direction centres and over a hundred radar-tracking sites. This was in fact to be the first large-scale wide-area computer network.

At a total cost of $8bn this was a huge undertaking but its real returns would be in the ideas that were generated and inspired by those who worked on the ground-breaking (or more accurately air-probing) project.

For example SAGE was the first to use screens, some 150 Cathode Ray Tube (CRT) monitors with light pens; prior to this entries and outcomes had been via switches, lights and punched cards. The use of screens would be adopted by those that came behind them.

The Systems Development Corporation (SDC) was formed as a systems engineering group for SAGE. When IBM designed a system for the US Strategic Air Command, its AN/FSQ-32 or Q-32 solid state computer was installed at SDC, this group went on to originate compiler and operating software including a time-share system.

SAGE pushed the development of computer software into many new innovations that took advantage of an early series of subroutines that acted as a sort of compiler and ran to 25,000 instructions; huge for 1955.

The SAGE computer hardware developments soon prompted the first mass-produced computer, the IBM 704 Electronic Data-Processing Machine in May 1954.

It is believed that IBM veered away from using the word 'computer' for its 700 series because this word had become too heavily associated with the UNIVAC. Yet this calculator took up a whole room and needed its own air conditioning plant.

It operated on the stored-program approach, solving a problem or processing data by following a set of instructions previously stored in the machine's memory, which in the 704's case was high-speed magnetic core storage, replacing the Williams-Kilburn tube used on earlier models in the IBM 700 range. The string of magnetic core doughnuts meant the 704 could access any item in 12 millionths of a second! It also had magnetic drum storage; this approach was soon in use at Bell Labs and MIT where many developments in software evolved.

Many interesting individuals were involved with the 704 design – Gene Amdahl who would later set up in opposition with funding from Fujitsu; John Backus, who had worked on the SSEC and led the group to develop the FORTRAN language.

The SAGE air-defence network generated a need for reliable data communication and this led to the first mass-produced modulator-demodulator (modem) device in 1958. These Bell-produced modems connected all the radar bases and air bases to the command and control centres using acoustic modems operating at just 110 baud or bits/second. They chose to use dedicated lines but the technology would have worked across the standard phone network.

AT&T/Bell went on to design a phone using data signals rather than the original analogue system and released a modem for general use by 1960.

SAGE was the first large-scale computer network and therefore its impact in so many areas cannot be underestimated. In 1953 a piece of serendipity occurred on an American Airlines flight. An IBM salesman, R Blair Smith, sat next to the airline's president, C R Smith. Having the same surname (hardly remarkable!) prompted a conversation and the IBM man was very familiar with SAGE.

The airline had been working on something it had given the glorious name of the Magnetronic Reservisor, an electromechanical computer to move it away from its current manual card-index reservations' system. Routinely these reservations handled manually took the airline anything from ninety minutes to three hours!

This chance in-flight conversation led to IBM submitting a proposal leading to the development of the Semi-Automated Business Research Environment (SABRE), a computerised reservations system based on two IBM 7090s. It was first operational in 1960 at a development cost variously stated as between $40m and $150m; and that's in 1950s dollars!

IBM went on to develop similar systems for PanAm and Delta airlines and by 1968 their work was made more generally available as the Programmed Airline Reservation System, by then ported to the IBM System/360. It continued to evolve and by 1976 it was interconnected to travel agents too.

By the 1980s reservations were made available via both CompuServe and GEnie. In 2000 SABRE itself was spun away from American Airlines and today connects consumers to 400 airlines, 50 car rental operators, 35,000 hotels plus cruise lines, ferries and rail operators. All built upon a chance meeting - and SAGE.

Switching from valves to transistors

MIT's Lincoln Laboratory managed an effort to transistorise the Whirlwind. The first attempt was the TX-0 (transistorised experimental computer zero), pronounced 'ticks-oh'.

The TX-0 took up just a room where Whirlwind had needed a full building to itself. It had a range of input-output options; a Flexowriter; a paper-tape reader; a 12" (30cm) CRT screen able to display 512 x 512 points on a 7" square (16cm) area.

It was built at the Lincoln Lab by Wes Clark as the key logic designer and Ken Olsen as the engineer. Ben Gurly designed its display, the approach being the basis for his later design of the PDP-1.

In 1958 the TX-O was dismantled and moved to MIT where it took John McKenzie as operations manager a hundred days to reassemble and test it.

In 1958 John McCarthy at MIT developed the LISP language, the second high-level language ever created, which followed his earlier IPL (Information Programming Language).

LISP (List Processing) had first been inspired at a 1956 conference at Dartmouth College, which also inspired the development of Dartmouth's BASIC language; both were efforts focused on evolving software in to artificial intelligence.

The next development was to have been the TX-1 but it ran in to problems and so it was leap-frogged to consider a much smaller TX-2, also designed by Wes Clark and this was produced by 1958.

TX-2 was designed to speed up the arithmetic while maintaining reliability; it worked in 36-bit words and had a RAM capacity of 262,144 words. The TX-2 had even more input-output opportunities, flexowriters, paper-tape readers, magnetic-tape writers for storage, CRT screens, a high-speed printer, data links to other computers, an analogue to digital converter...

This was the first computer with a graphics capability, though it was still intended as a research tool for data-processing and scientific applications of a real time nature and not a product for sale.

Minicomputers

The first minicomputer was designed in 1961 at the Lincoln Laboratory by Charles Molnar and Wes Clark. This was the Laboratory Instrument Computer (LINC) designed for the US National Institutes of Health to work specifically with the analogue inputs and outputs from a host of bio-med laboratory experiments.

The tabletop computer, priced at over $43,000, was not inexpensive but compared with what else was available at the time this was a very significant development. The first LINC was available in early 1962 and around fifty of these were built, many by DEC as the subcontractor. The LINC had been placed securely in the public domain by MIT but this notion was not to last.

By then Ken Olsen had become disenchanted and quit before LINC's completion. He left the MIT team and with Charles Molnar and Harlan Anderson founded Digital Equipment Corporation (DEC) and used the work on the TX range to create a saleable product.

The American Research and Development Corporation gave DEC its initial venture capital funding of $70k and for this seedcorn investment was eventually to realise $450m; nice work if you can get it!

Much of the early running in mini-computing was to be made by DEC. Ben Gurley joined from the Lincoln Laboratory in 1957. He laid down the design in just three and a half months for its first computer, the PDP-1 (Program-Data-Processor) that was based heavily upon the TX-O and TX-2 experience.

Gordon Bell was recruited from MIT's Speech Computation Laboratory. Bell designed the input/output (I/O) for the PDP-1 launched in 1960.

RANDOM ACCESS MOMENT:
Bell described in 1972 something he termed his 'Law of Computer Classes'. In essence he suggested that the increase in capability and decrease in price would mean that every decade or so computing would evolve a new class of computer. So it proved to be, with mainframes in the '50s and '60s giving way to minicomputers in the '60s and '70s, then networked workstations and PCs in the '80s, web-server browser PCs in the '90s, portable hand-held PCs in the mid '90s, web services and cellphone PCs in the 2000s, and he forecasts that in the 2010s the new class will be based upon home and body networks.

DEC appeared to deliberately choose a name that avoided the use of the 'emotive' term computer. The PDP-1's stated goals were simple - a fast and relatively inexpensive system. Though at a price of over $100,000 with just 4,000 bytes of memory the word relative sounds something of a stretch, yet compared to the seven-figure sums of its predecessors this was probably justified. They sold only fifty units but it set DEC on its way in evolving the market in mini-computing.

Olsen outlined and then countered the established wisdom of the time,
'Computers are serious, you shouldn't treat them lightly. You shouldn't have fun with them. They shouldn't be exciting. They should be formal and distant with red tape involved. That was the atmosphere at the time.

...we believed computers should be fun. They were exciting. They could do so many things. The opportunities were just without bounds. This was a great motivation in building a computer.'

The PDP-1 was the first of the long-lived DEC PDP range of computers that moved the focus from mainframes towards the minicomputer.

But there was clearly no friction between the parties. Olsen donated the second PDP-1 to MIT's Research Laboratory of Electronics, where the Tech Model Railroad Club members would take it to their hearts and use it to pursue their diverse ambitions – and definitely to have fun with it.

DEC was approached by a Canadian Atomic Energy Research group to design something that would control an atomic pile by handling a whole series of equations, many of which could not at the time be well-defined. DEC therefore chose to design its PDP-4 to be more a process controller than a programmable computer, though their customers could customise them.

By 1963 the PDP-5 was launched as the world's first commercially produced mini-computer, and by 1964 this had evolved using the latest technology into the PDP-8, at a price tag of just $16,000. With its compact size the PDP-8 successfully opened up a whole new world of commercial applications. In its various configurations this 12-bit minicomputer went on to sell over 300,000 units.

DEC's success led to many minicomputer competitors springing up along Route 128 in Massachusetts - Apollo, Data General, Prime, Wang...

Olsen and the Family

DEC subsequently launched the PDP-11 and the VAX series in the 1970s, but by the mid-70s they started to be surpassed by lower-cost microcomputers. This did not stop Olsen from being named by *Fortune Magazine* as 'America's most successful entrepreneur' in 1986. Around that time he made an interesting comment that many have still not come to appreciate,
'Some people study computers and don't learn anything else. Computers are just tools to do something...'

Certainly there are those who would appear to adopt computing as an end in itself, almost a religious commitment to the mere tool.

Olsen is also famous for providing massive funding from his DEC revenues into a secretive organisation called The Family or The Fellowship; it is a powerful and curious mix of religion and politics.

The most overt activity of this group is the National Prayer Breakfast held every February for fifty years. Every president since Eisenhower has attended one, George W Bush attended in 2008 and said of The Family,

'The people in this room come from many different walks of faith. Yet we share one clear conviction: We believe that the Almighty hears our prayers -- and answers those who seek Him.'

In recent years the invited keynote speakers to the National Prayer Breakfast have been big-hitters – King Abdullah of Jordan in 2006, the director of the Human Genome Project in 2007 and ex-British Prime Minister Tony Blair in 2009.

The leader Doug Coe also regularly attends weekly prayer meetings at the US Senate, which leads many to question whether this secretive network of fundamentalist Christians has an undue influence over American policy.

One author John Sharlet suggests,

'The Family wants to "transcend" (political) left and right with a faith that consumes politics, replacing fundamental differences with the unity to be found in submission to religious authority.'

When they do reveal something of themselves, Coe and his group appear controversial. As an example, he strongly urges a personal commitment to Jesus Christ but often draws upon tales of the followers of Hitler and Chairman Mao to be some sort of metaphor for the commitment, the type of blind faith that he expects of his followers. Further, a number of US senators revealed to be involved in sex scandals were also found to be prominent in 'The Family'.

Olsen retired from DEC in 1992 aged sixty-six. DEC was eventually acquired by Compaq in 1998. Compaq then merged with Hewlett-Packard in 2002.

Space men

Things started to turn full circle as the computers that rocket science engendered and funded started to appear aboard rockets, and then several of the individual PC innovators flew into space too.

The GRiD Systems Corporation laptop was to be the first into space. One of its portables became known as SPOC (Shuttle Portable Onboard Computer) when it was used by astronaut John Young on a December 1983 flight.

Charles Simonyi (Xerox PARC and Office Suite at Microsoft) let it be known that he wanted to become a space tourist in 2006. He signed up for a ten-day trip to the International Space Station (ISS).

First he was trained and tested by the Russian Federal Space Agency. He flew aboard a Soyuz rocket in April 2007, with his return flight delayed giving him a full eleven days on the ISS. In March 2009 he took a second trip again using Soyuz to spend a further twelve days aboard ISS. While there he pursued another of his passions sending amateur radio messages back to a number of schools.

Richard Garriott, aka Lord British, a Brit born in Cambridge but living in Houston Texas where his father was an astronaut; his father flew on both a Skylab and a Space Shuttle mission.

Garriott got the PC bug about the same time as he encountered the book *Lord of the Rings* and the game Dungeons & Dragons. He started writing fantasy games and in 1979/80 while working at a ComputerLand store, produced one of the first role playing games called Akalabeth for the Apple II.

The owner of the store encouraged him to sell the game and California Pacific Computer Company, offered distribution. Together they sold 30,000 copies, with his earnings at $5 per unit used to enrol him at the University of Texas.

He subsequently developed Ultima and again it was published by California Pacific Computer Company. It was a big success, enough to buy a car and start investing in property and businesses. California Pacific went in to decline and disappeared by 1982. Ultima 1 attracted the attention of Sierra On-line and Garriott was signed to them for a 30% royalty. At its launch the Sirius-published Ultima II generated back orders in the tens of thousands - at $59.95 each.

Garriott was later to follow his father into space when he took a trip aboard a Soyuz craft. In October 2008 he travelled to and stayed on the ISS for twelve days. It apparently cost him $30m to become the sixth 'space tourist'. He was the second 'second-generation' space traveller; Sergei Volkov was the first having followed his father Aleksandr into space.

Lord English was only the second to wear the Union Jack on his kit, the first was Helen Sharman; Michael Foale, Nicholas Patrick and Piers Sellers, although British each flew under the American flag.

There was a complete reversal of roles when computers began to fund rocket research.

Elon Musk, a South African, was one of the innovators behind PayPal, the online payment service. Musk was one of those who really espoused the original dot.com boom; his first venture was Zip2 which he sold on to Compaq for $300m to be merged into AltaVista.

Musk used $100m of his funds to launch SpaceX (Space Exploration Technologies) in 2002. It set out to develop the Falcon 1 and Falcon 9 rockets and a spacecraft called Dragon with a goal of reducing space flight costs by a factor of 100.

In 2008 NASA granted Musk a multi-billion contract for twelve flights using the Falcon 9 to carry freight to the ISS, given that the Space Shuttle program was to be closed during 2011.

In September 2009 the Falcon 1 became the first privately-funded liquid-fuelled launch of a satellite into orbit. Musk has strong views,

'An asteroid or a super volcano could destroy us, and we face risks the dinosaurs never saw: An engineered virus, inadvertent creation of a micro black hole, catastrophic global warming or some as-yet-unknown technology could spell the end of us. Humankind evolved over millions of years, but in the last sixty years atomic weaponry created the potential to extinguish ourselves. Sooner or later, we must expand life beyond this green and blue ball - or go extinct.'

5 - PARC and ride – Xerox designs the PC

'Research is what I'm doing when I don't know what I'm doing.' Wernher von Braun

Xerox to rival IBM

In 1969 Xerox spent over $900m in stock to acquire Scientific Data Systems (SDS), an operation that had been supported by ARPA. Xerox planned this both as a move to enter the computer market and to seek to develop 'The Office of the Future'.

The two principals Peter McColough, the CEO at Xerox, and Max Palevsky of SDS were also somewhat blinded by the notion that their combined strengths would move them towards supremacy over rival IBM.

Even the BUNCH (Burroughs, Univac, NCR, Control Data and Honeywell) had lost over $150m in the '60s versus the $3.5 billion in profits recorded by IBM. So a plan to come close to IBM's success was something of a big ask. SDS had less than a 1% share of the US market at this point; under Xerox it was to fare no better.

In seeking to achieve their goals for the acquisition McColough concluded that they would need to expand their research capabilities with a new facility that was initially called the 'Xerox Advance Scientific & Systems Laboratory'.

By March 1970 Xerox decided it should be deliberately located away from its current copier research facility and so established itself in California. It was renamed the Xerox Palo Alto Research Center, or PARC, and located right at the heart of Silicon Valley within the Stanford Research Park.

PARC's prime mission was to define and develop 'The Office of the Future'; but PARC would in fact go on to define much of the approach for personal computing.

The intriguing thing in retrospect is that they essentially could have achieved both of their goals – a sincere rival to IBM and the developer of the Office of the Future – if they had followed through with the developments created by the PARC team.

Dr George Pake had a Harvard doctorate in physics. He became a professor at Washington University, its Head of Physics at the age of twenty-eight and later Provost of the University. He was appointed as the first director of Xerox PARC.

George Pake coined a term that the PARC team employed regularly. This was 'error 33' which described when a project failed because it required the prior success of another project; this earlier requirement not having been achieved inevitably created a knock-on effect.

Somewhere along the way in selling I learned and routinely used the term a '22 job'. It was used when you were double-handed in a sales pitch. The one not presenting was better able to see when the prospect did not get a point that was made. By mumbling that it was 'a 22 job' the more engrossed presenter could take the hint and try putting over the point in another way.

The PARC operation was initially planned by Pake to have three divisions: Computer Science Laboratory (CSL); Systems Science Laboratory (SSL); and General Science Laboratory (GSL). But this was later expanded to include: Learning Research Group (LRG) and Systems Development Division (SDD).

Gaggle of gurus

CSL was run by Bob Taylor but only as its 'acting manager'. Taylor had developed an encyclopaedic knowledge of the research scene while heading up ARPA's IPTO but Pake judged that he could not be appointed the actual manager because of his lack of personal research credentials. Yet of course his background proved vital in their being able to identify and recruit the right team.

Taylor, born in Dallas Texas, served in the US Navy during the Korean War and returned to the University of Texas to complete a degree in psychology. His early work was in brain research and after a poorly paid stint as a teacher he applied successfully to join NASA in 1961.

While there he became interested in computing when he met up with Doug Engelbart. He had channeled some of the funding for ARC from NASA and had also helped out with the presentation technology at the 'Mother of all Demos'.

Taylor also met up with J C R Licklider and this eventually led to his being lured to join ARPA and its IPTO operation, working under Ivan Sutherland.

Some mystery surrounds Taylor's work during the Vietnam War, but at just thirty-five years old he was given the rank of brigadier general based on his ARPA status. There he created a common approach in the 'theatre' and had built a computer centre in Saigon.

On his return to the States in 1968 he linked up with Licklider again to prepare an influential paper entitled *The Computer as a Communication Device*. Later as head of IPTO Taylor was in charge of the largest US budget for research. He was responsible for distributing funds to colleges and research laboratories around the USA and worked to encourage them to meet for conference sessions. From this role he became a key player in the development of ARPANET.

When he found that ARPA was being directed more towards military research he left, spending a year at the University of Utah before moving to PARC.

Safely installed at Palo Alto, Taylor was in a unique position to assess the leading lights and the most promising venues of development. He soon used his contacts' list to recruit an amazing team of individuals to join him at PARC's Computer Science Laboratory. Taylor at the centre provided the directional vision, and his relaxed style created an environment that encouraged debate.

His recruitment programme was greatly assisted by the location of the company and two pieces of good timing. The location meant there could be a strong collaboration with a host of graduates at Stanford which was precisely the right place to participate in projects like ARPANET.

Good timing played its part as PARC promptly benefited from the problems at Engelbart's nearby ARC, successfully recruiting a number of the latter's disenchanted team.

The SSL team at PARC soon had Bill English as head of the PARC On-line Office System team (POLOS), English had co-invented the mouse and co-authored the paper for the 'Mother of all Demos'. Jeff Rulifson who had been a key player for the programming of the NLS at ARC also joined the SSL team.

Better still for PARC the Berkeley Computer Corporation (BCC) demise came at just the right moment too. BCC had been granted monies from ARPA to develop its Project Genie time-share system based around an SDS 930 but it had run into difficulties. Taylor initially tried to broker a deal for the operation to be acquired as part of PARC, but when this failed to materialise he moved quickly to recruit a large number of the BCC project team.

This recruitment included Butler Lampson, an operating system designer, and Chuck Thacker, a hardware designer, both of whom would become Turing Award winners for their work at PARC.

They also hired Peter Deutsch who pops up in the PC story regularly, first as a teenager when he was part of the MIT TMRC scene, later as a key member of the Community Memory Project.

Small thinking – Alan Kay

Another key PARC recruitment came from neither of these two sources. While at ARPA and prior to ARPANET Taylor had developed a simple technique to ensure the dissemination of information from colleges and research centres. Many of these were working in similar areas but had no means of cross-fertilising their ideas.

Taylor's scheme was to assemble the players and give each the opportunity to present for an hour; their peers would then challenge the notions expressed. In this way Taylor, who felt he was not as technically brilliant as many of the presenters, but he could watch and gauge from the interchanges where gems might be found.

One presenter got a very rough ride at such a session; this was Alan Kay. He had turned up from the University of Utah where he was working with Ivan Sutherland. He presented his vision for a notebook-sized personal computer he called 'Dynabook'. Kay got short shrift from the critical meeting but he and Taylor had discovered they shared many views on where computing should lead.

Taylor recruited Kay to be the team's 'odd man out', a thinker-philosopher in residence. He did not disappoint, making this early observation about the team's approach,

'The best way to predict the future is to invent it.'

Kay graduated from the University of Colorado in maths and molecular biology, but in the '60s completed his Masters and PhD at the University of Utah, where he met up with Ivan Sutherland and was inspired by his Sketchpad drawing programme.

Kay worked on ARPA research into programming techniques and developed software he called 'FLEX', a flexible extendable language. Subsequently he developed the 'FLEX Machine', an early desktop computer. It drew both upon Engelbart's thinking to have a graphics user interface with a pointing device and multiple screen windows, and on Sutherland's work by adding high-resolution graphics and animation.

FLEX was one of the first devices designed to have an object-oriented operating system. But the work on these projects merely highlighted the pressing need for more research and innovation in the way the user would interface with a computer.

During this project in 1968 Kay met up with Seymour Papert and encountered his Logo language; he learned too of the LISP language. Following on from these meetings and projects Kay conceived the 'Dynabook', a computer that he designed for children – of all ages!

Despite the poor reception for it at the ARPA conference, its description was a pretty accurate prediction of today's laptops, tablet PCs and eBooks.

When Kay joined PARC in 1970 he was hoping that that he might develop the Dynabook, and help the company to invent the future. Kay had the notion that each project on the Dynabook should be considered as a piece of paper, each piled up on a desk with only the topmost fully visible. This would of course become the 'desktop' metaphor that we all now use on our PCs.

He next developed 'Smalltalk' in recognition of the new graphical environments that were being developed at PARC. He set out to provide the means to use these environments to the full as the central software component for his Dynabook. This was the first software language to be fully object-oriented and also the first to include the notion of overlapping windows.

Object-oriented programming (OOP) is intended to make the task of programming easier; though some argue that while it is easier to keep track, the approach usually adds to the program's complexity rather than simplifying it. OOP designs its programs and applications by referring to objects, which are coherent functions or procedures that may for example represent a user profile. The program need only reference the 'object' and then its discrete functions are directly addressed and useable.

This first manifestation of the language was usually referred to as 'Smalltalk-71'; after several changes it became 'Smalltalk-80' which was the first version to be released outside PARC. It was supplied to Apple, DEC, HP and others for evaluation. It would shape both the Apple Lisa and Macintosh computers.

An ANSI Smalltalk was established much later, in 1998, as the de facto standard for the language.

To the max – Lampson and Thacker

Butler Lampson graduated at Harvard and did his PhD at the University of California, Berkeley, where he met up with Chuck Thacker. They both became an integral part of 'Project Genie' and helped to develop the Berkeley Timesharing System on an SDS 940.

RANDOM ACCESS MOMENT:
this was the actual SDS 940 that had been used by Doug Engelbart's NLS, OnLine System, and later turned up as the host and heart of the Community Memory Project established by Lee Felsenstein.

In 1968 they left to co-found the Berkeley Computer Corporation which attracted some $4m in funding and gathered a group of high-flyers from Project Genie and other UCB teams, with others from JPL, UCB, SDS and even MIT. Sadly it failed to find sales and marketing talent so the development of a prototype computer and a raft of good software came to naught and it crashed.

Installed at PARC CSL, Lampson and Thacker soon became the central technologists who helped define many of the projects.

One of CSL's first challenges was to be political rather than technical. The team needed to acquire a time-share computer for its own internal use and they concluded that this should be a DEC PDP-10 so that they would be compatible with others on the developing ARPANET.

But of course Xerox had acquired its own computer system, the SDS, and politically they came under pressure to choose one of these and were refused the right to buy a PDP-10. However they found the SDS inappropriate for their use; they would need to develop a suitable operating system for it and that would have set back their progress by man-years.

There was an impasse until the CSL conclusion was to build its own PDP-10 clone. After all they had only been instructed not to buy a PDP-10 not that they could not build their own!

Chuck Thacker ran the task which lasted a year and completed in September 1972. The whole team rallied around to complete the project, often working well away from their chosen specialties, as an example the operating system specialist Butler Lampson worked on the central processor. It proved to be a great way for the team to develop a mutual respect for each other's skills and created a fellowship and organisation that Engelbart's ESP training had never approached.

As a reaction to the initial corporate refusal, the name they chose was something of a snipe at Max Palevsky, the CEO at SDS. They called the computer the MAX-C, which they innocently defined as Multiple Access Xerox Computer, but the Palevsky allusion was all too apparent.

This was no slavish clone of the PDP-10 as they had used the opportunity to update it radically with a new approach to memory and a means of using software microcode to replace hardware circuitry. Microcode was a system that they had used at BCC and that Kay had also implemented with his FLEX machine at Utah.

Émigrés Collaborate – English and Duvall

At PARC the SSL team set out to deliver on the second part of Engelbart's vision – collaboration. They established a networked series of computers based upon the NLS experience. The computers selected for this were Data General Nova 800s, rack-mounted 16-bit minicomputers.

Data General was founded in 1968 by Edson de Castro, Richard Sogge and Henry Burkhardt III. All three had been at DEC working with the PDP-8 and had concluded that it could be improved by becoming a single board minicomputer, but Ken Olsen did not agree. They left and with Herbert Richman of Fairchild Semiconductor founded Data General.

The Nova design was one of the first 16-bit minicomputers, using Fairchild MSI, medium scale integration chips. The Nova 800 was launched in 1969 at just $3,995 and was advertised as 'the best small computer in the world'. In fact a practical configuration raised the package price to $7,995; it was to sell around 50,000 units.

As ARC declined PARC recruited one group led by Bill English and Bill Duvall and they set about developing the PARC OnLine Office System (POLOS); perhaps the first project at PARC that most closely looked at the expressed goal of the office-of-the-future.

The SSL team sought to have a book-quality display on their screens but found this was more of a challenge than they expected.

Bill English had worked at ARC with Engelbart to help develop the first mechanical mouse and was the first to use one. At PARC he would help to develop the 'Hawley' electronic mouse, replacing wheels with a ball; it was named for the manufacturer, Jack Hawley who built them for PARC.

Doug Fairbairn spent the three years on the interactions of the terminal's screen, its keyboard and its mouse. Even the cord to the mouse was a major undertaking; it needed to be sturdy but without introducing its own movements to the mouse.

It was the software developed by Duvall that came in for most of the criticism as to use POLOS an operator needed to learn a series of arcane commands and key sequences; something that also applied to WordStar and other packages later.

The sharing process too was odd. The user would sit at a screen and the system would allocate an idle Nova for the task, but no-one 'owned' a Nova and there were no guarantees that an idle unit would be available.

From inside the team Larry Tesler was the most outspoken against these processes but perhaps the writing was on the wall when a Xerox subsidiary, a textbook publisher named Ginn & Co, went to PARC in 1974 to see if POLOS might assist with editing manuscripts or typesetting.

Its reviewer found it too complex for its team to master and suggested that not enough reality checks had been included in the project thinking. By 1975 it was clear that POLOS had been overtaken by a CSL development and the project was terminated.

Singing Alto – the first personal computer?

Flushed with their success with MAX-C, Lampson and Thacker moved on to fresh challenges. In mid 1972 in a report, entitled *A Personal Computer with Micro-parallel Processing,* Thacker used the whole MAX-C experience to define how he saw the next step.

Lampson and Thacker then approached Alan Kay and offered to build his Dynabook. In fact this project would lead instead to the launch of the Xerox Alto not the Dynabook, though Kay did describe it as an interim Dynabook. The name Alto was proposed by Bob Taylor based upon their location at Palo Alto.

Kay recognised that the technologies to develop a proper Dynabook could not be realised until closer to the end of the millennium. He saw the Alto as a vision or a rallying call for others who might later evolve a fully-fledged Dynabook.

The Alto was started in late 1972, as much as a reaction to POLOS as anything else. The CSL team felt time-share had had its day and agreed with Kay; they wanted to see computing power delivered into the hands of the individual.

The original plan was to develop just thirty Altos for the CSL and Kay's Learning Research teams to use. It was never intended as a commercial product.

Alto was one of the first truly personal computers, though some would argue it was more a workstation than a PC. PARC invested it with all its developments as they each reached fruition. It was originally designed to emulate a Nova and for convenience and speed it used many components from MAX-C; it even utilised monitors from the POLOS project.

When the first prototype was completed, they needed something to present on the screen. Alan Kay digitised the Cookie Monster from *Sesame Street* thus this became the first ever PC graphic!

The completed Alto had four parts - a floor-standing storage and processor box about the size of a two-drawer filing cabinet, a keyboard, a graphics mouse and a screen. This was all designed before microprocessors, so the processor box contained a custom-built transistor-transistor logic processor modelled around the Data General Nova 1220. It had two 3-megabyte disk drives.

The screen was a US letter-sized portrait-oriented screen of 8.5" x 11" (216 × 279mm) which was a little shy of the ISO standard A4 at 8.3" x 11.7" (210 × 297mm). It provided a display of 60 lines, 90 characters in length.

The keyboard was like a typewriter keyboard but while each key had a code that could be assigned, a series of key strokes could evoke a user-defined function. Alto could also respond to the length of time that a key was depressed, which was useful for game play.

The mouse had three black keys although they were known as red, yellow and blue!

Software was written initially in Basic Combined Programming Language (BCPL) that had been developed in 1966 by Martin Richards at the UK's Cambridge University. To increase its awareness and utility in 1967 he then wrote a BCPL complier for an IBM 7094 within the CTSS time-share system; while he was working at MIT on Project MAC. BCPL's appeal was in its portability and it soon emerged on a number of products.

The Alto's own OS had several interesting features. It could 'shed' some of itself to make room for applications and then recover those portions when required. Alto Executive was the file manipulation and program executive application that had a way of simplifying file names that could be up to 31 characters long. As the name of a required file was typed the system would suggest the full name once enough characters were entered and a simple press of 'Escape' would complete the name automatically.

Alto was quite slow but back then it was perceived to have the major virtue that the user had exclusive use of its power rather than sharing and having to allocate overnight time to get enough of its attention.

In 1978 Xerox donated fifty Altos to Stanford, Carnegie-Mellon, and MIT for use in research but Xerox management rejected two proposals to market the Alto as a saleable product. It later approved work on an Alto II but then rejected an Alto II word processor proposal. It must have been incredibly frustrating to have developed all this good stuff and not be permitted to release it to the market!

By 1978 2,000 Altos had been built. They were being used for document preparation on a local area network at Xerox PARC and by a number of campuses. The notional price for an Alto, if it had been able to be purchased, was $32,000.

The Alto focused a number of other minds to look for applications that would work with it; the BCPL program Bravo was one of these.

Bravo! - Simonyi's word processor

Charles Simonyi, born in Budapest, had an early encounter with computing during his secondary education. While working as a night-watchman at a computer laboratory, his role was to 'baby-sit' a Russian Ural II mainframe that had the habit of burning out valves. He seized the opportunity to be trained by one of the programmers and of course had ample time to try out his techniques each night.

Subsequently developing various compilers in Hungary, he approached a visiting Danish trade mission and was hired by A/S Regnecentralen, the first computer company in Denmark; they manufactured Data General Nova computers under licence. Simonyi was just sixteen!

RANDOM ACCESS MOMENT:
An Ames Research Centre team led by Mark Bolas did however originate a great deal of virtual reality innovation. In the late 80s Bolas founded Fakespace and this developed peripherals like the Pinch glove and the BOOM, binocular monitor.

After working there for eighteen months Simonyi moved to the University of California, Berkeley where he graduated and then transferred to Stanford. At some stage he worked at BCC alongside Lampson and Thacker during this period. From there he did not move directly to PARC, instead joining NASA's Ames Research Center on the ill-fated supercomputer the Illiac IV. The supercomputer used 256 processors in parallel and a system it called vector processing. By the time it was completed in 1976, well over budget, it could not match the Cray 1 for performance.

Simonyi moved to PARC in 1972. By the time he arrived at PARC he had developed, as his thesis at Stanford, something he named 'meta-programming'. This was a type of working process for better productivity where a software team leader would specify a program at a very high conceptual level and then a team would code the defined elements. He had first tried this with some undergraduates in a project he called 'Alpha'.

When he encountered Alto, Lampson had used the meta-programming approach to outline his concept for a text editor, but Simonyi chose to look further ahead and decided to write a word processing package, that very logically, having had an Alpha, this was called 'Bravo'.

He drew on previous work done at PARC by Jay S Moore using Interlisp to define the way in which a whole document might be economically held in memory.

Bravo was the first document-preparation software program to use multiple fonts with both upper and lower cases. It also introduced underlining and emboldening to fully utilise the bitmap display of the PARC Alto computer. This text editing system could direct the font, format the text, justify it, add margins, with the actual copy entered in either an insert or append mode.

It is regularly said that this was the first system to deliver WYSIWYG, What You See Is What You Get, although that term more accurately came to mean that what appeared on the monitor would be what came out of the printer. But as the PARC Alto monitor at this time was 72 dpi and the Xerox laser printer was working at 300 dpi this was not strictly the case. There was however one mode that approximated the way the page would look which perhaps justified that claim.

On the Alto this Bravo word processing became the killer-app for all those who had access to it. The display was not much appreciated by those users as it was felt it did not take advantage of all the Alto's graphic capabilities. Bravo was not a user-friendly general-market program, but of course the design of this word processing software was quite an achievement for its time.

Simonyi would later be recommended by Bob Metcalfe to join Microsoft where he would implement his concept of meta-programming and later preside over its move into applications such as Multiplan, Excel and Word.

Gypsy Mott takes off – Mott and Tesler

Tim Mott was a Brit working for the Xerox subsidiary and textbook publisher Ginn & Co. It was he who was asked to liaise with PARC to consider its manuscript editing and typesetting requirements.

Mott had been disparaging of POLOS and Bob Taylor challenged him to stick around and do something that would satisfy their requirements. Mott worked on this with Larry Tesler who had been the strongest internal critic of POLOS at SSL.

They looked at the rudimentary word processing packages that were starting to emerge on the market and felt that Bravo, while the best available at the time, was still rather deficient in user-friendliness terms.

In particular they disliked the concept of 'modes'. Michael Hiltzik in his very informative and entertaining book, 'Dealers of Lightning', quotes an amusing critique of these modes,

'...This involved a user who inattentively typed the word "edit" while in command rather than text mode: Typing "e" selected the entire document.

"d" deleted the selection, and "i" instructed the machine to insert in its stead the next character to be typed... at which point the user discovered that his entire document had been inalterably replaced by the letter "t"'

They set out to use the graphics capabilities of Alto more thoroughly; they created a better user interface that they called 'Gypsy'. There were only four completed Altos at the time they started. So Tesler and Mott worked out that possession was more than nine-tenths of the law, while 'their' Alto was in use it could not be reallocated. Sharing one Alto between them they each worked fourteen hours, with an hour overlap at the beginning and end of their sessions so they could hand-over; more importantly they held on to their Alto 24/7!

This creative tension produced many of the features that we all use today, dialogue boxes, cut-and-paste, drag-through and mouse double-clicking. Gypsy, because of its use of bitmapping graphics, was in fact the first truly WYSIWYG word processor.

Ginn & Co called its version CAE; perhaps Computer Assisted Editing? In 1975 the organisation had a $41m turnover with fifty-five of its 284 staff engaged in what they termed content editorial. They forecast that CAE might reduce costs by 15 to 20 percent. This was initially rather difficult to assess because of course they were encountering all the usual issues of any prototype system. This exercise was perhaps the first real-life utilisation of a PARC-developed technology.

Tesler would move to Apple and later to Amazon.com and Yahoo! Mott was a VP at Electronic Arts, co-founded Macromedia and later had an investment business and an IT outsourcing enterprise. Gypsy would re-emerge later with Dorado.

Networking from out of the ether – Metcalfe and Ethernet
Bob Metcalfe was at MIT where he worked on Project MAC and he also built the interface hardware to sit between MIT's minicomputers and the ARPANET. He earned his Harvard PhD while at PARC as he hooked up the MAX-C to the ARPANET.

As the networking specialist Metcalfe was therefore charged with a means of linking up the Altos. Taylor, like Engelbart, saw the future to be in providing individuals with their own computing power, but just as vitally they both saw much benefit would be realised if connected to a network so they could collaborate together.

Metcalfe knew only too well that ARPANET was not a solution because of the on-costs of the equipment to connect to it. Simonyi while at PARC had developed an approach called Simonyi's Infinitely Glorious Network (SIGnet) but Metcalfe thought this was also too complex. POLOS had modified a Data General Nova networking system but this was both complicated and unreliable. Metcalfe sought a low-cost reliable and expandable alternative.

The solution came to him upon hearing of the unusual approach used by the Hawaiian network ALOHAnet. It needed to operate across the mountainous archipelago of islands and could not go for a wired approach; it was decided to broadcast data through the air instead.

ALOHAnet had also developed a neat way to handle the situation when two computers tried to broadcast data simultaneously. A lack of acknowledgement from the receiving computer would cause the sending computer to re-send after a random lapsed time; random so they would not clash again. Metcalfe earned his PhD from Harvard for work with this sort of packet communication.

He realised that the ALOHAnet approach could provide the solution for an Alto network. In May 1973 he wrote a specification for a patent application and called it *The Ether Network*. But this would send data not through the air but through a passive cable.

A coaxial cable was the proposed 'ether' through which packets of data could be distributed. He suggested a similar random re-send routine if two Altos should try to send data at the same time, but by setting a finite number of attempts he surmised that it would not reach an overload situation.

Metcalfe met with David Boggs, a Stanford student who had been given the rather mindless part-time task at PARC of unpacking and testing the Novas for POLOS. They met when Metcalfe was developing an ARPANET connector for the POLOS Novas. Recognising Boggs' hardware skills he arranged that he be allocated to assist with Ethernet.

The two worked closely and under some pressure to develop the Ethernet card for the Alto by November 1973. They got together again to produce a paper in 1976 on the subject proposing it should be marketed as an integrated solution, but Xerox once again showed little interest in selling the system to others.

Metcalfe left PARC to form 3Com in 1979 and subsequently talked Digital, Intel and Xerox into jointly marketing Ethernet as a standard.

Ethernet is still today the most used approach for connecting computers in the same building. In 2003, thirty years on from its development, Ethernet provided 184m new connections in that year alone.

Dry copies

One of the most significant of PARC's achievements requires us to look across the continent at Xerox's original Wilson Center for Research and Technology based in Webster, New York; founded in 1960 and named for Joseph C 'Joe' Wilson.

Wilson was educated at the University of Rochester and Harvard Business School before joining his father's business, The Haloid Photographic Company; it had been founded back in 1906. The company was ailing until Wilson discovered Chester Carlson's Xerography process and threw the organisation into developing dry photographic copiers. Later the company name was changed to Xerox.

Xerography had been invented by Chester Carlson in late 1938. He was working in a patent office and came to appreciate that there were never enough copies of a patent specification. To get further copies was either expensive, by taking photo copies, or time consuming, by having them re-typed and of course re-checked.

He decided to try to find a way to create a machine that would provide low-cost copies in seconds. Carlson researched the various copying methods that existed then. He dismissed pursuing photography because this involved the physics of light and the chemistry of the materials. He realised that larger corporations had big teams and deep pockets working on the R&D for these techniques.

He chose instead to look at photoconductivity and electrostatics and to seek to combine these techniques into electro-photography. He chose to name it xerography based upon the Greek words *xeros* meaning dry and *graphos* meaning writing; thus emphasising that it would be a dry system, with no nasty chemicals and fluids.

Using initially a sulphur-coated zinc plate, his assistant Otto wrote on a glass microscope slide the current date and their location *'10-22-38 ASTORIA'*.

They eliminated much of the ambient light, and then rubbed the plate rapidly with a handkerchief to create an electrostatic charge. They laid the inscribed slide onto the plate and put it in a bright incandescent lamplight for a few seconds which neutralised the charge wherever there was no original image.

They then sprinkled the plate's surface with lycopodium powder, often used as photographic flash powder. Then gently blowing away the surplus powder they revealed a perfect copy of Otto's writing adhered to the plate by the residual electrostatic charge from behind the projected image.

It took four years before Carlson eventually received a patent for this process; in October 1942. But his work was far from over; another seventeen years had to pass before his product would be produced. He approached many of the big corporates of the day but no-one showed any interest.

For example IBM scoffed,
'The world potential market for copying machines is 5000 at most.'

Coming from the same company that reputedly forecast five mainframe computers as its world market potential this is perhaps unsurprising.

Eventually it would be the Battelle Memorial Institute, a private and not-for-profit science and technology development company, which gave him support.

Battelle had previously developed armour for tanks in WWII, in the 50s they had worked on 'Snopake' the correction fluid for typewriters, they had produced the first nuclear rod fuels for reactors, developed cruise control systems for cars and were influential in aspects of the first optical digital recorder that presaged CDs.

They took Carlson's idea and developed it until it could be sold on to the Haloid Company. It was Haloid that later became Xerox. Xerox had done a deal with Rank in the UK to create one of my early employers, Rank Xerox.

Their first product the Xerox 914 was released in 1959, the very first dry plain-paper copier. By the late Oughties the market, no longer exclusively controlled by Xerox of course, had grown into a document management industry of more than $112 billion and they estimate that by then more than 4 trillion pages had been printed on xerographic devices.

Carlson's biographer David Owen said,
'It gave ordinary people an extraordinary way of preserving and sharing information, and it placed the rapid exchange of complicated ideas within the reach of almost everyone...'

You see information processing and sharing aren't exclusive to computers. And don't these outcomes sound rather like the objectives that Douglas Engelbart had been seeking too?

Before Carlson died in 1968, he had given away more than $100 million to charities.

Optical Allusions – Starkweather and laser printing

Gary K Starkweather earned a physics degree at Michigan State University and later enrolled as a part-time graduate student at the University of Rochester to study optics. He joined Bausch & Lomb for eighteen months but was lured to Xerox and its Webster-based centre by the imaging technology it pursued.

His chosen field of endeavour had been building momentum but it provided him with a bumpy ride at Xerox. Back in 1917 Einstein had set out the theoretic grounding for the LASER (Light Amplification by Stimulated Emission of Radiation) and the MASER (Microwave Amplification by Stimulated Emission of Radiation) in his paper *On the Quantum Theory of Radiation*; although this is often described as something of a rearrangement of Max Planck's earlier law of radiation.

Down the years others moved the subject forward by confirming the techniques experimentally and defining and forecasting applications. But in 1960 Theodore Maiman at the Hughes Research Laboratory in Malibu California used a synthetic ruby crystal to develop the first functioning laser. The output beam of red light from the device proved very precise and controllable. Prior to this light had to be bounced around by mirrors, focused by lenses, and altered by prisms to achieve just a small degree of apparent control.

Starkweather's early work at Xerox a few years later in 1964 was based on improving the amount of light that might be applied in high-speed facsimile machines. Light sources like bulbs were largely uncontrolled; they also delivered unwanted heat with disorganised light and if that was not enough, the light was affected by the inherent colour temperatures delivered by the chosen filament.

RANDOM ACCESS MOMENT:
I worked for Rank Xerox in the late 60s and used one of their early fax machines. First you put in your document on to a cylinder and then phoned the recipient for him/her to insert a sheet at their end. You both initiated the send and sat back for three to five minutes as it noisily whirled around. The resulting document proved to be often unreadable or feint – but this was still evolving!

Starkweather decided the use of lasers and their much-more controlled light could resolve the issue with the fax machine - and it worked. He had focused on lasers and holography for his Master's thesis and now he set about looking at how lasers might work with the Xerox main thrust, a product line of copiers and duplicators.

But the management of the research centre saw this work as speculative, unreliable and moreover the very notion of copiers in the field with potentially blinding light sources was quickly dismissed as absolute folly. Worse, lasers were expensive devices as they were still in their infancy. As a result Starkweather was dealt with summarily and told to stop his work.

He realised however that the controllable light of a laser could be modulated to carry data and he saw the potential for generating an original document rather than scanning and producing a copy or a facsimile. He worked in his spare time with an old copier and the lowest cost laser, as his budget would not stretch further.

The company had the perspicacity to take up Carlson's invention, had successfully invested its future in it, had the patience to see through ten years of effort from development to market and had been rewarded by creating a major enterprise.

But clearly they had learned nothing from the experience and simply pooh-poohed Starkweather's thinking. His colleagues and managers saw only problems, never opportunities; his line manager threatened to remove his resources if he persisted.

In 1970 he saw an internal announcement about the formation of PARC and bludgeoned them into meeting with him to discuss a transfer, something that had very much been discouraged to prevent the Webster team all moving westward.

Fortunately he found a senior manager in charge of advanced product development, George White, who did have some appreciation and experience of lasers and it was he who arranged for his transfer.

Starkweather joined PARC in 1971 and this move would result in the most significant revenues the operation would earn from its many innovative developments.

Computer printers had mostly been designed to work with the ASCII character set, using seven of its eight bits to define a maximum of 128 characters – upper and lower case letters and a series of symbols. But lasers could define individual dots with enormous precision. Early devices could run at 300 dots per inch and therefore were not limited and could describe any character or graphic.

It was not an easy gestation if the final product was to be competitively priced, but Starkweather eventually came up with a mirror and cylindrical lens arrangement that he christened 'SLOT' (scanning laser output terminal) to write the image to the paper.

Other PARC-ies Butler Lampson and Ron Rider worked with him to develop another key component the Research Character Generator (RCG), to take the computer data and send it in a readable form to the laser. The RCG involved an enormous effort in defining all the required typefaces and any features like emboldening and italicising that might be required.

Xerox's first commercially available laser printer was produced as the Xerox 9700 in 1978; it could produce two copies a second, 120 per minute. But IBM had beaten them to the market with the IBM 3800 launched in 1975. It combined laser printing with electro-photography, but the IBM unit was a huge device intended only for those with very high print volumes.

The marketing planners at Xerox proved to be none too hot. First they forecast a market of around just three hundred units for its Xerox 9700 when reality would show sales of tens of millions over the next two decades.

The planners also predicted that the 9700 was likely to be used only by those making 200,000 to 300,000 copies per month. But the first units shipped were routinely doing one million. This level stayed true for the first 5,000 to 6,000 shipped units; some were recording 2,500,000 copies per month which essentially meant that they were in 24/7 use.

PARC's core mission was to develop the 'office of the future' and this would finally emerge as a combination of the development of SLOT and RCG, linked with the Alto computer and Ethernet.

Together these created an integrated solution which became known internally as EARS (Ethernet Alto RCG SLOT).

The first laser printer aimed at the office user was the Xerox Star 8010 released in 1981, but at $17,000 it was not well placed to create a large market.

The first with mass market appeal proved to be the HP LaserJet launched in May 1984; it had the benefit of IBM PC compatibility. Based around a Canon-built laser and HP software it retailed at just $2,995.

Starkweather would leave PARC in 1987 to join Apple and virtually single-handedly developed colour management technology and the 'Colorsync 1.0'. After ten years at Apple he joined Microsoft Research working on display technology.

A postscript coming first? – John Warnock

Another independent yet parallel development at PARC also proved to be a key step in building one of the PC killer apps. Postscript literally means a remark added at the end of a letter, but the Postscript we are interested in was an important precursor to the output of many letters.

Laser printing needed page description languages that could construct a page from high-level sources. The first approach was called 'Press'. This evolved into 'InterPress', which would eventually inspire Postscript and open the door to desktop publishing.

John Warnock gained his PhD at the University of Utah, to which much of the early progress in computer graphics can be traced. His PhD supervisors Professors David Evans and Ivan Sutherland challenged him to develop an approach to digitise a view of New York harbor such that this could be used with three screens to replicate the view from the bridge of a supertanker.

In 1976 he was engaged by Evans & Sutherland, a company founded by the two professors to pioneer computer graphics. Evans & Sutherland at the time was primarily involved in working with Rediffusion Simulation developing this type of simulator 3D visual software. Rediffusion Simulation was then part of a UK company related to the cable television, TV broadcast and rental television operator; in 1988 it was sold to Hughes Aircraft.

Warnock worked with a small team. John Gaffney led the effort to create a database of various 3-D image components; it held the coordinates and height of each geographical feature. Warnock himself developed the 'virtual machine' that would interpret the database entries and the simulator's views.

A subsequent project at E&S found Warnock and Gaffney working on a space shuttle simulation for astronauts to train them in the use of the shuttle-bay robotic arm. For this they developed a language similar to Forth which they called the 'E&S Design System'.

In 1978 Charles 'Chuck' Geschke interviewed and hired Warnock to join Xerox PARC. The two, Geschke and Warnock, were mathematicians rather than the free-booting computer scientists that PARC tended to attract. This appointment was the start of what would prove to be a long period of association between the two.

From 1979 to 1981 Warnock ran a team at PARC developing two key programs. Essentially he was seeking a language that would drive the Xerox laser printer; though he had decided from the outset that this language would be completely platform independent.

Working together with Martin Newell he enhanced the work done previously at Evans & Sutherland, this package providing a much larger database of graphic primitives. They called it 'JaM' which stood for John and Martin. It was a 'token-based' system, the tokens being interpreted and displayed in turn. This was operational on the Xerox Alto by 1981.

Bob Sproull and William Newman, also at PARC, evolved 'Press format' an independent system that could be used by raster printers to define a page.

Sproull, Newman and Newell all moved on from PARC, but Sproull returned in 1982 during a sabbatical from Carnegie Mellon University where he had been appointed a computer science professor. While at PARC Sproull, Butler Lampson and Warnock combined to work on integrating 'JaM' with 'Press format' to create a page image description language that Warnock called 'Interpress'. This was used to control the Xerox-developed laser printers.

The team's direct line manager, Chuck Geschke, tried to persuade Xerox senior management that Interpress should be launched as a commercial product, but yet again there was no interest. In 1982 Warnock and Geschke therefore decided to leave and formed Adobe Systems Inc; named after a creek running behind Warnock's house, not the sun-dried clay bricks.

Adobe applied the equivalent of twenty man-years of effort to the notions implicit within Interpress and developed an absolutely new approach called 'Postscript'.

WIMPs – opening the windows

Of course the most significant advance that PARC came up with from the panoply of progress was the development of something Engelbart had started to define. PARC developed it into a full Graphics User Interface (GUI) for the Alto computer.

The GUI is so familiar to all users today that the approach feels intuitive, yet of course it had to be evolved.

RANDOM ACCESS MOMENT:
The GUI might today be considered as a meme. Richard Dawkins invented the term in his book, 'The Selfish Gene'. A meme is a conceptual gene, a cultural idea that gets passed on from generation to generation rather like a gene. In this case it passes not via the cell structure, but instead from mind to

mind. Like the keystone of an arch, someone once had to invent the notion but it barely needs teaching today, as once seen the idea appears self-evident.

PARC first named the GUI notion as WIMP (Windows Icons Menus and Pointing) device. Of course Engelbart's mouse and bit-mapped screen were vital precursors; GUI might not have happened without this origination.

WIMP was a truly cooperative development. The team realised one of the problems with multiple windows was just how to deal with their overlaying one another. It was Alan Kay's desktop metaphor which proposed that, just as papers and files could be piled on a desk, the windows too should be stacked in a similar manner; each to be provided with a little overlap to move from one to the other by clicking on its edge.

The issues for display first became apparent with the development of Smalltalk-72 for the Altos. Dan Ingalls, from Harvard and Stanford, had worked on the implementation of Smalltalk and it was he, Larry Tesler, Bob Sproull, and Diana Merry who came up with a solution. The technical issue was how could the partly-concealed window-content be made readily available to be presented with a click?

The solution they came up with was 'BitBLT', usually pronounced as BitBLT and meaning bit block transfer. Essentially it created and stored bitmap versions of the content of each window so, whether moved, closed or opened, the content was readily available for the screen. The process made the movement between windows and the summoning of dialogue boxes smooth and intuitive for the user.

As a solo effort, Dan Ingalls later micro-coded BitBLT to operate with Smalltalk-76 and this version ran several hundred times faster. He would leave PARC for Apple, later moving on to HP and then to Sun.

WIMP or GUI and Smalltalk can be shown to have had a strong link to the development of the 'Objective-C' language that is today a preferred development language for the operating systems Mac OS X and for the iPhone OS. Objective-C was created by Stepstone, founded by Brad Cox and Tom Love in the early '80s.

Taking note – Kay and NoteTaker

Alan Kay was still searching for a route to create his Dynabook, though it had taken on other names across time, such as KiddiComp. In 1976 he inspired Larry Tesler, Adele Goldberg and Douglas Fairbairn to look at the concept afresh and the outcome was NoteTaker.

This was a direct descendant of Alto but with only a subset of its capabilities as he wanted it to be portable and laptop-sized. This project also used the evolving microprocessor rather than TTL circuitry. It was designed to have a floppy drive and a mouse and would use the variant Smalltalk-78.

The final styling for the NoteTaker looked more like a portable sewing machine than today's laptop. It was more accurately described as a luggable rather than a true portable, weighing in at 48 lbs (22kg). Just ten were built at an estimated cost of $50,000 each. This too was never offered as a solution outside PARC.

However the design certainly had an influence on both the Osborne 1 and the Compaq Portable designs. And this was what Alan Kay had planned; he treated each of the PARC computer projects like a concept car - more a vision or rallying call for others to evolve his fully-fledged Dynabook. When Apple launched its Macintosh he famously said,

'...the first personal computer worth criticizing...'

Which while something of an accolade also implied, 'Nice try guys, but you've won no coconut yet!'. Kay would leave PARC after ten years to be chief scientist at Atari for three years and then in 1994 he became an Apple Fellow.

Let's talk of dolphins and dandelions – D*

While the Learning Research team had been developing NoteTaker they found little of the past support they had previously come to expect from the Computer Science Laboratory. This was in part because it was working on the 'D*' products for itself, each an evolution of the Alto.

Much of the work with Alto used BCPL as its high-level language, but for this project the PARC team developed a new language, using the name 'Mesa', the name implying it was high-level.

Mesa was designed by Butler Lampson and Chuck Thacker based upon the ALGOL language and to run within the TENEX operating system; later it was micro-coded for the Alto. It was adopted as the PARC language of choice on a series of products beginning with the letter 'D' - Dolphin, Dorado and Dandelion; the generic name used internally was D* or dee-star.

Mesa was later to prove valuable in disseminating GUIs to other platforms and it influenced later software programs like Java, Modula-2 and Modula-3.

By 1975 the Alto had been in use for some time and its users had established that its major limitation was a lack of a virtual memory plus its constraints in terms of both size and speed. D* was the project that sought to remedy these matters.

Chuck Thacker created Simple Illustrator (SIL) one of the earliest Alto applications. It was a design program for laying out circuit diagrams and schematics so that the finished product could define the layout of printed circuit boards. He had drawn inspiration from Sutherland's 'Sketchpad'.

Thacker subsequently used SIL to design the boards for the D* and a program called 'Layout' that would stitch-weld the cards. D* was originally intended as a faster Alto, but it fell foul of the team's plethora of ambitions and its features tended to proliferate. This was where the lack of any real commercial ambition at PARC was perhaps most telling.

While it was intended as a personal computer the result ended up too big and too expensive to become a serious contender.

The Model D0, or Dolphin, was operational by 1978 using an Alto emulation and Alto software. It was still based on TTL logic, not microprocessors, and had a series of software problems.

Xerox's Systems Development Division (SDD) had at some stage planned to use the Dolphin at the heart of a new digital copier but when it turned out to be the size of a double wardrobe using five noisy fans, this proved impractical.

Much of 1978 was dedicated to virtually redesigning the whole product and a down-rated slower version D1, aka the Dorado, was ready by 1979. Some twenty-five of these were built using the prototyping stitch-welding approach, and production of three to four a month followed in 1982. Dorado operated with BCPL, Smalltalk, Interlisp and Mesa languages.

Birth of a star

In 1976 the Xerox SDD, under David Liddle started its own project, code-named 'Janus', quite separately. This project planned to realise PARC's original 'Office of the Future' goal.

SDD had a team at El Segundo in Los Angeles and another at the heart of PARC. Along the way this development became lured into the D* project and eventually led to the project named Dandelion. Dandelion was later renamed the Xerox Star, or to give it its formal title, the Xerox 8010 Information System; pedantically the 'Star' referred to its software.

Available from 1981 it had everything that PARC had worked on: a WYSIWYG GUI bitmapped display with icons and folders; a mouse; Interpress and print server; file servers; Ethernet; email; on-board text editor, graphics and spreadsheet applications; a screen with a two side-by-side US-letter page display.

Its base price was $16,000 per unit but its most common configuration required two or three Dandelions supported by filing and print server hardware to make the investment more like $50,000 - $100,000.

Never intended to be used as a stand-alone computer, it was none-the-less later sold as one and did manage a degree of success, largely due to its associated laser printer. Some 100,000 Stars were produced.

The Star was not promoted as a platform for third-party software developers to work with and of course nothing already out in the market could run on it.

It was quite slow and very expensive but its influence was huge on competitors' products such as Apple's Lisa and Macintosh, Digital Research's

GEM, Amiga's Lorraine and of course Microsoft's Windows and the Sun operating system.

Two of the Star team, Liddle and Charles Irby, left Xerox and developed the Star into an office product featuring animated graphics. The company they formed, Metaphor Computer Systems, was later sold on to IBM.

Geometrical progression

In 1975 the PARC SSL team had a new manager in Bert Sutherland, brother to Ivan. He held the firm view that a research laboratory needed to keep in touch with the outside world to remain focused.

Carver Mead was a professor at The California Institute of Technology (CalTech) where he had been a student. His relationship with a number of the Fairchild Semiconductor founders led to his working with many organisations on the West Coast.

As part of Sutherland's goal for the research laboratory, Mead was invited to make a presentation to the SSL team on the current status of integrated circuit design. Mead had been involved with the move from medium scale integration to large scale integration. At PARC he presented his views as to how very large scale integration (VLSI) could mean a major leap forward.

Robert Conway had been a mainframe designer involved at IBM Research in designing supercomputers. He worked with Memorex before joining PARC in 1973 after a sex change operation and subsequently named Lynn Conway.

Conway and Doug Fairbairn at PARC developed a long term relationship with Mead and with Caltech. Conway and Mead jointly wrote the first textbook on the subject, 'Introduction to VLSI System Design' which became a bestseller. They also initiated a course at Stanford to encourage designers to work with the techniques and technology.

In 1981 Jim Clark submitted a design he called the 'Geometry Engine'. Clark had earned his PhD at the University of Utah and caught the graphics bug. His design, developed with Marc Hannah, would simplify the drawing of both highly graphic images and three-dimensional images.

Working with PARC Clark took four months to realise his design. He sought and got venture capital and founded Silicon Graphics Inc in 1981.

Patently unprotected

The previous pieces are by no means a comprehensive review of what PARC achieved. It also came up with innovations in fibre optics, optical storage, encryption systems and Internet standards.

It was the lack of central management support and direction that led to dissatisfaction in the teams and the resultant departures became a regular feature.

So while Xerox received a proportionately small return compared with what it might have achieved given these significant innovations, its concepts would lead to the development of many other PC products and organisations.

The impact of this 'golden period' of research and its brilliant team was felt for many years to come. All of this makes the lack of patent cover so stunning. Xerox, originated from the concept of a patent attorney and aggressive in protecting its xerography patents, had done nothing to patent the GUI and the many other developments. Apple, Microsoft, Sun and others paid them no royalties.

One excuse offered was that Xerox's eye was firmly on a series of anti-trust actions in its copier business during the mid-'70s. Still it is very strange as I recall while working at Xerox myself there was a whole department with the task to make sure that Xerox, as a word, was never entered in any dictionary; the company was concerned that, like Hoover, Sellotape or Biro, the name and brand would become a generic term; in this they failed.

Much later when Apple and Microsoft locked horns legally over MS Windows conceptually looking very like the Macintosh GUI, Xerox did choose to enter the fray and took legal action against Apple. But the action was dismissed as too late, they lacked the evidence of the required diligence applied to bring the development to market, something that patent law requires.

6 - In patents we trust

Julius Sextus Frontinus, a prominent Roman engineer, said at the beginning of the first millennium, 'Inventions reached their limit long ago and I see no hope for further development.'

Commissioner of the US Patent Office, Charles H Duell, said in 1899, 'Everything that can be invented has been invented.'

Perhaps Xerox had its own reasons for being tardy in patenting its PARC developments but the computer, electronics and the PC businesses were seldom slow to act to protect its notions.

Keeping tabs

The old adage 'necessity is the mother of invention' has collected many attributions down the years but it can seldom have been more appropriately applied to the desperate need that the US Government's Census Bureau realised it faced on approaching the census of 1890.

The effort to find a solution started back at the 1870 census; this was the first census following the American Civil War and therefore the first to remove the questions regarding slaves. Charles W Seaton, who had been a serving officer in the First Vermont Sharpshooters, joined the Census Bureau and realised that a manual tabulation of the forms from its 38 million population would require some form of mechanisation. He set about inventing a simple machine to tally the returns and a matrix printing apparatus to assist with the task.

Herman Hollerith, a German-American statistician came up with a solution. He graduated in 1879 and briefly followed one of his professors into the Census Bureau. Here he saw first-hand the problems that had faced the 1880 census. The population was by then 50 million and the census computation took a full eight years to complete.

By 1890 it was calculated that the population would be 63 million and the task certainly was not going to get any easier. Hollerith's inventions were used during the 1890 census and saved the Bureau $5m while shaving two years from the expected timescale. He himself credits a girlfriend's father with his initial inspiration,

'He said to me there ought to be a machine for doing the purely mechanical work of tabulating population and similar statistics... ...his idea was something like a type distributing machine. He thought of using cards with the description of the individual shown by notches punched in the edge...'

His brief stint at the Census Bureau was followed by a year teaching at the MIT Mechanical Engineering Department where he began work on his tabulating machine in earnest.

Hollerith appears to have then been further inspired by the same device as Ada Lovelace (née Byron), namely the Jacquard Loom. This was developed way back in 1801; it used punched cards with rows of holes to define the complex weaving requirements for materials like brocades and damasks. Each hole drove a hook that located the warp threads so the weft would pass above or below it.

Hollerith worked on the same approach to carry data rather than mechanical instructions on punched cards. In 1884 he was working at the Patent Office when he applied for his first patent for the Hollerith Electric Tabulating System. In total he would achieve a career tally of thirty US patents and many overseas too.

Not everything went smoothly for Hollerith though. Around this time he also worked on other inventions and his planned electrical brake system for trains lost out to the Westinghouse steam-actuated brake.

His tabulating system, after various approaches had been tested, was a device to make and break electrical circuits by the presence or lack of holes in the cards that were fed through it. Of course another key 19th century development, the telegraph, had a rather similar approach but this was to transmit messages rather than count data.

The guinea pig for testing Hollerith's ideas was the City of Baltimore in New Jersey, it opted to use Hollerith's equipment to analyse its mortality statistics in 1886. The cards were hand-punched, each card representing an individual person and the holes used to detail the individual's location, ethnicity, occupation and the cause of death. The equipment also had an electrical device that sorted the cards into a variety of slots.

Development of Hollerith's design was refined by the experience of further applications. Next came the Surgeon General's Office and several other health departments but New York's Bureau of Vital Statistics was probably where the product achieved its final bedding in.

The Superintendent of the Census Bureau appointed to manage the 1890 census tried to lure Hollerith back into the organisation but by then he was far too engaged in his own developments.

Three systems were evaluated for this census: Hollerith's system, now with a keyboard to punch the cards mechanically; another inventor's slip system that was very hands-on using coloured slips; the third was a coloured card system that was equally dependent upon much manual effort.

Hollerith won the contract and processed the 63 million cards in just three months, which was two years ahead of plan and showed financial savings of $5m.

Unsurprisingly the system gained international acclaim. It soon managed censuses in the Austro-Hungarian Empire, Canada, Italy, Norway, and Russia in 1897 and the UK by 1911.

Not only did Hollerith start the business of computing he also set another major trend that many would later follow, litigation. In 1905 his patent expired, and he soon became embroiled in a damaging series of legal actions against the Census Bureau that had unilaterally decided to modify his equipment. The action failed.

Power plays

In 1907 the Census Bureau hired and funded James Powers, a Russian-born mechanical engineer, to produce an alternative to Hollerith's equipment to be based on mechanical rather than electrical sensing.

The Bureau assisted him in patenting this and Powers gained the majority of the contract for the 1910 US Census. One of his innovations was that using his equipment a key for every question was set before the card was punched; this did allow errors to be corrected more readily.

The cards were the same size, the holes circular and the formats were 21, 45 or 64 column; Hollerith had opted for 80 columns and square holes.

In 1911 Powers founded the Powers Accounting Machine Corporation and his equipment enjoyed early success with insurance companies. The British Prudential Assurance Company, then the largest in the UK, took over the British Powers agency and helped expand its UK business dramatically.

Facing this growing challenge it was vital that Hollerith open up new markets and in 1902 he negotiated for a company called The Tabulator Limited to represent his products throughout the British Empire; by 1909 this was renamed as the British Tabulating Machine Company (BTM). BTM would later feature in Bletchley Park's code-breaking tasks.

But as business got tougher his resultant high blood pressure was quoted as the reason for his business being sold in 1911 for $2.3m, Hollerith himself pocketing $1.2m.

Enter Charles R Flint, known as the 'father of trusts' based on his track record of assembling a number of major operations. Flint had worked to form US Rubber in 1892 by integrating a series of operations. This company was later to become one of the original twelve founding organisations in the Dow Jones Industrial Average, better known as Uniroyal.

Flint also formed the American Woollen Company in 1899 merging eight ailing mills. In the same year he assembled American Chicle Company from a collection of chewing gum companies. He was also responsible for the initial overseas sales of aeroplanes for the Wright Brothers. He was one very smart businessman

It was Flint who bought Hollerith's business and merged it with others to form the Computing-Tabulating-Recording Company. This was the merger of

Hollerith's Tabulating Machine Company with the Computing Scale Company of America and the International Time Recordings Company.

The organisation was renamed International Business Machines (IBM) in 1924.

Patronage and patents

Patents have been around a long time, as early as 500 BCE a Greek controlled city in Italy decided that,

'...all who should discover any new refinement in luxury, the profits arising from which were secured to the inventor by patent for the space of a year.'

By the 15th century these were being expanded. The inventor of a barge hoist for loading and unloading valuable marble in Florence was awarded a three-year patent. Thirty years later King Henry VI gave a UK coloured-glass maker a twenty-year patent.

Royal patronage was an alternate approach. In the 17th century Blaise Pascal was awarded exclusivity in France by royal patronage for his Pascaline calculator. King James I gave his authorisation to what became the King James Bible and established that patentable product had to be the result of new invention. Queen Anne, who gave her name to the cabriole legs used on the furniture of her era, added the requirement for patents to be submitted with a written description.

France had its own patent system that amalgamated the notion of royal patronage too, but this was of course swept away by its revolution and rewritten in 1791.

The USA had worked with the colonial powers' systems and after its revolution individual States were alarmingly adopting their own formats, until the first Congress agreed the Patent Act in 1790. Its first award of a patent was made on 31 July 1790 for a new potash production process.

Not only did Hollerith start the business of computing he also set another major trend that many would later follow, litigation. When his patent expired in 1905 he became embroiled in expensive legal actions against the Census Bureau that believed it had the right to modify his equipment. His action failed.

As a result, in 1907, the Bureau hired and funded James Powers, a Russian-born mechanical engineer, to produce an alternative to Hollerith's equipment based on mechanical rather than electrical sensing. The Bureau assisted Powers in patenting this in time for him to gain the majority of the contract for the 1910 US Census.

With strong competition the business got tougher and Hollerith's resultant high blood pressure was quoted as the reason for his business being sold in 1911 to C-T-R for $2.3m, Hollerith himself pocketing $1.2m.

Shift and shuffle

Manufactured products have a long record of successful patenting. Automated writing began with Henry Mill, an Englishman, who patented the first typewriter way back in 1714.

A little over a century and a half later, Christopher Latham Sholes produced and patented the first successful mechanical typewriter. It was not very user-friendly but introduced the QWERTY keyboard layout that we still use today.

But early computer software was not initially considered patentable. For example WordStar was the first to use CTRL-C to copy blocks of text, CTRL-X to cut them, and CTRL-V to paste them. Given the frequency that we use these short-cuts today, imagine if we had to remit a licence fee each time we did?

Till we meet again

James Ritty was an American bar owner, who opened his first operation in 1871 when beer was just a nickel a stein, a bucket cost fifteen cents. Ritty offered free food at the bar, with boiled eggs, sardines, cold meats, pigs' feet, pickles, pretzels, crackers and bread. Sounds like a deal!

By 1882 he had built up a bar called the Pony House in Dayton, Ohio. This was no ordinary drinking den. He commissioned woodcarvers to fashion some two tons of mahogany into a bar that is still on show in Dayton today. He offered drinking, dining and gaming, and the bar reputedly could satisfy other desires too.

It must have been quite a place. Located close to the railway station, it attracted many travelling salesman and across its years the bar claims to have served among others Buffalo Bill, the fighter Jack Dempsey and the gangster John Dillinger. By now Ritty had fashioned himself as a
'Dealer in Pure Whiskies, Fine Wines, and Cigars.'

But Ritty realised he was not in fact making as much money as perhaps he could, and should. His bar staff were pocketing far too much of the bar's takings and he kept trying to find ways to control this theft.

They must have left him some of his profits because it was while he on a steamboat trip to Europe that he came up with his first idea. Seeing a mechanism that was counting the revolutions of the ship's propeller he thought this might offer a solution to his problem.

Ritty engaged his brother John to develop a device. The first attempt resembled a clock that displayed what the bartender had entered, the hands showing dollars and cents instead of hours and minutes. It meant Ritty could sit at the bar and compare what he saw had been served to the customer with what was entered on the machine. But as a device it proved far too inaccurate.

The third attempt proved the breakthrough. There were keys to enter the amounts, though as yet no cash drawer, and of course it could not do the arithmetic to tot up a round. The 'barista' still had to do that mentally and enter the total.

In 1879 this was patented as Ritty's Incorruptible Cashier. He set up a small manufacturing plant to build these, the very first cash registers. He soon found running two businesses was too much for him and he sold the business to a china and glassware salesman who renamed it the National Manufacturing Company and then rather rapidly sold it on again in 1884 to John H Patterson . This time the name was changed to one we all recognise the National Cash Register Company (NCR).

Under Patterson the notion to include a cash drawer was added and also a bell to alert the owner when it was opened. There was also a paper roll to retain an audit of the day's transactions. This roll was punched within virtual columns so the amounts could later be summed and checked against the money in the drawer.

A visible indicator displayed what had been entered. This avoided the presence of any 'sweethearts', the name the industry coined for the deliberate under-ringing of an amount for a friend.

J W Allison of Liverpool, England saw the NCR and signed up as the first international agent when they established it could be modified to work in £sd.

Another inventor from NCR, Charles F Kettering, added an electric motor to the device in 1906. But from there until the 1970s these electromechanical devices stayed pretty much the same, although the machinery progressively became more compact and increasingly complicated as engineering skills allowed new techniques be included. Mechanical cash registers would eventually add up purchases, provide sales group analyses and produce punched-paper tape output.

Thomas J Watson drifted in to technology. His first job was as a teacher; he lasted just one day in the job. He took a book-keeping course but that did not last either. He started to sell pianos and organs for a hardware company; the sound you can hear is Babbage turning in his grave!

He later sold sewing machines, before hitching up with a dubious showman to sell shares in Buffalo Building & Loan. He invested his earnings from this in a butcher's shop, but his partner ran off with the proceeds and he lost the shop.

While at his butcher shop Watson bought an early NCR and it prompted him to seek work with the company. He joined NCR's Buffalo branch where the branch manager was said to have been extremely inspirational in setting Watson's management approach; he said he learned more from this individual than anyone else. The operation had a strong sales ethic and used the *NCR Primer* for its sales force to learn the best sales technique.

On becoming the top salesman in the East he was awarded the NCR agency in Rochester, NY, where he virtually wiped out the rival company,

Hallwood. He was then invited to work at the head office in Dayton where he rose to the role of manager of the sales and advertising departments of NCR.

He was remorseless in his approach, undercutting his rivals, and even setting up Watson's Cash Register and Second Hand Exchange in Manhattan to dominate the second-hand market and further establish his monopoly position. He copied this approach in Philadelphia and progressively expanded it across the United States.

At one of his NCR sales meetings in the mid 1890s, Watson came up with the motto that he used both there and later at IBM. 'THINK!' He explained, *'The trouble with every one of us is that we don't think enough. We don't get paid for working with our feet; we get paid for working with our heads. ...Thought has been the father of every advance since time began... "I didn't think" has cost the world millions of dollars.'*

Was this later the inspiration for Apple Computer's 'Think Different!' campaign?

Of course his approach, particularly to the second-hand market, was a flagrant abuse under US anti-trust law and in 1912 Patterson, Watson and thirty other NCR managers were indicted for it.

Watson had been quite verbose in writing about his policies and this came back to haunt him; he was given a $5,000 fine and a year's imprisonment. The sentences were appealed and, fortunately for all of them, Patterson's high-profile aid with the Great Dayton Flood of 1913 helped them to get the prison term overthrown.

NCR would dominate the cash register business for many years. It launched its model 304 – the first commercially available fully-transistorised business computer in 1958. NCR was acquired by AT&T in September 1991.

Simple as ABC

One of the most significant strands of USA development was led by Dr John Vincent Atanasoff, the son of a Bulgarian immigrant. He was prompted to enter the fray after becoming frustrated with his mechanical Monroe calculator as he prepared his doctoral thesis in theoretical physics.

Once he took his assistant professorship role at Iowa State College, he began experimenting with thirty Monroe calculators yoked to a single shaft and used IBM tabulators as slaved devices. In this he caused some consternation when he modified IBM equipment that was supplied only on a leased arrangement. In 1937 he developed an analogue calculator, but he came up against the same problem as Babbage and Zuse had done before him - the mechanical accuracy and tolerances of the equipment was just too poor.

As a result he turned his attention to finding an electronic solution. He traced the next step to concepts developed during a long night-time drive.

With the benefit of two small grants from the Agronomy department and the Research Corporation of New York City, and the help of a graduate student, Clifford Berry, from November 1939 he used the basement of the physics building to build the ABC (Atanasoff-Berry Computer).

Atanasoff had prepared a paper back in 1940 entitled *Computing Machines for the Solution of Large Systems of Linear Algebraic Equations*; it had attached drawings and he submitted this with the package sent to a patent lawyer.

Later he attended a meeting of the American Association for the Advancement of Science in Philadelphia during December 1940 where John Mauchly was talking on the calculations used in weather forecasting. Atanasoff talked with Mauchly after the meeting and he advised Mauchly of his work on building the ABC.

Atanasoff and Berry also visited the patent office while in Washington DC, where they were comforted by the assurance that their work was clearly new and therefore would be patentable.

In June 1941 Mauchly made a special visit to them in Iowa where he stayed with Atanasoff and reviewed the ABC computer and its design documentation in much detail. The ABC computer was first operational in 1942; however a war-time role for Atanasoff interrupted things somewhat and he left the patent filing to his university - and it failed him.

The ABC weighed 700 lbs (320kg) and took up 800sqft (74sqm) of space. It had 300 vacuum tubes applied to the arithmetic unit and a further 300 for memory and control. It used a mile (1.6km) of wiring. It was the first computer to be all binary.

ABC used electronics exclusively for its calculations and was the first to separate computation and memory; the memory was in the form of a pair of drums each with some 16,000 capacitors. It had two main failings. First, it required operator involvement during its processing. Second, its device for storing intermediate results, a mechanical paper card reader-writer, was very unreliable.

During 1943 Mauchly again visited Atanasoff to discuss his computing theories; deviously he never at any stage in these meetings mentioned that he too was working on building a computer.

Clifford Berry went on to obtain thirty patents with another thirteen pending, but he had something of an unhappy early life. When he was just eleven years old his father working for the Iowa Power Company was shot dead by a disgruntled employee who had been sacked.

In 1954 an IBM patent lawyer approached Atanasoff and Berry to object to the Mauchly-Eckert patent application by showing that the ABC computer represented 'prior art'.

While this was still under way (it was not concluded until April 1973) Berry apparently took his own life in October 1963. Atanasoff queried at the time whether he was in fact murdered!

Before they locked horns IBM had reached an accommodation with Sperry Rand and withdrew its action. However in 1967 when Honeywell received a demand from Illinois Scientific Developments for $250m in royalties they promptly took up the good fight and sought to challenge the patent.

The trial ran from 1971 to 1972 and lasted 135 days across nine months. 77 witnesses attended and a further eighty were deposed. Honeywell presented over 25,000 documents, Sperry Rand responded with some 7,000 of their own. The transcript ran to well over 20,000 pages.

Once again it was the ABC that was used as the basis of 'derivation'. But Honeywell also challenged the IBM-Sperry deal as an anti-trust violation, something that IBM's Watson would very much wish to avoid. In October 1973 judgment held that the ENIAC had drawn inspiration from the earlier ABC.

One facet of the judgement stated,

'Eckert and Mauchly did not themselves invent the automatic electronic computer, but instead derived that subject matter from one Dr. John Vincent Atanasoff.' US District Judge Earl R Larson.

This very significant ruling however received next-to-no attention as the Watergate scandal sucked up all the column-inches the very next day. President Nixon fired the 'independent' special prosecutor appointed to investigate the Watergate break-in and this led to the immediate resignation of the Attorney General and his deputy.

It is unclear if Honeywell, in their legal preparations, had predealt with issues at the end of the process and somehow precluded Atanasoff from attempting to levy royalty payments of his own if their patent objection was upheld.

Atanasoff certainly never sought to pursue licence fees from others for his invention.

EDVAC patent

Back in 1944, before the ENIAC was completed, the team had already conceived of a number of improvements that might be brought to the design for the future. One enhancement was to satisfy the requirement for a stored program and this led directly to the subsequent design of EDVAC (electronic discrete variable automatic computer).

The original budget for this was set at $100,000 but ended up escalating to more than $500,000 by the time it was delivered in 1949; EDVAC was not operational until 1951. Eckert and Mauchly were extremely frustrated when they came to patent the EDVAC too.

John von Neumann had also been consulting with the Moore School team. Neumann was another of the truly remarkable individuals attracted to contribute to the development of computing. Born in Budapest he was a child prodigy, achieving his PhD in mathematics at the age of twenty-two.

Moving to the United States in his late twenties, he went to Princeton and was one of the first four individuals invited to join the Institute of Advance Study (IAS); other alumni were Albert Einstein, Kurt Gödel, a leading logician, and J Robert Oppenheimer, known as the 'father of the atom bomb' for his Manhattan Project management. Von Neumann repaid their faith by becoming one of the preeminent mathematicians of his time.

His early work was in pure mathematics particularly in game theory, but he moved more to applied mathematics by the late 1930s. In particular he developed an expertise in the calculation of explosions. As mentioned previously, he brought to the Harvard I a series of calculations of implosions; this was after he had been recruited to the Manhattan Project. The Harvard team and its Mark 1 computer performed the calculations without realising they were for nuclear bombs.

Neumann persisted in his belief that the best way to explode the A-bomb was by using a series of explosive devices that were lens-shaped to compress the plutonium and set off the reaction. Others on the project considered this would not work but he persevered and his approach resulted in the Fat Man bomb that decimated Nagasaki. He went on to work on the H-bomb and after WWII on proposing how fission bombs might function.

All of his interest was at the very edge of the capabilities of computers of the time and it was inevitable that he would contribute to computer science. He developed some sophisticated techniques for both the ENIAC and the EDVAC. In June 1945 he published a paper outlining the new approach entitled, *First Draft of a Report on the EDVAC*.

In this paper he set out the proposed architecture for the computer, though many suggest that this was not original work but based upon the Eckert and Mauchly activities and also mirrored the thinking of Alan Turing and Konrad Zuse. Whatever the truth of this, the structure would subsequently be termed as 'von Neumann architecture' and consisted of a central processor and a random-access memory storage device to hold both instructions and data. It also used an arithmetic logic unit that operated the required inputs and outputs. This became generally accepted as the best way forward and most subsequent computers adopted this approach, albeit with more complex means of transferring data and instructions.

The draft's fairly wide distribution of what was supposed to be a top secret project put the information virtually into the public domain. The critical issue was that this document predated the Eckert and Mauchly patent filing by a year and this ensured their application failed.

The von Neumann draft report and some new University policies were used to seek to force Eckert and Mauchly to sign over their intellectual property, instead they decided to leave the Moore School.

They received a grant from the National Bureau of Standards for some related work and this gave them the financial encouragement to set up the Electronic Control Company in 1946. It was later to become the Eckert Mauchly Computer Corporation and this move would lead to the development of both the BINAC and UNIVAC computers.

Coining it in

The first patented interactive electronic game is accredited to Thomas T Goldsmith Jr and Estle Ray Mann at DuMont Laboratories, a television equipment manufacturer, based in New Jersey. Inspired by the radar displays of WWII, they developed a missile simulator that the 'patent' application defined as a 'Cathode Ray Tube Amusement Device'. They applied for their patent in January 1947.

In 1958 to entertain the visitors to an open day at a nuclear research base, Brookhaven National Laboratory, William Higinbotham developed an interactive game he called 'Tennis for Two'. Using an analogue oscilloscope, it was one of the first games to introduce screen graphics.

'Tennis for Two' utilised prior work on ballistic trajectories and displayed a side view of the game, where the 'ball' would curve over a net, bounce off the 'ground', hit the net and so on. The ball was designed to experience both gravity and drag through the air and a button was used to hit the ball and a knob to apply an angle, there was also a sound when the ball was hit. The game was used only twice and never patented.

Patenting games had clear benefits. Charles Darrow was a domestic heater salesman who, like many, lost his job in the Great Depression. At the time there had been a series of home-made board games that were played based around the buying and selling of property. These early prototypes had names like 'The Landlord's Game'; Darrow selected the much catchier name of 'Monopoly'.

Significantly Darrow hired an artist who came up with the bold iconic images used for the stations, the utilities, for Jail, Chance and Go.

Darrow secured the copyright for Monopoly in 1933 and patented it in 1935. He sold this on to Parker Brothers/Hasbro in 1936 and became the very first millionaire simply from designing a game. Hasbro claims that 750 million people have played the game, making it the most played board game in the world.

Ralph H Baer is often referred to as the 'father of video games' despite Higinbotham clearly having captured the principle first. Baer is given the title because it is said he created the video game industry; but this is an accolade perhaps he should more correctly share with Nolan Bushnell?

Baer, a German Jew who escaped to the USA, became a radio technician and in WWII worked in military intelligence while posted to London. Post-war he took a BSc in Television Engineering in Chicago. He worked with Loral, a New York electronics company and by the mid-50s was at Sanders Associates, a US defence contractor. Sanders was later purchased by Lockheed Corporation; today it is owned by the British BAE Systems plc.

Back in 1951 Baer first thought of using a television screen for purposes other than watching broadcasts. At Loral he was charged with designing a better television set and routinely found himself generating patterns on the screen as a test process. He wondered if this facility might be built into a set and used to give the viewer some potential for game play. Loral had no interest in this.

Fifteen years later and working for Sanders he was reminded of his earlier thoughts and produced a four-page outline of his refreshed idea. He did some early work on generating and controlling a point on the screen and then involved Bill Harrison in a development project to deliver the concept.

Their ideas evolved into an analogue game that could emulate ping-pong, football, volleyball and shooting. The head of Sanders R&D approved further time and spend to develop the idea. The outcome, in 1966, was the 'Brown Box'; named for the adhesive wood-grain cover of its case.

The Sanders organisation and Baer received the patent for controlling dots or 'sprites' on a screen. They hawked the idea around all the TV manufacturers and initially had interest from RCA but this soon ran out of steam. An RCA executive, Bill Enders, had however seen the Brown Box and when he moved across to Magnavox he proposed that they license the concept.

Baer also developed a 'light gun' peripheral for use with shooting games and he conceived plug-in cartridges to add sound effects and other updates, but he did not press on to patent this notion.

Magnavox called its game 'Odyssey' when it was first launched in May 1972. The first product was the 1TL200 based on an analogue design using discrete transistors and diodes; it had no sound and worked in black and white. The cartridges supplied were hardware, not software; they made different electrical connections to drive the variety of games, up to twelve of them. Coloured overlays were supplied to simulate screen colours.

There was widespread concern that this would only work with a Magnavox television. This was not actually true, but the product was only supplied via Magnavox dealers.

However this disadvantage was to some extent balanced by the participation of Frank Sinatra in its TV commercial. It sold 130,000 units across its two years of life, together with 20,000 light guns.

Sanders and Magnavox were to make millions from other video game manufacturers by enforcing Baer's 'sprite' patent.

The other progenitor of video games was Nolan Bushnell. A keen amateur radio enthusiast, he had worked at the Lagoon Amusement Park while at school and college and had been particularly taken by the arcade games there. His first business was in repairing radios and TV sets.

He played 'Spacewar!' while studying electrical engineering at the University of Utah and then met it again through a friend working at the Stanford AI Lab.

He and Ted Dabney were working at Ampex when they decided to bring Spacewar! to a wider audience through a new operation, Syzygy Engineering.

Syzygy is one of those useful quiz-question words - a word without an official vowel, like rhythm. It is an astronomy term with a series of definitions but essentially means a conjunction, usually of the sun and moon.

Bushnell broke with the subsequent established norms of the PC business; he used his daughter's bedroom as his workshop, not a garage!

Dabney developed the product while Bushnell looked for a manufacturer, eventually agreeing a deal with Nutting Associates, a company that had made mechanical coin-op games. Nutting was not at the time particularly successful and perhaps this was why it took on the speculative job. The result was Bushnell's first coin-op arcade game 'Computer Space', released in late 1971.

It was originally based around the use of an expensive off-the-shelf minicomputer but this proved too slow, so it was instead designed in hardware using more than seventy transistor-transistor logic chips and a 15" (38cm) black and white GE screen for display. This analogue approach radically reduced their costs.

The console styling certainly looked the part but its gameplay proved quite complex and it was not a huge success. However they did sell 1,500 to 2,000 units at a value of more than $3m, not bad for a start-up. Perhaps just as valuably, Bushnell learned about the target end-user for this sort of coin-op and it gave him experience with various locations to establish those that were most valuable.

Bushnell and Ted Dabney soon learned that the Syzygy name was used by a variety of other organisations and they renamed their company Atari Inc. The word is the equivalent of 'check' in chess for players of go - a game that Bushnell played to some standard. In Japanese 'atari' is also used when a prediction comes true.

Bushnell took on Al Alcorn who set out to design a driving game. But Bushnell appears to have been inspired by seeing an early demonstration of the Magnavox game in May 1972; he would later regret signing the visitor book for that Magnavox demonstration. Whether this changed his approach is of course uncertain but there was a change of direction away from the driving game and they came up instead with the idea for 'Pong'.

Recognising its value he again approached Bill Nutting at Nutting Associates who had worked with him on earlier projects and offered the product in return for equity in the organisation, but he was turned down. He considered that Nutting had not marketed Computer Space that well and was not too disappointed.

Alcorn was the designer of the coin-op Pong game though he was directed by Bushnell throughout the process. Along the way Bushnell had bought out Dabney who, nervous of the market, was more attracted to the company's other activity of servicing pinball machines.

They had a sincere advantage over the Magnavox team in that they could afford more and improved components that could not be envisaged within the planned retail price for the Odyssey. Alcorn came up with a distinctive sound for Pong and added spin if the ball was caught at the extremes of the paddle.

Bushnell had been lining up two companies to license the product but now decided to keep it for himself. He cleverly extricated himself from negotiations by letting each know that the other was no longer interested and this led to them both choosing to walk away – atari!

However Bushnell found funding his own production was not easy. Bankers pigeonholed the product along with pinball and that market was clearly associated with the Mafia. But eventually Wells Fargo came through and Pong was on its way to being the first mass-produced coin-op video game.

RANDOM ACCESS MOMENT:
As a Brit I find it pretty implausible that in these last two sentences I can mention two archetypal US 'institutions' popularised in films and TV, the Mafia and Wells Fargo. Both have had such a fictional impact on many and here they are popping up in a commercial video game development. Who would ever have had the courage to connect Dale Robertson, Don Corleone and Donkey Kong?

Atari market–tested its Pong in late 1972 at Andy Capp's Tavern, a helpful current client. Within a few days the bar owner called to say the unit was malfunctioning. Alcorn found that the mechanism had been jammed by the overload of quarters that had been inserted to play the game.

Atari sold some 38,000 coin-op Pong consoles but there were soon a large number of clones that make the estimated total sales somewhere over 100,000. It became the most popular arcade game of all time. It was the success of this coin-op game and later the home versions of 'Pong' that was the foundation of the video game business.

The coin-operated games market in the US by 1982 was worth over $6bn. As a result the US Mint had to increase the number of quarters, 25c, in circulation to enable these volumes. The appetite for new coin-op material was intense but the life of a game usually proved to be short. Any successful format was endlessly cloned and the claw cranes and pinball machines were edged to the back of bars, restaurants and arcades.

There can be little doubt that it helped the Magnavox sales of Odyssey as those who encountered the coin-op game would be motivated to wish to play it at home. But the patent obtained by Magnavox and Saunders would be back to haunt Atari later!

RANDOM ACCESS MOMENT:
Steve Jobs (later of course the co-founder of Apple) joined Atari as a technician for just $5 an hour; he became its employee #40. His brashness apparently led to Alcorn, his manager, scheduling him to work nights when he would be less likely to offend the rest of the team but this allowed his friend Steve Wozniak (also a subsequent co-founder of Apple) to come in out of hours and get free time on the games.

In 1976 Bushnell wanted to come up with a single-player version of 'Pong' that he had envisaged and called 'Breakout'. Al Alcorn set the task for Steve Jobs and offered him $750 to create the prototype but added an intriguing bonus of $100 for each chip that could be eliminated from the outline design.

Jobs knew that Wozniak had seen the Atari arcade game 'Pong' and been motivated to develop his own version with many fewer chips. Jobs had encouraged him to show it to the Atari engineers.

Naturally Jobs brought in Wozniak to assist and he successfully eliminated fifty chips. Jobs duly earned a bonus of $5,000, but reportedly paid Wozniak only half of the original fee, $375, for his work. Wozniak only learned of this from a book about Atari published much later in 1984; if he had learned this earlier perhaps Apple's future might have been different.

In fact his design was judged as too small for the company to use given its current manufacturing approach so Atari decided later to redesign it using more chips. Though Wozniak said he could find nothing in the finished product that was so very different from his gameplay design.

Free sheets to the wind

In the early phases of the personal computer market one of the first software killer applications proved to be VisiCalc. In 1978 an MBA student at the Harvard Business School, Dan Bricklin, conceived of the electronic spreadsheet. It was to have a major impact on the market and yet was never patented!

Bricklin was an early software visionary, another individual who transited through the hallowed turf of MIT. In 1969/70 he met Bob Frankston where they both worked on the MULTICS project, that influential early time-sharing system. Initially on leaving they worked in different parts of the developing PC business, but not before they had identified a desire to start a small business together.

Bricklin decided to study for an MBA at the Harvard Business School in 1978 believing this to be a sound preparation for founding a business. While there he conceived the electronic spreadsheet.

Having watched a professor while he developed a financial model on the blackboard, he noted how when parameters were erased or changed it was necessary to follow through modifying data across the rest of the model.

Douglas Engelbart of ARC had only recently demonstrated his mouse at Harvard and maybe as a result of this Bricklin found himself considering equipping his TI calculator with a mouse that could move between cells of a financial model. Amazing the stuff that goes through the mind in a boring lecture, but he went on to harness the thought.

The term spreadsheet already existed. The *Dictionary for Accountants* by Eric L Kohler first published in 1952 described a spreadsheet as a matrix of columns and rows of numbers completed manually. I remember using them in this manual format and the curse was that when you added all the rows and summed them and then added all the columns and summed them, you seldom got to the same result. An add-lister was essential because that way you could backtrack to seek out your errors. The modern non-printing calculators seemed to add more opportunity for error along the way.

Richard Mattessich pioneered computer spreadsheets in the early 1960s in a paper and several books. In *Simulation of the Firm through a Budget Computer Program* he included illustrations and even a program written in FORTRAN.

So perhaps it was not surprising that when Bricklin outlined his concept to various professors he received limited interest or assistance. However one of them did introduce him to Dan Fylstra, a student in the year ahead of him.

Before attending Harvard Fylstra studied computing at MIT and worked as an associate editor at *Byte* before becoming the founding editor of *Computer Dealer* magazine.

In 1977 Fylstra realised there was an evolving need for some organisation to analyse the new PC market requirements and support software authors through the development process. This organisation would forge a relationship with the new computer stores as well as the traditional retailers. Fylstra founded Personal Software, one of the earliest PC software publishing operations.

By 1978 Fylstra had joined with Peter Jennings selling games and other applications for early personal computers. Jennings developed MicroChess, designed originally on the MOS Technology KIM-1 computer. Fylstra was approached by Steve Jobs to modify MicroChess to fit the Apple. Based upon

Personal Software's new publishing approach, MicroChess became the first piece of application software managing to achieve sales of over 50,000 copies.

As a result of this history Fylstra convinced Bricklin to develop his software for Apple rather than, as he had planned, on a DEC minicomputer. He even loaned Bricklin an Apple to advance the development of his concept, originally called Calcu-Ledger.

In 1979 Bricklin looked to his old friend Frankston, an experienced computer consultant, to help develop his ideas. They formed Software Arts Inc and evolved the basic approach for a spreadsheet they renamed as VisiCalc (visible calculator).

The concept is implicitly understood by most PC users today but of course it had to be inspired and conceived initially. Bricklin's approach was to automate the frustrating cross-casting process. He recognised that by using a software interpreter the arithmetic could be assured.

Bricklin prototyped his idea on a time-share system and came up with a status line to display the value of a cell with its formatting and formula held behind it. The early limitations of the available PCs, their very simple screens and even simpler printers then necessitated a whole series of innovations.

One of these was the referencing of columns as letters and rows as numbers, rather than using text headings that would use up memory, screen and printer space. But perhaps more significant was the need to develop windows or panes to view different parts of the spreadsheet simultaneously on the inadequate screens.

He and Frankston tried valiantly to fit the software code for VisiCalc into the smaller and less expensive 16K Apple II, but found with some regret that it required the larger 32K version.

Its great attraction was that anyone, even without programming experience, could grasp the processes speedily and be writing and operating 'programs' within seconds; never for a moment realising that programming was what they were doing!

Fylstra negotiated to represent Software Arts and its VisiCalc for a 37.5% royalty on direct sales and 50% on any OEM (other equipment manufacture) business, ie sales to the computer manufacturers. VisiCalc was formally launched at the 1979 West Coast Computer Faire and the National Computer Conference in New York.

Benjamin Rosen was at the time a much respected commentator on developments such as VisiCalc. Later he would become a direct player when he venture-financed both Lotus and Compaq. Commenting on the launch in the Morgan Stanley *Electronics Letter* issued in July 1979 he remarked,

'... for the professional, the home computer user, the small businessman, and the educator, there is precious little software available that is practical, useful, universal, and reliable.'

Yet, he went on to say presciently of VisiCalc,

'...*VisiCalc comes alive visually. In minutes, people who have never used a computer are writing and using programs. ...VisiCalc could someday become the software tail that wags (and sells) the personal computer dog.*'

At $99.50 per copy, VisiCalc took off rapidly, and single-handedly took Apple with it. This very simple concept proved to be the first killer-app selling over 700,000 copies in just six years and giving home computers the first true business application.

For example, on an Apple II equipped with VisiCalc I was perfectly able to manage Prism Microproducts through its first year while it notched up a £10m turnover in low unit cost Sinclair ZX81 and Spectrum computers.

The Personal Software company achieved sales of just under $900k in 1979, close to $4m in 1980; its sales of VisiCalc alone reached $14m in 1982 and exceeded $22m in 1983.

Yet VisiCalc was never patented. In the USA in the late 1970s it was felt that software consisted merely of symbols and algorithms and that these were matters of fact and/or laws of nature, so they were not considered as appropriate material for patenting.

The advice the US Patent Office gave to the VisiCalc team was that they had a less than 10% chance of getting a patent awarded for software. Given the high costs involved and the poor chances of a positive outcome they proceeded relying instead on copyright and trademarking.

In the UK a different view was taken and the first computer software patent was granted in August 1966 for a product described as *A Computer Arranged for the Automatic Solution of Linear Programming Problems*. It was an invention using software to organise the memory management when handling algorithms in linear programming. By the late 1970s Europe also had the European Patent Convention that enabled software inventions to be patented, albeit in a roundabout way.

But it took until 1981 for first USA software patent to be granted.

This was the culmination of something of a personal mission on the part of Satya Pal Asija, an Indian immigrant to the USA who had developed a data retrieval program called SwiftAnswer, an acronym for special word-indexed full-text alpha-numeric storage with easy retrieval. The software was designed to allow a user without programming skills to ask in plain language for something to be retrieved. The software could overcome problems with the user's spelling, punctuation, grammar or syntax.

Satya Pal Asija wrote the software in 1969 and he was not content to rely upon copyright alone. He thought he deserved to be granted the same strengths as a hardware inventor. He studied law, particularly patent law, and took and passed his bar exams. He lodged his application in 1974 and it took him a seven-year process to get his patent.

Satya Pal Asija wrote in 1983 a book entitled How to Protect Computer Programs: A Case History of the First Pure Software Patent. In the preface he says,

'Copyrights, design patents and utility patents all have their place in protecting software. As a rule of thumb copyright protection is sufficient to protect a specific piece of code and a patent is needed to protect the underlying algorithm. Design patents are needed to protect programs embedded in integrated circuit chips because utility negates copyright protection for chips [notwithstanding mask works]. This is so because computer programs are authored, chips are designed and algorithms are invented.'

SwiftAnswer never amounted to much, but its successful patent meant that VisiCalc had missed its opportunity by just two years. By the noughties the USA was issuing some 40,000 software patents each and every year.

While these commercial organisations were vying to own their software, seeking to establish their intellectual property ownership there was to be a whole other strand that believed software should be free.

7 - New components for a new market – electronic developments

'All you need in this life is ignorance and confidence; then success is sure.'
Mark Twain

Stepping stones to the PC
Progress was frantic in the years following WWII in mainframe and minicomputing, but it was to be major component innovations in electronics that were preparing the ground for the move towards personal computing.

A Brit, John Ambrose Fleming, produced the first thermionic valve back in 1904, he called it the kenotron. The theory is that the hot filament or cathode, emits electrons and these are collected by the anode. This was a simple diode and it became known as a vacuum tube. Further electrodes placed in the tube could amplify the signal or switch it.

Early mainframe computers were based around a version of these vacuum tubes though they proved to have many issues. First they were hot, necessitating the cooling of the computers. Heating the valves and their subsequent cooling consumed a great deal of power. They were also to prove too unreliable a component to be trusted at the heart of a mainframe computer.

At Tokyo University Eiichi Goto had developed an alternative to the tube which he called the 'parametron', a means of using the stationary point in the peaks and troughs of an oscillation to define a binary 1 or 0. It was adopted by many Japanese computer makers because it meant products were cheaper and the parametron in use was much more reliable than a valve-based tube, although it was quite slow. The parametron would be surpassed by the next semiconductor development, the IC.

The first stepping stone towards PC was the transistor, made from a semiconductor material so that it could amplify the power applied, a low signal delivered gave out a much larger signal as its output.

The effect of semiconductors was first noted by Michael Faraday back in 1833. But semiconductors did not find application until the beginning of the 20th century in early radio sets. The notion of how a transistor might work had been published as early as 1925 and WWII certainly pushed research into the subject further along, but it was not until 1947 that Bell Labs nailed it and patented the concept.

The second stepping stone was to be the integrated circuit (IC) developed directly from the attempts to find a replacement for the vacuum tube. The IC is made from semiconductor material prepared as a thin wafer that can hold a complete circuit, a series of transistors and other circuitry, printed or etched upon its surface.

The IC was first conceived at the Radar Research Establishment in the UK in May 1952. Similar work was also pursued in Germany by Siemens but it was in 1959 that Jack St Clair Kilby at Texas Instruments and Robert Noyce at Intel perfected the idea.

Memory ICs were another key development that would make the PC viable, offering various formats of ROMs and RAMs that could hold software and data.

The third stepping stone was the MPU, the microprocessor unit that emerged in the early 1970s. However this was not originally created as a development path but more as a workaround, a development of convenience. Nonetheless it was the MPU that would set the personal computer market alight.

Tiny bells
The transistor was developed in 1947 by William Shockley, John Bardeen and Walter Houser Brattain at Bell Labs. The term transistor was formed from a contraction of the words 'transfer resistance'.

Shockley is an extremely interesting character. Born in London to American parents, he was raised in Palo Alto, California. He achieved his PhD right across the continent at MIT and then went on to join the Bell Labs in New Jersey.

Shockley's war-time work was to be engaged in radar and anti-submarine warfare, but towards the end of the war he was given a very unusual task. He was asked to estimate the likely losses of a US invasion of Japan.

After deliberation he concluded that such an enterprise would need to 'budget' for the deaths of up to ten million Japanese, with a loss to the United States of up to 800,000 dead plus several million additional casualties. It has been suggested that it was this Shockley estimate that had a direct influence on the decision to use the atomic bomb to bring the war to a much speedier and less costly end.

Post-war Shockley led a solid-state physics team at the Bell Labs to develop an alternative approach to the fragile and heat-generating vacuum tube.

Bardeen and Brattain succeeded in December 1947 with what they called their 'Type A' transistor. They found that two contacts placed adjacent to each other on a germanium slab would amplify the current applied to one contact by 100 times as it emerged from the other.

Shockley had worked together with Bardeen and Brattain but there was a lot of friction when the patents were eventually submitted. Shockley's main contribution to this development, the field effect principle, was found to have already been patented in Canada back in 1930. As a result the Bell Labs attorneys applied just for the work that had been contributed by Bardeen and Brattain, for what they now termed the 'point-contact transistor'.

In 1948 the European point-contact transistor was quite separately discovered by two Germans. Herbert Mataré and Heinrich Welker had both been involved in the German war effort to produce its own radar system. Mataré had worked at Telefunken on crystal rectifiers while Welker was seeking ways of purifying germanium in Munich. Post-war they had been hired by a Westinghouse subsidiary based in Paris to work on solid-state rectifiers.

Mataré pursued an effect he had noted with germanium during the war and came up with the same conclusion as the Bell team. Imagine the shock when they learned Bell had beaten them to it. Undeterred they launched the 'transistron' and many thousand were taken up by the French PTT.

In the meantime Shockley had been extremely unhappy with the Bell Labs patent decision. Instead of arguing against it he buried himself in work to seek out other approaches. He pursued what became called a 'junction transistor' which he demonstrated in January 1948 and subsequently patented as his notion; it was in production by 1951.

Bell Labs continued its research and established later that silicon was a better material than germanium; it could operate across broader temperatures and had less leakage. They created the first silicon transistor in January 1954 but went no further with this development.

A set of Bell émigrés pursued the idea at Texas Instruments (TI) and gained most of the credit for its silicon transistor that was released in April 1954. TI soon dominated the silicon transistor business.

Bell Labs set about the challenges involved in developing pure enough samples of germanium and silicon for these new inventions to be efficient. It also began licensing its developments to others, for example in 1952 gathering forty companies that each paid a $25,000 licence to attend detailed training sessions.

Transistors appeared in consumer products such as hearing aids in the early 50s.

But it was to be the transistor radio that fully publicised the technology. Texas Instruments and Regency had a major early success with the Regency TR-1 radio that was launched in October 1954 at just $49.95; they sold over 100,000 units. But the Tokyo Telecommunications Company, later to be renamed Sony, launched the TR-52 transistor radio in March 1955 at just $29.95 and cleaned up. It was not just about consumer products, soon transistorised mainframe computers were being designed and created too.

In the meantime Shockley had fallen out with Bell and moved back to California where, as part of Beckman Instruments, he soon established the Shockley Semiconductor Laboratory in Mountain View, six miles outside Palo Alto.

Into this operation he recruited a number of promising graduates including Bob Noyce and Gordon Moore. But Shockley proved extremely difficult to work with, on one occasion threatening to use a lie detector on the whole team over some relatively insignificant incident. Moore delicately described him as,

'...a rather unusual personality, very bright, phenomenal physical intuition, but with relatively little idea how to work with people.'

RANDOM ACCESS MOMENT:
Shockley's move to the area often leads to him being credited as one of the co-founders of Silicon Valley though actually its beginnings can be traced back to the formation of Stanford University in 1891 and the the Stanford Industrial Park in 1951 that prompted Eastman Kodak, General Electric and Lockheed to move in.

Certainly the momentum for Silicon Valley was established when Shockley, Fairchild and Hewlett-Packard founded their electronics businesses there. They were soon joined by Intel, NASA, Engelbart's ARC, Intel, Shugart, Xerox PARC - and where else would Cisco, Google, Netscape, Sun, Yahoo! Facebook and others choose to be based?

IC IC IC

Robert Norton Noyce and Gordon Moore, plus six colleagues, left Shockley - the man himself called them the 'Traitorous Eight'. They went on to create the second electronic 'stepping stone' - the integrated circuit.

The demand had shifted and now system builder were asking for better and less expensive ways of more readily interconnecting transistors.

The IC had been first conceived at the Radar Research Establishment in the UK back in May 1952. It was Geoffrey Dummer at the UK's Telecommunications Research Establishment (TRE) that presciently posited,

'With the advent of the transistor and the work in semiconductors generally, it seems now possible to envisage electronic equipment in a solid block with no connecting wires.'

Yet it took serendipity to move things forward. In 1955 a Bell Labs chemist called Carl Frosch had an accident. Some impure hydrogen gas caught fire in the fabrication process and the outcome was that the silicon he was working with was coated in a layer of silicon dioxide.

This accident led to the discovery that coating silicon wafers and protecting them in this way during the manufacturing process would avoid the surface pitting problem that had previously been evident. This soon became part of the process that was used to fabricate transistors.

Also in 1955 Bell Labs discovered a new application for the photo-engraving techniques were already used in the manufacture of printed circuit boards. They realised that a similar approach called photo-lithography could etch away at the photosensitive silicon oxide coating and in this way micro circuits might be described onto the silicon.

In 1957 it was Sherman Fairchild, the same Fairchild significant in the aircraft business, who would fund this team of eight with its $1.3m start-up requirement - and Fairchild Semiconductor was born.

Noyce had earned his PhD in Physics at MIT but earlier while at Grinnell College his physics professor had acquired two of the earliest Bell transistors; reportedly Noyce was hooked as soon as he saw them! After qualification he initially joined Philco where he was engaged in making transistors. He then moved to Shockley but when the group of individuals decided to make their exit he, at the age of twenty-nine, was appointed to lead Fairchild Semiconductor.

Their first objective was to commence a volume production of silicon transistors. This was the very thing that Shockley had chosen not to manufacture; he had wanted instead to pursue diodes. The new Fairchild team could not see a market for diodes, but knew that the military would buy plenty of silicon transistors.

Early work on producing components directly onto silicon had been achieved by RCA, where an oscillator in silicon was created. Bell Labs and IBM also developed techniques that could describe an electronic counter onto silicon. Japan's Ministry of Trade and Industry and Texas Instruments established something of a patent race to define a raft of devices that might be made in this way.

The young Fairchild team had remarkable success setting up crystal-growing, evolving photolithography and developing its manufacturing processes.

It was military and government contracts that made this semiconductor progress possible, only these institutions had the deep pockets to fund the huge investment required. They needed greater reliability and the ability for their applications to operate in harsh operating conditions. They pushed the fabric as they demanded ever-more sophisticated devices.

One of the co-founders at Fairchild, Jean Hoerni, developed something he called the planar process. This involved photographically removing the silicon dioxide coating using a film negative that protected or revealed the coating to the photolithographic process. Areas not etched off left the silicon oxide as an insulator and the 'doped' area which had cleared the coating away was the conductors. The circuits were completed by interconnecting the conductors with aluminium wiring.

The first silicon mesa transistor, the 2N697, was launched in 1958; named for its raised flat structure. It was subsequently selected for the guidance system of the Minuteman missile.

In 1958 Noyce at Fairchild worked on a photolithographic camera system that could create identical transistors on a single wafer. But all these were for devices with one specified purpose.

Noyce found he could photographically etch diodes, transistors, resistors and capacitors. He quickly filed for the patent for an integrated circuit (IC) on 30 July 1959. Noyce got the patent but was only credited with being the co-inventor, along with Jack St Clair Kilby at Texas Instruments.

Kilby had gone down a different route connecting the capacitors, transistors and resistors with fine gold wiring that he called 'flying wires'. He had beaten Noyce to it when his solid circuit concept was announced in March 1959.

Kilby had failed his entry exams to MIT by a 'smidge' and therefore graduated from the University of Illinois achieving his master's at the University of Wisconsin.

During WWII he concentrated on miniaturisation of radios to be used for jungle-warfare. In 1947 he worked at Centralab, Milwaukee on radio and television components and hearing aids. Here he was free to experiment as the electronics field advanced and in doing so earned ten or more patents.

He joined Texas Instruments (TI) in 1958. TI had also been early in the move from germanium towards silicon for its transistors and it was Kilby who saw how silicon might be used for ICs. He had joined TI to spend his time on miniaturisation and came up with his 'Monolithic' idea, which he described as,

'...circuit elements such as resistors, capacitors, distributed capacitors and transistors - if all made of the same material - could be included in a single chip.'

On 12 September 1958 he was able to demonstrate his first IC.

Fairchild believed Noyce's approach to be much more conducive for applications of mass production. The US courts agreed that Kilby and TI should have the patent for the IC but Noyce and Fairchild would hold the patent for the manufacturing process. Despite this it was Kilby alone who earned the Nobel Prize for Physics in 2000 for the invention of the IC.

In 1962-3 the upgrade to the Minuteman 2 nuclear intercontinental missile provided a sales breakthrough when it was concluded that it would be built exclusively with ICs because of their proven greater reliability. This provided volume sales of a broad variety of different ICs, and for this military application a high price was not an issue.

But ICs elsewhere met reluctance from engineers who had become used to buying a batch of components and building systems for themselves. Although they were being offered a turnkey system with ICs, they did not meet with instant approval.

To overcome the general market reluctance Noyce adopted a simple marketing technique. He offered their ICs at the same price as the individual components would have cost, without the hassle of the user having to assemble them.

This meant that initially he was offering ICs for sale at well below the current cost price but he assumed that if he could develop volume sales then they could close the gap and eventually reach profitability - which proved to be the case.

Burroughs and RCA were the first to use ICs in the construction of mainframe computers.

Another individual at Fairchild Semiconductor is worthy of note. Don Valentine, a New Yorker, who had worked on the West Coast while in the military and convinced his employer Sylvania, to move him to California in 1957. He joined Fairchild in 1959 and rose to become senior sales and marketing executive where he hired, among others, Mike Markkula (later of Apple) to take a marketing role.

In 1967 Valentine left for National Semiconductor which he described as more manufacturing-biased rather than scientific, much more interested in quality and price than the science. There they had no qualms about sourcing from the Far East. His role was to be the presenter for National to the financial market, and this clearly defined his next change of direction.

In 1972 he left to found Sequoia Capital, a venture capital operation. He pioneered the accumulation of funds from individual investors and institutions being applied to start ups, primarily in the electronics sector.

Sequoia went on to fund hundreds of operations including many major PC companies including Apple, Atari, Cisco, Electronic Arts, Google, LinkedIn, LSI Logic, nVidia, PayPal, Plaxo, Rackspace, Yahoo!, YouTube…

Moore's Law

In April 1965 Gordon Moore, as head of research and development at Fairchild Semiconductor, wrote an article in *Electronics* magazine to first air his views on the speed of semiconductor development.

Subsequently this opinion became known generally as 'Moore's Law'. It suggested that the equivalent number of transistors able to be included on a microchip would double every year. By 1975 he revised it to state that it would still double, but now only every eighteen months.

The subsequent facts certainly seem to have confirmed this:
- Texas Instruments produced the first silicon transistor in 1954. This was the base zero for Moore's Law - a single transistor;
- By the 1960s TTL quads or gates were being manufactured which contained effectively a set of 16 transistors;

- By the 1970s 8-bit microprocessors arrived with the equivalent of 4,500 transistors;
- By the 1980s, the 32-bit MPUs had an equivalent of over a quarter of a million transistors;
- The 1990s saw new 32-bit MPUs with the equivalent of over 3 million transistors;
- The 64-bit MPUs of the 2000s have the equivalent of almost 600 million transistors.

The development path was not just about increasing size, it was also about decreasing costs. Early Fairchild transistors each had a price tag of around $150, but sales volumes managed to progressively drive this down to a unit price of just a few dollars. Today for the same few dollars you can buy a 64-megabit dynamic random access memory (DRAM) with the equivalent of some 70 million transistors.

In April 2005 Moore rescinded his 'law', saying this exponential growth could not continue as the industry was soon to approach a fundamental barrier. The individual circuits would need to be reduced towards the size of atoms and at this size their fundamental behaviours and properties would change.

His law however acted as a valuable yardstick or mission statement, rather like President John F Kennedy's stated mission to put a man on the moon by the end of the '60s. As a result of this NASA and its contractors were able to resolve deadlocks and other decisions by asking which course of action would be more likely to achieve the mission objective.

Moore's Law did the same for the semiconductor business. Each of the industry players had to plan accordingly and recognize that if developments failed to match the timescale of the 'law' then they were falling behind and this could lead to disaster.

I'll Hoff and I'll puff

When Fairchild looked to appoint a new CEO without considering Noyce for the role, he and Moore decided that they should leave.

In July 1968 they rapidly raised $2.5m based upon just a single-page business plan document; well, their track record did speak for itself. They co-founded NM Electronics, for Noyce and Moore, but a year later it was renamed to become Intel Corporation, a name derived from Integrated Electronics.

Using concepts proposed by Ted Hoff, Intel produced the 1103 DRAM, a 1K-bit device that by 1972 was the world best-selling memory chip. It was at the heart of HP's 9800 series computers and quickly replaced core-type memory.

But perhaps more importantly Intel brought about the development of the third stepping stone of semiconductors, the microprocessor.

A microprocessor is the name applied to an IC that contains almost all or the entire series of functions for a computer's central processing unit (CPU), all on the single chip. In the case of the very first, the 4004, this was delivered on a 16-pin IC.

During the 1960s computers had been created from a series of IC chips, from ten through to hundreds, but miniaturisation had reached the stage where everything could be compressed into the one chip, not that this was presumed or developed as a natural process.

In fact, as we shall see, Intel's development of the 4004 was not the culmination of a dream, plan or any special breakthrough moment. It was the result of a simple 'work-around'. It was not even designed for a computer but was the response to a tough specification that Intel had received from a Japanese calculator company.

Busicom (Business Computer Corporation) had developed a plan for a calculator that required the use of twelve custom-built ICs. Intel was chosen to be the supplier of these ICs.

Intel's team of Ted Hoff, Stan Mazor and Federico Faggin was set the task of developing these twelve ICs but thought they could perhaps save themselves a great deal of time and effort if all twelve could be compressed onto one chip. They were seeking to cram the equivalent of 2,300 transistors into the device.

Busicom had been founded back in 1945 as the Nippon Calculating Machine Corporation where it had built up its business around the 'Odhner' calculator.

Odhner, a Swede, founded his company in St Petersburg, Russia in 1873 and from there produced a range of mechanical arithmometers. It is suggested that 'his' design was not original and in fact was based very directly upon the earlier Charles Xavier Thomas de Colmar Arithmometer.

Odhner first manufactured his calculators for Ludvig Nobel for whom he had previously worked. While there he had been involved with Nobel's business in manufacturing artillery shells, cannons, wheels and other products. Ludvig was the older brother of Alfred, the inventor of both dynamite and subsequently the notion of the Nobel Prize.

By the time of the Russian Revolution in 1917 Odhner had produced more than 20,000 calculators, but the St Petersburg factory was then promptly transferred into state control. He and his family moved production to Sweden, but still operated as Odhner.

The Soviets later moved the abandoned production facilities to Moscow and called their version the Felix Arithmometer. But this change of tack opened the door to many other companies around the world to seize upon an opportunity to compete.

In Germany a Braunschweig-based organisation acquired the patents in Odhner's calculator and developed the Brunsviga range, from the Latin version of the town's name. By 1912 it too claimed to have sold over 20,000 units.

Separately both Tiger and Busicom, based in Japan, established manufacturing based upon the Odhner design; millions were manufactured. In this unorthodox manner the many clones of the Odhner made it the most successful mechanical calculator.

Busicom sought to reduce its production costs and devised a calculator based entirely upon integrated circuits. The design called for twelve of them and they rather courageously approached Intel, a new and small operation that had only been running for a year. Busicom tasked them to make the designs in silicon, and contracted with them to produce some 60,000 sets over three years.

Prior to this, and through the early stages of the project, Intel's business was in producing memory chips. In 1969 its focus had been on producing the first 1k-bit dynamic memory, the 1103, and a 2k-bit 1702 EPROM, the world's first non-volatile, electrically programmable, UV-erasable ROM. They had no expressed desire or intention to become the microprocessor innovators that they unintentionally became.

At around the same time Intel had signed another custom-chip project for the Computer Terminal Corporation (CTC) Datapoint 2200 terminal. This project required some 100 TTL, transistor-transistor logic, components to be integrated into just a handful of chips. Marcian Edward 'Ted' Hoff proposed that this too might be achieved with just one chip.

Hoff was the individual charged with defining an approach for the Busicom proposal. He had attended Rensselaer Polytechnic Institute and during a summer job was inspired to achieve his first two patents. He gained his master's and PhD at Stanford and in 1968 was appointed Intel's Manager of Applications Research.

Hoff realised that producing the Busicom twelve-IC design was a pretty forbidding task for a rather small and very young team. Merely as an exercise in expediency he therefore drew on his previous CTC thinking and conceived a way in which the twelve ICs might be delivered onto just the single chip.

He realised that this would not in fact prove to be much more complex than the work on some of the current memory chips. Together with Stan Mazor, he prepared the product specification for this one-chip approach; it would then be supported with several memory and I/O, input-output chips.

Having gained Busicom approval for the approach they hired Federico Faggin as the leader of the team to design and develop this single chip.

Faggin was born in Italy where he worked at Olivetti. He had developed his own computer at the age of 19 in 1960. He had then worked for Fairchild in Italy on MOS ICs then transferred to its Palo Alto base in 1968. There he developed the first MOS silicon-gate IC, the Fairchild 3708.

Faggin joined Intel in 1970 and had only been in his role for two days when Masatoshi Shima, the Busicom engineer who was developing the calculator firmware, arrived at Intel from Japan.

Shima had planned just a short trip to check on the logic design of the single chip and to review the general progress of the project but was shocked on finding Intel had made little-to-no progress. He eventually stayed for seven months helping to drive the project forward.

Faggin and Shima completed what became the 4004 by late 1971. It was to become the very first microprocessor on a single-chip in production. The terminology used here is cautious because of the prior three-chip CPU secret development for the Tomcat aircraft.

The whole development could have become a Japanese exclusive product as the original agreement between Intel and Busicom ceded the Japanese company exclusivity for the 4004.

However Busicom was strapped for cash at the time and approached Intel for a lower price. This opened the door for Intel to suggest that this could only be achieved if they were to increase production volumes. Busicom could not buy any more than they were committed to and the only way forward was for Intel to be permitted to sell to others. Busicom agreed to give Intel back the rights to the 4004 product in return for Intel returning to Busicom the original development monies, circa $65k.

Dr Masatoshi Shima from Busicom was unimpressed by the technology itself. After they had completed the design he said

'I was not so excited when the 4004 became functional, but when the 4004 worked as the engine for a calculator with my program, I was very excited and happy, because my responsibility was to develop a calculator.'

So Busicom gave up control of the first single-chip microprocessor for $65k! Its position did not improve and it was bankrupt by 1974. Broughtons of Bristol later bought the brand and badged a number of products as Busicom Business Machines.

It was Faggin who insisted on changing Intel's product numbering system and defined a family of numbers for use with the chips developed for the project. The 4001 was a Read-Only Memory (ROM), the 4002 was a Random Access Memory (RAM), the 4003 was the input-output (IO) device and the 4004 was designated as the microprocessor.

The 4004 was a 16-pin device with the equivalent of 2,300 transistors. It was capable of performing 60,000 transactions per second. Intel launched the

4004 as its own commercial product in late 1971. The Microcomputer System 4-bit (MCS-4) was announced as an assembled 4001, 4002, 4003 and 4004.

All the documentation supporting the MCS-4 was produced by Adam Osborne, who would go on to make his own PC marque.

A personal computer urban myth is that the 4004 was included on NASA's Pioneer 10, or Pioneer F, the first craft to pass through the asteroid belt and make direct observations of Jupiter and later the first to depart our solar system. While NASA confirms that the 4004 had been considered they had concluded that it was just too new to be safely included.

But almost as soon as it was introduced the 4004 was updated and surpassed by the Intel 4040 which held 3,000 transistors and work at the same speeds; this 'upgrade' was introduced in 1974.

There is one thing worth noting about the 4004. Federico Faggin etched his initials FF into its design, rather as a painter autographs his masterpieces. If you find a 4004 that has some grey traces in its white ceramic component, then go straight to eBay; they are worth over $1,000 today. If you find one without the grey 'flaws' the value is halved, but still probably worth more than the product that you found it in!

In the meantime the 1201 chip being developed by Intel for the Datapoint 2200 task had experienced some delays, and then to cap it all was rejected by CTC.

However at some stage Seiko had approached Intel, interested in using the chip for one of its own calculators. Intel received CTC's approval to market this chip as an Intel product.

Introduced in April 1972, this development was renamed the Intel 8008. It was a 16-pin device with 3,500 transistors and, although it ran a tad slower than the 4004 and 4040, because it worked with eight bits at a time it had an overall speed advantage. It also had the capacity to address much more memory and other components.

Masatoshi Shima was hired by Intel to work on the upgrade of this MPU to the 8080 which was also launched in 1974. This was a 40-pin device that used the higher-performance NMOS (N-channel metal oxide semiconductor) technology. It had the equivalent of 5,000 transistors and was capable of handling 290,000 instructions per second.

With the arrival of the 8080, engineers in many organisations felt that they could now 'stop the bus' and get onto the microprocessor trip. As a result the 8080 became the basis for many early PCs – Micral in France, Scelbi's 8H, the Mark-8, the Altair…

Who was first?

Most observers credit Intel and its 4004 as the first MPU but Intel did not seek a patent for it because they thought it was just an extension of current technology.

Around the same time Fairchild, Motorola and Signetics were each being commissioned to create ever more complex and custom-designed integrated circuits that would inevitably lead to other microprocessor approaches.

Among the precursors to the MPU was Texas Instruments' development in 1971 of the TMS 1802NC, a 'calculator-on-a-chip'. That same year Pico Electronics and General Instrument also produced a single-chip calculator for Monroe for use on its Royal Digital III.

In 1974 the Intel SOC (system-on-a-chip) integrated the features required for an electronic watch including the transistors to drive an LED display into just one chip. Only four years earlier in 1970 the Hamilton Pulsar Wrist Computer digital watch had been released containing 44 chips at a cost of $2,100; the Microma watch using the TI SOC chip sold from 1976 at just $20. Soon SOC was applied to the Texas Instruments pocket electronic calculator which against intense Far East competition was selling at just $10.

Today both the Smithsonian and the US Patent Office state that Texas Instruments got there first with a computer-on-a-chip.

Gary W Boone and Michael J Cochran created a micro-controller in July 1971. It was designed for use in computer keyboards, TV and VCR controls, and other household and industrial applications and completed just a few weeks prior to the Intel 4004.

This original TI product had a number of problems but its concepts evolved into the 4-bit TMS 1000 which was commercially available from 1974. TI heralded the product as,

'...a microcomputer – the first integrated circuit with all the elements of a complete computer on a single chip of silicon.'

In 1990 there was a furore when the US patent office unexpectedly awarded Gilbert Hyatt the patent for the single-chip microprocessor. Hyatt had claimed he developed an MPU even earlier in 1968; though it was as a machine tool controller.

Intriguingly his business, Micro Computer Inc, listed among its investors Robert Noyce and Gordon Moore, the very founders of Intel. This patent office legal decision suggested that Hyatt would be due millions from the semiconductor manufacturers; he somewhat gloated at the decision,

'This will set history straight. And this will encourage inventors to stick to their inventions when they're up against the big companies.'

But his joy was extinguished in 1996 when TI fought and overturned the decision on the basis that Hyatt's device had never been implemented; in fact given the current capabilities that were to hand back then it would have been an impossibility.

Boone and TI were awarded the patent and as a result Intel and TI entered into various cross-licence agreements that called for Intel to pay royalties to TI.

In reality they were all beaten to it by Garrett AiResearch when it developed the Central Air Data Computer. This was developed by Raymond M Holt and Steve Geller as an electronic replacement for electromechanical computers specifically to be used on the US Navy F-14 Tomcat fighter.

The Tomcat's MP944 digital processor had all the attributes to be considered the first microprocessor though it was not single-chip and it was not a general purpose device having been defined specifically for its role.

It used a set of MOS (metal oxide semiconductor) chips to do its job, not just the one, and was operational in 1970. However the development for the US Navy was a secret and no general information on this could be released until 1998. As a result Intel and TI were left to squabble over authorship. When TI was eventually awarded the patent it was not challenged by Garrett AiResearch.

Later Ray Holt, part Cherokee Native American, formed Microcomputer Associates in 1975 and released the JOLT computer kit that emerged at the time of a flurry of kits and it had limited success.

8 - Kit and Caboodle - hobby computer kits

'Foolproof systems don't take into account the ingenuity of fools.' Gene Brown

During the '60s and '70s the big mainframe manufacturers had a distinct commercial interest in sustaining a mystique for their computers. They saw little value in making them more understandable or more available. They were perfectly happy with their huge price tags and margins, so it would not be they who would set out to develop the personal computer.

Senior managers in IBM for example seldom even had a terminal at their desks, believing this to be something for lower-level data processing staff members. In much the same way they saw early word processors as something designed for typists and secretaries. No desire here for distributed or personal computing.

So it was, to a large extent, that the PC would come from enthusiasts and hobbyists seeking to build their own computers. After all, they had built radio crystal sets and other electrical and electronic products, so why not build a computer?

PC Genesis

Edmund Callis Berkeley, a Harvard man, met computers at their very inception, having used the Bell Labs calculators and the Harvard Mark I.

In his chosen career as an insurance actuary with the Prudential he had produced a specification for the use of sequence-controlled computers at the insurance company. This exercise led to the company buying one of the first UNIVACs.

In 1949 he wrote *Giant Brains or Machines That Think* to describe the current state of the computing art. In this he proposed Simon as a compact and simple-to-use 'mechanical brain'; this was the in-vogue parlance for computers at the time.

For *Radio Electronics* magazine in 1950 and 1951 Berkeley published the plans for Simon based upon relay logic; it would cost less than $600 to build.

Two Columbia University graduates used the plans and produced the first working model. It had quite limited capabilities but some four hundred sets of plans were sold and one of Berkeley's declared objectives for it was,

'...Simon may start a fad of building baby mechanical brains, similar to the hobby of building crystal radio sets that swept the country in the 1920s...'

It took a few years but this prediction proved to be spot on.

Berkeley was back again in 1955 with a series of products. The first was Genius Almost-Automatic Computer (GENIAC) the 'almost' because it had no relays, tubes or semiconductors to operate a switch; the operator had to do the grunt work for it.

GENIAC plans cost just $19.95. It was an electrical device not electronic, and was intended as an educational toy; however it provided many with a first encounter with the concepts involved in computing.

He followed it up with TINYAC, Tiny Almost-Automatic Computer; WEENIAC, Weeny Almost-Automatic Computer; BRAINIAC, Brain-Imitating Almost-Automatic Computer.

Berkeley later helped to co-found the Association for Computing Machinery (ACM) – with Richard W Hamming.

Build your own computer

Heath Company, owned by Schlumberger, released the Heathkit EC-1 as a computer kit for under $200 in 1959. It was also available at a higher price fully assembled.

It too was analogue not digital. It looked and functioned more like a piece of instrumentation, but it set in many minds the idea that a low-cost personal computer might one day be achievable. In 1979 Schlumberger sold the Heath Company to Zenith Radio Corporation for $64.5m.

Claude Shannon, one of the great personal computer philosophers, in 1961 devised the Minivac 601 Digital Computer Kit as an educational device using electro-mechanical relays.

It was initially sold by the Scientific Development Corporation for just $85. The early units were taken up by educational establishments, to teach binary arithmetic and to illustrate how an assembler worked.

SDC then changed the colour and altered the switches to make it appear more businesslike and then raised the price to $479, advertising it as,

'The Minivac 601 is a unique digital computer - the small brother of huge electronic brains that are the new tools of science and industry.'

It sold several hundred of them to businesses that wished to learn about computing.

Scoping the d-i-y business

Stephen Barratt Gray, Computer Editor with McGraw Hill's *Electronics* magazine, was one of many who had been motivated in the 1960s to set about building his own computer. But he found there was a dearth of useful information on the subject.

'I realized there was much I could learn from building a computer. It didn't take long to find out how difficult it was just to get started. There were no kits, no "cookbooks." Computer textbooks usually contained partial schematics, but none told how to connect the various sections.'

So in May 1966 Gray wrote to seven electronics and computer trade magazines and to three hobbyist magazines, proposing the formation of a non-profit association for the interchange of ideas and the sharing of information on building computers.

Gray used a different term, 'amateur computers', and went on to found the Amateur Computer Society (ACS). The society uncovered a great deal of interest, attracting an inaugural 110 members from the United States and from five other countries - all male!

He explained that the task facing them was formidable,

'...in the mid-sixties, to build a simple computer accumulator, which could do no more than add successive inputs, using toggle switches for input and lamps for output, cost several dollars per bit. To build an extremely simple "computer" with four-bit words and without memory, and which divided the easy way (by repeated subtraction without shifting), could cost two or three hundred dollars.'

By November 1967 the ACS Newsletter ran a survey among its members asking for details of their projects and finished computers. The results are interesting.

'Most of those who returned the survey form planned on using core memory, the hardest part of the computer to get working... ...but few got core up and running...

... As to "cost so far," the range was from zero to $1,500, with an average (among those reporting a cost) of $650. For "estimated cost when complete", the range was from $300 to "over $10,000" with an average of $2,100.'

So this was not at this stage a low-cost hobby, and the products they were designing were apparently not particularly convenient either,

'Jim Sutherland, an engineer with Westinghouse in Pittsburgh, noted that his Echo IV took a year to build and would need ten years to program. Echo IV was seven feet long (2.1m), one and a half feet deep (0.46m), and six feet high (1.8m).'

Gray would become a regular contributor to *Creative Computing* the first title that was published targeting personal computer users. In 1992 he donated the ACS archives to the Charles Babbage Institute.

Open the show Hal

Our next player, Hal Chamberlin Jr, is often claimed as the producer of the first personal computer.

Homer Dudley at Bell Labs worked from 1928 to develop a keyboard-operated speech synthesiser called the 'Vocoder' that would analyse speech and then transmit it. It was an early attempt to take telephone voice messages and encode them to reduce the bandwidth requirements; it was patented in March 1939.

Dudley later produced 'VODER', or Voice Operating Demonstrator, a speech synthesis system. It was subsequently adapted to create SIGSALY for encrypting wartime messages in 1943. Alan Turing worked with Bell Labs on this exercise.

Experimenting with mainframe computers to produce music soon became a popular pastime. An early Ferranti in 1951 was used to play 'Baa Baa Black Sheep' and 'In the Mood'.

The Aussies claim that they got there first with the Council for Scientific and Industrial Research Automatic Computer (CSIRAC). Certainly this was the first digital computer in Australia - with 2,000 valves. It played the 'Colonel Bogey March' some months earlier than the Ferranti feat in November 1949. It is still on show at Melbourne Museum.

In 1957 Max Vernon Mathews at Bell Labs wrote a sound generating program he called 'Music' on an early IBM 704 mainframe computer. As 'Music 1' it later played a 17-second tune in New York City. This simple beginning was to inspire many others.

Peter Samson had noticed that MIT's TX-O mainframe computer had an audio speaker that provided a positive feedback to show it was running satisfactorily. Regular users could listen to the tones and establish where they were in their program. Samson developed a series of codes that would change the pitch of the speaker to make it play simple one-voice tunes. When in 1961 MIT got its PDP-1, Samson developed a four-voice program he called Harmony Compiler.

Also in 1961 John Larry Kelly Jr had developed his 'Vocoder' voice recorder synthesis system and applied it to an IBM 704 to play 'Daisy Bell', better known to most as 'Daisy, Daisy'.

The sci-fi writer Arthur C Clarke had been present visiting a friend on that occasion and he filed away the notion. When he worked with Stanley Kubrick on a movie expanding his short story 'The Sentinel', the memory re-emerged.

Centre stage in that movie, '2001 - a Space Odyssey', was the HAL-9000 computer. Who can forget that scene when the fictional artificial intelligence computer went rogue?

'Open the pod bay doors HAL.' 'I'm sorry, Dave. I'm afraid I can't do that.'

Dave has therefore to force his way aboard and disconnect HAL's memory as it comments, 'My mind is going'. As the computer's memory declines it starts to sing 'Daisy, Daisy'. The computer's name 'HAL' was queried by many as derived from IBM, but Arthur C Clarke commented on the computer's choice of name:

'As is clearly stated in the novel (Chapter 16), HAL stands for Heuristically programmed ALgorithmic computer. However, about once a week some character spots the fact that HAL is one letter ahead of IBM in the alphabet,

and promptly assumes that Stanley [Kubrick] and I were taking a crack at the estimable institution... ...As it happened, IBM had given us a good deal of help, so we were quite embarrassed by this, and would have changed the name had we spotted the coincidence.'

Another Hal, Howard 'Hal' Chamberlin Jr, while at college noticed that a punched card reader on the college's IBM 1360 photo-digital archival storage system generated significant radio frequency interference that played havoc with any nearby transistor radio.

He used this fact to run the cards through the reader using a Do loops program to play out *Daisy Daisy* on the radio as a tribute to the Bell Labs rendition; the Kubrick movie had yet to be released. As only six of the terabit (160 GByte) memory IBM 1360s were ever built this was not going to make him his fortune.

A year later in 1966 it was this Hal who designed what might be considered to be the very first personal computer built from scavenged bits of IBM core memory, logic cards and a paper-tape read/writer.

Later, his friend David B Cox worked with him on the development of the printed circuit boards (PCBs), to help to produce the PC. It was first demonstrated as the HAL-4096 in 1968 at the North Carolina State University Engineer's Fair.

HAL-4096 was later described in the ACS Newsletter of September 1972 and a full set of plans was made available for just $2.

Chamberlin and Cox had moved away from this by then and in February1971 they launched Technology Unlimited Inc where they developed a display word processor. After thirty months of trying to sell the WP idea to both A B Dick and Olivetti they sold the company and its product to Hendrix Electronics. Sadly for them, A B Dick later did buy the WP product from Hendrix and achieved sales of over $1bn for it between 1980 and 1984.

The duo went on to launch Micro Technology Unlimited in 1977 and concentrated their efforts on digital audio communication. In 1979, Chamberlin's book *Musical Applications of Microprocessors* became something of a 'bible' for those in digital audio.

Not a recipe for success

The Honeywell H316 pedestal model aka the Kitchen Computer, launched in 1969, is the other claimant for being the first personal computer.

It was produced as an exclusive product for Nieman Marcus. The Texas-based luxury department store is best known for regularly bringing the world a series of frankly implausible 'His & Her' luxury gifts such as 'His & Her' hot-air balloons at a little under $7,000, 'His & Her' airplanes at $176,000…

The H316 at $10,600 was a computer built-in under a butcher's chopping board that would store recipes. For an additional $100 some 1,000 recipes were available from Helen Corbitt - a famous cook and author, also serving as the director of Food Services at Nieman Marcus.

To use it would require a two-week course on understanding how to toggle the switches and interpret the binary light display. Unsurprisingly it appears that none were ever sold.

Meanwhile out West

John V Blankenbaker was in his first year of mathematics and physics at Oregon State University when he started to design a computer way back in 1949, but he put it aside.

Working as an intern at the National Bureau of Standards he encountered the first-generation mainframe SEAC (standards eastern automatic computer), one of the first electronic stored-program computers in the USA.

Later, while achieving his master's at UCLA, he worked at Hughes Aircraft Company where he was charged with the design of a business data processor; this project was subsequently shelved.

He went on to MIT to qualify in electrical engineering and then worked with a pioneering company that provided real-time solutions for the stock market.

In 1970 he was inspired by the development of the IC, integrated circuit, to found his own operation that would develop a small computer. It was sold fully-assembled, used transistor-transistor logic (TTL) and had switches for inputs and lights as outputs; it could manage a few hundred instructions per second and had 256 bytes of memory.

He called the company Kenbak, taken from the middle of his surname. The product was the Kenbak-1.

It was aimed at the education market with its first two units supplied to a private school at $750 per unit. But budgetary cycles and decisions proved protracted in this market. The operation eventually built just forty Kenbaks but this still made it the first commercially-available personal computer. He sold the rights on to CTI, a more general school and college supplier.

Blankenbaker continued to work in the business with several innovative computer designs for other companies until he retired in 1985.

Adding fizz to the proceedings

Steve Wozniak, later to design both the Apple I and Apple II, regularly got together across 1970-71 with a friend called Bill Fernandez.

They stayed up late drinking Cragmont cream sodas to build a computer using cast-off components that they had gleaned from nearby semiconductor companies. They worked in the garage of Fernandez's father, the then mayor of Sunnyvale.

They called their completed product the 'Cream Soda Computer'. One of their parents arranged for a local reporter to visit and produce an article about the device. But its future proved short-lived when its power supply blew while it was being demonstrated to the journalist.

It was Bill Fernandez who first introduced Wozniak to Jobs. The Cream Soda computer was the first 'knockings' of what would later become the Apple I. By then Steve Jobs was involved and it was to be his father's garage that they used.

Fernandez became the first employee at Apple, though for his work pass he was designated as #4.

Correspondence coarse

In July 1971 the National Radio Institute, an organiser of correspondence courses owned by the publishing house McGraw Hill, produced a home study course on computing.

They commissioned Lou Frenzel to create a five-part computer kit. This very simple device was called the NRI-832 computer and was designed in solid-state circuitry.

The course cost $503 and taught how to build this limited device. It had just 16 or 32 bytes of memory and used toggles and lights for input-output devices. It was however another of the early commercially available computer kits.

This 'Airfix-type' constructor-set market tested soldering skills rather than any computing knowledge and the kits seldom even had a keyboard. Any attempt at developing software skills was by definition pretty minimal too.

At this time, while kits proved popular with hobbyists, these users were often more interested in the process of creating a computer and less in what it might actually do for them afterwards.

Intel, followed by others, launched single-chip microprocessors, and it was these that opened the door for lower-cost and much more capable personal computer products to emerge.

These new products would harness a new marketing approach by linking closely with the many successful hobbyist magazines.

Served up with chips

Intel, soon followed by others, launched microprocessors, single-chip central processing units (CPUs) and this rapidly opened the door for lower-cost and much more capable personal computer products to emerge.

These new products would soon harness a new marketing approach by linking closely with hobbyist magazines. At this time, while kits proved popular with hobbyists, they were often more interested in the process of creating a computer and less in what it might actually do for them afterwards.

A Vietnamese immigrant to France, André Truong Trong Thi, emerged at the Institut National de la Recherche Agronomique (INRA) in Paris. It was to be a pressing need that fostered his development track - in this case a requirement to control hygrometric or atmospheric humidity, measurements.

The team at INRA had started with a minicomputer approach and would have liked to have used a PDP-8 but their application did not have the budget for this. They opted instead to develop their own personal computer around the Intel 8008.

The original team started in the de rigueur hut and moved on to become Realisations Études Électroniques SA (R2E); Truong Trong Thi was its chief executive. They developed the first commercial, and significantly non-kit based, personal computer called the Micral-N.

It was launched in 1972 with the first prototype ready by January 1973; it had all the modern attributes of a PC and it predated the Altair by around two years!

R2E sought applications for it such as process-control and road-toll booths where cost was not an issue and thus its price-point of 8,500 French Francs or c $1,300 was still attractive.

The Micral-N hardware was designed by François Gernelle with a small team. Philippe Kahn developed the software originally called 'Sysmic' but in 1978 renamed 'Prologue'. Some 90,000 Micral Ns were sold.

Despite the French government's ambition to foster a local computer industry, Kahn concluded that to be successful in this embryonic business he needed to be in the USA. He took a job with Hewlett Packard initially, then left later to form Borland in 1982.

Kahn would grow Borland into a $500 million listed business going head-to-head with Microsoft, Lotus and others. He would later launch Starfish Software, then LightSurf Technologies, where he is credited with developing the first camera phone. Later he founded FullPower Technologies which developed MotionX and MotionX-GPS for Apple's iPhone and iTouch.

R2E went on to develop systems around the 8080, 8088 and Z80 microprocessors, moving on from the boxy device with flick switches to include floppy-disks, keyboards, monitors...

In 1979 Groupe Bull bought R2E and the Micral product. Truong Trong Thi joined them as part of the deal. Bull's last version was the Micral 20 before it adopted MS-DOS as its standard for future products. Approaching 100,000 of these French personal computers were sold in total.

By most accounts Truong Trong Thi was late to the party and performed merely as the CEO of R2E, but it did not stop him seeking to be recognised as the inventor of the first personal computer. The courts in 1998 found that he was merely the entrepreneur of R2E and not the inventor, awarding that status instead to François Gernelle.

Truong Trong Thi left Bull and joined Normerel where he developed the Oplite personal computer; by 1988 Normerel was the third largest microcomputer company in France.

In 1995 at 81 years old he formed a company called APCT to work on cryptography. He was awarded the *Legion d'Honneur* for his work in computing; he died in 2005.

In the 1960s Mers Kutt was working at a university in Ontario, Canada, when he became frustrated by the need to prepare punched cards to load a program onto a mainframe. He sought another approach and produced the Key Edit, a device that allowed users to key in programs directly into the mainframe then edit the input.

Apparently having met with Bob Noyce of Intel he managed to acquire some early 8008 MPUs and set about building something that would be useful to dons and students at the university.

He then set out to develop a computer for personal use and formed Kutt Systems Inc. This work eventually led to the development of the MCM/70. This was a small desktop computer that looked something like a large calculator with an integrated keyboard and twin audio cassette recorders. A 14K ROM held the required software and one of the recorders was used as a virtual memory. In this way there was around 100k of memory with a battery back-up.

Disappointingly it had a Burroughs plasma display with a single line of 32 characters. Later it included a floppy-disc drive, printers, plotters, card readers and an RS232 interface; though RS232 was called SCI 1200 at the time.

Just at the point of launch the computer's name was changed to Micro Computer Machines (MCM) based in Toronto, Canada. It was launched in Canada in late 1973 then rapidly followed with launches in New York, Boston and a number of European locations.

What was significant was that on-board was APL (A Programming Language), an interpreter previously only available on mainframes – developed by Ken Iverson at IBM back in 1965. The team emulated the 8008 on an IBM System/360 using macros to simulate each 8008 instruction.

This attracted interest from business, scientific and educational users, selling for example to the US Army and to the NASA (National Aeronautics and Space Administration) Goddard Flight Center. It was not inexpensive at Can$4,950 for the 2K version without cassette recorder and Can$9,820 in its full glory; Canadian dollars were virtually equivalent to the US$ at that time. As APL was hot at the time with many universities around a third of their MCM/70s were sold into education.

MCM lasted as a company and as a product for just a decade but it was certainly one of the first true personal computers; certainly it was the first that was portable at just 20 lbs (9kg) and was the first to achieve some serious end-user applications thanks to its APL on board.

Much later Mers Kutt formed All Computers Inc and fell out with Intel when he claimed that Intel's Pentium and Celeron MPUs had infringed his 1993 patent.

In 2004 at 74 years old he claimed Intel should pay him $500m for the infringement. A bad-natured series of judgments and appeals eventually led nowhere for Kutt.

The Scelbi 8H was founded by design engineer Nat Wadsworth while working at General DataComm Industries where he became intrigued by the Intel 8008 MPU and decided to use it for his new product.

The company name derived from Scientific Electronic Biological and its computer could be purchased ready-assembled or in kit form; it was pronounced by the designers as 'Sell-Bee'. This was the first PC-based microprocessor available.

Promoted initially in the *QST* amateur radio magazine in March 1974, it later featured in *Radio Electronics* and *Byte* magazines.

Wadsworth and his colleague Bob Findley would leave employment after coming up with the design. They clearly found the task was onerous and at just thirty years of age Wadsworth had a heart attack, but recovered to complete the project.

As a kit it cost $565 with 1K of RAM, random access memory, with a further 15K of memory offered for the princely sum of $2,760! There was no high-level language capability but Wadsworth produced a book teaching the use of its assembly language and giving machine code techniques for the product.

The *QST* advertisement received a great response but Wadsworth then had a second heart attack which forced him to scale down his ambitions; as a result the Scelbi faded away. Not a quitter, while in hospital he wrote a book on machine language programming with the 8008 that sold over 1,500 copies at $20 a shot.

'Altogether we sold about 200 computers, half assembled, half kits.' Half were Scelbi-8H hobby computers... ...the rest, differing mainly because of more memory (up to 16K), were Scelbi-8B business computers...'

'For that time, we had a very sophisticated system, a complete system. We had a tape cassette interface ... We had a CRT based on an oscilloscope, and Teletype interface, and we developed a combination monitor, editor, and assembler in ROM.'

Scelbi began to develop software products to support the 8H and the 8B, but which were put in book form: our editors, monitors, and assembler. We sold thousands of copies. After the success of those books, we went on to modify them for the 8080, for the Altair, the IMSAI, whatever was out at that time.'

... The first two were written by Bob Findley. The first was for the 8080, patterned after my [Wadsworth's] machine language programming book. What we had was an engineer's handbook that presented the instruction set and utility routines... ...That was an extremely successful book. Tens of thousands of the cookbooks have been sold in virtually every edition we put out. It became a classic.' Stephen Barratt Grey.

The Scelbi was rapidly pursued to market by an initiative from Jonathon Titus. Titus was doing his doctorate in Virginia and often used a PDP-8L to develop his programming skills but became frustrated wanting a computer of his own; he set about building something.

He bought three 8008 chips at $125 each, and built a set of boards. He developed a panel with switches and indicators that could be used to program the unit, painstakingly bit by binary bit.

From this experimentation he developed the Mark-8 computer which he shipped to both *Popular Electronics* and *Radio Electronics* magazines. It was *Radio Electronics* that featured it on the July 1974 cover.

The basic approach used was odd in that users were expected to buy the plans and boards but then had to acquire the rest of the components themselves; it was not that simple to assemble either. Nonetheless 7,500 sets of plans were sold and a few hundred board sets were shipped out. Its popularity was strong leading Hal Singer to launch a *Mark 8 Newsletter*.

But six months later *Popular Electronics*, smarting from its competitor's success, would work with another maker to launch something to trump the Mark 8.

The Ohio Scientific Superboard II, a single-board computer, was released in 1978. Based on a 6502 MPU it had 4K or 8K of memory and a ROM-based BASIC. It had a 24 line x 24 character video output and at $279 was very good value for money.

It was also available fully-assembled in a case with 16K of RAM and a 5.25" floppy drive at around $1200. The product sold through well.

British kits

If you look on the Internet for background in this market you see endless repetition of the same old stuff from site to site and a great deal of it is plain wrong.

There are also quite a few holes that emerge where there is no champion for a particular piece of hardware or software, holes that seem to glare at you and challenge your own memory. Let's attempt to remedy some of this.

For example history and the Internet are unkind to the Newbury Labs Newbear Electronics 77-68 computer kit which was a bare board with a Motorola 6800 launched in 1977. In truth its major merit was that it was probably the first UK kit; it was heavily publicised among the hobbyists of the time.

In late 1977 a UK company was formed called Nasco, for 'North American Semiconductor Company'. The plan was to import some of the many USA products appearing on the market.

It certainly made some headlines at the time with the Nascom 1, though there are those who suggest that this move was more about raising sales of Z80 MPUs - similar to Chuck Peddle's approach at MOS Technology with the KIM-1 and 6502.

A total sales figure of between 200 and 400 units was forecast, and this was achieved in just days after the launch. Unfortunately the manufacturers of the keyboard could only supply 400 pieces and a keyboard at the right price point had to be rapidly re-sourced.

I recall specifically going to a West London show to see the Nascom-1 as my potential entry-level purchase, but its promotion and promise seemed out of step with its reality in the flesh. Perhaps this was my first understanding that I wanted a computer that would do things, rather than simply a bare kit to build one, my soldering skills have always been meagre.

Nascom-2 followed with the ambition of adding a bus, the device within a computer to interconnect components – that had been developed in the UK to avoid paying any royalty for the established S-100 bus; this was not a success.

The company ran into funding problems and in 1981 and was bought out by Lucas Logic, part of the car and electrical components group. The new operation Lucas Nascom redesigned the bus as the '80-Bus' and launched a short-lived Nascom-3.

Some of the Nascom concepts and products lived on through Gemini Microcomputers Ltd that developed British-made computers in Amersham, Buckinghamshire. Gemini did not really espouse the personal user and should not be confused with Coleco's Gemini, the Atari VCS clone.

Issued in 1983 the Galaxy used the Nascom 80-bus. It had two Z80A MPUs, one operating as the computer and the other as the video processor. Its selection of the 80-bus ensured that users had access to a range of expansion board opportunities.

Its Enigma (no connection!) was a CP/M based, twin Z80A model designed to transfer files between computer platforms. In the days before Microsoft dominance this alone proved worthy of the £1,695 price.

In 1979 the Compukit UK101 microcomputer was released as a 6502-based kit, also available ready-made. As a kit it cost around £229. It featured as a part-work across four issues of the UK *'Practical Electronics'* magazine - August through November 1979. It was however essentially a straight lift of the Ohio Scientific Superboard II. As a result the north London operation ran in to a deal of flak and lost momentum.

Newbury Laboratories was largely state-owned producing some innovative products and the company was granted the inside line to become the supplier of the BBC computer. However it was decided not to tender against the specification. They were having problems with ULAs (uncommitted logic arrays) and sold the designs on to Grundy.

Based in Teddington and Cambridge, Grundy Business Systems had been planning its own CP/M based computer but took the Newbury designs to develop the NewBrain computers.

The AD, based on the Z80A, sold at £229 when released in 1982. Grundy sold over 50,000 units, largely to the educational and industrial/scientific sectors and with some success in the small business sector too thanks to its choice of the CP/M OS. An ANSI BASIC and a Pascal compiler were also available. There was particular success in selling in to the Netherlands.

So it was less of a surprise when in 1983 Tradecom International BV bought Grundy Business Systems from its receivers in order to fulfil a contract to supply schools and colleges in the Netherlands. The deal was satisfied directly from existing stocks and though there was talk of a new production facility in India nothing came of this.

But these were all just starters before the main course in the UK personal computing banquet.

Second-rate star goes nova – the Altair

The first PC product that really took off came appropriately from Micro Instrumentation and Telemetry Systems (MITS) - appropriate because as its name suggests the company was founded to market electronic rocket kits to hobbyists.

Ed Roberts, who was born in Florida, started out on a medicine course at the University of Miami but his interest in electronics saw him switch over to electrical engineering.

A US Air Force scheme assisted him through college and as a result of this he was posted to the laser division of the Weapons Laboratory in Albuquerque. Roberts met Forrest M. Mims III, Stan Cagle and Bob Zaller and they decided to use the skills developed while there in a commercial business.

Their rocket kits proved to be a bit of a damp squib but Forest Mims had developed a good relationship with hobbyist magazines for promotion of their ideas and this would later prove useful.

Mims had written pieces for *Model Rocketry* magazine and later had an article accepted for the much larger 400,000-readership *Popular Electronics*. He was keen to become a full-time writer and some years later would successfully sell over seven million copies of a series of around thirty hobbyist books through Radio Shack stores.

In 1970 Lee Solomon, editor of *Popular Electronics*, visited MITS and this led to the magazine promoting the 'Opticom LED Communicator', a device that allowed voice to be transmitted over an LED light beam across hundreds of feet (30+ metres).

Roberts later bought out his colleagues and set about designing a kit for a calculator. This was based upon a six-chip set produced by Electronic Arrays. The MITS 816 four-function calculator was featured in *Popular Electronics* in late 1971 as a kit for $175 or fully assembled at $275. By March 1973 revenues were running at $100,000 per month; he had amassed over a hundred employees.

In 1973 MITS promoted an advanced calculator, also carried in *Popular Electronics*. Called the MITS 1440, it sold at $200 as a kit or $250 assembled. They later offered a 'programmer unit' that could be connected to either of the calculators to give a capacity of 256 programmable steps.

However the introduction of low-cost pocket calculators to the market meant that at retail Roberts could buy a competitive calculator at prices well below his product's component costs. His operation had gone $300,000 into the red and he now desperately needed to find a new product.

Fortunately for him two hobbyist magazines were having something of a battle; *Radio Electronics* had taken the lead with the Mark-8 computer kit and also the SwTPC 'TV Typewriter', a basic video terminal that displayed two pages of 16 lines by 32 characters. But both of these products were little more than simple circuit diagrams provided for the hobbyist who needed to buy all the components and then assemble them according to the instructions provided.

Lee Solomon wanted to up the ante in the two magazines' battle and offer a much stronger computer kit. He learned from Mims that Ed Roberts was working on an 8080-based computer and they soon reached agreement that it could become the cover article for *Popular Electronics*.

Given the magazine's agreement Roberts was able to get an additional credit line of $65,000 from the bank and he set about delivering a suitable design.

The first problem was that he believed the target end-user price should be under $400, yet in small quantities the Intel 8080 chip alone was priced at $360. By committing to one thousand he found he was able to get that price down to $75.

The product was originally codenamed the 'PE-8', for Popular Electronics 8-bit, but the two parties sought a more striking name.

Two stories circulate as to how they came up with 'Altair'. One version is that Solomon's 12-year-old daughter suggested the name because it was the

planet where Star Trek's USS Enterprise had headed in that evening's episode. The other suggests that an editorial team came up with,
'It's a stellar event, so let's name it after a star.'

But if the latter is true then it seems a strange choice in that they picked such a second-rate star – our own Sun or Sol is obviously our brightest star, then in rank there are Sirius, Canopus, Arcturus, Vega, Rigel and even Betelgeuse; all are much brighter than Altair.

But the product came down to earth with a bump when Roberts' first and only prototype was lost by Railway Express when despatched to New York for the magazine to review and photograph.

An empty box had to be mocked-up for use on the front cover of the January 1974 edition of *Popular Electronics*. The headline said,

'PROJECT BREAKTHROUGH!
World's First Minicomputer Kit to Rival Commercial Models... "ALTAIR 8800." SAVE OVER $1000.'

So this quantum leap in the progress towards PCs was founded upon a completely empty box from an over-extended company that was flirting with bankruptcy,

'Plus ça change, plus c'est la même chose.' Written by Jean-Baptiste Alphonse Karr back in 1849, loosely translated to mean 'the more that things change, the more they are the same'. Or much more tersely, a recent trip to Cambodia uncovered the most popular tourist T-shirt epigram said simply, 'Same. Same.'

Roberts calculated that he needed to sell two hundred of Altairs to break-even, although he promised his bank manager that they would sell four times as many in the first year. On its launch he was pleasantly surprised to receive over one thousand orders in the first month.

However this meant there was no chance that MITS could live with the promised 60-day delivery. Unashamed Roberts threw even more resources at it, offering it as a kit or assembled by mail order through both *Popular Electronics* and *Radio Electronics*, with the 1K memory version at just $375.

At this price MITS could only achieve a little better than a break-even on the computer, but he believed success would be achieved by virtue of the on-sales of a series of planned profitable add-on boards. Many of the original line-up of promoted cards however failed to materialise and they ran in to technical difficulties with one of the most popular, the MITS Dynamic RAM board.

Fortunately for Roberts his very enthusiastic customers were quite prepared to wait while MITS got its act together. The RAM cards were reduced in price from $264 to $195 as an apology. And, eventually, they managed to build and deliver 5,000 Altairs by August 1975.

Despite all this enthusiasm the entry-level Altair was a pretty unedifying piece of kit. You could only program it by flicking switches on its panel, entering one byte at a time to define in digital 1s and 0s one of the instruction set or its associated data. The processor would then cycle through each entered byte to run the program. Invariably it would find a glitch in the entered information, even if it did run then the only feedback was by way of lights displaying the result on a bland panel.

Yet this was the first product to achieve any sales volume, in part because of the use of the 8080 which gave it its real potential. The product was also remarkable for being delivered with a computer bus, later to be renamed the 'S-100 bus', which rapidly became widely adopted as the industry standard, permitting MITS and other suppliers to offer a series of plug-in expansion boards that would add utility.

But the real impact was in those whom it would inspire. The Altair opened the floodgates to a huge pent up demand.

9 - Worshipping at the Altair

The computer was born to solve problems that did not exist before.' Bill Gates

One of the less famous Homebrew club members was Steve Dompier; he had been infected with the 'PC disease' when he met 'Eliza' on an HP time-share computer. This was a pseudo-therapist program developed in 1963 by an MIT professor, Joseph Weizenbaum. It responded to the user's comments in a way that made it seem like they were actually involved in a dialogue.

Dompier had later purchased a teletype terminal in order to play a 'Star Trek' game remotely but then he heard about the Altair. He ordered and received a catalogue and trumped up $4,000 to order the 'full monty' - disk drives, add-on cards the lot.

MITS responsibly wrote back to point out that he had sent too much money as a number of the modules were only at the planning stage; in truth of course it was all yet to be completed. Apparently they did have some scruples about the parts they had only put in the catalogue to provide the full 'mugs-eyeful'.

It was a measure of the degree of interest and enthusiasm that many potential owners were prepared to send money, usually several hundred dollars, to this organisation – an organisation that no-one had heard of before, that was situated in the 'middle of nowhere', that had no track record or experience and that was, had they but known it, none too far into its production process - and broke!

This was completely at odds with the mail order principles that the US postal regulations expected to be maintained. Normally an American consumer would demand his money back but these hobbyists wanted the product and were prepared to wait for it.

Dompier decided to go further; he went to see for himself what was going on with his order. What he found was not at all reassuring - a small two-office set-up, a handmade company sign and a secretary fielding calls from irate customers who were demanding their products. MITS had orders worth over a million dollars and was struggling to fulfil any of them.

Two other Homebrew members, Harry Garland and Roger Melen actually received the Altair kit #002. But the pair later founded Cromemco in 1974, naming the company after the Crowthers Memorial dormitory at Stanford. The Cromemco Systems I, II and III were launched from 1976 onwards. These used the S100 bus and either an 8080 or Z80 MPU they ran on CP/M or Cromix, its own UNIX version.

Yet another insistent kit customer parked outside the Altair premises in an RV, camper van, and waited until he was rewarded with the Altair serial-numbered as #003. He stayed outside darting in and out of the MITS office for direct advice as he built it.

Dompier left Albuquerque with a bag of components and over the next few months received more sent in instalments. When he attended that first Homebrew meeting he was still waiting for parts for his Altair which when completed proved to be serial number #004. He would later co-author the software for the SOL computer.

So it might be assumed that the kit Albrecht received must have been Altair #001, though I have found no confirmation of this surmise anywhere. Whatever, the Homebrew members certainly were among the very first to get Altairs.

Establishing fundamentals - BASIC

One way of adding value to the Altair was in the software language offered to its users, and BASIC was a prime candidate.

BASIC stands for Beginner's All-purpose Symbolic Instruction Code. It was developed back in 1963/4 at Dartmouth College in New Hampshire by John George Kemeny and Thomas Eugene Kurtz.

Kurtz, US born, had held various computing roles at Dartmouth eventually as director of the Computer and Information Systems program; its aim was to create information systems' leaders for industry.

Kemeny was Hungarian-born, his family having escaped during the German invasion of 1940. He worked on the Manhattan Project at Los Alamos, alongside John von Neumann and others. He was Einstein's mathematical assistant when he returned to Princeton, later moving on to Dartmouth's Department of Mathematics, rising to become the department head and later became president of the college.

Kemeny proved influential upon John McCarthy, helping him gain a Sloan fellowship which he used to go to MIT where, at the heart of 'hacker-dom', he was the teacher who developed the LISP language and made a number of advances in artificial intelligence.

Kemeny and Kurtz worked with the LGP-30 (Librascope General Purpose, or Precision), an early drum-memory desktop computer which was sold and maintained by a Royal Typewriter Company subsidiary, Royal McBee. It had been designed by Stan Frankel.

RANDOM ACCESS MOMENT:
You could be forgiven for thinking this LGP-30 sounds a pretty unremarkable computer, but besides being the birthplace of BASIC it had several other claims to fame.

Mel Kaye was a programmer and hacker, in the MIT sense of the word, who worked on the LGP-30, writing in hexadecimal machine code (respect!). The Royal sales team requested a demonstration piece of software for use at exhibitions and he created a Blackjack program. But they complained that it was too scrupulously fair, their customers would lose, and they insisted he rewrite it so they would more often win; Kaye initially refused but eventually gave in to the company's pressure.

The same type of computer was used by Edward Lorenz on weather forecasting models. He identified that very small effects could have a major impact; his work defined the 'butterfly effect' - a simple fluttering could set off a chain of reactions with long term and major global impacts.

Kemeny and Kurtz had cooperated to develop the Dartmouth Time-Sharing Service (DTSS) for the college and went on to create BASIC, an amalgam of their knowledge of FORTRAN II and ALGOL 60. The intention was that students from outside the science faculties might then be better able to use computers and the DTSS.

The two Dartmouth men decided to make the software available royalty-free so it could become widely adopted. However it rapidly became marginalised by being called 'Dartmouth Basic', at a stroke opening the door to other versions.

Later in 1983 Kurtz and Kemeny founded a company called True BASIC Inc and created 'True BASIC' as an updated version of the original language.

BASIC was quickly introduced by manufacturers like DEC for the PDP mini-computers and Data General for the Nova. Hewlett Packard used it as the basis for HP Time-Shared Basic. Progressively it had changed its nature from being a compiler and to becoming more of an interpreter. This was the format that Gates had in mind when he approached MITS.

Opportunity knocks at the gates

Paul Allen saw the *Popular Electronics* issue announcing the Altair and showed it to Bill Gates, then just nineteen years old. They saw the opportunity to provide a BASIC interpreter for the product. This would allow users to enter instructions almost in clear language and the software would do the conversion to the machine code that the Altair required for its operation.

Gates and Allen believed that whoever got there first would be in good shape to take advantage of what they believed would be a growing market in personal computers, and they went for it. With these two young guys' help, MITS was able to introduce the Altair BASIC in 1975; this was to be the very first Microsoft product.

Gates and Allen met with Ed Roberts of MITS, who showed some interest in the idea but not necessarily any sort of firm commitment. Who can blame him when they had no apparent track record, but then neither did he!

Gates was convinced that whoever produced the first such software package would be in a very strong position to dominate the market. Lacking a sample of an Altair, they started by creating an 8080 simulator on the PDP-10 to which they had access. They rushed to complete the language within the very restricted 4K of memory of the Altair.

Bill Gates had an early introduction to programming from the age of thirteen. The Lakeside school he and Paul Allen attended had the foresight to raise funds to offer students access to computers by buying time from General Electric for use of its PDP-10. But Gates and his schoolmates used up all the time that was available far too quickly.

A new arrangement was made by the school with the Computer Center Corporation (CCC) but this too was abused when the students managed to crash the computer several times and eventually broke into the computer's systems to alter their logged usage time so they could get more access than they were allotted.

They were discovered and banned from using the computer. This prompted four Lakeside students, including Gates and Allen, to form the Lakeside Programmers' Group and to seek out early applications on which they could apply their programming skills.

The very first application they found had them back with CCC; the group was asked to assist with tightening security, in return for unlimited computer access - a 'no-brainer' for Gates and his crew. CCC later had problems and went out of the business by 1970.

Other opportunities came along when the group was approached by Information Sciences Inc to write a payroll program and for this they were promised royalties on sales of any packages they produced. Shades of things to come!

The group also did work for TRW, a defence contractor, eliminating the bugs in its computer system. All these tasks expanded their access to computers, developed their knowledge and confirmed their desire to get in to the business of computing.

An interesting development came about when they learned of an application used by traffic engineers and local governments; simple rubber tube devices used pneumatics to count passing traffic.

The system recorded the number of axles of the passing vehicles and recorded it onto a 16-bit paper tape device. The standard at the time used on Teletype machines was 8-bit and this traffic device output could not be read directly into readily available systems. Instead various third parties were hired to manually work through the tapes and provide the data for a fee.

Gates and Allen believed they could automate the process and persuaded their schoolmates to transcribe the tape onto computer punched cards. Via Allen's father they then gained access to the University of Washington's computer to process the flow analysis. In this way they managed to undercut the existing suppliers of the service.

But they sought a more elegant approach and decided to develop a microprocessor-based device that would read the tapes directly. They had no hardware or engineering skills so approached a friend of a friend, Paul Gilbert, who was an electrical engineering student at the University of Washington.

Gilbert based the approach upon the Intel 8008 MPU and took much of a year to develop the device. His brother Miles Gilbert designed the logo for the resultant business, Traf-O-Data. This was founded with Gates owning 43% of the equity, Allen with 36% and Gilbert with 21%.

I can find no article on the reasoning for these very odd percentages. If Allen was the one developing the emulation and Gilbert the one doing the hardware, why then did Gates get more, and why 43%? If it was that he was providing the funding then why did he not seek the ratio 51-49 in relation to the others? Why 21% for the hardware designer and not 20 or 25%?

The really interesting point for us is that while the Traf-O-Data computer did not yet exist, how could they develop the software other than to wait on the finished product? This was what prompted Paul Allen to try out computer emulation on a PDP-11, which would later prove to be the approach that they adopted with confidence when they developed BASIC for the Altair 8800.

Computer emulation had been developed at IBM by an engineer called Larry Moss. He wanted to run software from earlier mainframes on the IBM System/ 360 and developed a package for it to perform as if it was the earlier computer. He decided that emulation sounded better than simulation, the word implying that, while it ran the earlier software, it did so with the improved performance of the 360.

On the PDP-11 Gates and Allen, writing in assembly language, created and tested the Traf-O-Data in parallel with the hardware development. Unfortunately at the demonstration of the first unit the reader failed and soon after this the State of Washington offered to run the analysis for its cities at no charge, thereby effectively eliminating the traffic-logging requirement. Yet the experience was to prove invaluable.

So when Paul Allen saw the Altair 8800 on the front cover of *Popular Electronics* with the headline 'World's first microcomputer kit to rival commercial models' they already had all the required knowledge to seek out MITS and make their bold approach to become the first supplier of a BASIC language for it.

The really remarkable fact was that they delivered this successful software language without ever having seen an Altair 'in the flesh'.

Gates wrote the code and Allen prepared the emulation on a PDP-10; eight weeks later Allen was able to demonstrate it to MITS. He delivered the software output from punched paper tape in March 1975. He did not even have enough money to pay for his hotel room and Ed Roberts of MITS had to sub him.

The first demonstration crashed but a second tape ran successfully. The very first operation was not brain surgery; they simply typed in '10 print 2+2' then 'Run' and got back the answer '4'. Compelling, heh?

They signed a licence deal with MITS, for shipping Altair BASIC in 4k or 8k versions. They received $3,000 up front, plus $30 per sold copy of the 4k version and $35 per 8k version. It was intended that MITS would eventually own the rights in the software once $180k of royalty payments had been paid.

This Altair or MITS BASIC was the very first computer language made widely available on a personal computer. Perhaps because of the royalty costs it was far from inexpensive at $150 a pop, but Roberts suggested this was set high to assist with the sales of add-ons. The cost would be dropped to $75 if you bought a memory expansion board; if you purchased this together with an input/output board then it dropped to just $60.

It was however Monte Davidoff, while a student at Harvard who produced the floating-point arithmetic for the Altair BASIC.

Paul Allen moved from a role at Honeywell and took the role as a VP and director of software development based at MITS in Albuquerque; Bill Gates was appointed a 'software specialist'.

Gates later dropped out of Harvard and with Allen founded Micro-Soft, initially based in Albuquerque to be convenient to the Altair headquarters.

Initially the company name did have that hyphen, with the equity divided as to 60% Gates and 40% Allen. See what I mean? These are perfectly sensible percentages, unlike those used at Traf-O-Data.

But there were mixed messages coming from the founders at this early stage. On the one hand they had formed Microsoft declaring that their objective was

'...a computer on every desk and in every home, running Microsoft software...'

Today we know that this is precisely what Microsoft became, but back in 1976 it was high ambition for an operation still very much feeling its way.

Despite this belief, Microsoft offered to sell MITS all its rights and intellectual property ownership in 8080 BASIC for just $6,500. Fortunately for them Roberts refused the deal which allowed them to retain ownership and develop it for other products.

At the end of 1975 Microsoft had just three employees, Gates, Allen and Ric Weiland, a school friend, and the business had earned just $16,000.

By 1976 MITS was selling some 1,000 computers per month and launched the Altair 680b based upon the Motorola 6800. Microsoft agreed to produce a 6800 Basic for the Altair 680b but for this MITS insisted this was not to be based on a licence arrangement and instead agreed a fixed fee of just over $30,000.

Altair's success prompted the first microcomputer convention, the 'First Annual World Altair Computer Convention'. It was held at a hotel in

Albuquerque and is remembered most significantly for Bill Gates using the occasion to launch one of his many attacks on software piracy.

The ingenuity of the early user meant that Gates and Allen did not do as well as they might. First users would club together and buy a single copy of BASIC and then distribute it among the 'co-op' purchasers, with tongue firmly in cheek some called this 'multi-user Basic'.

It became apparent that there was a deliberate catch inserted into MITS BASIC so that it could not be used on other 8080 products. Users identified the 'trap' and resolved it, distributed copies of the 'open' version became known as 'New Jersey Basic'.

Gates was incandescent in his speech and also wrote a series of tirades about the immorality of software piracy. But hadn't he himself essentially pirated Dartmouth Basic?

Ironically it was the broad familiarity gained for it by this widespread piratical distribution of the Microsoft-generated Basic that later allowed it to step up and become the de-facto standard.

Roberts found he no longer enjoyed the work and in May 1977 negotiated to sell MITS to its magnetic tape interface and disk interface supplier, Pertec Computer Corporation. He made $2m and later returned to college to complete his degree in medicine in 1986 at the age of forty-five.

Pertec believed that in buying MITS it had also acquired the rights in BASIC but after various legal activity it had to conclude that it had not.

Pertec continued to manufacture Altairs until 1978, and eventually moved on to develop its own microcomputer product based on the Intel 8085. This was the PCC-2000; it also developed a series of mini-computer business products. Pertec was later purchased by Triumph-Adler.

At the end of 1978 with $1.3m in annual revenue, thirteen staff and no external investors to worry about, the two Microsoft founders moved the operation back to their roots in Bellevue, Washington State.

Microsoft had forged ahead with its work on BASIC variants, for example netting $150k from Xerox for developing a stand-alone disk-based BASIC.

In April 1979 Microsoft's 8080 BASIC won the *ICP Million Dollar Award*, the first time this was awarded to a piece of microprocessor software rather than a mainframe computer. It all stemmed from Altair BASIC!

When Roberts died in April 2010, Bill Gates travelled to his bedside. Acknowledging Microsoft's debt to him, he and Allen said,

'We will always have fond memories of working with Ed.'

Software without charge

In seeking to create this version of BASIC for the Altair, Gates did not have the field to himself.

Dennis Allison, in the computer science faculty at Stanford, had been challenged by his friend Bob Albrecht to produce a TinyBASIC for the Altair. Albrecht sought a BASIC that could work with the small memory (circa 2-3K) that was all that was available on the current personal computers.

Albrecht was founder of the People's Computer Company and member of the Homebrew Computer Club. He had long held the belief that computers should be made available to all. He realised that it was through products like the Altair that this might just come about.

In December 1975 Albrecht and Allison released the code for TinyBASIC as a three-piece part-work freely available via the *PCC* quarterly journal. This then was the prompt for two computer hobbyists from Texas, Dick Whipple and John Arnold, to create and send Albrecht a useful TinyBASIC interpreter.

Albrecht and Allison went on to launch *Dr. Dobb's Journal of Computer Calisthenics & Orthodontia*, later renamed more simply as *Dr Dobb's Journal*. In its May 1976 issue TinyBASIC's code was made fully public domain. The Dobbs came from a contraction of their first names Don and Bob.

So it was by no means clear that a BASIC for the Altair would provide any sort of income opportunity, what with both Dartmouth and TinyBASIC being available fully royalty-free and free-of-charge.

Thus Gates has been routinely attacked down the years by those who propose that public-domain is the correct way to go for software.

They also served - Altair boys

The Altair had the market to itself during 1974 and the first half of 1975 but protracted deliveries allowed others to see a market and move in on them.

During 1975 there was a host of alternative competitive kits launched.

Wavemate released the Jupiter II computer kit and later followed this up with the Wavemate Bullet, a CP/M computer based on the Z80 MPU.

Daniel E Meyer founded DEMCO in 1964, the name based on his initials. It was later renamed as SwTPc (Southwest Technical Products company), it released its M6800 computer kit in November 1975.

Microcomputer Associates released the JOLT computer kit in December 1975. The founder and designer was Raymond M Holt. It was based on the 6502 MPU and sold at $249 for a kit or $348 fully-assembled. By the late 1990s Holt was finally permitted to discuss his work at Garrett AiResearch with the innovative CADC (central air data computer) for the F-14 Tomcat development.

Michael Donald Wise of Sphere Corporation launched the Sphere I computer kit in June 1975 at $650. Sphere was based in Utah and produced one of the first PCs to include a keyboard and a monitor. For this reason it was later selected by *Byte* magazine as the first true personal computer.

RANDOM ACCESS MOMENT:
Few agree with Byte's statement, but this does open a debate as to which was the first. Perhaps it comes down to what you mean by a personal computer? If it is the fact that it gives more personal access to computing then MIT's LINC in 1962 is perhaps the first. The French Micral N has a claim as the first to feature all the major attributes of a PC in 1972. Xerox's Alto that same year had all the modern features that we expect today. If it is the first to be in broad distribution to personal users then it was probably the Altair in 1974.

Sphere did create one of the standards that we still all use today- it was the first to introduce the Ctrl-Alt-Del routine to reboot without powering down the PC. Sphere sold around 1,300 units, half as kits, half assembled.

In May 1978 Wise founded A-Systems Corporation that developed an *Accounting Software for the Construction Industry* package.

In 1975 Roberts had used the term 'personal computer' applying it to the Altair, but in fact the reality was that once the kit had been successfully assembled it could not do a great deal.

Box shifters – Byte shop

It was also the Altair that set the scene for the whole business not just by selling via mail order but also by developing a retail market.

In July 1975 Dick Heiser was prompted to form 'The Computer Store' in Santa Monica, Los Angeles to sell Altair computers, peripherals and expansion boards. Its actual name was Arrow Head Computer Company and it was the first ever computer store.

Paul Terrell took a novel approach to these new start-up microcomputer makers. He signed a dealership arrangement with MITS, and later with other makers, to promote and sell the products throughout northern California in return for a 5% commission on all sales achieved in the territory, whether he sold it directly or not! He later founded 'Byte Shop' in December 1975 and soon had stores along the West Coast. *Byte* magazine had been founded in September 1975 by Wayne Green.

Byte Shop grew in to a large international franchise operation that ended up making its own Byte 8 computer, only available through its own stores. The Byte Shops were later sold to Logical Machine Corporation for $4m.

Terrell would later work with Pete Kauffman and Howell Ivy of Exidy Inc, an arcade coin-op video game operation, to develop the highly graphics-oriented Exidy Sorcerer home computer in 1978.

Even later Terrell would establish Computer Mania as a rental operation for computers and software, but subsequently the US Congress outlawed the rental of software for piracy fears.

Filling the gap – Processor Technology

The initial MITS sales philosophy was to sell the Altair computer for virtually break-even prices and then to make profit from the sale of expansion boards.

At launch it proposed it would have two memory boards (1K and 4K), parallel interface boards, two serial interface boards (RS-232 and Teletype) and an audio cassette interface board.

There were specific problems with the 4K memory board but it was perhaps the overwhelming sales success of the computer itself that meant all attention was focused on getting the computers built and shipped; this opened the door to others.

For its own purposes the Altair had provided for expansion through its bus structure and card slots so it could later supply additional product. This approach would soon be adopted as the industry standard S-100 bus which meant many other companies could set out to supply standard expansion cards that would work across a number of platforms - the Altair, its clones and other CP/M products.

Bob Marsh and Gary Ingram founded Processor Technology in April 1975 and it was the first to offer compatible expansion boards that could be used directly with the Altair.

Processor Technology soon had a 4K memory expansion board priced at $255 versus the assembled Altair version at $338.

Its VDM-1 (Video Display Module) became for a while the standard video display system for S-100 systems; it could generate upper and lower case lines of text which offered either a black-on-white or white-on-black composite video image.

Processor Technology also made a Computer Users' Tape Standard audio cassette interface.

These and other cards were soon available for the Altair, IMSAI, Polymorphic and SOL platforms.

When IBM launched the IBM PC in 1981, it followed a similar approach with its Industry Standard Architecture bus. The IBM launch team recognised that it could not, within the constraints of IBM, develop all the required cards so it threw the door open to others. It repeated this with its PS/2 launched with the Micro Channel Architecture bus in 1987.

IMSAI and Computerland

Bill Millard, an ex-IBM employee, founded the software operation System Dynamics in 1969 but this ceased operations three years later leaving him in debt. He was left with the belief that software would be easier to sell if offered with a computer; but he realised that this required capital.

He started a new business in 1972 called IMS Associates Inc (information management services), a computer consultancy and engineering operation that dealt mostly in the area of software. A series of successful custom contracts allowed him to amass some capital.

IMSAI was one of the early operations that managed to attract a large number of motivated individuals who were inspired to go on to play other roles in the personal computer market.

Millard himself went on to launch Computerland. Ed Faber, another ex-IBM-er and IMSAI's director of sales, structured IMSAI as a retail proposition and subsequently he ran Computerland.

Seymour Rubinstein the IMSAI marketing manager took the chief programmer Rob Barnaby with him to form MicroPro International as they launched WordStar. Glen Ewing one of the chief engineers had previously worked alongside Gary Kildall at the Naval Postgraduate School in Monterey, California

It was to be clients whom Millard had successfully worked with on software and engineering tasks that challenged him to enter the computer manufacture business. In 1974 he was approached to supply a product to replace electromechanical accounting equipment. This was his first opportunity to develop a fully rounded product with hardware and software.

Another request wanted him to develop a system for General Motors new-car dealerships which would network five workstations and share the use of a central hard disk drive. The contract for this charged Millard to develop the product but the client would retain exclusivity for the auto market, IMSAI permitted to sell its product to all other sectors.

The price negotiated and the credit line established proved to be too low. It was realised, perhaps a tad late, that only a microprocessor approach could keep the project within plan; sourcing boards and components from traditional minicomputer suppliers had proven not to be viable.

A lot of time was spent trying to achieve a system based around the Intel 4004. It was only when the 8080 microprocessor was launched that there was a product with real potential for the application with which they had been struggling.

When the Altair was launched, it first aroused and then dashed their hopes. They tried to acquire some Altairs but delivery proved to be too long-winded. They were not offered a credit line by Ed Roberts and delivery time was quoted at 90 days. The notion both of pre-payment and delays led them to decide that perhaps after all they should and could produce something themselves.

Significantly it was decided to build the product to be Altair-compatible and as they were coming to the subject freshly they sought some significant improvements too. The Altair was mirrored so closely that the result is often suggested to be the first 'clone' PC.

Launched by an advert in *Popular Electronics* as the IMSAI 8080, it received a good reception in late 1975, largely from the hobbyist market. For the operating system they took a licence with Digital Research for CP/M, the software developed by Glen Ewing's old colleague Gary Kildall.

By the end of 1975 IMSAI had shipped just fifty units via direct mail during December, in the same year MITS had shipped 2,000 Altairs.

A common problem in the early market was that designers and builders rushed a product to market with a mail order proposition and only then realised they needed retailers; invariably pricing had not been set to leave a suitable margin. These early players had seldom needed to run a business plan or establish a robust pricing policy.

In 1976 IMSAI was one of the first to fall foul of this, realising a little late that it needed retailers and dealers. First the price was raised from $439 to $499 to allow for a margin, and later from $499 to $599 to give a more realistic percentage to get dealers onside.

By the end of 1976 the Altair had 25% of the market, IMSAI had gained 17%, Processor Technology's SOL and SwTPC each had 8%: the rest of the market was divided between makers such as Cromemco, Digital Group, MOS Technology, Ohio Scientific, Polymorphic...

In 1977 IMSAI designed an integrated product, the VDP (video data processor) range. Its code was the VDP-80 and it consisted of a microcomputer with 32k of RAM, a 12" screen, a keyboard and a floppy disk drive at $6,995.

IMSAI shipped around 20,000 units between 1975 and 1978, but became bankrupt by 1979 with debts of $1.9m, for example owing Microsoft $60,000 in licence fees for BASIC and FORTRAN.

Former employees did acquire the trademark and continued its manufacture, selling a further 2,000 units between 1979 and 1986.

Millard threw his efforts into establishing the 'Computer Shack' retail franchise in 1976 in partnership with John Martin-Musumeci. But a shot across the bows from Radio Shack saw it renamed 'ComputerLand.'

It grew rapidly from $1.5m in sales through 24 franchises in 1977 to 147 stores and $75m in sales by 1980. When IBM decided to sell its PC only through IBM stores, Sears Business System Centers and Computerland, the organisation really took off.

By 1984 Forbes magazine identified William Millard as the 27th richest man in the USA. By 1985 ComputerLand was the world's largest chain with over 800 outlets in more than 20 countries, approaching $1.5bn in sales.

But by then, while successful, the franchisees were none too happy about being excluded from going public and were disappointed by poor investment from the franchisor. Three hundred and fifty of them combined to take action against Millard's holding company.

Millard was also said to have diverted monies and resources from IMSAI to form Computerland and he was pursued successfully by an investment group. They achieved the conversion of a promissory note in IMSAI into a 20% holding in Computerland and were also awarded $115m in punitive damages forcing him to sell out his interests in the retail operation.

He moved Ed Faber back in to run the business, sold his 52% for $80m, and retired to Saipan, a tax haven. The buyers later sold the operation on to Merisel for $150m, when two years earlier it had been valued at $1.4bn.

Kits by catalogue - SwTPc

Southwest Technical Products Company (SwTPc) founded back in 1964 in Texas as the Daniel E Meyer Company, offered to supply assembled versions of the kits that appeared in the hobbyist magazines. Perfect for those who could not bother to raise the enthusiasm or the soldering iron to make them for themselves.

Renamed SwTPc in 1967, for the next four years it offered its own kits through hobbyist magazines, for example its ASCII keyboard kit for $40. It also supplied the kits in support of some fifty *Popular Electronics* articles.

Meyer expanded this market to the point where he had a 32-page catalogue largely featuring audio kits. He then worked with other designers to promote their products. Most notably in 1975 SwTPc launched Don Lancaster's CT-1024 computer terminal kit, aka the 'TV Typewriter' as featured in *Radio Electronics*.

SwTPc launched microprocessor kits based around the Motorola 6800 MPU and later the 6809 and augmented these with a range of terminals evolving from the TV Typewriter.

The SwTPc 6800 was its first computer product sold from 1975 to 1979. Based on the 6800 MPU it was priced from $395 for the 2K memory version. Software was supplied in-house and by Technical Systems Consultants of Indiana. SwTPc was also an early advocate for open-source software publishing a catalogue of material obtained free of any licence.

Homebrewing the SOL

Processor Technology Corporation was founded in April 1975 which did precisely as I suggested earlier and named its computer kit after the brightest of our stars; the SOL terminal computer was designed as a kit or a fully assembled PC.

The SOL-20 was designed by Bob Marsh, Lee Felsenstein and Gordon French, all members of the Homebrew Computer Club. It had been of course French's garage that provided the location of the club's first meeting.

The SOL-20 was launched in June 1975 and opted to use Intel's 8080 and it included an S-100 bus. It was priced at $1,649 as a kit or $2,129 assembled. Version III at over $5,000 came with a monitor, disk drive and BASIC.

Some 10,000 units were manufactured through the late 1970s. It was based on the Altair or S-100 bus; in fact it was these new suppliers that changed the name to S-100 as they had no desire to refer to it using a competitor's name.

This explosion of personal computer kits and assembled units and in particular the development of the S-100 bus led directly to many companies stepping up to develop a range of suitable peripherals to expand the capabilities of the otherwise quite inflexible and ineffectual systems.

Earlier Processor Technology was active in producing standard expansion boards. It was also the first company to offer bundled software. This was provided on audio cassette, one side had the program in the Computer Users' Tape Standard format and the other the Kansas City Standard.

Getting it taped – Kansas City and CUTS

As the installed base of personal computers grew exponentially there was a growing need to find something for them to do. Many early users were motivated by the notion of low-cost computers, many buying them as kits and gaining all their joy in their assembly.

But now that assembled PCs were flowing freely via mail order and through a growing number of specialist retail outlets, a new user started to emerge; one who actually wanted the PC to do something.

The vital first steps of the PC market had been taken by enthusiasts and hobbyists who were in all honesty probably happiest when their computer did not work. But this was not the sector that was going to take the business on to the next stage.

This next wave of users would be lured by software that could make personal computers sing and dance. This was not the simple software language that Microsoft had been focused upon, but software that would drive the new array of devices and peripherals that could be connected to a microprocessor.

When you ran a program on early computers you needed to load the application from a device and if you wanted to retain the result of the program it had to be output to a device, because of course everything was lost when you switched off.

Paper tape was soon discarded as inappropriate and with time the ideal solution would emerge as the floppy disk drive, but initially priced at more than $1,000 they were really a feature of the late '70s.

So in the mid-1970s *Byte* magazine decided to act and sponsored and promoted a meeting in Kansas City, Missouri to look at creating a standard for what was economically available right then - the tape cassette player-recorder.

The magazine suggested that someone needed to create a standard for writing data to and from a standard audio cassette so computer software and data could be loaded and saved easily. *Byte* commissioned Don Lancaster, who had designed the 'TV Typewriter', to outline a design and with this interested parties were attracted to discuss how it might be developed.

Lee Felsenstein was one who rose to the occasion. It is suggested that Felsenstein was much inspired by Ivan Illich, who though half-Jewish became a Catholic priest as well as a philosopher and social commentator. Perhaps encapsulating some of his thinking, Illich once said,

'Man must choose whether to be rich in things or in the freedom to use them.'

Certainly Felsenstein had a social conscience about the impact of technology. He would be involved in a series of developments like the 'Penny Whistle' modem and the 'Tom Swift Terminal' in 1974.

In 1975, having seen the Altair launch, he followed through on his early ideas to co-design the Processor Technology VDM-1 video display module board that rapidly became a standard; he then worked on their SOL-20 computer. In 1980 Felsenstein was commissioned to design the Osborne 1.

So Felsenstein was one of those who turned up at the *Byte* magazine Kansas City meeting. He and Harold Mauch of Percom Data Company jointly rose to the challenge and produced what later became known as the Kansas City Standard. It operated at just 300 baud (symbols or pulses per second) which proved to be more reliable than higher speeds, but of course it made for a rather arduous load and save process.

Computer Users' Tape Standard (CUTS) was subsequently developed by Processor Technology to operate at 300 or 1200 baud. The Compukit, Nascom, Altair, KIM and Ohio Scientific equipment all selected CUTS.

In the UK the Tangerine Microtan 65 used a 300 baud CUTS system or its own 2400 baud approach. Acorn Computers used 1200 baud CUTS on the Atom, Acorn and BBC Micro.

The Sinclair computers went with a tone modulation approach for the ZX80 and ZX81; this operated at very slow baud rates – but then the memory capacities back then were so small that none of us really noticed!

While these audio cassette systems were perfectly fine for the early PC systems with their limited memory and capacities, they could not begin to deal with the volumes of data that the increasingly voracious personal computers began to demand.

Disk jockeying – Shugart and Ernest

In 1971 3M introduced a ¼" magnetic tape drive and cartridge suitable for desktop computers but the negative issue with tape was that you had to sequentially run along its length to reach the material you required.

IBM developed disk technology simply as a means to load the software required to boot up its mainframes. A disk system allowed you to run around the disk as on an old record player or you could jump radially across the face of the disk to reach a particular point much more rapidly.

Alan Shugart started his career at IBM, cutting his teeth on the IBM 305 RAMAC (random access method of accounting and control) launched in 1956. This was the first commercial computer with a moving-head hard disk, the IBM 350, and the system sought to offer real-time applications. The drive had fifty, double-sided, 24" surfaces that could store up to 5 million 7-bit characters. It was large at 60" (152cm) tall, 68" (172cm) wide and 29" (74 m) deep and weighed over a ton (tonne).

Shugart rose through the IBM Direct Access Storage department to become its product manager and in 1971 he ran the team that launched the 8" diameter floppy disk, the 23FD, a flexible plastic disk coated with iron oxide on just one side.

Initially it was read-only and suitable only for loading programs or data. By 1973 IBM had developed the 33D drive that was double-sided and could be used to read and to write with a capacity of 400k bytes.

Though IBM developed the floppy disk they never sold the drive as a distinct product and the market was left to others to exploit.

In 1973 Shugart left IBM, worked briefly at Memorex, and then formed his own Shugart Associates where he launched the SA901 an 8" disk drive that was fully compatible with the IBM 33D.

In that same year IBM changed the point of attack by launching the first Winchester hard drive. The designer, Kenneth Haughton, gave it this name because it was originally planned to have two 30-megabyte spindles; the most famous Winchester hunting rifle was the Model 1894 also known as the 30-30. When it was finally launched it offered either 35 or 70 megabyte options, but by then the name Winchester had stuck.

The first Winchester was the IBM 3340, it used air to suspend the read/write head some 18-millionths of an inch above the recording surface. Announced in March 1973 the drive had four x 8" disks to give it a massive 70 megabyte capacity. This approach progressively became the industry standard.

In 2002 IBM sold off its disk drive operation to Hitachi.

In 1976 Shugart developed the 5¼" mini-floppy drive for the microcomputer, a market requiring something much more compact. It had a price of just $390, a capacity of 110k and was a great success.

Larry Boucher led the team at Shugart Associates also developed the Shugart Associates System Interface (SASI) though this did not launch until 1981. SASI set the standard for the means of connection and transference of data between a computer and disk drives and other peripherals.

Boucher and several other engineers left Shugart Associates in 1981 to form Adaptec Inc specialising in helping products to work via connectors in data, audio and video. They took SASI forward and evolved it into SCSI (small computer system interface) pronounced 'skuzzy'; although the word small is misleading as it went on to become the standard for all sizes of computer.

SCSI was used by the likes of Amiga, Apple, NCR and Sun; and it remains a standard in various further evolved formats. Other systems like Parallel ATA, or IDE, SATA, Serial ATA, USB and FireWire were also introduced and each took a segment of the market.

At Shugart Associates designers also set out to develop a small business system, but Shugart himself fell out with the venture capitalists and the operation was sold on to Xerox.

With Finis Conner, Syed Iftikar, Doug Mahon and Tom Mitchell he then launched Shugart Technology; this later changed its name to Seagate Technology with Shugart as its CEO. In September 1981 the Seagate IPO raised $25m.

To minimise the capital requirement of this new operation they outsourced their production to Matsushita and this gave the Japanese a kick-start to grow and to become the largest disk drive maker in the world.

Outside his work Shugart was an interesting character in his later life as he took a shot at politics. First he tried, and sadly failed, to get his Burmese Mountain Dog, Ernest, elected to the US Congress in 1996.

Then he was part of a move that tried in 2000 to arrange that California ballot papers would have as one of its choices a 'none of the above' option. Priceless!

10 - Wait for ages, then three come along – Apple I, PET and TRS-80

'There are only two industries that refer to their customers as "users".'
Edward Tufte, a Yale professor

No longer just a hobby

The transition from kits and hobbyists to a proper business happened in something of a rush. New products appeared that were full-grown off-the-shelf purchases that could actually do things! Three major entries emerged from completely different directions - a dreamer, a distributor and a dealer.

The dreamer was Apple, from the early hobbyist-enthusiast scene, as it stepped up to the plate and launched a serious product.

The distributor was Commodore, a business equipment operation. It saw PCs as a new market sector that was just a step-function away from its current market of selling calculators.

The dealer was Radio Shack, a retailer that saw the PC as a new big-ticket product range to be sold through its existing 3,500 outlets.

Apple - Early Wozniak

Menlo Park is a city in San Mateo, California that covers just over 17 sq miles (45 sq kms), although 42% of that area is taken up by water. At the turn of the millennium there were just over 12,000 households and a population that is rather small for a city, just under 31,000 souls.

When you learn that Joan Baez, Stevie Nicks of Fleetwood Mac and Jerry Garcia of Grateful Dead all made their homes there, it perhaps conjures up an image of an affluent, quiet, restful place – assuming that these artistes do their playing out on tour and not in their garages.

But Menlo Park is adjacent to Stanford University and is the location of the Stanford Research Institute. This has made it many times more significant than simple statistics might suggest. It would later be home to Oracle and Google.

In the early '70s Bob Albrecht, of Dr Dobb's and TinyBASIC fame, had formed the People's Computer Company in Menlo Park. It was also there that the Homebrew Computer Club first assembled in March 1975.

Steve Wozniak was of course a keen hobbyist who had been drawn along to the first Homebrew meeting. With an IQ of 200, Wozniak had become inspired and well-versed in electronics at an early age by his father, an engineer.

At school he routinely won science competitions, one of these for a device he built to show the atomic structure of all 92 atoms in the periodic table. He later explained that he had thoroughly learned all of the features of a diode to make this circuitry work.

For another competition he produced a tic-tac-toe, or noughts and crosses, device completely designed around the capability of logic circuits. Earlier we saw that Bill Gates wrote a tic-tac-toe software program in 1968 at the age of thirteen, yet Wozniak had built his hardware device when he was a year or so younger!

In the eighth grade, at 13-14 years old, he developed a rudimentary computer that he called an Adder/Subtractor. It was a complex device consisting of 100 transistors, 200 diodes, 200 resistors with relays and switches. It used switches to enter two binary numbers and select add or subtract, following which a series of lights presented the solution.

At high school Wozniak, a shy guy, often used his technical skills and practical jokes to compensate for his lack of social skills.

He focused mainly on hardware, though his first foray into software proved to be very educational. He was getting a day-per-week work experience at Sylvania, the consumer electronics company, where he learned to program.

He consumed a FORTRAN manual and as his very first task set himself the tough old chestnut of the Knight's Tour challenge. The task is to move a knight chess piece with its strange moving routine, two forward and one to the side, to take just 64 moves to visit all 64 squares of the chessboard.

Wozniak, with some assistance, set out to keypunch his program to work out a solution. His approach was a process of elimination to establish the correct start point. He loaded the software but nothing appeared to happen.

However the Sylvania team studied the matter and suggested that his program may have put the computer into a loop, an infinity loop; coincidentally the name of the street in Cupertino where Apple has its headquarters today.

On further investigation Wozniak calculated that the program as he had written it would take longer to run than the universe had existed to date!

Cream Soda computer
At college Wozniak again ran into trouble when his programs proved to have used so much time-share that he had consumed five times the level of the computer science department's annual budget.

He was on much safer ground when he came across a DEC PDP-8 manual which he read thoroughly and then challenged himself to redesign the computer using his, by then, broad understanding of electronic circuitry.

He acquired other minicomputer manuals and on paper and in his mind he worked on improved designs that would use fewer chips. He could not afford actually to pursue any of these notions but he remained confident that his designs would work and represented an improvement on the originals.

He took a sabbatical year from college, working as a programmer at Tenet, an operation developing a minicomputer system. While there one of the Tenet team acquired some chips for him. He and a friend, Bill Fernandez, used these to build the Cream Soda computer. This had no screen and no keyboard, programs were entered by punched card and results had to be read from a series of lights.

This had most of the features of the Altair and other early kit systems yet was built without a microprocessor. Sobering that it would take five years for the MPU-based kits to arrive and yet they would offer no more than the Cream Soda computer.

A local reporter, whom Wozniak's mother arranged to review it, stepped on a lead at the end of the interview, the device shorted - and was no more. But his work with Fernandez did connect him up with Steve Jobs. On meeting they experienced one of those moments when two minds collide. They discovered they were both working on projects, they were both pranksters and they shared many of the same aspirations for computing.

Phreaking out

Back at college he was inspired by an article in *Esquire* magazine about phone phreaks, a contraction of phone and freak. These were the direct predecessors of the negative form of computer hackers, who explored loopholes in telecom systems to get free calls or occasionally simply to report these flaws to the PTT; Wozniak was of the latter persuasion, at least initially.

A Bell Systems Technical Journal in 1960 entitled *Signalling Systems for the Control of Telephone Switching* had rather obligingly revealed how this might be done. This and other articles of the time opened up the network to the phreaks.

Exploring the potential Wozniak built a 'blue box', a device that generated a tone and emulated the specific codes used by the phone company to make free phone calls. Another illicit device at the time was a 'black box'. This was developed by others to allow them to receive free calls fooling the equipment into believing that no call had in fact taken place.

Wozniak produced his device just because he could. It was his friend Steve Jobs who convinced him to build it for sale to fellow Berkeley students. The precedent of their relationship was set!

Wozniak was a keen prankster and reputedly once used the device to call up the Vatican City. Imitating Henry Kissinger's accent, the Pope was woken to take the call!

In 1964 AT&T began monitoring calls to try to catch the phreakers, but it was the introduction in the early 1990s of separate data and signalling channels that really slammed the door on them.

Working for others

After college, in early 1973 Wozniak took a job at Hewlett Packard where he was employed on designing scientific calculators.

Prior to this he was the proud owner of an HP 35 scientific calculator that allowed him to throw away his slide rule. At HP he was designing the future of scientific calculators and really appreciated that this was a company that really respected and treasured engineers.

But he maintained his own projects. Having been introduced to the ARPANET he designed a form of teletype system he called the Computer Converser that allowed him to use his home television as a video terminal. Seeing the arcade game Pong he developed his own version with many fewer chips and Steve Jobs, who was then working at Atari, encouraged him to show it to Atari engineers.

Atari offered him a job but he was content staying with HP for the time. Later Steve Jobs called him to assist with a new arcade game called Breakout that Atari wanted, and they wanted it developed in four days. The two Steves delivered and it was while working on this project that Wozniak conceived a novel approach to generating colour on a screen that he would later use in his design of Apple II.

Own designs – Apple I

In March 1975 the fateful inaugural meeting of the Homebrew Computer Club was held in Gordon French's garage. It was to some extent inspired by the launch of the Altair 8800 and it brought together some remarkable young men.

Wozniak was invited by a friend and attended because he understood the meeting was to be about video terminals. He was somewhat disappointed when they talked mostly about the Altair which he considered to be no more significant than the Cream Soda computer he had built five years earlier. He had not pursued his project further after it had shorted, as it was clear to him that its capabilities were limited.

Someone at the meeting handed out the technical specification of a clone of Intel's 8008 microprocessor and when Wozniak analysed this later he realised what the MPU was about, and just how he might use it. He concluded he need not buy an Altair; he could build his own and he set about doing just that.

He looked around for an alternative to the expensive Intel unit and found that as an HP employee he could acquire a Motorola 6800 MPU for just $40. His HP experience with calculators led him to establish that he needed a small piece of software he called Monitor and this he located in a ROM that would start up his computer promptly and have it ready to program. The Altair and others had a complicated and time-consuming delay while a program was loaded.

Perhaps more importantly he decided his computer should also come with a keyboard and a screen. As Wozniak said in his autobiography *iWoz*,

'Every [micro]computer before the Apple I had that front panel of switches and lights. Every computer since has had a keyboard and screen. That's how large my idea turned out to be.'

Selling fruit – Jobs and Wayne

Jobs wanted to form a company to sell the computer and he came up with the name Apple Computer based on his recent return from a commune in Oregon in which he had some interest; it was located in an area where there were a number of apple orchards.

Apple was of course the pre-existing name of a number of the Beatles operations, most notably Apple Corps Ltd and Apple Records formed back in 1968, and they would later take exception to the usage.

The two needed cash so Wozniak sold his HP 65 scientific calculator for $250 and Jobs sold his Volkswagen van for $1,500 to raise the necessary seedcorn capital. Then the two Steves together with Ronald Wayne formed Apple Computer - on All Fools' Day, 1st April 1976.

Wayne had worked with Steve Jobs at Atari and it was he who drafted the partnership agreement, designed and drew the first Apple logo and he also produced the Apple I user manual. He was awarded a 10% equity holding, each Steve having 45%. Wayne, a little older than Wozniak and Jobs, had some business experience under his belt and it was agreed that he would be the referee if there should be any dispute between the other two.

It was this previous business experience that caused him concern when things started to expand a little too rapidly for his taste. His own partnership agreement made him jointly and severally responsible for any debts, and also agreed that he would be working for no salary. Fresh in his memory was how he had spent two years paying off creditors for a previously failed business in slot machines.

In later life he indicated that the two Steves were 'whirlwinds' whom he feared he could not match for pace. When the team picked up a big order that needed to be financed he decided to pull out and sold back his equity holding in April 1976 for just $800. Though Wayne is quoted as saying he had no regrets, he surely must have had some sleepless nights as he saw the organisation grow.

RANDOM ACCESS MOMENT:
Perhaps only Pete Best, the original drummer with The Beatles, would have been able to appreciate just how he felt.

Best joined the Beatles as they went off to Hamburg, he was the only one who could speak German; he helped them hone their skills only to be dismissed by Brian Epstein. Epstein then approached Tommy Hutchinson, drummer with the Big Three, who as a friend of Best refused the role, he helped out though until Ringo Starr was able to join them; the rest is someone else's history to write.

Best was dismissed on 16th August 1962, the very next month The Beatles recorded 'Love Me Do' and by February 1963 they were greeted by thousands of screaming fans to the US where they featured on the Ed Sullivan Show.

Back to Ronald Wayne, he sold his 10% for just $800 in April 1976 only to see the success of the Apple I, then to watch as 7,000 Apple IIs were sold in 1977. Within three years they were turning over $100m. How must he have felt when its IPO (initial public offering) in December 1980 sold out 4.6 million shares in minutes, valuing the company at $1.8bn? Of course the Beatles would return frequently in the Apple Computer story, but we are getting ahead of ourselves.

Wozniak as an employee of Hewlett Packard, did much of the Apple development while working there, making regular use of the facilities. He felt morally obliged to offer them the product, but HP politely declined reportedly for a fairly obscure reason - as the Apple used a domestic TV, the HP management foresaw problems if the selected television did not work with the computer.

The real reason may have had something to do with the fact that HP had its own Project Capricorn; the codename for an MPU in development. This later resulted in its HP-85, a large yet portable calculator that looked a lot like a PC, with a keyboard, a small screen, a thermal printer, a tape drive and HP BASIC built in.

Jobs then had a stroke of luck, or perhaps it was in fact down to exceptional negotiating skills?

Taking a byte – Paul Terrell and the PO

Paul Terrell, another Homebrew Computer Club member, started out as a marketing and sales agent for the MITS Altair 8800. In June 1975, in return for his promotional activity, he negotiated to get a 5% commission on every Altair sold in northern California – whether he was personally responsible for the sale or not.

On the strength of this in December 1975 he launched one of the very first PC retail outlets, The Byte Shop, located at Mountain View in California.

He soon found he had hit on something that attracted the interest of others and quickly signed up more outlets on a franchising arrangement. By March 1976 his retail business had been incorporated as Byte Inc.

The two needed each other - Apple wanted distribution and Terrell needed product to fuel his burgeoning empire. The two Steves had shown the Apple I prototype to the Homebrew Computer Club and then Jobs took it to the Mountain View store. Terrell already had computer kit offers from many early players, and his interest was very much focused on a finished product.

The outcome was that Terrell in July 1976 gave Jobs a purchase order for fifty Apples and agreed to pay cash on delivery. Wozniak had priced the Apple I at a retail of $666.66, not as some subtle reference to the Anti-Christ, just a simplistic approach of $500 plus a third mark-up. They could build the Apples for just over $200 and would sell them to Terrell for the trade price of $500.

Jobs was quick to see that this could provide them with the needed funding. He presented the deal to a parts supplier and requested 30-day credit terms against the security of the purchaser order, giving him and the Apple team those thirty days to assemble the units and collect their money from Byte Shop.

The parts distributor spoke with Terrell directly to get his confirmation of the validity of the PO, and once he received it Apple and Byte Shop were off and running. Terrell added his own power supply, keyboard, monitor and case and sold it as a complete system.

The end of the beginning – divest?

Wozniak was twenty-five and employed, Jobs was twenty-one and still living at home, neither took a salary, the work was done in Jobs family garage, there was no rent. They used two high school kids Chris Espinosa and Randy Wigginton to assist, so they had virtually next to no overhead.

Total production of the Apple I was to achieve around two hundred units, and it very much set the scene for the PC business.

RANDOM ACCESS MOMENT:
by 2008 it was estimated that just thirty to fifty of these Apple Is remain extant, each commanding an average value of $15,000, but Apple fans being so committed there have been reports of one fetching $50,000 at auction.

This was no run-away success, around 175 Apple Is had been sold by 1977 mainly on a hand-to-mouth basis to Byte Shop and other retailers in Northern California. However another Homebrew-inspired team was selling its Processor Technology SOL-20 and achieving sales of more than this each and every month.

So at this early stage the future of Apple as an organisation was very much in the balance. In late 1976 Stan Veit the owner of the Computer Mart in New York was offered 10% of Apple for $10,000 but he concluded he already had a use for all his capital.

RANDOM ACCESS MOMENT:
Stan Veit should not just be passed by in that last paragraph; he too was something of a pioneer. He had been a technical writer at Bell Labs and elsewhere and then wrote the manuals for Time Sharing Resources. When the Altair was launched he formed Computer Mart as one of the first computer stores and he was the third store to be appointed an Apple dealer.

Veit continued to write several books and many magazine articles, later becoming Computer Editor at 'Popular Electronics' magazine, then joining Ziff Davis as Technical Editor for Computers & Electronics and for one of the first online magazines on CompuServe. He moved on to become founding Editor and Publisher of 'Computer Shopper' which he grew into the largest magazine in the world. He sold the publication to his erstwhile employer Ziff Davis.

About the same time Commodore was shown the Apple II and declared an interest in acquiring Apple in its entirety but Steve Jobs had valued the company up into six figures and wanted a salaried role for each of them as part of any deal. There was no serious progress made at this high price.

Ripening – Mike Markkula

The Apple team was looking for investors. They wanted to evolve the Apple I into an improved Apple II and this would require some serious funding.

Based on the success of the Apple I, Steve Wozniak and Steve Jobs approached several venture capitalists. Some suggest it was Nolan Bushnell or Al Alcorn of Atari who connected them up with Mike Markkula; others say it was a referral from another venture capitalist, either Regis McKenna or Don Valentine or both.

Markkula had worked at Fairchild Semiconductor and then Intel as a Vice President of Marketing. He made a personal fortune when he sold his accumulated stock options, retiring at just thirty-two years of age. However the introduction was made, it was Markkula who subsequently provided them with $250k to fund the building of a thousand Apple IIs.

In 1977 Markkula supplied $80k to buy a third of the Apple equity and $170k as loan capital. Surely this must have been one of the best investments of all time?

Given his funding they incorporated as Apple Computer Inc in Jan 1977, moved to offices in Cupertino and quickly commenced the expansion of the Apple I into a full-blown product.

Markkula was not just a financier; he brought a much needed level of professionalism to Apple. He presided over a raft of changes to the thinking, for example he created Apple's very first business plan.

But it went further. He immediately started the work to ensure there was patent cover for innovations, he declared that Apple should become marketing-led as an organisation and he also made it clear that he wanted to see the Apple II developed as a home computer.

Markkula's declared goal was for Apple to expand rapidly enough to become a *Fortune 500* company. He also insisted that to make this possible Wozniak should promptly leave his employment with Hewlett Packard and work full-time at Apple.

Keeping up appearances – Apple II
Wozniak was again solely responsible for the functional design of the Apple II computer.

Jobs wanted the look and feel of the Apple II to be different, to be more like a home appliance, to be a complete ready-to-use computer and not a hobbyist product. The case was defined by designer, Jerry Manock who was hired by Jobs just nine weeks before the product's launch at the West Coast Computer Faire.

The case was to have a sleek look, more like a calculator or typewriter. It had no obvious fixing, all the screws came from the underside, and the top could simply be lifted to insert additional cards; usually the monitor sat on top of that flap.

The case was made in polyurethane using a reaction-injection moulding process. The quick and inexpensive approach proved however to be somewhat irregular and a number of the Apple II cases required hand finishing by sanding the joints. The paint used was also inconsistent in terms of its adherence to the case.

Later production moved over to an acrylo-nitrile-butadiene-styrene plastic which did not need finishing or painting; it proved to be both smoother and harder wearing.

An Atari engineer, Rod Holt, was approached to develop the power supply as analogue circuitry was not one of Wozniak's skill sets. The heat from the power supply needed to be dissipated, so this and the expansion card slots determined the height of the case. But the rest was all Wozniak.

Adding colour – Apple II
One of the first innovations was that Wozniak designed the Apple II as the first PC to offer a colour display. Apple I had been created with the capacity to handle colour but he did not follow through for that product. The colour approach grew from Wozniak's earlier terminal design. He said of the Apple II colour facility,

'... *it took only two chips...* '

In fact Apple II had half the number of chips he had used on the Apple I.

But Wozniak wanted the graphics and text capability inbuilt on the Apple II to really make the most of that colour facility. He also wanted it to play games and this required the addition of sound and games paddles to the product. He included a cassette connector so that data and programs could be saved and loaded. He also added expansion slots for up to eight cards though at the time they only projected an immediate need for two, a printer and a modem.

He wrote and included a built-in BASIC that would be there at start up. Late in the design he realised he had to add graphics to this, so it could run a version of Breakout that he had written in BASIC. Subsequently, prompted by Markkula, Wozniak developed an elegant approach to drive a 5.25" disk, the Apple Disk II.

With the Radio Shack TRS-80 Model I, the FCC regulations on radio frequency (RF) interference had proven to be something of a challenge, and it was to prove a particular problem for the Apple II.

Place a portable radio on top of a microwave oven and switch both on and you will see an example of the issue; the RF given off by the microwave interferes massively with the radio. Many early products sent a lot of spurious signals around the house or office, so the USA's FCC looked for a safer and more 'democratic' approach to the use of its airwaves. Perhaps because of the plethora of radio and television stations, or as likely because of its more litigious nature, the rules in the United States were strict and enforced.

At that time in the UK and Europe there was only a set of recommended levels of RF signals from devices. These were not legal limits, just advised levels and there was no 'police' force.

Apple had maintained the idea that it wanted users to be able to connect with a home TV set rather than be obliged to buy an expensive monitor; so it needed to supply an RF modulator to provide the appropriate signal. But the modulator they developed gave off too much interference and this threatened to delay Apple getting to market while it achieved the necessary FCC approval.

Apple took an unorthodox approach. The Apple II would be supplied without a modulator, but one would be offered to clients by a small specialist company as a separate supply. The small company selected was M&R Electronics, run by Marty Spergel, a fellow Homebrew Computer Club member.

The agreement had Spergel supply RF modulators to dealers as an accessory; the Sup'R'Mod retailed at $30. Apple forecast that Spergel should expect perhaps fifty unit sales a month, but his eventual volume of sales was over 400,000 units.

Going to market – Apple III and an IPO

Steve Jobs always had an eye for marketing and he appointed an agency that had previously handled the marketing for Atari, Byte Shops and Intel. The McKenna Agency gave the commission to a young art director called Rob Janoff who, motivated by the fact that the Apple II was the first PC with colour, came up with the famous apple silhouette with a bite taken out. It had a striking six-stripe rainbow logo that linked directly to the hippy culture of the day.

All this meant Apple II at $1,298 stood out as a serious contender when it launched in April 1977 at the West Coast Computer Faire in San Francisco.

This exhibition was the brainchild of another Homebrew member, Jim Warren, also of 'Dr Dobbs' fame; quite a large guy it was quite a shock to see him roller skating around the show. They were all there: Apple, MITS Altair, IMSAI, Processor Technology, Cromemco, DRI and its CP/M, Sphere, Vector Graphics, Polymorphic Systems...

Thanks to the launch of the Apple II the company achieved sales of over $750k in 1977. The next year, as it was the only PC with VisiCalc, it recorded further stunning growth to $8m.

1978 proved quite significant for Apple. At the start of the year at the winter Consumer Electronics Show it demonstrated its Apple II disk drives and interface cards for most of the available printers of the time; both were significant developments that drove even more sales.

With success under its belt Apple was able to attract Chuck Peddle away from Commodore, but he lasted just a few months, not at all happy with the ethos that he found inside Apple. He promptly moved back to Commodore.

As the Apple III was being completed Apple launched the initial public offering of its shares and created some 40 millionaires overnight.

The Apple IPO took place on 12 December 1980, underwritten by Morgan Stanley and Hambrecht & Quist. It was forecast to be placed at $14 per share, but opened at $22 and closed that first day at $29, valuing the company at $1.8bn. It had generated more capital than any other operation since that achieved by the Ford Motor Company some twenty-four years earlier.

At the end of that day's trading Jobs' share was valued at more than $215m, Markkula's shareholding was worth over $200m, and Wozniak who had designed the Apple computer was worth $115m+.

Many of the team had also been awarded stock options at a notional $4 so they also received valuable Apple windfalls. Those who had received options before April 1979 had been awarded founders' shares which had subsequently been multiplied by a number of stock splits so that each was worth 32 shares at the IPO.

Wozniak was unhappy that only salaried staff had been awarded stock options and created the WozPlan allowing around eighty of the hourly-paid technicians and others to buy some of his shares at advantageous rates, though of course they had missed out on the stock-split multiplier.

Following its IPO Apple had 800 dealers in North America and a further 1,000 overseas. By 1983 Markkula's prediction proved accurate as it was ranked at 411th on the *Fortune 500*.

But it was earlier, in 1979, that a fateful meeting took place. Jobs, Wozniak and several others of the Apple team were prompted by Jef Raskin to visit the Xerox PARC facility. There they saw, among many other developments, its graphics user interface and mouse.

What they saw inspired them so much that they offered PARC an option on 100,000 shares at the pre-placement price of $10 per share in return for its Apple design team being granted three days of access to the PARC thinking and developments. The Apple Lisa and Macintosh products were the outcome of this fateful meeting.

The beat goes on – Apple Corps
Meanwhile Apple's development of such a significant business attracted the unwelcome attention of The Beatles.

About this time a British barrister, when asked to identify the group by the judge in another court case, reputedly described it in this rather pompous and out-of-touch manner,
'I believe they are a popular beat combo, m'lud.'

But this beat combo owned its own label, Apple Records, and its holding company was Apple Corps. In 1978 it sued Apple Computer for infringement of its brand. It took until 1981 for the two parties to resolve a one-off payment of $80,000 to grant the right to use Apple with computers. But the agreement also stipulated that Apple Computer would not market audio or video products with any recording or playback capabilities.

There was clearly no inkling at Apple about the forthcoming MIDI protocol (Musical Instrument Digital Interface) launched only three years later in 1984, or the multimedia systems that would become essential for PCs later in the 1980s and certainly there was no consideration of iTunes or iPods way back then.

As a result Apple Computer and The Beatles would meet in court regularly on each matter.

Military titles – Commodore from typewriters to calculators
Jack Tramiel was the original founder of Commodore. A post-WWII Polish immigrant to America who had not only survived the ghettos, he had actually transited through Auschwitz at one stage. He was moved on to a work camp near Hannover, from where he was liberated in April 1945.

He emigrated to the USA and joined the US Army where he gained useful business equipment repair skills and experience. Upon leaving the army to form his first company he sought a military name for it, but finding that many had already been taken he eventually opted for Commodore.

In 1953 he founded the Commodore Portable Typewriter Company as a repair operation but then sought relationships with Czech manufacturers. Realising the USA's restrictions on imports was an issue he subsequently set up Commodore Business Machines in Toronto, Canada to get around this.

He also took over a typewriter business in Berlin in order to have his own products manufactured. Having formed this complex operation his progress proved slow as low-cost Japanese models were starting to flood the markets.

He switched his focus to dealing largely in mechanical adding machines and calculators. This was a successful move and in 1962 Commodore International debuted on the New York Stock Exchange.

However in the late 1960s this market too was assailed by the Japanese. Tramiel moved again, this time into electronic calculators.

Commodore produced its first electronic pocket calculators based around a Texas Instruments (TI) chip with an LED display.

RANDOM ACCESS MOMENT:
The Commodore design was only overtaken technically by Clive Sinclair some years later when he significantly reduced the calculator's size.

Sinclair Radionics was also to reduce the power consumption of its unit when Chris Curry (later of Acorn Computers) and Jim Westwood (who went on to design the Sinclair Spectrum among other products) realised that the calculator's power need not be on permanently and could instead pulse regularly with the device contentedly holding power between pulses.

But this time the damaging competition for Commodore came from much nearer home as chip prices tumbled and TI launched its own low-cost calculator ranges. The real issue was that Commodore held large stocks of calculators that had been sourced at an earlier, much higher price point.

In the mid-1970s Tramiel used an infusion of new capital to purchase operations to secure his supply lines. He bought Frontier, a chip maker, and MDSA, a display supplier.

Perhaps most significantly Commodore bought MOS Technology which was having issues of its own. As part of the deal it also acquired Chuck Peddle. Chuck Peddle, a Canadian, had worked at General Electric and was involved in defining electronic cash registers as well as credit-card operated gas, or petrol, pumps.

This led nowhere so he joined Motorola in 1973, where he was a key part of the MC6800 processor design team. But Peddle became unpopular for seeking a low-cost alternative to the 6800 price-point of $300, an alternative that would better fit many applications they were encountering.

Peddle and others therefore moved from Motorola to found MOS Technology Inc where a new approach achieved better yields and enabled them to drive its microprocessor prices down to $25. Its planned 6501 microprocessor was designed to be completely pin-compatible with the MC6800 but was halted when Motorola lawyers came after them claiming infringement.

The financial owners of MOS Technology basically walked away and gave the operation over to the management team who eventually paid Motorola $200,000 to settle the matter.

All this simply inspired Peddle and Bill Mensch to produce a very much improved version named the 6502.

To promote the 6502 processor, Peddle designed the TIM-1 (Terminal Input Monitor) and KIM-1 (Keyboard Input Monitor). Quite unintentionally these became the world's first single-board computers which quickly enjoyed success; tens of thousands were sold to hobbyists, engineers and colleges.

Through these products Peddle met with many early pioneers. For example, a meeting with Steve Wozniak and Steve Jobs at a trade show led to the design of the first Apples around the MOS 6502 in 1976.

KIM-1 was very limited with a small hexadecimal keyboard and six LED displays. However as the device could separately address every element of each of the six seven-segment displays it proved quite versatile. It was later offered with 'TinyBASIC' and also had the first implementation of 'MicroChess'.

Commodore had in fact been purchasing the majority of MOS Technology's calculator chips. When the calculator market crashed the supplier started to wobble and almost inevitably Commodore acquired it.

Acquiring a mascot. PET
On arrival as a Commodore employee Chuck Peddle was quick to suggest to Tramiel that, as the market in calculators was coming to an end, they should enhance his KIM-1 design to become a full computer.

This resulted in the launch of the Commodore PET 2001 (Personal Electronic Transactor). PET was an inspired choice as a name as it overcame any technophobia that it might otherwise have encountered.

This was a significant moment in the development of the PC. This was the first time that a serious business was setting about designing a product; not the usual hobbyist with a dream and a soldering iron.

Peddle had previously shown his design approach to Radio Shack as a potential retailer for the product but, unbeknownst to him and to Commodore, it had already seen a working model of its own internally-developed product.

Where previous devices had simply attached a keyboard to the electronics, the PET took a new and comprehensive approach. It came fully assembled within a smart moulded cabinet and it was supplied with a built-in screen, a calculator-like keyboard, a data cassette unit and a series of peripheral edge-connectors. It meant users needed only to plug it into the mains and they were off and running.

To create the PET's monitor design Peddle had read and used a book by Adam Osborne that described how to build your own television. But when it was initially switched on the image was upside down which had them quickly thumbing back through the book to remedy things.

RANDOM ACCESS MOMENT:
I recall that with the PET I bought I was much taken by its range of graphic symbols. For example I found it offered each playing card suit symbol and I remember producing a bridge convention card on it. Today you usually have to fiddle around to find playing card images somewhere deep in the 'symbol' subset.

PET's early keyboard came in for much criticism but it is worth recalling that at this stage there was no standard for a keyboard. *Byte* magazine fought a battle right up until 1985 to get the market to agree a standard layout and just what symbols should be included on it.

The Commodore BASIC was produced by Microsoft as a ROM-based implementation. Microsoft and its founders at the time were still rather young and green and apparently Peddle negotiated a single and very low perpetual licence fee with Gates for unlimited use on any Commodore MOS 6502 based products. Though Peddle has always refused to announce the actual sum paid.

The PET was first shown as a prototype at the winter Consumer Electronics Show in January 1977 and the first production unit was produced for the summer show. It therefore beat both Apple II and the Radio Shack TRS-80 to the market.

Being a serious business, Commodore assessed the dealer interest that its launch had provoked and was the first organisation in the PC market to require its dealers to prove they had a proper retail operation. They had to show a track record and a credit history and they were expected to have an engineer and workshop facility to back up sales activity.

Compare this with the earlier players who, only after launch, realised that they needed their pricing to include a sensible margin for the retailer and then sold to anyone who asked to buy. Commodore also had the nous to work the educational markets and also to approach the major retail household names.

The PET at just $495 provided to be a turnkey solution that was highly appropriate for schools where many of its sales were subsequently made. The price soon hiked to $595 for the 4k model, the 8k version was $795. Although I recall to my cost that when it reached the UK the $ price was almost doubled to become the same number in £s.

Early production was constrained in 1978 but some 25,000 PETs were sold creating a revenue of around $20m. The PC market had grown up.

A second victory – VIC-20

Following on from the success of the Commodore PET the company decided to develop more computers.

The Apple II was taking off during 1979 and Jack Tramiel was eager for something to present at the winter CES in early 1980 that would have a competitive price point. In the event it was actually the summer CES before it was ready.

The unit Chuck Peddle had been working on for the purpose ran into problems and instead plans were based around something designed by Robert Yannes, a young engineer at MOS Technology, of course by now owned by Commodore. Yannes had worked at home to create what he had called the 'MicroPET'.

By all accounts it became a bit of a hybrid, much more about using what parts they had to hand rather than designing the dream machine. It used 1K RAM chips merely because Tramiel wanted to remedy an overstock position. Its video chip was something MOS Technology had designed for another display purpose but, failing to find a ready market for this product, they decided to use supplies of this MOS Technology video interface chip, or VIC, on the new product.

It was intended to call this product by its internal project name 'Vixen' but on learning that in German the word would be pronounced either as '*Wichsen*' or '*Ficken*', meaning 'masturbate' or 'f--k'.

So the product took on the video-chip name instead and became the VIC 20; the '20' is usually assumed to refer to the total of 20K of ROM aboard. The name was shortened in Germany to the VC-20 and presented as the Volkscomputer or people's computer.

The MicroPET was also based on the 6502, and the computer design was hastily expanded to include all the required features. It had the facility for only 5K of RAM but this was overcome by placing a further 16K inside games cartridges.

Scott Adams was contracted to produce a series of five adventure games for the VIC-20, all text-only games; these achieved over $1.5m in sales.

In 1981 an outside team was contracted to create the VIC Modem which at $99 was the first sub-$100 modem; it was sold at this price with a bundle of free tele-computing services from The Source, CompuServe and Dow Jones, worth $200.

With all of its compromises the Commodore VIC-20 became the first computer to sell one million units. It achieved this by January 1983 and went on to sell 2.5 million units in total!

VIC-20 also gained popularity as a controller of sensors, for robot step-motors and in theatre stage management.

Many industry individuals met computing first with a VIC-20; one significant individual was Linus Torvalds, the Linux inventor.

Further promotion – Commodore 64

During 1981 Commodore's chip-making subsidiary MOS Technology created the chips required for the next generation product. Jack Tramiel again asked that they marshal their plans to have a product ready for the winter CES, in January 1982.

The project name for this new computer was originally 'VIC-40'. It was based on a 6510 MPU and a VIC-II graphics chip providing 16 colours and its sound interface device which was a 3-channel 8-octave audio chip. It had the latest BASIC 2.0 and Tramiel insisted it had 64K of RAM. It had RF and composite video so could be used with a domestic television or a monitor for higher quality images.

The Commodore 64 hit the market in spring 1982 at just $595. This low price was only practical because of the vertical integration of Commodore and MOS Technology; at the time the Apple IIe cost $1,200 and the Atari 800 was $899.

Commodore drove its marketing powerfully. It also established traditional retail outlets for its products. In January 1983 it offered $100 rebate to anyone trading out another console or computer. Some suggest this was one of the contributing causes of the 1983 video console crash.

As a result, between 1983 and 1986 around 2 million units were sold each year in the USA, only ever surpassed by combined sales of IBM PC and its clones in 1985.

This market share prompted the release of some 10,000 software programs, games, commercial applications and utilities for the CBM 64.

Commodore is also credited with establishing a computer art sub-culture known as the 'demoscene' where artists showed off their skills and versatility in creating audio-visual presentations, squeezing every last feature from the computer - rather like the early MIT hackers had done many years earlier.

The Commodore 64 had a much tougher ride in the UK where it was priced at £399 and had to compete with the Sinclair ZX Spectrum at £175, the BBC Micro from £299 and the Amstrad CPC464 at £249 for its green and £359 for a colour screen.

A family of 64s emerged later. An Educator 64 was created by putting the 64 into a PET case with a black & white monitor. This package was well received versus the Apple II in schools and colleges.

The SX-64 was the first Commodore colour portable with a built in 5" screen. This was joined by a sleeker 64C styled on the new 128 model. Later still a C64GS games console was launched in Europe, though this proved unsuccessful.

In its life the Commodore 64 became the top selling PC selling over 30 million units before it was finally discontinued in 1995.

Retailing computers - Tandy

Way back in 1919 Norton Hinckley and Dave Tandy started the Hinckley-Tandy Leather Company to supply leather and other goods to shoe repair shops around Fort Worth. After WWII the rationing of shoes led to the preferential supply of leather to the military so Tandy's son, Charles David Tandy, took the business into more of a general leathercraft operation.

Hinckley was dropped from the company name and it became Tandy Leather Company. By the mid '50s there were more than sixty stores in over thirty states.

Founded two years later than Tandy in 1921, Radio Shack was created in Boston by brothers, Theodore and Milton Deutschmann; they had emigrated from London. Their plan was to exploit the amateur radio or ham radio sector and early success was based upon their supply of military surplus equipment. The company was named after the room on a boat where the radio equipment was stored - it was hoped to imply something of a professional-to- amateur customer crossover.

By the 1940s Radio Shack had a small chain of shops with a mail order catalogue operation and was branching into the hi-fi business selling own-label products. It ran into trouble in the 1960s and was heading for insolvency when Charles D Tandy acquired the operation for $300,000 and renamed it the Tandy Corporation. Tandy had caught the electronics bug.

Stores were initially given the implausible name of 'Tandy Radio Shack and Leather' but by the mid-1970s the non-electronics side of the business was discarded. Tandy Corporation expanded the number of Radio Shacks in the USA and launched both in the UK and Australia as Tandy.

RANDOM ACCESS MOMENT:
What's in a name? Radio Shack, they weren't shacks and they sold more than radios. In the UK we had Radio Rentals and the one thing they did not do was to rent radios. Though Selfridges did live up to its name!

In the mid-70s Radio Shack scored strongly with the CB Radio enthusiasts. CB had perhaps one of the most dramatic adoption curves for a product, from 0% to 20% in just a few years at the start of the 1970s. Given this fillip, Tandy's range of products expanded broadly.

In Tandy's West Coast operation, Don French, one of its buyers, was watching first-hand as Silicon Valley exploded exponentially around him. He suggested that Radio Shack should consider entering the PC market. John Roach the VP of Manufacturing was on a visit to Silicon Valley and he and French called on National Semiconductor on a 'fishing trip'.

While there they had a fateful meeting with 24-year-old Steve Leininger, another Homebrew Computer Club luminary, who was at the time developing TinyBASIC for National's SC/MP microprocessor (Simple Cost-effective Micro Processor), pronounced scamp; SC/MP would be the basis of the Science of Cambridge MK14.

They tried to get Leininger's contact details while there but National Semiconductor refused to release them. By chance, later that same evening, they met up with him again while he was working at a Byte Shop. Impressed they invited him down to Fort Worth where he was hired on the spot.

Initially it was proposed to launch a kit computer, but soon Leininger was charged with developing a complete turnkey personal computer system that could be sold through Radio Shack at a marketable price - and in volume.

This was new thought at the time - the design of a full-featured PC that would be produced in volume and handled and supported by a large and successful retail chain. The original goal was that it should be created to sell at a $199 price point.

Trash sells – TRS-80

Leininger worked alone, not in a garage but in an old saddle factory in Fort Worth, to develop the TRS-80 (Tandy Radio Shack) personal computer; undeservedly known by many as the Trash-80.

He based it around the Zilog Z80 microprocessor and it featured a full-size keyboard, a monitor and a cassette deck. At its eventual $599 price-point it would represent the most expensive item in the Radio Shack inventory.

The TRS-80 was launched in August 1977 at a press conference in New York City which proved to be a bad choice of date and venue. The *Fuerzas Armadas de Liberación Nacional Puertorriqueña*, or Puerto Rican Armed Forces of National Liberation, chose that very day to set off two bombs in NY City. These were in a Defense Department facility on Madison Avenue and the Mobil building on East 42nd Street and resulted in the loss of one life.

In addition the terrorists warned that bombs were also placed in the World Trade Center and the Empire State Building; 100,000 office workers had to be evacuated. A total of eighty false-alarm calls were made in the demand for independence to be granted to Puerto Rico.

It was impossible for Tandy to command much press attention against that busy headline-making day.

The initial production run for the TRS-80 was set at 3,500 which was also the number of Radio Shack and Tandy stores. Its president realised that if the product did not sell through, then at least it would still able to run each store's inventory.

Any fears proved groundless when 10,000 units sold in the first month!

The video monitor was not particularly exciting. Initially supplied as white-out-of-black and later green-out-of-black, it displayed just 16 lines of 32 or 64 characters.

The TRS-80 could however differentiate between upper and lower-case characters in its memory, although initially lower case could not be displayed. This apparently saved $1.50 in parts which would reflect in a retail impact of $5. When the target price was $199 this saving was of course significant.

Later this was resolved by a $59 upgrade that enabled lower-case to be displayed on the monitor. The Radio Shack TRS-80 III was launched with fully integral lower-case by 1980; by comparison it took Apple until 1983 on the Apple IIe to have a standard lower-case system.

The keyboard on the Model I also contained the motherboard but this was found to have something of a bounce problem; one keystroke would deliver a multiple display of the character to the screen.

Initially printing was a further issue as it required the addition of a relevant expansion interface that was relatively expensive, priced from $299. This was due to the card being rather comprehensive and quite sophisticated. It offered an increased memory of 48k and provided a floppy-disk controller able to handle up to four drives. It provided a parallel printer port as well as a serial RS-232 port, plus a further cassette port and even a real-time clock. All of this was in the one card.

Later Radio Shack introduced a much simpler printing-only interface and also a low-cost electrostatic screen-grabbing printer.

Getting basic - TinyBASIC and Microsoft

The TRS-80 Level I BASIC was derived from public-domain software written by Li-Chen Wang. Called Palo Alto Tiny BASIC it was the fourth version of Tiny BASIC to appear in the Dr Dobbs May 1976 issue. Its use of short commands needing a little less than 1.8K of memory made it very suitable for small-memory computers.

Wang also published a Star Trek game in the People's Computer Company newsletter in July of that year. He wrote the code for the TRS-80 'Exatron Stringy Floppy' controller launched in 1979. This was a credit card sized sixteenth-of-an-inch continuous loop tape which proved to be faster and more reliable than a standard audio cassette and was later used by the VIC 20 and Commodore 64.

Leininger had worked with Wang's Tiny BASIC and selected it for the TRS-80. His version had a few additional Tandy-produced input-output features and was supported by a very good manual.

This was unusual. Most PC manuals of the time appeared to be a last-minute thought and they tended to be initially patronisingly simple and then without warning jump into the esoteric, exhibiting little user friendliness!

Level II BASIC was later released as a Microsoft-derived version which had to be somewhat squeezed into its 12k ROM, although Microsoft also offered a Level III version that could be loaded via the on-board tape cassette drive to bring it back to the full 16k level.

The TRS-80 team worked hard and attracted a wealth of software from small independent producers who either designed or ported across arcade games, business applications including VisiCalc, utilities, a bulletin board system and even an operating system called TRS-DOS.

Government interference – FCC regulations

The Federal Communications Commission (FCC) is the authority in the United States that creates and enforces the use of the airwaves throughout the entire radio frequency spectrum. In October 1979 it issued a new set of rules for personal computers.

The TRS-80 Model I was found to emit significant RF interference and on investigation it was declared to be in breach of the FCC regulations. The model was therefore phased out after a Tandy board decision in January 1981; but not before some 200,000 units had been sold in its short four years of life.

This was a big issue for the time. Apple had circumnavigated it by not supplying its own RF adaptor. Tandy had to stop production of its successful product and many subsequent products had a metal foil bag placed around the whole PCB in an effort to minimise the effect.

There was a further major problem with power supplies. Some of this was a European problem caused by PCs sold with US-supplied transformers that had only enough iron in them for the US 60Hz requirements; they overheated or melted when used with 50Hz supplies.

Jet setting – PET Jet, berms and Flight 191

These three early and significant jet-setting PC makers made heaps of money and quite naturally they used some of this to acquire the ultimate 'boys' toys'. These proved not to be without their hazards.

Commodore, with bases around the world, soon purchased what they called the 'PET Jet', a seven-seat private aircraft. In September 1980 a fire broke out midflight; it was ablaze for forty-five minutes before the plane could land. Jack Tramiel, VP Dick Sanford and other senior executives were aboard and fortunately they were merely shaken but unharmed.

Steve Wozniak crashed while flying his Beechcraft in February 1981. The aircraft has some provenance. A version of it was involved in the incident that killed Buddy Holly, Ricky Valens and the Big Bopper in 1959. In 1964 Jim Reeves perished in a Beechcraft too, and twenty years later Randy Rhoads, a guitarist with Ozzy Osbourne, died in a Beechcraft crash. In 1984 Robert Moriarty buzzed through the legs of the Eiffel Tower in one without mishap. Having said all of the above, some 17,000 have been built and flown uneventfully for a considerable number of hours.

Wozniak crashed his Beechcraft during take-off and was adjudged by the authorities not to have been fully qualified. It was suggested that his unfamiliarity with the aircraft, led to him stalling it and hitting a perimeter berm.

He survived physically unharmed but subsequently suffered amnesia and was forgetful about many things in his life. Once he was back to normal he took the opportunity to walk away from Apple and returned to fulltime education and completed a degree course.

But even if they did not fly their own private aircraft these high-distance PC travellers were still at risk.

Don Estridge, who led the IBM PC launch team, was rewarded with a series of promotions which in typical IBM-style moved him away from the team that he had built. In 1983 he was approached by Steve Jobs to become president of Apple. He was offered a sign-on of $1m, $1m a year and $2m to buy a house. Estridge rejected this proposal. Apple lured John Sculley from Pepsi Cola instead.

By 1984 Estridge was a VP of Manufacturing at IBM. Sadly in August 1985 he and his wife died when the Delta flight 191 crashed at Dallas-Fort Worth, he was just forty-eight and left three young daughters. By that time the division he did so much to shape had sold over a million IBM PCs.

Slow penetration

But all these early efforts and initiatives to bring us the PC resulted in worldwide sales across that first decade, 1968-78, of only 200,000 personal computers, with a total sales value of under $500m.

The world's population at the time was 4.3 billion; this meant that very few of them had ever encountered a PC by 1978 and only a minuscule four thousandths of a single percentage point of the globe's population had actually bought one!

The USA's total population was then 215 million people, living in 77 million households. Even if all 200,000 PCs sold had been ring-fenced and distributed only within the USA, and all to consumers, then this would mean just one fifth of a percentage point in household penetration was achieved across the decade.

This was not so surprising when comparing the price of those early PCs with the average price of a house. In the UK an average house in 1968 cost £4,000, quadrupling by 1978 to £16,000; in the USA the price doubled from $25,000 to $50,000 in the same period.

The average annual income in the UK was £1,500 and although this rose by more than 3.5 times across the decade it was still only £5,500 by 1978. The average in the USA would double from $8,000 in 1968 to $17,000 in

1978. So on both sides of the Atlantic individuals and households were certainly able to become more conspicuous in their consumption across that decade.

However the early Apple I was priced at $666.66 which was 5% of the median USA income for the decade. This represented a significant investment decision for many - over two and a half weeks gross pay. If we take the early habit that $s meant £s for imported American products into the UK, then the cost represented almost 20% of the median UK gross income, or over ten weeks salary.

Anyone at the time might have looked at these statistics and wondered if the PC was set to become a significant development. Most would think twice before applying resource and time to something with such a small potential in terms of application; could it ever be worthy of the investment?

This first decade did however see Intel and other semiconductor manufacturers founded and they had started to climb up their 'hockey-stick' graphs. It was a time when a plethora of new products, peripherals and software were conceived and tested – although to be honest they were generally found wanting! But fortunately the enthusiast sector was never daunted by a little lack of utility or a few setbacks.

The first PC decade also inspired a number of the eventual market-shapers and shakers. It was half-way through this decade, in 1973, that a certain William F Gates, then 18, declared to a friend at his Lakeside Preparatory School,

'I'm going to make my first million by the time I'm 25.'

So it was very much the 'springboard' period that ended with many of the key players in place and many concepts tried and tested.

Comparisons are studious

However to see just how impressive that growth in PC usage is one needs to consider several other well-used products.

The first television was demonstrated back in the mid 1920s; by the end of 2003 the CIA World Factbook reported that there were 1.4 billion televisions in the world. This means that the all –pervasive television took twice as long as the PC and the Net to reach the one-billion-in-use figure.

The very first automobile was built in 1885 by Karl Benz. Run time forward more than one hundred and twenty years and we find a global market still very much in love with the automotive industry.

Around the world we buy just over 70 million new vehicles each year, and in total there are 806 million, or 0.8 billion, cars and light trucks currently in use on the world's roads! Thus the automotive industry took three times as long to reach only 80% of the PC usage. In this case it is not just about market penetration. Bill Gates pondered the technical progress of the product when he said,

'If General Motors had kept up with technology like the computer industry has, we would all be driving $25 cars that got 1000 mpg.'

Bill Gates was also quoted in 1980 in an interview with *Microcomputing* magazine:

'There's nobody getting rich writing software that I know of.'

By 2009 he was named as the wealthiest person in the world! Microsoft was the largest technological corporation and the world's third largest company overall behind PetroChina and ExxonMobil. Proving that ending a sentence with a preposition is not that much of a hindrance to progress!

11 – Games people play

'Where is the "any" key?' Homer Simpson, in response to the message, "Press any key"

The majority of early PC users wanted speedy gratification for the purchase and many therefore turned to games. Many PC developments would emerge from the efforts applied to stretch the technology to offer ever more complex games.

Games in many forms had of course been around for a long time - games to pass time, games to challenge the individual, games to pit two or more against each other, games of strategy, games of chance.

Belligerent games – early computer war gaming

It was obvious that computers could be applied to games-play from a very early phase and once again belligerent military requirements led the way.

The first computer-based war game was developed in 1948 on a Univac 1 at John Hopkins University. By 1953 it had become the first computer simulation of military operations. John Hopkins, based in Baltimore, has been a leading US university regularly recording massive R&D spends each year. At that time it was appointed the US Army's Operations Research Office (ORO).

In 1950, George Gamow, a consultant to ORO and physics professor at George Washington University, invented a manual mathematical game called 'Tin Soldier'. This was the first game for analytical rather than tactical operations.

He went on to produce the first digital computer game called CARMONETTE, (Computerised Monte Carlo Simulation) which, unexpectedly given its name, simulated tank and anti-tank battles - not casino games. It was played from 1956-1960. The Mark II version from 1960-1965 added the dimension of infantry. Later versions included helicopter support, communications and night vision.

Of course the US Navy had enjoyed war games for many years too, but these had usually been played out manually on charts. During WWII a machine was used to assist in submarine tactics but this too was a mechanical aide rather than a gaming device.

The University of California designed a combat training system for the navy in 1945. This led to the later creation of the Navy Electronic Warfare Simulator in 1957/8 and from this a Navy War Games Program was established.

The US Air Force was of course predisposed to the notion of computer assistance given its use of flight simulators. In 1951 it established the

Advisory Board for Simulation, later changed to become the Institute for System Research. With the University of Chicago it looked at flight control systems and eventually from these roots developed its astronaut training program.

By 1957 the USAF had an Air Battle Analysis Centre running high-level simulations and war gaming was introduced at the Air Force Academy. Of course soon it also had SAGE, not a game, but a real-time analysis of the North American airspace for homeland security.

For war gaming and simulations the USAF went instead to a contractor, the RAND Corporation headquartered in Santa Monica. RAND was formed in 1946 as a research project, within Douglas Aircraft Corporation, for the US Army Air Forces. One of its first reports was *Preliminary Design of an Experimental World-Circling Spaceship* which was based on the potential for use of man-made satellites.

In 1948, as a 200-person team supported by the Ford Foundation, it became the RAND Corporation,

'an independent, nonprofit research institution committed to exploring the most complex and consequential problems facing our society'. RAND Corporation website

It is more usually referred to as a 'think tank' though that term was later applied in the 1960s. It insisted that it was always non-partisan, pursuing no agenda other then R&D. Its purpose was defined as,

'To further and promote scientific, educational, and charitable purposes, all for the public welfare and security of the United States of America.'

On its formation in 1948 the then Secretary of War and Commanding General of the Army Air Force, Hap Arnold, wrote:

'During this war the Army, Army Air Forces, and the Navy have made unprecedented use of scientific and industrial resources. The conclusion is inescapable that we have not yet established the balance necessary to insure the continuance of teamwork among the military, other government agencies, industry, and the universities. Scientific planning must be years in advance of the actual research and development work.'

One theme that RAND followed was developing all sorts of simulations and games. Saw was a war game in 1948 and 1949, by 1953 it became Straw, and by 1958 it was Swap. They also designed an inventory management simulation called Monopologs.

RAND was also responsible in the early 1950s for a system called COW (Conference of Wargamers). This allowed twenty individuals to role play twenty independent states in a war game. Its parameters were too weak to be of much value, but the exercise proved that there was the potential for computer systems like these, they just needed more development. RAND later developed Sierra in 1954 for the US Air Force, also to simulate limited war scenarios.

In 1955 RAND originated the prototype Air Battle Model I which was to be used to train and practise the response to a nuclear war. RAND became the leading organisation for man-machine simulations with a whole raft of systems including Flight Operations Planning and in 1961 Strategic Air Planner, both for Strategic Air Command. There were also simulations for the likely impact on civilians with MUSTARD and QUICK COUNT.

Business entrepreneurs are of course never slow to see an opportunity and the American Management Association approached RAND and others to develop a business version of these simulations.

The first fruit was The Top Management Decision Simulation running on an IBM 650 computer. This was given to twenty large corporate presidents in May 1957. With their feedback this was made into a game that by March 1958 was being played by 350 corporate executives and a number of business schools.

Games with mainframes

The first patented interactive electronic game is accredited to Thomas T Goldsmith Jr and Estle Ray Mann at DuMont Laboratories, a television equipment manufacturer, in New Jersey.

Inspired by the radar displays of WWII they developed a missile simulator that the patent application in January 1947 defined as a *cathode ray tube amusement device*. Users could control a dot on the screen but the scenarios or targets were achieved by placing overlays in front of the screen. Only a few handmade prototypes were ever built.

The early mainframe behemoths were funded by the government and military authorities, they were enormously expensive to build and maintain. The universities were only just rising to the challenge of creating new graduate courses for those who would be allowed to tend them.

But human nature is indomitable and individuals would soon find ways to access and modify the mainframes. They were tweaked and tested in ways very different to their intended purpose.

In 1949 a game called Bouncing Ball was developed for MIT's Whirlwind computer, though it had no interactivity.

Early 1950s Ferranti computers were often used for games. In March 1950 Claude Shannon devised a chess programme for one. For the Festival of Britain a Ferranti Nimrod was programmed to play both forms of NIM, a subtraction game, using its display lights; NIM deriving from Old English or German for 'take'.

In 1952 Alexander 'Sandy' Douglas used the Cambridge Electronic Delay Storage Automatic Calculator to play noughts and crosses (Tic-Tac-Toe); he called his game simply 'OXO'

In 1958 to entertain the visitors to an open day at a nuclear research base, Brookhaven National Laboratory, William Higinbotham designed an interactive game named Tennis for Two. Using an analogue oscilloscope, it was one of the first games to introduce screen graphics.

Tennis for Two utilised prior work on ballistic trajectories and displayed a side view of the game, where the 'ball' would curve over a net, bounce off the 'ground', hit the net and so on. The ball was designed to experience both gravity and drag through the air; a button was used to hit the ball and a knob turned to apply an angle. There was also a sound when the ball was hit. The game was used only twice and never patented.

When the TX-0 arrived at MIT its users were among the first to experience controlling a computer with a terminal rather than merely feeding it punched cards. This inspired the creation of early games like Mouse in the Maze and Tic-Tac-Toe using its screens and light pens to advantage.

Mouse in the Maze allowed players to define a maze using a light pen on the oscilloscope and then set loose the mouse. A simple blob on the screen represented the mouse which would set off around the maze in search of cheese, some other screen blobs. Some versions added a glass of martini as an alternative goal. Tic-Tac-Toe also used a light pen to play the classic game, what we Brits call noughts and crosses.

In 1969 Ken Thompson was the co-designer of the UNIX language but that year he also developed a video game called Space Travel which was ported to GECOS and later to a PDP-7. It showed a representation of the solar system that the user could negotiate with a space ship to view the scenery and attempt to land on the various moons and planets.

Board games on a computer

John McCarthy, a teacher at MIT, set out to devise a chess game on MIT's IBM 704. The program had originally been written by him in FORTRAN which needed to be compiled before the computer could use its instructions.

The task was taken over by Alan Kotok, a TMRC member, and a group of other students in 1959. Kotok switched the approach to part FORTRAN and part assembler and developed the necessary algorithms.

The work went on for a number of years and spanned several generations of MIT computers and students, eventually being operationally demonstrated in 1962. In truth the exercise was probably more about the joys of having a computer calculate and make moves and there was little real chess thinking or strategy involved.

Some years later Ricky Greenblatt, another MIT hacker, took up the chess challenge, by then on a PDP-6. He was actually a chess player and was not satisfied by merely simulating a game. He created a program that could set out and win a game. Between 1965 and 1966 he wrote and developed Mac Hack aka The Greenblatt Chess Program. The Mac related to MIT's Project MAC, not Apple.

Its version VI could play chess to tournament standard and they registered the PDP-6 as an honorary member of the game's state and national associations. In 1967 it played in four tournaments winning three games, drawing three and losing twelve. It was later ported to the PDP-10.

Hubert Dreyfus, an academic, had publicly attacked these attempts to have computers play chess as being a pointless exercise and had suggested that no computer could beat a ten-year old. But when he was challenged to face Greenblatt's program he promptly lost.

Spacewar!

Slug Russell, Wayne Witaenem and J Martin Graetz came together at MIT, initially working on statistical calculations with an IBM 704. When MIT's TX-0 arrived they were among the first to experience controlling a computer with a terminal rather than merely feeding it punched cards.

But it was to be the PDP-1 that inspired these TMRC members to produce the 'Spacewar!' the first shoot-'em-up game.

Russell, an E E 'Doc' Smith sci-fi fan, had foolishly announced his intention to other club members that he would develop a space battle game - foolishly because it meant his fellow hackers pressured him until he actually completed it.

Russell's game had two rocket ships discernible by their different shapes each able to fire a torpedo. If the torpedo blip coalesced with a rocket on the screen then an explosion was created. Each player started with 31 torpedoes and a rudimentary, random, background of stars had been added. There were four simple controls: rotate clockwise, rotate anticlockwise, accelerate and fire.

The general practice among these hackers was one of complete openness in their software. They were each committed to allowing others not just to see their work, but to take it forward if they could make neat improvements or clever add-ons.

Russell's torpedoes were originally designed to run out of steam with distance and also had some randomness in both their speed and direction. One hacker soon changed them to make them run true.

Peter Samson decided that the star background should be accurate and painstakingly created a real star chart, displaying all the major stars that would actually appear above their location in the night sky. Dan Edwards then added a 'sun' that introduced a gravitational effect that could pull the ships to disaster, yet its gravitation was able to be skilfully used to slingshot a rocket to add speed.

Shag Garetz added a facility that allowed a player to avoid an opponent by disappearing off in to hyperspace. But this had to be a feature of last resort as when the rocket re-emerged a new location was selected at random and this might be right next to the sun where the user could not escape its gravitational pull.

Others developed joystick controllers and the video game business was essentially born following this series of hacks. DEC found that Space War! was a perfect routine to test their products at installation time and soon every PDP was shipped with a public domain version of Spacewar!

In 1971 Bill Pitts and Hugh Tuck at Stanford University installed one of the very first coin-op games at a student union building. It was a version of Spacewar! called Galaxy Game and it ran rather extravagantly from a PDP-11. The hardware investment of $20,000 would have taken a long time to be recouped given revenues of just 10 cents per game or three games at 25 cents. A year later it was modified to manage three or four consoles but by then the market had moved on. This game has survived and is on show at the Computer History Museum at Mountain View in California.

In 1971 Mike Mayfield and high school friends developed a text-based game using a time-share SDS Sigma 7 at the University of California, Irvine. He purchased an HP-35 scientific calculator that led to him popping in and out of Hewlett Packard's office for advice. The HP team let him loose on their HP 2000, unusual for its time in that it used BASIC, in return for his developing a version of Star Trek for their minicomputer.

HP issued the Star Trek game as part of its public domain software. But it really took off when David Ahl, working in the education department at DEC, found the HP2000 game, ported it into DEC BASIC-PLUS and distributed it within a DEC user newsletter.

Later in 1973 Ahl collected together a whole suite of programs in a book called '101 BASIC Games'. He had modified many games himself, including Star Trek which for the book he called *SPACWR*. This book sold over a million copies and the game was ported onto many new PCs as a result. Ahl would later launch *Creative Computing* magazine.

In 1974 Bob Leedom updated the code extensively and created Super Star Trek on a Data General Nova. Leedom wrote it up in the *People's Computer Company* magazine and Ahl featured it in his later book called *BASIC Computer Games*. In 1974 Leedom proposed to his employer that they should develop a lower-cost version of the PDP-8 for c$5,000; they dismissed the idea as foolish.

Super Star Trek proved to be one of the most important games after it was ported into FORTRAN and C programming language and included as part of the package on all IBM PCs in the early 1980s.

Gaming for money

MIT's *The Tech* newspaper of February 1961 reported that one of its mathematics department instructors, Edward O Thorp, had used its IBM 704 to analyse the casino game of 'Blackjack'.

He visited over eighty casinos in Nevada and studied the different rules that each applied. In fact he found over a hundred variations – so do make sure you check before you start!

Thorp then produced a study paper entitled *A Favorable Strategy for Blackjack*. He calculated that the casino rule variations could change the expectation of winning or losing by a minuscule .005%; so apparently no startling revelations for all that diligent effort.

But with access to a high-speed computer he was able to improve on earlier studies that had been severely limited - using calculators. He was able to show that Blackjack had the least favorable odds of all the casino gambling games.

Rather more surprising was his conclusion that if you noted all the 5s had been used from the packs in the game the odds of winning would increase by over 3%.

Progressively less significant, but still delivering a favorable outcome for the player, were if all the 4s and 6s, 3s and 7s or 2s and 8s had gone – and there I was worrying about the aces and court cards!

He advocated using minimum bets until any of the above numbers had been used up and then to switch over to maximum wagers.

Play with enthusiasm

The burgeoning PC and console business was voracious for content. This would lead to a plethora of authors and software houses emerging. But at the beginning it was rather more about individuals with a compelling interest.

They developed software to pursue both their hobbies and their computing, not as a business opportunity, but a means of expanding their enjoyment.

Will Crowther a programmer with Bolt, Beranek & Newman, was also a potholer and his enthusiasm for caving inspired him to produce the game Adventure.

He had come to know a cave system in Kentucky rather well. The Mammoth-Flint Ridge Cave is the longest known in the world at 110 miles (177km); though it may in fact be even longer as connections with other cave systems are constantly being discovered. It is both a World Heritage Site and a Biosphere Reserve thanks to an endangered sightless albino shrimp living in its waters.

So this provided rich material for Crowther's interactive textual game called either Adventure or Colossal Cave Adventure when he wrote it in 1975/6. He modelled his game particularly on the Bedquilt entrance to the system and was so faithful in his descriptions that those that had become familiar with the game were later able to navigate the sections in reality.

In 1976 Don Woods, a programmer at Stanford AI Labs, came across the open-software game on a computer. He was a hacker who had contributed to the Jargon File and to The Hackers' Dictionary. Raphael Finkel at Stanford produced the Hacker's Jargon File.

RANDOM ACCESS MOMENT:
An extract from the original Hacker's Dictionary, BELLS AND WHISTLES n. Unnecessary but useful (or amusing) features of a program. "Now that we've got the basic program working, let's go back and add some bells and whistles." Nobody seems to know what distinguishes a bell from a whistle.

Finding Crowther's game Woods decided to contact him in a novel manner; he went on to the ARPANET and sent an email to crowther@sitename; site name was a generic for all sites on the network. He received a response.

Woods, with Crowther's agreement, extended the game and as he was a Tolkien fan he added elves, trolls and magical objects. The game was distributed on the Internet and became popular, particularly on the PDP-10.

While one person was pursuing an enthusiasm, others saw it as a business opportunity. One of the early independent software companies was Infocom, founded in June 1979 by a team of MIT faculty members and students, including Joel Berez Marc Blank, Dave Lebling and Albert Vezza.

The Infocom team suggested they had been inspired directly by Will Crowther's Adventure. They developed a LISP-like language called ZIL (Zork Implementation, or Interactive, Language) which enabled them to design games on a virtual computer called the Z-machine.

The completed code could then be simply ported to a broad variety of current PCs or consoles. ZIL created a better 'relationship' with the user by allowing more of a dialogue format rather than the limitation of instructions to stark two-word, verb and object, orders.

The Infocom team used its approach to first produce a text-based adventure game called Zork. In 1980 it was released for Apple II and TRS-80.

Zork was hacker-speak for an unfinished piece of software; they had initially considered renaming their finished product Dungeon, but by then Zork had stuck. It was set in an underground labyrinth; each year new versions were launched.

They went on to develop a series of other text-based games, including in 1984 a successful *Hitchhiker's Guide to the Galaxy*, co-produced with Douglas Adams himself.

The declared intention of Infocom had been to use the revenues from games to build a business software library. To achieve this they developed a database product called Cornerstone, but this did not prove to be the start of their planned empire and in June 1986 they were taken over by Activision.

Another enthusiast who did reluctantly espouse commerce wrote what became the Microsoft Flight Simulator series.

But this was not Microsoft stepping out of its comfort zone of operating systems and languages; it was more because Bill Gates had developed an interest in flying.

Bruce Artwick while an electrical engineering student at the University of Illinois at Urbana-Champaign had also been engaged in research in the Aviation Research Lab. His thesis was on 3D graphics in relation to flight simulation, using one of the first UNIX installations on a PDP 11. After graduation he wrote several papers on 3D graphics while working at Hughes Aircraft in California.

By 1977 he developed his ideas on a 6800 MPU based PC and wrote several magazine articles. An editor indicated that readers were interested in buying it from him and he set up SubLogic; he was soon offering Altair and IMSAI versions.

It was when he launched an Apple II version and a TRS-80 version that both IBM and Microsoft approached him; he opted to sell a licence to Microsoft for an IBM PC version and received a very early IBM PC on which to develop the software. Microsoft Flight Simulator 1.0 was released in 1982.

MS Flight Simulator can probably claim to be the 'game' that has the longest history of being constantly available on sale; the Microsoft team kept it updated and evolving from 1982 until 2009.

12 - Video game consoles

A computer once beat me at chess, but it was no match for me at kick boxing.
Emo Philips

Coming home

By 1974 the Atari team set out to develop a home version of Pong. A chip expert, Harold Lee, had proposed that a single-chip approach was possible a year earlier and he worked on this with Al Alcorn and Bob Brown. They created a single chip that would provide the game, on-screen scores and sound.

But when it was shown at the New York Toy Fair to a fanfare they received no orders at all. Fortunately a buyer at Sears saw the game during a round of meetings before the show and expressed interest in an exclusive deal. Given little success at the fair, Atari returned to Sears who made good on an exclusive deal for 150,000 units with Sears agreeing to be responsible for all the promotion.

Bushnell achieved the necessary $10m funding through Don Valentine who had co-founded Sequoia Capital in 1972 and would go on to provided venture capital to many Silicon Valley companies.

The home version of Pong was sold in 1975, exclusively by the retailer, as the 'Sears Tele-Games system'. At $100 it just flew off the shelves. But this success soon attracted the attention of Sanders Associates and Magnavox and Ralph Baer persuaded them to take action against Atari and the clone makers.

Bushnell's signature in the visitor book for the early Odyssey demonstration in May 1972 showed that he had seen that product before starting Pong and this weakened any argument that Atari might mount. This together with forbidding potential legal costs led to Atari agreeing a $700,000 retrospective licence fee.

The success of Tele-Games attracted a whole host of Pong-variant home game consoles. The market exploded with an enormous selection of largely Far East produced devices flooding the market. By enforcing Baer's patent, Sanders and Magnavox were to make millions from these clone makers.

One major home-Pong competitor of note was Coleco; this was the Connecticut Leather Company founded in 1932 by Maurice Greenburg to sell leathercraft kits. Post-war Coleco moved into plastics, moulded swimming pools and toys, but in 1976 it launched the 'Telstar' a Pong-clone with three games.

Space remained a recurrent theme in games systems, but perhaps they should have considered that both Telstar 1 and 2 communications satellites crashed and burned after seven months and twenty-four months respectively?

Coleco went on to launch fourteen different systems across three years, all based around General Instrument's 'Pong-on-a-chip'. Supplies of the chip were scarce but as Coleco was an 'early-booker' it managed to get supplies and break even.

In 1974 Videomaster was one of the first in Europe, and the very first in the UK, to launch home versions of Pong. For five years it introduced a series of around fifteen different games systems. The first was the VM 577 which used discrete circuitry to generate the game; dedicated Pong chips were not yet available.

One of its founders, Cameron MacSween, was often seen around the exhibitions resplendent in full kilt with gun dog. The Videomaster business was sold to the conventional games organisation, John Waddington Ltd. MacSween later ran Prism France.

At the end of the decade and into the early '80s a number of companies banked the royalties due to Sanders and used the money as a fighting fund to overthrow the sprite patent; they eventually succeeded in the effort.

Not that Baer will have been much concerned as in 1978 he subsequently developed an electronic game based upon the classic 'Simon Says' principle. The colourful and noisy Simon game challenged users to recall and repeat an increasingly complex set of sequences – this was a massive stand-alone hit.

Atari hired Cyan Engineering, a design agency run by two ex-Ampex guys Steve Mayer and Ron Milner. It was charged with researching and forecasting where the video game business might be headed next. They were certainly inspired by several early '70s developments.

Of course they looked at Ralph Baer's development that became the Magnavox Odyssey with its coloured overlays and hardware cartridges; but this was already surpassed.

In 1976 Fairchild Semiconductor launched a games console, originally called the Fairchild Video Entertainment System (VES) and later renamed the 'Channel F'. This console was the first manifestation of the Fairchild F8, a two-chip 8-bit MPU; later used by NewBrain too. The VES console had two built-in Pong clones, Tennis and Hockey, and offered additional ROM-based videocarts.

Hewlett Packard also used ROM cartridges with its HP 9830 desktop computers and Texas Instruments later provided GROM cartridges with its home computer launch. So cart games were certainly something of a vogue.

Cyan came up with a proposal for a flexible video game console named the Atari Video Computer System (VCS), later referred to as the Atari 2600.

This was launched in late 1977. A badged version, the Sears Video Arcade, was supplied as an OEM (other equipment manufacturer) deal to the retailer/mail order company, perhaps in recognition of the two operations' earlier relationship with the domestic Pong game.

The Atari VCS was supplied with two joysticks and a Combat cart at $199, and in the final quarter of 1977 they sold 250,000 units.

Having moved production of the unit to Hong Kong they sold 550,000 in 1978 but 800,000 had been preordered and this would put pressure on finances. Bushnell eventually resolved matters by selling Atari for $28m to Warner Communications. He went on to use his wealth and freedom to set up an organisation to support and fund Silicon Valley start-ups.

By 1979 Fairchild had backed out of the market, just as the games console proved to be the must-have Christmas present for the family. Atari sold one million units.

In 1980 it acquired a licence for Taito's original coin-op Space Invaders game and sold two million units turning over $2bn. With 4 million units sold in 1981 and 8 million in 1982 Atari can be seen to have securely put the notion of programmable games and computers onto the agenda of most households.

But in 1983 the market crashed, and Atari lost $538m. Warner split the operation in two, retaining as Atari Games the arcade side of the business and selling off the home games division to Jack Tramiel, the founder of Commodore.

Intelligent television

In the late 1970s Mattel was the biggest toy company in the world with Barbie and Ken being among its most significant products. It was also successful with a range of hand-held electronic games. It formed Mattel Electronics to enter the games console market and in 1979 launched Intellivision, a shortened form of Intelligent Television, which included a whole series of innovations.

Ed Krakauer was the CEO. Don Daglow was one of the design team; he had devised a series of simulating and role playing games and would later create Stormfront Studios that later sold 12.5 million games.

Intellivision was promoted as,

'The most exciting entertainment system since television itself.'

It used a General Instrument CP1610 MPU, so claimed it was the first 16-bit games system; the mathematical registers were 16-bit, though the CPU and cartridges used only 10-bits. It also had an add-on IntelliVoice system to synthesise speech.

There was a very clever controller with a 16-way disk-shaped joystick and a small keypad that used a graphic and colourful overlay to customise the purpose of the buttons; in this way it offered more control of the software.

It launched with sixteen carts, featuring sports (Soccer, NFL Football, Baseball, Tennis, Basketball, Hockey, Golf and Skiing), shoot 'em ups

(Armor Battle, Sea Battle and Space Battle), gambling games (Poker/Blackjack, Roulette and Backgammon) and a 'Maths Fun' cart.

Intellivision offered downloadable games which were lost once the system was switched off and later worked with GI to develop a cable-download process too.

The true innovation was that 'an elegant Keyboard Component' was planned for launch in 1981, into which the Intellivision could be slotted to turn it in to a full home computer. This would enable the user to,

...learn languages, develop personal exercise programmes, plan your family budget... ... You'll even be able to talk to it!'

But the keyboard never materialised as planned. A rather late de-tuned version was issued to placate any potential legal action over the failure to deliver the promised feature.

RANDOM ACCESS MOMENT:
Working at ACE, a Dixons Group subsidiary, I helped to launch the unit into the UK to some success. One of its best games was American Football but in the UK the rules were not that well known. I recall having to learn about these to write the manual for a UK user. Later Channel Four in the UK started to carry games from the NFL and this helped disseminate the awareness of the rules.

Mattel eventually sold three million Intellivisions in the product's life.

He all, he all, he always told me that

Coleco launched its games console system, ColecoVision, in August 1982, based on the Zilog Z80 MPU. It came with arcade-standard graphics and eventually some 150 games cartridges were available for it.

There was also an 'Expansion Module' enabling the console to run all the existing Atari VCS titles as well. Atari tried to seek a judgement for infringement but failed.

There was little doubting that the licensing of Donkey Kong, included with the console sale, was the basis of its success. Coleco's Eric Bromley was head of design for games and struck a deal when he happened upon the Nintendo game in Japan. He reached an agreement to pay $2 per cart provided he wire-paid $200,000 there and then to secure the contract. Even then he had to mount a rearguard action when Atari sought to outbid him later.

The 'port' of the popular Donkey Kong was so good it drove sales of 500,000 units over the fourth-quarter of 1982, passing the million-unit sales mark in 1983 before the crash later that year. It went on to pass two million unit sales and ten million carts in total before finally exiting the home electronics business.

Spurred on by the failure of Atari's legal action regarding the expansion module, in 1982 Coleco also launched a direct Atari VCS clone called

Gemini. It had improved 8-way joystick controllers and it bundled Donkey Kong, versus Atari still offering the by then rather tired Combat. Sears offered a version and a video game club was formed by Columbia House, mirroring its vinyl record club.

The Coleco Adam home computer launched in October 1983 appeared to be a well-timed move to shift from games consoles. It could either be purchased as an add-on to the ColecoVision or as a stand-alone computer at $600. Adam came with a monitor, cassette reader/writer and a letter-quality printer together with all the ColecoVision carts which to be used via a cartridge slot.

This caused grief as Donkey Kong was being offered on what was a computer and Coleco had only acquired the rights from Nintendo for the games console market - Atari had the licence for computers.

However the console and its daisy-wheel printer had technical problems which meant the product was withdrawn for the important fourth-quarter 1983 season and it never really recovered from doubts about its reliability

In 1985 Coleco had launched the lucrative 'Cabbage Patch Kids' and withdrew from home electronics.

The video console crash of 1983 stopped or delayed a whole series of developments while manufacturers licked their wounds. But by the end of that decade video consoles were coming back with new technology, boasting PC-like speeds and capabilities.

For all the family – Nintendo NES
Nintendo charged Masayuki Uemura to develop a design of what it called the Famicom (Family Computer) and Atari was targeted to become the US OEM for it. But at each meeting between the companies, the console crisis was unfolding and the personnel at Atari kept changing as its problems ratcheted up. Nintendo's decision to license Donkey Kong to Coleco also did nothing to assuage the friction between the parties.

Instead Nintendo chose to sell the Famicom only in Asia, launching it in July 1983; it became the top selling console in Japan for 1984. Nervous of the USA market it applied its technology instead to a series of coin-op games that allowed it to build a range of software with credibility.

As the dust settled in the United States the Famicom was renamed the NES (Nintendo Entertainment System) and announced at the summer CES in 1985. It was launched in October 1985 supported by eighteen software titles. Nintendo was cautious and test-marketed it first in New York, offering sale or return terms, but soon it had sold over 100,000 systems in that trial alone.

By 1986 it was a big seller, featuring the coin-op mascot Mario the Plumber in the Super Mario Bros game. By 1990 it had outpaced all other console systems, achieving almost 62 million units sold in its lifetime. But its 8-bit MPU was beginning to look a little tired.

Megabucks – Sega Master System

Sega also launched several cartridge-based consoles in Japan, including the SG-1000, for Sega Game, which was designed by Hideki Sato and launched in July 1983. They also produced the SC-3000 as a computer for beginners which actually outsold the SG-1000.

To compete with the Famicom it launched the Mark III in October 1985; this was backwards-compatible with the SG-1000. But it was not introduced to the USA market in the aftermath of the console crash there.

By 1986 Sega could see the NES success and was ready to respond with a revised Mark III that it called the Sega Master System. But it had not watched Nintendo that well. The competitor had successfully espoused third party software developers through its NES and had signed agreements to keep these developers exclusive to themselves!

The Sega Master System was launched some seven months after the NES, albeit with superior graphics and sound. Sadly it could offer only a tiny catalogue of games, mostly ports from its coin-op software; these were 'tired' compared to NES. It had reached Europe by 1987 where it did achieve something close to parity with Nintendo.

Sega tried two early 'mascot' characters but neither really managed to rival Nintendo's Mario. The first was Opa-Opa, a little spaceship, but the one with a little more success was Alex Kidd.

The image of Alex Kidd was a sort of monkey-boy, usually described as being fourteen years old - though monkey-boy years were said to be different to those of humans. Alex Kidd was an orphan living on Mount Eternal on the planet of Aries or Miracle World. He featured in six games and later had cameo roles as a playable character in games like Sega's Superstars Tennis. This game achieved the second best sales performance for Sega achieving 13 million unit sales.

Nintendo still commanded some 90% of the USA market, so internally Sega's attention had already turned to the next generation, a 16-bit games console based on the Motorola 68000; the Sega Mega Drive was launched in 1988 in Japan.

In the United States they could not use that name so it was called the Genesis there and sold at just $189 in 1989. Elsewhere it was successfully launched as the Mega Drive during 1990. This was Sega's most successful console, in part because it had come up with a more striking mascot.

The USA launch of the Genesis had gone well given that it was now supported by a broad range of software from either coin-op ports or new material such as Arnold Palmer's Tournament Golf.

But Nintendo still dominated and worse it was soon to launch its own 16-bit Super NES. So Sega ran an internal competition and briefed its agency to come up with a strong mascot to be used to assist marketing.

Naoto Ōshima's Sonic the Hedgehog emerged the winner. Sonic was defined as a fifteen-year-old blue anthropomorphic hedgehog able to run faster than the speed of sound. Sonic was the star of a series of games from 1991 onwards, inspiring spin-off merchandising, comics and even a feature film. The Sonic series of games have sold over 150 million copies.

Help also came in the shape of Trip Hawkins at Electronic Arts. The organisation had always stayed clear of game consoles, preferring to produce PC software, but now it agreed to produce games for the Genesis. As a result Sega developed a caché in sports games.

Counter blow – Nintendo SNES

Nintendo realised they had to counter Sega. Masayuki Uemura, who had designed the original Famicom, came up with the Super Famicom which was released in Japan in November 1990; in August 1991 it was launched in the United States and in April 1992 across Europe.

The initial production run of 300k units sold out in less than a day. This was assisted in part because it had retained all its third party software developers for this new product.

The chaos the launch caused resulted in the Japanese government asking Nintendo to only release its new products at the weekend. That other great Japanese institution, the Yakuza organised crime syndicate, began showing so much interest in this commodity product that Nintendo scheduled its deliveries during the night too.

Launched as the SNES (Super Nintendo Entertainment System) in the United States and Europe it was bundled with a bundled Super Mario World. In South Korea it was launched as the Hyundai Super Comboy. Nintendo also sought further to control its software market by having regional lockouts, both physical and electronic.

New horse in the race – PC Engine and TurboGrafx

Two brothers, Yuji and Hiroshi Kudo, established Hudson Soft Ltd as an electronics and CB-radio business on the Japanese northern island of Hokkaidō. When Nintendo's Famicom was released their company produced and launched several profitable games for it.

Hudson Soft also created operating systems for other Japanese computers and a plug-in keyboard for the NES that was released only in Japan.

In 1985 it decided to create its own game console and came up with one of the smallest; it was a very elegant and the Guinness Book of Records listed the PC Engine as the world's smallest games console.

They presented this product to Nintendo but were rejected and then worked with NEC, renaming it the NEC PC Engine and releasing it in October 1987, successfully beating Sega's MegaDrive to market and taking a strong market share in Japan.

When they took it to the United States two years later, as the rather inelegantly named TurboGrafx-16, the video was boosted and the memory four times greater. Despite the use of that '16' in its name this was an 8-bit system; the reasoning was that it had 16-bit video. But they made the mistake of trying to use its successful Japanese software with no attempt to Americanise it.

In fact Hudson Soft negotiated only exclusive software supply deals and this severely limited the third party developer route, everything had to come via Hudson Soft; although they did manage to arrange some ports from Konami and Namco.

As a result they were trying to sell the console to the US market with unfamiliar software; Sega with its MegaDrive/Gemini system could issue games that had already earned a local reputation through coin-op use.

When Mortal Kombat was brought to the console, both Sega and Nintendo had versions; Sega went without any form of censorship, therefore creating lots of controversy – and PR! NEC missed out.

Hudson Soft had also developed a special memory card for the product called a HuCard, more the size of a playing card than a cartridge. The same approach had been developed for the MSX with a smaller version called a BeeCard. In its normal format HuCard was supplied in a jewel case and had an 8 MBit capacity.

In 1988 NEC released the first CD-ROM player as an add-on to the system; it was the first product to have one.

After some early promise in the United States the console bombed, and never really made it into Europe. For the USA market NEC had ordered 600,000 units from several Taiwanese sources but sold only 250,000 of them.

Nintendo and Sega battled for dominance through the early '90s, with Sega routinely using advertising to knock Nintendo. But Nintendo being the first to offer Capcom's Street Fighter II was a significant riposte. Street Fighter had been designed back in 1987 by Takashi Nishiyama and Hiroshi Matsumoto.

Nintendo tried to control its developers by having a strict policy of approving all releases, limiting each developer to just five releases each year and insisting they did not offer a title to another console for two years. Acclaim breached this policy first by deciding to launch for both consoles, and the others followed them.

Nintendo sold over 49 million units of the SNES, discontinuing it in the United States in 1999 and Japan in 2003. By comparison the NES sold almost

62 million units, the Sega Mega Drive/Genesis just under 30 million and the TurboGrafx-16 just 10 million units.

Serious new player – Sony comes to play

Back in 1986 Sony had applied its latest CDi technology in a liaison with Nintendo to create a CD-ROM version of the SNES. The company's earlier systems had a rewritable disc which made more it more prone to being erased and had little security against piratical copying.

Sony planned to deliver its own version of the SNES using its new CD-ROM, but behind the scenes Nintendo could not reach agreement on a split of revenues with Sony. It felt that the earlier contract had given too much power across to Sony. So when Sony announced the details of its console, the very next day it became clear that Nintendo had moved across to a Philips technology.

The Sony president was none-too-pleased about this and appointed Ken Kutaragi to use their experience to develop a Sony console. In an early manifestation some 200 Play Station units were created from this aborted Nintendo project, but Sony soon suspended this approach.

Kutaragi worked on to develop a new product, which they called PlayStation, contracting it to one word. The design was created by Teiyu Goto. However there was not a widespread belief in the project among senior Sony executives; in June 1992 it came to a showdown meeting.

The outcome was that Kutaragi was moved to Sony Music, an autonomous though Sony-owned operation, where he was permitted to continue his work. PlayStation was launched in December 1994. It was the first successful disk-based system and became the first console to sell over 100 million units, in under ten years from launch.

Phil Harrison, a Brit, was hired to work with developers and publishers. Harrison had previously been with Mindscape as a games designer. In 2005 he would become the president of Sony Computer Entertainment Worldwide Studios in charge of development at thirteen studios around the globe.

Armed with its 3D capabilities and easier CD-ROM production facility, Harrison soon signed up Electronic Arts and Namco to the PlayStation cause. A year before he left Sony there was a portfolio of just under 8,000 titles for the PlayStation and these had sold over 960 million units; he moved to Infogrames in 2008.

To assist its developers Sony produced a Net Yaroze version, costing considerably more than the consumer console but permitting the development of applications and games. It was less sophisticated than the full-blown development software.

Handing out more fun – handheld consoles

Along the way most of the consoles also launched handheld game versions.

The handheld market actually started way back in 1977 when Mattel launched Auto Race and followed it up with Mattel Football. Auto Race was pretty crude using very simple symbols on a basic LED screen, but it was the first electronic handheld game; it accumulated $400m in sales.

In November 1979 the first true handheld console was the Milton Bradley Microvision with a plug-in cartridge system. Its small screen and limited software catalogue gave it a short life; it was dead by 1981.

Subsequently Bandai, Coleco, Entex and Parker Bros all entered this market.

From 1980 Nintendo launched a series of Game & Watch units. The designer was Gunpei Yokoi who was inspired on watching a bored businessman playing with an LCD calculator on a bullet train. His notion was a unit that played a game but displayed a clock in the corner of the screen, with an alarm feature too. Each unit played just a single game. There were eventually 59 units released across eleven years and over 43 million of these extremely simple devices were sold.

Yokoi went on to design Nintendo's Game Boy, launched in April 1989 and reaching the USA by July, Europe by late September. It was launched at $89.99.

It had just four buttons (A, B, Select, Start) and a directional pad. There was a port that could link two Game Boys for head-to-head play initially with Pokémon and later as a networking port.

Part of Game Boy's success was based on bundling Tetris with the game, which proved so compulsive.

Game Boy Color followed in October 1998 as a response to the Atari Lynx. Game Boy and Game Boy Color sold a total of 119 million units.

Game Boy Advance was launched in March 2001 in Japan and by the next month into the USA and Europe. This sold more than 81 million units.

Atari seriously entered this market having had a number of earlier projects in this sector. Initially they looked to produce both a handheld Breakout and Space Invaders but these came to nothing.

A company called Epyx had developed the Handy Game and sought investment. Atari acquired it on the basis that it would do the manufacturing and Epyx would handle the software. The outcome was the Atari Lynx, launched in September 1989. It had a real edge, given its colour LCD screen.

But it needed six batteries to give just four to five hours of playing time; Game Boy gave 10-12 hours with four batteries. Its price at $189.95 and a short supply line for Christmas 1989 consigned it to achieving low sales figures.

Lynx II was a cosmetic facelift at a new price point of $99 but still it could not break the Game Boy grip on the sector. Lynx sold in total somewhere between 2 million and 5 million units depending on whom you believe.

In 1990 NEC issued a handheld that derived from the TurboGrafx-16, called the Turbo Express or PC Engine GT (Game Tank). At $249.99 it was far from inexpensive and it soon earned the name the 'Rolls-Royce of Handhelds'. A significant benefit was that it could play all the TurboGrafx-16 HuCard cartridges.

It had some capacitor problems that led to a loss of sound and some of the pixels in the display often failed. It had just a three hour battery life. It never really took off selling just 1.5 million units.

In October 1990 Sega released the Game Gear in Japan; it reached most of the rest of the world the following year. It was a portable version of the Sega Master System so it was easy to port games to the Game Gear cartridges.

It also had colour, but to counter it being more expensive than the Lynx and having a worse battery life, the Game Gear had a good software catalogue. Almost 400 titles were launched for it, but the perception was still that it was short on titles.

It did not really take off in Japan. Its price at $149.99 versus Game Boy at $89.99 also constrained sales elsewhere. It took second place in the sector but still made some impression, selling 11 million units.

In late 2003 Nintendo let it be known that it was working on a successor to the Game Boy. Its DS (Developer's System) was launched in November 2004 in the United States and Japan, reaching Europe the following March.

It was backward-compatible with the Game Boy Advance though playing this software it of course used only one of its two screens. Significantly there was no regional blocking - any DS would play any cart.

For DS software its lower screen was a touch screen operated with a finger or a stylus. It had stereo sound and its carts were slimline compared to earlier systems. Battery life was ten hours.

The Nintendo Wi-Fi Connection, launched in November 2005, offered online gaming to coincide with the launch of Mario Kart DS. The Download Play feature also enabled multi-player gaming with another DS user located within 60 feet (20m).

The Nintendogs cart was a real-time pet-care program. The user could pet the dog and groom it, throw balls and Frisbees, take the dog for a walk – all a lot more easily and less messily than in real life! That's perhaps why it sold over 23 million copies, only beaten to second place by the evergreen New Super Mario Bros.

By the end of 2010, Nintendo had sold over 144 million of its DS units. It was the best-selling handheld console of all time and second best selling video game console overall – behind the PlayStation.

Five-a-side – 5th generation consoles

Just when you might have thought that PCs would take over the games console business by exercising one of many software attributes, the console makers upped the ante with new products.

Atari reentered the console business when it launched Jaguar in November 1993. It aimed to surpass the Sega Mega Drive and the Nintendo SNES with more power; it was designed with a 64-bit processor and was a fifth generation console.

Designed to outshine the fourth-generation consoles, in reality it would be forced to compete with the fifth-generation consoles Sony PlayStation and Sega Saturn which came along all too soon.

The Jaguar had its roots in Flare Technology and its founders Martin Brennan and John Mathieson. They left Sinclair to form Flare where they worked on the development of a computer to be competitive with the Amiga and Atari ST.

Konix, a UK peripherals' maker, approached Flare and proposed that they work jointly to produce the Konix Multisystem. They developed this 16-bit console for release at the February 1989 International Toy Fair. However it ended up with a limited memory to keep its costs low, and the advanced chips it used required complicated programming to get the most from them.

Konix was in financial difficulty, the computer's launch was delayed and then terminated; Konix had run out of cash.

The technology developed by Flare was sold off to Bellfruit, and the Flare team started to look for the next project. Atari had watched with interest and proposed the closure of Flare and the founding of Flare II for which Atari would provide the funding.

Flare II started work on two consoles, 32-bit and 64-bit, but progress was quicker with the latter and the 32-bit console was shelved.

Atari Jaguar was launched at $249.99 but it suffered from a small software library. Even after reducing the price its sales proved slow; by the end of 1994 they had sold only 100,000 units. The next year saw the introduction of new Sega and Sony consoles which reduced the sales even further.

By the end of 2005 only 125,000 units had been purchased despite a great deal of promotion. When Hasbro acquired the Atari rights in the late 1990s it declared the Jaguar to be open source, encouraging homebrew development; some developers finished earlier work and a few produced new material for it in this format.

In 1991 Trip Hawkins, ex-Apple marketeer, created the notion of The 3DO Company, a joint venture between his Electronic Arts software operation and AT&T, LG, Matsushita, MCA and Time Warner. The goal was to develop an interactive multiplayer games console.

The 3DO console was designed by Dave Needle and RJ Mical of New Technology Group. Needle and Mical had been part of the design team for the Amiga Lorraine. Initially the 3DO company offered the design to Panasonic and later to Goldstar and Sanyo in return for a royalty on each console sold.

It also planned to take a royalty on each game sold. At just $3 per unit paid to 3DO this was a significantly better deal for games developers than the normal arrangement with Nintendo or Sega.

The Panasonic version was launched in the United States in October 1993 but its high price at $699 and severely limited third party software support meant this was a big ask in a crowded market. It was discontinued in 1996.

3DO was reconfigured to become a third party software developer.

Sega launched the Sega Saturn in Japan in November 1994. This was a 32-bit system, a fifth generation console, and it launched six weeks ahead of PlayStation. It sold 170k units on the first day.

The president of Sega USA proudly proposed that it would be launched in the US on Saturday 2 September 1995. But subsequently Sega learned that the PlayStation was coming just one week later. So the launch was rushed forward to May 1995 at the E3 show. It was released in Europe in July 1995.

The rush meant they held meagre stocks and the surprise was not well received by third party software developers who suddenly had to revise or rush their project planning. Sega also changed the fundamental primitive in its software from a triangle to a quadrilateral; this added a layer of problems as most industry development tools were based upon the triangle.

The Saturn had a complicated design employing two CPUs; rumours suggest the second was added as a riposte to upstage news of the PlayStation. However it came about, it made making the most of the hardware very tough for software developers.

Launched at $399 it appeared expensive, as Sony had let it be known that the PlayStation would be on sale at just $299.

It sold 9.5 million units in total but lasted only until 1998 in the United States and Europe, running through until 2000 in Japan.

Sony launched the PlayStation in a fit of pique when Nintendo switched horses on a joint development at the eleventh hour. In the United States the Saturn had sold 75,000 units by the time the PlayStation launched in December 1994, but the PlayStation sold 100,000 units directly upon its release.

Nintendo announced its 64-bit console, the Nintendo 64, in 1995; it was available in Japan and the United States in 1996 and Europe in 1997.

This console was quite late to market but had the benefit of using developments by SGI (Silicon Graphics) and MIPS Technologies to deliver

3D graphics. Jim Clark of SGI had first offered the notion to Sega, who had passed.

The Nintendo 64 was the first Nintendo console to officially support online gaming. In the United States 500k units were sold in four months and it would eventually sell almost 33 million units worldwide.

As Nintendo 64 joined the fray the Saturn slipped to a distant third place. The competition between the three led to Sony and Nintendo dropping their pricing but the complexity of the Saturn design meant very few savings could be made.

Coming later to the product, Europe made its decision based on the United States market's relative successes and the Saturn never really took off there.

Sega lost $268m with the failure of Saturn and had to lay off a third of its workforce. It needed to placate its third party developers and be better prepared for the next generation.

Sony's PS One was released on 7 Jul 2000 as a cosmetic reworking of the original PlayStation; initially it outsold all consoles including PlayStation 2, its replacement that experienced some early production difficulties.

Around this time Apple designed the Pipp!n, a Macintosh derivative product as a games console; named for a smaller relative of the McIntosh apple.

Apple worked with the Japanese toy maker Bandai to produce and launch it, during 1995 in Japan and 1996 in the USA. It was the Apple Bandai Pipp!n in the USA and the Pipp!n Atmark in Japan.

Priced in the US at $599, it was more a low-cost computer than a high-end console. It did poorly in the market as it received no third party software support. Less than twenty titles existed for the USA market and some eighty or so in Japan.

Bandai made fewer than 100,000 and sold just 42,000 of these before stopping production in 1997. Katz Media Productions also tried to launch a version in Europe called the KMP 2000, but made only 5,000 units.

Six of one - 6th generation consoles

Sega's sixth generation console, the Sega Dreamcast, was launched in November 1998 in Japan and reached the United States and Europe in 1999 - before PlayStation2, Xbox and the Nintendo GameCube.

Sega put two competing teams onto the task of developing this next console. Tatsuo Yamamoto's team went for the Hitachi SH4 MPU and 3Dfx graphics and was internally adjudged to have won the competition. The 3Dfx operation leaked the project to the market as it was shaping up for an initial public offering, so Sega went instead for the Hideki Sato design using a VideoLogic VR2 graphics chip.

Microsoft worked with Sega for two years to develop an OS for Dreamcast, a version of Windows CE, but it was only ever used on some software titles and was not adopted as the OS for Dreamcast.

In the USA it created a record by selling 225k units in the first 24 hours, and 500k in the first two weeks, but deliveries were protracted. It did however overhaul the Nintendo 64 sales.

Dreamcast lasted as a product until 2001 in the United States and 2002 in Europe. Hideki Sato in the meantime had risen to the role of president of Sega and it was he who withdrew the company from the console business, pledging it instead to concentrating on software for the future.

PlayStation 2 was released in March 2000 in Japan, reaching the United States and Europe later that year. It competed directly with Dreamcast, GameCube and Xbox.

The PlayStation system used full-size DVDs, which meant it could also be used to play back standard DVDs and audio CDs. The PlayStation 2 inspired the development of homebrew emulators to allow it to use past software developed for the Atari VCS, BBC Micro, CBM 64, GameBoy…

It sold 980,000 units on its day of launch in Japan. However early lack of availability saw PS2s being sold via eBay for $1,000.

It recovered from this and was the fastest console to reach 100 million unit sales - in under six years. It became the best-selling console of all time, achieving some 146 million sales by the end of 2010.

In 2010 the Sony BRAVIA KDL22PX300 television set was launched with a PlayStation 2 onboard.

Nintendo's sixth-generation console arrived in Japan in September 2001. This was the Nintendo GameCube (NGC). It was launched in November 2001 in the United States and May 2002 in Europe.

It used the NGC game disk, a mini DVD, for storage and games. The NGC also offered on-line gaming through use of its broadband adaptor and modem.

It failed to achieve the market leadership of earlier Nintendo consoles, not standing up against the PlayStation and Xbox, yet it still sold approaching 22 million units. It was discontinued by 2007.

In November 2001 Microsoft, having collaborated with Sega on the Dreamcast development, itself entered the console fray in the USA with the Xbox; it took until 2002 for it to be released in Japan and Europe.

Seamus Blackley, a game developer, was part of the team that developed Xbox. He joined Microsoft in 1999 from Dreamworks Interactive where he had produced a Jurassic Park game. Blackley was originally hired to work on Direct X, a collection of APIs to enable PC multimedia applications and most specifically games. He wrote the original Xbox proposal and helped assemble the team.

It is suggested that the product name was originally intended as the Direct X box, given much of the team had been engaged on that project, but it was later simplified following focus group research.

Based around an Intel Pentium III, the console had an on-board hard disk drive allowing users to rip audio CDs onto the hard drive. Its clunky controllers were widely criticised so a smaller, lighter versions were released.

Microsoft acquired Bungie and was able to use *Halo: Combat Evolved* as an early come-on and this proved to be a killer app. Having sold five million copies in five years it was natural that Microsoft launched it for Windows and MacOS too.

The Halo 2 sequel became the highest grossing release with sales worth $125m on its first day; it went on to become the worldwide biggest selling Xbox game.

By 2002 Microsoft had earned second place in the console market, displacing Nintendo. By 2006 it had sold 24 million Xbox units, two-thirds of these to the USA market.

Late in 2002 Microsoft added Xbox Live as an online gaming service. This attracted 250,000 sign-ups in its first eight weeks. By mid-2004 it had a million subscribers, growing by mid-2005 to two million, by mid-2007 this had grown to three million and by mid-2009 it had over 20 million subscribers.

Sony responded in late 2002 by releasing the PlayStation Network Adapter to promote its own version of online gaming.

In Japan in December 2003 Sony launched the PSX, essentially a PlayStation that also operated as a DVD burner and a digital video recorder. It received limited interest and was not released elsewhere.

In November 2006 the PlayStation Network (PSN) was launched as an online service that also enabled multiplayer gaming. In Japan it offered the opportunity to purchase electronic money in the form of PlayStation Network tickets to establish credit for buying items through the network. As this rolled out internationally it became a PlayStation Network Card system.

In April 2011 the PSN system was hacked and 77 million user profiles, purchases and passwords were put at risk. Sony advised US users to obtain credit reports and freeze their credit cards in case they were attacked. During May the company progressively restored their service.

Lucky seven - 7th generation consoles

Microsoft and Nvidia were in dispute on the pricing of the chipset used in the Xbox and this led to Nvidia in 2005 halting production of the processor; Microsoft rapidly changed horse to launch Xbox 360.

In February 2003 Microsoft had assembled four hundred developers seeking to get support for the next generation of Xbox. They also recruited Peter Moore, formerly president of Sega of America.

Given the research feedback, a Power PC processor was soon selected for the new product. As this was the same MPU as an Apple Power Mac G5 developers could emulate their software on the Mac.

The Xbox 360 was a seventh generation console launched on 22 November 2005 in the United States, reaching the rest of the world before year's end. In fact by launching in thirty-six countries in the first year it set a record for console launches.

The launch team members were each given special editions of the product with a unique faceplate stating 'I made this'. Chronic short supply led to some 40,000 Xbox 360s being promoted on eBay, amounting to some 10% of the total supplied at that stage.

To fully support online gaming Xbox Live was onboard and it offered Windows Media Center multimedia. Xbox Live itself was updated to create two tiers of service - Silver which was free to any Xbox 360 buyer, and 'Gold' which offered online gaming at $49.99 pa.

In 2006 the Xbox Video Marketplace service offered movies and TV shows for rental or download; it also provided streaming for various networks such as ESPN and for the UK's Sky Player.

The system had a number of technical problems, leading to Microsoft in 2007 having to take a charge of $1 billion against its June 2007 results for potential returns of the system. Microsoft extended the warranty on the Xbox 360 to three years to calm criticism.

Given its head-start on Sony and Nintendo, it was the market leader for the first half of 2007. In 2010 a slimmer version dubbed Xbox 360S was launched.

Some 50 million Xbox 360 units have been sold to date and, as mentioned earlier, they have some 30 million Xbox Live subscribers.

In November 2006 Nintendo launched its seventh-generation console, the Nintendo Wii designed by Ken'ichiro Ashida.

It was backward compatible with the GameCube software. The disc drive would accept the 8cm GameCube disks or the 12cm Wii discs which gave it plenty of software at launch.

The Wii name has been given a series of unconvincing explanations by Nintendo,

'Wii sounds like 'we', which emphasizes that the console is for everyone. Wii can easily be remembered by people around the world, no matter what language they speak. No confusion. No need to abbreviate. Just Wii.'

I cannot help wondering whether during development and before the wrist strap was introduced someone let the Wii remote fly, and said Wii?

The Wii remotes significantly offered a new dimension in play. It used an infrared detection system and an accelerometer to impart motions in three dimensions to the console and the software was therefore much more realistic in its response.

The Wii certainly took the market by storm with unit sales rising every quarter since launch. It considerably outsold its two prime competitors, the PlayStation 3 and Xbox 360.

While console makers usually expect to make a loss or perhaps to wash their faces on console sales then make this up on ensuing software sales, the Wii was actually sold with a net profit realised on the console itself.

In July 2007 the Wii Fit with the Wii Balance Board was launched; this finally offered a realistic and valid means of using a games console to keep fit. Its other games get the user away from a desk and require them to physical effort too.

By the end of 2010 almost 85m units were sold. There have been rumours of an HD Wii to follow soon.

Rather belatedly in November 2008, with the PlayStation 2 still going strongly, Sony arrived with its seventh-generation console, the PlayStation 3. In Japan over 80,000 units sold on the day of launch.

In the United States there were a number of problems experienced when it was first available. Some of those queuing to buy were robbed. Outside a Best Buy store queuers were shot at; four people were hit, including a reporter. The police used pepper balls to settle down another crowd waiting outside a Circuit City store. Sixty prospective purchasers who queued to find there were only twenty units available got into fights. It's only a game!

PlayStation 3 was offered with 20 MByte at $499 or 60 MByte hard drives at $599. Its Blu-Ray disc system meant it could be used for watching DVD films; though problems on supply of these this did delay the European launch.

The PlayStation Network service ensured that online gaming was better managed; the earlier approaches had left much of this task to the software developers.

From 1997 the Sony PlayStation's DualShock analog controller had two vibrators to give action feedback in games. Nintendo had a similar system but it used batteries; the Sony version took power down the cord avoiding the need for battery replacement.

In 2007 the DualShock 3 added wireless capability and a Sixaxis capability;

RANDOM ACCESS MOMENT:
Sixaxis is one of the few palindromic PC products!

As the name implies, it can detect three-directional and three-rotational movements. Initially the vibration was removed because of fears that this interfered with the movement sensors. Later it was re-instated.

In September 2010 Sony launched the PlayStation Move, a wireless movement-sensing wand controller. A camera in the PlayStation Eye monitors the wand's movements. The Sony campaign said 'This Changes Everything'.

The bright globe at its end can show any of a large number of colours; in fact it looks at the screen graphics and selects a colour not to clash with the action.

13 - The second wave – as PCs abound

'I've noticed lately that the paranoid fear of computers becoming intelligent and taking over the world has almost entirely disappeared from the common culture. Near as I can tell, this coincides with the release of MS-DOS.' Larry DeLuca

John Vincent Atanasoff was finally recognised by a court in 1973 as the 'creator' of the modern mainframe computer, overthrowing the Eckert and Mauchly patent for ENIAC. It is poignant that this was at the very time the personal computer first struggled out of its primeval slime.

It is difficult to trace the chronology of the early offerings because of course each contender likes to be considered the first and usually claims this to be the case.

Winston Churchill stated:
'History is written by the victors'
Many of the early participants were not to become the victors and so are now more curiosities than recognised players in the process but they did serve to create an environment in which the PC would emerge from wild ideas and take form.

During the early PC decades most of the issues for the new technology were not yet full-blown but certainly all the important matters were being discussed and developed. This was the vital insight phase when the various steps of innovation were being thrashed out in silicon, plastic and wood.

Candy and Colleen
We last looked at Atari as a games supplier, first with arcade coin-op systems and then with home consoles. But they entered the PC business too.

Cyan Engineering was co-founded by Atari and Steve Mayer. It was later renamed the Atari Grass Valley Research Center, and became a research consultancy focusing on the Atari VCS games console.

Atari had calculated that the VCS would have just a three-year life, though it actually lasted for four times as long. Cyan advised Atari that a replacement should be in design almost before the VCS was released. Mayer was later subsumed into Atari as VP of R & D working closely with its new CEO, Ray Kassar.

During the development programme of this new product the Apple II, PET and TRS-80 were released and so Kassar directed the team to shift objectives towards creating a home computer for Atari, not a console.

The VCS was designed only to display sprite graphics and so major changes to meet this goal were to add text capability, insert a BASIC software and include a whole raft of new connectors and peripherals.

Research identified two sectors that might be exploited. The low-end product was named 'Candy' and the high-end 'Colleen'; named for two secretaries on the team; perhaps best underlining that these were much simpler times! Announced late in 1978 these products were available from late 79. Joe Decuir had been a key developer of both the VCS and Colleen.

Candy was designed as a 'games-turbo' console and became the Atari 400, designated thus because it had 4K of RAM. It was based on the 6502 MPU and supplied with a low-cost membrane keyboard.

Colleen became the Atari 800 with 8K of RAM; it had slots to add further RAM, ROM carts and a full keyboard.

However as memory prices were descending, in accordance with Moore's Law, both in fact were supplied with 8K of RAM at launch. As capability increased and prices decreased, eventually the 800 sold as standard with 48K.

Both had only 8K of ROM and the Microsoft BASIC of the time needed 12K, so they tailored Atari BASIC to fit these units. The 400 outsold the 800 and was the more successful in achieving a broad software library.

One issue Atari encountered in trying to handle the computer business as it had the games console market, keeping much of its software proprietary. This merely served to exclude many independent software developers from getting behind the products.

Both units ran in to trouble with the FCC on signal leakage from their RF modulators and had to be modified with an aluminium frame to act as a shield. This approach in turn limited the capacity for adding expansion boards, and as a result any add-on memory had to be achieved via a cartridge.

A mellowing of the FCC rules later allowed home computers to use enough shielding to avoid interference with other devices rather than be built to stop every 'particle' of RF leakage.

The combined sales of the Atari 400 and 800 exceeded that of the Apple II each year from 1979 to 1983, but then sales dropped away for the next two years until they were both discontinued in 1985.

Atari moved forward with a plan to upgrade the 400 and 800 which it called Sweet 8 and Sweet 16 but in the event these were combined and released as the Atari 1200XL in early 1983. There was never a PAL version so it did not reach the UK. It offered no improvements over the 800 and was discontinued within a year.

Bullish approach – Hi-Toro to Amiga

Jay Miner developed the ICs for the Atari VCS display hardware, known as the television interface adapter. In 1982 like many other members of the team who were becoming frustrated at Atari, he left to set up a competitive operation.

He had been urging Atari to develop new chips but they were content to stick with what they had. With David Morse he formed Hi-Toro as a chip design operation. Three Florida-based dentists financed the project.

Initially Hi-Toro created games and joysticks for both the VCS and ColecoVision. To gain more publicity they came up with the Joyboard, a floor-located device that the player stood upon in order to control the game. Essentially the normal directional controls of a joystick were located beneath a board so the user leaned to direct the game. This was something Nintendo would upgrade for the Wii Balance Board launched in July 2007.

But Hi-Toro's real objective was to develop a console chipset around the 68000 MPU. When this was to hand it renamed the company Amiga and the product Lorraine.

Carl Sassenrath had joined Amiga from HP in 1983. He developed a multitasking operating system for the PC which was well ahead of the field.

Comings and goings – Atari v Commodore v Amiga

In the meantime Atari developed a whole new family of XLs – the 600XL, 800XL, 1400XL and 1450XLD – but it walked in to a double Commodore whammy.

First Jack Tramiel of Commodore went after Texas Instruments in a price war; he was probably still smarting from what they had done to his calculator business. Atari got caught up in the crossfire.

Then Commodore introduced the VIC20 and CBM 64 which upstaged the new Atari XL computers at the worst possible moment, just when Atari's video console market had also 'hit the wall'.

Atari was losing $1m each day!

In the meantime Jack Tramiel was pressing for the Commodore board to agree to produce a new 32-bit machine. He fell out with the main shareholder over this decision and was fired on Friday the 13th January 1984. On leaving he founded Tramiel Technology with his sons and started looking around for a product.

Tramiel met with Amiga as it had become general knowledge that its protracted development period had left it short of funds. Discussions fell through when he made clear that he only wanted the Amiga technology and not the team.

Amiga did however do an interim deal with Atari who gave it $500k in return for a one-year exclusive on its chip design.

It was ironic, on so many different levels, when it turned out to be Jack Tramiel who ended up buying the Atari console and home computer business from Warner in July 1984. By then it was only losing $10k per day.

Essentially Atari Inc was no longer an entity after Tramiel created a new vehicle called Atari Corporation. He went through the old Warner operation firing people and terminating projects as he sought a way forward.

He soon discovered the deal between Amiga and Atari and the clause that if Amiga did not deliver their chipset to Atari by 30th June 1984 it would forfeit both the company and the chipset to Atari Inc.

Atari had been planning for the chipset to form the basis for a product codenamed Mickey and designated internally as the Atari 1850 XLD.

The Amiga team heard that Tramiel was about to take over Atari and, knowing its deadline was not going to be achieved, approached Commodore. Commodore agreed to acquire Amiga in its entirety and judged that this would invalidate any outstanding contracts. Besides Atari Inc was no more!

Just to be sure Commodore supplied a cheque for $500,000 to repay the funding Amiga had received from the old Atari. This was made out to the new Atari Corporation in an attempt to bring an end to the matter.

In August 1984 Tramiel took legal action against both Amiga and Commodore to stop them using the technology he judged now to be his; he succeeded in delaying progress until late 1984. The legal action rumbled on until the spring of 1987 when a closed decision was reached out of court, but Amiga was by then securely part of Commodore.

The Commodore Amiga 1000 launched in July 1985 was based upon the Lorraine and upgraded by Jay Miner. It had an advanced approach to video, graphics and sound to make it one of the first truly multimedia computers.

RANDOM ACCESS MOMENT:
At its previews in January 1984 it notably adopted a regular theme for computing when it demonstrated on the screen a red-and-white chequered bouncing ball, known as the boing ball. It was first used by the Whirlwind computer team in the 1950s; Commodore itself used it in demonstrations at a 1978 CES event. But the smooth rendering of the Amiga highlighted its custom graphics.

In search of excellence – Atari XE and ST

Under Tramiel's stewardship Atari went on to launch the Atari 65XE and 130XE (for XL-Expanded) in 1985.

At the same time it launched the Atari ST (Sixteen Thirty-two) in reference to the 68000 MPU's 16-bit external bus and 32-bit internal bus. The ST was securely targeted to vie with the Apple Macintosh which was then only available in black & white, while the ST offered colour.

The ST had 512k of RAM with a double-sided double-density 3.5" floppy drive. It used the GEM GUI. It was also the first PC to offer MIDI (musical instrument digital interface) a system that enabled computers, synthesisers, sound cards, drum machines and other musical instruments to work with each other, controlling the volume, pitch and tempo of any music.

The Atari 520ST became widely known as the Jacintosh. Though the ST series never reached the sales levels of the Macintosh it did sell over 2 million units between 1985 and 1993.

Texas hold 'em - a case study of its time

I had been there at the early stages of this market and used an early Intellec MCS 80 microprocessor development system for a cash register development - I wanted to be part of it all. I rather presumptuously wrote to Robb Wilmott, then CEO at Texas Instruments UK, stating that I believed they would be doing something in the personal computer space and, if true, I wanted to be part of it.

Robb of course denied that there was any such plan but then asked me to travel down to Villeneuve-Loubet, near Nice in France, to meet with someone there.

As a result of that trip in 1978 I was appointed Personal Computer Manager in TI UK's Consumer Products operation. I was part of a pan-European team that was to finalise the research on a series of microcomputer products. There was to be a home computer, an executive computer and a business computer.

Early on I was sent to Lubbock Texas where the TI personal computer development was being managed. I also met my first working robot at Lubbock, a mail distribution device for its one-floor plant. It followed a UV spray on the carpet and would arrive at various assigned position where it would beep. Those at that 'mail stop' would take their mail and insert anything that needed forwarding.

The Consumer Division I joined soon launched a series of 'learning products'; these were the Little Professor, Spelling B and Speak 'n Spell, used to drill arithmetic and spelling with fun calculator-sized devices.

The team also launched the Starburst, the first analogue digital watch. This was developed when research showed that we do not look at a watch to establish the precise time; what we really want to know is whether we are late or how long we have before we need to be somewhere else. An analogue watch gives a picture of time; the fact that it is precisely 10:21 is of little interest.

One of our key roles was to research precisely what potential users of our home computer might find appealing in the way of software. Apple, Atari and Commodore had developed some serious software with CP/M. VisiCalc, WordStar and Dbase II, but most of these were small business applications. If the market was to be truly 'personal' then other applications were needed for these products.

The TI European team ran coordinated research which, among other things, recruited the general public straight off the street, showed them the potential for a home computer and asked what was of most interest from a list of proposed applications,.

Remember that the vast majority of the general public at that time had never encountered the notion of a home computer. We also tested them for sensitivity to various likely price points. They were asked to place a series of consumer products in order of 'desire-to-buy'. This was done firstly before they were told anything of the home computer and then again after they had received a brief introduction to the likely features.

We needed to understand which of the household adoption curves the home computer might follow? We hoped this would be similar to the colour television where a strong rental proposition ensured that the UK take-up was rapid, but it still took five years from the first colour broadcast to reach a penetration of 17% of households – a figure that would be perfectly acceptable for our goals. Or might it instead follow the dishwasher that had been around for over a decade before it reached a mere 2% penetration. We sincerely hoped that it would better this.

Following this exercise we recruited the top people in the hot subjects that research had identified as key.

For foreign language tuition software we worked closely with Linguaphone, the taped-language course providers, seeking new features for their established approach. But this is one of those classic research failings. Everyone says they would like to learn a new language to a researcher as it makes them sound serious and sensible. But when it comes down to it the British are extremely fortunate to be allowed to be lazy linguists.

The other laudable application was of course health and fitness. We worked with TV guru Dr Magnus Pyke, famous back then for waving his arms around as he explained things, and with a senior doctor from the British Heart Foundation to develop an approach for a health and nutrition package.

We considered linking this to an exercise routine. I recall we looked at the various calisthenics routines of the time, the Canadian Air Force version was the favourite. In retrospect it took right up until the noughties for WII Fit to realise anything useful in this application area.

We studied all sorts of other things that turned out to be non-starters too. For example a system similar to the Kitchen Computer sold by Nieman Marcus, storing recipes and calculating the required ingredients for a given number of diners. A logical application if you are academically looking for suitable uses for the PC, but I am unaware of anyone ever using it for this; perhaps the odd celebrity chef may have created a database of recipes somewhere for regurgitating in the next book, but I know of no sizeable market that exists for such a package.

Our attention kept coming back to games.

The home computer project later became known as the TI 99/4. TI had no problem defining its hardware approach as it was able to see the earlier contenders and learn from their relative successes and problems.

The home computer was based upon TI's own TMS 9900 microprocessor with its own TI BASIC supplied within a ROM. It had a colour video output delivering sixteen colours at a 192 x 256 resolution. There was an RS232 serial interface with optional joysticks, a cassette drive, a 5.25" floppy disk drive, a thermal printer and an expandable bus. But at an initial launch in June 1979 the price of $1,500 did not prove particularly competitive.

Yet a great deal was learned in this development phase. First off, the American-built units used a power supply based upon the US system of 120 volts running at 60 Hz, hertz, or cycles per second. The UK and Europe operate on 220-240 volts and at 50 Hz. Aeroplanes and ships use a system based upon 400 Hz as this higher frequency allows them to use less iron in the transformer thus reducing the weight of devices.

Though the difference between 60 and 50 Hz sounds insignificant, the reduced amount of iron of the 60Hz designed system meant the power supplies tended to overheat when used in Europe; often they became too hot to touch. In fact the power supplies generally proved a problem on the early products - overheating, failing and in some cases even 'minorly' exploding.

But it was evident from the outset that software was going to be the key issue; it would make or break the project.

One of the cornerstones of the TI home computer project was that the software would be based upon GROM (graphics read only memory) plug-in software that was a new concept then but today we would all recognize from games consoles.

But this was its Achilles heel. When Sinclair and others launched their products they used a low-cost audio cassette. Although there was no comparison in terms of speed, capability or software security, the price differential proved to be a significant barrier to home users and for educational users adopting GROMs.

In developing the software there was also a more subtle effect created by that 50-60 Hz frequency difference. For the programmer's convenience much of the early software was written using the power supply 'clock' to define screen motions. This meant a space game received from the USA was far too easy in the UK, the 50/60ths reduction in speed made it quite slow. Our 'personal bests' were impressive but head for the United States and they were mediocre.

We were possibly working on one of the first truly pan-European projects and we learned that we needed to advise the software teams that that they must maintain all of the text in one part of the software to facilitate the ease of translation. It was also established that there needed to be 25% more space in the part of the GROM for the almost ridiculously long (to an English eye) words required within the German versions.

TI's personal computer project rather fell apart when it first shelved the TI 99/7 executive computer and then the business computer. This left just the TI 99/4 home computer as its offering.

The software approach developed for it, the GROM memory, would some years later prove to have been a good approach but at the time of launch with memory sizes still very limited most users were content to work with the lower-cost cassette-loaded approach.

The corgi that roared – Mettoy Dragon

After Texas Instruments I became consultant sales & marketing director for a launch by Mettoy, a toy manufacturer wishing to enter the PC market. On the face of it, it too had all the credentials to succeed - established distribution with mass merchandiser and mail order operators, for its Corgi brand of replica cars.

In the early 1980s Mettoy's core toy business started to record heavy losses. Its sales director explained that because all cars were by then mostly wind tunnel designed, ie samey, there were no longer distinctive marques to become of interest as collectible Corgi models.

Peter Katz, the CEO, decided it was going to move in to computers and as its selected plant for this was in Swansea, Wales, the choice of name Dragon Data Ltd and the Dragon computer seemed obligatory, clearly hoping some of the magic of *Y Ddraig Goch*, the red dragon of Wales, might rub off on it.

Launched in August 1982, the Dragon 32 was often compared to the Apple II and the TRS-80 Color Computer in its appearance. It was full of the right features, supplied with a full 32K of RAM, sporting a full-size professional keyboard, with RF output to a domestic television in nine colours and with a five-octave range of sound suitable for music and speech synthesis. It had Extended Microsoft Color BASIC, supplied with a hefty 160-page free manual.

We announced it as using a 6809E processor pointedly saying,
'... *a great advance on the original 6502 – still used by PET, Apple, Atom, Atari 400, BBC Micro, VIC 20.*'

A sign of the era was that the keyboard was guaranteed for 20 million depressions as opposed to the slightly dodgy keyboards of other current systems. We also stressed it used both upper and lower case letters and that someone able to type would find it much more comfortable and easy to use.

Initial sales were good and a much-delayed Dragon 64 followed but by then I was moving off, now embroiled with Micronet 800, Prism and Sinclair.

Dragon was refinanced later in 1982 with Mettoy retaining only 15.5%, the rest being taken by venture capitalists such as Pru-Tech, an investment arm of Prudential Assurance, and the Welsh Development Agency. Some

40,000 Dragon 32s were sold but with its production capacity capable of 5,000 per week, growing eventually to 10,000, there was something of a mismatch!

A deal was later struck with the Tano Corporation in New Orleans to manufacture the Dragon for North America and the Caribbean. But Dragon Data did not last long. Its production line was purchased from the receivers by a Spanish company, Eurohard SA. I heard, though cannot confirm, that this company later sold on the production line to a Chinese company - they would certainly have appreciated the dragon motif!

Approaching the spectrum – Clive Sinclair

Clive Marles Sinclair was born in Richmond, Surrey in 1940. His grandfather was a naval architect working on mine sweeping technology. He played a role in the towed glider approach to clearing mines called a 'paravane'. Maybe this was the inspiration for Clive's first invention as a child; he designed a submarine.

But through school he often took jobs at electronics companies and was drawn progressively in that direction. Still at school he wrote his first paper for *Practical Wireless* magazine.

At eighteen years old he designed a small transistor radio kit he called Model Mark I. He planned to sell 1,000 a month of these kits to hobbyists through advertising in relevant magazines. At nineteen he published, *Practical Transistor Receivers, Book 1* and went on to produce a whole series of books at Bernard's Publishing and for Bernard Babani publishers.

He spent much of the 1960s working for United Trade Press on *Instrument Practice* magazine where, as technical editor and assistant editor, he wrote regularly on miniaturisation technologies; this clearly became his ambition – to produce small, mass-produced products.

In July 1961, aged twenty-one, he formed Sinclair Radionics Ltd and through the '60s developed a series of printed circuit boards and radio kits. In 1963 the Sinclair Slimline kit was being sold at 49s 6d (£2.47) and he followed this up in 1964 with the Micro-6, advertised as the world's smallest radio. About the size of a matchbox, it had an adaptor to allow it to be worn on the wrist. By 1967 his Micromatic took over the 'world's smallest radio' mantle.

While working as a journalist he had access to products submitted for review and developed his knowledge of the main suppliers and components. He acquired reject components and repaired these to use in his own products. For example in 1965 he released the Stereo 25, a hi-fi pre-amp product, but when his supply of reject components dried up he had to halt production.

In 1966 he first took a look at television and developed plans for what was claimed to be the 'world's first portable television', but the costs would have been prohibitive so the Microvision was not produced or released.

Stereo Sixty followed in 1969 and was the most successful audio product for the company. Also that year his radio kits MAT 100, at 7s 9d (37.5p), and MAT 200, at 8s 6d (42.5p), were designed to work with small deaf-aid batteries and these also achieved some success. He undertook his own quality assurance of these products. By the 1970s they were making a profit, £85k from £563k turnover in 1971 and £97k from £761k in 1972.

During the 1970s his attention moved to calculator design and the 'world's first slimline pocket calculator', the Sinclair Executive was released in 1972 at £79.95 (the UK had decimalised by then!). It was a four-function calculator with LED display and was much admired for its style. It was one of the first to be battery-powered rather than requiring mains supply. In 1973 he launched the Executive Memory at £24.95 and this drove turnover that year to more than £1.8m.

In 1975 he followed up with the Sinclair Scientific at £99.95; the HP equivalent was closer to £400. In 1977 came the Scientific Programmable at £29.95 and the Sinclair Sovereign, a small-run niche product supplied with gold or silver plating.

In 1975 Sinclair moved into electronic watches with the launch of the Black Watch with an LED display. It was available as a kit at £17.95 or fully built at £24.95. The LED display had to be pressed to display the time; it was heralded for its design but there were both battery and accuracy problems.

Chris Curry, later to found Acorn, joined Radionics in 1966 and remained there until Clive invited him to move across to a new company, a renaming of an off-the-shelf company Sinclair had acquired much earlier. This was Sinclair Instrument Ltd formed in 1975.

In 1976 the Microvision television design was dusted off and revised and the Microvision TV1A/MON1A was released for sale at £99.95. Supply exceeded demand and 12,000 surplus units were sold off cheaply, largely responsible for a £480k loss on the year. The second model Microvision TV1B fared no better and the technology was sold on to Binatone, a UK-based importer/distributor.

Meanwhile Sinclair Instrument Ltd launched the Wrist Calculator. In 1977 the company was renamed Science of Cambridge Ltd, the only time Sinclair's name was not used in the company title.

British apple? – NEB funding for a UK PC

The UK's National Enterprise Board (NEB) acquired 43% of Sinclair Radionics for an injection of £650,000. The NEB was one of Harold Wilson's government thrusts to get more public ownership of British industry.

The NEB sought to support the creation of a British competitor for the Apple and it provided funding to investigate an approach in 1978. At the time it had ownership in both Sinclair Radionics and Newbury Laboratories.

The proposed product appears to have started as a Sinclair Radionics project, though it had a joint-venture feel to it with Clive Sinclair directing, and the hardware designer, Mike Wakefield, and the software designer, Basil Smith, both working from Newbury Laboratories.

However Radionics was damaged by the television project and Sinclair his attention more to Sinclair Instrument Ltd with plans for his own computer.

The NEB project was moved across to Newbury Laboratories, a maker of VDUs and printers; the idea was developed into a series of computers including a portable. In 1980 two main models of the NewBrain computer were announced – the Model A which used a monitor or TV set for display and the Model AD which had a small one-line 16-character vacuum fluorescent display. There was also a customised version called the Model M, specified by a pharmaceutical client.

The Newbury team and the project was soon sidelined when the UK government shifted attention to the BBC that planned to launch its own computer in association with a proposed new TV show, The Computer Programme.

Quite separately Ian Williamson approached the Sinclair operation with a computer product he had developed. Its design was based upon the National Semiconductor SC/MP (simple cost-effective micro processor) and used parts salvaged from another Sinclair product. This would form the basis for the Sinclair MK14 microcomputer kit.

Chris Curry tried to convince Clive Sinclair to progress it as a product but they took up the offer from National Semiconductor to design it for them. Of course as a result it used all National Semiconductor components; National had offered to produce the PCB too. Williamson, who had prompted the approach, was edged out, receiving no contract or involvement in the ongoing project.

The MK14 was launched in 1978 at £39.95 plus VAT; other kits at the time were priced much nearer to £200. Around 50,000 units were sold.

Yet, like most kits of the time, it offered little utility. It had small memory and an 8 or 9 character seven-segment red LED display output. Its appeal was more about building the computer to learn about microprocessors than any subsequent application, though others did develop software for it. This lack of utility inspired articles by *'Personal Computer World'* and *'Practical Electronics'* advising users how to expand and use it.

Jim Westwood worked at an electronics store owned by Bernard Babani, Sinclair's publisher, and he joined Clive as an engineer. From 1979 Westwood was charged with design work on the ZX80 and he later became Sinclair's chief engineer working on most of the subsequent Sinclair products.

The UK's *Financial Times* in May 1979 predicted that personal computers would fall in price to less than £100 in the next five years. In under a year, in February 1980, by opting to use a home television as the screen and a cassette tape recorder for loading and storage of data the Sinclair beat that price barrier.

The ZX80 was launched as 'world's smallest and cheapest computer' at £79.95 as a kit or at £99.95 fully assembled. It was based on the Zilog Z-80 microprocessor with on-board Sinclair BASIC. Significantly, at a time when most were looking to the Far East for production, this was built by Timex at its Dundee, Scotland plant, forming part of what became known as the Silicon Glen.

Software was loaded from a cassette player. Now, it is time to 'fess up. Come on, did you paint the volume position on your cassette recorder with Snopaque (promoted as liquid paper)? I certainly did. Once you found the 'sweet spot' to load and save, you did not want to lose it.

The company changed its name in November 1980 to Sinclair Computers Ltd and in March 1981 to Sinclair Research Ltd when it launched the ZX81 with a stronger design approach as a £49.95 kit and £69.95 finished product. It was sold not just as a mail order product but it was offered through a few major multiple retailers.

By March 1982 the company had turned over £27m with profits in excess of £8.5m. The next month it launched the ZX Spectrum at £125 for 16K of RAM and £175 for the 48K version.

Through a Prism – Sinclair distribution

It was my turn to have the de rigueur 'PC garage' moment - well two of them in fact.

I had met and founded a business with Richard Hease the publisher of *Sinclair User* magazine who effected a meeting with the man himself. It was organised to discuss Micronet 800 but unbeknownst to us he had just had a shipment of ZX81s turned away by one of his retail clients and was feeling vulnerable; this had happened to him with his calculators too.

The outcome was that with a 'back of the envelope' agreement I agreed we would become his exclusive UK distributor outside his direct mail operation and five named multiple retailers.

We knew the new ZX Spectrum was imminent and, although we had no arrangement regarding the new product, we judged that if we called ourselves Prism, Prism Microproducts Ltd in full, then we could 'suggest' that the best place for someone to get a Spectrum was obviously through a Prism.

I had agreed to take a thousand ZX81s a week plus a proportionate number of the associated accessories and software. When Clive called me to say that the first week's delivery was ready, I made a quick decision.

I was working in London and living 60 miles (100km) away in rural Bedfordshire, in fact not that far from Cambridge which was Sinclair's base of operations. I said they could be delivered to my home and I called my wife telling her to expect a panel van to arrive with delivery guys and asking her to get them to put the boxes into our garage.

I got home late to find my wife, daughter and son were quite cross with me. First there was only one driver who came with the stock and he proved to be none too helpful offloading it. Secondly I had completely misjudged what 1,000 x ZX81 boxes and their related material might look like. They had filled our quite generous double-length garage, a bedroom, the hall and various other parts of the house and the family had operated as unpaid warehouse staff!

The first week was like something from the Minder television series with me cast as Arthur Daley (for non-British he was a rather dubious south London market-trader dealing in grey goods). People were arriving at our home at all hours of the day and night and taking away stock in a variety of vehicles, mostly private cars.

We decided we needed a more professional approach. Our offices were established in Islington, North London, and we were renting car parking space in a nearby large building that had been converted to parking from being a warehouse. It had an inner section that could be locked off so we rented this for the second week's shipment. However no insurance company would give us cover on what they judged as a pretty insecure building in what was then a slightly dubious area.

I had to sleep in my car inside the car parking area, not so much sleep of course as I jumped at every noise from that creaky old building.

After some weeks of paying our 'PC garage dues' we could finally afford a proper warehousing service.

We signed up large numbers of retailers and turned over £1m in a matter of a few weeks, and sold over £10m in Sinclair product in our first year.

One and a half million ZX81s were sold in total, many of these through Prism. They were offered with 16K RAM expansion packs and a thermal printer using an aluminium-coated paper. It was the software range and these additional packages that were the reason I misjudged my original garage requirements.

We upgraded our contract to include further products. So that in April 1982 we also distributed the ZX Spectrum, a colour 8-bit Z-80 computer at £125 for the 16K and £175 for the 48k version. It came supported by a huge range of cassette-based software and this established it as a great success.

Despite early delays in sending out orders, between 12,000 and 15,000 Spectrums were sold every week. This soon added up to millions in sales as the computer was rolled out in over thirty countries. Prism hit £30m turnover in year two and £50m in year three.

Going global

Sinclair signed a deal with Timex to form Timex Sinclair and to break into the huge US market. Timex was already its main manufacturing source at its plant in Dundee. This new operation was based around a Timex plant in Portugal, taking advantage of some of the lowest labour rates in Europe.

It launched the TS1000 based on the ZX81, the TS1500 based on the ZX Spectrum and a TS2068, a ZX Spectrum with a cartridge port to seek to take on games consoles. Initially it went well with sales of 600,000 units in 1982, but sales slowed and it was all but over within three years.

We formally applied for and received the distribution rights for Sinclair in France. We did this with one of the co-founders of Videomaster, Cameron MacSween, one of the early home Pong and video game console makers. Cameron, a Scot, had met and married a French woman and taken dual nationality. This meant he could operate as our *president directeur générale* using his French nationality, with us content that we were dealing with a Scot.

In May 1981 Sinclair signed an exclusive distribution deal in Japan with Mitsui for the ZX81. Mitsui was a major importer of British goods including Jaguar Cars and Burberry products

Prism the distribution operation had merged with Hease's publishing interests. Two of Prism's magazines were joint ventures with Pat McGovern's CWCI operation, already by then one of the world's largest publishers in electronics and computing, today known as IDG (International Data Group).

IDG declares itself now as the world's largest technology media company reaching 200 million technology buyers in ninety-two countries. Its founder, McGovern, is listed in the Forbes 400.

McGovern worked at the *MIT Tech* newspaper while at college and after graduation was editor of *Computers & Automation*, one of the first computer magazines. With a friend he then formed IDC (International Data Corporation) in 1964 and launched the *Computerworld* newspaper in 1967.

In 1971 the US Table Tennis team was competing in Japan when they were unexpectedly invited to go to China. The Chinese often used sport as a diplomatic mechanism – they have the slogan, 'Friendship First, Competition Second.' This was the first time an American sports delegation had entered China for twenty-two years.

As a result of this first 'ping-pong initiative' President Richard Nixon visited China in February 1972. Pat McGovern went along and met with the Beijing Science and Research Institute. Supported by China's Ministry of Trade and Industry, they jointly launched *China Computerworld* newspaper in Mandarin Chinese.

In the early '80s McGovern advised us that this magazine had a 100,000 print-run and it was estimated that each copy was read by some 1,000 readers until the ink literally came off the page; such was the interest in computers behind the lifting bamboo curtain. He asked what Sinclair was doing about China?

In turn I asked Clive and the upshot was that we were granted distribution rights for China. Another back of an envelope deal that had awarded us a third of the world's population!

McGovern's arranged for Hease and myself to visit China in 1982. We walked through the Hong Kong border and had to list every item of equipment, jewellery and cash we had on us; then we were driven on the back of a pick-up truck to Shenzhen. Shenzhen had already been designated a special enterprise zone but it was closer to its origins as a fishing village than today's status of some 9 million population with a Hong Kong-like skyline.

We travelled on to Shanghai and Beijing with a guide and translator supplied by McGovern, Sai Man Hui. Simon, by now we had anglicised Sai Man, eventually got cross with our hosts' constant delays and told them to put up or shut up. They came back a little later with a contract neatly typed out in Mandarin Chinese.

The contract had to be translated onto audio cassette for us by two interpreters so we could have some confidence as to what it actually said. It called for us to send 500,000 semi-knock-down Sinclair ZX81 kits which they would assemble and, most significantly, they would keep them all for internal use.

Imitation is said to be the sincerest form of flattery, though I'm not sure that Clive saw it that way when the ZX81 was cloned in South America, in both Brazil and Argentina.

Silicon Fen

Cambridge and the fenlands just north of the city soon became superheated with Sinclair, Acorn, Tangerine, Oric, Camputers, Enterprise and Jupiter Ace hailing from there.

Journalists, having seen the Scottish electronics' production phenomenon become tagged Silicon Glen, soon adopted the term Silicon Fen for this area.

Chris Curry had moved across to Science of Cambridge for Clive Sinclair and was the one to propose the MK14 computer kit product. Curry had drawn on a friend, Hermann Hauser at Cambridge University, for assistance through the project.

Perhaps hedging his bets as he saw Sinclair's mounting problems with the National Enterprise Board, the dire state of the calculator market and the failure of the Black Watch, Curry moved to set up his own operation in 1978.

The company was called CPU Ltd (Cambridge Processor Unit) and his partner was Hauser. Hauser was born in Vienna but came to the UK at the age of fifteen to study at an English language school. He returned to graduate in Physics at Vienna University, and then arrived back in Cambridge for his PhD.

CPU initially took on a consultancy project with Ace Coin Equipment to develop a microprocessor-based fruit machine, or one-armed-bandit. It was based on the SC/MP at first, but then it was switched over to the MOS Technology 6502.

CPU later formed a subsidiary called Acorn Computers Ltd. Apparently the reason given for the name was in part that it would appear before Apple in any alphabetical listings. Acorn initially produced a series of microprocessor products.

Acorn System 1 was designed for engineering and laboratory use. It was based on two cards with a keypad, a cassette interface and an LED display for output. At just £80 it did attract some hobbyist interest too. Acorn System 2 rejigged it into a 19" (480mm) rack-mountable format and included BASIC. System 3 added a floppy disk controller, System 4 a second drive and System 5 had a faster MPU.

Curry completely severed his role at Sinclair when it became clear that Clive Sinclair would not take the MK14 project any further. Once Curry was full-time at Acorn in 1979 it launched the Acorn System 75 based upon the SC/MP processor and designed specifically to be an improvement upon the Sinclair MK 14.

Another Cambridge University PhD, Andy Hopper, formed Orbis Ltd as a joint venture with CPU. They had plans to take the Cambridge Ring networking system to the general market.

Andy Hopper, born in Warsaw Poland, took British citizenship in 1964. He worked with Maurice Wilkes at Cambridge University Computer Laboratory to design this local area networking system that could theoretically connect up to 255 nodes, computers and peripherals. Based on DEC VAX minicomputers it could transfer packets of information at 10 megabits per second. By 1980 Hopper helped increase this speed with the 'Cambridge Fast Ring' to 100 megabits per second.

Orbis was acquired by Acorn in 1979 and Hopper went on to help with a number of Acorn projects.

The Acorn Atom was launched in March 1980 to go head-to-head with the Sinclair ZX80. It was a version of the earlier Acorn System 3, a 6502-based product with the disc drive replaced by a cassette interface; it had a keyboard and Atom BASIC.

Atom sold in kit form at £120 with 2K of RAM and 8K of ROM, or fully assembled at £170; with the maximum RAM and the floating point ROM it was over £200.

Splitting the proton – the BBC Micro

Acorn was developing the Proton as its next generation computer when a TV ratings battle broke out which helped give Acorn a huge uplift in sales and profile.

The ATV channel, the UK Midlands independent commercial station, ran a documentary series around a book produced by Dr Christopher Evans of the National Physical Laboratory. The show was called *The Mighty Micro: The Impact of the Computer Revolution* and it set out to provide a forecast of the future. The six-part series was aired posthumously as Dr Evans died from cancer at forty-eight years old in 1979.

These programmes had a major impact and generated questions in the House of Commons. The British Government announced its MEP (microelectronics education programme) project that would run from 1980 to 1986 exploring how computers might be used in schools to give the UK a head-start in computing.

The organisation was run by the Council for Educational Technology, who utilised Prestel to communicate its objectives. The MEP team also used Telecom Gold as an email service, a service that would also be superseded by the Internet.

The UK Government also developed a *Computers in Schools* project setting out to install one computer for every thirty schoolchildren, but parent teacher associations and home purchases soon exceeded this conservative goal.

As part of the reaction to *The Mighty Micro* the BBC planned to air its own show *The Computer Programme* which would review all aspects of hardware and software as the basis of a computer literacy project. BBC Enterprises saw a revenue opportunity and decided to badge a personal computer which could then be featured in the series. The BBC Engineering department was charged with the design of the computer.

As the BBC is government-owned, the UK's Department of Industry insisted the selection should be British and pushed for it to be supplied by the Newbury Laboratories. The DOI set the specification virtually to that of the Newbury product. But Newbury declined the opportunity and the TV shows were delayed by six months as the BBC met and spoke with Sinclair, Acorn and others.

Acorn already had its project to develop the Acorn Proton underway and Curry negotiated for the BBC to change its specification a tad so it could fit his product.

It was launched as the BBC Microcomputer towards the end of 1981 and was promoted by the TV series from 1982 onwards. Demand far exceeded supply, leading to delivery delays and much friction.

Its BBC BASIC had an education bias and was a powerful interpreter for its time. It had a number of advantages over the Microsoft BASIC being used by most other PCs at the time. It offered hi-res graphics, four-channel sound and an extensive series of input/output possibilities.

There were two BBC Microcomputers, both 6502A-based - the Model A with 16K of RAM at £299 in late 1981 and Model B with 32K at £399 released in 1982. The product was built robustly and rapidly gained acceptance as an educational computer adopted by a large number of UK schools.

Parents who sincerely wanted their children to get ahead and who knew little or nothing of computing (ie most of them back then!) saw the BBC Microcomputer as an investment they just had to make.

A broad range of software was generated and 1.5 million units were sold.

Acorn did not achieve a monopoly in education as the Research Machines 380Z was also well thought of and achieved a significant share.

Sinclair responded by offering a half-price deal, just £60 for a ZX81 and 16K RAM; over 2,000 schools took up this low-price offer.

RANDOM ACCESS MOMENT:
At Prism we caught the bug of linking a computer to a television programme when we met with the ITCA (The Independent Television Companies Association), the body that brought together all the independent television franchise holders in the UK; it is now called the ITV Network Ltd.

They were keen to top the BBC with something better than the BBC Microcomputer and 'The Computer Programme'. We had early success in suggesting the way to do that was to create an 'executive computer' that would be portable and offer personal productivity in your work for a large organisation or your own small business. We proposed a system with all the BBC benefits that could also be used at home.

There was an immediate acceptance of the name chosen for this product. The 'Wren' has a strong British significance, both the architect and the bird, and the latter carried with it a sense of compactness too.

We were familiar with a design team at Transam Microsystems and they had already developed some ideas when we took the ITCA deal to the table. They completed the design and we launched a 25:75 Transam/Prism enterprise choosing Thorn EMI Datatech as our manufacturer. We had worked with them on our modems and by now Sinclair was double-sourcing with them too.

At launch in 1984 the Wren was really a luggable rather than a portable, weighing 26 lbs (12kg). It had an elegant 7" amber screen and a neat way of sliding forward over its keyboard for security during transportation. It came with CP/M and 2 x 5.25" floppy drives.

Being Micronet 800 savvy it was fully Prestel compatible with a 9600 baud modem on-board and a whole raft of connectors. It was sold with subscriptions to Micronet 800 and Telecom Gold.

We included the Perfect series of applications - PerfectWriter, PerfectCalc, PerfectFiler and a neat graphics user interface we developed ourselves called Executive Desktop that booted at start-up showing a series of paper-shaped icons for fast access to launch each application. We also added a diary system, phone book, notebook and a card index system linked to an auto-dialler.

We offered a 16-bit upgrade card to counter suggestions that Lotus and 16-bit software might overtake us. We had a colour output and a Winchester drive.

We priced it at £1,000, about the same price as Osborne 1, with our CP/M Plus version being rather better than theirs at the time. We also developed a stock-financing and rental basis for our dealerships. We forecast 2,000 sales per month.

We had many meetings defining the TV shows that might show all of this to advantage but the ITCA failed to come through to anoint the Wren as the ITV Executive Computer and without that endorsement the Wren failed to fly.

Electron storm – Acorn Electron

About the only problem the BBC Microcomputer had was its price; it was quite expensive if you stopped to make comparisons. The Acorn Electron was introduced as a lower-cost though slightly detuned version of the BBC Micro.

Launched in July 1983 the Acorn Electron was aimed at those who could not afford the BBC Micro for Christmas that year.

RANDOM ACCESS MOMENT:
I still have a framed copy of an original Jak cartoon that appeared in the Daily Express on December 24th 1983. It has a child being shaken by a department store Santa Claus in his grotto saying, 'A train set! A train set! You'll have a ****** computer like everyone else!'

Unfortunately the Xmas deadline was largely missed by Acorn and it was a little too detuned to stand up against the Sinclair Spectrum and Commodore 64.

This effectively weakened Acorn so Olivetti was able to acquire it in 1985. Curry left to form General Information Systems, an organisation focusing on networks.

Hauser became Vice President for Research with Olivetti to manage their laboratories in the USA and Europe. Hopper too became a vice president for research with the Italian company. The two obtained funding and co-founded the Olivetti Research Laboratory' at Cambridge with Professor Hopper as its director, researching computing and telecommunications.

In 1988 Hauser invested £1m of his own cash in to the Active Book Company and later sold this on to AT&T in 1991. It was renamed EO, derived from the Latin word for 'Go'; Hauser became chairman of EO Europe and its chief technical officer.

In April 1993 the company launched the AT&T EO Personal Communicator, a PDA with wireless communications rather similar in approach to Apple Newton. It achieved some major corporate clients yet still failed to attain its targets and ceased operations in 1994.

During 1990 Hauser presided over ARM (Advanced RISC Machines) being hived off from Acorn. Acorn went on to launch the Archimedes based upon the ARM RISC MPU. Later it launched a laptop too but it never recaptured the heady days of the BBC Microcomputer.

Urbane spread

The Fens delivered a number of other products. Tangerine Computer Systems formed in 1979 by Dr Paul Johnson and others; he was joined later by Barry Muncaster. The operation initially created a VDU kit that achieved much acclaim, then launched the Microtan 65 a 6502-based kit computer selling for under £80 as a kit. They designed a follow-up, the Tangerine Tiger, but this failed to materialise.

Tangerine had some success producing Tandata Prestel terminals, which we sold with both Electronic Insight and later with Micronet 800.

Tangerine then spun off a new operation called Oric Products International Ltd. The Oric-1 was launched in 1983. It looked a lot like the Sinclair Spectrum, though 6502A based, with 16k at £129 or 48K of memory at £169. That year it sold over 200,000 units, with a quarter of these going to France where it became the country's top selling PC.

The Oric Atmos followed it in 1984 with a 'proper' keyboard and upgraded software but this failed to catch the imagination. Planning to produce an IBM PC-alike and an MSX computer the company ran out of time and went in to receivership in February 1985. The receivers did do deals with a Yugoslavian and a Bulgarian company to manufacture Atmos-alikes but this was effectively the end of Oric.

In 1982 yet another Cambridge-based company called Jupiter Cantab Ltd launched the Jupiter Ace. This was a Forth programming language computer. The founders were both émigrés from Sinclair, Richard Altwasser and Steven Vickers. The Jupiter Ace, called the Ace 4000 in the United States, was very like the ZX Spectrum with a Z80 processor and similar appearance, rubber keypad... It was competitive at £90 but there was only a mono video output and Forth proved not to be of particular interest; the company went in to receivership late in 1983.

The Fens were not finished. Camputers produced the Hohn Shireff designed Lynx computer, a Z80A-based computer launched in 1983. Coming late to the market the Lynx did have a number of improvements over its competitors but its pricing was high at £225 for a 48K version, £299 at 96K and £345 at 128K. It still managed to sell around 30,000 units before ceasing trading in June 1984.

In 1984 Nick Toop, who had worked previously on the Acorn Atom design, and Dave Woodfield got together to design a games-centric computer called the Enterprise. The Z80A-based computer had a joystick on its full-sized keyboard and came as a 64K or 128K version. It had a 256-colour 672×512 pixel video output and a plethora of connectors. Its BASIC ROM could emulate the Spectrum and thus they claimed all the Spectrum software as compatible; briefly we offered it for sale at Prism. In total they sold around 80,000 units, with apparently some 20,000 finding their way to Hungary where it developed a cult following.

But what of Oxford, Cambridge's arch rival university-city?

Founded by Mike Fischer and Mike O'Regan, Research Machines focused on the educational market. It launched its first computer in 1977. There was originally intended to be an RM 280Z kit version but this was never shipped. The 380Z assembled version was Z80A-based. The series ranged from a unit with 16K memory and a cassette-based system selling for £965, to a dual 8" floppy disk version with 56K of memory and CP/M for £3,266. This was followed by the Link 480Z in 1982.

Research Machines was perfectly placed and at one point was virtually offered the BBC Microcomputer contract on a plate but they chose not to take it on as they feared it was too big a project for them.

However this slightly cautious approach paid off in the sense that the company is still operating as a profitable venture today. It grew itself carefully into an international operation in learning technologies and educational resources, offering services to examination boards, professional awarding organisations and government agencies.

There were also several notable UK Midlands' players. Applied Computer Techniques (ACT) formed in 1965 to manufacture computer hardware. Based in Birmingham it suggested that it built every component of a PC other than the silicon.

Its first foray into supplying finished product was not met with much success but in 1982 it released the US-designed Victor 9000 computer in the UK and named it the ACT Sirius 1. It was not IBM PC compatible and quite expensive at £2,754, yet it still managed a good degree of success in the UK and Europe.

The Victor 9000 was designed by Chuck Peddle who together with Chris Fish founded Sirius Systems Technology in 1980; they were funded by Walter Kidde Inc. In 1982 Sirius acquired the calculator and cash register operation from Kidde and was renamed Victor Technologies.

ACT was not alone in importing the Victor 9000. An operation called DRG Business Machines in Weston-Super-Mare also imported it directly and sold it as the Victor 9000.

In September 1983 ACT launched the Apricot PC, aka the ACT Apricot. It was an 8086-based computer, still not fully hardware-compatible with the

IBM PC but it could run MS-DOS and CP/M. It had Word and Multiplan onboard, Lotus 1-2-3 was available too.

By 1984 ACT launched the Apricot PC Xi with a 10 MByte hard drive. That same year they added the Apricot Portable. There was also a shot at the home market with the Apricot F1 but this was not successful.

In 1985 ACT changed its name to Apricot Computers and launched further products in its F series together with the XEN aimed to compete directly with the IBM PC AT.

Mitsubishi acquired Apricot in 1990 to be more competitive in its home market, still using the name Apricot into the late noughties.

In 1983 Richard Austin and Bob Hitchcock formed Evesham Technology initially to sell Amstrad computers. It soon added to its range with many other components and products, including Commodore 64, Olivetti PC and Atari ST.

It then launched the Vale range of computers changing the brand to Zydec in 1992. The organisation developed a chain of nineteen retail outlets and was an approved supplier to educational establishments.

When the British Government withdrew its home computer initiative in 2007 Evesham was left exposed and went into administration. A Dubai investment company took an interest though the retail shops were closed. Evesham was renamed as Geemore Technology Ltd. The restructuring did not make the operation any more interesting and it was finally shut down in March 2008.

In 1984 the Taiwanese company Tatung announced that its Tatung Einstein would be built in Telford in the UK. This was a Z80-based computer priced at £499, designed in Taiwan. Remarkably some 5,000 units of the Telford production were actually shipped from the UK to Taiwan!

It looked and felt like a business computer but was aimed at the sophisticated home user; unfortunately the high price condemned it to a relative lack of success.

One giant leap – Sinclair QL

Sinclair beat both the Apple Mac and the Atari ST to market with its project initially named ZX83 and then later ZX84. This was planned as a portable with an integral flat-screen CRT monitor.

However when it was launched in 1984 it was switched to being a desktop computer the QL (Quantum Leap). This was the first PC based on the Motorola 68000 series, with a 68008 at its heart, 128k of RAM and two on-board Sinclair Microdrive tape-loop cartridge drives.

It beat the competitors to market because frankly it was not ready - no working prototype existed. Using its normal approach Sinclair first promoted the product as a 28-day delivery mail order proposition, but the first shipments started to trickle through after three months.

By May 1984 the order book for QL had exceeded 13,000 units and £5m yet only a few hundred had been shipped. The UK's Advertising Standards Authority (ASA) rattled sabres at Sinclair as this was hardly the first time that Sinclair had provoked its code of conduct in terms of extended deliveries. The ASA forced Sinclair to open a special bank account where monies received was retained outside the company's direct control. The company also shipped the delayed units with a free cable by way of apology.

The QDOS operating system was not really ready and this was only resolved by the addition of an EPROM 'dongle' to be attached for it to function.

Those who got early units soon found there were problems in the SuperBASIC; the Microdrives proved unreliable too.

Sinclair was awarded his knighthood in 1985 , the same year that production of the QL was suspended, largely because the IBM PC had by then become the de facto standard for the business market that QL had espoused.

Portability - Psion

Psion was founded in 1980 as a software house working closely with Sinclair. David Potter was the founder and chairman of Psion which derived its name from Potter Scientific Instruments, but as PSI was already used the 'on' was added.

Initially Psion produced software for the ZX80, ZX81 and ZX Spectrum computers. It had a very popular Horace series (I recall 'Horace Goes Skiing' was a big seller), plus generic themed programs like Chess, Chequered Flag and Flight Simulator.

When the Sinclair QL was in development Psion PLC worked closely with Sinclair producing a series of applications for it - The Quill word processor, the Abacus spreadsheet, the Easel graphics software and the Archive database. These were subsequently released as an MS-DOS port called PC-Four.

As the QL was being released Psion entered the hardware market with the Psion Organiser, the world's first handheld computer or PDA (personal digital assistant). The design would be echoed later by the Blackberry. It came with a Hitachi 6301 8-bit processor, able to store phone numbers and addresses while maintaining a calendar.

There was a compact 6x6 keyboard with the alpha keys arranged in A-B-C order (not QWERTY) and a single row LCD mono display. Innovative and protected by patent was the way it used EPROMs for data storage. But removing them and putting them under a UV lamp to erase them was none too convenient.

The Psion Organiser II followed in 1986 with increased memory capacity, a two-line display and alternative data storage media like EEPROMs and RAM packs. Given the increased memory it came with built-in applications such as a diary and an alarm clock. There was also a BASIC system called Organiser Programming Language (OPL) that compiled the entered code.

Its features and portability won it some major clients including the retail variety chain Marks & Spencer using it for stock management and the UK employment services using it for benefit calculations.

In the 1990s the Psion Series 3, or SIBO (Sixteen Bit Organiser), and the 32-bit Series 5 moved on to a QWERTY keyboard and a clamshell design with an upgraded OPL language. This revised OPL was the predecessor of the Symbian operating system used by many smartphones.

In 2000 Psion acquired Teklogix International Inc, a Canadian company specialising in wireless data, data management and real-time data collection primarily in the logistics business. Purchased at £240m, or Canadian$544m, the merged organisation became Psion Teklogix Inc.

Sugar craft - Amstrad

Alan Michael Sugar was born in the East End of London. Leaving school at sixteen he was soon selling car aerials, intercoms and other electrical items from a van.

In 1968 he formed Amstrad (A M Sugar Trading) to operate initially in the audio and hi-fi business. The company went public in 1980 and entered the PC market in 1984.

The first computer product was the Amstrad CPC series (colour personal computer) based on the Z80A and targeted to compete with the Sinclair Spectrum and Commodore 64 home computers. It developed a following and inspired a number of magazines aimed at its users.

In September 1985 it launched the Amstrad PCW (personal computer word processor) range which was primarily sold for the word processing package 'Locoscript' for use at home or in a small business. Locoscript was produced by Locomotive Software, a UK software house that produced much of the Amstrad software.

At just £399 in the UK and $799 in the USA it included a printer and was available with BASIC and CP/M. It represented a very competitive package.

It was initially sold exclusively by Dixons Group in the UK. Some 700,000 units were purchased in the first two years propelling it to a 60% share of the UK market and 20% share in Western Europe. In total 8 million units were sold in its thirteen years of manufacture.

In April 1986 Amstrad acquired the name Sinclair and all the rights in its computers including all unsold stocks for just £5m; merely selling through those stocks proved to be worth more than the sum paid. Amstrad went on to launch two new Sinclair computers the ZX Spectrum +2 which included an on-board cassette deck and the ZX Spectrum +3 with a built-in 3" Amstrad floppy drive.

Sinclair Research Ltd continued as an R&D business, initially innovating in wafer-scale integration, telephony and satellite receivers. From the 1990s its prime activity has been in bicycles - the Zike, the Zeta and the A-bike folding bike.

Amstrad went on to manufacture low-cost PC clones. In 1986 the PC1512 with the GEM GUI was priced at £399; it took a 25% share of the European market. It also had several early portable PCs.

Later models were less successful. The PC2000 series had some hard-disk problems. Entry into games consoles with the GX4000 in 1990 had limited success too. But by then the company was refocused and had become a significant supplier of Sky satellite television set-top boxes and communications products.

Amstrad acquired Viglen in 1994, a British company formed back in 1975 specialising in the education and public sectors. The business was rearranged such that the satellite boxes and comms side of the business became Amstrad plc. This segment was later sold to BSkyB in 2007 for £125m and Sugar stepped down as chairman.

Viglen retained the computer side of the business and was chaired by Sugar until he handed over the reins to Claude Littner in 2009.

In 2000 Alan Sugar was knighted for services to business. In 2005 he was selected to be the host and taskmaster of the UK version of *The Apprentice*, first popularised in the United States by Donald Trump.

However he was not always right with his forecasting. Sugar famously spoke scathingly of the Apple iPod in 2005, in an echo of his style in *The Apprentice* saying that by Christmas it would be,

'...*dead, finished, gone, kaput...*'

In June 2009 he became the business advisor and 'enterprise tsar' to Gordon Brown's Labour government and was awarded a peerage becoming Lord Sugar, Baron Sugar of Clapton; a year later Brown's government failed to be re-elected.

14 - The East enters the fray
'Simple things should be simple; complex things should be possible.' Alan Kay

Of course during this period we were also witnessing a massive growth in the tiger economies and as part of their planning they certainly did not ignore PCs.

Fuji with the FUJIC computer had been the first computer in Japan but any PC interests they had thereafter were concentrated into computer media. It was the second Japanese mainframe, the TAC designed by Tokyo University and Toshiba, that was to have a powerful PC heritage.

A light in the east - Toshiba
Toshiba was founded in 1939 when two long-standing organisations came together. One had been engaged in telegraphy from as early as 1875 and the other had been a manufacturer of incandescent light bulbs from 1890. Tokyo Electric and Shibaura Engineering Works combined to form Tokyo Shibaura Denki and this title was the source of its brand name.

Toshiba was the first Japanese company to develop radar systems, and this was perhaps why it was the company that helped Tokyo University design the TAC valve-based computer. Toshiba followed up with Japanese firsts in transistor televisions, microwaves and colour video phones.

In 1959 it launched a transistorised computer for business called the TOSBAC-2100; this had 5,000 transistors and 10,000 diodes. Toshiba was to have a long history of semiconductor innovation and is in the world top twenty semiconductor manufacturers.

It launched the JW-10 word processor in September 1978, using *kana* and *kani* symbols to computerise the preparation of Japanese documents. In 1982 it released the Pasopia 16 which offered true Japanese language operation.

In May 1984 came a computer based upon Microsoft's MSX operating system. This was the HX-10, though it was also called the Pasopia IQ in Japan. It enjoyed some success but of course MSX proved to be a cul-de-sac.

Toshiba developed an early clamshell laptop PC in 1985, the T1100, which it claimed to be 'the world's first mass-market laptop'. It had a mono screen, a floppy drive and a somewhat crowded keyboard. The T1000 followed in 1987 mirroring the look and feel of the IBM PC Convertible. The T3100 (aka J-3100) in 1986 and the T1200 in 1987 added a hard drive.

A notebook called the T1000SE or 'Dynabook' (not to be confused with Alan Kay/PARC's use of this name) was released in 1989. Toshiba also launched a very compact or mini-notebook Libretto computer in 1997; it ran Windows 95, had a TFT screen and a hard drive.

Later the Toshiba main line of laptops was the Satellite and Satellite Pro series.

By 2009 Toshiba was ranked the fifth largest computer manufacturer in the world, behind HP, Dell, Acer and Lenovo.

Elevating the argument - Hitachi

Hitachi was founded back in 1910 to build a five horse-power induction motor. It was based in the village of Hitachi, from which it took its name. It expanded into other electrical components and then to turbines, locomotives (including carriages for the *Shinkansen* Bullet Train) and elevators.

In 1957 Hitachi developed the HIPAC MK-1 computer, not for the computer itself but simply as a device with which it could calculate the likely sag and tensions in power lines they were managing.

Perhaps prompted by this, in April 1960, the leading designers of the early Tokyo University TAC mainframe computer, Kenro Murata and Kisaburo Nakazawa, left to join Hitachi. By May 1963 they had designed and built HITAC 5020 a general-purpose computer; HITAC 5020 units were later delivered to Japanese universities and NTT, Japan's PTT (postal, telephone and telegraph company).

In 1977 Hitachi and National Semiconductor negotiated an alliance with one of its contracts to manufacture IBM-compatible mainframe computers for Itel, an equipment leasing company. These compatibles were branded Advanced Systems and had great success, some two hundred units sold for $73m in a short time.

Itel ran into trouble when technology changes, both real and threatened, made clients hold off purchasing. National Semiconductor acquired Itel and renamed the product as NAS (National Advanced Systems).

IBM's initiatives in semiconductors and its publicity for the IBM PC conspired to put pressure on NAS, Amdahl and other IBM compatibles. Worse, IBM sued National and NAS for infringement. In 1983 NAS ceased manufacture of IBM compatibles and sold Hitachi products instead.

Hitachi launched the 8-bit Page Master MB-6880 in September 1978; it had all the attributes of a PC. It could use an RGB monitor or domestic TV, it played games, had simple sound and could be programmed in BASIC. The Level 3 MB-6890 added Japanese language capability by 1980.

In 1982 the Hitachi MB 16001, part of the 16000 Series, was released as a 16-bit business computer with MS-DOS on-board and the ability to be used with COBOL and FORTRAN.

By 1983 Hitachi had its B-Series personal computers, the B-16 offered word processing, graphics, financial management and used for control systems including managing robots.

In January 1999 the operation was renamed Hitachi Data Systems.

Building mountains - Fujitsu

After much experimentation with the parametron the next Japanese computer development was managed by Fujitsu and it would grow into a global player.

Fujitsu Ltd was founded in June 1935 and though it was clearly part of a *zaibatsu* it still emerged from WWII able to produce the FACOM 100 computer in 1954 and grow into Japan's largest computer company by 1980.

In 1974 Fujitsu launched its M-Series of mainframe computers which were IBM compatible.

Of specific interest to the PC story is that in March 1977 it launched the LKIT-8 and NEW LKIT-8 hobby kit computers; its first foray away from mainframes.

In May 1981 the Fujitsu FM-8, using the 6809 MPU, was one of the first to have a 64 KBit DRAM; it was similar in appearance to the Radio Shack Color Computer. The FM-8 was Japan's first personal computer; FM stood for Fujitsu Micro. A home computer FM-7 version and an advanced FM-11 business series were added in November 1982.

In 1983 a range of business PCs called the Fujitsu Micro 16 was launched based on the Intel 8086 with an expansion card Zilog Z80. In 1984 the FACOM K series of desktop computers also addressed the business market and grew into a family of products through the late '80s and early '90s.

From 1989 it manufactured a PC by the unlikely name of FM Towns (Fujitsu Microcomputer and Towns). The 'Towns' was for some reason a contraction of the name Charles Hard Townes, a winner of the Nobel Physics Prize for quantum electronics. It had a large number of options with a GUI OS of its own.

Fujitsu fully understood the need for good software support and at one stage worked with Richard Garriott to port the Ultima games to the platform.

But they chose to discontinue FM Towns in favour of the FMV series; launched in October 1993, these were IBM PC-AT clones.

Back in 1971 Fujitsu became involved with Mers Kutt's Key-Edit product and through this it developed relationships with both ICL and Amdahl; these were later to prove significant.

Fujitsu acquired 80% of the UK ICL business in 1990 and, through its Pete Bonfield, negotiated to acquire over half of the Russian company KME-CS (Kazan Manufacturing Enterprise of Computer Systems) in 1991. It renamed ICL as Fujitsu Services in 2002.

Fujitsu had invested in Gene Amdahl when he left IBM and built his 470 V/6 computer in one of its plants. In 1997 Fujitsu acquired the Amdahl operation.

In 1999 Fujitsu Siemens Computers was formed with its German partner of many years. It bought out Siemens in November 2008 and later sold off its hard drive business to Toshiba in October 2009.

Today Fujitsu operates in seventy countries with a turnover in excess of $50bn. It has a strong server business, its notebook and tablet PC ranges branded Amilo and Lifebook and a broad range of scanners. It also has a strong IT consulting business.

Transistor radios to world domination - Sony

Masaru Ibuka started a radio repair business in 1945. With his partner, Akio Morita, he founded Tokyo Tsushin Kogyo KK or Tokyo Telecommunications Engineering Corporation in May 1946.

They used various brand names for their products but, finding Americans were unable to pronounce them, the company name was changed to Sony, from *sonus* the Latin word for sound They appreciated the fact that phonetically Sony resembled the American term for a young lad, 'sonny'.

Ibuka travelled to the United States and acquired a licence from Bell Labs for its transistor technologies. Both Regency and Texas Instruments beat Sony to the market with the transistor radio, but the Sony TR-55 sold in real quantities from 1955. It used five transistors created in-house and its style was modelled on the look of the dashboard of a Lincoln car.

For the Sony TR-6, launched in May 1956, the cartoon character 'Sony Boy' promoted the product; an ancestor of Mario and Sonic? The market in transistor radios in the United States grew from around 100k in 1955 to over 5 million a year by the end of the '60s.

Of course down the years Sony developed many other products, notably the Walkman and Discman; and it is known for standards battles with the Betamax, Compact Disc... It also enjoyed much success with its PlayStation consoles.

Sony launched computers during the 1980s but only for the home market and it withdrew from the sector by the end of that decade.

Its prime entry into the PC space was therefore not until 1996 when it globally launched the VAIO range. This was originally defined as video audio integrated operation, but since 2008 was redefined to mean visual audio intelligence organiser. Some comment that the way the VA is shown is an analogue wave and IO of course is accepted to mean input-output. Your choice!

The early laptops used the Sony XBRITE displays to give a very crisp and clear image. Sony was also the first with LED backlit screens in 2005 and the first to offer Blu-Ray writable discs with the AR series in May 2007. The TZ series in 2008 included an early solid-state drive. Sony also manufactures a range of desktops using the VAIO branding.

Sony has suggested it plans a touch screen VAIO portable to work with the PlayStation Network, perhaps targeting the iPad space?

Self-propelled - Sharp

Sharp began back in 1912 as a small metals factory in Tokyo. One of its early successes was the Ever-Sharp propelling pencil, from which it later took its corporate name.

The 1923 earthquake killed over 100,000, destroyed large parts of Tokyo, Yokohama and other areas, and made over three million homeless This left Sharp looking for a new business and this it found in radios, manufacturing them from 1925.

Sharp worked on ultra shortwave technology in WWII and was in a good position to produce the first Japanese prototype television in 1951. Its licence with RCA the next year allowed it to create three TV sets for its domestic market. NHK began broadcasting in February 1953 and Sharp made the first commercially produced TV set, the TV3-14T.

Sharp was soon involved in a broad array of consumer electronic products. It was ready with colour television as Japan launched four colour broadcasters in 1960. In 1961 it created Sharp Central Research Laboratories to investigate future electronic projects.

During the 1960s it expanded operations to some eighty-seven countries distributing transistor radios. It was the first Japanese producer of a microwave oven, it was an innovator in solar power and it was also active in health care technologies.

Sharp never became involved in mainframe computers. It was to be the Tokyo Olympics in 1964 that pushed it to develop the CS-10A, the world's first all transistor-diode electronic calculator. This rapidly became a busy sector, Sharp's website stating that,

'...Manufacturers rushed into a field that was soon crowded with 33 makers offering 210 different models. This intense competition... ...was called the "electronic calculator war".'

Calculator developments led it into semiconductors and other electronic components. It also claimed the world's first IC-based calculator with the CS-31A launched in 1966. In the late '60s it established itself in Germany and the UK; it already had a US presence.

It was active in LSI and ELSI (extra large scale integration), operating under licences from Rockwell. Using LSI technology it launched the QT-8D Microcompet calculator. This move to electronics was formally acknowledged in 1970 when the company was renamed the Sharp Corporation; dropping the word 'electric' from its name.

In the early '70s Sharp launched a range of electronic cash registers and the HAYAC-3000 stand-alone computer terminal. It also entered the photocopier market.

Its innovations in LCD technology also saw the launch of LCD calculators such as the EL-805. By 1975 it had shipped its ten millionth electronic calculator; two years later it launched a credit-card sized sensor-touch electronic design.

Also in 1977 it launched the Shoin WD-3000 Japanese word processor, an electronic translator and a voice-activated calculator.

In 1978 Sharp formally entered the PC market with the MZ-40K and MZ-80C kits, only ever released in Japan where they took some 50% of the market.

In 1979 outside Japan Sharp released a fully-assembled MZ-80K which had a similar approach to the Commodore PET and Tandy TRS-80. It had 48K of RAM, an onboard screen using simple graphics and a cassette tape reader/recorder. It came in three memory sizes (20K, 36K and 48K) and worked with BASIC, Pascal and FORTRAN. Its downside was a squared off non-standard keyboard. At just £500 it did well in Europe selling over 100,000 units.

A business series called the MZ-80B was created from the consumer range but with more serious keyboards, graphics etc. Sharp also launched an IBM PC-AT alike, the MZ-8000 series.

Sharp's television division then entered the market, to some extent in competition with its own computer division when it launched the XI Series between 1982 and 1988. It had one oddity; instead of offering BASIC in a ROM it had to be loaded from disk. But this led to a series of computers called 'clean machines' which made the entire RAM available for non-BASIC programming. Of course given its origins it also offered RGB colour.

Sharp is also known for its range of pocket programmable calculators and computers produced from 1977 onwards. Today it is difficult to find much mention of PCs on its site or its approved history.

Coming down the line - NEC

The Nippon Electric Company was founded in August 1898 but took on its more familiar NEC name in 1983. Initially its business was in telephony, with early contracts for the Japanese phone system. It began exporting switches to China from 1904 and to Korea from 1908.

Its early fortunes were linked to government plans for telephony. The 1923 earthquake destroyed four NEC factories and wiped out thirteen Tokyo telephone exchanges. A British company Automatic Telephone Manufacturing Co had the rebuild contract but NEC partnered with it, gaining valuable technology transfer arrangements.

It also went into the radio business following the earthquake, initially importing Western Electric product but soon making its own broadcast and receiver equipment.

WWII saw two of NEC's plants acquired for military developments; its foreign relationships shut down. Two plants were bombed to destruction and another heavily damaged. Post war it was almost necessary to start again from scratch.

By 1950 the company was a significant player in R&D into transistors. By 1958 it had produced the NEAC-1101 and NEAC-1102 mainframe computers using the local storage system of the parametron. By 1959 the transistorised NEAC-2201 was launched. The next year it was heavily dedicated to IC developments.

In August 1978 NEC launched the TK-80 computer d-i-y kit and for which it later offered expansion boards. In May 1979 it launched the PC-8001 which came as a series of components; the CPU was built into the keyboard and this could be connected to a CRT display, a floppy drive and an acoustic coupler.

By the early '80s NEC was involved in LSI and VLSI development. Its first PC was the 8-bit PC-8800 series in 1981. The PC-9801 launched in October 1982 was the first of the 16-bit PC-9800 series and this scored well in the Japanese business market. A detuned version of the 9800, called the PC98LT, was the first Japanese laptop. By October 1989 it had its PC-9801 notebook, aka 98NOTE.

NEC worked with HudsonSoft to produce the PC-Engine games console for its home market and the TurboGrafx-16 for the US market.

The NEC MobilePro handheld computer series was first launched in 1997 and these have stayed current with regular updates.

Its Versa range of notebook computers and PowerMate desktops and hybrids have also kept them current.

NEC produced its first supercomputer the SX-2 in 1986. From 2002 to 2004 it could boast the world's fastest supercomputer as a result of a Japanese government initiative to simulate global climate models to investigate global warming. This was the Earth Simulator Computer based on the SX-6; it achieved 35.86 TFLOPS; this was surpassed by IBM's Blue Gene/L in September 2004.

Timing it right - Seiko/Epson

Seiko was securely in to watches but inevitably as these became electronic the company dabbled in computer watches and other portable devices such as crossword solvers; however it would not focus on PCs but instead on computer printers.

In 1942 the founders assisted a local clock shop, Daiwa Kogyo Ltd, to set up as a maker of watch parts for one of its subsidiaries, Daini Seikosha. The two parties later jointly set up a factory to make Seiko watches. This was later renamed Suwa Seikosha Co Ltd which developed the Seiko innovations.

This operation set up a subsidiary Shinshu Seiki Co that soon had the task of producing a printing timer to support the Seiko Group when it was appointed the official timekeeper for the 1964 Tokyo Olympics.

This became the basis for the launch in 1968 of the world's first mini-printer, the EP-101 (electronic printer). It was soon offered with many electronic calculators. In June 1975 the operation was renamed Epson, said to derive from 'son of the EP'.

By June 1978 Epson had launched the TX-80, an 80-column dot matrix printer, just in time for the PC explosion; it was selected for the Commodore PET and others. In October 1980 an improved MX-80 became the top selling US printer.

In July 1982 as the operation's name was formally established as Epson Corporation it launched the HX-20 - the first handheld or notebook computer, released in November 1981. A4-sized with an LCD screen, 16K or 32K of RAM, Epson BASIC and built-in microcassette drive and a thermal printer, it weighed just 3.5 lbs (1.6 kg).

In June 1984 the SQ-2000 (called the IP-130K inside Japan) was the first commercial inkjet printer to reproduce the 96-character ASCII set in eleven different type sets.

In 1985 the Suwa Seikosha Co. and Epson Corporation merged to become Seiko Epson Corporation.

Epson developed the Micro Piezo inkjet technology and in March 1993 launched the 360 dpi Epson 800 inkjet printer (called the MJ-500 inside Japan). This was followed in 1994 by a 720 dpi colour inkjet called the Epson Stylus Color.

The company's language for controlling the printers, ESC/P (Epson standard code for printers) became widely adopted as a standard. The name derives from the escape sequences used in formatting. Today it has been overtaken by Postscript and PCLs (printer command languages).

Other Japanese players – Canon, Matsushita, Mitsubishi, Oki...

Matsushita was founded in 1918 to manufacture electrical domestic products, though its production of a bicycle light and the founder's enthusiasm saw it diversify into bicycles.

Like other Japanese brands it moved into radio in the '30s and television in the '50s. Its Technics hi-fi brand grew strongly too but for some reason it was not lured in to computing.

It was only in 1990 that it launched its first notebook computer, the Panacom PRO NOTE and today it has the Toughbook laptop; but it never became a big PC player.

The Toyota Prius uses Panasonic battery technology. In 2008 it acquired Sanyo. Apropos of nothing, Sanyo means three oceans - Atlantic, Indian and Pacific. The freshly combined operation turns over $110bn.

Oki was founded in 1877 when it reverse engineered Bell's telephone and started making its own from 1881. It is still innovative in that sector, for example working with Bell Labs in 1975 to produce the first car telephone system.

Oki produced the OPC-1 (Oki parametron computer) in March 1959. It had quite a mix of technologies using 6,000 parametrons, 130 vacuum tubes and 300 transistors.

In May 1980 Oki launched an 8-bit business PC, the if800 series Model 10 and Model 20. The Model 30 was launched in 1981 with CP/M. By April 1983 it had added a 16-bit Model 50 and in January 1985 the 16-bit Model 60.

In 2004 it produced the IP Convergence SS9100 Server and in 1996 the Center Stage NX5000 comms server to carrier standards.

Today it is best known for ATMs and printers.

Canon launched two MSX-based PCs in 1983, the V-10 and V-20, but subsequently remained in its prime business of cameras, copiers and printers.

Mitsubishi Electric launched what would be the industry's first 16-bit computer, the MULTI 16 in 1981. It used an 8088 MPU using CP/M 86; it had hi-res colour graphics and a 5.25" double-sided double-density floppy drive.

It could run BASIC, COBOL and FORTRAN and was launched with Multiplan spreadsheet and MULTIPLOT drawing. Mitsubishi had arranged for a broad set of other software applications. But it did not sustain interest in the sector.

Ricoh might just have entered the PC business with its photocopier strengths having gobbled up many competitors from back in my Rank Xerox days – Gestetner, Nashua, Rex-Rotary, Lanier, Savin, Danka… But it stayed just to one side of it with DocumentMail, an SaaS document management series of solutions.

Taiwan- Acer, ASUS, Quanta…

Sitting just 100 miles (160km) off the coast of China, Taiwan has a chequered history. Japan routinely seemed to have designs on it and occupied it during WWII.

In 1949 the ousted Kuomintang Chinese government fled to Taiwan and took all China's foreign currency and gold reserves. Even with these assets, in 1962 Taiwan was only ranked economically among minor African nations. Its 23 million population is certainly industrious and by the late noughties it had become a tiger, a major player in global economic growth.

With others, Stan Shih and his wife Carolyn Yeh founded an operation called Multitech back in 1976, changing this to Acer Inc in 1987. It started out making electronic components but also presented itself as a consultant in the use of microprocessors.

Its business in DRAMs, licensed from TI, provided a strong foundation that was used to transfer the company into the manufacture of PCs and laptops. By 1993 it turned over $75m, and grew this considerably to $3.2bn in 1994 with a profit of over $200m.

During 1995 Acer continued this growth, overtaking Dell, HP and Toshiba to become the ninth largest PC manufacturer in the world.

That same year it launched the Aspire PC, its desktop series for home and small business use, and the Predator series for gamers.

Wistron Corporation was spun-off from Acer in 2000 as a manufacturing operation. It concentrated on designing notebooks, desktops, servers for others.

AOpen was formed as an Acer subsidiary in December 1996 and had its own market listing in 2002; most recently it has concentrated on energy-saving products.

On 23 January 1997 Acer acquired TI's mobile computing business. At that time it was the world's seventh largest PC brand and the fourth largest PC manufacturer. As Shih stated, this was not just about the technology but also the team in terms of R&D and sales & marketing skills.

The Acer Veriton range is for business use with a broad range from towers to notebooks. It also launched notebook ranges using the TI brand names TravelMate and Extensa to target this market. From 2003 it had a licence to use the Ferrari name with several of its PCs and from 2006 became an official sponsor of Scuderia Ferrari.

In January 2008 Acer acquired Packard Bell. The company had nothing to do with Hewlett Packard or Ma Bell, but was founded back in 1926 in Los Angeles to operate in radio, television and military electronics. In 1961 it developed its own computer based on Turing's NPL Pilot ACE design. An Israeli investment team acquired the brand in 1986 and launched a range of IBM PC compatibles.

In March 1996 Packard Bell acquired Michelangelo Data Systems from Groupe Bull, with Bull and NEC taking a share in it. From then until mid-1996 Packard Bell held market leadership in the USA until Compaq took over that status.

In September 2006 Packard Bell was acquired by John Hui. Hui had owned eMachines but had sold this on to Gateway back in 2004.

In August 2007 Acer acquired Gateway for $710m and in January 2008 it had negotiated to own 75% of Packard Bell too.

In July 2008 Aspire One, a subcompact notebook was launched, though this is produced for it by Quanta Computer, another Taiwanese company. By 2009 it was the world's second largest computer manufacturer and Gartner states it to be the number one in notebooks.

Acer launched the Acer Tablet designed to work with Android in 2010. In November of that year the Acer Itonia was announced as a further tablet development with a dual touch screen.

Wayne Hsieh, Ted Hsu, MT Liao and Th Tung founded ASUS in Taiwan in April 1990. The name ASUS is said be derived from Pegasus, but by dropping the 'Peg' they would be assured of a better alphabetic position in catalogues.

It is quoted on the Taiwanese exchange as well as London Stock Exchange, yet production is largely Indonesian based. It manufactures components for Apple, Dell and HP.

It entered the mobile phone business in 2003 and the PDA/smartphone business in 2007.

In 2007 it launched its own super lightweight Eee PC netbook using Linux and an Intel 900 MHz Celeron M processor. The three Es stand for 'easy to learn, easy to work, easy to play'. By autumn 2008 it had shipped 1.7 million units.

In 2008 it shipped 50% of the 104 million motherboards produced globally; of its competitors, ECS delivered some 20 million, MSI 18 million and Gigabyte 16 million. In May 2008 a problem was uncovered in that ASUS motherboards had a glitch with Windows XP; this was fixed by December 2008. The 2009 turnover was $21.2bn.

Quanta Computer, founded in 1988, has produced notebooks for among others, Acer, Apple, Cisco, Compaq, Dell, Fujitsu, Gateway, HP, Lenovo, Sharp, Sony, Sun and Toshiba.

In 2005 Quanta became the original designer and manufacturer of the XO-1, defined for Nicholas Negroponte's OLPC project, 'one laptop per child'. The project is a non-profit notion supported by AMD, eBay, Google, Red Hat and others. It draws on the thinking of Alan Kay and Seymour Papert,

'It's an education project, not a laptop project.' Nicholas Negroponte.

OLPC planned to sell the XO-1, sometimes called the CM1 (children's machine), in 250,000 unit lots to Third World country governments so they might free-issue them to the children via educational establishments. It kept prices low by using flash memory rather than a hard drive and the open-source Fedora Linux OS.

It was planned at launch in 2006 to cost $188, but then to drop to a $100 price point in 2008 and to have a $50 price by 2010. However the economic downturn reduced OLPC funding and the price therefore stuck quite resiliently at $199. A G1G1 campaign promoted the notion of 'give one and get one', one for you and one for a Third World child. Fewer than 100,000 took up the G1G1 deal in 2008.

OLPC needed 3 million unit sales to make the effort viable. In 2007 deals were signed with Mexico, Peru and Uruguay; in 2008 with Colombia, Ghana and Peru; in 2009 with Rwanda, Sierra Leone and Uruguay; in 2010 with Argentina and Peru. Almost 2 million laptops have been distributed through the scheme.

The G1G1 scheme has seen laptops delivered to Afghanistan, Cambodia, Ethiopia, Gaza, Haiti, Mongolia, Rwanda and a number of Pacific islands.

Compal Electronics was founded in Taiwan in 1984 and was soon producing laptops for Compaq, Dell and HP. It is today the second largest contract laptop manufacturer, to Quanta, and by 2010 had shipped a little under 50m notebooks. Production facilities are in Taiwan, mainland China and South Korea.

Founded in 1987, Elitegroup Computer Systems was yet another Taiwanese motherboard maker that has recently developed laptop systems too. Micro-Star International is also a motherboard and video card maker.

Korea – Daewoo, Goldstar, Samsung

Korea you might have expected to emerge with key players in PCs and there is little doubt that each of Samsung, Daewoo and GoldStar have on occasion attempted to enter the market.

Samsung is Korea's largest conglomerate. Formed in 1938 as a small trading company largely in foodstuffs, it entered the electronics business in the 1960s with television and telecommunication products. It has become the world's largest producer of memory chips and the second-largest chip maker; after Intel.

In August 1996 Samsung acquired 51% of AST Research for $162m. US-based AST was founded by Albert Wong, Safi Qureshey and Thomas Yuen, the name being their first name initials, and it manufactured expansion cards for the IBM PC.

Daewoo produced computers and other consumer electronic products in the 1990s before it went bankrupt in 1999.

LG (Lucky GoldStar) was founded in 1947 and became the second largest Korean corporation. It would later try to suggest in advertising that LG means 'life's good'.

It produced the first Korean radio set and its electronics division is today the world's second largest TV manufacturer. It is the third largest manufacturer of mobile phones.

In 1994 LG made the first 3DO console, but now seems to content itself with computer monitor manufacture.

China – Great Wall, Founder, Lenovo

Today's Chinese Academy of Sciences of Beijing was established in 1949 as the National Academy of Natural Sciences. As part of an ongoing programme it often launched commercial enterprises.

One of these creations was founded in November 1984 by Liu Chuanzhi under instruction from the Academy of Sciences.

It was part of the vanguard of Chinese businesses moving in to Hong Kong prior to it being handed back to China (1st July 1997); it founded its own operation there in June 1988.

The company was known as Liangxiang inside China but adopted the name Lenovo for the overseas market in November 1989. The name is apparently a contraction of legend and novo (new).

Lenovo first started making computers in 1990 and funded its growth by going public on the Hong Kong exchange in February 1994 with a P/E of almost 14. It was an early market leader in the domestic market but this was changing and in the five years 1989 to 1993 the percentage of locally manufactured computers sold in China declined from 67% to 22%.

The other Chinese players rushed to secure their positions in the face of this onslaught.

Founder Technology Group initially did a deal with Dell and grew its business to be one of the top ten world PC suppliers while remaining in the top two in its domestic market. Great Wall allied with IBM and Sitong with Compaq. At the time Lenovo only had 12% of its business in computer equipment.

Yang Yuanqing was given a key appointment in 1994, to run Lenovo's computer department and he is usually credited with turning around the company fortunes. He attended Shanghai's Jiatong University and went on to do a postgraduate course at the Chinese Science & Technology University.

He was assisted by a strengthening home market with over 40% of Beijing households saying they wished to buy a PC within a year and another 45% with the desire to buy within two years. A decade earlier I had travelled through China with *China Computerworld* magazine backing and even then we could see that an enormous demand was building.

Lenovo set about creating the E-Series (economy) and by 1999 it had an 8.5% market share across the Asia-Pacific.

By 2002 Lenovo had created a supercomputer and was the first Chinese company accepted into the Beijing Olympic Partner Programme.

In December 2005 Lenovo did what would have previously been unimaginable and bought IBM's PC business.

At the CES in January 2011 it announced the Lenovo Enhanced Experience 2.0 which booted up twenty seconds faster than any other PC.

Many Chinese companies manufacture computers and notebooks that were branded with western names. For example Foxconn Technology produced computers and then became the prime Apple iPod manufacturer.

Russian revolutions – MIPT, LEMZ, Elektronica, Pentagon, Kraftway

Pyotr Kapitsa, subsequently a Nobel winner for his work on superfluidity, wrote to Stalin in 1946 proposing there was a need for an institution to maintain and develop research into defence matters for the Soviet Union.

In the event the Moscow Institute of Physics and Technology (MIPT), often referred to as the Russian MIT, was founded, initially as a department of Moscow State University. It became independent in 1951 and is the highest Russian authority for the physical sciences. Boris Babaian and Sergei Lebedev were alumni of MIPT.

The first computer kits in Russia appeared in hobbyist magazines. In 1983 the Micro-80 appeared in the Russian *Radio* magazine as a d-i-y kit with an 8080 and some two hundred ICs. The following year the same magazine launched Radio-86RK and this proved to be much simpler with fewer than thirty ICs. The magazine's final offering was the Orion 128 that ported software from the Sinclair ZX Spectrum to achieve some popularity.

In 1987 *Modelist-Konstructor* magazine published plans for the Specialist computer kit. It had good graphics but did not really take off.

In 1988 *Young Engineer* magazine launched its very simple kit, the UT-88.

During the 80s the ES PEVM was produced in Minsk as a clone of the IBM PC.

In 1983 the USSR Ministry of Radio commissioned LEMZ to clone the Apple II. LEMZ was previously a motor car manufacturer but it was when production moved to more electronically-minded plants that it took off. This effort designed the Agat computer which became much used in Soviet schools. Though priced cheaply, this still represented an investment of twenty months of the average Soviet salary.

In 1985 the Elektronica BK series was launched. It was designed by the NPO Scientific Center which at the time was the leading Soviet microcomputer design centre. It was the only official Soviet mass-produced home computer. It was quite costly and soon overhauled by the Soviet Spectrum clones.

In 1989 a group of Russian enthusiasts produced the Pentagon home computer, a clone of the ZX Spectrum 128. It was copied right across the USSR and became very popular. The ATM Turbo was introduced in 1991 as an enhanced ZX Spectrum clone. Many others clones existed - the Hobbit, the Scorpion…

The KME-CS (Kazan Manufacturing Enterprise of Computer Systems) was another USSR player; it was acquired by Fujitsu in 1991.

Kraftway, founded in 1993, worked closely with MIPT. Today it manufactures home and office computers, and servers.

15 - Getting serious – IBM's entry

Ken Olsen founder of DEC in 1977 said, 'There is no reason anyone would want a computer in their home.'

The seventy stone gorilla is roused - IBM

The PC business was growing up and the market was beginning to come together. Those who had originally dismissed the PC as merely a hobbyist fad could now appreciate its potential; the old traditional computer companies began to take it more seriously.

The number of PC users also meant it was becoming viable to invest the large monies and time required to innovate in software. Major retailers were naturally attracted by a product that it was believed would fly off the shelf.

The 8-bit PC products and their software applications were soon to become just 'two-bit' when 16-bit processors and IBM entered the market.

From the very early days of personal computers there was always a degree of paranoia about IBM. Just when would the world's largest computer manufacturer turn its attention towards the personal sector?

It was assumed that this would be happening soon and often the question was answered with a knowing nod and a reiteration of the question,

'Where does a 70-stone gorilla sit?' The correct response being, 'Wherever it chooses!' Anon

IBM was a large, slow-acting corporation, extremely long-lived with a long memory of previous short-lived escapades. It was somewhat akin to a stately elephant plodding along, apparently unaware of the personal computer sector which was the frantic equivalent of a hummingbird.

It did not need low-cost fast-changing products to come along and disturb its stately progress and virtual monopoly of the mainframe business. Its R&D was specifically designed to lag just a little behind others, allowing any dust to settle and waiting for issues and problems to emerge before it was prepared to take action.

Within its own offices few of its senior management thought there was any merit in having a terminal on their desks, seeing this as something for mere data processors and secretaries to use.

It was also very unlikely that any of them had ever wielded a soldering iron - they were in the business of data processing. Computers were merely the current devices of choice to crunch that data; they were not interested in computers per se.

But the label IBM still proved sufficient to propel its PC into perhaps an undeserved market leadership. In part this was due to one of the first viral marketing campaigns of which I was aware. Using an established rhetoric tactic of FUD (fear, uncertainty and doubt) they managed to get people to recite,

'Nobody ever got fired for buying IBM equipment.'

Surely this came from an IBM marketing department? Certainly Gene Amdahl of Amdahl Corp railed at IBM for using the tactic against Amdahl as early as 1975.

The tactic ensured many corporate buyers would propose that, while they may well have assessed other products favourably, they were more likely to get approval from senior management for the IBM brand.

The approved IBM history says that its first personal computer was the IBM 5100 Portable Computer introduced in September 1975, but at $20,000 it was securely a business and scientific product, not very personal at all, and at 55 lbs (24 kilos) it was not particularly portable either.

The 5100 used the IBM System/370 operating system; a BASIC interpreter was available together with a ¼" tape cartridge and a 5" screen with a 64 character display.

The successor product in 1978, the 5110, moved from conception to production in just ninety days, confirming the team's confidence that it could move quickly if necessary.

The IBM 5120 followed - a larger, more expandable desktop system. The division sold tens of thousands of these and this was what gave the internal independent business unit the credibility to be permitted to take its next step.

Whether or not the 5100 can be considered a personal computer is moot, but it certainly was the first of a dynasty. The 5110 and 5120 were soon followed by the 5140 PC Convertible Computer, the 5150 IBM PC, the 5155 Portable Computer, the 5160 PC XT and the 5170 PC AT.

RANDOM ACCESS MOMENT:
At the turn of the millennium a series of postings to a number of bulletin boards was made by a 'John Titor' announcing himself as a time traveller from the year 2036.

He described his time machine as being rather Back-to-the-Future esque, built into the rear of a 1967 Chevrolet Corvette convertible. He explained that it would be CERN and its Large Hadron Collider that would uncover the secrets of time travel.

Titor suggested he had been trying to warn us of the threat of CJD (Creutzfeldt - Jakob disease). He described a future US 2004 civil war that would break the USA into five smaller units; he talked of a 2015 nuclear attack by Russia.

But intriguingly he suggested that one of his missions was to acquire an IBM 5100 and take it back to his time to translate various computer codes and debug problems that had emerged in the computers of the future. UNIX at the

heart of all operating systems of the future had just two years before a flaw would cause havoc.

An IBM-er confirmed that the 5100 did actually have a little-known facility to emulate and debug System/360 and other mainframes.

There had been three or four internal attempts from individuals and teams pushing for IBM to enter the personal computer market, before there was any success.

In 1973 IBM went through something of a change when Frank T Cary became the new CEO. He split the operation into IBUs (independent business units) with some autonomy to pursue their individual sectors.

IBM Entry Level Systems

One such IBU was IBM's Entry Level Systems division based in Boca Raton, Florida. It was managed by Bill Lowe, a career-long IBM-er and often heralded as the 'father of the IBM PC'.

Lowe's IBU task was to come up with products to move the brand into new sectors, to be a nursery for new mainframe opportunities.

The PC project sat outside the normal IBM corporate ethos. It was done in such a hurry, managed in less than a year and bizarrely no proprietary control of any of the component parts of the product was maintained.

Lowe reviewed what the Altair and others had achieved and the multi-million dollar businesses they had generated. In 1979 he produced a market analysis identifying both a business and a consumer sector.

He proposed either IBM should acquire one of the currently active companies (he went as far as suggesting this might be Atari) or that it should develop its own approach. The company's Corporate Management Committee was receptive and asked for a prototype to be developed.

Bill Syndes was put in charge of twelve engineers to develop the prototype. The software lead, Jack Sams, had recently been involved in the System/23 Datamaster development and the internal creation of a BASIC. The lack of that software for the project had delayed progress heavily and it was largely for this reason that when the prototype was presented to the management committee it was proposed they acquire CP/M and BASIC externally. The planned development haste was another reason it was decided not to produce the OS and languages in-house.

Its bus specification mirrored the Datamaster format and was openly published to attract others to develop expansion cards for the IBM PC. In fact they would have had to publish it anyway because of an anti-trust resolution in the 1950s.

The prototype and approach were approved and a new IBU was formed in July 1980 at Boca Raton in Florida under the Project Chess code name and located functionally within the Entry Systems Division.

The team was given the right to breach all the normal IBM processes and told that it had just one year to come up with a PC.

Management books of the time took great interest in such clearly stated missions. President J F Kennedy had told NASA to put a man on the Moon by the end of the '60s. This directive helped to focus the mind, the team asking itself which course was the more likely to achieve that objective, and then selecting that route.

IBM's team of twelve was initially headed by Bill Lowe, but having originated the people and the approach he was promoted elsewhere within IBM before the project finished. He was allowed to select his own replacement and he chose Don Estridge, a Floridian who had been in the army and at NASA before joining IBM.

The new IBU drew in the plant manager at Boca Raton, Joe Bauman, to assist with manufacturing. Mel Hallerman from the IBM Series/1 minicomputer team joined as chief programmer.

Project Chess set out to do the impossible in IBM terms, create a new product in around a year. The IBM PC or 5150 would launch in September 1981.

The challenge was judged as fair, but a one-year deadline made it essential that they acquire technologies and software rather than take the time to develop them in-house. Here was another breach of the IBM norm. In the past it had always tended towards internal development, just as it preferred to promote from within too.

The product took on the codename Acorn, clearly implying the great oaks that this entry-level PC might grow for IBM. Acorn Computers in the UK was already founded back in 1978, but its Electron was not released until 1983 so there was no evident clash at the time in this project-name selection.

For speed a pre-existing monitor already developed by IBM Japan was selected together with an appropriate Epson printer.

The monitor was from the earlier IBM Datamaster project. It was assessed as a product that would not require a specialist installer; it was virtually plug-and-play. Work on Datamaster had been running for several years before Project Chess and the Acorn; it came to market just a month before the IBM PC.

The team almost selected a processor developed internally, one used for the IBM 801. The 801 was named after the building in the Thomas J Watson Research Center where John Cocke experimented to find improved performance for IBM computers; he would win a Turing Award and a Presidential Medal of Science for this work.

The 801 processor was a very early RISC (reduced instruction set computer). RISC used primitives to work with compilers and make the most of the architecture of the computer. This CPU would perhaps have been a good choice for them. It was certainly more powerful than the eventual choice and had a more advanced operating system than the DOS that they would come to use; and it was their technology!

The need-for-speed for the planned development necessitated an 'open-architecture' approach so third party developers would be encouraged to populate the required range of optional extras which would expand sales of the PC; without IBM having to do this for itself.

In an early conversation with Bill Gates at Microsoft, Jack Sams indicated that they were looking for Microsoft to supply an operating system for an 8-bit MPU. Gates recommended that instead they leapfrog the current 8-bit microprocessors and go straight for a more future-proofed 16-bit approach.

It would appear that the design parameters were still a tad fluid in that they proved readily willing to be swayed in a single conversation with a third party supplier. The Intel 8088 16-bit processor was selected.

Software sourcing for the IBM PC

The first and most important requirement to use the personal computer was of course a software language and two of these rather led the way.

Perhaps the best known is BASIC. The original BASIC (Beginner's All-purpose Symbolic Instruction Code) was developed at Dartmouth College in New Hampshire during 1963/4 by John Kemeny and Thomas Kurtz. It was brought to a wider audience when Microsoft developed the Altair or MS BASIC which permitted non-computer users to tackle programming and achieve a rapid progress.

In 1971 Niklaus Wirth, while at ETH Zürich, the Swiss Federal Institute of Technology (that had 'fostered' Konrad Zuse post WWII), created a teaching language called Pascal. Wirth later spent four years as assistant professor at Stanford and two one-year sabbaticals at Xerox PARC. Pascal became very popular as a general-purpose programming language.

Wirth was prolific, developing other languages such as Algol W, Euler, Modula and Oberon. In keeping with many in the business he published 'Wirth's Law' which stated that,

'Software is getting slower more rapidly than hardware becomes faster.'

Microsoft was formed from its fast reaction to the Altair launch, and set out to become the very first supplier of a BASIC language. It then built a business through seeking licence payments.

Paul Allen worked directly for MITS while Gates looked at expanding the business by creating the routines that would permit BASIC to be made available on floppy disk and then developing BASIC for each of the other microprocessors and systems as it was launched, starting with Altair, IMSAI...

One of the early deals was with General Electric; Gates licensed 8080 BASIC for a fixed sum of $50,000. In these early heady days they split the proceeds with MITS. Later they did not do this for other platforms because each BASIC required changes to suit its host, so they judged this to be another product beyond that licensed to MITS. Another school friend Marc McDonald joined as a programmer to be the first formally paid employee.

By late 1976 Gates finished a semester at Harvard and returned as company turnover reached $100,000, this trigger also prompted Allen to leave MITS and work full-time at Microsoft. They re-formalised their business arrangements as 64% Gates, 36% Allen – yet again a rather unusual equity split!

This work on other systems inevitably led to a falling out with MITS that by then had over 200 employees and a turnover in excess of $6m. But the operation was still not secure, Pertec Computer Corporation signed a letter of intent to acquire MITS for $6.5m in December 1976.

The purchase was as much because it was felt it would give Pertec the ownership of the BASIC software and it soon sought to stop Microsoft taking any more OEM deals. The Pertec-Altair deal was completed in May 1977, Ed Roberts himself earning $2m. The argument about licensing BASIC was resolved by an arbitrator in September 1977 – in Microsoft's favour.

During 1977 the Apple II, TRS-80 and Commodore PET were released and by 1978 each had also opted to offer a Microsoft version of BASIC.

Wozniak wrote a simple integer BASIC for the Apple II, they paid Microsoft a fixed $21k to add floating-point and cassette extensions and from this had created a Microsoft-defined AppleSoft BASIC. This proved not to be Microsoft's best deal when AppleSoft was issued on more than a million Apple units and represented just two cents per copy to the authors.

Radio Shack's TRS-80 had a Level I Basic produced in-house based around TinyBASIC, but they licensed Microsoft to product a Level II version that was customised to fit within its 12k ROM.

Commodore directly licensed a Microsoft BASIC from the outset.

In the late '70s Microsoft expanded its repertoire and introduced Microsoft FORTRAN for CP/M, FORTRAN-80, COBOL for CP/M and COBOL-80 language compilers.

It was therefore ready and able to support IBM and the PC.

Yet Microsoft's future was still in the balance at this phase of its development. For example in 1978 there was a meeting held between Gates and Gary Kildall to discuss the potential for a merger of Microsoft and DRI, a coming together of languages and operating systems, but they could not reach an agreement.

In 1978 Microsoft celebrated its first $1m turnover year by moving back to the founders' roots, from Albuquerque to Bellevue, just across Lake Washington from Seattle. The move was in part because it was finding it tough to hire programmers to work in Albuquerque; by then they had just twelve employees.

In August 1979 Ross Perot of Electronic Data Systems (EDS) met with Bill Gates and discussed the potential for EDS to buy Microsoft. Perot would become 'famous' when he mounted two campaigns to become president of the United States. Both times he was unsuccessful, losing to Bill Clinton in 1992 and again in 1996.

Perot, a Texan, attended the US Naval Academy and served in the navy until 1957, when he joined IBM as a salesman and came to realise that the corporate clients often had difficulty with the recruitment and management of the appropriate staff needed to run a new IBM computer installation. He tried to get IBM to respond to this requirement but they were not interested.

He therefore left the company and founded Electronic Data Systems in 1962 to offer data processing services to IBM clients. He invested $1,000 and within four years had amassed a massive fortune.

EDS offered operations support, systems integration and management consulting - a full concierge service for IT. It was not an easy sale. Thirty years later his setbacks in the race for the presidency were as nothing for someone who in his EDS organisation's early days lost out seventy-seven times before managing to finally win a contract. In 1965 EDS had further success when it created a service to process claims for Medicare and Medicaid.

EDS went public in 1968 with its shares growing tenfold at its launch. In 1979 EDS appointed a president and so Ross Perot, its chairman, was able to take the air and look around; hence the discussion with Gates.

The parties were both open to a deal. Gates saw the opportunity with EDS as an entrée to a world of large corporate clients. Perot saw Microsoft as one of a number of acquisitions in the PC sector. Gate's mother saw the deal as a chance for her son to go back to Harvard and complete his degree.

Gates was very taken by Perot's patriotism, his office festooned with flags and paintings. The EDS logo also featured an American eagle; Perot used the motif in his attitude to recruiting staff,

'...eagles don't flock, you have to find them one at a time...'

So there was clearly one point of contact between the two men, they both gave much attention to the quality of their teams.

The two have different memories of the price that was discussed back then. Gates suggests he was not really interested in selling but when asked sought something between $6m and $15m, which was an ambitious P/E for a small operation just recording its first year achieving $1m in revenues.

But Perot reported that he recalled the price requested was $40m to $60m and so naturally he was not interested; he did identify his regret later when he saw what Microsoft had become.

Operating systems

By 1981 the software team had incorporated without the hyphen, as Microsoft, and it was manoeuvres with IBM that ensured, when it introduced its IBM PC, there was Microsoft again centre of stage.

But it was not just programming languages that the PC would need; it would also require an operating system (OS). The OS boots on start-up to manage the hardware, software and input-outputs within a consistent framework.

IBM had already met and mastered this requirement for mainframe computing. The concern was how to squeeze what was required into a personal computer?

Early tasks with mainframe inputs and outputs, buffering, data processing and file management were at first rather wastefully embedded forming part of every piece of unique application software. This of course lengthened the code and in a number of ways complicated the production and management of software. An operating system would concentrate all of this in one place for speed and economy.

In 1955 a group of IBM 701 mainframe users in Los Angeles got together to form the SHARE User Group to exchange information and experience with languages and operating systems.

It created the Share Library where source code was retained and readily available between the members. This approach was an important early influence on the later desire for open-source software. Today SHARE is incorporated as a non-profit organisation with some 2,000+ IBM clients and 20,000 members.

In 1959 this group released the SHARE Operating System (SOS) as an improvement on an earlier General Motors system with which the group had been working.

SOS provided a standard operating system for the IBM 704 and it was then expanded to fit the 709. IBM then ported it as IBSYS (IBM system), an amalgam of FORTRAN and SOS that could work with the new transistorised mainframes the 7090 and 7094.

By 1964 IBM had released the OS/360, an operating system designed to work across the whole System/360 series of products.

All the mainframe companies developed their own operating systems. UNIVAC had EXEC, GE had GECOS or GCOS (general comprehensive operating system) DEC had TOPS-10...

The notion of a transportable operating system had yet to come of age.

Initially the much smaller personal computers tried to handle this requirement with a simple ROM-based program called a 'monitor'. But as disks and other peripherals were added to the PC configuration the requirement grew for a full operating system to harness and release all the potential within the hardware and, just as importantly, provide software developers with a framework within which to deliver their ideas and skills.

Gary Kildall was another individual who set out to enable microprocessors to be more than simple electronic control devices and to take on the attributes of a full-featured computer.

As a result he developed one of the earliest and most widely adopted PC operating systems; he called it CP/M.

He had originally been planning on a career in teaching but was drafted into the US Navy and found himself posted to the Naval Postgraduate School in Monterey. From here he was just a short drive from Silicon Valley and caught the 'bug'.

Given this enthusiasm he bought an early 4004 MPU and learned how to program it. He developed his understanding by working on his days off as a consultant at Intel. After national service he returned to the University of Washington and completed a doctorate in computer science.

As part of this he developed a concept called data-flow analysis, a process that gathered information about the likely values to be calculated at various stages of a program. Armed with this 'scoping' the compilers can then maximise a program much more readily.

Kildall also worked on software to control the new floppy disk drives that were emerging. As a result of this early work Intel was prepared to loan him 8008 and 8080 systems. He used these in 1972 to develop one of the first high-level programming languages for use with Intel MPUs which he called PL/M (programming language for microcomputers). PL/M was developed initially to drive the Intellec MCS 8 system.

PL/M drew upon many other languages, including Algol and XPL, but significantly it was optimised for the microprocessor, allowing it to address directly any location in its memory, any input-output location and the processor interrupt flags.

Kildall went on to form his own operation together with his wife, Dorothy McEwen. Initially they used the grandiose name of Intergalactic Digital Research but later simplified this to Digital Research Inc (DRI).

During 1973/4 Kildall wanted his software to enable him to connect up a Shugart floppy-disk drive to his Intellec-8. This updated software became CP/M, which originally stood for 'control program monitor' but during trade-marking, the name changed to 'control program for microcomputers'.

Back in these early days many developments were derivative, not to say plagiarised, and in the case of CP/M much of the development work had been done upon a DEC mainframe. It was therefore heavily influenced by DEC's TOPS-10 operating system (timesharing total operating system).

Developed in 1967, TOPS-10 was a fast and competent operating system that allowed the efficient sharing of available memory. Today it is best-known however for spawning three major initiatives - DECWAR, one of the first multi-player computer games; Forum, a forerunner of chat rooms; and CP/M.

RANDOM ACCESS MOMENT:
It was the TOPS software that set file names with a three-digit extension to define the type of file that we still all recognise today.

This proved to be another one of those moments when some of the PC innovators came together and cross each other's paths. The resulting creative tension fired a number of imaginations, driving ripples right across the PC pond.

Kildall, as a graduate thesis advisor in the US Navy, mentored an individual who went on to become another significant PC player, Gordon Eubanks. Eubanks master's thesis developed a BASIC compiler called BASIC-E, which Kildall promptly integrated into his CP/M development process.

Eubanks was later lured to work as a consultant for IMSAI while still serving in the US Navy. His company, Compiler Systems, produced CBASIC for IMSAI, the first implementation of BCD arithmetic (binary coded decimal). Some suggest the 'C' derived from 'sea' because he was posted to a submarine while he wrote it; though in fact his submarine was being overhauled in Vallejo for over a year of his posting, allowing him to complete his software project.

When his submarine finally sailed his mother ran the business and it was she who hired George Tate, who would later feature with dBASE. In 1981 Eubanks' business was sold to Kildall at DRI as part of a thrust into application software.

Applying BIOS

CP/M was first implemented upon the Intellec MCS 8 system and in order to run the CP/M routines Kildall managed to get Al Shugart at Seagate to loan him some 8" floppy disk drives.

Originally written for a single-user 8-bit microprocessor, CP/M when combined with an S-100 bus rapidly became the inspiration, and de-facto standard, for many early PC and software developers.

But this would only occur if DRI accommodated CP/M to fit a bewildering and ever-growing array of freshly released PC systems. IMSAI was the first in line, as it was using an 8080 MPU it naturally sought out DRI to provide it with the operating system.

It was the pressing need from a growing number of makers that led to Kildall developing a simple and effective approach.

Much of the specifics of CP/M he placed into a segment he called BDOS (basic disk operating system); this managed the CP/M file system for example. A separate segment was the CCP (console command processor); CCP was loaded from ROM and would often be overwritten by any application software but it was automatically reloaded when the application was closed.

The other basic building block of CP/M he called BIOS (basic input/output system). BIOS did precisely what the name suggested and provided the vital connection between the software and the specifics of the current hardware that it was to operate upon.

BIOS was effectively an interpreter between CP/M and its host PC ensuring the software could recognise individual keyboard key-strokes, could enable the writing and reading to and from floppy disk sectors, the buffering of data and so on. BIOS promptly became a fixture on all PCs that followed this development; it was instantly adopted for example by IBM when it entered the market.

In this manner Digital enabled software authors to produce a program that was fully and simply transportable across a whole range of microprocessors and PCs.

Software authors rapidly realised that if they wrote in CP/M this would open up a much bigger market potential than writing in any machine-specific operating system. Progressively any new PC system builder concluded that it should not bear the time and cost of developing its own operating system but adopt CP/M and harvest all the existing software programs by default.

The early versions of CP/M were not without snags, for example if you changed disks the system would not automatically 'see' that you had done this and would still be expecting to find the previous disk's directory. If you made the mistake not to manually have it re-read the new disk then you got a fatal error message back for your forgetfulness.

Even so CP/M was implemented on many early systems because it took so little memory and was largely bug-free. It was used on the Altair, the IMSAI, Osborne 1 and, with an add-on Z80 card, it could be used on an Apple II. Later still it was used by the Commodore 128, by Research Machines, on Acorn's BBC Micro, on later versions of the Sinclair ZX Spectrum and on the Amstrad PCW - to mention just a few.

Perhaps as importantly, CP/M was the vehicle selected by two of the most significant early applications, WordStar word processing and dBASE database management systems. Later versions of VisiCalc also ran in CP/M and Turbo Pascal was another spreadsheet system that debuted with CP/M; it would subsequently become Multiplan and even later evolve into Microsoft Excel.

By 1978 CP/M was implemented on every 8080 and Z80 system and this eventually meant some 500,000 personal computers operated the software. But DRI's heavy and necessary concentration on 8-bit processors meant it proved slow to develop a 16-bit version. It belatedly started work on CP/M-86 to remedy this.

RANDOM ACCESS MOMENT:
Not all operating systems proved to be quite such a success. The Japanese consumer electronic giants sought a standard for their home computers and lit upon MSX, said to mean either Microsoft Extended BASIC or Machines with Software Exchangeability

MSX was conceived by the Microsoft ASCII VP, Kazuhiko Nishi, in mid-1983 and it had the early support of software developers such as Konami, Sega, Taito and Hudson Soft. Microsoft ASCII was an overseas sales office for Microsoft set up with an established publishing company.

Nishi's proposal attempted to create a standard for 8-bit home computer makers. His thinking was to avoid the blood-letting of the all-too-fresh battles of the Betamax and VHS standards for video recorders.

The standard initially met a good reception. It was adopted by Spectravideo in the USA, by Philips of the Netherlands, GoldStar in Korea (Samsung and Daewoo followed later) and a who's who of Japanese companies - Canon, Casio, Fujitsu, Hitachi, JVC, Mitsubishi, National Panasonic, Pioneer, Sanyo, Sony, Toshiba, Yamaha, Yashica-Kyocera. Even a Kuwaiti company, Al Almayeh, joined the party.

MSX was specified around a pre-existing Spectravideo SV 318 and was defined to use readily available components. Of course they would use MSX BASIC from Microsoft, usually with the Zilog Z-80 MPU, a standard TI graphics chip, a GI and an Intel I/O controller. MSX units usually used a proper keyboard rather than the then popular 'chiclet' form.

It came too late to make a real impact in the States and Western Europe and never made it as a global standard. Some 5m units were sold with MSX on board, many to Eastern Europe and Brazil.

As the Apple II only sold 6m units and the Atari 8-bit computers only 4m it was not however globally insignificant; though the Commodore 64 sold over 17m units.

The standard later had a small revival in the noughties, but never really caught on.

Selection process for the IBM PC

IBM's secretive Acorn product had a rushed deadline and of course it needed available software to annexe all the current software out there.

IBM assessed that the required software was readily available in the marketplace and drew the obvious conclusion that what they needed to do, given their haste, was to acquire an existing operating system and software language.

CP/M was the most attractive OS of the moment with widespread adoption and a host of third party software released based upon it.

Perhaps because Microsoft produced a hardware card that enabled CP/M to function with the Apple II, the IBM team was somehow confused because they first called at Microsoft to acquire the operating system for Acorn.

Gates must have wanted to bite off his tongue but he did correct the error and direct them to meet up with Kildall at DRI.

The IBM-ers duly turned up at DRI and were apparently unprepared to talk until a very one-sided NDA (non-disclosure agreement) was signed.

Dorothy Kildall was reported to be alone at the office when they came calling; Gary has been variously described as away from the office using his light aircraft for fun or, in some accounts of that day, he was using it for a business trip. Whichever it was, he wasn't there and in his absence Dorothy refused to sign the document without his advice and input.

Kildall himself reported that they did meet later but he concluded that he was too busy to take on the task. Still further versions of the tale were that the non-disclosure agreement was indeed signed but then progress was halted when IBM required a one-time payment arrangement and Digital demanded its normal ongoing licence arrangement.

Whichever it was, failing to make effective progress at Digital, IBM returned to Microsoft. Gates was clearly prepared to sign the non-disclosure and to get into a proper discussion with them. Once the NDA was signed the IBM team outlined the Chess project and the plans for Acorn.

IBM's other purpose with Microsoft was to acquire a ROM-based BASIC which of course was known as Microsoft's forte. This was when it became clear to Microsoft that IBM was seeking an 8-bit solution.

Gates recommended they should instead adopt a 16-bit processor approach and this opened up a new 'can of worms' for IBM, and somewhat conveniently a new front for Microsoft to exploit. It knew that at the time CP/M had only been released for 8-bit microprocessors.

Microsoft was certainly aware that Digital was working on a 16-bit version called CP/M-86, targeted at Intel's 8086 and 8088 microprocessors. But IBM's own NDA had insisted that signatories should not release any proprietary information of which they were aware, so Microsoft had sufficient reason not to mention this knowledge.

It is unclear whether IBM had ever been made aware of this by DRI. They may have been informed and simply assessed that they were unlikely to reliably hit the tight deadlines with an uncertain completion date for CP/M 86.

Microsoft had no such OS product, but Paul Allen knew of another operating system produced by a nearby organisation called Seattle Computer Products (SCP). It was originally called QDOS (quick and dirty operating system). It had been written in just two months and was later renamed more elegantly the 86-DOS.

SCP had been in the S-100 expansion board market and then developed one of the early computer kits based around the 16-bit Intel 8086 microprocessor. But they found that sales were slow because of the lack of an operating system. To them DRI appeared to be taking its own sweet time about getting its CP/M-86 developed to address this market.

Tim Paterson, then a bright 24-year old, was charged by SCP to develop its own version. He certainly based his QDOS upon CP/M but also diligently set about enhancing it where he saw shortcomings, in particular in file management.

He had met microcomputers while at Seattle University and had a roommate whom he influenced to buy an IMSAI 8080 - that he could then use. He took a job in a local computer store where he met Rod Brock of SCP as the store retailed his S-100 cards. Regular meetings led to him being appointed a consultant at SCP. Paterson is quoted as saying about the OS task that he was given,

'I was waiting for Digital to come out with CP/M-86. I thought they would have it real soon. If they had beat me I wouldn't have taken the trouble. I had always wanted to write my own operating system. I've always hated CP/M and thought I could do it a lot better.'

Microsoft agreed to supply IBM with both an operating system and BASIC; this was a major departure for them and broke an unwritten belief that had been held by Kildall, that DRI did the OSs and MS did languages.

Microsoft initially paid for a non-exclusive licence for 86-DOS from SCP and directly contracted Paterson himself to accommodate it onto the IBM PC; of course without identifying it as such. A few months later Microsoft bought out all the rights to it from SCP for just $50,000. The resultant OS was named MS-DOS by Microsoft and supplied on a non-exclusive basis to IBM as PC-DOS.

When SCP realised that Microsoft had acquired its OS for the IBM PC and watched the massive revenues they were achieving, it took legal action. Microsoft eventually settled this with an additional $1 million payment.

Gary Kildall's company DRI also claimed that the MS-DOS and PC-DOS infringed its CP/M operating system. They had finally come up with their 16-bit version CP/M-86 and merely used the threat of legal action to reach an agreement with IBM for them to offer CP/M-86 as an alternative operating system to MS-DOS/ PC-DOS on the IBM PC. But with MS-DOS priced at $60 and CP/M-86 System at $170 this proved a pyrrhic victory.

There was a third OS offered with the IBM PC that few recall; this was UCSD Pascal P-System, a platform-independent system. Offered at $450 with next to no application software available for it there can be little surprise that it never really featured too heavily in the charts.

Microsoft was dominant as the supplier of both the IBM PC's MS-BASIC and MS-DOS. Because of this central role with these two key items of software it also required Microsoft's involvement in every decision on the hardware as well.

Whether it was the keyboard format and layout, the way the graphics were formatted, the way it generated and handled sound - all these features needed to be handled by the OS. In fact Gates indicated that as a result they ended up making many decisions for IBM along the way.

Intriguingly Microsoft was recompensed for its consulting role and of course had licence revenues from its software, but it was not judged worthy of being invited to the formal launch of the product.

Launch of the IBM PC

The IBM PC was launched using a Charlie Chaplin advertising campaign; perhaps unconsciously seeking to distance itself from its tag 'Big Blue' by using the 'little tramp'? It appears that this was the first personal computer that actually had the term PC as a part of its name.

Its marketing had to be all new too as its mainstream business had been predicated on its sales and engineering personnel developing a regular face-to-face relationship with its customers. At the price of the PC this would not be practical.

It was H L Sparks that was charged with selling to retailers, both new consumer electronic outlets and more traditional multiples and departmental stores.

At the IBM PC announcement on 12 August 1981 competitors tried to suggest that it was insignificant. John Roach, the president of Tandy, said,

'I don't think it's that significant... ...there is nothing that IBM has presented that would blow the industry away.'

Tandy was to be effectively gone as a PC contender by the end of the '80s.

Apple took a tongue-in-cheek full-page advert in the Wall Street Journal saying,

'Welcome IBM. Seriously.'

The use of truncated sentences in Garamond font became a fad at Apple. By 1983 the PC and its clones would be selling three times the number of Apple IIs.

So despite its hasty conception, its open architecture, its thin capabilities and the scoffing of its opponents, the market reception far exceeded even IBM's ambitions for it.

The internal forecasts were that perhaps 240,000 units might sell across an assumed five-year lifespan; in fact it lasted for six years. Before launch its own staff pre-ordered 30,000 units for themselves and a presentation made the day before its formal launch to a dealer conference in Toronto generated around 250,000 unit orders. On launch day a further 250,000 units were ordered.

At the end of calendar year 1981 Radio Shack was the market leader with a 20% share, Apple had 17% and IBM in just four months had sold 13.500 units to earn a 2% share. During 1982 IBM shipped between 150k and 180k units taking a 19% share, already a serious challenge to Radio Shack selling 215k units and Apple at 300k. By 1985 the PC peaked at a little over 50% of the market.

The IBM PC or 5150 did have a professional look and feel. It was supplied with a good keyboard, based on its Datamaster 'sister', and it had a professional monitor. But it had limited memory and initially loading and saving was only via cassette.

Though it was a 16-bit computer it was not as capable as some of its 8-bit rivals. The basic 16k version was $1,565, but if you wanted 64k, a floppy drive and monitor it would set you back $3,000. A full business configuration with twin drives and a printer was around $4,500.

The IBM PC at launch was not a very competent product but it achieved an opening of the PC floodgates by finally making it legitimate for IT departments within large corporates and institutions to purchase a personal computer. All those DP managers who had probably bought a PC personally were now able to buy them on behalf of their organisation because IBM gave it the patina of respectability.

IBM saw its PC merely as a short-term entry-level product that would build awareness and business for its more serious computer products, and it was to some extent caught unawares by its success. The departure from the normal approach of in-house development on technologies it controlled had been replaced by an open architecture which permitted the clones to move in.

The IBM market assumptions for its PC had several flaws.

It believed that its market was small businesses or off-line departments within a large business and that these would have a single task in mind. No multitasking was built in to the IBM PC capabilities. This became rapidly evident as wrong thinking; independent software developers did come up with neat ways around the problem within their own packages.

It had also developed a new ISA bus for the IBM PC, meaning the plethora of S-100 expansion cards were not compatible. It may just have been that IBM saw this as a benefit, some degree of control, but it also involved a high degree of risk. Would third parties develop for it?

By launching primarily with PC-DOS 1.0 on-board it was launching without any back catalogue of software which users might draw upon, though CP/M was offered as an option in an attempt to harness its large library. At launch IBM had negotiated to have a VisiCalc version available and Captain Crunch's (John Draper) EasyWriter followed a little later.

Back in June 1980 IBM's Office Products Division launched the Displaywriter text processor. This was an MPU-based product consisting of a typewriter-like keyboard, a CPU box, floppy drive and printer with a capacity for 100 pages of text.

It had a 50,000 word dictionary for spell checking, it could indent, justify and underline and mail merge - all very novel at the time. It cost $7,895 or could be rented at $275 per month. The on-board software was then repackaged as a Displaywrite word processing package for the IBM PC.

Throughout 1982 software and peripherals were announced for the IBM PC as it picked up some momentum. It was also in 1982 that IBM learned the anti-trust action taken against it way back in 1969 had been dismissed as 'without merit'. They must have been feeling pretty good!

In a move to secure its supply and access to future technology, IBM acquired a 12% interest in Intel for $250m in December 1982. Intel was coming under pressure at the time from Japanese competition in a market that was shrinking. But as the market improved and Intel shares rose sharply IBM sold much of its holding during 1986 and 1987 realising a sizeable profit.

In January 1983 Lotus 1-2-3 was released and rapidly became the 'killer app' for the IBM PC. Its integrated spreadsheet, graphics and database was the first PC software advertised on television and it drove PC sales forward.

So now the 70-stone gorilla had eventually emerged and taken its seat at the PC table; this led to others being inspired to enter the PC market. This was greatly assisted by the fact that IBM had gone for an open architecture and much of its approach was based around off-the-shelf technologies.

Sending in the clones - copyrighting a ROM?

Before we look at how the IBM compatibles and clones were able to supplant the PC original it is useful to consider a precedent that was fought out in the US courts when Apple took Franklin Computer Corporation to task.

Joel Shusterman had established a major Apple dealership in the Philadelphia area and was joined there by two experienced computer engineering individuals, Russell Bower and R Barry Borden. They set about designing their own computer.

Franklin launched the Ace 100 and Ace 1000 systems as copies of the Apple II and Apple II+ computers; the computers' printed circuit boards and the content of the ROMs was virtually identical to those of the Apple.

Apple was able to see and show that large parts of the Franklin ROM software had been a straight lift of the Apple code. For example the name of one of its programmers, John Huston, and the term AppleSoft had even been replicated within the Franklin software.

Franklin admitted to the copying; how could it do otherwise? But it countered strongly. It suggested that as the software was in machine code it was an engineering item and not a written document that could be copyrighted.

It stressed that a ROM is a three-dimensional device not a two-dimensional printed document and that it was unreadable directly by human beings. It postulated that an OS is an idea and ideas could not be copyrighted.

It also maintained that by not being permitted to make its computer compatible Apple would be adversely limiting the market potential of software authors and expansion card makers who had Apple-compatible products.

In short it embroiled the action in the antitrust laws of the USA which protect market competition against any anti-competitive actions.

The District Court for the Eastern District of Pennsylvania found in Franklin's favour. But three days later, in the United States Court of Appeals for the Third Circuit, Apple had this overturned and established that programs and operating systems whether in a ROM or elsewhere were able to be copyrighted.

In 1984 Franklin paid Apple $2.5 million in damages for copyright infringement of the OS used on the Apple II and agreed to cease selling the cloned OS by April 1.

Undaunted Franklin came back later with the Ace 2000 and Ace 500, copies of the Apple IIe and Apple IIc; it would also launch several IBM PC clones.

Franklin Computer was eventually harried out of the business, filing for Chapter 11. It emerged from this in February 1985, when Morton David became chairman of the board and presided over it becoming one of the largest players in hand-held electronic products.

In 1984 VTech (Video Technology) a Hong Kong based company issued the Laser 128 computer as a clone of the Apple IIc with an increased expansion potential.

Apple took legal action against VTech too. But the Far East company was able to show that it had 'reverse engineered' the software. This is a process of looking at what each of the processes achieved and then recreating it without in any way using the Apple code itself.

VTech was greatly assisted by the fact that it was able to license the AppleSoft BASIC, a foundation of the Apple software, from Microsoft and this minimised the amount they needed to reproduce. VTech defeated Apple in the courts.

Sears Roebuck marketed the VTech products strongly and it proved so successful that Apple moved to counter it by introducing the Apple IIc Plus. VTech responded in turn with its Laser 128EX and Laser EX2.

Apple later had some success when the International Trade Commission issued a USA exclusion order on the importation of Apple-alike computers manufactured in Taiwan.

But all these actions were being watched very carefully by those who were thinking of producing clones of the IBM.

Columbia and Eagle

If you wanted to build a clone of the IBM PC then you would wish it to work with all the pre-existing and third party hardware, expansion cards, peripherals and software that had been developed by third parties for the platform.

Yet the only thing on the IBM PC that was proprietary was the BIOS (basic input/output system). BIOS was originally a work-around developed by Gary Kildall to make his CP/M readily portable to different systems. IBM's BIOS connected the operating system with the unique configuration of the hardware of the IBM PC.

IBM was not offering to sell the contents of its ROM; its BIOS was copyrighted as they knew it was its only unique element. The Apple v Franklin judgment had stopped anyone ripping it off. But copyright is granted as specific to the actual code itself so if you could write your own that would emulate all the functions without actually copying IBM's code then you would be on to a winner!

The cloning of the IBM BIOS proved to be an obvious opportunity for Microsoft and this would open up new OEM deals for MS-DOS; this also drove sales for the increasing number of Microsoft languages and applications.

So once again Microsoft being among the first was significant, particularly once they had burned off the other two OSs. The first of these, UCSD Pascal P-System, was expensive and cumbersome. Defeating the other, CP/M, with its software back catalogue was rather more of an achievement.

Initially the Microsoft OEM deals were conventional in that the PC manufacturer contracted for a DOS that would be named for the host PC, but Microsoft soon switched its approach and insisted that the manufacturer call it MS-DOS.

Microsoft further assisted the process by promoting the notion that programmers could use its APIs (application programming interfaces) set within MS-DOS so that software authors could apply them in preparing any applications for the IBM PC.

In June 1982 Columbia Data Products launched the first compatible PC, the MPC 1600 (multi personal computer). This copied almost all the features of the IBM PC. It used IBM's published structures and reverse-engineered the IBM PC's BIOS to be fully compatible.

At just $2,995 it cost $1,500 less than the IBM PC. It was a clone but it also offered advances on its host with 128K RAM versus the IBM's 64K; it had eight expansion slots versus IBM's five; two of these on the IBM were also reserved for use with the video and disk controller cards. The Columbia MPC 1600 also had floppy drives, a parallel and two serial ports - all optional extras with the IBM PC.

Columbia sales were over $9m in 1982; it had an initial public offering at the beginning of 1983 and finished that year with revenues of well over $50m. But by 1985, as others made this clone market crowded and competitive, its shares crashed and it was delisted with its name and assets being sold to a private business. This new operation moved in to producing small computer system interface software for others.

Eagle Computers already had a business in CP/M based computers when in 1982 it launched a close copy of the IBM PC named the Eagle 1600. This used MS-DOS, included hard disks and had a massive 640k of RAM.

It was not a full clone as it used an 8086 MPU, the IBM PC's 8088 was 16-bit internally but had only 8-bit capability for its external interfaces; Eagle's 8086 was full 16-bit throughout.

Eagle's initial public offering in June 1983 was not at all smooth. On the day of the IPO, Eagle president Dennis Barnhart was already living the dream. He had been lunching with a yacht salesman and after the meal he crashed his new Ferrari and was killed.

The underwriters withdrew the IPO and refunded all investments. It was brought back to the market several months later but its value had been radically reduced.

IBM enjoined Eagle in a legal action claiming infringement of its BIOS. Eagle and others settled out of court and Eagle set about rewriting its BIOS. It never really recovered from the setback and by 1986 was out of business.

It was not just North America that was cloning. In 1983 Olivetti launched its IBM PC clone, the M24. It proved to be extremely compatible at a time when many clones were not. It could run both Lotus 1-2-3 and Flight Simulator; these were often used as clone yardsticks at the time.

Reverse engineering - Compaq, Phoenix, Zenith

Compaq Computer was a company that approached cloning differently. It was formed in February 1982 by three ex-Texas Instrument senior managers, Rod Canion, Jim Harris and Bill Murto; each put in $1,000 capital.

They originally founded the operation to build a disk drive for the IBM PC but the funding for this particular enterprise fell through. With subsequent investment from Ben Rosen, the writer of newsletters and venture capitalist, they pursued a personal computer of their own; Rosen became their chairman.

The very name Compaq identifies their objectives exactly; it was based upon the words compatibility and quality; though some suggest this was stated as an afterthought. It sought 100% compatibility with the IBM PC so the product would work with all the hardware, peripherals and software out there. Without these it could see there would be a real barrier to uptake of the new computer; with full compatibility it would be off and running.

A team of software programmers was given the task of reverse engineering the IBM PC BIOS code. It cost many man months and over $1 million to get it right, but they made it; this effort ensured there could be no IBM legal action.

The Compaq Portable was announced in November 1982 with the stance that it would not only be fully compatible but also a tad cheaper than the IBM at $2,995. It was a luggable, in the Osborne mould, which gave it another unique selling proposition against the IBM.

Sparky Sparks was one of the first six senior managers at the IBM PC Company involved in its marketing, but he had soon become the distribution supremo. Compaq lured him to join them and offer dealers a slightly improved margin. Sparks established some 1,800 dealers for Compaq.

Compaq was also to recruit a number of key people from the IBM PC team including Jim d'Arrezzo and Ross Cooley; together with Sparks, the three are often cited as the powerhouse that drove the Compaq success.

Compaq sold around 50,000 computers in its first year turning over $111m, the highest first year revenue recorded in US corporate history.

But to pigeonhole Compaq as merely a clone-maker would be unjust.

It built on this good start with the range of Deskpro desktop PCs. It worked closely with Intel and in 1986 beat IBM to the market with the Deskpro 386, the first 80386-based PC; it was three-times faster than anything IBM had delivered.

Compaq then set about launching a server product. It concluded not to use the IBM MCA bus (micro channel architecture) and with HP and others developed an alternative called EISA (extended industry standard architecture). The Compaq Systempro server was its first server launched in late 1989 with EISA aboard.

In the early 1990s it added the Presario range, featured and priced to go after the home and executive markets at a retail cost of less than $1,000.

Compaq would go on to acquire Tandem Computers for its server series in 1997 and Digital Equipment Corporation (DEC) in 1998. Its progress and acquisitions made it the second largest computer manufacturer in the world. Compaq also became the youngest firm to be listed in the *Fortune 500*.

It was acquired by Hewlett Packard in 2002 for $25bn.

Phoenix Technologies Ltd was formed in 1979 by Neil Colvin, appropriately named as his previous employer had gone out of business and he had hired others from the company to form this new operation.

Originally it acquired a licence from Seattle Computer Products (the QDOS people who originated what became MS-DOS) for its 86-DOS operating system and created platform-specific OSs based around this.

Phoenix too set a team of programmers to produce a BIOS that was untainted by the IBM code but it did not want to produce its own PCs; instead it sold its BIOS ROMs to those who did want to produce a clone.

Zenith Data Systems (ZDS) was formed as a subsidiary of Zenith Electronics after it acquired the Heathkit business in 1979. Heathkit had developed the H-100 computer kit and ZDS created a fully-built version named the Z-100 in mid 1981.

ZDS later partnered with Microsoft offering all its languages with the Zenith computers and soon was making IBM PC compatibles.

Zenith took the USA market leadership in both 1987 and 1988 as a result of its deals with the US IRS and then the US Air Force. It was acquired by Groupe Bull for $511m in October 1989; in March 1996 Packard Bell in turn acquired Zenith.

Action and reaction – the PC XT

Suddenly a compatible IBM PC became a commodity product. You no longer needed to buy an IBM per se which was any way often short on supply - and much more expensive. You could purchase a clone and it would operate with everything that was available for the IBM PC. This was great news for expansion board makers and software writers too, as their market universe expanded rapidly.

So IBM's only proprietary item had offered them little protection; they had to start innovating to stay ahead of the clones. But now the principle was established they would be constantly harried by innovative companies emulating each of their steps.

Clearly IBM would not rest on its laurels and it quickly responded, maintaining a very non-IBM pace to its introduction of new products. It split its team into three, one to develop the PC XT, one the Peanut or PCjr and the other the Circus or the PC AT.

First the PC itself was beefed up to become more of a business computer. In March 1983 the IBM PC XT (extended technology) aka the model 5160 was launched

Still based around the 8088 MPU, it came with PC-DOS 2.0. The original 128k of memory at launch was soon further expanded to 256k. It had a better graphics card and it included an internal 10 MByte hard drive for $4,995.

One of the appeals of the XT was that it apparently had eight expansion slots, whereas the 5150 had just five. In fact the extra three were taken up by the disk drivers (a floppy and a hard disk) and its Async card. Also slot eight proved not to be standard, it was prepped for use as a terminal and as a result some cards would not work in it.

Slot eight was in fact designed so that a version of the XT named the 3270 PC could be offered as a low-cost terminal to mainframes at just $4,290.

Another variant, the PC XT/370, was launched to emulate the System/370 which was IBM's 1970s mainframe successor to the 360 range.

This launch succeeded against competitors and by December 1983 it passed a milestone as one million IBM PCs had been sold.

In a direct response to Compaq and others, IBM launched its own portable IBM PC, the 5155 in February 1984. Based on the 8088 MPU it used the PC XT motherboard.

It was also introduced with PC-DOS 2.0, having twin floppy-drives and an amber display. It was a luggable pluggable; it weighed 30 lbs (13.6kg) but it had no batteries so needed a mains supply. A few tens of thousands were sold and it was eventually discontinued in 1986.

A PC for peanuts – PCjr

Sticking with the 8088 MPU, IBM next released the IBM PCjr or model 4860 in November 1983, though it was not actually available until spring 1984. The 'jr' meaning junior of course, it was to be a 'lite' PC. This ran PC-DOS 2.1, had a floppy-drive and addressed the educational and home computer markets. It was available in 64k and 128k versions at just $669 or $1269.

It was intended to be fully compatible with the PC but this proved to be not entirely the case because of its limited memory; in fact it proved less compatible than many other manufacturers. Less than 50% of the pre-existing software worked on PCjr, and this did not include WordStar, Lotus 1-2-3 and Flight Simulator!

PCjr had better screen management, and for its consumer credentials it included 16-colour graphics, 3-voice sound, two joystick ports and two ROM cartridge slots. It had an IR wireless or wired keyboard and a lightpen port, which was later used for an optical mouse. But damagingly it proved even slower that the original PC.

The PCjr used what we in the UK call a rubber keyboard and the United States call a 'chiclet' keyboard. It is made using a single slab of moulded rubber to form all the keys. In the US it was thought to resemble chewing gum, hence the name. This made it appear even less serious. The approach of course avoided a slew of components and mechanical elements but it proved unpopular as the feel was not positive. The PCjr version also encountered some technical problems.

Some business users bought it as a low-cost PC only to find that it was not interchangeable without buying a Tecmar Systems expansion card to make up for its lack of a direct memory access controller (DMA). This lack of DMA also meant when the floppy drive was running the keyboard was disabled!

Its price was twice that of the Commodore 64 or the Atari 400 and 800 and the home market proved tough to penetrate even though it had the attraction of being a 16-bit PC. The Apple IIe and IIc, the Atari ST and Commodore Amiga soon followed and further exposed the PCjr strategy as flawed.

PCjr was in real trouble when the Apple Mac was announced to a flurry of interest in January 1984. Soon the 1,400 appointed PCjr dealers in the USA were reporting that they had not even sold through their initial 25 unit stock allocations.

At a meeting in April 1984 the IBM chairman John Opel announced that the PCjr would get a makeover and admitted it was not performing to forecast levels. He also defended its position against Apple by saying,
'We expect to keep our technology leadership.'

Others were less kind. William Bowman of Spinnaker Software said,
'We're just sitting here trying to put our PCjrs in a pile and burn them. And the damn things won't burn. That's the only thing IBM did right with it - they made it flameproof.'

That meeting was also significant in that it marked the end of an IBM dynasty. The PCjr was ailing and Thomas Watson Jr had reached the mandatory age of retirement which was seventy. By then he and his father had served at the pinnacle of the corporation for seventy years!

The industry, presumably prompted by IBM, had forecast a sales range for the PCjr of 250,000 to 480,000 in the first six months. When this was not happening IBM offered a free exchange of the keyboard; this exercise made clear that at that point they had sold only 60,000 units.

PCjr lasted in production for just a year; IBM had had its first PC flop. Intriguingly however Radio Shack was undaunted when it decided to clone the PCjr with its Tandy 1000 and this did prove to be relatively successful.

Let's have another try – PC AT

During 1983 to 1984 a range of graphics user interfaces (GUIs) started to emerge - user-friendly systems like the Xerox Star, VisiCorp's VisiOn, DEC's GEM and the Apple Mac OS. Windows was beginning to make its tortuous route towards the market and IBM had to respond to this; its DOS was beginning to look archaic.

In August 1984 IBM moved its PC product radically forward launching the model 5170 or IBM AT (advanced technology). The AT was the first in the series to have real business and scientific capabilities; yet it had no GUI!

This new PC was based on the Intel 80286 MPU and initially ran at 6 MHz, later increased to 8 MHz; it was thus five times faster than the XT and came with better features.

The MPU's real virtue was that it had multi-tasking built in and, better still, it was able to work with the software developed for the 8088. IBM also upgraded the bus for the AT while maintaining it as backwards compatible with the PC and XT.

It came with PC-DOS 3.0 in two versions. The model 1 had 256K of RAM, two floppy drives and a colour screen. Model 2 had 512K of RAM with one floppy drive and a 20 MByte hard drive; the software enabled file-sharing. The hard drives did have some early problems but this was resolved by changing the drive to a new 30 MByte version.

The launch of the AT was the last occasion that IBM was able to set the pace with a specification. From thereon the PC truly became a generic commodity product and took on a life of its own, quite outside IBM's control.

Aware that this was happening, IBM had sought to trademark the name AT, but the clone makers adopted and popularised the term 286 to represent the series of products that were launched to mirror its capabilities.

In 1985 IBM appointed a new CEO John Akers. By August that year the need for local area networking of PCs was becoming clear and IBM chose not to go with the evolving standard, Ethernet. Instead it developed its own Token Ring. Shielded twisted pair cables connected up PCs that were arrayed in a ring format; messages had a prefixed control token to identify them and this was passed around at 4 Mbits per second. This was promoted as superior to Ethernet, but the latter evolved more quickly and took the market leadership.

IBM, during the mid '80s, published its SAA (Systems Application Architecture) standards seeking to enable software to operate across its platform, from PC to mainframe. It later learned that businesses wanted portability across different manufacturers and launched Open Blueprint to propose how this might be managed.

It was all getting personal – PS/2

In 1987 IBM tried to regain the PC initiative by developing its third generation product, the IBM PS/2 (personal system). It launched four models – Model 30 using a fast 8086 MPU, Models 50 and 60 with the 80286 and Model 80 with the 80386. Pricing ranged from $2,595 up to just under $11,000.

It was a big ask because they needed to ensure it could still work with all the prior PC XT and AT software and peripherals to take advantage of the wealth of material already available. It was supposed to be launched at the same time as a new IBM owned OS/2, but this was late.

This compatibility objective gave it a split personality, using two quite separate BIOSes. Compatible BIOS allowed it to be backward compatible with the pre-existing material, Advanced BIOS offered access to the new and improved OS/2 features.

A new 32-bit bus was developed for the PS/2 series called MCA (Microchannel Architecture) but this meant that there was no backward compatibility with expansion boards from the PC XT and AT.

Unfortunately they also tried a sequential launch and the first PS/2 was released with only part of the MCA capabilities, saving some for a later v2.0 launch; this meant the PS/2 was slow. Other shortfalls would later be uncovered like poor grounding and a limit on the number of input-output addresses.

There was a further complication with MCA when IBM expected developers to pay royalty on any cards they created for the PS/2 and then expected them to back-pay for any they had made for the PC, XT and AT!

The clone industry simply stuck with the ISA bus approach where there had been no control. A 'gang of nine' clone makers (AST, Compaq, Epson, HP, NEC, Olivetti, Tandy, Wyse and Zenith) got together in 1988 and developed their own EISA (extended industry standard architecture) bus that was fully compatible with XT and AT boards.

OS/2 also had a difficult birth. IBM was disenchanted that it had permitted Microsoft to retain the rights in DOS that had proved so lucrative for the software company. It saw PS/2 and OS/2 as an opportunity to introduce some proprietary control over the PC operating software.

In August 1985 IBM and Microsoft signed a joint development agreement to produce this next generation of OS for the PC. Significantly this time the software would be owned and managed by IBM; Microsoft would not be empowered to license it to third parties.

Prior to the Microsoft agreement IBM had considered developing its own OS internally and even looked at a Linux approach. They initially called this CP/DOS (control program DOS). The project was slow to bear fruit, in part since of course Microsoft dragged its heels somewhat because of its own plans for Windows.

But things moved rather rapidly now. OS/2 1.0, released in April 1987, had multitasking as a central plank of its design but it was a text-mode only product; it had no GUI at a time when the market was very much demanding one.

When OS/2 1.1 was released in October 1988 it had a GUI, called Presentation Manager. This release also enabled more complex and higher capacity disk drives to be controlled by the OS. But just as the Macintosh Mac OS had proved to add so much overhead to the programmer's task and learning curve, so too did this GUI. Independent software developers were turned off by this time premium.

The OS/2 1.1 Extended Edition was an IBM-only version that offered a data manager, a relational database, and a communications manager with a mainframe terminal emulation.

OS/2/1.2 followed in May 1989 and introduced more file naming-flexibility and better disk operations; it added Ethernet and TCP/IP (transmission control protocol/internet protocol) capabilities.

The pressures between IBM and Microsoft grew, particularly when Windows 3.0 proved to be the first successful manifestation of that software. Windows started to be bundled with many new PC clones and this helped to make it a great success.

IBM was by then preparing to launch OS/2 1.3, the first all-IBM version, and starting to plan for OS/2 2.0, the first truly 32-bit OS. But it became extremely concerned that monies given to Microsoft for OS/2 development were being applied to its own Windows development.

It was concluded that IBM press ahead itself with OS/2 2.0 and Microsoft would look at OS/2 3.0, a platform-independent network server version; the latter would eventually be the basis for Microsoft's Windows NT.

But by then Windows was already on its way to market dominance.

16 – Getting into Apple-pie order
'Never trust a computer you can't throw out a window.' Steve Wozniak

Apple III problems
At the end of September 1980 (Apple's 1979-80 financial year) showed that it had sold 79,500 Apple IIs and turned over $117m; with a 10% net profit. In December 1980 it launched the Apple III and projecting a continued success it mounted its very successful initial public offering.

The Apple III was the outcome of Apple's Sara project; it was the first Apple computer not been designed by Wozniak. Instead it was conceived by an ever-changing organisation where management and marketing was progressively taking over from dreaming and designing.

It decided to respond to the launch of the IBM PC by creating Apple III as a business computer and it certainly came up with something that was a clear improvement on the early IBM PC.

It also managed to remedy some of the architecture and operating system issues of the Apple II. For example the DOS 3.3 system on the Apple II needed specific peripherals to be placed in specific slots for them to work. The Apple III's DOS was named Apple SOS (pronounced 'sauce') to make it expandable and it had a more competent Apple III Business BASIC, with a subsequent option to add UCSD Pascal.

Being keen to link the Apple III to the breadth of software that evolved for the Apple II, the company came up with a compromise. The Apple III could either utilise all of its features or it could be switched down to emulate the Apple II for use with pre-existing software. But this was an either/or option; you could not use an Apple II piece of software and apply the new features of the Apple III to it as well.

Apple III also had a planned systems utilities program for configuring the system and the manipulation of files. There was also Selector III to launch applications, but neither was completed.

A young organisation called Quark Engineering was formed by Tim Gill and Mark Pope at Denver, Colorado in 1981. They initially designed a word processor for the Apple II and Apple III called Word Juggler and went on to develop Catalyst to allow users to run applications software from a floppy disk, just as Selector III had been intended to do.

But the real issue the Apple III encountered was that the first batch, some 14,000 units had a 'robotic' problem. The automatic insertion of chips onto the boards did not push them in firmly enough and this led to a raft of problems for users. At one point Apple even advised its customers to pick up the Apple III and drop it onto the desk to try to remedy the problem.

It was also established that during the flow soldering of the components the solder would sometimes create a bridge between components that were not intended to be connected. Add to this the fact that for aesthetic reasons Steve Jobs insisted that Jerry Manock the designer should not include any air vents on the Apple III, this decision too led to overheating problems.

The first 14,000 units were exchanged for new ones with new boards. The redesign and relaunch were all completed professionally and reasonably promptly, but a computer product seldom gets a second chance. Apple III was tainted by this episode and never really recovered from it.

At its high price points from $4,340 to $7,800, users expected perfection straight from the box. Of course if it was a business that was relying on the computer then any problems like these would lead to the consideration of other suppliers.

The final production total was just 65,000 units before it was discontinued in April 1984. This did however serve to extend the life and variants of the Apple II which was no bad thing.

Apple visits PARC and designs the Lisa

Fortunately there was another development in process at the Cupertino base of Apple. This had started back in 1978 within the Personal Office Systems team; the project was named Lisa.

The official history of Apple says this stands for Local Integrated Software Architecture but as Steve Jobs' first daughter Lisa was born that year you might wish to draw your own conclusion?

While Steve Jobs presided over the project initially, many engineers learned that he was a difficult person with whom to work. To Jobs' chagrin it was therefore John Couch who was selected to take over the Personal Office Systems team and to manage Lisa. Couch was an ex-Hewlett Packard engineer who had joined initially as Director of New Products, working directly for Jobs.

It was Mike Scott, Apple's then president, who appointed Couch to the role. Couch went on to develop Lisa with a team featuring such Apple luminaries as Bill Atkinson, Trip Hawkins, Rich Page, Jef Raskin, Wayne Rosing, Larry Tesler... Some 90+ people would work on the Lisa project; many would later become big PC hitters in their own right.

Raskin had been at Stanford's AI Lab and spent a lot of time at Xerox PARC; he was also a professor of visual arts at UCSD. He went on to develop Swyft, a laptop PC, and was prolific in writing on the subject of the computer-human interface. He would become a real catalyst for the Apple Mac.

Bill Atkinson had been a student of Raskin, qualifying in computer science. He was close to getting his PhD in neurochemistry and created software graphically to present CAT (computerised axial tomography) scans.

Raskin lured him to Apple where his first role was to write its Pascal language; he was to be significant in both the Lisa and Mac teams.

Trip Hawkins would leave Apple to found Electronic Arts, later still he launched a video console business, 3DO, and a mobile video game development company called Digital Chocolate.

Rich Page (shouldn't he have centred his career in desktop publishing?) would later join Jobs at NeXT Computer.

Rosing started with DEC and Data General, became the director of engineering on Lisa, and would later join Sun where he worked on the Java language, before moving on to Google.

Tesler's pedigree was PARC. At Apple he worked on both Apple Lisa and Apple Newton, then would later move on to both Amazon.com and Yahoo!

John Couch presided over a development that owed a lot to his old employer and its HP 3000 minicomputer series, a product that originated in 1973 and stayed current for over thirty years. Lisa was originally quite closely defined around providing a low-cost PC with HP 3000-like capabilities.

Jef Raskin wrote the Integer Basic Manual for Apple II as an outside consultant and received the second-ever Apple II with which to do his work. He joined Apple and during his time working in the Lisa project team, it was he who urged the team to visit Xerox PARC.

Commercially the then world's leading personal computer maker Apple came face-to-face with the world's best think tank on computer science Xerox PARC. At last someone would set about doing something with the PARC concepts which would move from pure research into commercial products.

The Lisa team could not fail to be inspired by the visit. It was no surprise that Steve Jobs subsequently arranged a 100,000 pre-IPO share-option deal with Xerox to gain them additional time and access at PARC; though Raskin's reward for this was to be edged from the Lisa team by Jobs.

The team proceeded to implement the concepts they had seen at PARC to their Lisa product. It rapidly became a more expansive and expensive product. Fifteen of the PARC team moved across to Apple. But rather like the Xerox PARC products, Lisa became perhaps too expensive by being less market-driven and more of a features Christmas tree.

PARC showed them its concepts but it had never needed to think through its ideas to becoming a commercial product, it was left to Apple to perfect the approach.

Bill Atkinson pressed for and succeeded in getting the team to adopt the concept of emulating paper upon the Lisa screen. This meant it would have a white background, as did the Xerox Alto; before this time we had been offered only green or orange screens. But white screens tended to have a noticeable flicker and this had to be eliminated.

They also freshly commissioned a mouse, but what should it look like, how many buttons did it need? The PARC version originally had three coloured buttons, but later this was reduced to two - one to select, one to expand the selection.

Jerry Manock the Apple designer tried more than a hundred shapes and sizes before they lit on the one adopted; Tesler market-tested a number and concluded one button was the way forward, with single and double-click options.

Lisa was already planned to have a bit-mapped graphics output; now with PARC notions fresh in their mind they added in both the windows concept and icon-driven selections. With these they had a remarkable product that would be a step-function ahead of anything else on the market.

The Lisa team developed the click, drag and drop routines that we all know and use today. They created the method of resizing windows. These features bore the PARC gene but were also somehow pure Apple. For various reasons the menu bar was placed at the top of the screen it was necessary to flip the PARC notion of pop-up menus and create a drop-down alternative.

The team needed to define how the graphic user interface would deal with 'drawing' windows to sit in front of each other on the screen, particularly how to handle the portion of a window that sat behind another.

Atkinson and Andy Hertzfeld came up with LisaGraf which was soon renamed QuickDraw, a two-dimensional set of APIs (application programming interfaces). QuickDraw used coordinates to define the position and content of the screen and each window within it. Its coordinates sat between the pixels on a screen, such that a required pixel was drawn to the right and below this imaginary coordinate position. This was present in Mac OSs right the way up to OS X 10.3.

It was realised quite late in the day that the whole GUI needed an 'executive' which they called Desktop Manager to organise the Lisa's work surface; this user interface was initially written by Bill Atkinson.

Each new development had to be produced and tested; one of the driving principles of Lisa was that it could be used straight from the box.

There was very little available application software as it had no compatibility with any prior Apple or PC. Though it was shipped with seven packages – LisaWrite, a word processor; LisaCalc a spreadsheet; LisaGraph for charting; LisaList, a sort of brain mapper for managing ideas and tasks; LisaProject, a network analysis and PERT planner; LisaDraw a drawing program; LisaTerminal for communicating via modem, but, with the benefit of hindsight, quite significantly for a business computer it had no networking feature.

The twin Twiggy 5.25" floppy drives proved slow and unreliable, and these were soon replaced by two Sony 3.5" drives. On the face of it the 68000 processor was rated at five times the speed of the then current Apple IIe; it still used the aged 6502, but the OS and other features made Lisa perform much more slowly.

Apple spent $50m on the hardware and $100m on the software to create Lisa. It was launched in January 1983 with the headline,
'Apple invents the personal computer. Again.'

It was a truly remarkable computer, but it failed as it ended up as far too cumbersome. This contributed to it being too slow and it was also rather expensive at $9,995. Reputedly fewer than 100,000 were sold.

In 1989, to be assured of a tax write-off, Apple dumped 2,700 unsold Lisas into a guarded landfill site in Utah.

So Apple, who had set the PC world alight with the Apple I and Apple II, was then burned by both Apple III and Apple Lisa. Fortunately help was close at hand.

Jef Raskin defines and names the Macintosh

Jef Raskin had been edged out of the Lisa project, despite being the person who had arranged for the team to visit Xerox PARC where they had received their inspiration. Undeterred he continued to champion the notion of an easy-to-use and less-expensive personal computer within Apple; while the Lisa development seemed to get ever more complex and more expensive.

He presented his thoughts to Mark Markkula and was initially asked to look at a games console project, but later he gained the go-ahead to develop and expand his thoughts for a computer.

It was Raskin who came up with the name Macintosh based upon his favourite type of apple. The McIntosh, cultivated for its red colour, was a variety grown mostly in eastern North America.

He added the extra 'a' to avoid a clash with McIntosh Laboratory, a maker of high-end audio equipment. But that tweak was not enough for them to get trademark approval. Eventually Apple had to pay for a licence from the audio company which has been variously reported as costing either $100,000 to 'much more' than this.

Raskin envisioned the Macintosh as a $500 retail product. He wanted it to be portable as he planned that the product would be so indispensable to owners that they would want it with them at all times.

Raskin asked Bill Atkinson to join him in defining the hardware but he was too committed to Lisa. Burrell Smith had become interested early in MPUs and had had a brush with the Homebrew Computer Club in the mid '70s. Wishing to join Apple he found the only role available was that of a repairman for the Apple II. He said he had fixed around a thousand of them before Bill Atkinson recommended that Raskin recruit him to the nascent Mac team.

Andy Hertzfeld had bought himself an Apple II and developed software for it. He sold one of his programs to Apple and Jobs offered him a job.

Raskin lured Hertzfeld to become the third member of the Mac team. He notably worked on the software throwing an all-nighter to get it to display its first ever graphic image of Scrooge McDuck.

Even Steve Wozniak was attracted to the project, giving part-time support to the Mac team until his flying accident took him away for a protracted period.

So intriguingly all this meant the Macintosh sat well beneath the corporate radar, and as a result was more akin to the development of Apple I and II in its approach with dreamers defining them rather than being a product of the marketing machine that Apple had become.

This had its downsides too. If Raskin and his team put their heads above the parapet then they would run the risk of cursory cancellation. In fact the project was quite routinely axed but then reinstated.

Steve Jobs had been with the Lisa project through all the early phases and was a very vocal critic of the Mac project, calling it a stupid idea; perhaps this was why he later termed it 'insanely great'?

But this all changed when the Apple president Mike Scott had his Black Wednesday in February 1981 and fired half the Apple II team without first gaining board approval. As they were now a quoted company this was not acceptable behaviour and he was deposed in March.

All this internal attention and blood-letting could not have been timed more unhelpfully as it was of course taking place in the months leading up to the IBM PC being announced.

Markkula took over as president and he soon bounced Jobs from the Lisa project. Reviewing Raskin's work afresh Jobs turned his attention to the Macintosh project bringing his personal Xerox PARC revelations to the product. The two, Jobs and Raskin, had clashed at Lisa and were now set on a course to do so again with the Macintosh.

Raskin had unwisely written to Mike Scott just six days before his Black Wednesday gaffe criticising Jobs' management style or rather questioning if he had one at all. He suggested this was the opinion of the whole team, but subsequently he was the only one forced out; one too many pops above that parapet.

The Raskin Macintosh would have been more of a PDA, perhaps Newton-like, but now it would radically change direction.

After Apple, Raskin dedicated his energies to plans for the human-machine interface and produced a firmware card, SwyftCard, for the Apple II with an integrated applications package called SwyftWare.

Jobs takes the helm – redefining the Macintosh
The Macintosh project now proceeded under Jobs and it brought out the best in a whole team of individuals worthy of comment; the project developed

momentum. Even while Raskin was still present Jobs began to insert new members onto the team.

He added people like Jerry Manock, the industrial designer who had worked on Apple II and Apple III. Manock was given the task of creating a look-and-feel for the Macintosh that would make it portable, approachable and visually appealing.

From 1982 Manock was assisted by consultant designer Hartmut Esslinger and his company Frogdesign, a German operation based in Mutlangen, Baden-Württemberg. Frogdesign had produced exciting designs for Wega, for Sony and for Louis Vuitton and was appointed at a fee of $1m per year to transform Apple's design strategy and turn it into a recognisable global brand.

Esslinger evolved what was called the Snow White Design, it had a way of using vertical and horizontal stripes on the product casing both to conceal cooling slots and to make the case appear smaller, even if not quite dwarf-sized.

The White in the name had nothing to do with colour. In fact the design moved the products towards either fog (off-white) or platinum (light grey) colouring rather than the previous beige.

It was the implied seven (as in dwarfs) motif that provided the name; it was to be applied across seven products. However this effort was delivered for the first time on the Apple IIc and would miss the first Macs. Esslinger later broke his Apple contract to assist Jobs when he left to found NeXT.

Jobs also challenged Burrell Smith to design the Mac around the Motorola 68000 MPU, the same one used by Lisa. Under Raskin, Smith had based his first designs around the 6809E. Smith achieved the upgrade and with his design skills achieved a means whereby the Mac would run twice as fast as the Lisa.

Jobs is said to have believed that at last here was an Apple that he himself could be said to have 'designed'.

Bruce Horn was a student who had been engaged from the early age of thirteen with the Learning Research Group at Xerox PARC, where a team led by Alan Kay had developed the SmallTalk language. Horn worked with Larry Tesler (later a member of the Lisa team) in the development of graphic elements of the NoteTaker, a portable device using SmallTalk with a bitmap touchscreen display and mouse.

On the Mac team Horn was challenged primarily with producing Finder with the task of bettering Lisa's desktop manager software. The Finder was to be the first port of call for users, to open, save, copy and move files around and of course to find them again. Its problem was that it had to interact with every other file and yet not become so unwieldy in itself so that it might interfere with performance. He also produced the resource manager and worked on other Mac innovations.

Andy Hertzfeld qualified in computer science at the Ivy League Brown University, based in Providence, Rhode Island. Following through at the University of California, Berkeley he bought himself an Apple II in 1979. Joining the company his first role was to develop the firmware for SilenType, Apple's first printer. This was actually the Trendcom Model 200, badged as an Apple product. Hertzfeld also produced the first 80-column card for the Apple II.

For the Mac team Hertzfeld produced much of the system software, what became known much later as the Mac OS (Macintosh operating system), the engine of its graphical-user interface. The system part of the Mac OS very deliberately eliminated the command line that was the only prior means of talking with computers, making clear that it could only be operated graphically.

Hertzfeld would later leave Apple and write Switcher which he sold back to Apple. This permitted the Mac Plus in 1985 to load multiple applications and switch between them from the menu bar; the applications needed no direct modification. This later evolved inside Apple to become MultiFinder.

Jobs brought Randy Wigginton across to Mac; Wigginton was one of the very earliest Apple team members. Wigginton had been given lifts to the Homebrew Computer Club by Wozniak and was present when the Apple I was first shown there. He was also one of the four-person team who got the Byte Shop Apple I order assembled and despatched from Steve Jobs' garage.

Wigginton later worked on the Apple II ROM software and wrote demo BASIC programs. He was responsible for the floating point mathematics in the Applesoft BASIC, and some critical Disk II routines; at one time he was charged by Markkula to come up with a competitor to VisiCalc that Apple could own outright.

Quite a team!

Strength in depth – the Macintosh team

Having seen the problems experienced with Apple III the Mac team wanted to be sure it would get software developers on side with its new PC. The process it adopted was to appoint 'Apple evangelists'. Guy Kawasaki in the Mac marketing team is credited with this notion.

Mike Boich was the first, charged with demonstrating the Macintosh to software developers and getting them to commit to writing software for the platform. He was succeeded by Alain Rossmann, who later married Joanna Hoffman another Mac team member.

They gathered support but the developers faced real problems because the process of programming on the Mac was quite arduous. Worse, the internally produced MacWrite and MacPaint were so elegant that the bar had been raised extremely high; developers were somewhat daunted by this.

As a thirteen-year-old Chris Espinosa tried to get his computer-time fix in Byte Shops and found the best way not to be thrown out was to develop software for the store. He cut his teeth on the Altair and IMSAI. Jobs came across his software and he and Wozniak took Espinosa to the Homebrew Computer Club, his mother often going along to keep an eye on him.

Espinosa later helped debug the BASIC for the Apple I and was the fourth person who helped deliver that first Apple I order with Byte Shops. He attended the University of California, Berkeley where his freshman advisor was Andy Hertzfeld. Of course he was going to join Apple!

He played a role in the marketing and documentation for Mac. Espinosa stayed on at Apple, involved in many projects, and often speaks at the annual Worldwide Developers' Conference.

Larry Kenyon, now part of the Apple III team, had strong experience with enabling the Apple II to talk with peripherals such as printers. Hertzfeld invited him to join the Mac software team. Late in the project he was challenged by Jobs to bring down the lengthy thirty second start-up delay of the Macintosh. He managed to rework the software to save 10% of this. Jobs suggested each user would save this at every start of the Mac; multiply it by all the users and this was to be of huge significance.

Joanna Hoffman studied anthropology, physics, and linguistics and was pursuing a PhD in archaeology. Her regular use of an Apple in her archaeological work led her to decide she was not going to spend any longer on the past but wanted instead to look to the future. She became the fifth member of the Mac team. For the first year Hoffman was the only individual charged with marketing of the Mac.

Hoffman defined the 'bible' for the Mac team, the *User Interface Guidelines*, which they all had to follow; for example this defined how menu bars and dialog boxes were to look.

Later in the project she was shouted down by Jobs when she suggested the Mac needed a hard drive. It meant that when she later prepared the Mac launch business plans she had to use an Apple III with a ProFile hard disk. This was still inadequate despite it having ten times the capacity of the original Mac drive. It should have been a QED moment to hint at what might happen later; but no one heeded it.

Susan Kare was at high school with Hertzfeld. She was an artist and graphic designer with a PhD from New York University and worked at the Museum of Modern Art in San Francisco. She was lured to Apple by Hertzfeld where she worked on developing pixel art to deliver fonts and tools for the Mac.

The icons that became such a part of the Mac's appeal were Kare's creations using a 32 dot x 32 dot canvas - the smiley Macintosh that was there at the start up, the paint pot, the lasso, the trash can, the bomb. These helped to define the art form ever since.

Rather than pay a licence for existing fonts Kare developed a whole string of them for Apple. She made them similar to the major fonts and available in upper and lower case, emboldened, italicised, outlined or shadowed. These were named for cities - Chicago, Geneva, London, Monaco, San Francisco...

Kare would leave to join Jobs at NeXT and later as an independent designer worked for both Microsoft on Windows and for IBM. She designed the playing cards for the Microsoft Windows 3.0 Solitaire game and icons for IBM OS/2. Even later she designed icons for the Facebook Gifts feature. Quite a CV!

To add to the magic of the Mac, Jobs introduced some intriguing innovations to the production technique. A highly automated plant used robots to insert components and it adopted the 'just-in-time' Japanese approach where component stocks were kept to an absolute minimum.

To deliver the Mac this mighty team burned itself out under the autocratic rule of Steve Jobs. Jobs wanted to beat Lisa to market and the original business plan was to launch in 1982 at a price point of $1,500 and to sell some 50,000 units a month.

It was then postponed and planned for release in 1983. It was not in fact announced to the press until October 1983, under an embargo until January 1984. The '1984' TV advert launched it on 22nd January 1984 with the 128k Mac plus MacPaint and MacWrite included for a limited period, priced from $1,995 to $2,495.

It took two and a half months to ship the first 50,000 units and just 100,000 units were sold across the first six months.

Anyone seeing the Mac, and MacWrite and MacPaint in particular, could feel the significance of what had been achieved. I remember spending days playing with the font options in MacWrite and trying to create works of art with MacPaint. It was instantly enthralling and compulsive.

But the early Mac had problems. Despite all the brilliant work and the startlingly innovative ideas, it proved slow and lacking in capacity. Its single disk drive meant just copying a disk was a nightmare.

While the point and click on the icons was simplicity itself, its constrained capacity necessitated the constant insertion and removal of the object and target disks, the amount it could handle at each switch was so tiny. *Byte* magazine quantified this in a review as requiring some fifty disk exchanges to copy a full disk, the exercise requiring twenty minutes of prestidigitation.

The memory on the Mac was heavily earmarked by the OS and the Finder to allow their immediacy which was so key to the Mac concept, but this should have alerted the team to have built-in more memory to compensate. It was for this reason that the Lisa had an on-board 1,000K, compared with just 128k on the Mac.

Of course the Mac drew every letter individually pixel-by-pixel, so MacWrite was limited to well under ten standard pages before a document exceeded the capacity of a disk. If only Hoffman had pressed for the hard drive and mentioned her planning exercise with the Apple III that had rapidly exceeded the ProFile hard disk! But the Mac as designed did not have the capability to add a hard drive!

Jobs had been adamant that the Mac needed only 128K. This was later attributed to an over-reaction to having watched the Lisa get too large and expensive. In fact, despite his command, Burrell Smith had chosen to ignore Jobs and fortuitously designed it to be expandable to 512K.

During the launch Jobs himself had used an artificially inflated Mac to show it off to advantage, not quite the Fat Mac as the 512K version would be termed when released in September 1984. Surely this demo requirement should have indicated that the product needed extra capacity?

Not so much insanely great as insanely grating!
According to Steven Levy in his book *Insanely Great* and Jack Schofield of the UK's *Guardian* newspaper, it was Alan Kay, of PARC fame and later an Apple fellow, who was moved to write a criticism of the Mac that he headed,

'Would you buy a Honda with a one-gallon gas tank?'

In September 1984 the 512K Mac was introduced to resolve some of these problems, but at $3,200 retail this did little to lift the product's fortunes.

With Macs beginning to accumulate in warehouses, in November 1984 Apple launched the ultimate 'puppy dog sale'. The theory is that if you leave a puppy with someone overnight, they cannot bear to be parted from it by morning. Of course this presupposes that it has not chewed all your furniture and piddled all over your carpet!

The 'Test Drive a Macintosh' campaign was successful in persuading 200,000 individuals in the USA to take home a Mac for a free 24-hour trial. I cannot establish how many of these stayed put, but during December Apple was able to announce that the 250,000[th] Mac had been sold and 270,000 had been sold in that calendar year. Remember the busplan had proposed 50,000 a month so even this good late result reflected just 45% of their busplan.

RANDOM ACCESS MOMENT:
December 1984 was when Apple announced the sale of its two millionth Apple II.

A new dimension in software - Mac software

A clear requirement of the time was a suitable word processor for the Mac and for this it chose to look in-house. Randy Wigginton was charged with delivering this key application package for the Mac; it was called MacWrite.

It proved to be a nightmare for Wigginton and his two-man team, Don Breuner and Ed Ruder, since all the features that the Mac offered to make the user's life simple and straightforward combined to make the programmer's task significantly tougher.

This was in fact true for all programs with the Mac, but there was a whole extra layer of pain for a word processor package. Before this there had been no WYSIWYG to contend with, no font choices, no variation in the size or style of the characters, no mixing of text and images.

Add to this that the program was being written while many of the other elements of the Mac were still far from firm - not just macro things like the OS and Finder but even down to the way that files could be named and handled. It also had to be written to work with a dot matrix printer, the Apple ImageWriter; a badge-engineered and modified C Itoh Electronics 8510 printer.

Jobs saw that they were struggling and covertly ran a parallel project, just in case. This was later released as WriteNow.

Wigginton left Apple in September 1981 to form his own operation, Encore. It was from there that he did eventually deliver MacWrite for the Mac and in the late '80s a spreadsheet called Full Impact that was marketed by Ashton-Tate.

The team also sought a drawing program for the Mac. The earliest of these had been MIT's T-Square in 1962 and of course Ivan Sutherland's Sketchpad in January 1963. Apple could also draw inspiration from many sources closer to home, in particular work at PARC that they had witnessed.

Dick Shoup and Alvy Ray Smith produced SuperPaint as a computer painting program at PARC in April 1973 (not to be confused with Silicon Beach Software's use of the name in 1986 for the Mac). William Newman followed with Markup in 1975 as a bitmap graphics editor for the PARC Alto.

Patrick Baudelaire and Bob Sproull used Sutherland's Sketchpad as inspiration for both their Draw and SIL (simple illustrator programme) in 1976. Bill Bowman and Bob Flegel produced another program called Flyer in 1976, written in SmallTalk for the Alto.

Flyer in turn inspired Dan Silva to develop Doodle in 1981 which was used on the Xerox ViewPoint, a successor to the Xerox Star launched in 1985; it was branded as Free-hand Drawing. Silva joined Electronic Arts in 1983 where he wrote Prism, a drawing development tool, and later developed it into DeluxePaint for the Amiga and IBM PC.

Whatever inspirations were drawn, the task fell to Bill Atkinson when he crossed the house from Lisa to join the Mac team. He had developed QuickDraw for the Lisa but came to accept that it was going to be too expensive as a product to set the world alight. His work had earned him the coveted title of 'Apple fellow' which allowed appointees to select for themselves the projects upon which they would bestow their skills.

Building upon his experience with QuickDraw, Atkinson chose to work on the package that would best show the spirit and capability of the Mac's GUI. He developed MacPaint, a bit-mapped graphic drawing program launched with the Mac in January 1984. Using QuickDraw, a graphic drawn in MacPaint could be cut and pasted across to MacWrite.

Atkinson went on to design and implement HyperCard in March 1985, the first popular hypermedia system. This was written with SmallTalk and Logo as an authoring system able to link unformatted information by using hyperlinks.

VisiCalc had proven invaluable in building Apple II sales, so one of the first requirements identified was a suitable spreadsheet for the Mac.

To provide this application they turned to Microsoft and signed a deal in January 1982 for the development of a series of applications. These would include Multiplan a spreadsheet, MacGraph a business graphics program, and MacBASIC a BASIC interpreter.

The contract decreed that Microsoft, in being given access to the Mac plans, would not be allowed to market similar software until after 1st January 1984.

Microsoft already had a product originally developed for the CP/M platform called Multiplan. This was a VisiCalc competitor designed by Charles Simonyi, ex PARC. From this root it developed a version to fully use the Mac's GUI features, still called Multiplan and this was first shipped in April 1984.

Multiplan lasted a year before it was replaced by Excel. Then in a move that Microsoft had used with Altair and perfected with IBM, it rapidly rescinded its deal with Apple to permit Microsoft to offer these products on to others.

The evangelists' work too was bearing fruit. In November 1984 Lotus Development launched a GUI version of the Lotus 1-2-3 called Jazz for the Macintosh 512K. This was an application suite offering spreadsheet, database, graphics, word processing and communication software priced at $595. It was followed up in January 1985 by Microsoft Word 1.0 and FileMaker.

Also that month marked a marked triumph for the Mac team over the Lisa team when the Lisa 2/10 was renamed as the Macintosh XL, soon popularly interpreted to mean ex-Lisa. It ran the Macintosh operating system instead of the original Lisa OS, but would last as a product only briefly - until April.

So finally some software was available but the Mac had yet to find its own killer application.

The Apple Macintosh launch

It was 1984, but we got the month wrong. It was not 'a bright cold day in April', in fact it was Friday 13th January 1984. However we did kick off our presentation as the 'clocks were striking thirteen'- well it was 13:00. We were launching Nolan Bushnell's Androbot personal robots into the UK.

Unbeknown to us, nine days later Apple would also use the George Orwell novel *1984* as its inspiration for the Macintosh launch television advertisement; it aired during the third quarter of Super Bowl XVIII. (For the record, the LA Raiders beat the Redskins in Florida.)

This was the one-minute advertisement that prompted Mark Markkula, Apple's chairman, to ask Steve Jobs and John Sculley,

'You mean you really want to show this?'

Produced in Shepperton Studios in the UK and directed by Ridley Scott, the budget was $900,000. It was aired only twice but delivered an enormous impact, achieving free runs on news channels and comments in the print media - just imagine what YouTube could have done with it?

At first an Apple spokesperson said it was not planned to be anti-IBM but was in fact an attack on conformity and a celebration of the triumph of originality. Although Steve Jobs, previewing it in late 1983, said it was trying to convey that,

'It appears IBM wants it all. Apple is perceived to be the only hope to offer IBM a run for its money.'

So things had clearly changed in the two years since Apple's Wall Street Journal advert on the announcement of the IBM PC which rather tongue in cheek had declared,

'Welcome IBM. Seriously.'

The IBM PC had little originality and yet managed to take the majority of the market; now it demanded more respect. Apple was desperate to throw a spanner in the mechanism, and the advert showed an athletic archetypal Californian blonde throwing a hammer through the image of a conservative East Coast patrician. Most people watching the advert had no problem at all in recognising that the Big Brother character represented IBM.

In fact Anya Mayor, the blonde actress, was British; she later starred in Elton John's video *Nikita*. Big Brother was David Graham, also a Brit, who voiced Daleks, and characters from Thunderbirds to Peppa Pig. He also appeared in many classic UK TV series *Callan, Danger Man, The Saint, Softly Softly, The Avengers, The Bill...*

Apple's final strapline for the TV advert that introduced the Mac computer was,

'On 24th *January, Apple Computer will introduce Macintosh. And you'll see why 1984 won't be like "1984".'*

Jobs' discomforter

As the Macintosh killer app was being sought, the recriminations within Apple were only just getting up a head of steam.

Apple again took advertising time during the 1985 SuperBowl broadcast, this time to promote Macintosh Office. It depicted businessmen in blindfolds going over a cliff like lemmings to a background tune of *Heigh-Ho*.

Not quite having the subtlety or pizzazz of the '1984' advert, this cost Apple $400k to produce with an air-time cost of $800k.

RANDOM ACCESS MOMENT:
the Apple 'lemmings' advert reminds me uncomfortably of a campaign I presided over for the Mettoy Dragon 32. We had used the term 'family computer' so that the warm cuddly word, family, would counterbalance the technical term 'computer'.

We noticed everyone at the time had a brochure with a similar beige box pictured on the front and we wanted to do something different. It was a time when parents were feeling their children would be disadvantaged if they did not have a PC.

So what was our idea for a sales brochure to potential Dragon retailers? A headline that said, 'What will happen if you ignore the family computer market?' We had commissioned some poor actor, dressed smartly in shirt and tie, to have fried egg all over his face. The brochure is beside my keyboard as I write this and I cringe to think that we had ever considered it as a good idea.

But the 'lemmings advert' promised new Macs; that did not materialise. There were just a few, mostly unremarkable, products launched by Apple in support of the large ad-spend. The first was the Macintosh XL, which was in fact a renamed Lisa and had a very short life span. Next came the much-delayed AppleTalk networking solution and finally the LaserWriter. Though the LaserWriter was later to become significant, at this stage with a price-point of $6,995 it was not an immediate success.

There were plans in 1985 to release the Big Mac (how did they avoid legal action from McDonalds?). It would be built around a 68020 MPU and was conceived as UNIX-based with a new Apple Desktop Bus. It was termed as a 3M machine. Nothing to do with Minnesota Mining and Manufacturing but instead used to mean a PC with a megaflop of processing power, a megabyte of memory and a million pixel display. Six prototypes were built, each exhibiting a number of problems, and the project was never followed through.

It did not achieve 3M levels but perhaps it was part of the inspiration for NeXT?

It was at this stage that Wozniak finally made his break with Apple. He had come back to work as an engineer after recuperating from his flying accident with a sabbatical and a venture into organising festivals.

While working at Apple he became frustrated with the ever growing number of remote controls that consumer electronics spawned in the home. He tackled the problem in his inimitable style by creating a universal programmable remote control.

He named his company CL 9, after he had considered moving into the site of a failed restaurant called Cloud 9; that name was already taken so CL 9 was an alternative. The programmable remote was called Core and at its heart was his old faithful, a 6502 MPU. It could be connected to a computer by serial interface and had a timer; it allowed the user to manage all sorts of home consumer products.

The Core was patented and Wozniak originally asked Frogdesign, the Snow White designers, to develop the case for it. However Jobs would not allow them to work for CL 9. The CL 9 business, products and patents were sold on in 1988.

The next sign of unrest occurred at a board meeting where Sculley made Jobs step down as general manager of the division responsible for the Macintosh and replaced him with Jean-Louis Gassée.

Back in 1977, the headhunters Heidrick & Struggles had identified John Sculley as a likely candidate to become the Apple president, at the time he was president of Pepsi-Cola USA. Steve Jobs had challenged Sculley to come and run Apple by asking the question,

'Do you want to spend the rest of your life selling sugared water, or do you want a chance to change the world?'

Sculley was the manager who introduced the Pepsi Challenge campaign that gained market share from Coca-Cola. He was to apply the same fmcg (fast moving consumer goods) approach at Apple. His ten years of stewardship grew the company tenfold, and he famously edged out Steve Jobs along the way. In 1987 he was the top-paid executive in Silicon Valley earning $2.2m pa. He once said,

'The future belongs to those who see possibilities before they become obvious.'

But then in 1987 for *Playboy* magazine Sculley also forecast that the Soviet Union would land a man on Mars within twenty years - the Soviet Union lasted four years and still as yet no footprints from any nation have appeared on the red planet!

Now Sculley had lost patience with and unseated Jobs. Shortly after this, at an executive meeting held prior to Sculley taking an overseas business trip, he confronted Jobs over rumours of a mutiny planned to take place during his absence.

Jobs declared he thought Sculley should leave but got little support from others on the board. As a result Markkula supported Sculley and removed Jobs from any formal role at Apple.

On Friday 13th September 1985 Jobs announced he was leaving Apple with plans to build his own 3M computer to focus on the higher-education sector. He also advised that he was taking five Apple executives with him to the new company.

RANDOM ACCESS MOMENT:
Fear of thirteen is triskaidekaphobia. This apparently derives from the duplicitous Judas Iscariot being the thirteenth to sit at the Last Supper. Fear of Friday the 13th is normally referred to as friggatriskaidekaphobia or alternatively paraskevidekatriaphobia; it is also suggested to derive from the crucifixion of Jesus Christ on a Friday.

I wonder if there should not be a word for someone who does things on significant days - like William Shakespeare, who was apparently born and died on St George's Day. As there is some doubt as to precisely who he was and even how he spelled his name, I am unsure how we know his birth and death dates? If there is such a word then it should certainly be applied to Steve Jobs, who co-founded Apple on All Fool's Day and left it on a Friday 13th.

Six months later in May 1986, a further exodus of the Mac team members, including Burrell Smith, Andy Hertzfeld, Alain Rossmann, Mike Boich and others, to found Radius. The company specialised in products to enhance the Mac - processor upgrades, graphics accelerators, TV and video capture cards. In March 1995 it became the first licensed Apple clone manufacturer.

But in the meantime this meant that Apple had lost both its founders and many prime dreamers in under a decade!

Writing the next chapter – Geometry and 3D Silicon Graphics

Intriguingly the major PC players were not early to adopt the ARPANET or the Internet because this was seen to have been designed for mainframe users.

Instead the PC makers were concentrating on advancing their own products and solutions for their market. This period did see some remarkable PC developments.

Jim Clark attended the University of Utah where he was grounded in graphics and as a PhD student worked with the Evans & Sutherland team, following in some august steps like those of John Warnock, who achieved his doctorate five years earlier and went on to co-found Adobe.

In 1981 while an electrical engineering associate professor at Stanford Jim Clark, with Marc Hannah, designed the Geometry Engine as part of a scheme developed by Lynn Conway and Carver Mead as an outreach VLSI project from Xerox PARC.

Clark spent four months at PARC on his VLSI design and in 1981 attracted venture capital from the Mayfield Fund to co-found Silicon Graphics Inc (SGI) with Abbey Silverstone (I wonder just how he was named after a significant bend in the British F1 racetrack?) and seven graduates and research staff from Stanford.

Silverstone graduated from the University of Illinois and worked at PARC on the Alto project; he also developed the packaging design for the Xerox Star 8010.

Initially SGI specialised in 3D graphics display terminals based around the Geometry Engine; they allowed speedy resolution of the geometric calculations to create 3D images. In 1984 the first products were the IRIS 1000 and 1200 (integrated raster imaging system) which worked alongside a DEC VAX to independently manage the display.

Initially it had a motherboard from Stanford that had been used by Sun, and added this to a 68000 MPU and the standard Multibus. The terminal evolved and by the time of the release of the IRIS 3130 was capable of full 3D animation and rendering.

SGI developed the IrisGL (graphics language) to give users ready access to the advanced graphics features of the system.

SGI then moved over to using the MIPS RISC chip and the UNIX System V operating system on the workstation IRIX that could run up to 64 processors and deliver fully realised 3D graphics. It was next drawn to the MIPS R4000, the first 64-bit RISC microprocessor.

MIPS Computer Systems was founded in 1984 by another Stanford Research team, headed by John Hennessy and Dr John Moussouris. It set about developing the RISC (reduced instruction set computer) microprocessor chips. The R2000 and R3000 MPUs proved very successful and the company had a strong initial public offering in 1989. But as it was developing the next series, the R4000, it was attracted by the dream of developing its own computers using RISC technology. MIPS soon ran in to trouble funding these two tracks of development.

To secure its supply SGI acquired MIPS in 1992 for $333m and renamed it MTI (MIPS Technologies Inc), a subsidiary of SGI. The SGI IRIX 6.2 was a 64-bit product that used the R4000 MPU. In the 1990s SGI decided to espouse the new Intel Itanium processor and it hived off MTI; but the Itanium was much delayed and this did not assist SGI's progress.

RANDOM ACCESS MOMENT:
In 1991 SGI joined with a group of other manufacturers that included Acer, Compaq, DEC, Groupe Bull, MIPS, Microsoft, NEC, Olivetti, Siemens, Sony, Wang... They believed that RISC would create the potential for a better price performance. But perhaps they were also motivated to try and weaken Intel's powerful position in the MPU market, and at the same time challenge Sun's workstation dominance.

They defined a MIPS-based architecture with either Windows NT or the SCO UNIX operating systems and proposed the way forward with an agreement on 'advanced RISC computing'.

The group had all sorts of political wrangles, but when SGI bought MIPS and Compaq withdrew from the consortium the whole initiative simply fell apart.

The Iris GL had so many add-ons and changes by 1992 that SGI updated it and released OpenGL as a low-cost licensable product to be maintained as the standard by a cross-industry group. This meant OpenGL became the 3D graphics standard, only Microsoft (*quelle surprise!*) choosing to go its own way.

SGI went on to make other acquisitions that on the face of it looked like sensible moves, but some of its follow-through proved none too clever.

Wavefront Technologies was founded in 1984 by Bill Kovacs, Larry Barels and Mark Sylvester to develop computer graphics software for Hollywood. It created Personal Visualiser to permit Silicon Graphics computers to run its rendering software in 1988. It later developed the GameWare development software for use with the Atari Jaguar.

Alias Research, founded in 1983, developed Maya software to handle 3D modeling and animation.

In February 1995 SGI acquired Alias and Wavefront and merged them to become Alias|Wavefront. They paid some $500m for the two companies yet in June 2004 sold the merged company on to a private equity firm for only $57.1m. Within a little over a year this had been sold on again to Autodesk for $182m.

In 1996 SGI merged with the supercomputer manufacturer Cray Research for $740m but it was unimpressed by the latest Cray, the CS6400 which was a SPARC-based supercomputer.

It sold its Superservers division on to Sun for what was widely reported to be between $50m and $60m. The product CS6400 was the basis for the Sun Ultra Enterprise which developed a whole series of workstations and servers. Sun called the deal the 'best investment since Microsoft bought DOS'.

SGI spun off the Cray elements of its business into an operation it called Cray Research; this was then sold in 2000 to Tera for $175m - $35m in cash and one million shares.

Later still in September 2000 SGI bought Intergraph Computer Systems for its series of ZX10 Vizual workstations and servers, featuring 2D/3D graphics, but this never really took off.

By the end of our fourth PC decade SGI had filed for Chapter 11 bankruptcy twice and was eventually acquired in 2009 by Rackable Systems for just $42.5m, to become Silicon Graphics International.

3M computing - Sun Microsystems

The first 3M computer (one megapixel display, one megabyte of memory and a speed of one MIPS, million instructions per second) was developed when a graduate student at Stanford designed a personal CAD workstation in May 1982 for the Stanford University Network; the name became Sun-1.

Andy Bechtolsheim was born in Germany, spent some time in Rome, then returned to Germany. Studying engineering at the University of Technology Munich, he won a Fulbright Award scholarship and at the age of nineteen moved to the United States.

He achieved his master's in electrical engineering at Carnegie Mellon and enrolled for a joint electrical engineering and computer science PhD course at Stanford.

Bechtolsheim had become frustrated waiting for computer access time at Stanford and designed the Sun-1 based on the UNIX operating system with built-in networking. It was Vinod Khosla who wanted to turn the product in to a business.

Khosla was born in Pune, India and rather similarly had gained a degree in electrical engineering in Delhi and then a master's at Carnegie Mellon, but he chose Stanford Business School for his MBA. In 1980 he founded a CAD company called Daisy Systems which specialised in electronic design automation.

Together with Stanford man Scott McNealy and UC Berkeley student Bill Joy, the team founded Sun Microsystems in February 1982; Khosla was the first chairman and CEO.

McNealy had been working as manufacturing director at Onyx Systems that had started out building Z-80 CP/M systems but graduated to producing a Zilog Z8000 16-bit microprocessor-based UNIX system. He would later become the Sun CEO.

Bill Joy was prominent in Berkeley Software Distribution (BSD) a UNIX derivative used by many workstations. He developed the 1BSD for a PDP-11 as an add-on to the UNIX 6th edition in 1977 and improved this with 2BSD a year later when he wrote the 'vi' text editor and the C shell, both of which have become a standard routine in subsequent Unix systems.

Sun hit profit in its first quarter in summer 1982 creating 68000-based UNIX workstations for financial organisations and telecom companies. It based these on its own UNIX operating system called SunOS. In 1984 Sun introduced NFS (network file sharing) processes and released this licence-free to ignite the general take-off of PC networking from 1986 onwards.

To put this into context, NFS was launched at the same time as Fidonet was issuing its inter-BBS, bulletin board system, approach and a year before the Internet's file transfer protocol was fixed in RFC #959 (request for comments).

Sun had its initial public offering in 1986 and was one of those fortunate enough to ride the Silicon Valley dot-com wave and the euphoria for dot-com launches as every one of these operations would require workstations and servers.

The same year Vinod Khosla was appointed a partner of the venture capital organisation, Kleiner, Perkins, Caufield & Byers.

In 1987 Sun developed SPARC (scalable processor architecture). Like RISC its philosophy was that simpler architecture would result in improved performance. SPARC machines were usually based on the SunOS or Solaris (later OpenSolaris), though NeXTSTEP, Linux and various BSDs have also been used.

By 1988 Sun had become the market leader in workstations. That year it also exceeded $1 billion in sales revenue.

In 1987 Sun developed an alliance with AT&T, the notional UNIX owners, to create a UNIX business computer. They worked together to merge the current market leading UNIX software systems (BSD, System V and Xenix) to create the Unix SVR4, System V Release 4.

In 1991 James Gosling and others working at Sun commenced a project that resulted in the programming language Java. Originally based on UCSD Pascal and used with a smart television remote control; like Wozniak's CL-9.

Named 'Oak' it was switched to a more object-oriented approach, based on C and C++. The objective was a virtual machine that would ensure software portability. This inspired its motto of 'write once, run anywhere'. It was subsequently somewhat randomly renamed as Java.

First released as Java 1.0 in 1995, Netscape promptly incorporated the facility to run Java applets inside web pages and this proved extremely popular. Applets had first been used by Apple Computer in AppleScript in 1995. They are small specific-task applications, or plug-ins, that run within a larger program.

With Netscape, Oracle and then IBM getting behind Java, Microsoft did what it often does and followed.

The Java Community Process was formed in 1998 to manage the process for interested parties to be involved in defining future features or versions of Java. In 2006 much of Java was released by Sun as open-source software under the GNU general public licence.

In 1992 it upgraded its SunOS to Solaris which was designed with the SPARC workstations in mind. It used SVR4 and integrated an OpenWindows GUI and open network computing features.

Sun faced a trend for clients to move towards a cluster of low-cost Linux-based servers rather than using the more sophisticated Sun servers. It therefore introduced several new series of low-cost servers as the backbone for business networking; by 1993 it had shipped its millionth system.

However when the dot-com bubble burst in 2001 Sun was hit hard as hardware demand dried up. Its shares were literally decimated and it was forced to lay off staff and close some of its manufacturing resource.

Back in August 1999 Sun acquired StarDivision for its StarOffice suite and the source code for this was released in 2000 in an effort to wrest away Microsoft Office's control of the market. Sun went on to espouse the open-source software movement by donating 1,600 of its patents to the community and offering open-source applications like its StarOffice and OpenSolaris.

Sun acquired MySQL in January 2008 from MySQL AB of Finland. This open-source relational database system was developed by Monty Widenius. While working with a colleague in a data warehousing business he had begun work on MySQL, the My apparently being his daughter's name. Sun paid $1 billion in total consideration to enter the $15 billion database market.

In 2009 Sun and Oracle reached an agreement and in January 2010 Sun was acquired for $7.4 billion and renamed Oracle America Inc.

More 3M - the NeXT big thing

Steve Jobs, while still with Apple, helped create the Apple University Consortium which offered faculty members, students and their institutions to acquire Apple equipment at a discounted rate. This led to a large number of campuses choosing Mac; by early 1984 the consortium had been responsible for $50m in Apple sales.

In support of the consortium Jobs met many senior university individuals. It was one of these, Paul Berg, who asked Jobs to develop a 3M computer at Apple. Berg was a Nobel Prizewinner for Chemistry and currently working on recombinant DNA. He needed this level of performance for him and his students to make any real progress.

In 1985 the Mac team ran into some difficulties with delays on the release of upgraded Macs, hold-ups on its efforts to break in to the business sector with Macintosh Office. Amidst stock write-offs Sculley removed Jobs from his role and this led to his departure in autumn 1985.

Jobs promptly formed NeXT Inc, later to be split into NeXT Computer Inc and NeXT Software Inc. He assured Apple that his new company would not compete with it but took with him a group of Apple personnel. Apple took legal action to stop him using his knowledge from his time with it but this eventually petered out.

NeXT's target was the higher education market and the development of the 3M computer.

It must have looked promising because Ross Perot's interest was attracted. He had also discussed acquiring Microsoft back in 1979. He had continued to grow EDS and then in 1984 sold a controlling interest to General Motors for $2.4 billion.

In 1987 Perot invested $20 million in NeXT for 16%, at a stroke making the fledgling business worth $125 million. The team set out to create a computer workstation with the power that Berg had identified but at a price that students could afford.

Paul Rand was contracted for $100,000 to develop the brand image; he had done the same for IBM, UPS and others.

Rich Page of the Lisa team led the hardware development of the first offering.

Avie Tevanian joined the team from Carnegie Mellon University where he had worked on the development of the Mach kernel, valuable for operating system development for use with distributed computing. He developed the NeXTSTEP operating system.

The team delivered the NeXT Computer in October 1988 at a retail price of $6,500. Built into a magnesium case created by Frogdesign, its shape instantly had it unofficially known as the Cube.

Its software was particularly appreciated. Based on multi-tasking UNIX, it added a Display PostScript WYSIWYG GUI that allowed users to avoid the complex syntax of UNIX. It also had C-based object-oriented programs. This powerful combination drove others soon to follow suit.

It was not quite a 3M PC in that while it did have a massive 8 megabytes of memory and close to a million pixels of grayscale display (in fact just 0.93m); it achieved only 265 KFlops of processing from its 25 MHz 68030 MPU. Later, faster versions using the 68040 were released. It had a 400 dpi laser printer which was patently sharper, particularly with half-tones, than pre-existing 300 dpi models.

It used advanced VLSI and had the first built-in digital signal processor to handle the complex algorithms and other mathematical operations for conversion of audio and video material. Ethernet was built in, multimedia email, CD-quality sound...

The NeXT Computer did sell into research establishments and perhaps most notably one was used by Tim Berners-Lee at CERN where it became the first World Wide Web server and web browser. John Cormack used a NeXT to design Wolfenstein 3D and Doom games.

Canon's magneto-optical drives were first used on the NeXT computer. These were much less expensive than the hard disk and the media was lower cost too, the equivalent of 320 of the then current Mac disks. But they proved not to be very reliable.

However the relationship prompted Canon in 1989 to buy in to NeXT. The investment from Canon's perspective was as much about getting access to the NeXTSTEP operating system for its own workstations. It paid $100m for a 16.67% share; this meant that NeXT was now valued at $600m.

From 1989 NeXT expanded beyond the higher education sector and was sold through a reseller, BusinessLand, to selected markets at a retail of $9,999.

Though the production facility was created to be capable of manufacturing 150,000 NeXT PCs per year, only around 50,000 were ever sold and production was stopped in 1993. In part this poor performance was due to the lack of third party software, although at its second launch in 1990 it had Lotus Improv and WordPerfect.

NeXT decided to concentrate its attention on marketing its powerful software. NeXTSTEP was ported to the IBM PC and its clones and enjoyed a good deal of success among banks and US agencies, including ARPA and the CIA. It then worked with Sun Microsystems to modify its NeXTSTEP operating system, removing the Mach kernel to produce OpenStep which was used with new Sun systems.

Further development produced OpenStep Enterprise which was a Windows NT version. NeXT also produced WebObjects, a web server package that created web applications; despite its $50,000 price point this achieved some high profile clients, with the BBC, Dell and Disney among its users. It is still used by iTunes Store and the Apple website.

Late in 1996 NeXT was purchased by Apple, paying over $400m in cash to investors and 1.5 million Apple shares to Jobs himself. The attraction was the NeXTSTEP software which was purchased to integrate into and update the Mac OS; it still lives on in Mac OS X.

Though NeXT and NeXTSTEP had a short existence it was to be the platform that Tim Berners-Lee used to develop the World Wide Web.

In what must have seemed a sweet victory during 1997 Jobs was appointed as CEO on a pro-tem basis and by 2000 this was altered into a permanent role.

17 - Clever GUIs – PCs get user friendly

We don't have a monopoly. We have market share. There's a difference. Steve Ballmer, Microsoft

Software driven – Microsoft evolves

By the end of 1979 Microsoft had turned over $2.4m, with some 28 employees.

In March 1980 it released its first piece of hardware, the Z-80 SoftCard for Apple II, which enabled CP/M-80 versions of COBOL and FORTRAN to be used. This opened up the Apple to a range of software applications that helped its cause enormously.

Microsoft also bought a licence for CP/M at $50,000 for it to be distributed with the SoftCard. It sold at $349 with both CP/M and Microsoft Disk BASIC; some 5,000 were sold within a few months of launch, around 100,000 units across its five years of life.

Microsoft also purchased a UNIX licence from AT&T in 1979 and developed using this its XENIX OS for 16-bit computers. It was announced in August 1980 and sold as a commercial proposition, compatible with all UNIX software and running with Intel's 8086, Motorola's M68000, Zilog's Z8000 and the DEC PDP-11 minicomputer.

By the end of 1980 and before the IBM deal was to bear any fruit, Microsoft had expanded to have forty employees and sales were over $7.5m. All this had derived from the fateful day when they decided to produce BASIC for the Altair.

But of course the critical moments in 1980 were the meeting with IBM, the purchase of QDOS and the hiring of Tim Paterson to create MS-DOS from that software. By the end of the year it had contracted to supply IBM with PC-DOS, BASIC, an Assembler, Pascal, COBOL and FORTRAN, and, most significantly, within the deal it was permitted to offer MS-DOS to others.

Microsoft also decided to move into applications during 1980 and from the following year Charles Simonyi and his team worked on a spreadsheet program called EP (electronic paper). This would become Multiplan, launched in 1982.

It was developed using Microsoft's own 'pseudo code C' that allowed the program to be easily ported. It did not do well against Lotus 1-2-3 and was later replaced by Microsoft Excel; for Mac in 1985 and for Windows by 1987.

The following year the organisation entered the games market. Microsoft Adventure was written by Gordon Letwin, one of the original twelve Microsoft employees from the Albuquerque days who therefore held shares in the company at the time of the initial public offering. Microsoft Adventure was released in 1981 as a port of the Colossal Cave Adventure and it later became the first game released for the IBM PC.

For his work on Adventure, Letwin received a royalty; he was the only person within Microsoft to receive such a deal for work done while employed at Microsoft. Later Letwin would also lead the OS/2 operating system work at Microsoft.

It continued to go well for Microsoft as in late 1981 it signed its first licence deal, worth $1m, with Hitachi for Basic v5; this was also known as GW-BASIC (gee whiz). GW-BASIC was a dialect first developed for Compaq. Its graphics features certainly justify the gee whiz tag, or it may have been named after one of the programmers who worked with it, Greg Whitten. Conspiracy theorists even suggest it might have even been for Gates, William!

Microsoft Flight Simulator took off in 1982 selling a million copies across the next decade. Also during that year the Microsoft Consumer Products division, managed by Vern Raburn, released two TRS-80 apps, Typing Tutor and Microsoft Adventure.

RANDOM ACCESS MOMENT:
Bill Gates has certainly created some personal friction with his opponents. Some even suggested he is the Antichrist because if you sum the ASCII character values of his name thus - B = 66, I = 73, L = 76, L = 76, G = 71, A = 65, T = 84, E = 69, S = 83, I = 1, I = 1, I = 1, it totals to 666 - the number of the beast. Though for my taste the letter I being counted as 1 is a bit of a fudge. Some point out that the ASCII characters in WINDOWS 95 also total to 666!

But this form of arithmetic could be applied to others. 'George Bush' using the numerology of Hebrew letters also adds up to 666 – so are we to believe both presidents with this name are Antichrists?

666 is itself an extremely intriguing number in that it is the sum of the first 36 integers (1+2+3+4...+35+36). It is therefore the sum of all the numbers on a roulette wheel; I knew I was playing with fire betting on that game!

It is also the number created by placing the first six Roman numerals in descending order DCLXVI. Of course if you use all seven roman numerals you get MDCLXVI or 1666 the infernal date of the Great Fire of London.

666 is also the sum of the first 144 digits of Pi - come on, own up, who was sad enough to work that one out?

Fear of 666 is hexakosioihexekontahexaphobia. Ronald and Nancy Reagan moved to Bel-Air, Los Angeles in 1989 and quickly had their house number changed from 666 to 668. There were also some concerns expressed by pregnant women who did not want children born on 6/6/6, the 6th June 2006.

Yet Kabbalists believe the number represents perfection in creation as the first six stands for the number of days God took to create the world, the second for the six cardinal directions (N, S, E, W, Up and Down) and the third six represents God in their religion.

Remorseless growth - DOS

The release of IBM PC DOS and MS-DOS proved a quantum leap for Microsoft; by the end of 1981 it had a team of 128 and had turned over $16m.

Of course this was not without strains on the organisation, which was still being run by Gates and Allen who had no experience with the organisational nightmare they had created.

To deal with this, in June 1980 Gates encouraged his school friend, Steve Ballmer, to leave Procter & Gamble and join Microsoft as his assistant. Ballmer had been an assistant product manager at the consumer goods company while attending the Graduate School of Business at Stanford.

Subsequently Charles Simonyi had been prompted by Bob Metcalfe to join Microsoft, from Xerox PARC in 1981. His 1976 paper *Meta-Programming: A Software Production Method* was clearly of great appeal to an organisation needing to manage a growing number of staff members and projects.

Simonyi looked after Microsoft's applications strategy, starting with Multiplan and later with Word and Excel. It was he who came up with what he termed a 'revenue bomb', which was a virtual machine on which they could develop a program and then port it to any platform, maximising return on effort.

Microsoft was incorporated in June 1981 as a privately-held company with Gates as president and chairman, Allen as executive VP. The equity was still all held in house with Bill Gates at 53%, Paul Allen at 31%, Steve Ballmer at 8%, Vern Raburn at 4%; Charles Simonyi and Gordon Letwin each had 1.5%. Those strange percentages again! Who had the other 1%? Unless there were fractions of %ages smoothed out in this researched list.

The defined goal was to become the 'IBM of software' which was, perhaps subconsciously, rather more accurate than intended. Thomas J Watson Sr was always keen that IBM was not the first in a field, preferring instead to let the pioneering dust settle before making a move. This was precisely what Microsoft had done, using Dartmouth BASIC to create its original Altair language, acquiring QDOS to create MS-DOS and, as we shall see, following the PARC and Apple GUIs well trodden route to develop Windows.

Of course to have IBM's dominance of the market Microsoft would need to expand its applications catalogue and in the process overtake the current dominance of Lotus and its 1-2-3 spreadsheet. It would also have to displace WordPerfect and dBase in their sectors too. It was the move towards GUI-based PCs that would present an opportunity for it to do just that.

In the meantime, by March 1982 Tim Paterson completed MS-DOS 1.1 and promptly quit Microsoft in April 1982 to return to Seattle Computer Products (SCP). He stayed there only briefly before leaving to form his own operation, Falcon Technology.

For their work on the development of DOS both SCP and Falcon were granted royalty-free rights by Microsoft. In April 1986 Microsoft acquired Falcon to recover its rights for around $1m and in December 1986 it paid SCP $935k to buy back its rights too; of course SCP had already been recompensed for the acquisition of its original QDOS.

MS-DOS was launched in two versions in May - 1.1 for the IBM PC, enabling the use of larger 320 Kbyte double-sided floppy drives, and 1.25 released for the IBM compatibles.

Microsoft also licensed DEC with a DOS for the Rainbow 100 series. Completely out of character this was agreed on a flat fee basis of just $95,000.

As the company grew to tackle these increasing markets Steve Ballmer urged Gates to bring in senior management help and in June 1982 he hired James Towne as president.

Towne had been VP and general manager at the Tektronix instrument division. Tektronix was founded straight after WWII based upon the founder's invention of a triggered oscilloscope. It was the leading electronics manufacturer in Oregon but was heading in to a period of reorganisation and staff reductions.

Towne was a forty-year-old, married with children. While this added some maturity to the organisation it put him completely at odds with the rest of the Microsoft team; here was someone who had a life outside the company. He lasted just a year.

Microsoft launched the Multiplan spreadsheet for Apple II, the IBM PC and the Osborne I in August 1982. It was able to be launched simultaneously across each platform as a result of Simonyi's pseudo-code C and virtual machine. This represented a huge saving in time and effort.

In September 1982 Gates appointed another Tektronix manager to look after PR for Microsoft. This was Pam Edstrom who lasted just two years before she left to form her own PR agency.

C Rowland Hanson was hired in 1983 to oversee marketing and in particular to build the Microsoft brand. The thirty-one-year-old had been with Neutrogena, a premium health and beauty products company, where he had experience in brand creation and management of global products.

At Microsoft he ran focus groups and other exercises but realised early on that the brand in this organisation was Bill Gates himself whom he set out to promote widely.

This brings to mind the widely-used, yet apparently anonymous, advertising agency ditty,

'When the client moans and sighs, make his logo twice the size.

When the client's hopping mad, put his picture in the ad.
If he still should prove refractory, add a picture of his factory.'

Time magazine in 1982 had made the personal computer its '*man* of the year'. But the business media was a tad confused about quite how to respond to the two Steves at Apple as role models; both were college drop-out Bohemians, not the usual fare of business magazines.

Hansen set about establishing Gates as the acceptable corporate face of the PC and managed to get him a front cover of *Time* in 1983.

In the meantime Microsoft was spreading its wings. Back in 1978 it had established its first overseas operation in Japan through an exclusive agent, Microsoft ASCII; though this was terminated in 1986 after the Microsoft IPO. It established its first European venture in Belgium with a representative company, Vector International and established its own operation in the UK, France and Germany.

At the end of 1982 it had 220 employees and around $24.5m turnover.

By 1983 it was hailed as the world's number two software company, but as it was still growing at 100% a year the top slot was very much in sight. DOS v2.0 was released in March 1983 which proved to be five times the size of DOS v1.0, containing some 20,000 lines of code.

In 1983 Paul Allen was diagnosed with Hodgkin's disease. His treatment of radiotherapy and bone marrow transplant was successful but he never returned to Microsoft, though he retained his board position until late 2000. In 1984 he founded Asymetrix that spent a long time in R&D producing several software products ranging from screen savers to 3D graphics programs.

Nonetheless, by 2008 Allen was one of the richest people, ranked as #17 in the *Forbes 400* with his wealth valued at $13bn. In 2011 Allen published *Idea Man: A Memoir by the Cofounder of Microsoft* and appeared with it to be seeking greater recognition for his efforts, suggesting,

'I was the idea man, the one who'd conceive of things out of whole cloth. Bill listened and challenged me, then homed in on my best ideas to help make them a reality.'

Allen also revealed in these memoirs that when his illness was diagnosed Gates and Ballmer had tried to reduce his shareholding; they both subsequently apologised.

With Towne gone and Paul Allen on leave of absence, Gates hired in Jon Shirley in August 1983 as president and chief operating officer, a role he was to retain until he retired in 1990; at that time he was worth over $100m for his efforts. He remained on the board until November 2008.

Forty-five years old when he was hired in 1983, Shirley had been VP of computer merchandising at Tandy. Gates and he had routinely met to negotiate for Microsoft products to be used with the TRS-80 and Model 100 portable. It was Shirley who professionalised the management of Microsoft, improving accounting controls, driving down manufacturing costs and changing the approach to distribution…

In March 1983 Microsoft diversified to create Microsoft Press and release books in support of its technologies such as *Exploring the IBM PC*, *The Apple Macintosh Book*...

Multi-Tool Word was launched in April that year, later to be renamed more simply Word, and in May Microsoft launched its own mouse. The two came together in September with Microsoft Word launched at $375, optionally supplied with the mouse for $475.

Also in 1983 Microsoft began work on Odyssey, a spreadsheet to rival Lotus 1-2-3, which would eventually be released as Excel.

Symbiotic relationships – Microsoft and GUIs

Microsoft Windows was its first operating system to feature a graphics user interface (GUI) but its birthing was a rather complex story.

Of course the notion of the GUI was evolved at ARC and then PARC, building upon the original concepts of Bush and Engelbart.

But not everyone got it; one mystified IBM-er was quoted as saying,

'*What I saw in the Xerox PARC technology was the caveman interface, you point and you grunt. A massive winding down, regressing away from language, in order to address the technological nervousness of the user.*'

In July 1981 Xerox launched the Star workstation that pulled together all the PARC features and its Alto computer experiences. Priced at $16,000 the Xerox Star was not a serious consumer proposition; further, a normal configuration would require two or three Stars plus supporting server equipment and cost between $50k and $100k. Later stand-alone versions were made available though only 25,000 were sold.

But it was the Star that took the PARC GUI public.

In 1986 Berkeley Softworks developed GEOS (graphic environment operating system) and this brought GUIs to the early home computers like the Commodore 64 and other 6502-based systems. It later became GEO Works and by 1990 it was releasing GEOS for the IBM PC.

Its founder was Brian Dougherty who had written games for the Mattel Intellivision and then cofounded Imagic that was a victim of the 1983 video console crash.

The name GEOS was later reapplied to become a suite of application software; it came with GeoPaint and GeoWrite application software. GeoPublish and GeoCalc packages were soon added. Dougherty stated that his own business was completely based on these Geo packages.

GEOS was later updated for the Commodore 128 and the Apple II. It became the third best-selling OS behind MS-DOS and MacOS.

Quarterdeck Office Systems was founded in 1981 by Therese 'Terry' Myers and Garry Pope; they named it for the address of Myer's rented apartment at Marina del Rey. Yet another PC business that started in a garage!

Myers focused her attention away from the PC limelight and sought to stay under the radar of the big players. Quarterdeck produced the DESQ utility program, a valuable system that allowed the IBM PC to switch readily between applications.

So much for anonymity. In 1983 the Computer Dealers' Exposition voted DESQ as the 'software of the show'; Quarterdeck soon attracted $5.5m in venture capital.

Microsoft was deep into the development of its Interface Manager, which would later become Windows. IBM was shown early versions of this but was not interested. This was in part because IBM was developing TopView to offer the same multi-tasking facility that Quarterdeck had originated. IBM planned for its software to have windowing too. On its announcement in August 1984 the sales in DESQ slumped and dealers started to return unsold copies; DESQ was priced at $395 and IBM's TopView was announced at just $225.

TopView was announced to coincide with its PC AT, though it was not quite ready. They had judged that multitasking would be essential to harness the increased power of the 80286 MPU at its core; though TopView was designed to work with all x86 MPUs.

At this time IBM also introduced its program information files (PIF) that defined how files should be run under multitasking, the prime function being resource management. But the promised windowing did not materialise; instead TopView was text-based.

Microsoft had looked at acquiring Quarterdeck but Gates, realising that TopView had damaged it, lowered his original offer and this was rejected. This proved to be good news for Quarterdeck when it became evident that TopView was not able to offer the promised GUI-windows facilities and subsequently flopped.

The IBM launch and Microsoft opportunism served to focus Quarterdeck's attention and it launched DESQview in 1985. This updated program included many TopView features like PIF files; it had a form of GUI and did offer a series of windows. In April 1989 Quarterdeck received a US patent for the technique.

Initially priced at $99.95, it proved a winner. The next year it was voted *Infoworld's* 'best new idea'. Microsoft continued to have delays in its evolution of Windows and this allowed Quarterdeck to sell over 700,000 units of DESQview across two years.

However Quarterdeck was badly affected by a slowing in MS-DOS utility programs in 1998 as Windows finally bit back; it was to be acquired by Symantec. A Quarterdeck utility product called CleanSweep assisted the removal of unwanted programs; this was relaunched by Symantec as Norton SystemWorks.

At the human interface – Interface Manager

In the meantime Microsoft licensed the GUI and the Star's desktop-style approach from Xerox. In September 1981 it started work on Interface Manager as a first move towards the development of a GUI. In part this was enabled as an approach because Intel had developed chips that operated with DOS and also with a GUI.

During April 1983 Microsoft presented a 'sleight-of-hand' demo of its far-from-ready Interface Manager to IBM. It showed overlapping windows and ran multiple applications - something that would not in fact appear when Windows 1.0 was launched some thirty months later. But IBM again expressed no interest.

Apple and Steve Jobs had separately negotiated a deal with Xerox PARC for access to its GUI thinking, and in return granted Xerox an amazingly advantageous deal on pre-IPO shares in Apple. The first fruit of this deal, and the first GUI in the PC market was the Lisa in May 1983. But at $9,995 and given its speed problems and dodgy drives it did not set the world alight.

The next GUI software available on the market came from the VisiCalc people, VisiCorp. It was called VisiOn and was launched in December 1983. It was mouse-driven, used a bit-mapped display and multiple windows as a graphical environment. It was priced at $495 but required a mouse at a further $295.

VisiOn was launched with a software suite consisting of a spreadsheet, a graphics package and a word processor, but to buy the whole totalled $1,765. Worse, to operate it required 2.2 M-bytes of hard drive, which meant you needed to buy a 5 M-byte drive. Together with its controller that put the total spend up at $7,500; though this was of course still 75% of the cost of Apple's Lisa.

Privately Microsoft showed what it was now calling Windows to IBM again in November 1983. It was Rowland Hansen who proposed the name change from Interface Manager. But yet again it received no interest as IBM was by then already committed internally to its own TopView GUI.

Nothing to lose, in November 1983 Microsoft announced its intention to launch an operating system using a GUI called Windows. Gates promised it for April 1984 and forecast that by the end of that year it would be used by 90% of IBM compatibles. In fact it was two years before Windows was shipped, but this announcement provoked something of a maelstrom at Apple.

Microsoft's announcement had quite deliberately pre-empted the Apple Macintosh launch, planned for two months later in January 1984. Microsoft was fully aware of this because the product would include its Mac BASIC and also offer Microsoft Multiplan.

Worse still from Apple's viewpoint, the IBM PCjr was announced that same month with MS-DOS 2.1 aboard. All Apple's promotion was prepared to highlight its superiority over the earlier MS-DOS and now suddenly the PC world had shifted on its axis.

Sand in your eyes – Microsoft and the Mac

Microsoft had received a very early Macintosh prototype unit directly from Steve Jobs and was provided with access to some of the source code so it could develop the required applications for the Mac. Internally at Microsoft this top-secret project was referred to as SAND, for Steve's amazing new device.

This cooperation was a smart move by Microsoft in that it gave it direct experience in GUIs, somewhat at Apple's expense. This it could apply to its own Interface Manager activity, all at a time when it had to accept that the PC/MS-DOS platform was not yet able to compete.

Jobs was concerned that Microsoft might become a competitor for the GUI and therefore first insisted they reach an agreement that Microsoft would not release any software that worked with a mouse until after the first shipments of Macintosh. However the contract was based on the then belief that the Mac would be launched in September 1983, and of course this date had slipped. Apple had not allowed for this eventuality and now it had come back to bite them.

Neil Konzen had been given the task of developing Microsoft's Mac applications. Konzen started work with Microsoft while at high school and was a key individual who had worked both on Simonyi's pseudo-code C and on the system software for the Z80 SoftCard; he was also personally a keen Apple user.

Andy Hertzfeld at Apple liaised with Konzen and became increasingly disturbed by some of Konzen's questions that appeared to fall increasingly outside the scope of what he might need to know for the development of the application software.

Hertzfeld put on record the content of the resultant meeting following Microsoft's announcement. Hertzfeld said Jobs demanded that Gates come to Apple HQ and explain this breach of their agreement. Gates turned up alone to be confronted by ten of the Apple team. Jobs, with something of a bullying reputation, forcefully accused him of ripping Apple off, betraying his trust and stealing from them. The diminutive Gates quietly and calmly replied that there were in fact two ways of looking at the matter. He suggested it was rather as if they shared a rich neighbour, Xerox, and that when Gates broke in to steal his TV set, he found Jobs had beaten him to it.

But of course it was Apple's bravado about the Mac launch date embedded in the contract with Microsoft that meant its complaints were founded upon sand; ironically the very name Microsoft internally designated for the product.

Apple did wring a concession from Microsoft to hold fire on Excel for the PC and to concentrate efforts instead on Excel for the Mac.

Jockeying for position – GUIs, Microsoft and Apple

But the GUI wheel kept on turning. Tandy launched the Deskmate in 1984. This was a keyboard-driven GUI that depended heavily on function keys; it did not have overlapping windows. It was not really stable as a program until its v 3.05 in 1992.

Amiga launched Workbench in 1985 as a GUI file manager and launcher to work with the Amiga OS.

Microsoft countered these initiatives in May 1984 by shipping developer kits for Windows to software authors and encouraged them to support the upcoming Windows OS.

DRI, the CP/M originators, demonstrated its GUI in late 1984; it was called GEM, for graphical environment manager and launched in February 1985. It was to have its best success with the Atari ST computer series and with Amstrad IBM PC compatibles.

Lee Jay Lorenzen joined DRI from Xerox PARC and first produced GSX (graphics system extension) as a suite of graphics routines useful for charting within CP/M. GSX then became one part of GEM when linked with the user interface elements.

Apple sued DRI and was successful in having it remove certain components and to be forced to relaunch as GEM/2. But the software's real downfall was that DRI failed to get any third party software developer support for GEM.

In October 1984 Microsoft was back showing Windows to IBM yet still achieved no interest from Big Blue.

In January 1985 Microsoft showed Jobs the Excel spreadsheet software that was pledged to be initially Apple only, but by then Jobs was committed to Jazz, being developed by Lotus for the Mac.

Lotus 1-2-3 swept in to existence in 1983 and achieved over $50m in sales that first year; this had trebled in 1984 to over $150m. Mitch Kapor had stepped down from the presidency and the new incumbent was Jim Manzi. But it was Kapor who was approached by Gates for merger talks and they thrashed out a draft heads of agreement.

Gates was of course eyeing the Lotus direct sales force and saw this as an at-a-stroke opportunity to realise his goal of being the top dog in software. Kapor was up for it, having been offered a role in Microsoft. However Manzi, a management consultant, could not see how he would fit in with Microsoft's highly technical team; he therefore scuppered the deal.

Over the spring/summer of 1985 Jobs was himself in the process of being removed by Sculley from his role as head of the Macintosh team having been accused of fermenting insurrection. He was soon to leave to establish his approach and team to create NeXT.

Ever the opportunist, in June 1985 Bill Gates wrote to John Sculley outlining why he believed the Mac was not the hoped-for success and proposing the solution that the Mac OS should be licensed to Microsoft and three or four others so it would gain market credibility, it would also harness partner innovation and distribution and help it to become the de rigueur new standard for PCs.

Gates went on to suggest whom they might approach, suggesting in an ideal world it would be AT&T, DEC, HP, TI or Wang. He also put forward a 'more realistic' list which might be 3M, Burroughs, CPT, Kodak, Motorola and Xerox... He even suggested some European candidates such as Bull, Olivetti, Philips and Siemens.

Sculley was intrigued enough to charge Chuck Berger with doing the rounds of these potential licensees, those Microsoft had proposed and others that his team identified. It went well, and the interest led promptly to letters of intent from Apollo, AT&T, DEC and Wang.

But then Jean-Louis Gassée, who had taken over the Macintosh and Lisa teams from Jobs, successfully overthrew the notion. He was confident that their software could not be matched and this would derive good and profitable hardware sales.

At the back of Gassée's thinking was of course the fear that Microsoft was securely in the IBM PC camp and had a vested interest in keeping MS-DOS sales lively. But this rejection merely gave Gates more incentive to complete Microsoft Windows.

At the June 1985 year-end Microsoft had turned over $140m, with profits of over $30m and employed a staff of 910.

In the autumn of 1985 Microsoft announced it would set up its first international production facility in Dublin, Ireland and that it had shipped its one millionth copy of Multiplan. Notice that all of this was achieved before Windows!

Steamy windows – Microsoft Windows at last

Windows 1.0 was finally launched at COMDEX in November 1985, and first shipments were made straight after it on 20th November, selling at $99.95 per copy. It was not yet 'fit for purpose', it still had bugs and proved slow.

But Microsoft was adopting an approach to its products that it termed 'launch then improve'. I guess this was a slight improvement on the early PC hardware manufacturers who often tended to 'launch then create'.

At Apple, Gassée was jubilant; he felt Windows was not going to be a real competitor to Mac. In truth Windows 1.0 was much closer to the GUI originally developed back at PARC and had few of the enhancements that Apple had wrought in developing the Mac. Gassée saw it was a weak GUI with very clunky, consisting of tiled windows that could not overlap each other.

But Sculley had a different reaction. He believed the implementation had used Apple proprietary material; it had an almost identical menu bar, drop-down menus and many other features that were virtually identical. It even bundled Write and Paint, just as Mac had done with MacWrite and MacPaint. At this time Apple was a $1bn turnover operation, Microsoft a mere $140 million 'upstart' and he was not going to sit back and let it steal 'his' material.

An Apple lawyer was despatched northward to take legal action against Microsoft. Microsoft was shocked as it believed it had its deals in place with Apple and Xerox for the use of the GUI technologies. Neither wanted a protracted legal battle. Microsoft was moving towards its initial public offering. Apple needed all its attention focused on making the Mac a success; Apple III and Lisa were still all too fresh in their memories.

In the event Microsoft threatened to remove its support of the Office applications for Mac and Sculley capitulated. He gave Microsoft a non-exclusive, non-transferable, worldwide, royalty-free and perpetual deal for its Mac GUI in present and future software packages. In return Microsoft agreed that its software had indeed derived from Lisa and Mac and committed to more software support for the Mac, including a deal that would see Excel as a Mac-only platform until October 1986. This was signed on 22nd November 1985, just two days after Windows 1.0 was first shipped - Microsoft must have had a good chuckle!

Sculley then officiated over a back to basics period, dropping the Big Mac and a planned UNIX-Mac. By happenstance this coincided with the DTP effect on Mac sales and he was praised for his skilled management of the turnaround of Apple.

In March 1986 under pressure from employees to realise their share options a Microsoft IPO placed its shares at $25.75 and raised $61m.

RANDOM ACCESS MOMENT:
Sticks and stones – MS-DOS aficionados often dismissed the Apple Mac OS as WIMP - nothing to do with failure to outwit Gates, but based upon windows, icons, mice and pointers interface. When Windows came of age as Windows 95, Apple fans would chant 'Windows 95 – Apple 85' and Apple itself would lump all its Windows-based competition into one dismissive name of WINTEL (Windows-Intel).

Another GUI contender emerged in 1986 from Berkeley Softworks, a small start-up company. Its principal Brian Dougherty had worked on games development for the Mattel Intellivision and was part of the team at Imagic.

He formed Berkeley Softworks originally to create Sky Trap, a computer to be built into the back of airline seats. It was for this application that he developed a GUI called GEOS (graphic environment operating system).

He and his team had been used to the meagre resources of the Atari VCS 2600 and Mattel Intellivision and came up with a very compact approach which would suit the aircraft application very well. But airline deregulation stymied Sky Trap when the airlines moved to seek weight and fuel savings.

GEOS was therefore adapted for the Commodore 64 and 128; it was later bundled by Commodore with the C64C. The success of Commodore products briefly propelled GEOS to second place in the GUI market behind the Mac OS, and third in the generic OS market behind MS-DOS and Mac OS - pretty remarkable for a small operator.

In the meantime Windows 1.0 flopped and attracted little third party software. Aldus PageMaker was in fact the first but not until January 1987. Of course it was the very small Windows installed base that discouraged software authors from doing anything to remedy this.

Gates dismantled the Windows 1.0 team and fielded his 'striker' Neil Konzen, the individual who had worked cheek-by-jowl with Apple on the Mac applications and that had spooked Hertzfeld with his questioning.

Konzen was set the task of enhancing Windows and he did. His new version Windows 2.0 was released in November 1987. It delivered overlapping windows, icons, added multitasking and was available with in-house and third-party software support.

Microsoft's own Word and Excel were supported with pledges from Aldus with PageMaker, Corel with Draw and Microtek the Taiwanese scanner manufacturer, all planning to deliver on Windows 2.0 applications.

Sculley was once again to send in the lawyers. Without warning, in March 1988 Apple charged Microsoft with abusing its GUI copyrights in no fewer than 189 listed ways. For good measure Apple also enjoined Hewlett Packard for its New Wave graphical desktop environment, a Windows 2.0 program being prepared for its launch in 1989 but that had been previewed in 1988.

Microsoft countersued. This had the benefit for Apple of making PC clone makers and software developers wary of committing to Windows 2.0 while the subsequent action unfolded. But once again Apple was to prove guilty of not having read the small print in a Microsoft contract.

RANDOM ACCESS MOMENT:
It does make you ponder just what you are agreeing when you tick something unread, to suggest that you have read, understood and agree the terms and conditions when you buy a Microsoft package. It is just too dull to read through the clauses.

As if to prove my point, a UK games retailer called Gamestation on 1st April 2010 changed its website terms and conditions to say it owned the customer's soul in perpetuity. 88% of their customers happily ticked without query, the 12% that did check it got a £5 voucher for spotting the joke. Gamestation, the 21st century Mephistopheles, then sent the following email to the 88% of Faustians,

"Little did you realise that upon your last purchase from Gamestation.co.uk you also granted us a right to claim your humanity... ...To avoid future fatalities, always check the terms and conditions.

However, as Gamestation customer services conjurer I have been informed by HR that this little clause of mine is, apparently, not playing fair. So I'm releasing you from your part of the soul bargain."

I have to admit that I am surprised to discover that as many as 12 per cent of people read the terms and conditions. I had assumed that everyone ignored them.

So did you notice it above in the list of terms of the 22nd November 1985 deal between Apple and Microsoft? That it included the notion of perpetuity? Well Apple had not and they believed they had signed a deal that was just for Windows 1.0 so on this basis their current complaint proved to have no foundation.

Fifteen months later in July 1989 the judge ruled that 179 points on Apple's list were permitted by the agreement and the other ten were ideas that could not be copyrighted anyway. Apple did not give in easily and appealed. They eventually took the case to the Supreme Court, but it would not even hear the appeal.

By August 1993 Microsoft had won.

RANDOM ACCESS MOMENT:
perhaps it is sobering to ponder just what the PC business would have been like had Microsoft lost the case. While many bemoan the dominant force they were to become, I recall the early days before Microsoft Office where it was virtually impossible to distribute a letter or spreadsheet with anyone else. They were on WordPerfect while I was on WordStar, they were on Lotus and I was on VisiCalc and so on...

Mac fans were shocked by the series of legal proceedings. They were particularly stunned that Sculley had given the Mac GUI away in return for a spreadsheet and a word processing package; surely there were more than enough of those in existence?

But in 1988 Microsoft and Apple did finally find some common ground. Somewhat sadly the unity was based upon their mutual hostility for Adobe that seemed to keep turning them both down.

Apple wanted to stop paying big money to Adobe for PostScript software and hoped to develop its own solution. Microsoft bought a PostScript clone called TrueImage and licensed it to Apple. Apple reciprocated by licensing Microsoft its font format software TrueType, and they proceeded jointly to attack Adobe's monopoly.

Fresh openings – UNIX to Linux

While these commercial organisations were vying to own their software and squabbling over intellectual property, there was a whole other strand of the software market that believed software should be free.

We saw how AT&T, the Bell Labs owner, developed the UNIX software. It had been granted a unique position in the USA with its monopoly status in telecoms but this came at a price.

In 1956 in an anti-trust settlement it agreed to being excluded from the computer business. So from 1975 AT&T released the sixth version of UNIX to education and research establishments and to the US government at a nominal charge of $150 for the manuals and a tape of the source code.

Through the late 1970s three major versions of UNIX appeared; each had many variants. It became the OS of choice for academic users and this in turn allowed them to cooperate on experiments and systems because of the compatibility of their software.

When Ken Thompson and Dennis Ritchie presented a paper on UNIX in 1973, Bob Farby at the University of California Berkeley requested a copy of the system and students at the university began working on it. In 1975 Bill Joy and Chuck Haley created a line editor called 'ex' and a Pascal compiler for it. Pursued for copies of their version they launched it as Berkeley Software Distribution (BSD). The second generation of BSD added a WYSIWIG text editor called 'vi'.

In 1979 DARPA decided to standardise its operating systems on UNIX and Bill Joy submitted a proposal to use the third generation as the standard. He received the contract and established the Computer Systems Research Group; it developed what became known as UNIX BSD. It continued to improve the system adding TCP/IP in 1984, and Domain Name Server in 1986.

By 1989 a new version was released that avoided any AT&T code so a licence was no longer required from the telecoms company.

Back in 1979 AT&T had decided it should commercialise UNIX and established UNIX System Laboratories as the vehicle to pursue this goal. In 1983 AT&T was back in the courts as the Bell monopoly was ordered to be broken up, but this in turn released it from the constriction of the 1956 agreement and allowed it to make UNIX a chargeable product.

In 1983 it announced UNIX System V Release 1 as its first approach, collecting together various enhancements and seeking to earn from its development. This move was not well received by the open-source fraternity who tended to update existing UNIX programs rather than buy the new version.

As a result the industry was confronted with two chargeable versions, System V from AT&T or BSD UNIX. Having grown used to not paying, the users applied their energies behind the development of a third major group UNIX Open Systems.

In 1987 AT&T formed an alliance with Sun Microsystems who were marketing BSD Unix and they jointly set about unifying the two commercial systems; as part of this they launched UNIX SVR4 in 1989.

The open systems people responded in alarm and created the Open Systems Foundation with a free-from-licence version called OSF/1 in 1991. A European group also released another open version X/Open.

AT&T did not achieve too much for itself by its various moves and sold UNIX System Laboratories off to Novell who in turn assigned the rights to X/Open. Novell later disposed of its ownership in UNIX to the Santa Cruz Operation (SCO) in 1996. SCO initially marketed System V but eventually chose to merge the OSF version and X/Open into The Open Group making the system freely available.

But by the late '90s the attention moved from UNIX to gnus and to penguins.

Copyleft and GNU
Richard M Stallman was one of the hackers who had been let loose at the MIT AI Lab in the early 1970s; formally he was employed there as a programmer. While at high school he had worked for a summer with IBM on FORTRAN and APL, and after high school with PL/1 and an IBM System/360.

The MIT AI Lab ran a PDP-6 and PDP-10 at the time with its OS being the hackers' Incompatible Timesharing System. From 1963 the Lab, and by that I mean that almost everyone who worked there had participated, they produced an ongoing text editing system called TECO (tape editor and corrector). The word 'tape' was retained long after the tape device was used on a Friden Flexowriter; later the 'T' was used to mean 'text'. TECO was perhaps the most used text editor until 'vi' was created.

Stallman visited the Stanford AI Lab in the early '70s and encountered what was called an E editor, built on WYSIWYG principles. He set about updating TECO soon after. TECO was still inherently designed around tape editing and had no random editing capability; Stallman by 1981 had added this facility. He rewrote a series of pre-existing hacks, for example the Control-R routine that automatically refreshed the screen at each editing keystroke; significantly he added the facility to work with macros.

This was called EMACS (editor macros) though some comment that a nearby regular haunt may have been the inspiration - it was an ice cream parlour named Emack & Bolios; Stallman dismisses the notion. EMACS remains popular to date with the more technical programmer and vies successfully with 'vi'.

Stallman's hacker principles were clear when he explained,

'EMACS was distributed on a basis of communal sharing, which means all improvements must be given back to me to be incorporated and distributed.'

Stallman would work in pursuit of his belief that users had the right to copy, alter and to redistribute software.

RANDOM ACCESS MOMENT:
One of Stallman's notable hacker exploits was in 1977 when MIT set up the Laboratory of Computer Science and insisted on password access. Stallman hacked everyone's password and emailed the decrypted password to every user. He proposed that they change their passwords to empty strings (ie no password) so usage could not be logged; 20% of the faculty took up the suggestion, but passwords did eventually win the day.

James Gosling in 1981 wrote the first UNIX EMACS editor called Gosling EMACS. Written in 'C' and with Lisp-like add-ons it was initially released as proprietary software.

As a hacker Stallman became disturbed by the AT&T UNIX machinations and the motivations of others in the space; he set about coming up with a free version of the software:

'Starting this Thanksgiving I am going to write a complete Unix-compatible software system called GNU (for GNU's Not Unix), and give it away free to everyone who can use it. Contributions of time, money, programs and equipment are greatly needed...' Richard Stallman posted this on 27th September 1983.

In 1984 he resigned his position at MIT so his work could not be claimed as copyright by MIT or by its main sponsor DARPA. Much of the software was co-written by volunteers in their spare time and some unkind individuals suggest that GNU has yet to release a stable version even at today's date.

In 1985 he founded the Free Software Foundation as a non-profit charity thus avoiding the payment of tax. The funding was largely achieved from sales of CD-ROMs of the 'free' software that it developed.

His first project was to take the Gosling EMACS and rewrite it with a true Lisp interpreter; GNU EMACS was released by the GNU Project in 1985. He also wrote the GNU C Compiler.

All of the GNU software was distributed licence free via the GNU General Public Licence; Stallman used the term 'copyleft' to define its aims. The licence permitted anyone to upgrade and modify it provided that they made the new code public. It is today the most widely used free software licence.

His definition of free software however was quite loose in that he explains it means freedom and this does not mean zero-priced software. He described himself as a software freedom activist.

GNU was taken up by a number of commercial organisations who would provide free software but commercial and technical support was chargeable.

Cygnus Solutions was a group of those supporting the GNU development, using the promotional device 'making free software affordable'. Cygnus for example developed the BFD (binary file descriptor) or occasionally defined as 'big f-----g deal'. This permitted some fifty different file formats to be used with twenty-five different processor platforms.

Presumably Cygnus was selected as much because its name contains the letters 'gnu'. Cygnus was later to be merged into Red Hat.

The only people who have anything to fear from free software are those whose products are worth even less.' Quote by David Emery

Tux the penguin - Linux

UNIX was expensive, priced such that it was of little interest to the PC fraternity and prohibitive for educational establishments; all of this of course assisted Windows to permeate far and wide in the meantime.

One organisation in the 1980s the Association for Progressive Communications (APC) did develop a distributed networking approach for users to use UNIX on simple low-cost PCs.

'For those of us who have access to it, the internet has become an essential part of our daily information and communication needs. However millions of people still do not have affordable, reliable or sufficient connectivity. APC believes the internet is a global public good. Founded in 1990, we are an international network and non-profit organisation that wants everyone to have access to a free and open internet to improve our lives and create a more just world.' From the APC Website.

Andrew S Tanenbaum, an American-born Dutchman, while based at the Vrije University Amsterdam in the Netherlands decided he would develop a UNIX clone for the IBM PC and its 8086 MPU. He explained that he wanted his students to be able to study and work with a 'real operating system'.

Developed in 1987 he called it Minix (Mini Unix). It was based on a BSD Unix licence, with just 5,000 lines of code as its kernel. It certainly developed a huge amount of interest, for example Minix inspired a USENET group which rapidly added some 40,000 subscribers. He also wrote *Operating Systems: Design and Implementation* and made available 12,000 lines of code written in 'C' and assembly languages so programmers could get right into the heart of it.

A student at the University of Helsinki was using it and sought to make changes so it would not be solely a teaching tool, but Tanenbaum rejected the idea out of hand, and the student was forced into making a decision,

'Hello everybody out there using Minix - I'm doing a (free) operating system (just a hobby, won't be big and professional like gnu) for 386(486) AT clones. This has been brewing since April, and is starting to get ready. I'd like any feedback on things people like/dislike in Minix, as my OS resembles it somewhat... ...Any suggestions are welcome, but I won't promise I'll implement them :-) Linus', posted to the Minix newsgroup 25 Aug 1991.

Linus Torvalds, a 21-year old second-year computer science student wrote a new kernel using the available GNU tools and issued his software, under the GNU general public licence. Torvalds called it Freax, a contraction of free, freak and the 'x' from Unix, but the Helsinki University of Technology server administrator convinced him to rename it as Linux.

The software was released as a copyleft product named Linux 0.01 in September 1991. Torvalds picked a penguin called Tux as its logo and mascot, though apparently his first encounter with a real penguin resulted in him being bitten when he tried to pat it!

Within a few months a hundred programmers were actively communicating with Torvalds via Usenet and contributing fixes and hacks; within a year a fully functioning Linux was ready.

Tanenbaum was unimpressed,
'Be thankful you are not my student. You would not get a high grade for such a design.'

By 1993 there were 20,000 Linux users, and by 1994 some 100,000; the code had then grown to consist of some 170,000 lines.

Putting a hat on it – Red Hat

Bob Young, a Canadian, and Marc Ewing, an American who graduated from Carnegie Mellon University, got together in 1994 as Red Hat Software to sell Linux product. Ewing was renowned for wearing a red hat as he moved between classes. He was recognised as an expert in computing matters and many at CMU were told to 'ask the man in the red hat' if they had a problem.

The pair's Red Hat Linux was soon offered free but there was a charge for any support. By March 2002 it combined UNIX and Linux packages so they resembled more of a suite of software à la Windows, culminating in what they called the 'Red Hat Enterprise Linux'.

When Red Hat went public in mid-1999 it recorded the eighth largest first day gain on Wall Street. Not bad, an operation selling free software valued at $3bn! It was looking to raise between $60m and $72m but achieved $84m. With these proceeds it acquired Cygnus Solutions three months later.

RANDOM ACCESS MOMENT:
Carnegie Mellon University has featured heavily in thePCstory but we should just pause to include mention of Edward A Feigenbaum who as his PhD thesis developed EPAM (Elementary Perceiver and Memorizer) a computer

program that is based on his theory of learning and memory. This and later work he did with Raj Reddy in artificial intelligence systems earned him the sobriquet the 'father of expert systems'.

Red Hat and other initiatives ensured that Linux became one of the fastest-growing operating systems. It was adopted by many businesses simply to avoid the Microsoft licence fees and supported by many developers who successfully ported it to many platforms and who quickly ensured it was compatible with any new processors and other hardware releases.

RANDOM ACCESS MOMENT:
In 1996 the Los Alamos Labs used Linux to connect sixty-eight PCs to become one huge parallel processor to work on nuclear shockwave analysis. The approach cost only $150k to put together and the result was a device that could achieve 19 million instructions a second, making it the 315th most powerful computer in the world.
   In 2001 the US Government planned for its four supercomputing centres to join up 3,000 processors using Linux to create 'Teragrid', a mega computer capable of 13 teraflops (trillion calculations) per second.

Linus Torvalds did not become a billionaire, but appears to have few complaints,
'If you want to travel around the world and be invited to speak at a lot of different places, just write a Unix operating system.'
   He is also quoted as saying,
'Software is like sex: It's better when it's free.'

Is it catching? Viruses and malware

Two years after Ray Tomlinson developed email, Bob Metcalfe at PARC developed the Ethernet. The connecting up of equipment and users became very much the order of the day. But it was not just email spammers who had illicit designs for this new interconnectivity.
   It was John von Neumann's fault! He produced his *Theory and Organization of Complicated Automata* back in 1949 and in 1966 published the *Theory of Self-Reproducing Automata*. This identified how a software program might replicate itself. Once the notion had been defined it was not long before it was applied to various nefarious purposes.
   Based upon von Neumann's theories, during the 1950s the Bell Labs team would often play a game called Darwin for which an area of the IBM 7090 was set aside as an arena. Within this arena two or more opponents would insert a software routine that would replicate itself and in doing so would try to erase its opponent's routine from the arena. But one of the game's creators

Robert Morris Sr. brought the fun to an end when his program appeared to be unbeatable.

In 1971 Bob Thomas at BBN also experimented with a self-replicating program named Creeper. He produced it on a PDP-10 using the TENEX operating system and it spread via the ARPANET. It would reveal itself on the remote computer by stating,

'I'm the creeper, catch me if you can!'

It did not replicate itself within the host but instead would jump from computer to computer announcing its arrival at each host and erasing itself from its previous location. The Reaper program was later created to seek it out and to delete all instances of Creeper.

A number of sci-fi writers loved this notion and expanded on it throughout the 1970s. In 1972 Michael Crichton's *Terminal Man* described a computer that would dial random numbers until it reached another computer and then inject a program so that the recipient computer would do the same, seeking an exponential and inevitable takeover of all available computers.

The same year David Gerrold's *When HARLIE Was One* introduced an AI computer called HARLIE (human analog replication, lethetic intelligence engine) that was threatened by its human protagonist with being switched off. It countered by creating a virus, the first use of the term, to infect other computers and discredit its human minder.

RANDOM ACCESS MOMENT:
The word 'lethetic' caused me some problems. It did not come up on my Sharp Electronic Dictionary and Googling was not much help either. It seems to be taken from the Greek where 'lethe' means forgetfulness or forgetting. In Clayton Koelb's book 'The Incredulous Reader', he uses alethetic reading to indicate texts that comply with the currently established academic norms, so lethetic implies it is outside the norm. The context appears to be the fear of texts that threaten to overthrow the established view and change the world. My brain hurts!

The use of the term virus is often credited to Frederick Cohen in a PhD treatise produced in 1984 when he saw the similarity to biology in the way a program might embed itself in another. Cohen himself credits his teacher with the term, but both were securely post-HARLIE.

Published in 1975, *Shockwave Rider* by the UK writer John Brunner, drew upon the forecasted futures in Alvin Toffler's *Future Shock*. It featured a fugitive who had super computer skills, by accessing a computer from any phone booth he was able to change his identity. It introduced the term 'worm' for a program that could insinuate itself through a computer network.

Canadian sci-fi writer Thomas J Ryan published *The Adolescence of P-1* in 1977. The main protagonist developed an artificial intelligence that he called

The System. It used telecom links to seek out other computers and have them establish their own P-1 areas. Each P-1 would then learn, adapt and exchange its discoveries with other P-1s. This was the first notion of a virus that would attempt to control a remote computer's operating system.

Fact following fiction

By 1974 the first Wabbit virus was released. This did not replicate between computers but duplicated itself using the inherent 'fork' operation within a computer. It was called Wabbit because of the pace at which it reproduced, rapidly overwhelming the capability of the computer to cope and usually requiring a complete reboot to overcome it.

John Walker has solid programming credentials as the co-founder of Autodesk Inc and the co-author of AutoCAD. But before this in 1974/5 while working for UNIVAC he created an improvement for the popular Animal program. This program would try to guess the animal the user had thought of by asking a small number of questions. He was overwhelmed with calls for copies of this new version and must have taken umbrage at all the time it was taking him.

He wrote another version of it with a second hidden program known as Pervade. While the user was playing Animal, Pervade would replicate itself in every directory the user could access. It was not malicious and was written with care so as not to damage other files and not to penetrate beyond the user's access rights.

It spread widely until a new release of UNIVAC's operating system changed its directory structure and managed to stop the process. This is considered to be the first Trojan Horse virus, though it was not termed such at the time.

Darwin and Creeper later inspired Core Wars. These wars established a virtual computer called MARS (memory array redcode simulator) that operated within the memory of the host rather like Darwin. Again the plan was for a user to create a software 'organism' that would battle and overwhelm its opponents within a defined arena. It was launched as a game in the mid 1980s and classes of 'warriors' emerged that were just as complex as in any Dungeons & Dragons game. Bombers, evolvers, imps, replicators, scanners, silks, vampires and others were launched and despatched to do battle in a virtual battlefield.

In 1981 Elk Cloner was released by Richard Skrenta, a high-school student who would later work at Commodore, UNIX System Labs and Sun. It attacked Apple II computers by spreading itself via the Apple DOS 3.3 operating system whenever it wrote to a floppy disk. It was only on its fiftieth activation that it would announce itself by displaying a poem that commenced *'Elk Cloner: The program with a personality...'*

In 1986 two brothers from Lahore, Pakistan, suggested they had inadvertently created the first IBM PC and MS-DOS virus epidemic. Basit and Amjad Farooq Alvi were writing medical software and created a routine that they believed would protect their copyright from those trying to abuse their ownership. The routine infected the boot sector of a 360K floppy disk and this slowed down the drive by infecting a few disk sectors.

The routine was called the Brain virus because the affected floppy volume label showed '©Brain'; this approach inspired a number of variants.

In 1987 a fresh infection called Stoned emerged from New Zealand. It attacked PC-AT hard disk drives and an infected PC would show the text,
'Your PC is now Stoned!'

Another version was Bloody! In a tribute to the Tiananmen Square protests and the bloody outcome in Beijing, China, it displayed the text,
'Bloody! Jun, 4, 1989'

IBM responded to these early viruses by coming up with some anti-virus tools and forming the High Integrity Computing Laboratory team in 1987. This team pioneered the computer virus epidemiology approaches that are used today.

Vermicelli

But the infection that put the subject into the limelight was released in November 1988 by a 23-year old programmer called Robert T Morris, intriguingly he was the son of the chief scientist at the National Computer Security Center.

He was at Cornell University but to cover his tracks launched the infection from MIT - where he would later become a professor!

His purpose was to establish how many computers were connected to the ARPANET at the time; it replicated itself using a variety of loopholes. The program was a worm that would arrive at a computer and check to see if it was already present, if not it would then clock up another on its counter.

The problem was that Morris had prepared for computer administrators seeking to bar the program's access by making it randomly try again on one in seven rejections. This 14% re-try proved too high a frequency and the Morris worm replicated itself repeatedly and rapidly infected 6,000 computers on the ARPANET.

There is some evidence that this was 10% of the estimated 60k computers which were at that time attached to ARPANET. It was also estimated that the damage to each system through the enforced downtimes was from $20k to over $500k each; there was thus a possible total impact of somewhere between $10m to $100m.

Morris was the first to be charged under the 1986 US Computer Fraud and Abuse Act. Eventually receiving a $10,000 fine, he served three years on probation and was committed to many hours of community service.

In 1987 the Jerusalem virus was first detected, named for where it had first been encountered. This was a worm-type virus that would sit in DOS, adding around 2K of code to .exe files each time they were used until eventually they become too large to load.

But where it was really sinister was in the way it brought to life any latent paraskevidekatriaphobia (or friggatriskaidekaphobia). On every Friday 13th after 1987 it was set to delete all files executed since infection.

Earlier Suriv viruses had done something similar; Suriv2 on April 1st and Suriv3 on Friday 13th.

The Jerusalem virus hit first on Friday May 13th 1988. It peaked in terms of worldwide presence by 1990-1991 but as Windows became more prevalent it was in decline by 1994. This was largely because Windows would very evidently underperform when infected and users would be prompted to repair or re-boot to dispose of it.

Immunisation

John McAfee, the founder of McAfee Inc rather unwisely said in 1988,
'The problem of viruses is temporary and will be solved in two years.'

I bet he is grateful that he was wrong with this forecast. Twenty years later the company turned over $1.6bn for antivirus software and computer security products.

Back in 1982 Gary Hendrix obtained a National Science Foundation grant and founded Symantec to investigate AI and database programs. In 1984 it was acquired by C & E Software, run by Denis Coleman and Gordon Eubanks.

Eubanks wrote E-BASIC while at college, then while in the US Navy produced CBASIC for the IMSAI and sold this on to Microsoft. He subsequently worked at DRI with Gary Kildall.

Still called Symantec, with Eubanks at the helm, it first launched 'Q&A' an integrated database and word processor in 1985. This was followed by a range of utility programs. It then acquired Peter Norton Computing Inc in 1990. Norton had developed several utilities but with its anti-virus program was not faring well against competitors.

This acquisition by Symantec tripled revenues within fifteen months and Norton AntiVirus became the established market leader. A series of high-profile acquisitions built the organisation into a $6bn revenue operation by the late noughties with anti-virus representing around a third of its business.

Symantec did have some early problems when its Indian call centre would rather too freely suggest that a caller was contaminated and sell an online immunisation; it was unclear whether this was company policy or just local enthusiasm.

RANDOM ACCESS MOMENT:

I cannot quite remember when this emerged, but I remember all too vividly that there was a popular email going around at about this time. When opened it showed my C: drive dialogue box with all its actual current contents. Then a message popped up saying 'Confirm erase all files'. Alarmingly they then proceeded to disappear one by one from the screen. No matter what I did I could not stop it and was reduced to sitting there watching all my disk content steadily erased. Then a message popped up saying 'Just imagine if this had been real' and it prompted you to buy protection. It made its point very graphically, but I imagine it being withdrawn after several heart attack and mental anguish legal actions.

Other companies including McAfee have built a strong business in this sector; the McAfee VirusScan program was early in offering an enterprise-wide product. In February 1997 McAfee was also responsible for detecting the first virus used with Linux. Today a number of server-based programs are also available from a series of suppliers.

But as the World Wide Web evolved a whole new series of security and privacy issues emerged including control of cookies, parental locking, managing adware and spyware. Many companies sold add-ons or separate programs to combat or offer these applications initially, before the market moved to more integrated approaches.

One specialist application came from the Kaspersky Labs in Moscow, Russia in 1997. The Kaspersky Anti-Virus program offered protection from malware (short for malicious software) with Windows, Mac OS X and Linux.

Malware is a vast and ever-growing sector. In 2008 estimated Symantec the rate of release of malware exceeded that of legitimate applications; but then of course it was in its interest to make this sound an overwhelming threat.

Not to in any way diminish the defence against malware that today includes viruses and worms, Trojan horses, adware and spyware, crimeware that seeks to grab your identity, rootkits that seek to get administrative control of your PC...

Ad-Aware from Lavasoft for example originally offered a means of alerting the user when a website being viewed with Internet Explorer was tracking non-essential information. Later more protective versions of Ad-Aware simply blocked these, added spyware and malware routines and offered an anti-virus component too.

In 1992 Grisoft in what was then Czechoslovakia launched the AVG (anti-virus guard) program. In 1997 it released AVG as an anti-virus and Internet security program to the UK and Germany; it was available in the United States the following year.

By offering an AVG Free Edition the company promoted itself extremely well and achieved over 100 million users by the end of the noughties. It is tenacious in trying to switch users from its free edition to the latest chargeable version, but it is still possible to persevere and only use the free program.

Like most such battles the two sides win some and lose some - the malicious author manages to circumvent current controls and the anti-virus programs counter with a response.

18 - Communicating by computer
Sir William Preece, then the Chief Engineer of the UK Post Office, said in 1878: 'The Americans have need of the telephone, but we do not. We have plenty of messenger boys.'

Linking television and computers
It did not take long for computing and television to be connected. These two high-value family purchases were initially located remotely; the television was the centrepiece of the lounge and the computer was often tucked away in a corner of the study or a bedroom.

The first services that sought to connect the two were similar text-based, on-screen information sources, both originating in the UK.

Teletext was a service that utilised the spare lines on the UK's 625-line television broadcast system. These lines were usually tuned to be set off the edge of the screen's viewing area and were therefore being wasted.

Teletext transmitted a sequential series of pages of text within these spare lines that at first were read using a plug-in adaptor. Soon the electronics were built-in to larger-screen television sets as a standard feature. The two UK television networks offered competing services.

The BBC (British Broadcasting Corporation) had an enthusiastic director of engineering, James Redmond, who drove the launch of the teletext service in September 1974. He was supported by an editor, Colin McIntyre, and a small team of nine. It was called Ceefax, phonetically derived from see facts.

The IBA (Independent Broadcast Authority) responded with its own Oracle service later. The name was rather inelegantly justified as standing for Optional Reception of Announcements by Coded Line Electronics. I am not sure why IBA felt the need to come up with this definition as it was such a good name in its own right – as in 'ask the oracle' or as its own marketing suggested, 'page the oracle'.

The two services were initially incompatible but two years later they agreed on a single standard. It was called WST (world standard teletext) and remains the European standard. It had a little success in the USA which had adopted a more complex system NABTS (North American broadcast teletext standard).

In fact these two teletext services were underwritten by the UK government when in the early 1980s, lobbied by BREMA (British Radio Equipment Manufacturers' Association), it provided incentives and easy terms for UK households to buy or rent large-screen televisions with teletext built-in.

This was founded on the belief that UK manufacturers had an edge in producing these large sets and so was seen as a smart way to support home industry without appearing to restrict imports. As a result manufacturers, retailers and renters concentrated attention on these large sets, just as consumers concluded that they wanted the compact sets being delivered by Sony, Hitachi, Panasonic and others!

Teletext services offered around 200 pages of latest news, business news, weather reports, sports results and TV schedules. But as the pages were delivered one by one the access times were lengthy.

When these government initiatives expired, Teletext was improved, expanded and speeded up; it was the backbone for subtitles for the deaf. Before the Web took off, Oracle created quite a reputation in accessing last-minute travel deals, though extreme patience was necessary to wait through many cycles of sending pages. Oracle was closed at the end of 1992 and replaced by Teletext Ltd. BBC's Ceefax was planned to disappear on the replacement of analogue television in 2012.

The arrival of the Web and the improved ways of referencing TV program schedules by expanded newspaper features and listings magazines took their toll. 24-hour news channels and smartphones feed us news and reviews.

VideoPlus codes (VCR+ in the USA) assisted users to programme their video recorders and this too had an impact. More recently TiVo digital video recorders provided an electronic catalogue with easy programming and series links; these finally surpassed any need for teletext. In the UK, TiVo is better known as Sky+.

Viewdata

The other on-screen text service was Viewdata, a much more interesting system that actually delivered many of the features of the Web.

It was designed by Sam Fedida, based at the UK's Post Office Research Station originally at Dollis Hill and then later at Martlesham Heath, Suffolk. He too was inspired in 1968 by Licklider's article *The Computer as Communications Device*. This said,

'In a few years men will be able to communicate more effectively through a machine than face to face...When minds interact, new ideas emerge.'

Unlike Paul Baran, Lick Licklider, Ted Nelson and other visionaries of networked computers, Fedida was a development engineer in the UK's Post Office, which then also ran the telephone system; his focus was therefore naturally based more around the phone network.

Fedida saw a way of getting information to consumers and businesses using the two items they already possessed - the television and the telephone. Though in fact back then a single television in the household was usually in the corner of the lounge and the telephone often some distance away out in the hallway.

He first demonstrated his approach in 1974; this led to the launch of Prestel, a contraction of press telephone in 1979. In August 1980 the Post

Office received a patent for 'information handling system and terminal apparatus' which in the late 1980s it tried to suggest gave them rights to all hyperlink systems. This application was pretty presumptuous and it ultimately failed.

When privatisation was forced upon the Post Office it split its postal service from its telephones, British Telecom took Prestel to its side of the house.

On screen Prestel was very similar to teletext with 24 lines of 40 characters, supporting seven colours and rather blocky graphics. The top line was reserved for the page number, the information provider's name and the charge for the page; the bottom line was reserved for system messages. So in fact the medium was reduced to just 22 lines of 40 characters.

Pages used the V23 system to send data outward at 1200 bps and receive messages back from the user at 75 bps. Prestel formed the basis for the subsequent adoption of the CEPT Videotex European Standard; several of the standard's elements in retrospect appear to be deliberately written to exclude new USA PCs such as the Apple II and Commodore 64. If so this did not achieve its aim to support European contenders versus US 'invaders'.

Prestel really showed an edge over teletext connecting the home television to the home phone so the capacity and the speed of text pages were 'limitless' - not quite true as the capacity was limited by its page numbers 0 to 999,999,999.

What was interesting however was that the system allowed the information provider to set a price for accessing certain information pages; initially from £0.01 to £9.99. Better still the Post Office, and later BT, with all its mighty accounting strengths would bill and collect the sums. Payment was assured in that few would risk having the telephone cut off for non-payment.

The Prestel organisation rushed around and signed up many corporates to provide the information. In particular the subject of travel was an early success for the service.

Prestel adaptors were initially acoustic couplers to allow a home phone to communicate with the Prestel centres. The services offered were mostly the same fare as appeared on the teletext services – news, sport, weather...

Prestel did lure the consumer reviewer *Which?* onto the service and had many other planned initiatives. It grew to some 15,000 users of which only 2,000 were consumers so it proved not to be that big a market.

But this was a technically innovative system that seemed to ignore those interested in technology. I felt it should be talking directly to the technical market and devised something called Electronic Insight, which set out to provide a comparison database of all electronic products available at the time.

I had personally already invested heavily in my Atari VCS, Commodore Pet and an Apple II. I had attended most PC shows and developed good contacts with the various Apple User Groups. For example I was close to

BASUG (British Apple System Users' Group) and had been supplied free of charge with a host of utilities and games developed by users royalty-free.

Through them and contact with Prestel itself I managed to get a meeting of all those considering telesoftware and bulletin boards in the UK. We all looked enviously at The Source and CompuServe in the USA!

There were two telesoftware standards being promoted at the time and this meant that we were in limbo while they slugged it out. The meeting agreed that this was daft and we decided we would all go with the CET (Council for Educational Technology) version - we were off and running!

The user groups gave their agreement to our putting their public domain material up onto Electronic Insight for free downloads, and we started discussing what we might offer in terms of chargeable downloads. With £9.99 being the maximum per Prestel page we quickly looked at how to spread the code across multiple pages.

I bought myself a Bishopsgate terminal and spent interminable hours in a back bedroom creating simple text-based telesoftware pages. It was amazing what could be produced in those 22 lines of 40 characters with limited graphics. However I still bear the scars - I am convinced it was the large flashing cursor and the many hours I spent looking at it that left several 'floaters' in my eye.

For the initial revenue source I planned the sale of advertising pages within the service - £125/page/annum or £500pa for four text pages plus a response page, all designed on the Bishopsgate. Within this price updates were offered four times a year and a quarterly report of the accesses achieved.

The brochure proudly proclaimed 'Comment to Commitment – in 8 easy steps'. It showed eight screens – a news page announcing the 'ABC' computer, a page detailing its features, a page comparing it with other PCs, a link to the 'ABC' Company itself, its page on benefits and selling points, a list of local stockists, a link to the local retailer and finally a response page to order the computer using a credit card.

The user was locked inside the avuncular British Telecom system and the use of credit card numbers was not seen as a risk back then - unlike on the Web later. Users would be unlikely to default on payments and lose their phone service!

Remember this was developed well before the Internet was mooted.

Micronet 800

I launched Electronic Insight at Mullard House in Central London in March 1980. After my presentation the usual group of journalists pressed me for more material than was in the press release and brochure. One was persistent and while not being rude I was a bit brusque as he kept saying he wanted to do what I was doing.

The next day that individual, Richard Hease, asked his secretary to call me and explain that he was the chairman of EMAP's (East Midlands Allied Press) Computer and Business Press. Now he had my attention!

Hease had worked at IPC as a journalist, but left to establish *Practical Computing* which he promptly sold back to IPC for a sizeable sum. He went on to launch *Computer Management, Computer & Video Games, Educational Computing, Which Computer?, IBM User, DEC User, Sinclair User, Acorn User...* - pretty much all the titles that had presaged and helped the early UK PC industry move forward.

We met and spent the day talking. We shared the same views as to what was going to happen next in the PC sector and promptly formed a new company called Microrental London Ltd - something Richard had created off-the-shelf but which had not yet traded.

EMAP bought Electronic Insight from me and I joined the board of its Telemap operation. Bizarrely this was setting out to be a Prestel information provider in the gardening and horticulture sector. EMAP was strong in the magazine sector of gardening so this was a natural approach for them, but hoary-handed, calloused and green-fingered gardeners struck me as being the least likely to come from their greenhouses or market gardens to sit down and start working at a keyboard.

With EMAP's strengths we negotiated a special status with Prestel and soon turned Electronic Insight into Micronet 800. The 800 was our home page for the service; it was subsequently used on every English car I have had since because I soon acquired the custom vehicle registration plates RSD 800.

At the time Prestel had identified two major projects it felt were capable of opening up its service - Micronet 800 and the Nottingham Building Society.

The building society planned an online banking service called Homelink on Prestel, in cooperation with the Bank of Scotland. The idea was to use this online approach in place of opening an expensive series of retail outlets as its competitors had done or were doing.

It was felt that the reduction in overheads would allow the addition of fruitful new services. This never really happened but in the pecking order at Prestel it was mentioned in every one of their announcements and feted as the 'new great shiny thing'; for us, it felt a little like we had to skulk in and out of the tradesmen's entrance to get a hearing.

Both of the services were CUGs (closed user groups) which meant some of the main features were only available to those who subscribed and received the relevant access to those closed pages.

Micronet 800, with the resources of Prestel and EMAP behind it, set out to be much more ambitious. We offered a turnkey solution to connect all leading PCs of the day to Prestel. But to make Micronet work we needed a series of solutions for each PC, not just a modem but also the required connectors and software to customise it to the host PC.

On the software side this was where user groups came up trumps and provided us with software for pretty much all the PCs out there.

A major advertising and direct mail campaign claimed most of today's Internet benefits for Micronet 800,

'Today, we talked to our user group, booked our holiday, zapped nine monsters, checked the football results, bought two games, looked at share prices, learnt some French and conquered the universe!'

The campaign went on to say that it was possible to send instant messages and use electronic mailbox services.

We were significant in Prestel terms, signing more than 30,000 subscribers to Micronet 800 by 1985. Prestel at its peak achieved only a total of 90,000 users. And our subscribers were particularly active - we were getting over a million page views per week.

Sound familiar? There we were in the early '80s offering all the benefits that the Internet and World Wide Web would offer much later. Yes, we were constrained in terms of display graphics, but in no way in terms of imagination or service potential.

Minitel

Meanwhile across the channel in France there was a simple way to get the huge penetrations that we had sought for Prestel.

In 1979 Gérard Théry, Director General for Telecommunications in France, announced it would fund the free issue of low-cost viewdata terminals by the simple expedient of offering phone users a straight choice, the usual bulky white telephone book or a Minitel terminal.

By getting into volume production it could drive down the cost of the terminals and by the end of the 1980s some five million were in use across France. Another four million users were said to have accessed it with Web-enabled devices and this made it the most successful network prior to the Web.

Minitel was originally a joint venture between the UK's British Telecom and France's PT (*Poste, Téléphone et Télécommunications*) service; the latter was going through a similar privatisation phase as it became separated into France Télécom and La Poste. It used the same V23 system as Prestel, operating at 1200 bps outward and 75 bps back.

The basic service was actually called Télétel, but the first trial service became known as T3V because it ran in Val de Bièvre, Velizy and Versailles; with time it became better known as Minitel. Its 3615 and 3617 telephone prefixes were broadly advertised by the information providers.

The Minitel 'dumb' terminal consisted of a screen, a keyboard and a modem; later there were printers that could be attached to the system.

It offered a full telephone book and search service, and access to air and rail reservations, mail order companies and other information sources. There was also a message board service.

It too had the weight of the national telecom organisation behind it to collect charges reliably, and for this reason was trusted with credit card transactions.

By 1994 Minitel had 25,000 services using its medium and some seven million terminals in use. Minitel rapidly replaced Louis Pouzin's Cyclades service and, depending on your point of view, it either delayed France's adoption of the Web or prepared its users more fully for adopting it.

Many feel the former, playing to the Chauvinist fears perhaps best outlined in Jean Jacques Servan-Schreiber's book *The American Challenge*.

Minitel-like services did appear in other markets, as CommunityLink in the USA, AlexTel in Canada, Telecom Eireann in Ireland, Viditel in The Netherlands ... but it was never significantly successful in any of these.

Though due to be closed in 2009 Minitel found its directory enquiries service was still being used a million times each month, so the service continued.

Getting connected - modems

We have seen how the thrust towards the PC was about moving away from large central computers and time-sharing and towards the principle of giving individuals their own independent computing power.

These personal computers brought with them new applications, new opportunities and new levels of personal productivity. But perversely they really came of age when they started to interconnect with each other for collaborative working and better communication.

Systems for networking computers had been around for some time and predated the general move towards the Internet protocols of TCP/IP.

For example IBM had the SNA (systems network architecture) from 1974; this was a series of communications packages enabling computers and peripherals to 'talk' between themselves. DEC too had the DECnet from 1975, launched to interconnect PDP11s.

It was natural that there would be interest in finding ways for interconnecting PCs in a similar manner.

The first means of having PCs talk with other devices was the modem (modulator-demodulator) that used the modulation of a carrier signal to carry a digital message. The modem modulated the signal when sending a signal and demodulated it on its receipt.

The most common early modem used an acoustic signal in the voice-band range to send its message across a standard telephone line in place of a caller's voice message. These were usually defined by the amount of data it could send in bits per second, or by the number of bauds (pulses per second) it could achieve. The word baud comes from Emile Baudot, an inventor from the days of telegraphy.

In fact the first requirement for a modem had been in telegraphy, when there was a need for teletype machines to talk with each other across a standard telephone line rather than a more expensive leased line. George Stibitz (Bell Labs, Model K kitchen computer and Complex Number Calculator) first demonstrated this in 1940 when he connected a New Hampshire-based teletype with a computer in New York across a normal phone line.

The SAGE air-defence network generated a need for a mass-produced modem in 1958. The Bell-produced modems connected all the radar bases and airbases to the command and control centres using acoustic modems operating at 110 baud. Dedicated lines were used but the technology would have worked just as well across the standard phone network.

AT&T Bell launched a phone using data signals rather than the original analogue system and also released a modem for general use in 1960.

The first widely used standard was the V21 standard, operating at a full-duplex 300 bps or baud rate; this was launched by Bell Labs in 1962. Of course PTT companies like Bell were still very much operating as a monopoly, particularly with anything electrically operated that was going to be connected into their networks. There was little incentive for others to look at this technology.

However a route around this was discovered using acoustic couplers. These were not physically connected directly to the PTT network and instead used two cups to fit over a handset to send and receive audio messages.

A legal decision in the USA in 1968, the Carterfone decision, changed this matter. The Carterfone, developed by Thomas Carter, was able to patch someone on a two-way radio (including a CB radio) through to someone on the public telephone network.

There ensued a 'turf war' between the Federal Communications Commission (FCC) and AT&T. The FCC had approved the Carterfone to be connected into AT&T's network provided it caused no harm to the network. This was upheld by the legal decision.

But AT&T tried to frustrate this by making the process to ensure there was no damage to its equipment a very complicated and expensive one - but the door was now ajar. Most users chose to use an acoustic coupler into the 1980s to avoid the hassle.

In 1976 in Chicago Casey Cowell, Paul Collard, Steve Muka and others formed a company to make modems. They also followed the PC formula and started their business in a garage!

They funded the operation with just $200 to build a keyboard and acoustic coupler - and achieved $50,000 turnover in the first year.

For a company name they looked to the Asimov robot short stories for inspiration. Asimov had a fictional mega-company called US Robots and Mechanical Men and they opted for the name US Robotics, though there never appeared to be any ambition to produce robots. The name was later truncated to USR.

Paul Collard who designed the modems was raised and educated in the UK. He attended Sussex University earning a degree in applied physics. His wife hailed from Chicago and it was while working at the University of Chicago's Computation Center that he met the others with whom he formed USR.

For want of agreed standards, USR developed its own protocol HST (high-speed transfer) which was a 9600 baud service; this was later expanded to 14.4k and 16.8k.

In 1984 the company moved to a proper factory space as it achieved an 8% share of the overall modem business, though it supplied close to 50% of the higher-speed modems.

USR continued to innovate down the years, bringing the first 56k modem to the market for example. When it was acquired by 3Com in 1997 it had a 25% share of the USA market. 3Com and USR combined had a $5bn turnover.

In 1981 Hayes Communications introduced the Smartmodem. Dennis C Hayes qualified from Georgia Institute of Technology and in the mid 1970s worked for the National Data Corporation; it handled credit card authorisations and electronic funds transfers. Hayes was employed to investigate offering NDC clients a modem connection.

He found several types of modem available at the time. There were some that entailed the user manually dialling, attaching an acoustic coupler once the carrier signal was reached and manually disconnecting at the end of the call. Or there were auto-answer versions that tended to be used at the host computer end.

There was also the internal type of modem including the most popular solution for an Apple II, the Novation Apple-CAT II. Connected to the motherboard, this modem allowed the computer to control the modem directly and, for example, enabled the computer to 'listen' for a busy signal.

But Hayes found none that could do all these things automatically. From spring 1977 he produced hobbyist modems. The first was the 80-103A, a 300 bps modem compatible with Bell's 103A system that worked with S-100 bus PCs. It sold for just $299.

By early 1978 he and his colleague Dale Heatherington were able to quit their NDA jobs to form D C Hayes Associates in Atlanta, Georgia. By 1979 they launched the Micromodem 100 for S-100 bus PCs and Micromodem II for the Apple II. The Micromodem essentially provided a modem, an autodialler, a serial and a parallel interface, plus an FCC-registered coupler that did away with an acoustic coupler.

But as the TRS-80 and Atari 400/800 were launched it became obvious that a more general approach was required. The RS-232 serial port came to their rescue; it was a 25-pin standard connector for modems to PCs that rapidly became the standard serial port for PCs. The Recommended Standard 232 defined the electrical characteristics of the port, its size, the pin out connections, the timing and the meaning of the signals passing through it.

Hayes and his team developed the Smartmodem as an external modem that would connect via the RS-232C. They established two modes for it. There was a data mode whereby the modem modulated and sent data received from the computer, and there was a command mode where it interpreted the message from the computer as commands to hang-up, dial a number and so on. Some thirty different commands could be handled by any operating system. It worked with both pulse and Touch-Tone phones; its built-in audio monitor made clear when a busy line was encountered.

Heatherington came up with the command string '+++ ' (three plus symbols followed by a pause) that was so unlikely to be needed naturally that it could be used to alert the modem to switch between modes. The significant little pause after the triple + was important as it guarded against accidental mode switching. Hayes patented this approach in 1985 and charged other manufacturers $1 per modem for its use; many termed this the 'modem tax'.

The Hayes Smartmodem was launched in July 1981 at $279. It was the first modem to give the PC complete control of the phone line. It was also significant for being completely independent of the PC platform. When bulletin board services became available the Smartmodem sales really began to take off.

By 1982 the Smartmodem 1200 giving full 1200 bps was launched at $699. When the CCITT introduced the V22bis standard for 2400 bps Hayes launched the Smartmodem 2400 at $549 in 1985. But cloning Hayes became a popular pastime and competition rapidly drove prices down, by 1987 the market price for a 2400 modem was just $250.

Hayes was slow to launch any faster modems and this left the door open for a competitor.

At Prism Microproducts we started out providing Prism-badged acoustic coupler modems for our Micronet 800 Prestel-based service but soon graduated to smarter modems.

I recalled during my time at Dixons Group that we had secured supply of the Signetics games chips for the Acetronic MPU 1000 games console; though this was to prove a pyrrhic victory when Atari cornered Space Invaders.

So at Prism we used a similar approach and tried to monopolise the early supplies of single-chip modems. We designed the Prism Model 1000 and

2000 modems that were packaged with the required leads and software for each PC as Network Adaptors or Prism Comms Packs. These single-chip integrated modems were manufactured for us by several suppliers - Thorn EMI Datatech and Pace being the most significant.

With these single-chip modems we were able to drive down the entry price considerably; in 1983 the Prism Modem 1000 cost £69.95 for a full duplex V23 system. The 2000 was a software-controllable version at £94.95.

The Comms Packs were low-priced too as they were based upon hobbyist solutions. As an example, versions for the BBC Micro were offered with an RS423 connector with software either on cassette at £14.95 or as a ROM at £19.95. The Apple II/IIE version was a disc, either connected via the games paddle port for £29.95 or with an expansion card approach at £49.95. We also had solutions for the IBM PC, ACT Sirius and Apricot, the Commodore 64, Tandy Model I and III...

Of course the top selling UK PC of the time was the Sinclair ZX81 and this proved to be the most elusive solution. We ran a competition challenging the user groups, with a big cash prize (well £1,500) for coming up with a way of connecting the ZX81 to Prestel – and they succeeded.

Based on our ZX81 solution we created a Sinclair Spectrum version, the Prism VTX5000 modem, which early in 1984 was the *Personal Computer News* 'peripheral of the year'. By this time we had an approach using dBase II Run-Time so users could download viewdata pages and process the material on the page. We also offered an off-line email preparation system so that the message was sent upon logging on.

We soon added a rental proposition for the ZX Spectrum. For just £11 per month a user received a Prism VTX5000 modem worth £99.95, a year's subscription to Prestel (then £20), a year's subscription to Micronet 800 that we priced at £32, one hundred free Spectrum programs and hundreds of free and discounted software downloads, email software worth £19, special hardware offers every quarter, plus latest news and views provided by the EMAP editorial team.

It also allowed the user to turn a Spectrum into a terminal to the PSS (packet switching system). The software we offered hit all the targets we had identified – games such as Quest, Death Stars, Void, Battle on Hoth; educational offers included an introduction to computing, Spiders an adding game, Touch Type to develop typing skills; and there were utilities programs such as Cogitate to assist memory, Bill to manage utility costs, VATPROG to calculate value added tax returns...

By 1983 there were over nine hundred information providers on Prestel with almost a quarter of a million pages. Micronet 800 had added over 30,000 users onto the Prestel service. But Prism soon became preoccupied by the immense sales volumes of ZX81s and Spectrums and by then videotext was being stalked by the Internet and dub-dub-dub.

Telebit was founded by Paul Baran, as we shall see he was the inventor of packet switching. He founded Packet Technologies to investigate interactive TV systems but lit upon a way of developing a high speed modem and created Telebit.

In 1985 Baran developed the Trailblazer modem based on a 68000 MPU; it was one of the first to achieve better than 9,600 bps. It was based around its own packet ensemble protocol (PEP) which was capable of 18k bps, though it could achieve this only in one direction.

However the Trailblazer was expensive, largely because of its on-board MPU. Telebit kept current with a variety of speedier models that espoused the emerging standards and soon moved to providing digital modems. Trailblazer was well received and used by the UUCP/bulletin board community.

Telebit later ran into some difficulty when the FastBlazer was promised to have a fax facility which did not materialise. This led to it merging with Octocom. The new management consolidated its Net-based activity in California but moved modem development to Octocom in Massachusetts for overhead savings

Cisco Systems bought Telebit for $200m in 1996 to acquire its digital modem technologies; the analogue modem side was spun off and run by its management as Telebit Incorporated.

Towards the ARPANET

It is important to get some terminology sorted out. Today we tend to use the words 'Internet' or 'Net' and the word 'Web' as being completely interchangeable terms. But these are in fact distinctly different developments that formed separate strands of the evolution.

RANDOM ACCESS MOMENT:
As we review the slow and serendipitous progress of these networking systems it is important to keep in mind the most significant fact - no individual or organisation ever sought a patent on any of the concepts or coding involved and therefore no ownership was implied or acknowledged.

Talking between computers was tough as each early manufacturer's system was so very different; there were no standards making it easy to pass messages between them. Early computer users such as academic institutions and research agencies crafted their own customised hardware and software.

ICL in the UK was created by the merging of a number of other companies and inherited a nightmare as it needed to support an array of different systems with absolutely no compatibility. IBM too met the same problem and dealt with it to a large extent by moving towards a common IBM System/360 approach.

RANDOM ACCESS MOMENT:
I was taught at some stage that there were six main buying motives for any product or service, though often a buyer would mix and match several of them. These were made easy to remember by use of the term SPACED - security, performance, acceptability, convenience, economy, durability. But the lesson came with a vital seventh motive that should never be overlooked. This was 'fear' - fear of being outmoded or overtaken is a really big motive.

The USA experienced fear following the USSR's launch of Sputnik. The pressure was on to find a means of sharing material and notions within local networks and between locations. At this time yet another concept emerged, that there needed to be a plan for a network able to survive a nuclear attack.

In the aftermath of Sputnik, President Eisenhower presided over spending more than a billion dollars on research and development. Secretary of Defense, Neil H McElroy, had no military connection prior to taking the role; in fact he had risen through the Proctor & Gamble to become company president.

Back in 1931 working on the Camay brand he had introduced the company's brand management approach. He also initiated the notion of promoting the company's products through 'soap operas'. As Secretary of Defense, McElroy quickly got himself worked up into something of a 'lather' ordering up all manner of missiles.

McElroy appointed Roy W Johnson to run ARPA. Johnson was a VP from General Electric Corporation who had been active in a recent decentralisation exercise at the company; McElroy had met Johnson while at Proctor & Gamble. Johnson agreed to a two-year term and also accepted a drop in salary from $61,000pa to just $18,000pa to run ARPA; however he did get to keep his GE shares.

Almost immediately the space program elements were then moved across to the new agency NASA (National Aeronautics & Space Administration) and a new Director of Defense Research & Development was appointed. This left ARPA potentially without a role, but fortunately it soon reinvented itself and survived.

By 1962 a small division within ARPA was established, attracting a meagre 10% of its total budget. It was the Information Processing Techniques Office (IPTO) and Joseph C R 'Lick' Licklider was the individual headhunted to run it.

Licklider was keen on engineering - a model aircraft builder as a child, a renovator of motor vehicles through much of his life - but at college he turned towards psychology and psychoacoustics. The latter subject required complex calculations meaning he inevitably became interested in IT in order to achieve his goals. He had become part of the team at MIT that had set up the Lincoln

Laboratory. While there he worked on the human factors of the SAGE (semi-automatic ground environment) air defence system.

SAGE led directly to the development of what was then the world's largest computer, the IBM AN/FSQ-7. Fifty-two of them were built and linked to manage three combat centres, twenty-four direction centres and over a hundred radar tracking sites. This was the very first large-scale wide-area computer network.

Via his papers and then while at IPTO, Licklider provided an inspiration that started the real process for others to emerge and be funded.

Licklider inspired and annexed the energies of two key individuals, Ivan Sutherland and Bob Taylor, who in succession took over the reins at IPTO.

The plethora of projects that IPTO was by then funding, were located right across the breadth of the United States, and this highlighted the need for ways to link incompatible computers for research teams to converse and inspire each other. This was initially achieved by using leased-lines to connect to remote mainframes, but something smarter was clearly becoming necessary.

This was perhaps most obvious to Bob Taylor, located in his Pentagon office where he had three different terminals connecting him with the CTSS at MIT, SDC in Santa Monica and Project Genie at University of California, Berkeley. Each was completely autonomous, with its own log-in procedures, and there was no means of interconnecting them. He despaired at the prospect of a proliferation of terminals as evermore projects were supported.

Taylor proposed to his IPTO line manager that a network was required and was given a million dollars to pursue the idea. He and Thomas Marill first outlined a tender document entitled *Cooperative Network of Time-Sharing Computers* and realising his lack of knowledge he set about luring Larry Roberts to come and resolve an approach.

But one of the issues the two encountered was not a technical matter; once again it was fear. If the various sites were connected and each had full access to the others' computers, how could they be assured of security for internal confidential information?

There has always been a healthy paranoia in remote computing. This is driven by fear that some smart individual could circumvent any reasonable security features to gain access to the 'crown jewels' or, worse, a disgruntled individual could wreak havoc of another sort.

This fear was strongly articulated at an ARPA gathering of funded researchers in 1967 when Roberts outlined his plans to connect them all up. More helpfully the meeting also outlined the technical issues of linking computers, each of which used a different operating system.

Wesley Clark, an erstwhile colleague from Lincoln Laboratory, listened carefully and later privately proposed a solution to Roberts. His idea was to place a small routing computer between each target computer and the network.

This interface message processor (IMP) would handle communications to and from the network. Each IMP would talk the same language and therefore have full compatibility around the network and between other IMPs. However each IMP would then need a proprietary approach for talking to and from its host.

The IMP provided what was often called a 'gateway' that translated material into and out of a network; most importantly it also acted as a physical buffer to maintain the integrity of each mainframe to avoid becoming too readily accessible to others.

The notion of the ARPANET was born.

Making networks manageable

The next issue faced was how to handle the potential traffic through this network. At the time two prior approaches existed as a potential model - the telegraph system and the telephone network. Both had proponents who suggested they were an earlier form of the Internet!

The telegraph used a copper-wire network to send Morse signals. It started in 1843 when London Paddington station was connected by cable to Slough in Buckinghamshire (now Berkshire) less than twenty miles away. Progress was speedy, with a submarine cable connecting the UK to France by 1845 (properly operational from 1851). Ireland was connected in 1853 and by 1854 the Ministry of Defence was able to send and receive telegraphs directly to the theatre of the Crimean War. The first transatlantic connection was in 1858.

RANDOM ACCESS MOMENT:
Although the telegraph system and its Morse code seem archaic today, it was amazing what could be achieved before the advent of electronics and microprocessors. In the early 1990s I visited the BT Museum and saw the Electrophone system. It was a small mahogany table with a series of headsets that could be connected by telephone to a theatre or music hall. Victorian Londoners could get live cable entertainment piped to their homes in 1895. On Sundays they could listen remotely to a sermon! The French and Hungarians had similar systems that served to set the scene for later radio broadcasting.

The telephone network was introduced in the UK in 1876 with the first directory published in 1880. This too was based upon analogue systems and each call committed two wires, aka a twisted-pair or copper-pair, which provided a fixed connection between the two callers. This was a synchronous system where both ends were connected for the duration of the call and of course the users were both fully aware of the process.

But this was terribly wasteful as for large periods of time there was nothing being said but the line was being reserved for the call until it was terminated - to the exclusion of other users. Worse, the telephone networks on both sides of the Atlantic were run by monopolies that were more concerned with securing the status quo than innovation.

One matter that needed to be considered was the bandwidth requirement for these new data networks. Bandwidth is the maximum amount of information, usually expressed in bits per second, which can be handled by the connection.

RANDOM ACCESS MOMENT:
the telephone network was of course originally built for voice messages only. As soon as data and multimedia was to be sent then the bandwidth was under huge strain. For example, hi-fi sound needs a dozen times the bandwidth of voice and video needs 30,000 times the bandwidth.

A skilled operator transmitted Morse code at 0.005 Kilo-bits per second, the very first modems reached 0.11 Kbit/s, ADSL broadband in the year 2000 achieved 12,288 Kbit/s. By 2008, the GPON G.984 (gigabit passive optical network) fibreoptic service could run at 2,488,000 Kbits/s.

A common misapprehension about the birth of the Internet is that it was built so the USA military command and control could survive a nuclear attack. This notion derived from the work done by Paul Baran who joined the RAND Corporation in 1959.

There was a very real concern at the time that a misunderstanding between the superpowers could be disastrous. They both had nervous fingers hovering over a nuclear trigger and if command and control should fail in a crisis there would certainly be catastrophic results.

RAND calculated in 1960 that a stand-alone cable network with nationwide reach to all its command centres and launch sites would need to be buried very deeply to withstand a nuclear attack. RAND calculated this network would cost over $2bn and Baran was asked to seek out a lower-cost solution.

He was first drawn to the existing network of small AM radio stations that criss-crossed the USA; might they not be annexed in a crisis in order to relay commands or messages? While the military felt that the president speaking to calm the nation might well use this approach, for full control much more reliability of connection and bandwidth was needed.

Baran therefore looked for another solution and came to some useful general conclusions. The first was that the problem of network redundancy was somewhat counter-intuitive in that each node of the network needed only three connections to other nodes to be robust enough for the job.

He also realised that the network could not be based on an analogue system as, for example, the signal within telephone networks deteriorated across distance. If the network were to route around areas of damage it would need to travel large distances without loss of quality. He concluded that it would have to be a digital network.

His other great idea was to chop a message into small chunks that he called, rather straightforwardly, message blocks. These small parts of a message could fly speedily around the network without overloading it.

Nodes would treat each block like a 'hot potato', the name of Baran's algorithm, and select the best route to its intended destination, choosing for example to route around damaged parts of the network. Each block would have a sequence code so on arrival it could be reconstituted in the correct order for the recipient. An error checking system would identify when the recipient received corrupt or incomplete messages and request a re-send.

In his 1962 report *On Distributed Communications Networks* Baran defined a network supported by 1,024 switches, or nodes, to deliver its blocks via small towers using low-power microwaves. The nodes had back-up provided by petrol-driven generators, each equipped with a 200-gallon (750 litres) drum of fuel buried beneath the site to power it for three months if there was no grid-supplied electricity.

RANDOM ACCESS MOMENT:
in the late 1980s I visited the Société Européenne des Satellites (SES) headquarters in Luxembourg. It operated the Astra geo-stationary satellites that today deliver most of Europe's satellite television channels.

Little Luxembourg has always been at the forefront of European cross-border broadcasting. It started Radio Luxembourg back in 1933 as the first cross-border broadcasting station. This rapidly took a 50% share of European listening, with some 2m listeners from the UK finding its lowbrow material less dismal than the BBC fare. With 208 Radio Luxembourg in the 1950s/60s being the forerunner of pirate radio, we all strained at night to hear top records as the signal faded in and out.

Radio Television Luxembourg (RTL) is Europe's second largest TV, radio and production company, second only to the BBC. Today it broadcasts forty-five TV and thirty-two radio stations to eleven countries and is one of the world's leading producers of TV content.

So of course RTL rapidly entered *the satellite TV business and early relationships with movers and shakers including Rupert Murdoch, Silvio Berlusconi and others assured it of a strong position in Europe. It has so many transmitters that its power consumption per capita is three times that of the UK, with a 125th of our population!*

When I visited SES it appeared to have followed some of Baran's thinking. It needed to demonstrate a high sense of responsibility, because a terrorist takeover of the HQ today would gain control of 2,500 radio and television channels and reach 125 million households right across Europe and Africa. It was explained that the centre was capable of running autonomously during any siege by virtue of diesel generators buried beneath the site with reservoirs of fuel to last through many decades of glorious isolation.

NPL names it – packet switching

Baran's approach was designed for a nuclear-surviving system but it would later be applied to ARPANET. While his development would have been perfect for ARPA's IPTO requirements, it was buried deep under bureaucracy and by Ma Bell's self-interested disinterest.

Embarrassingly, IPTO needed to learn of Baran's work via the British. It was also a Brit who gave message processing its name.

Quite independently and with no knowledge of Baran's work, the UK's National Physical Laboratory (NPL) came up with a similar solution for the data network problem. As Head of Computer Science at NPL, Donald Watts Davies sought a way for computers to intercommunicate.

He was a product of Imperial College who in WWII had worked on the atomic bomb project at Birmingham University under the code name Tube Alloys. There he used armies of computers, but these were the human kind, equipped with calculators. After the war he took a second degree in mathematics at Imperial and was lured towards computers as machines.

He joined NPL in 1947 and set about emulating what was happening in the USA campuses - where Aiken had the Harvard Mark I underway, Eckert and Mauchly were developing ENIAC at the Moore School and John von Neumann was working at Princeton. The race was on for NPL to produce the ACE (Automatic Computing Engine) designed by Alan Turing, recruited from Bletchley Park.

But ACE rapidly became bogged down in the processes at NPL. Turing left for Manchester University, which together with Cambridge University was to take up the computing baton for the UK.

Davies was not involved in this and in fact for the time would have been accumulating some valuable airmiles - if they had existed back then. He spent a year at MIT in the mid '50s and his role in the mid-'60s took him to a conference in California and he took the opportunity to visit Dartmouth to see the work on the BASIC language. He also visited MIT and RAND to learn about their time-sharing systems.

Davies settled back at NPL to contemplate the problems of computer communication. He looked at the other pre-existing network, the telegraph and its message-switching approach. The telegraph met the problem of how to route and handle heavy traffic by using a manual process in which telegraph offices relayed messages between themselves.

When the service introduced teletype terminals with punched paper tape reader-writers the system was a little more automated. They developed the 'torn-tape' system process where a received message was output onto tape, torn off the machine and then inserted into another teletype to be relayed onward.

Davies considered the message switching approach when he realised that any long messages tied up the process blocking all other users. He then applied the notion of time-sharing to the process and concluded that the way forward was to slice up the network's facilities between users. This led to the reasoning that the messages needed to be broken up into packets to be sent in segments and then reassembled.

Initially he called these segments 'short messages' but they soon became 'packets'; apparently this was because the word packet would translate into other languages more easily. So it was Davies who provided the ultimate name of the technology, 'packet switching', even if Baran had the idea earlier.

Baran and RAND decided not to patent or have his concept classified as its merit was in its ability to defuse any misunderstanding between the two superpowers; if it was plagiarised that would be good news.

Only after his own 1965 paper was published did Davies learn from the UK's Ministry of Defence, that Baran had pre-dated him. But Davies happily referenced Baran in all future papers about this thinking. Significantly Davies pressed on at NPL to define and design a functioning packet switching network; this was all in hand by 1967.

One of Davies team, Roger Scantlebury, attended an Association for Computing Machinery (ACM) meeting in Gatlinburg, Tennessee; he was there to present a paper on their plans. Also presenting there was Larry Roberts of ARPA, outlining the early thinking on what would become ARPANET.

It was in this roundabout way, attending the NPL presentation, that ARPA became aware of packet switching; it had not heard of Baran's work directly. But it was very quick to act, soon hiring Baran himself as a consultant to develop packet switching as the basis for ARPANET. From this the public data network X.25 protocols for packet switching across wide area networking would emerge.

Build it and they will come – bidding for the ARPANET work

It was at the implementation phase that ARPA fell back on Kleinrock's earlier work. The telecom community was initially none too impressed by the notion of packet switching and it was only by demonstrating Kleinrock's theoretic work on networks that they could be persuaded to become supportive.

Elmer Shapiro of SRI called a meeting in mid-1968 to discuss the proposal for a network and invited representatives from potential early users. It was one of those 'dangerous' meetings whereby if you turned up then you ended up with a role.

By the end of the year Shapiro produced *A Study of Computer Network Design Parameters,* drawing on the work of Baran, Davies and others. From this Larry Roberts and others at ARPA were able to conclude the proposed IMP specification.

When ARPA went to tender for the IMPs they identified well over a hundred potential suppliers. IBM and CDC were quick to reply, but showed no interest in working with them.

In fact only twelve organisations were to respond positively, hardly the overwhelming endorsement of the concept that might have been expected from the pioneering computing operations.

Larry Roberts had indicated to BBN that ARPA was to fund a network and its team therefore invested time and effort in preparation to place it in a strong position for submitting a bid. It was the most positive bid, a 200-page proposal that essentially outlined the Internet. It was no surprise in January 1969 when BBN won the $1m contract to supply the IMPs.

The BBN team was led by Frank Heart who gathered several interesting team members, among them Will Crowther, potholer and Colossal Cave game author, and Bob Kahn a significant player in the ARPANET story.

BBN chose the Honeywell DDP-516 for the IMP hardware. The DDP-516 was originally designed by the Computer Control Company Inc which been acquired by Honeywell in 1966. It had a rugged design, modified to work with up to four local host computers and up to six other IMPs across leased lines.

The UK's NPL network was originally planned to be based on a Plessey product but, when this was cancelled as a project, they too selected the same Honeywell hardware.

The first four ARPANET sites were selected and BBN set about delivering the IMPs for these within a year. But this was only one part of the job.

While BBN was charged with delivering the Honeywell IMPs and their means of communication, no individual or organisation had been appointed to consider how the IMPs would talk with the host computers themselves. More surprisingly no thought was being applied to what applications might then be developed for this inter-networking.

It was those who attended Shapiro's meeting who had to evolve an approach. Essentially of a group of graduate students from around the selected sites, they were left to take up this 'slack'. Initially these were Steve Crocker and Gerald Deloche at UCLA, Bill Duvall and Jeff Rulifson at SRI and Steve Carr at Utah.

It was Steve Crocker who formally announced their presence in what would become known as RFCs (requests for comments); this was part of what he said in RFC #1,

'The software for the ARPA Network exists partly in the IMPs and partly in the respective HOSTs. BBN has specified the software of the IMPs and it is the responsibility of the HOST groups to agree on HOST software. ... I present here some of the tentative agreements reached and some of the open questions encountered. Very little of what is here is firm and reactions are expected.'

RFC notes evolved to be produced by anyone at any site, and they were urged to issue them expediently rather than wait for them to become polished. Initially these were typed and hard copies were circulated to ARPA, BBN, SRI, UCLA, UCSB (Santa Barbara) and Utah; as the ARPANET came on stream they were created, issued and archived online.

It was RFC #3 that provided a name for this informal team; they called themselves the Network Working Group (NWG). Jon Postel at UCLA became the RFC editor allocating the next number and archiving each RFC as it was issued; they were never modified or rescinded but could be superseded by a subsequent RFC. Postel served in the office for almost thirty years (1969-98). Following his death, his obituary was circulated in October 1998 as RFC #2468.

A similar ad hoc arrangement evolved when UCLA began to prepare for the receipt of its IMP #1. Another graduate student, Mike Wingfield, stepped up and built an interface to connect the IMP with the Sigma 7 host computer. Steve Crocker and Vint Cerf, another UCLA student, wrote the necessary software. They were greatly helped by having been involved in preparing the submission of one of the other IMP bidding companies

Limited interest was garnered from the industry and support was provided only by graduate students; not the most promising birthing!

BBN had a setback when the first Honeywell, or IMP 0, arrived and it did not work!

It was UCLA that issued a press release announcing the ARPANET in July 1969, though its IMP did not arrive until August 1969. On arrival it was scarily found to have been packed upside down! But the selection of a hardy computer was fully justified when this was found to have caused no damage and early in September they were able to get the IMP #1 and their host 'talking' together.

They had to wait until October for IMP #2 to arrive at Doug Engelbart's ARC at SRI and for it to be connected with the SDS 940 that also ran the team's NLS system. They initially used a 50 Kbit circuit for this. By 1972 this would be replaced using X-25, the standard established for wide area networks (WAN).

Kleinrock asked graduate student Charley Kline to send the first packet between the two IMPs in October 1969. At each end they used a headset with a normal phone connection so they were connected in this way as the attempt was made.

Trying to enter 'LOG IN' Kline entered 'L' and received confirmation that it was received at SRI, he then entered 'O' and which again was confirmed, but when he tried to enter the 'G', the system crashed at SRI. So the first ever network transmission was an unintended greeting 'LO'. The problem was quickly resolved and LOG IN was achieved at the second attempt.

The continental US nodes were soon inter-connected by 56K modems, while Hawaii was connected through a satellite link.

ARPANET going international

Of course air traffic control and aerospace security systems had been communicating internationally and so had banks, but the first 'public' data network connections to go trans-border were in 1973.

The first international ARPANET connection was to an unlikely location - Kjeller in Norway, 25 km outside Oslo. This was the base of the Telenor Research Centre and also the first nuclear reactor not belonging to one of the major nuclear powers (USA, USSR, UK, France and Canada).

This came about as a result of techniques that Texas Instruments evolved to monitor nuclear tests using seismology. NORSAR (Norwegian seismic array) was established in 1968 for its proximity to the Soviet Union. It sent required seismic data via the Nordic satellite station in Tanum, Sweden back to the SDAC (Seismic Data Analysis Center) in Virginia.

In June 1973 the first terminal interface message processor (TIP) was located at NORSAR. TIPs were a 1971 add-on to IMPs and provided a direct ARPANET connection back to the SDAC. IMPs, by then Honeywell 316s, had a price tag of $50k. Adding a TIP at $70k allowed the connection of up to sixty-four terminals. The Norwegian satellite link was via a 9.6k modem.

From 1970 onwards there was conversation about connecting ARPANET with Donald Davies' NPL network but politics intruded as the UK government was more interested in connections to the EU than to America. Therefore Davies was steered by the UK government to look instead at the European Informatics Network.

It became evident that it would not be difficult to link a UK node as part of the NORSAR approach, but it was not the National Physics Laboratory that was to be connected.

Instead in July 1973 the University College of London (UCL) was selected to be the first UK ARPANET node. It had good credentials - it ran the UK's

Computer Aided Design Centre (CADC), and had a direct link to the Rutherford High Energy Laboratory (RHEL), which boasted what was then the UK's largest IBM 360/195 computer.

Larry Roberts provided the funding for both the TIP and the transatlantic link so that UCL could be connected. Peter Kirstein at UCL set about getting the rest of the funding by suggesting that computer science departments in the UK would be able to interconnect.

But the UK's Science Research Council would not provide the funding for this. The dithering meant that Norway's Kjeller connection ended up being direct to the USA and the UK node had to meet the additional cost of a high-speed link to Norway. This was cobbled together with support from the Post Office and NPL; but they agreed to fund it for just one year.

When the TIP arrived at Heathrow the UCL team found it was faced with both import duty and VAT charges. As the TIP was said to be merely on loan the import duty was easily avoided, but it still needed to guarantee the VAT charges. It is just so wonderful to be British; we do love routinely to shoot ourselves in the foot! The UCL/RHEL link was operational by November 1973.

A shaky start, but the UCL node really advanced when it later achieved Ministry of Defence funding for 1974 to 1976; by 1975 some forty academic research groups were connected. Queen Elizabeth II formally opened the UK link to ARPANET in 1976 at the Royal Signal and Radar Establishment (RSRE) in Malvern.

In September 1973 a conference was held at the University of Brighton and as part of the proceedings it was decided to choose another route to demonstrate the ARPANET. It used a satellite link to Goonhilly Downs, near the Lizard peninsula in Cornwall, where an ARPANET node was established. This was landlined to UCL and from there to Brighton. Goonhilly had built Arthur, the world's first parabolic satellite communication antenna, for use with Telstar back in 1962.

It was not all about highbrow applications. Leonard Kleinrock used this Goonhilly link when on returning to his lab from Brighton he called back via the ARPANET to Larry Roberts who was still there. They used TALK, a program that split the user's screen in two and allowed a typed dialogue. Kleinrock asked for someone to bring back his forgotten razor.

At UCL Pål Spilling of the Kjeller team worked with Peter Kirstein and Vint Cerf testing and refining the transmission control protocol (TCP).

An alternative French approach - Cyclades

Throughout history the French have always sought to develop their own style and the ARPANET was to be no different. Still smarting from local company Bull being taken over by Americans in the 1960s, the French wanted their own network system; this was of course all happening before Minitel.

The Institut de Recherche d'lnformatique et d'Automatique (IRIA) funded several local manufacturers and research institutions to develop its own packet-switching approach.

Louis Pouzin had been involved with both MULTICS and the CTSS time-share system at MIT and also with the early ARPANET. With this experience he was a natural choice to be asked to develop a way of connecting the French government departments. This was to a large extent against the wishes of those departments as each wanted to guard its own turf and approach.

Work started in 1972 and the name Cyclades, from the name of the scattered Greek island group, was selected as being symbolic of the task. Pouzin was in a position to dispassionately examine where he felt the ARPANET had blind spots or weaknesses and he concluded it was in its over-reliance on hardware.

He named his system's packets 'datagrams', a contraction of data and telegram, and his means of transmission was to be called Mitranet, based upon the Mitra 15 computers that were used. But the French are very active in maintaining the purity of their language and the word 'net' is not French. It became CIGALE, the French word for cicada. This was because of the chirping sound that the early users heard through use of a small speaker as an audio reassurance that a datagram had passed.

Pouzin's innovation was in the software that encapsulated the datagram so the hardware need not concern itself with the delivery. The ARPANET IMPs ensured packets were sent and received sequentially, Pouzin's datagrams could become muddled along the way but the software was able to sort them out at the other end.

The system was successfully linking sixteen universities by 1973, but in 1974 there was a regime change in the French government and the new broom decided computing should be an industry run without government support.

In 1976 the French PTT company developed Transpac as an X.25 service and held the monopoly on data transmission. The PTT used this status to have any support for Cyclades removed; by 1981 Cyclades was dead.

Pouzin's work did however bring about change. He paved the way for host computers to take responsibility for their own packets and not leave this to the network operator; it was this approach that was to prevail within the Internet.

Networking software - Vint Cerf and TCP/IP

Vint Cerf is often referred to as the 'father of the Internet'; certainly he was there at its birthing and played a number of key roles.

He earned a maths degree at Stanford and joined IBM for a short while but then went to UCLA for his master's and doctorate. While there he worked with Kleinrock setting up the software for the first two nodes of the

ARPANET. Also at UCLA he met Bob Kahn who was working on the hardware side of the ARPANET.

By 1970 the NWG team had produced the network control protocol (NCP) as an operating system controlling the creation, transmission and reconstruction of packets through the network; this was the system's 'backbone'.

In the early 1970s Cerf was an assistant professor at Stanford and his graduate students developed the needed core protocol for the ARPANET to manage its messages as a network of networks; by 1972 Cerf had become chair of the International NWG.

Cerf collaborated throughout with Bob Kahn who was on the East Coast having a spell at Bell Labs and a professorship at MIT before working on the IMPs at BBN.

In late 1972 Kahn was working with IPTO and spoke at the International Computer Communication Conference in Washington DC. In RFC #371 he described his aim,

'I am organizing a computer communication network demonstration to run in parallel with the sessions. This demonstration will provide attendees with the opportunity to gain firsthand experience in the use of a computer network. The theme of the demonstration will be on the value of computer communication networks, emphasizing topics such as data base retrieval, combined use of several machines, real-time data access, interactive cooperation, simulation systems, simplified hard copy techniques, and so forth. I am hoping to present a broad sampling of computer based resources that will provide attendees with some perspective on the utility of computer communication networks.'

While at IPTO Kahn saw that this plethora of networks was going to become an issue. He worked with Cerf to develop a means whereby the networks might be interconnected with the host computers being responsible for their own reliability, rather than it all coming back to the network operator.

The two published a paper in May 1974 entitled *A Protocol for Packet Network Interconnection* which was described as an internetworking protocol using packet-switching among the nodes to share resources. This defined TCP/IP. Now the ARPANET had grown up and was ready to birth the Internet

Transmission control protocol (TCP) required the development of internet protocol (IP) to handle the packets or datagrams themselves by encapsulating them in an envelope that routers could pass around. The May 1974 paper described how the combination of TCP and IP could form an internet protocol suite. This fundamental software could have all sorts of other protocols built around the stable base.

Through the late '70s and early '80s Cerf was with DARPA providing funding to those working on the TCP/IP technologies.

In 1983 Paul Mockapetris, at the behest of Jon Postel, developed the domain name system (DNS); this was published in RFCs #882 and #883. The DNS provided a translation of the recognisable website names into the numeric code that was required to identify the host computer from all those on the Internet.

In the mid-80s Cerf became VP of MCI Digital Information Services in charge of the engineering of MCI Mail, the first commercial email service on the Internet. MCI had prospered when AT&T was broken up and grew rapidly to become responsible for more than 15% of the American market.

MCI Mail operated on the principle that users used a modem to call it up. It handled three sorts of onward messages - email, telex or a hard copy to be snail mailed. The latter would be laser printed and send by the US postal service for a price-per-page fee; this proved attractive to many users who could only afford lower quality dot matrix printers for themselves.

More recently, among many other roles, Cerf was on the board of ICANN (Internet Corporation for Assigned Names and Numbers), the non-profit operation founded in 1998 to manage the assignment of domain names and internet providers. It took over the role from various government departments and the Internet Assigned Numbers Authority (IANA).

He also worked with the NASA Jet Propulsion Laboratory to develop the Interplanetary Internet. This has the aim of creating an Internet for planet to planet communication, the large distances requiring a different protocol to deal with the spans and higher incidence of errors.

The Internet was to become the 'network of networks' but the Interplanetary Internet was planned as the 'network of Internets' - is this not Licklider's 1962-defined intergalactic computer network?

Kahn became the director of IPTO and was responsible for funding the Strategic Computing Initiative, a $1bn ten-year spend on artificial intelligence and a forlorn effort to ensure that Japan's fifth-generation computing research did not leave the USA lagging behind.

The US response to Japan ensured one early change in that the 1984 Cooperative Research Act enabled consortia to be formed in the USA; this was something that had been previously illegal in the United States.

The major resulting consortium formed largely by mainframe manufacturers was the Microelectronics and Computer Technology Corporation (MCC). It was led by Admiral Bobby Ray Inman who had been both director of the US National Security Agency and deputy director of the CIA. Although it did good work on system architecture and design, smaller faster microelectronics, intelligent systems and distributed computing, it was wound up in 2004.

We British were not immune from Japano-phobia at the time. Our Alvey programme also looked at AI and knowledge-based systems, man-machine interfaces, parallel processing and natural-language software.

Working with the network - FTP, Telnet, Mbone

The hardware and the networking were now in place and the first applications were developed by the NWG; neither became a killer app but both were essential stepping stones needing an operating system.

These NWG applications were FTP (file transfer protocol) which as its name suggests was a system for sending files between hosts, and Telnet that allowed a user at one site to log on to a host computer at another location.

Telnet was originally defined in 1972. With ARPANET it first worked with Network Control Protocol but on 1st January 1983 it was transferred across to TCP/IP. This was the date that many refer to as the starting point of the Internet proper.

File transfer protocol (FTP) was first published by Jon Postel on the MIT MAC team in Feb 1971 as a means to copy files between computers with a different OS and file structure; it was defined for use with MULTICS and PDP-10s. It was the subject of many ARPANET RFCs but was heavily revised for use with ARPANET by Jon Postel in 1980 and was modified again in 1985.

It had two distinct parts. The first was a control connection that started once the user was logged on and wanting to run an ftp session. As its name suggested it controlled the interaction between the user and remote computer. The second part was the data connection and this actually transferred the file/s and any directory listing. Thankfully today this sits somewhat invisibly inside the browser.

ARPANET was now ready for expansion and by December it had connected four locations, adding in the University of California, Santa Barbara with its IBM System/360 and the DEC PDP-10 at the University of Utah .

By mid-1970 there were ten nodes across the USA. But these pioneers had little appreciation of what they had started. The original BBN design was for a maximum of sixty-four computers connected to one network. Today we have millions of computers and hundreds of thousands of networks all interconnected.

In 1992 Stephen Casner, Steve Deering and Van Jacobson launched Mbone (multicast backbone), a free system that sat as a virtual network on top of the Internet enabling multicasting of audio and video. The first major user were the Rolling Stones in November 1994 when they multicast a concert from the Cotton Bowl in Dallas. Clearly Mick Jagger was fully up to speed when he said,

'I wanna say a special welcome to everyone that's, uh, climbed into the Internet tonight and, uh, has got into the M-bone. And I hope it doesn't all collapse.'

A spammer in the works – eMail and spam

It was in late 1971 that Ray Tomlinson was to develop the ARPANET's killer app. email; although email was not invented by him - it predated the Net.

In 1965 MIT's CTSS system first offered users of its time-share system the facility to send and receive messages. Systems Development Corporation (SDC) provided this facility on the AN/FSQ32 around the same time. The SAGE system too gave the facility from 1966 onwards. But this was just between users while they were connected to the same computer.

Tomlinson while working at BBN using TENEX on a PDP-10 was familiar with this sort of email process called SNDMSG which allowed a user on the computer to compose, address and send messages to another user's mailbox.

He had also worked with CPYNET which was a file transfer program for networks. He concluded that CPYNET could send a mailbox message just as it did a file and he developed an append routine to make this possible. But he needed to distinguish between local SNDMSG activity and the messages he wanted to append to CPYNET and send outwards from the local network.

It was Tomlinson who came up with the previously little-used '@' symbol to separate the name of the users and the computer on which they were connected to define the remote recipients. This was a very good choice, but it did run into one problem since MIT's MULTICS used the '@' to erase the current line of code/instruction when an error was made. So on entering an email address MULTICS users would have a tough time of it.

He first tested it between two computers that were right next to each other; their only connection was via ARPANET. He suggests the first message was probably simply QWERTYUIOP or something equally anodyne. But the process was included in the 1972 release of TENEX and soon remote emailing became popular.

RANDOM ACCESS MOMENT:
It is interesting to see how new technologies are first formally applied. Samuel Morse in 1844 officially opened his telegraph system with the biblical quote 'What Hath God Wrought'. Alexander Graham Bell in 1876 used his first telephone circuit much more practically saying 'Mr Watson - Come here - I want to see you.'

Many suggest that Thomas Edison in 1877 first recorded the human voice when he sang 'Mary had a little lamb', though he was in fact predated by seventeen years. He was beaten to it by Frenchman Edouard-Leon Scott de Martinville who invented the phonautograph that implausibly etched sound waves into paper coated with soot from an oil lamp. In 1860 he captured a short blast of a female singing 'Au Clair de la Lune'. The first computer music was 'Daisy Daisy'.

In 1938 Chester Carlson simply recorded the date and location for his first Xerox with '10.-22.-38 ASTORIA'. In 1969 NASA and Neil Armstrong had the 'One small step...' quote ready.

But compare these with the 'LO' at the first ARPANET connection and Ray Tomlinson's probable 'QWERTYUIOP' for the first email; both clearly missed the great import of the moment.

During 1972 the FTP protocol was being settled by the ARPANET community and Tomlinson's process was modified by Larry Roberts who updated READMAIL to RD. Barry Wessler then updated RD to become NRD and Marty Yonke merged Tomlinson's SNDMSG with NRD and called it WRD; this added a help function to the reading and sending processes. Finally John Vittal added an automatic answer routine and called it MSG. In 1973 MSG put email right at the heart of the developing networking service.

In 1976 OnTyme, one of the first commercial email services, was launched; but it was a little early and ran out of 'tyme' before enough potential users were attracted to the service.

Sadly it took only six years before unsolicited bulk emails or spam emerged. The term 'spam' is said to be derived from the famous *Monty Python* Viking sketch in which the featured café's menu consisted largely of canned luncheon meat and the skit was punctuated with the Vikings singing 'spam, spam, spam, spam...'

Gary Thuerk, working in the DEC marketing team, mailed a message in May 1978 to every ARPANET address he could find on the US West Coast; these were listed in a published directory. The sender was 'THUERK@DEC-MARLBORO', inviting them to a presentation of the latest DECsystem-20 computers; there were around 400 spammed recipients!

This was however quite a mild offence; to be kind, perhaps it was in fact the first viral marketing message? However today it is estimated that 80% of all emails sent are spam or junk emails. And this is not likely to go away, given that the FBI in 2007 said criminal spammers netted more than $239m from their annoying campaigns.

By 1982 the protocols were updated so email no longer piggy-backed on FTP but had its own SMTP (simple mail transfer protocol) arrangements.

Initially emails were text-only but by 1996 the protocols were changed to permit multimedia content to be attached to an email with an add-on named MIME (multipurpose internet mail extensions), co-developed by Nathaniel Borenstein.

Neither email nor Usenet were planned strategies or conceived as key elements of their host technologies. Both were happenstance developments -

email merely an aside to ARPANET, and Usenet an inadvertent benefit of a UNIX updating technique. But email and newsgroups became the killer-apps as the Net evolved.

In 1988 Steve Dorner released the Eudora email client software for both Windows and the Mac, working also with the OSs for Newton and Palm. It was originally released as open software but later split its offering into a free Light version and a chargeable Pro option.

RANDOM ACCESS MOMENT:
One study published in 2005 by King's College, London University, suggested that high email, mobile and text usage could be damaging to the IQ.

These messages constantly interrupt thinking and they liken the challenge of balancing your current task against dealing with a new message as being as damaging as losing a night's sleep.

Experiments on 1,100 people found that it could lower IQ by ten points, while taking cannabis drops it by only four points. Worse, a third of those tested believed that it was now acceptable to break off and take a call or email during meals and face-to-face meetings. The experimenter said it was 'a recipe for muddled thinking and poor performance'.

19 - Keeping connected

'...there are already a million monkeys on a million typewriters, and Usenet is nothing like Shakespeare." Blair Houghton

PC Interconnections – Xerox PARC networking

PCs evolved standards for connecting up with peripherals such as hard drives, printers and modems. But in small and medium enterprises the pressure was soon turned towards seeking ways to connect PCs more effectively.

LANs (local area networks) were to some extent popularised by two British developments.

Donald Davies worked at the National Physical Laboratory and focused on developing a wide area network like the ARPANET, though at NPL the close physical location made it feel more like a local area network. It has claims to being the first ever local area network; way back in 1971.

By the late 1970s the work of Maurice Wilkes with EDSAC led to the development of the Cambridge Ring and this too became a LAN approach adopted by many European academic institutions.

However in the mid 1970s Xerox PARC developed the PUP (PARC universal packet), one of the earliest internetworking protocols which handled the packet creation, routing and delivery around a LAN.

It was of course aware of the early knockings of the TCP/IP Internet protocols being developed, but PARC wanted to press on and implement a system internally to form part of its planned 'office of the future' initiatives. Bob Metcalfe and Edward Taft published the PUP specification.

PUP was best considered as the equivalent to the IP component of TCP/IP. PUP was a tad smaller than IP at 554 bytes, integrating an 8-bit network number, an 8-bit host number and a 16-bit socket number into its network address; IP used 576 bytes.

PUP used a gateway information protocol (GIP) for routing, though this would subsequently change into the routing information protocol (RIP) that is at the heart of most LAN and WAN (wide area network) systems; RIP was first defined in 1988 in RFC #1058.

PUP used both the Telnet and FTP applications. Its implementation meant that it became influential on the thinking that went into the TCP/IP definitions.

By the early 1980s PUP had transmogrified into Xerox Network Services (XNS), providing general network and routing services. The protocol allowed remote printing and filing as well as file and message routing. Of course in keeping with other Xerox PARC developments it was never sold, but very influential.

XNS influenced the OSI (open systems interconnect), an industry-wide effort to agree networking standards; however it never achieved agreement and was eventually overtaken by TCP/IP.

Squeezing messages down the phone line - ISDN

In thinking about networking we should not overlook the PTTs (postal, telephone and telegraph companies). They were also beginning to sit up and notice that more of their clients wanted to send data across networks and they decided this should be via the PSTN (public switched telephone network).

In 1988 ISDN (integrated services digital network) was introduced as a new standard for mixing voice, data, fax, video and other messages through PSTN lines. This premium line enabled better quality connections between packet switched networks and one of its early targets was those desiring access to the Internet.

It meant a user could use just one telephone line for a variety of services and obviate the need to buy further lines.

Hawaiian approach - ALOHAnet

At the University of Hawaii it was not really an option to use the PSTN or any form of cabling between Hawaii's many islands. It opted instead to connect the seven colleges spread across four islands by the use of amateur radio.

Norman Abramson, a Bostonian, studied physics at Harvard, gaining his master's at UCLA and a doctorate in electrical engineering at Stanford. He worked at the Hughes aircraft company before joining the faculty at Stanford and the University of California Berkeley. A very keen surfer, he approached the University of Hawaii and became professor of electrical engineering and computer science.

Abramson's research was initially in radar and digital communication. He acquired funding from Larry Roberts at ARPA. With a team in the late '60s he developed a computer networking approach and a radio packet switching system, or perhaps more accurately packet broadcasting system. Naturally, being in Hawaii, the name chosen was ALOHAnet which went live in June 1971.

The system used a central hub in Honolulu to broadcast out to all nodes simultaneously on one radio frequency (413.475 MHz) using a 9,600 baud radio modem. Each node communicated back to the hub on a second radio frequency (407.350 MHz). The beauty was that the radio service was permanently open, ready to send or receive data without any on-costs being incurred. The hub was inspired by the ARPANET IMPs and based on a Hewlett Packard HP2100 minicomputer.

The name given to the hub was that of the Hawaiian mythological forest-dwelling little people said to predate the Polynesian occupation of the islands, the *ka poe Menehune,* it was named the Menehune.

Abramson used packet technology for his messages to be distributed but he faced the same issues as with the cabled packet switching systems - what happened if two nodes were transmitted at the same time and clashed? Packets were all the same size with a 32-bit header, a 16-bit parity check, 80 bytes of data and a further 16-bit parity check.

He might have overcome this by having each node use a separate frequency but then the network would have an update issue every time a new node was added. A second approach would be to have each node allocated certain time slots but this was inefficient, wasting slots when a node had no message to send for example.

It was resolved by developing carrier sense multiple access (CSMA); the packets would be sent when they were ready. The Menehune would then re-transmit the packet so the node could listen to hear if it was correctly received. Not hearing it back would lead to a retransmission. This was also the case if any errors were detected in the echoed packet. These resends would be timed randomly by each node to ensure they did not just keep clashing.

The approach used by ALOHAnet did have its downside as it meant the network could only utilise a maximum 18% of its theoretic capacity, otherwise the clashes and resends reach a logjam, or as they called it a 'congestion collapse'.

In 1972 Abramson met with Larry Roberts at ARPA:

'At one point during the meeting, Roberts was called away from his office and Abramson noticed a blackboard listing sites awaiting IMPs along with delivery dates. He picked up a piece of chalk and added 'the ALOHA system' to the list with the date of 17 December. He had planned to discuss this with Roberts when he returned, but the conversation turned to other things and Hawaii's IMP was never raised. Abramson had forgotten all about it 'when about two weeks before the December 17 date, we received a phone call from the group charged with the responsibility of installing the IMPs asking us to prepare a place for the equipment.' Gillies and Cailliau in How the web was born.

The IMP was duly installed on 17 December connecting the ALOHAnet nodes into the ARPANET via satellite; this was the very first non-ARPANET network connected into that service.

Abramson later developed a satellite version of ALOHAnet called PACNET, the first packet-broadcasting satellite network that connected up many Pacific locations.

ARPA saw the military applications of the radio-based ALOHAnet and used the approach to develop battlefield radio and also satellite networks. Abramson's work was also significant in paving the way for laptop and smart phone remote connection into networks.

The randomising re-send approach of ALOHAnet certainly inspired Bob Metcalfe when he was developing Ethernet. His modified version became known as CSMA/CD (carrier sense multiple access, collision detection).

Ethernet and 3Com
Bob Metcalfe was at Xerox PARC when he developed his Ethernet approach for local area networks. But like many at PARC he became disillusioned about the apparent lack of desire to market and develop his invention. He left to co-found 3Com in 1979.

The 3Com name was based on highlighting its three areas of interest - computers, communication and compatibility.

In the mid 1980s 3Com launched the EtherSeries Ethernet adaptor cards for the IBM PC, the VAX and others. The cards used the Xerox XNS protocols but named them as EtherMail for email, EtherPrint for printing, EtherShare for file sharing and Ether-3279 for IBM terminal emulation.

By 1982 almost a hundred companies had been licensed to build Ethernet products though fewer than twenty had announced a product.

In 1986 3Com negotiated a sale to Convergent Technologies, formed by a group of Intel and PARC émigrés back in 1979; it had developed a series of workstations. The deal was called off by 3Com at the eleventh hour and two years later Convergent itself was acquired by Unisys.

Another means of interconnecting computers came with the advent of routers. Effectively of course the first routers were the ARPANET IMPs, sitting there between the hosts and the packet switching network to ensure inter-compatibility.

In 1972 the International Network Working Group (INWG) was formed and chaired by Vint Cerf to consider how further networking technologies might be advanced in various countries and across a variety of different forms of network.

The goal at INWG was to establish a common technical standard to allow any computer to connect with the ARPANET. However Cerf was soon cooperating with Kahn to define TCP/IP protocols and the INWG and its goal was passed on to the International Federation for Information Processing (IFIP).

An approach was created that owed a great deal to Cyclades in that the router would not be concerned with ensuring messages were accurately and timely delivered - that was to be the host computer's obligation.

The router was defined by INWG as having a series of network interfaces. One of these network interfaces received the inbound packets where each was processed and stored, then forwarded to a second network interface for onward transmission.

Based upon its work a series of different routers were subsequently developed; many early routers were actually minicomputers dedicated to the purpose.

In 1974 Xerox PARC created simple routers for use with its PUP system. In 1975-6 BBN developed the first router suitable for use with internet protocol using PDP-11s. By 1981 MIT and Stanford researchers had developed a series of multi-protocol routers, though once TCP/IP became widespread these were unnecessary.

In 1987 3Com purchased Bridge Communications, which claimed to have shipped the first ever commercial router. The acquisition broadened its market from simple network cards into selling a range of routers. Although it would subsequently come under pressure from Cisco and exit the high-end router business in 2000.

By 1997 3Com had merged-cum-acquired US Robotics, the modem maker and by then owner of Palm Inc. It tried to use this base to get into the DSL (digital subscriber line) business, which was the basis for broadband distribution of data across the telephone network.

In 2010, Hewlett-Packard acquired 3Com at $7.90 per share, valuing the operation at $2.7bn.

Thinking different – AppleTalk to Airport

In 1984 as it launched the Macintosh, Apple entered the networking fray with AppleTalk which was a set of protocols for networking Macs. It was part of the Macintosh Office project to enable a Macintosh to share printers and disks. This project was however iced in 1986, but the successful Apple LaserWriter continued to use AppleTalk.

Naturally Apple had not taken the route adopted by others, ie the Xerox XNS and Ethernet services. Instead it took a novel approach in that the system had a series of protocols. LLAP (LocalTalk link access protocol) and later AARP (AppleTalk address resolution protocol - not the American Association of Retired People!) were used by the host to generate a 4-byte network address. Its name binding protocol (NBP) would map the network addresses to the names that users applied themselves. Chooser would then display a list of equipment on the local network in groups - Macs, printers and servers...

Later AppleShare was released; it used AppleTalk as its default network system as a file server. But soon Apple had little option but to espouse the all-conquering TCP/IP standard and by the time of the Mac OS X v10.5 AppleTalk had disappeared altogether.

But AppleTalk had been a real contender, inspiring many systems to enable cross-platform networking.

Sun developed the TOPS Teleconnector that allowed cross-platform use of AppleTalk. For just $59 it facilitated a mixed network of Macs and PCs, equipped with TOPS, to talk with each other.

The open-source system Netatalk enabled computers using BSD and Linux operating systems to use Apple Talk. Netatalk was developed by the Research Systems UNIX Group at the University of Michigan.

Columbia University came up with Columbia AppleTalk Package (CAP) which enabled AppleTalk to work with SunOS, IRIX and other UNIX varieties.

Even Windows NT and other releases up to Windows Server 2003 came with the facility to use AppleTalk.

Apple would later launch AirPort in July 1999 as its local area wireless network approach (AirMac in Japan). It operated at 11 Mbps and was upgraded to AirPort Extreme in January 2003 operating at speeds of 54 Mbps.

Network operating system - Novell

The Eyring Research Institute was founded in Provo, Utah in 1972 as a non-profit making organisation. It worked closely with the Brigham Young University and consulted closely on its patent policy. The institute assisted many new businesses - WordPerfect was just one notable example.

Four Eyring employees - Dennis Fairclough, Drew Major, Dale Neibaur and Kyle Powell - left to form Novell Data Systems in 1979. Initially this was to manufacture CP/M based computers but it did not work out.

In 1983 Novell Inc was formed as a software company, with Ray Noorda as CEO. Its first product was indeed software; it was ShareNet, a multi-platform NOS (network operating system). This was based on an extremely simple and clever concept - it used file sharing rather than disk sharing.

Novell utilised the Xerox PARC network protocol XNS, and its own internetworking packet exchange (IPX). The software evolved and was later renamed NetWare.

But Novell was also famous for developing an early server. The term 'server' is a rather vague one in that it can be applied to many applications but in each the server is a computer, often a PC.

It might be a printer server to where a number of PCs send print jobs and it then drives the printer. It might be a database server that handles queries from a number of PCs and provides the requested data. But most often it is a web server where the server sits between PCs and the Internet looking up pages for user PCs.

RANDOM ACCESS MOMENT:
Servers, our quiet servants, sit patiently waiting for our enquiries, usually 24/7, and this led to some concerns at the end of the noughties.

Research suggested that by 2008 2.5% of all USA energy consumption was consumed in running servers, with another 2.5% applied to the cooling systems that the servers necessitated. It was suggested that by 2020 servers would be consuming more world energy than air travel!

Novell later developed a 6800 MPU-based server using twisted pair connections arrayed in a star configuration. The server software used Novell-DOS which was similar to PC-DOS and MS-DOS; this had to some extent been made possible by its acquisition of DRI in 1991. Another acquisition, that of Excelan, also gave it access to a range of high-value Ethernet cards that it was able to sell at low prices.

This approach gave Novell the lion's share in business servers during the 1990s. Prior to the coming of Windows NT Server in July 1993, Novell was able to claim a 90% share of PC-based servers.

In 1993 Novell purchased the UNIX Systems Laboratories from AT&T to have headline rights to UNIX. It also purchased WordPerfect and the Quattro Pro program from Borland, but later sold this on to Corel.

By 1996 Novell had started to espouse the TCP/IP standard and moved away from its own IPX.

Routers – Cisco and Telebit

Bill Yeager, while at Stanford's Knowledge Systems Laboratory, developed the first multiple-protocol router in 1981. Yeager obtained his degree and master's in mathematics before opting to pursue software engineering for his doctorate.

A married couple, Len Bosack and Sandy Lerner, licensed Yeager's concept and founded Cisco Systems in San Francisco. They developed the Yeager design to become the first to sell multiple network protocol routers. However as internet protocol grew in importance the multiple protocol facility became somewhat less important.

In 1990 the company was quoted on NASDAQ but Lerner was fired shortly afterwards and her husband left with a $200m pay-off with which they set about generously spreading to various charities before later divorcing.

The company continued to grow through acquisition and development, and by 2000 it was among the world's most valuable companies with a capitalisation of $500bn. By the end of the noughties this had fallen back to a little over $100bn.

Baran's Packet Technologies operation failed and many of the team gravitated to Telebit. One of these was Mike Ballard who became the Telebit CEO in 1986 and president in 1992.

Ballard led the team that developed NetBlazer; this was the first dial-on-demand Internet router. It looked rather like a modem, but was based on an

80386 PC, with some added custom software and an Ethernet connection that could work with TCP/IP; later it was upgraded for Novell's IPX, AppleTalk and other protocols.

Network Forums - Usenet

A researcher at Bell set out to resolve the need for updates and problem resolution for the plethora of UNIX-based computers within AT&T. But he inadvertently created a whole new series of network applications.

Mike Lesk was the individual who came up with a process whereby Bell's central research computer connected with or called up the many computers in various departments to manage updates directly. The program was UUCP (UNIX-to-UNIX copy program). By 1979 UUCP was included as part of all new UNIX shipments.

UUCP was seized upon by Jim Ellis and Tom Truscott, students at Duke University, to form the basis for them to interconnect computers and receive updates of news and newsgroups. Their first approach was NetNews which was produced with Steve Bellovin at the University of North Carolina. The program allowed the connection of computers to acquire any updates within designated files and folders.

This first version was very slow so Truscott and Steven Daniel rewrote it in the high-level C programming language. This was called News version A but it became popularised as Usenet.

The process involved the user logging on to a computer and using a 'news reader' to reference areas of particular interest in a précis form; anything of interest could then be requested in full. The computer to which the user was connected would access the requested material from wherever it was resident and pass it on to the enquirer.

The material within a newsgroup was moderated to keep it pertinent and easy to use. A structure emerged with time whereby the more powerful Usenet host computers took a key role in handling the traffic.

Significantly Usenet was not owned by any individual or organisation. There was no central network manager but just a whole series of volunteer (ie unpaid!) moderators. It also switched the approach established by ARPANET – in this case the users decided what information to access and to which groups they wished to subscribe.

In 1981 Matt Glickman and Mark (later becoming Mary Ann) Horton developed the News version B software which permitted unmoderated newsgroups. Initially there were just these two forms of newsgroups, the 'mod' ones which were moderated and 'net' ones which were not.

Progressively it was necessary for more categorisation of the subject-based newsgroups or forums within a hierarchy of topics. The first seven of these were 'comp' for computing, 'misc' for miscellany, 'news' for news, 'rec' for recreational, 'sci' for science, 'soc' for society, 'talk' for chat rooms…

ARPANET had been available only to those in the colleges and research agencies serving the US military, but Usenet was available to all those with access to UNIX-powered computers. Usenet did not log a user on to a remote computer it was simply a medium for exchange of data, news and views.

The University of California Berkeley subsequently 'connected' the two network types by creating a means of taking the forums into the ARPANET and posting content out to Usenet newsgroups.

From three sites established in 1979 it grew to fifteen in 1980, 150 in 1981, 400 in 1982 and over 5,000 by 1987.

By 1988 there was a growing controversy about the quality of the dialogues on the sites, for example the content of the articles in terms of the language used. There was also a tendency arising for individuals to direct hostile remarks at other users; this became known as 'flaming' or 'bashing'.

Moderated sites were quite particular and fought against these trends. Those who did not wish to be corralled like this developed 'alt' sites where anything and everything was permitted.

Two of the earliest alt sites were alt.sex and alt.drugs. One user could not bear the suspense and launched alt.rock-n-roll and the genre was on its way.

Bulletin boards

But there was yet another networking development path afoot.

Back in the 1970s there were a series of initiatives to use the cataloguing and cross-referencing skills of computers and this followed a quite separate evolution from the military funded ARPANET.

Other organisations with an interest in computers learned of the ARPANET and its benefits and wanted those benefits for themselves.

Lee Felsenstein and others acquired access to an SDS 940 and in 1973 set up the Community Memory Project with its notable terminal outside Leopold's Records used as an electronic bulletin board where all manner of material was promoted and disseminated.

It evolved a language for non-computer users to be able to post and reference the material it contained. But this was on a local directly-connected system, unlike the Usenet system for forums that operated remotely.

The work of Ward Christensen and Randy Seuss created yet another means for distributing files, information and communication between multiple computers. The two met as members of CACHE, the Chicago Area Computer Hobbyists' Exchange.

In 1977 both were running with the CP/M operating system and looked for a way to transfer files between themselves. Christensen wrote a program which he called MODEM and which was made available to the CP/M users group. The members were free to modify it and they regularly did.

A friend of Christensen, Keith Petersen, modified it to include various upgrades including error-correction. This version was the XMODEM which soon became the basis of the file transfer protocol that inspired so many derivatives. It required both computers to have the MODEM/XMODEM installed and then they could connect by using telephone handsets with acoustic couplers.

By 1978 Christensen and Seuss were finding the process frustrating as it all too rapidly exceeded the capacity of their floppies. Snowed in by the great blizzard of that year, Christensen fancied a hack. They decided to create a networking approach, something Christensen had encountered through his membership of PCNET, a primarily-Californian club.

They came up with a hardware/software combination they named CBBS (computer bulletin board system) and published details in *Byte* magazine.

The original hardware was assembled from pre-existing material; it used a PC kit with an 8080 MPU and S-100 bus, an 8k memory board, a Processor Technology VDM, a Hayes hobbyist modem card and two floppy drives. Eight EEPROMs held the CP/M, video display and other software.

Of course these were early PC days and so the material on the BBS was simple ASCII text and ANSI art. The service was a one-user-at-a-time system so once the modem was engaged no-one else could use it; and of course with the 110 and 300-baud modems of the late 1970s the whole process was very slow and ponderous.

But it was the vital inspiration for the bulletin board systems that followed; and not just used for transferring files and data, but for forums and chat rooms, news and bulletins, online games...

Usually a BBS was set up by an enthusiast more as a hobby than a business; it was usually a local service taking advantage of the USA telephone principle of no charges for local calls.

As modem speeds increased to 1200 baud, BBSs emerged for almost every early PC. Until the World Wide Web emerged fully in 1996 the BBS approach was very popular, spawning three new monthly magazines in the United States.

One notable BBS was the WELL (whole earth 'lectronic link), established in the Bay area of San Francisco in 1985 by Stewart Brand and Larry Brilliant.

Brilliant was a physician who formed Network Technologies International and approached Brand with the idea of launching an operation to host a public computer conferencing system.

Brand had originated the *Whole Earth Catalog* as a counter-culture publication back at the end of the 1960s. The catalog had wide-ranging articles and promoted a collection of products and services. It was largely based on inspiring independent lifestyles by providing not just information on how to do so, but also case studies of those leading them.

The Whole Earth name came from Brand's earlier lobbying of NASA to release a photo of the globe or the whole earth that it was said to possess. Brand believed this image to be iconic and illustrated how we were a single system sharing a single resource. Steve Jobs said of the publication in 2005,
'... one of the bibles of my generation. It was created by a fellow named Stewart Brand not far from here in Menlo Park, and he brought it to life with his poetic touch. This was in the late 1960's, before personal computers and desktop publishing, so it was all made with typewriters, scissors, and Polaroid cameras. It was sort of like Google in paperback form, 35 years before Google came along: it was idealistic, and overflowing with neat tools and great notions.'

Prominent among the editorial team were Matthew McClure and Cliff Figallo who had been members of The Farm. Steven Gaskin had led a party of sixty vehicles across the United States speaking on respect for the earth and non-violence. He and some 300+ hippies, from San Francisco initially, bought 1,000 acres of land in Tennessee to establish The Farm as a commune.

In 1985 Brand and Brilliant launched the WELL, reached by dial-up, as a series of bulletin boards and online discussions. WELL was one of the first dial up ISPs (internet service provider) in the early 1990s.

Its BBS was based on a leased VAX computer using UNIX and a PicoSpan conferencing program. Users paid $8 per month and $2 per hour. It divided itself into forums that it called 'conferences' reflecting users' interests and 'topics' running particular threads. There was also a general public area.

It was through WELL that Mitch Kapor and others met and communicated to create the Electronic Frontier Foundation - a non-profit organisation that supported the freedom of individuals in the digital community.

Another BBS of note emerged in 1988 after several years of gestation. The Big Sky Telegraph was founded to connect rural teachers and develop skills in using online services for the access of information and knowledge. The founders cite Toffler's *Future Shock* as an inspiration that was triggered by the arrival of the IBM PC, Apple II and low-cost faster modems.

Dave Hughes, aka the 'cursor cowboy', was a retired US Army colonel who taught himself about computers at the age of forty-nine and established The Little Red Electronic Schoolhouse BBS. Frank Odasz contacted Hughes and the dynamic duo evolved the notion of the Big Sky Telegraph to connect a hundred rural one-room schools in Montana. It took four years to raise the required funding.

Hughes built the system on an IBM 386 PC using UNIX and they started with ten one-hour training sessions entitled *Microcomputer Telecommunication Basics*. This was eventually disseminated across nineteen states and some 900 rural teachers. The catalogue of courses expanded to around 700 lessons by 1995.

In early 1989 the City of Santa Monica launched its PEN (public electronic network) service: perhaps the first operated by a local government.

Ken Philips headed the city's computer department and PEN was initially intended to link citizens with the city's services. Prior to this they were usually run by academe, or in one notable case in Japan by a chamber of commerce.

PEN placed a number of public terminals in libraries and other public offices. The service stored a wealth of accessible local information. It offered email facilities and also an area where teleconferencing could be used to discuss local issues. It was intended to be a local-government to local-citizen communication process but it rapidly moved itself to being citizen-to-citizen too.

There was one early and unexpected application coming from it being free to users. Homeless people were able to use the teleconferencing to highlight their requirements and this led to an action group setting about resolving these issues.

The group was called SWASHLOCK for showers, washers and lockers – three of the most pressing needs. Some 3,500 users (from among the 96k population) were operating on PEN by mid 1991.

Fido

But these BBS services were autonomous networks. They desired interconnectivity but connection costs for what were largely one-man-band hobbyists were far too high.

While living in San Francisco it was Tom Jennings that developed the next key step in the process. He used the CBBS system and developed Fido, his own BBS software. The name derived from a homebrew PC he had built previously; it was such a mishmash that someone referred to it as a mongrel and it became Fido.

Fido was not just a straightforward BBS system; Jennings wanted it to operate with a network of BBSs too. FIDOnet arranged for messages to be sent between FIDO BBSs using a store and forward system, whereby the user collected all the messages it detected and then those not reaching their ultimate destination BBS were forwarded onwards.

Subsequently the network established a hierarchical structure with certain users being defined as 'gateways' that would consolidate traffic which was more conveniently allocated to regions and zones.

Jennings also sought to define the network to make the most of the USA free local call service and avoid incurring any network charges. However as FIDOnet grew into an international service this became increasingly untenable.

By 1984 there were two Fido BBSs operational, one in the Bay area and one in Baltimore. The software was made freely available and growth was rapid - forty by the end of 1984, over a thousand Fido BBSs by the end of 1986.

In 1991 Fido had 10,000 BBSs worldwide and more users than the then Internet.

Tim Pozar produced a piece of software called UFgate, presumed to mean UUCP to Fido gateway. He had been writing routines called fidouucp.exe and uucpfido.exe for file exchanges between Fido and the Internet and got together with John Galvian and Garry Paxinos who were working in the same area.

They pooled resources and tested their thinking to develop UFgate, enabling the two services fully to interconnect.

EUnet

But the UNIX and UUCP developments were not just a US phenomenon. UUCP was also seized upon by users in the UK, the Netherlands, Sweden and Denmark and they cooperated to create EUUG (European UNIX Users' Group) in 1982; this later grew into EUnet International Ltd (European UNIX Network).

RANDOM ACCESS MOMENT:
In 1984 there was a new Usenet site formed called Kremvax which purported to be moderated by the USSR President Chernenko. Those who spotted its founding date of 1st April were not fooled for long. The joke was generated by Piet Beertema of the Dutch National Research Institute for Mathematics and Computer Science, but it did mean that six years later when a genuine Russian site (demos.su) was launched there had to be a great deal of reassurance that it too was not a joke.

In 1988 EUnet was interconnected with the ARPANET via the Amsterdam Mathematics Centre and ARPANET use soon spread through the European research community.

Also in 1988 Ben Segal at CERN (Conseil Européen pour la Recherche Nucléaire) the European organisation for nuclear research, linked its TCP/IP activity by adding routers to the EUnet. This gave CERN its access to the ARPANET which proved to have such a major impact later.

Secret connections

ARPANET set the scene and developed the techniques to hasten the advent of the Internet, but it required developments elsewhere to take it from the military and military-funded academic sectors.

By 1982 the paranoia within the US Department of Defense, largely based upon fears of hackers, led to it splitting off its own secure network, MILNet (military Net) from the general ARPANET.

Both networks were designed by BBN and a series of gateways were established to allow email to pass between the two nets. Later in the decade MILNet became four separate networks at varying levels of security clearance and these were known as the DDN (defense data network).

By the 1990s a broad global series of military networks had been established at different security levels. There were two primarily used by the Department of Defense. One was NIPRNET (non-classified internet protocol router network) known as nipper-net. The other was the clearly separate, or as the US military termed it 'air-gapped', SIPRNET (secret internet protocol router network), referred to as sipper-net.

The intelligence community created JWICS (joint worldwide intelligence communications system), its own independent network for top secret material.

By the mid 1980s ARPANET was being phased out and that might well have been the end of the road had it not been for the coming of PCs and the parallel development of other networks to ensure that this did not happen.

No military purpose

Not all colleges and research agencies worked for the US Department of Defense and therefore they were not part of the ARPANET. Their computer departments were not slow in realising that those who were connected were gaining an edge on them.

In 1980 the National Science Foundation (NSF) awarded a $5m grant to CSNet (computer science network) to connect the nation's computer science departments. It was created as a network of networks and included the ARPANET. The first step was that three departments Wisconsin-Madison, Purdue and Delaware were given ARPANET nodes.

DARPA and Vint Cerf gave their support but CSNet had to become self-sufficient within five years. As a result users' departments had to pay for connection to CSNet. Early discussions therefore looked for a low-cost way forward and Dave Crocker, a graduate student at Delaware University, proposed it start with a telephone-relay email service; this became Phonenet.

The universities of Delaware, Purdue and Princeton were operational on Phonenet by 1981 and it grew from there. Twenty-four sites were connected by 1982, eighty-four by 1984, by then both computer science and engineering departments were joining.

The first to be connected internationally was from Israel, followed quickly by Australia, Canada, France, Germany, Korea and Japan.

This led to a network gateway being established between CSNet and the ARPANET, and to enable this activity the TCP/IP software was provided free to CSNet.

BITNet

Another non-military network emerged from yet another group of universities.

Ira Fuchs at the City University of New York set out to exploit the IBM network software program RSCS (remote spooling communications subsystem) which allowed information transfer and communication using its VM (virtual machine) operating system.

Fuchs connected his NY computer to his friend Greydon Freeman and the Yale computer during 1981. They called it BITNet (because it's there network), it being RSCS of course. Later it was referred to as 'because it's time…'

It used leased phone lines and modems and hosts agreed to allow access at no charge. A tree structure where each host had just one connection between them kept the network simple. It was founded on the principle of a cooperative with no central manager. It was more like USENET than ARPANET in that all files were stored and forwarded across to the user computers.

Its prime application was email based on the IBM VNet and LISTSERV software and the exchange of files, but they also developed the first 'instant message' service, formally Interchat Relay Network but usually called BITNet Relay.

BITNet launched other innovations including *VM/COM*, an electronic magazine published by the University of Maine.

Bruno Chabrier and Vincent Lextrait, French students at the *École Nationale Supérieure des Mines de Paris*, created a text-based adventure game in 1984 called MAD (multi-access dungeon). MAD was the first MUD, or multi-user dungeon game. It became so popular that it maxed out the bandwidth of BITNet several times and after two years the college was asked to remove it from the system.

This was initially only available to IBM owners but soon RSCS emulation was available with other computers too, including VAX and UNIX. By 1982 twenty institutions were interconnected using this approach; a year later there were over sixty nodes and a waiting list of many other universities wishing to join.

Supported by IBM, BITNet expanded its reach to South America and in 1983 into Europe as EARN, to Canada in 1984 as NetNorth, India as TIFR, the Middle East as GulfNet, and in to Japan as ASIANet. Eventually it connected some 3,000 nodes and 450 universities and research institutions.

In 1988 BITNet and CSNet merged and its management was handled by CREN (Corporation for Research and Educational Networking).

BITNET II was developed in 1987 to give a higher bandwidth, but the Internet was already having an impact and it had faded away by the end of the millennium.

Janet

BITNet developed its European arm the EARN (European academic research network). This was based in Paris and had some success but the Internet with its UNIX and TCP/IP slowly superseded it.

The UK developed its own network. The situation had become confused with British Telecom developing an X.25 network, UCL still used its gateway to the ARPANET; the Rutherford Appleton Lab had an EARN/BITNet gateway, the University of Kent Computing Lab had a UUCP service, and Manchester, Bristol, Edinburgh and Newcastle also had their own networks.

A British government funded joint network team was formed to develop a unified system and to develop the protocols for the host of platforms to be interconnected. It opted for X.25 and developed JANET (joint academic network); it went live in 1983 connecting fifty sites with a 9.6 Kbit/s service.

All further and higher education organisations and the research councils were progressively connected to JANET. By the 1990s it was the fastest X.25 service in the world with the backbone running at 8 Mbit/s and access links at 2 Mbit/s.

Intriguingly it adopted a mirror-image naming system from that used by the the Internet and instead used UK.AC.CAMBRIDGE.XXX rather than xxx.cambridge.ac.uk

A series of nineteen regional network operators managed the connection to schools, colleges and universities.

In 2011 Janet (UK) also became responsible for administering the .ac.uk and the .gov.uk domains.

RANDOM ACCESS MOMENT:
the .uk Internet domain is the fourth most popular top-level domain after .com, .de, an
d .net, with some 8.5m registrations at the end of the noughties. But when the Internet came to deciding what we should be, in fact the use of '.gb' was proposed; it was the pre-existing use in JANET of '.uk' that prevailed.

I have heard what I assume to be an urban myth that the UK government had to pay the Ukraine silly money for us to get the .uk designation!

It was supposed to be illegal to use .uk alone; it should be .co.uk or .gov.uk or .ac.uk. But several government agencies managed to do so before Nominet UK was established to enforce the rule. The Ministry of Defence has mod.uk, the National Health Service is nhs.uk, and the British Library is bl.uk.

Disbursement

The US Government knew it had achieved what it wanted with the ARPANET and desired to divest itself of the management of what had rapidly become rather more than it had anticipated.

It had already split off military and secret parts onto MILNET, NIPRNET, SIPRNET and JWICS. Now it looked around for someone else to take up the public baton.

In the mid '80s the NSF (National Science Foundation) was planning five supercomputer centres - the Cornell Theory Center at Cornell University, National Center for Supercomputing Applications at the University of Illinois at Urbana-Champaign, the John von Neumann Center at Princeton University, the San Diego Supercomputer Center at UCSD the and the Pittsburgh Supercomputing Center. The NSF had also developed CSNet.

In 1984 the NSF charged Dennis Jennings with connecting these five supercomputer sites via an NSFNet (National Science Foundation network). He concluded that he would use TCP/IP for the purpose and that the NSFNet would not just connect the five centres but operate as a backbone to the existing CSNet and other regional networks.

The most likely choice of router was BBN's Butterfly Gateway but the team instead went for a product it called Fuzzball.

In 1986 the centres at Illinois and Cornell were the first connected. Remarkably, given their supercomputer goals, this was operated at just 56 kbps, but then multimedia applications had yet to take off so messages were largely textual. NSFNet flew, doubling in size every seven months.

In 1987 Ed Krol at the Illinois centre was funded by the NSF to write his *Hitchhiker's Guide to the Internet*. He explained that this was because he was fed up with telling everyone the same story!

In 1988 the NSFNet lured some 170 other networks to connect with it and this was effectively the time that the Internet went fully public. By 1989 CSNet and BITNet merged as part of this process.

Finally in 1990 the ARPANET was officially dissolved and as the '90s progressed a whole new phase of commercialisation of the Internet ensued.

20 - Slavery without shame – Robotics and AI

'In the fifties, it was predicted that in 5 years robots would be everywhere. In the sixties, it was predicted that in 10 years robots would be everywhere. In the seventies, it was predicted that in 20 years robots would be everywhere. In the eighties, it was predicted that in 40 years robots would be everywhere...'
Marvin Minsky

The Ministry of Truth and Androbot
It was 13:00 on Friday 13th January 1984, not 'a bright cold day in April' that we launched the Androbot range in a series of press and dealer presentations. We hired the London Hippodrome, just off of Leicester Square. Peter Stringfellow had just acquired it and completed a major refit to install the most amazing laser and light shows; we were the first to use it for a commercial event.

We watched the show in rehearsal but it still wrought a visceral effect when the 13,000 watts of sound and 100,000 watt light show were in full flow. Reporting the launch, *Audio Visual* magazine very briefly mentioned us but waxed more lyrical about the £3m (1984 £s) spent on creating the venue.

There was even a rocket that glided above the stage, and naturally we selected space themes as the sound track. One of the highlights was when we played *Thus Spake Zarathustra*, the Richard Strauss music inspired by Nietzsche's book, but which for many shall forever be linked to the movie *2001: A Space Odyssey*.

As the evocative music played, the stage opened and a section raised from the depths, the lights went wild, the dry ice billowed its clouds, the lasers picked out the faces of Topo and Fred as they rose from the ground. The BBC, not known for hyperbole, described it on prime-time news as a 'cosmic experience'. One of the BBC outside broadcast engineers went on record to describe it as 'better than the launch of the Space Shuttle'.

Topo and Fred were Androbots. Nolan Bushnell is more famous of course for founding Atari, though in reviewing the cuttings of our UK launch, I see *Leisure Electronics Trader* described him as Noel Bushnell and *Marketing* magazine as Norman Bushnell – a very belated sorry, Nolan!

Nolan did not rest on his laurels after Atari but created Catalyst Technologies, a venture capital operation with a difference. If you had a good idea then Nolan would set you up in an office with equipment and staff, so you could concentrate on delivering your idea as a product to market.

This had happened with Androbot. Walter Hammeken and Jack Larson, also ex-Atari, had worked up the notion. Hammeken later moved off to pursue industrial robots, while Nolan funded these personal robots. They were first seen at the Las Vegas CES in January 1983 and we were launching in the UK a year later in what Nolan termed the year 1AB.

Nolan shot down the PC killer apps by pointing out that fewer than 10% of Americans ever sent a letter and therefore had little need for a word processor, a tiny percentage of people could understand or would ever need a spreadsheet, but he believed that everyone would like someone readily prepared to go and get a beer from the fridge, or to do the ironing. He saw robots as slaves without the guilt!

RANDOM ACCESS MOMENT:
Representing Androbot for the UK we got to know Nolan and can confirm his then description of himself as a 'space cadet' was perfectly valid. My favourite story is of his Catalyst Technologies operation, where he set up a micro-waved network between the offices so he could talk with those he was funding.

But while they had a fixed camera, rather like the webcams used today, he had a headset and pocket-clipped keypad for his camera to track. So while they had to sit fixed in front of cameras he could pace up and down with the technology keeping him in shot.

He also had quite an office that could be switched between themes. The best for me established a twilight simulation with low general lighting, point lighting on the desk and the background sound of cicadas.

Robots in history

Robots have been present as a notion since the beginnings of civilisation. As long ago as 3,500 BCE the Greek myths talked of intelligent machines. Hephaestus, the god of fire, was described in Homer's Iliad as creating young serving girls from gold. For King Minos of Crete he produced a bronze statue that patrolled the island to protect it from an invasion. Even in these first mentions in literature robots were clearly defined as servants of Man.

By legend Pygmalion, the king of Cyprus, created a statue of a woman, Galatea, he prayed to Aphrodite (wife of Hephaestus) to give the statue life, she did and Pygmalion married her.

Down the years there have been many automatons and devices, mostly intended for general entertainment, though of course each stretched the mechanical principles of the day.

Around 350 BCE Archytas of Tarentum, a Greek born in Italy and one of the originators of mathematical mechanics, is said to have built a mechanical pigeon that was able to fly, probably using steam power. It is unclear however whether he used some sort of guide wire or if it actually flew.

The Egyptians were content to hide priests inside statues to simulate robots as divine messengers. The Jews have legends of 'golems' which were little men (or homunculi) made from clay that were invoked to protect the community.

In 1495, Leonardo Da Vinci is credited with the first automaton design of a human figure - who else? This followed on from his Vitruvian Man drawing and anatomical enquiries. The definition of an automaton is a 'self-propelling machine'.

Hans Bullman, a German, is credited with creating the first android in 1525; this was a robot with human appearance.

There was also a Middle Ages fashion for creating talking heads.

Other automatons such as water-driven clocks appeared in Babylon and again in Greece; the Chinese created a whole mechanical orchestra. There were also notable Arab, Indian and Japanese inventors.

A famous robot was Jacques de Vaucanson's Digesting Duck (canard digérateur) created in 1738. He built it as an entertaining demonstration to raise funds for him to pursue his work. Made from copper with 4,000 mechanical parts, it drank water and ate grain, digested and voided it; it could also move, wag its tail, flap its wings and quack. Some suggest the eating and defaecating was something of a fraud and that it would ingest the food into one container and eject faeces that had been prepared earlier.

The term robot itself comes from a 1920 play by a Czech writer, Karel Čapek. The play was *Rossum's Universal Robots* in which a Brit called Rossum manufactured robots to relieve humankind of the drudgery of work. They were made a little too smart and overthrew their human masters and took over the world for themselves.

The word robot derives from the Czech *robota* which is translated as worker, though with the suggestion of being more a slave or serf than that word might generally imply. Čapek credits his brother Josef, an artist and writer, as proposing its use.

Isaac Asimov, the sci-fi writer, is credited with the term 'robotics' in 1941.

Yet another MIT contribution came from Norbert Weiner. He was another child prodigy - graduated at eleven, earned a BA in mathematics at fifteen, and then switched his attention to the study of philosophy. At twenty he travelled to Europe to study under some of the great thinkers including Bertrand Russell in Cambridge, England.

In WWII Weiner worked on automating anti-aircraft guns and this led to him and colleagues developing the concept of what would become cybernetics.

In 1948 Norbert Weiner founded the field of cybernetics and coined the name which was based on a Greek word translating to steersman, pilot or governor. It is the study of animals (including humans) and of machines, looking at communication and developing theories of control and feedback.

This was originally applied to anthropology but as electronics evolved it was increasingly used for devices.

He went on to contribute significantly in robotics, computer control and automation.

Industrial robots

Much of the early robotic development focused on arms and legs.

An early arm was the Rancho Arm, developed in 1963 at a Californian hospital as a prosthetic device; it had six joints to simulate a human arm. In the same year Stanford University acquired one and became the first to connect a robotic arm to a computer.

By 1969 Victor Scheinman, a Norwegian, had developed the Stanford Arm which was the first electrically-powered and computer-controlled arm. By 1974 it was capable of assembling a Ford Model T water pump. Though how many Model Ts were still extant is unclear.

One of the earliest robotic hands was developed by Rajko Tomovic at the University of Belgrade in 1965. It had pressure-sensitive switches to give it a sense of touch. David Silver at MIT created the Silver Arm in 1974; this also had pressure-sensing.

In 1968 Marvin Minsky developed a twelve-jointed arm that could extend around corners. Controlled by a PDP-6 this became known as the Tentacle Arm.

Ichiro Kato built the Wabot-1 in 1973 at the Waseda University in Tokyo. It had all four limbs - WL-5 legs and WAM-4 hands. It could speak in Japanese and had a range of sensors to map distances and directions. By 1984 the Wabot-2 was a musician robot able to read a score and play a keyboard. The WASUBOT in 1985 was able to play a concerto.

Hitachi's WHL-11 was capable of walking on flat surfaces from 1985 but it took a whole thirteen seconds per step in order to keep its balance.

But much of the real progress early on was made in industrial applications.

George Charles Devol Jr considered going to MIT but was drawn instead to creating his own operation. In 1932 he first dabbled in the technology of movies with his United Cinephone Corporation looking at novel ways to put sound on to film, but realised larger organisations were more likely to succeed. He did install amplifiers at the Cotton Club and enjoyed watching the jazz stars of the time.

But he was prolific; he came up with lighting innovations for garment plants, controls for printing presses, packaging plant, and automatic photoelectric tollbooth counters for the New York World's Fair.

Around the time of WWII he joined Sperry Gyroscope to explore some of his ideas in radar. He developed proximity devices for use with laundry presses then set up another company of his own to look at electronics and radar test equipment. In WWII he produced jamming devices for the US Navy.

Post-war he established Devol Research Associates, working with memory, magnetic recording, sensors and even high-speed printers. He also developed a microwave product to vend hotdogs.

His experience across so many different products and production processes inspired him to find ways of automating tasks and he obtained the first patent for an industrial robot, he went on to own thirty or forty related patents. His system was called universal automation, shortened to Unimation.

In 1956 Devol met with Joseph F Engelberger and the two advanced the industry together. When he sold his rights in 1961 to Consolidated Diesel Electric Corporation a subsidiary was established using the name Unimation Inc.

Engelberger, as president of Unimation, developed Devol's ideas into creating a proper business in industrial robots and producing Unimate, the first industrial robot. Thus it is Engelberger that is heralded as the 'father of industrial robotics'.

In 1961 Unimate had its first installation at General Motors where it handled hot die-cast parts. It went on to be used in the manufacture of television sets. It stored its faithfully followed instructions in a drum memory.

It was of course this industrial robotic path that led to exploration of harsh environments with robotic submersibles, robotic spacecraft, and moon and planet surface rovers. They were also applied to more delicate detail work including robotic bomb disposal devices and robotic surgery. I guess you might even consider cruise missiles and predator drones to be robotic in principle too.

Today the International Organization for Standardization defines an industrial robot in the published standard ISO 8373,

'an automatically controlled, reprogrammable, multipurpose, manipulator programmable in three or more axes, which may be either fixed in place or mobile for use in industrial automation applications.'

This definition has also been adopted by the International Federation of Robotics and the European Robotics Research Network (EURON).

By the late noughties most estimates suggest there were a million industrial robots in use in the world with some seven million 'service robots'. The latter term is used for a robot other than those engaged in manufacturing, operating in part or fully autonomously to provide services useful to the well-being of humans, plant and equipment.

The startling thing perhaps is that this is not one of the USA's more successful areas. Half of the world's robots are in Asia (30%+ in Japan), a third in Europe and only 16% in the USA.

Tortoises and Turtles

W Grey Walter, American born though educated in Britain, worked at the Burden Institute in Bristol, England using an EEG machine to research alpha and delta brainwaves. During WWII he applied this knowledge to radar scanning and to guided missile systems.

In 1948/9 he developed Elmer and Elsie, two small mechanical tortoises that used their three wheels to reach an identified light source and when required to find a power source to recharge themselves. Their behaviour resembled that of an insect or animal. He demonstrated three of his second generation of robots at the Festival of Britain in 1951; several of the tortoises are still extant at London's Science Museum and at the Smithsonian.

He used analogue electronics to mirror brain processes to see if these devices might be able to develop any sort of self-awareness; they did not.

In the 1990s a Bristol team used the remnants of a tortoise and approached W J 'Bunny' Warren who was still working at the Burden Institute, coincidentally when the first lobotomies were ever performed. Warren had designed and built the originals and he helped to produce Ninja and Amy. These were demonstrated at the Second European Conference on Artificial Life in Granada, Spain in July 1995.

Back to the 1960s. The drive was on to try to add 'senses' to equipment - cameras to see, sensors to touch. The effort was applied to see how much intelligence might evolve from providing machines with these attributes. John McCarthy at MIT was the first to use the term 'artificial intelligence' for this discipline. He set up the AI Labs at MIT in 1957 and later at Stanford University in 1963.

It was soon realised that cameras and sensing devices could be added but of course we do not see with our eyes, we see with our brain. It was not the act of seeing but the discernment that was difficult to emulate.

One standard experiment that was set testing sight systems was the black box, where tools were put into a black painted toolbox. While a human had no difficulty in selecting a required tool from a glimpsed view of it beneath a jumble of others, this proved very difficult for a computer. It had to 'see' the tool in full 3D, and try to identify any familiar contour - all to be achieved in low light conditions.

Seymour Papert, a South African based at MIT, adopted a similar analogue to Grey Walter in creating the American equivalent of the tortoise, a turtle. Papert was educated in South Africa and the UK; he previously worked at the UK's National Physical Laboratory (NPL) while also active in the Socialist Workers' Party and its publication *Socialist Review*.

At MIT his specialism was learning theories, particularly as they might be applied to schools. As part of his thinking at Bolt, Beranek & Newman (BBN) he helped develop LOGO in 1967, this was a functional programming language. The LOGO name was based on the Greek *logos* or word because it was aimed to be more linguistic than mathematical. Its first implementation was on an SDS 950, written in LISP.

Papert built educational robots to exploit and demonstrate his LOGO programming language. The first US turtle, called Irving, was built at BBN in 1969. This was a floor-roamer with an umbilical; there was no wireless or IR back then. Later versions were produced as tabletop devices.

LOGO used simple instructions like LEFT 60, FORWARD 50, for the turtle to rotate 60-degrees leftward and advance 50 'steps'. Therefore REPEAT 4 (FORWARD 50, RIGHT 90) described a square. It could also learn expressions or macros; thus TO SQUARE, REPEAT 4 (FORWARD 50, RIGHT 90) meant the use of the term SQUARE in future would give the same effect.

LOGO was often used in early video games so a shape could be set as a 'sprite' and then moved around the screen using LOGO geometry.

Fictional robots

But this short chronology of robotics is completely inadequate without giving credit to fictional robots; don't forget that even the term robot came from fiction!

Certainly books, comics, plays and movies have done as much to drive robotic development as has pure research. Our imaginations wrought fabulous skills and futures for robots that were simple to create in movies using an actor in a suit.

Isaac Asimov was perhaps the person who most popularised the notion of robots; certainly he is the one who challenged our thinking about how a robot would fare given the whim and self-interest of mankind. It was he who drew up the Three Laws of Robotics,

'1 – a robot may not injure a human being or, through inaction, allow a human being to come to harm. 2 - a robot must obey the orders given it by human beings, except where such orders would conflict with the First Law. 3 - a robot must protect its own existence as long as such protection does not conflict with the First or Second Law.'

But then Asimov spent many years and many hundreds of pages showing how, despite this apparently simple series of three laws, robots could still create mayhem.

Fritz Lang's *Metropolis* in 1927 portrayed a beautiful female robot used to mesmerise humans and ferment revolution against the heartless brutality of the sci-fi city. Also heartless was the Tin Man in *The Wizard of Oz* of course. Andromeda in *A for Andromeda* had her construction plans transmitted from the stars; scientists following these decoded plans turned out to be a big mistake for humankind.

Amusing to consider that before CGI most fictional aliens and robots were bipedal humanoids thus making the required costumes and acting more straightforward.

Of course, *The Terminator* movies' T-800 and T-1000 hunter-killer robots reached back through time to change history. Neither should we forget the *Transformers*.

But not all robots were portrayed as aggressive. Robby the Robot in *Return to the Forbidden Planet* was based on Shakespeare's Ariel from *The Tempest*. Robby was unable to cause harm. The robot in the TV series *Lost in Space* was a guardian too, constantly calling out a warning - 'Danger, Will Robinson!'

C3PO and R2D2 in the *Star Wars* series provided light relief, K9 in *Doctor Who* was cute; all three were benign. Twiki in *Buck Rogers*, Crichton in *Red Dwarf* were amusing foils and supports to their stars. KITT in *Knight Rider* was the more intelligent sidekick to the human star, the Hoff. Even *Teletubbies* had Noo-Noo.

Fictional robots were usually accorded intelligence and progressively personality. Johnny 5 from the *Short Circuit* series was a powerful defence weapon that developed an independent personality. David the robot in *Artificial Intelligence; AI* examined the problems of a robot with intelligence and the power to love. David was placed in an emotional maelstrom of a family whose human child recovered from a coma and exhibited sibling rivalry, within a society that was turning against robots.

Douglas Adams' Marvin the Paranoid Android was a robot equipped with GPP (genuine people personalities) technology. Marvin was miserable because he had a brain the size of a planet, 50,000 times more intelligent than a human, but it was being used for mindless tasks like parking cars.

These all fed researchers with notions, but reality was tougher than fiction.

Defining robots

This then was the backcloth for those who realised that a robot might be created as a form of mobile personal computer, a personal robot. But just what might it do?

A few months after our Hippodrome UK launch of the Androbots the embryonic industry assembled at the first International Personal Robot Congress & Exposition held in Albuquerque in April 1984.

Keynote speakers included Nolan Bushnell and Joseph F Engelberger; Isaac Asimov was linked remotely to provide a teleconference address. Prism was interested as a member of the fledgling British Personal Robot Manufacturers' Group.

Much time at this event was dedicated to defining what a robot was and what it might do. It was Engelberger who resolved an extensive debate at the congress on what a robot was, by suggesting,

'If you pay your dues to the Robotic Institute of America then your product is definitely a robot.'

There had been a fad around this time for 'show robots' – simple mindless devices that would dance and gyrate to attract attention or appear to have intellect and engage in conversations by virtue of a concealed human operator. But this show called for robots that actually did something!

One approach discussed at Albuquerque was to consider the robot as a pet, as then the question of what it could do might be largely avoided. Nobody asks what your dog or cat is doing for you when it lies on a rug in front of the fire. We accept these creatures into our homes in return for what are often the most tenuous signs of affection and intelligence.

The robot as a toy was considered too. In the late nineties and noughties both these ideas really took off as a concept.

But there has always been an anthropomorphic tendency in robots.

The first day's proceedings saw Asimov's keynote coming from New York using AT&T's relatively new teleconferencing facilities. His key theme was that he felt there was little value in trying to make machines act, think or look like humans.

For example, computer intelligence was particularly good with numbers - being fast, accurate and never tiring - while we humans are slow, inaccurate and easily fatigued. In fact humans have a powerful history of avoiding mathematics by using fingers, an abacus, paper and symbols, slide rules and computers - anything rather than our brains.

Humans, Asimov felt, were better designed for intuition, insight, imagination and creativity. As an example of our insight, Newton had intuitively guessed at the density of Earth but it was eighty years before Cavendish could scientifically prove him correct.

Asimov considered it a waste of human ability to bother to become computer-like with numbers, just as it was a waste of machine intelligence to mimic mankind. They could at best be poor copies. Instead he proposed a symbiosis, a combination of man and his computer or robot to bring about something greater than the abilities of the component parts.

This prompted much debate as to whether the robot should become a supra-portable PC that would be an encyclopaedia, dictionary, thesaurus, calendar and calculator. But surely there ought to be more?

Personal Robots

Step up Bushnell and others. Nolan maintained that 'fun sells'; he wanted to cast the robot as a pet and a companion,

'Many people own a dog, and wish that it could speak English... ...Many lonely and perhaps senile people need to be reminded to take their medicine.'

Bushnell ignored Asimov's concerns about anthropomorphism, and designed the Androbot's look very carefully. He explained that part of the appeal of Mickey Mouse was that the relative size of head to body was that of a one year old child, an age that research indicated drew out the most powerful parental urges. TOPO had those same proportions and a very distinctive face.

The Androbots came in three formats. TOPO (from topographic) was designed as a development device. It would faithfully rotate and move as commanded using its two drive wheels and a system that started slowly and accelerated gently so it would perform very accurately on all flat surfaces.

It was driven by a PC via an IR device built into its head; but key to its approach was its electronic architecture being designed to allow hardware and software developers access to add their own arms, own applications, sensing devices...

FRED (the friendly robotic educational device) was an Androbot that performed as an educational turtle. Driven by a keyboard or joystick, it was able to draw and perform routines.

BOB (brains on board) was a TOPO with its own built-in computer thus not requiring external computing power. Nolan at his launch of Androbot used the term 1AB for 1984; this in his parlance meant one year after BOB. I still have my small brass version of BOB with '1AB' proudly inscribed on its back.

Also available from 1982 was Heathkit's HERO-1 (Heathkit educational robot). Naturally, being Heathkit it was available as a kit or ready-assembled. It's 'head' (not humanoid) could rotate by 350 degrees to align its sensors without rotating the whole robot.

Of course these personal robots were a very long way short of developing any sort of real autonomy, and certainly had no sort of local intelligence (sorry BOB!). They merely carried out human instructions.

RANDOM ACCESS MOMENT:
One of the most remarkable speakers at Albuquerque was a disabled guy whose premise was that disabled people better understood robots because they experienced life with a sensory or movement deprivation. The speaker showed his gritty character as he went on to say,
'Twenty years ago I would have been considered a cripple, ten years ago they would have more kindly called me handicapped, today I'm even more simply described as disabled. But I hope in a few years that I'll be considered as a guy who likes a challenge!'

Honda's R&D department started work on a range of robots from 1986. The E-Series from 1986 to 1993 essentially experimented with robotic legs.

The Honda EO was demonstrated in 1986 and simulated human walking, though each step took around five seconds to complete. Subsequent versions became faster and had more degrees of movement in the legs. By 1993 E6 was able to negotiate obstacles and climb stairs.

RANDOM ACCESS MOMENT:
Back at that Albuquerque conference one speaker pooh-poohed the need for robots to climb stairs. He suggested that the robot could haul itself up a banister rail and when it wanted to come down it could check that no-one was on the stairs or below, then just throw itself down - its construction would be arranged to allow for this sort of 'self-abuse'.

Honda's P series released from 1993 to 2000 added arms and developed a progressively more humanoid look and feel. Honda only demonstrated these from the P2 onwards with its first 'outing' in 1996. It was the Honda P3 that attracted the attention of the Japanese authorities.

METI, Japan's Ministry of Economy, Trade and Industry, got together with NEDO (New Energy and Industrial Technology Development Organization) and AIST (National Institute of Advanced Industrial Science and Technology) to found the Humanoid Robotics Project. The project was supported by Kawada Industries and Kawasaki Heavy Industries.

Kawada was founded back in 1922 as a blacksmiths company. It had previously worked with the University of Tokyo to develop the H6 robot in 1999 and the H7 in 2000.

The Humanoid Robotics Project acquired three Honda P3s and from these Kawada developed the project's HRP-1 through HRP-4 robots by adding new features. The HRP-2 Promet had a unique ability in that it was able to stand up from lying flat on the floor; either from its back or its front.

In 2000 Honda revealed the Asimo (advanced step in innovative mobility); Honda denied it had anything to do with Asimov and his famous three robotic laws.

It was child-sized (120 cms tall) and looked a little like an astronaut. Asimo was remarkable for its capability to move. Its arms had three distinct joints, the wrist and shoulder each having movement in three directions and the elbow adding a seventh. The hand itself had movement in the fingers and thumb. Its legs had joints at the groin with three directions, the ankle with two and the knee with one.

Progressively additional features were added to Asimo. A camera in its head assisted with local movements and interaction. It could respond to hand gestures, recognise faces and distinguish sounds. By use of the Internet it could be used to regurgitate news and weather reports.

An Asimo costs around $1m to make and so it is unsurprising that only around 100 units were ever made.

In 2001 Fujitsu entered the market with the HOAP-1 (humanoid for open architecture platform). This was much smaller at just 17" (50cm) high and worked with RT-Linux to allow simple reprogramming.

Fujitsu also launched the Enon in 2005, implausibly standing for exciting nova on network, it was sold as a personal assistant at $60,000. It could navigate, pick up light items, shake hands and had limited speech recognition and speech synthesis.

A Vietnamese company called TOSY started development in 2005 of the Topio range (Tosy ping pong playing robot). In 2011 the Topio 3.0 stood 1.88m tall with 39 degrees of movement. It had in-built AI routines to recognise fast-moving objects and improved its skills with time. It could successfully play table tennis against a human.

Also in 2005 Aldebaran Robotics from Paris, France developed the Nao robot. With 21 degrees of movement in 2011 it took over the RoboCup soccer competitions from Aibo. Aldebaran worked with independent developers and announced its plan to sell its robots in 2011.

In 2008 MIT collaborated with Xitome Design and Meka robotics to develop Nexi. Nexi could roll around on a pair of wheels, but the real innovation was in the way it expressed itself facially and with its body and hands. Its neck had four degrees of freedom and it moved its eyebrows, eyelids and chin to create various clear expressions. It was defined as a mobile, dexterous, social robot: in demonstration it was definitely a 'she'.

In 2010 the Dextrous Robotics Laboratory at NASA, part funded by DARPA and General Motors, developed the Robonaut, intended for space walks. Before Robonaut the use of robotics in space was largely based upon manipulating and moving large objects. The Robonaut R2 was equipped with over 350 sensors; it had twelve degrees of freedom in its hand and used telepresence for human remote management of some of its tasks. Robonauts could use a Segway for movement.

A Robonaut joined the International Space Station during 2011 to perform humanoid tasks alongside human astronauts. Another plan, Project M, proposed sending a Robonaut to the Moon.

Artificial Intelligence and robots

Isadore Jacob Gudak was born in London to Polish parents, later anglicising his name to Irving John Good.

Good completed his doctorate at Cambridge while working as a cryptologist with Turing's team at Bletchley Park during WWII. He also collaborated with Donald Michie and Max Newman on a series of ciphers that formed part of the development of the Colossus computers. Post-war Good followed Newman and Turing to the University of Manchester where he was part of the Manchester Mark 1 team before moving on to GCHQ.

He is best known for his theories of what he called ultra-intelligent machines. He was not entirely positive about his work and sounded quite strident when he said,

'The survival of man depends on the early construction of an ultra-intelligent machine.'

He proposed that this work would lead to a 'technological singularity', a moment when machines would eventually take over,

'Let an ultra-intelligent machine be defined as a machine that can far surpass all the intellectual activities of any man however clever. Since the design of machines is one of these intellectual activities, an ultra-intelligent machine could design even better machines; there would then unquestionably be an 'intelligence explosion,' and the intelligence of man would be left far behind. Thus the first ultra-intelligent machine is the last invention that man need ever make.'

Marvin Minsky, co-founder of MIT's AI Lab, must have agreed too when he said,

'It's ridiculous to live 100 years and only be able to remember 30 million bytes. You know, less than a compact disc. The human condition is really becoming more obsolete every minute.'

From 1963 MIT was involved in what John McCarthy had termed as artificial intelligence. It was seen how the norm for computers was to slavishly fulfil their programming with no facility to look for alternative approaches or short cuts. AI set out to develop programs that would learn from past activity and adapt their approach accordingly.

By the 1980s those in computing were experiencing heady times - anything could be built now, couldn't it?

As a result in 1982 the Japanese MITI (Ministry of International Trade and Industry) gave a hurry-up call to all developers of computers and robots by suggesting that instead of copying the products of the West they should force ahead with a fifth generation computer project focusing on the development of a supercomputer with artificial intelligence. This should be completed within a ten-year timeframe.

This concept of generations appeared to dismiss the purely mechanical gears and relay phase and assumed that the first generation computers were those using vacuum tubes developed in the 1940s and early 50s, the second were transistor-based from the mid 50s to mid 60s, the third were based on integrated circuits in the late 60s and early 70s and the fourth were the microprocessor-based computers from the early 70s onwards.

The fifth generation computer they suggested would be a step-function beyond, developing artificial intelligence with parallel processing, logic software, and perhaps using superconductors and nanotechnology...

On the software front there were also five generations; once again the manual switches and dials phase seems to be disregarded. Machine code was therefore considered to be the first generation with the user having to learn the limited functions by rote and perhaps use hexadecimals to enter instructions. The use of symbols and routines specific to the computer constituted the second generation with assemblers that could write the machine code for you.

By the 1970s third generation software was represented by the introduction of high-level languages such as FORTRAN, COBOL, BASIC, PASCAL and C which allowed the user to concentrate on what was required, and leave it to the program to achieve this. These early generations used compilers and interpreters to assist the process of course.

Fourth generation software assisted the user to create specific applications; this includes packages like SQL and TeX.

The fifth generation would seek not to be algorithm-driven but instead use logic to solve any problems applied to it.

McCarthy at MIT was part of the AI team within Project MAC led by Marvin Minsky; this was later formalised into MIT's AI Lab in 1970.

By then John McCarthy had moved on to establish the Stanford Artificial Intelligence Laboratory (SAIL). This was operational by 1966, it had been funded based on his advising ARPA that it could build a thinking machine within a decade.

The lab was merged into the computer science department in 1980. By the time the Japanese MITI plans were formalising, McCarthy was obviously feeling less positive when he said in 1978 (already two years beyond his promised decade),

'...*human-level A.I. might require 1.7 Einsteins, 2 Maxwells, 5 Faradays and 0.3 Manhattan Projects.*'

The Japanese project was undeterred; it was co-funded by a number of the large and successful Japanese manufacturers. The Japanese ministry established the Institute for New Generation Computer Technology (ICOT) as the vehicle for this research. It was all set out very logically, it would run the project for three years of R&D, then four years to build the various components and subsystems and a further three years would be required to prototype the product.

The director of ICOT was Kazuhiro Fuchi; he assembled a 40-strong team from among the Japanese PTT and the eight supporting commercial organisations. They set out to create a large-scale knowledge database to be rapidly accessed by inference programming techniques.

They used Prolog-based high performance workstations and built a parallel processor. It worked on logical inferences at incredible speeds; they claimed it could achieve up to 1G LIPS (logical inferences per second) when 100k LIPS was the current norm.

Prolog was a logic programming language developed by French computer scientist Alain Colmerauer, later a professor of Computer Science at the University of Marseilles.

The West was terrified - after all the Japanese had already readily taken over most of the consumer electronics market. The USA responded with the Strategic Computing Initiative and the MCC (Microelectronics and Computer Technology Corporation). The UK had the Alvey Programme. In Europe there was ESPRIT (European Strategic Program of Research in Information Technology) and also the ECRC (European Computer Research Centre) in Munich. The buzz words soon became 'parallel inference machines'.

The Japanese plan spent $450m without achieving its main goals. This and other equally expensive initiatives certainly contributed to new understanding in many fields but no artificially intelligent computer emerged – at least to my knowledge!

Robotic pets and toys

Though there was no real progress in AI with robots there have been a number of entrepreneurial and engineering advances to provide robots with some semblance of 'intelligence'.

The Tomy toy company was early in launching a whole series of toy robots under the title Omnibot and designed by Tony Kyogo.

Pets have been a persisting theme. Clearly not at all an AI device, the Tamagotchi was introduced in 1996; the name comes from the Japanese word *tamago* meaning egg.

It was designed by Aki Maita of Bandai and Akihiro Yokoi of WiZ Co and resembles a brightly coloured stop watch. Once switched on an egg appears; this soon hatches and its gender is announced. The user names it (up to eight characters) and then has to maintain its health and well-being.

The user effectively becomes the owner or parent and the device is quite demanding. Initially there was no pause feature and this led to all sorts of problems. Children were taking their 'pets' to school so that they would not die during school hours.

If the owners were not routinely careful the character would become truculent and if abandoned would die. If cared for, it would go through five life stages and could even mate with another Tamagotchi; the offspring always being twins, with one allocated to each parent.

Some 70 million were sold by 2008 and its success prompted many other products.

Caleb Chung and Dave Hampton developed the Furby in the late '90s and sold the idea to Tiger Electronics, who launched it in 1998.

Furby was described as an owl-like robot that spoke a language called Furbish. The user could then add English words to its vocabulary; eventually twenty-four different language versions were offered. This learning ability gave it a pseudo-AI implication.

It had very simple movements; its eyes and mouth opened and closed, its ears moved and it could lift itself off the ground. It was suggested that this was 'dancing'!

Furby was launched at just $35 but its popularity led to shortages and a price hike; some users were prepared pay over $300 to get one. Close to 2 million units were sold by the end of 1998, and 14 million the next year - over 40 million units sold in total.

The more advanced and physically larger Emoto-Tronic Furby range was launched in August 2005 with added voice recognition and a whole series of facial expressions to add to its appeal.

Tiger Electronics later launched Poo-Chi, a dog robot. This had pre-recorded sounds, could express emotions with symbols in its eyes and could sing one of a rather strange and eclectic collection of six songs; the *Wedding March, de Camptown Races, The Star-Spangled Banner, When the Saints Come Marching In...*

A rather more serious robot was Sony's Aibo launched in May 1999. It was designed originally by Hajime Sorayama as a dog robot; later versions were designed by Katsura Moshino.

The dog responded to the spoken word and could assess its environment as it walked around. It made noises composed by the Japanese DJ/composer Nobukazu Takemura.

Sony free-issued its R-CODE language and a programmer's kit that permitted reprogramming of the Aibo. This inspired many to use Aibo as a low-cost device for AI experimentation. Aibos were also used in the RoboCup soccer competitions within a special four-legged league.

Silverlit Electronics of Hong Kong also launched a dog robot in 2000; it was called the i-Cybie and distributed by Tiger Electronics in 2001. It was very similar in appearance to Sony's Aibo.

There were some battery life problems and despite a relaunch in 2005 it never really took off. However a group of i-Cybie owners added a computer port to their units so it could be reprogrammed.

In March 2005 the iDog (eDog in Germany) was manufactured by Sega Toys and distributed by Hasbro. It responded to music from an iPod or MP3 player by flashing its LED lights and dancing to the beat. It came in various colours and even had a range of clothing!

The team went on to launch iCat, iFish, iTurtle and iCy (a penguin-like version).

The Korean company Dasarobot launched yet another dog-like robot in 2006; it was modeled on a bull terrier called the Genibo. When released it cost $1,500 and came with movement sensors, a master's voice recognition system and a hundred voice commands; it could exhibit emotions, for example when stroked.

Another Hong Kong based company, the WowWee Group Ltd was founded by Canadian brothers Richard and Peter Yanofsky in 1982. It made various OEM and own brand developments in remote control animals.

Peter Yanofsky saw Mark Tilden featured on the Discovery Channel talking about his work in robotics at the Los Alamos National Laboratory. They hired him as a consultant just before WowWee was taken over by Hasbro in 1998.

Tilden joined the operation full-time in 2001 and started work on Robosapien; the relationship with Hasbro was poor and Yanofsky bought the operation back from Hasbro in 2003. Robosapien was released in 2004 and sold over 1.5m units in less than six months.

Robosapien was supplied with a remote control with twenty-one buttons that could be programmed to create up to sixty-seven different command sequences. The robot could walk or dance and grasp or throw items with its hands. It had a broad range of sounds and tunes. What made it interesting was the low price together with the open architecture that positively encouraged modifications and add-ons.

Follow-ons include the Robosapien v2, the Spidersapien, Femisapien, Roboboa, Roboquad (4-legged spider-like), and Homersapien (yes as in Homer Simpson!); plus the Roboreptile and Roboraptor.

In 2007 the company launched the Dragon Fly a remote controlled wing-flapping robot and followed this with a helicopter, the Bladestar.

21 - Number crunchers – spreadsheets, dbases and accounting

'The real danger is not that computers will begin to think like men, but that men will begin to think like computers.' Sydney Harris

The clue is in the name of course – computer. Many of the first applications that took off for mainframes, minicomputers and personal computers were those that would count, compute, calibrate, calculate, cost and cast numbers. In most cases with the right software the computer can do these functions more quickly, tirelessly and accurately than we can. In this application area several killer apps would emerge.

Forecasts and what-ifs - spreadsheets

Dan Bricklin was an early software visionary, another individual who transited through the hallowed turf of MIT. In 1969/70 he met Bob Frankston where they both worked on the MULTICS project, that influential early time-sharing system. Initially on leaving they worked in different parts of the developing PC business, but not before they had identified a desire to start a small business together.

Bricklin conceived of the electronic spreadsheet while studying for an MBA at the Harvard Business School in 1978 as he watched a professor develop a financial model on the blackboard.

In 1979 working with his friend Bob Frankston, and assisted in terms of distribution by Dan Fylstra of Software Arts they created VisiCalc the killer-app for the early Apple computers.

Selling 700,000 copies in just six years and giving home computers the first true business application. Yet as we saw earlier this was never patented.

Ed Esber was an ex-IBM-er instrumental in the 1970s in making that corporation seriously consider the new microprocessors coming from Intel, Motorola and others. He was also tasked at IBM to look at using the PC to control home energy costs.

But the bug caught him and he joined Texas Instruments at Lubbock in 1978 to be in product marketing for its PC plans. Just like me as TI UK's personal computer manager, he did not stay long and joined Personal Software where he worked on the distribution and marketing of VisiCalc and its growing range of applications VisiFile, VisiWord, VisiPlot, VisiTrend…

Given just how vital VisiCalc was to the Apple II, it must have been evident to the organisation a major software battle would be to become the spreadsheet of choice for the new IBM PC.

VisiCalc, as the Apple II killer-app, was keen to maintain its market position and worked quickly to modify VisiCalc to fit the IBM product.

This was tested on a prototype unit with no casing and no identification. Internally it was named the 'Florida computer system' - a suitable name for an IBM product from Boca Raton in Florida.

They succeeded in porting VisiCalc to the IBM PC but therein lay the problem. It was not developed directly for the IBM PC but merely modified to fit it. This made it slow, unresponsive and unable to take advantage of the 16-bit MPU and other features of the new product.

The market had moved on since the original invention. Now MBA courses proliferated and students on these courses were computer literate, still frustrated by the speed and costs of time-share and keen for the right package on this new PC. They were also demanding more sophisticated applications.

Along the way Personal Software released 30% of its equity, achieving over $500k, and renamed the organisation as VisiCorp in 1982. As we saw earlier, VisiCalc was never patented which allowed others in to the sector. It would be acquired by Lotus that had taken the spreadsheet notion and created the IBM PC 'killer app'.

Keep it in context – Context MBA

Others were of course drawn towards the IBM flame. Context Management Systems based in Torrance California developed an omnibus or integrated package approach called Context MBA, eventually to be priced at $695 when launched in mid-1982.

This was a massive five-in-one package, offering a spreadsheet, graphics, database, word processing and communications. It had an early implementation of windows so a spreadsheet could be open in one as a graph of a selected series of cells was shown in another. Each cell in the spreadsheet could contain up to four pages of text rather than a limited number of characters.

But the development was a tad confused by nervousness as to which OS might emerge the victor on the IBM PC - would it be DOS or CP/M-86?

So Context decided to hedge its bets and wrote its software in UCSDp (University of California at San Diego pseudo). UCSDp was designed so software could be written in PASCAL, a high level language, and the UCSDp would then port the code into a variety of systems. But this all-things-to-all-people approach made it ponderously slow, any scrolling or screen refreshing proved very painful, recalculations of the spreadsheet took a significant time that would frustrate users.

Context president G H Hoaxie argued that the integration of features and other enhancements transcended its slow speed - but the market thought otherwise.

Context MBA was first launched on the Apple III six months before Lotus, but this Apple product never really took off. A later version the Context MBA 1.2 was issued for the IBM PC but like VisiCalc is was not designed directly to take advantage of the PC features or architecture.

Context did what it could to speed it up and in one version added communications, Hoaxie, quoted in *Info World* on 24th January 1983, said,

'Communications is the unique feature. Now the user can dial up a remote computer, download information and convert it into the spreadsheet format.'

This is something we take for granted today from the Internet but that was where it was first offered with a simple process.

Also a routine was included in the software that called for an inordinate frequency of disk accesses. The slowness of UCSDp, its not having been directly written for the IBM PC, the busy-disk approach and the coming of Lotus 1-2-3 all combined to sound its death knell.

You've been framed - Framework

But this was not quite the end. Robert Carr, Context MBA's author, went on to write Framework, an integrated package for Ashton-Tate.

Carr and his friend Marty Mazner founded Forefront Corporation in 1983. In July they approached Ashton-Tate and outlined plans for Framework as a suite of programmes that worked via a number of frames, each being a process such as a spreadsheet, WP, database, charting, email etc. Most importantly this was not a series of stand-alone modules with a family feel. This was a truly integrated package.

A deal with Ashton-Tate took just days to be finalised. It agreed to fund the development in exchange for having exclusive marketing rights. The founders and a team of six wrote it in C to run on DOS; this took ten months and it was launched in March 1984.

The frames were controlled by FRED (frame editor) which was written in Lisp. FRED might be viewed as a simple form of GUI. Further FRED permitted for example that a cell in a spreadsheet could be its own frame, opening up a new file.

In 1985 Ashton-Tate acquired Forefront and its team. While they continued to originate through version II in 1985, v III in 1988 and v IV in 1991, it appeared that its marketing of Framework was very much reduced compared to that it did for its successful dBase.

Carr's product would battle with Lotus Symphony and Microsoft Works for what proved to be quite a small part of the market.

Lotus blossom – Lotus 1-2-3

Sales and marketing of VisiCalc were handled by VisiCorp itself, the new name for Personal Software. To handle the new market requirements Ed Esber saw the way forward as the development of a linked range of solutions.

For example products like VisiPlot, a 'bolt-on' to VisiCalc, was licensed. It enabled the user to plot graphs and charts from data held in a VisiCalc file. There was an inbuilt module named VisiTrend to provide statistical analysis routines. However the transfer of data between them was not simple; it had to be exported and then re-imported. These programs had been written internally by Mitch Kapor and Eric Rosenfield while working at Personal Software.

Kapor was a New Yorker with broad interests. While at Yale he was both the music director and programme director of the university radio station. He went on to be disc jockey on a Connecticut rock-station, where he became keen on transcendental meditation (TM).

While working for his master's in counselling psychology Kapor maintained an interesting mix by teaching TM while also working as a computer programmer. He attended a master's course at the MIT Sloan School of Management but did not graduate. There he met Rosenfield who was finding a program he was using to be very heavy going.

Developed by MIT this was software called TROLL. It is still in use today by banks, government agencies, colleges and corporates for econometric modelling and statistical analysis. Based around a database engine it had a suite of tools to manipulate, simulate and estimate equations. As Rosenfield was running it on a time-share computer the time it took him was proving very costly.

RANDOM ACCESS MOMENT:
Troll is also a term used in Internet circles to mean someone who is deliberately provocative in posting left-field or controversial views to fish for emotional responses. For UK readers to understand the usage they need to appreciate that what we call trawling, in US English is spelled trolling.

To assist Rosenfield with his work Kapor wrote TinyTROLL on an Apple II. Clearly working with TROLL really was not very easy as a similar approach to that of Kapor was prompted from by David Lilien also drawn to the Apple II colour graphics capabilities when he produced MicroTSP. Professor Steven Hall called his software Reg-X when developing yet another version.

When Kapor joined Personal Software he was able to use his work on Tiny TROLL to use this approach to the VisiCalc software, and from this he produced the VisiPlot package.

He promptly licensed the rights in the software to VisiCorp who marketed it at a retail price of $249.95, though of course the dealers had a 60% margin and bought it for just $100. This still left him 37.5% royalty as a significant sum per copy, earning around $500,000. This was a phase when VisiCorp was keen to move towards owning its own products and so it negotiated to pay Kapor $1.2 million to own VisiPlot/VisiTrend outright.

Of course he took the money. His licence fees had been good but Kapor knew the spreadsheet authors were earning many times more than he. While working with VisiCorp he was fortunate enough to see the prototype IBM PC and decided to reinvest most of his windfall into developing a spreadsheet for it.

He wanted his program to have an edge and decided to create a package to be a spreadsheet, a graphics program and a word processor. His background in meditation provided the name, Lotus; the goal of a three-in-one package gave it the brand name, Lotus 1-2-3. The company was founded by Kapor and Jonathan Sachs with funding by Benjamin Rosen.

Lotus had the major benefit of seeing and using Context MBA before its own launch. It was the slowness of Context MBA that led Jonathan Sachs, Kapor's partner, to conclude that they should not include a word processor in 1-2-3, as his investigation suggested this was what added considerably to the lack of pace with Context.

As a result of the evaluation, Lotus 1-2-3 changed its thinking and decided the third element would be a database, rather than the original notion of a word processor - so spreadsheet, graphics and database it was. The two Lotus individuals split the work in what was then a reasonably novel manner. Kapor defined the goals and system requirements while Sachs actually wrote the software.

Sachs had quite a pedigree too; he had been a FORTRAN programmer at MIT and spent several summers working at the Jet Propulsion Laboratory on the Mariner IV satellite. For MIT's biomedical centre he wrote the STOIC (stack-oriented interactive compiler) language, a dialect of FORTH. He also worked on a COBOL system used for a point-of-sale terminal - for one of my erstwhile employers Sweda.

While working at Data General he saw a demo of VisiCalc presented by the designers themselves and was asked to clone it for Data General minicomputers. He acquired an Apple II and a VisiCalc manual and, operating as Concentric Data Systems, he wrote a spreadsheet program called SuperComp. It was distributed by Access Technology with Sachs retaining rights in the source code so he was later able to develop it for DEC and to begin to think about CP/M versions.

Kapor had by then formed a company called Micro Finance Systems and was exploring spreadsheets too. Sachs joined him and produced a prototype spreadsheet written in the C language. Once they acquired an IBM PC Sachs set about rewriting it in 8088 assembly language.

Sachs compared writing in C with writing in the 8088 assembly language and found it some five times faster. The eventual outcome proved much smaller in code, so C it was to be. He also learned that writing to the screen memory buffer of the IBM PC made the screen refresh more quickly.

These decisions were crucial as they meant Lotus 1-2-3 was optimised to the IBM PC. Compared with VisiCalc and Context MBA it became the clear winner.

Lotus forecast that 1-2-3 would achieve sales of $1 million in its first year, but it actually achieved $54 million; not the greatest advert for someone designing and selling a forecasting software package, but one that was easily forgiven!

Super-calci-fragilistic - SuperCalc

Once on the slippery slope it just does not get any easier. VisiCorp, buffeted by Lotus in its bid for the IBM PC sector, had neglected the CP/M market.

Richard Frank and a team of CDC émigrés formed Sorcim to pursue Frank's CP/M products. At a poker evening they ran into Adam Osborne and Lee Felsenstein who were working on the Osborne 1 and wanted a CP/M BIOS - as one does!

But Osborne was also interested in sourcing a spreadsheet. He felt he was not getting far with VisiCalc so asked if Sorcim would produce one for him.

Martin Herbach led the development which was launched as SuperCalc in April 1981. It received a great response; selling 250,000 copies within eighteen months and routinely took 15% of the market.

It ended up being ported to 150 different platforms, mainly in the CP/M camp. SuperCalc had some big advantages. To the bemusement of Kapor it was all run from one disk, and it was the first spreadsheet to resolve circular references iteratively.

SuperCalc2 for CP/M followed in April 1983 and for CPM/86 a month later; sales rose to over $7m.

In 1984 a round of sourcing (sourcing for Sorcim!) secured $9m through the venture capital company Alex Brown & Co. But using $1m of this for a promotional campaign achieved little improvement in sales. The company did nothing to expand beyond the CP/M scene and failed to see the writing on the wall. Further it developed no other applications.

In spring 1984 Sorcim asked Alex Brown & Co to find a buyer, which it did. Computer Associates, a serial acquirer and today one of the largest independent software corporations of the world and a *Fortune 5000* company, acquired Sorcim in 1985 for $27m.

The success of Lotus 1-2-3 and Sorcim dealt a series of deadly body blows to the future of VisiCalc - the original killer app was having a slow death all of its own.

Getting it all under control - databasing

The other major number-crunching application for the early computers was in databasing.

Mainframe computers largely dealt in data processing on a case-by-case, product-by-product basis. But by the late 1950s there was pressure from those working in software to find some means toward gaining standardisation.

In April 1959 an influential two-day conference was organised; this was CODASYL (conference on data systems languages). This attracted an industry-wide group to define a standard programming language to be used across many different computers.

The Department of Defense agreed to fund some of the objectives outlined at CODASYL; its 'celebrity' Grace Hopper served as a technical advisor to the group.

RANDOM ACCESS MOMENT:
Rear-Admiral Grace Hopper has many claims to fame working on both the early Harvard Mark 1 and UNIVAC computers. But perhaps is most famous for something that happened on the Harvard Mark II in September 1947. It stopped working for no obvious reason. The team dismantled it to see what was wrong and they found a moth caught between the contacts of Relay #70 in Panel F that was interrupting the connection. The dead moth was sellotaped into the operations log for the unit, the entry saying very simply,
    'First actual case of bug being found.'

Grace Hopper's Flow-Matic language was to be one of the foundations of a new language. Other influences were to be IBM's COMTRAN language (commercial translator) a business alternative to the scientific FORTRAN, and Honeywell's FACT language (fully automated compiling technique).

By the end of 1959 this sub-committee had defined COBOL (common business-oriented language). COBOL was early in introducing the use of a more straightforward language than machine codes and assemblers that had gone before.

CODASYL was also to prove significant in databases.

Charlie Bachman gained a PhD in mechanical engineering and also pursued an MBA. However his career was forged in software engineering, first with Dow Chemical where he rose to become data processing manager.

Later working at General Electric in the 1960s, Bachman developed IDS (integrated data store) which was one of the very earliest databases. It was termed a navigational database management program. Navigational databases typically use paths and pointers for users to find any desired record. Hierarchical databases are somewhat similar but have a more formal tree-like structure.

The IDS program prompted CODASYL to create a List Processing Task Group in 1965. Renamed the Data Base Task Group in October 1969 it defined a standard way for COBOL to handle databases; this was known as the Codasyl approach or the Codasyl data model.

CODASYL, based on COBOL, was soon adopted by IBM as its Programming Language 1, a key part of the System/360. GE followed with the IDS and a derivative the Honeywell IDS/2. Univac had DMS-1100 and DEC the DBMS32.

Bachman went on to produce dataBasic, a language that added database facilities to the BASIC language for time-share users at GE.

Cullinane Corporation was founded in 1968 by John Cullinane and Larry English. Its business approach was to scour the IT departments of major organisations and seek out any unique software packages, then propose that they would represent these as pre-packaged offerings to others on a shared revenue basis.

This was quite a ponderous process, so to make ends meet they needed to write and sell some of their own utilities first. One such success was Culprit, a simple report writer, later renamed DP Auditor which give it a second and somewhat larger popularity.

The operation's main thrust bore fruit when it was approached by Naomi O Seligman on behalf of B F Goodrich, the aerospace manufacturer. At Goodrich it had successfully ported some software to an IBM and Seligman asked if Cullinane wanted to represent this product.

In 1973 the Cullinane team threw all its resources at this to produce IDMS (integrated database management system). It enjoyed a great deal of success and achieved a who's who of blue chip clients.

The degree of copying and plagiarism back in those mainframe days was remarkable. For example Cullinane sold the code to ICL in 1976 where it was promptly ported to the ICL 1900 and 2900 series. And then ICL went on to enhance it and sell it on, with no shred of shame, as the IDMSX.

In 1978 the operation changed its name to Cullinet Database Systems Inc, went public and became the first USA-listed software-only company. Hambrecht & Quist assisted in its initial public offering in April 1982; it was to become the first software company valued at $1bn. It was also the first IT company to take a Super Bowl advert - not Apple.

In 1979 it successfully integrated financial and manufacturing applications within the IDMS, launching it into the enterprise resource planning scene. It used this and the experience gained from several acquisitions to develop the Information Center Management System.

Six months after the IPO, IBM launched the 4300 series and its sales force suggested IDMS would not run on this series, and that users should use the IBM IMS/DL1 database which would be integrated into all future IBM software releases.

Cullinane found a simple solution to run it on the 4300 and added in its integrated data dictionary (IDD) to restore faith and sales. IDD was an IDMS database itself to keep track of definitions of the database fields etc.

The organisation changed its name again in 1983 to Cullinet Software and it addressed the PC market with an integrated package it called Goldengate. Sadly it did this before Windows and thus had to invest heavily in handling all sorts of different PC configurations which was expensive; it never really took off against Lotus Symphony.

But by the mid-1980s some 2,500 licences had been issued under the Goodrich- Cullinane agreement. The operation still had a $50m fund to use creatively. David Chapman was appointed as a new CEO to handle this. He chased acquisitions to position them in the minicomputer market while neglecting the mainframe business where they progressively lost out to others with relational database systems.

Cullinane was sold to Computer Associates in 1989 for $289m. CA's shares were lifted by a factor of ten on the announcement of this particular acquisition; it still sells and supports a version of IDMS.

Close relations – relational databases

Relational databases allow a data set to be 'searched' using each item's component elements within the data to give the user more insight into and ready access to the contents.

Of course the data might be representing products and components, human resources lists or financial records; the database software does not care. It can store, manipulate and report on the whole or sets within the whole.

The term relational database was first used by Edgar Codd at IBM in 1970. Codd was a Brit born on the Isle of Portland, which is connected by Chesil Beach to the mainland Jurassic Coast of the south of England.

His 1970 paper *A Relational Model of Data for Large Shared Data Banks* defined the basis of relational databases where the data tends to be assembled in spreadsheet like rows and columns but related fields in different sheets can use a join-function for advanced enquiries.

Yet Codd's approach was not adopted by IBM until action by its competitors finally chivvied it into action. The first commercial relational database was developed by Honeywell as part of the MULTICS project; launched in 1977 as the MULTICS Relational Database Store.

IBM was content with its Information Management System and IMS/DB products. These were developed specifically for the Apollo program back in 1966 in conjunction with Rockwell and Caterpillar. IMS was used for example to track the parts involved in building the Saturn V rocket and the Apollo spacecraft.

When IBM did finally realise it needed to upgrade IMS it still chose to ignore Codd's work and launched a research project called System R, developed at the then IBM San Jose Research Laboratory; today it is the IBM Almaden Research Center. System R's first client was the engine maker Pratt & Whitney in 1977.

When IBM sought a multi-user version for System R again Codd was not given the task. IBM ignored his Alpha language and went instead for yet another IBM internal development.

This was a system developed by Donald D Chamberlin and Raymond F Boyce called Sequel (structured English query language) though this name was found to clash with a Hawker Siddeley product and was recast as SQL (structured (or System) query language). SQL became the de facto industry standard particularly when it was adopted as both the ISO and ANSI standards.

IBM could have had the field virtually to itself with its headstart of IMS/DB and SQL but it proved remiss in not developing a version for Windows or UNIX; it was this that left the door open for others. Worse, its general release of the papers describing System R attracted the sort of people who could and would do something about it.

IBM launched its first mainframe database product to use SQL as the DB2 system in 1983; although Oracle had released an SQL program a little earlier.

DB2 has been upgraded down the years with Viper in 2006 and Cobra in 2009 and it is still a regularly-used program today, ranked second to Oracle and ahead of Microsoft SQL Server.

In 1973, Michael Stonebraker and Eugene Wong at the University of California Berkeley came across the System R material. They already had funds for a research project and using this they took SQL and set out to create Ingres (interactive graphics retrieval system) as an open-source relational database system.

Needing further funds they were disappointed that neither DARPA nor the Office of Naval Research would support them. They cobbled the funds together from a series of other sources.

Successive teams of students and staff worked on Ingres which was planned for the UNIX and DEC platforms rather than for mainframes. The code was released for a nominal fee and around 1,000 copies had been issued by 1980.

These copies went to a number of colleges that were subsequently prompted to develop their own database systems. For example Jerry Held and Karel Youseffi received a copy while at Berkeley and moving to Tandem Computers with some ex-Project R team members used it to develop NonStop SQL in 1987.

Others inspired by Ingres and Project R were more significant prime movers - Oracle, Sybase and Informix.

In the meantime Codd continued working on relational databases until a series of decisions eventually made his role at IBM untenable.

Along the way he came up with a new name for his thinking - OLAP (online analytical processing). This set the ground rules for multi-dimensional analysis of data and relational management reporting, today known as data mining.

OLAP gathered elements from navigational databases, hierarchical databases and relational databases. It permitted faster and more complex analysis, its output often being displayed in a matrix or a pivot format.

Though quite separately, the first OLAP product was actually developed in 1970. It had nothing to do with IBM and was well before Codd had coined the phrase.

Expressing oneself – IRI and Express

Jay Wurts, while an MIT student doing coursework, realised he spent much of his time formatting and reformatting the collected data rather than doing the analysis that he set out to achieve. Spreadsheets were not available to him!

He developed an approach to hold the data multi-dimensionally on a computer and this allowed all sorts of manipulation and what-ifs to be applied.

His professor, John Little, and others joined him in forming a company called Management Decision Systems (MDS), based near to MIT. The program was called Express then later renamed as Mainframe Express. This was one of the first packages that used the term DSS (decision support system), allowing business forecasting and analysis.

Professor at the University of Iowa Gerald Eskin, market researcher John Malec and computer specialist William Walter came together in 1977. They identified how bar coding of consumer products might provide a new approach for consumer marketing. They achieved the necessary funding through contracts signed with major manufacturers like Coca Cola, Kraft, Proctor & Gamble...

The previous system was typified by Adtel, a company that issued retailers with a diary to be manually completed (hopefully accurately) with the results laboriously analysed.

The company founded by this threesome was Information Resources Inc (IRI). They saw they could automatically scan product sales and turn around the research more speedily using a computer. Today the InfoScan service provides weekly analysis from more than 2,500 supermarkets, 500 drugstores and 250 mass merchants. In 1980 its BehaviorScan put scanners into homes, growing this to some 15,000 households in eight cities by 1983.

IRI had its IPO in March 1983, when shares immediately went from $23 to $43. By 1984 *INC* magazine listed it in the Top 100 fastest-growing USA public companies.

It sought a better way to distribute the results that had traditionally been by hard copy. Instead IRI chose to use Express database files. The usage of IRI gave MDS a headstart with other fmcg companies and it soon dominated the sector. In 1985 to expand its business IRI acquired the MDS company and its products.

It grew the applications for the technology and in the mid-80s Express was updated to operate in C language and ported to the IBM PC as pcEXPRESS.

Prompted by its new owners subsequent versions were launched using C and VisualBasic, for example to give it GUI features. Express MDB was launched for UNIX and other platforms. Express was sold on by IRI to Oracle in 1995.

Codd later consulted with Arbor Software in the development of the Essbase system (extended spread sheet database), patented in March 1992. Arbor had been founded earlier in 1991 by Bob Earle and Jim Dorian, both with prior experience in business analysis software.

The Essbase objective sought to overcome the limitations of spreadsheets like Lotus 1-2-3 and Microsoft Excel by adding a multi-dimensional storage system. This link of spreadsheet and database assembled a series of unrelated files that could combine to generate report outputs, using a spreadsheet.

This of course made Essbase less a relational database and more something of a multi-dimensional database system. It was initially available with IBM's OS/2 but Windows and UNIX versions soon followed. It tended to group data into hierarchies and had a wizard called the Essbase Application Manager allowing users to develop their own applications within the program.

Arbor was keen to develop partnerships with other software developers and published APIs (application programming interfaces) for them to use to bring their own ideas to the piece.

In 1995 Arbor was listed on NASDAQ and this enabled it to acquire AppSource, an organisation that had developed a useful OLAP viewing and presentation tool. Arbor Software merged with Hyperion in 1998.

Financial databasing – IMRS to Hyperion

Robert Thomson, a Scot, worked in banking in London and the United States and decided to create a financial look-up service using PCs rather than mainframes. In 1981 with Marco Arese he founded Information Management Reporting Services (IMRS) to pursue this goal.

Its first product was Micro Control, a financial management program launched in 1982. Venture capitalists introduced Thomson to James A Perakis who was also working in a financial information business, Interactive Data Corporation. He joined the company in September 1985 and set about creating a sales force for Micro Control - at $75,000 a pop they certainly could fund a team.

By 1987 Perakis took over the helm from Thomson as president, though Thomson remained on the board. They soon acquired Hoechst Celanese and its Financial Application Solution to Analysis and Reporting. Between them these two packages represented the market leadership in financial reporting. With 5,000 installations at some 400 corporate clients IMRS turnover exceeded $20m.

In 1989 Windows was chosen as the vehicle for its new OnTrack; at the time the court was still out as to which OS to follow - DOS, OS/2 or Windows? OnTrack brought its service to the uninitiated user. Now anyone could use it to obtain a corporate or financial report. One feature of OnTrack was hypertext and this was said to be in part the inspiration for the naming of the next product.

IMRS went public in 1991. Also in that year it launched a Windows version of Micro Control, by then holding an 85% market share of the sector; it re-named it Hyperion.

As the company shaped up to go public it chose the Hyperion name for the company too and in February 1995 it became Hyperion Software Corporation. Its growth through this period was remarkable from $66m annual sales in 1993, to $137m in 1995 and $222m in 1997.

In 1998 it merged with Arbor Software Corporation. Arbor shareholders had 40% and Hyperion 60% of the shares of the new Hyperion Solutions Corporation.

The two operations and products were swiftly integrated, though not without experiencing several problems. The combined operation was huge, valued at over $800m with 1,800 employees located across twenty-six countries serving 4,000 clients in over forty countries.

Hyperion took the Essbase OLAP notions and created a series of applications. Its product line-up became the Essbase OLAP Server, Hyperion Pillar which was a budgeting tool, Hyperion Enterprise which provided financial consolidation reports and Hyperion Tools, for presentation and reporting. It spun off AppSource from the main operation.

At the end of 1999 it had a turnover of $425m. In the new millennium it set about creating web-based packages, Hyperion Financial Management and Hyperion Planning.

Along the way it founded a new sector called BPM (business performance management); today it is known as EPM (enterprise performance management).

It continued to make a number of major acquisitions but by the end of 2002 while turnover had increased to $528m it recorded a loss of over $31m. However as scandals like Enron led to corporates seeking better financial management Hyperion was well-placed to return to profitability. Oracle acquired Hyperion for $3.3bn in 2007.

Consulting the oracle – Ellison and Oracle

Larry Ellison was born to single mother Florence Spallman in New York City but he was brought up by his aunt and uncle in Chicago. He was not to meet his mother again until he was forty-eight years old. His surname came from his adoptive parents who on immigration to the USA took it from the famous landing point, Ellis Island.

This was quite an unlikely start in life for someone who would go on to acquire a personal wealth of $28bn in 2010. At that time he was the sixth richest person on the planet!

He attended the University of Illinois but left in his second year. A subsequent short attendance at the University of Chicago introduced him to computer design and he moved to California. At the Ampex Corporation, Ellison worked on a project for the CIA where he created a database named Oracle (optional reception of announcements by coded line electronics).

Ellison was made aware of Codd's 1970 paper and of the IBM System R by Ed Oates, who joined Ampex from IBM together with Bob Miner. The three formed SDL (Software Development Laboratories) in 1977.

Ellison funded the formation himself with a personal investment of just $1,400. He set out initially to make his product compatible with IBM's System R but because IBM insisted on keeping its code secret this became impractical.

He therefore went it alone, selecting the C programming language so the product would be easily portable across platforms. In 1979 the company name was changed to Relational Software Inc and it moved to Menlo Park.

Its first release based upon SQL was Oracle 2 to imply that the product had already been through a process of de-bugging and market testing - perhaps it had at the CIA? Its first client was the Wright-Paterson Air Force Base that ran Oracle 2 on a PDP-11.

In 1981 Umang Gupta joined the company as a VP and general manager; he produced its first business plan. In 1982 the company was renamed once again to Oracle Systems to link it more directly with its main product. In 1984 Sequoia Capital supported Oracle with much-needed funding and in the same year it ported its software to the PC with an MS-DOS version.

By 1986 revenues were $55m and new versions, including one for the Mac, backed by an applications division grew this tenfold in three years; by 1989 Oracle Systems was turning over $584m.

But in the following year it ran in to trouble with a loose sales bonus arrangement that had its team being paid against client's future expected sales. This also led to its misquoting revenues to the market and facing shareholder action for misleading data. As a result Oracle laid off over 400 members of its team, some 10% of the whole, in order to avert possible bankruptcy.

In the early '90s it also came under pressure from Sybase that through technological advances had overtaken it in the sector. But then fatefully

Sybase took its eye off the ball, concentrating instead on its acquisitions and mergers.

From the mid-90s Oracle was not deterred by the Sybase experience and maintained a busy buying programme that saw it acquire over sixty organisations and their products over the next fifteen years, including Express in 1995, Hyperion in 2007 and in April 2009 Sun Microsystems too for $7.4 bn.

Just prior to the Sun acquisition it jointly launched the Sun Oracle Database Machine, defined as the world's fastest platform for any database application.

Today it has over 300,000 clients including every one of the *Fortune 1000* companies and operates in 145 countries.

Developing SQL - Sybase

Sybase was formed in 1984 by Bob Epstein, Jane Doughty, Tom Haggin and Mark Hoffman. I find it somewhat disappointing to learn that it initially operated from Epstein's Berkeley home, not his garage!

Its Sybase SQL Server relational database management system for UNIX was tested during 1986 and formally launched in 1987. Sybase then reached an agreement in 1988 with Microsoft to develop SQL Server for OS/2 together with Ashton-Tate; Ashton-Tate dropped out of the project in 1990.

Sybase and Microsoft had an agreement to develop SQL Server for Windows NT; it was launched in 1992 and referenced as v4.0. The relationship broke down in 1993 and Sybase chose to sell its Windows-based database software to Microsoft.

Microsoft of course had access to the Sybase code and went on to launch its own versions, v 6.0 being the first all-Microsoft development.

In 1996 Sybase, to avoid ongoing confusion, changed the name of its product to the Adaptive Server Enterprise and concentrated its efforts on UNIX.

Additional products including the Sybase Open Client/Server Interface drove sales to $56m in 1989. Its launch in 1992 of the System 10 family of products, which assisted organisations in a state of flux between mainframes and client/server systems, provided all users anywhere on the evolving network with ready access to the latest changes within the organisation.

It was the Sybase acquisition of PowerSoft and the PowerBuilder object-oriented programming language that took the corporate eye off the database ball. They did grow PowerBuilder to around 100,000 users by 1998 but Sybase was to some extent diverted from its core database business. In May 2010 the German company SAP AG acquired Sybase for $5.8bn - in cash.

Running the marathon – ISAM to Informix

Yet another database player emerged when Roger Sippl and Laura King developed a small relational database for their employer Cromemco, one of the early S-100-cum-CP/M contenders.

They worked with an IBM database technique called ISAM (indexed sequential access method) where each data entry was captured together with its indexing so, although entry is slow, retrieval is quick and easy. The program was created as part of a report-writing application.

Sippl and King left to form Relational Database Systems in 1980 and came up with Marathon, a 16-bit version of the program. They went on to develop the Informix (information on UNIX) program in 1981 and Informix-SQL in 1985; success with these led to a change of name to Informix Software.

After a slow start Informix rode the rapid growth of UNIX and SQL to an IPO in 1986. It too then went on an acquisition trail subsuming Innovative Software's Smartware and WingZ, and Illustra's Datablades.

By 1994 Informix had surpassed Sybase and also become Oracle's sternest opponent. This led to Larry Ellison of Oracle and Phil White, CEO of Informix, having a vitriolic and highly public battle for hearts and minds; Oracle had won out by 1997.

It was Informix mismanagement and other internal problems that progressively weakened it. As a result Walmart, one of its largest clients, prompted IBM to acquire the Informix database technology and its 100,000 users in 2001.

The other Informix products were floated off into Ascential Software, but this too was acquired by IBM in 2005. Both became part of the IBM Information Management Portfolio.

Vikings and foxes – PC databasing

The early PC market was quick to realise that a PC database system would sell. A very early player in 1977 was WHATSIT? apparently meaning 'Wow! How'd all that stuff get in there'. It was designed for an Apple II with CP/M by Lyall Morill of Computer Headware and formally launched in 1978 by Information Unlimited Software at the West Coast Computer Faire.

This most significant early PC database application had its roots in the Jet Propulsion Laboratory (JPL).

JPL is a NASA field centre based near Pasadena; it eschews manned flight and focuses instead on the development of robotic spacecraft. The facility is manned and managed by Caltech, the California Institute of Technology.

In the 1960s Fred Thompson and Jack Hatfield cooperated to improve Retrieve, a Tymshare program they were using to manage a database of calculators. This led to them evolving the program JPLDIS (jet propulsion laboratory data information system) for its UNIVAC mainframe.

This FORTRAN-based program on a Univac 1108 was presented as a paper during a 1973 Univac Users' Group and a National Science Foundation meeting on *Data Storage and Retrieval*.

Jeb Long inherited the project and was charged with carrying on the development of JPLDIS after Hatfield left the JPL. He was responsible for a number of space program software developments for the Mariner and Viking missions.

It was still securely the era of copying or borrowing ideas of others. When Wayne Ratliff developed a database program for his personally assembled IMSAI 8080 kit computer he thought nothing of leaning heavily upon the JPLDIS in creating his program.

Ratliff first encountered computers when he used a CDC 6400 to assist him in designing a car. He created programs to look at engine choice and the effect of this on the centre of gravity and was thus able to estimate suspension requirements.

While completing his degree and for a total of thirteen years he worked in aerospace with the Martin Marietta Corporation where his first title was 'computer', an echo of earlier times when a computer was indeed a person who computed, rather than a device. He avoided serving in Vietnam based upon the significance of his programming skills. Instead he worked with COBOL-based war games that focused on logistics called LOGEX.

While at Martin Marietta, he operated as a contractor at JPL on the Viking project and wrote MFILE, a data management program for the Viking Lander.

Ratliff purchased an IMSAI kit and took a whole year assembling it, only to find like all IMSAI users that he had created something with little utility. Undeterred he added a keyboard and other I/Os and calculated that in the end he had spent some $6,000 on his finished computer.

The company had an American football pool in which employees tried to identify the winner of a match and also forecast the point spread. To this end Ratliff would pore over the Monday morning statistics in the papers. In 1978 this task inspired him to write a database program, and he was keen to try to do this in a natural language.

Ratliff's Vulcan – the evolution of dBase

He set out basing the approach on his MFILE work but found that JPLDIS had more of the simplicity required for a PC. He named the program Vulcan, apparently inspired by Star Trek's first officer Mr Spock. Where JPLDIS handled 200 fields the original Vulcan used just sixteen.

It took him eighteen months to complete; twice he lost three months waiting on a floppy disk drive repair. In October 1979 he promoted the product as Software Consultation Design and Production in *Byte* magazine, offering the package for just $50.

George Tate and Hal Lashlee created a company that started its life as a home-garage operation. They formed Software Plus Inc (SPI) publishing *Discount Software,* an early mail order catalogue run from Tate's garage. Later they also formed Softstream Inc as a software distributor.

Tate and Lashlee approached Ratliff and negotiated exclusive rights to Vulcan and re-tasked SPI as a software publisher. The team jointly improved the user interface and made it more suitable for use with a TV screen or monitor. They promptly raised the price to $695 and renamed it.

SPI's marketeer, Hal Pawluck, came up with two notions. First he suggested Ashton-Tate as the organisation's name, despite there never having been an Ashton; although Tate did subsequently use the name for his pet parrot!

Pawluck also decided the first issue of the product should be named dBase II to imply it was a long established and evolved product - just as with Oracle, there had never been a dBase I.

Pawluck created some intriguing advertisements. One used the headline 'We all know bilge pumps suck', earning the ire of the maker of the pump pictured in the advert, but still catching the eye.

In fact dBase II was both a programming language and a database. As a language it used very simple commands such as find, list, use... It was somewhat similar in its approach to VisiCalc in that the software was designed to allow those with no programming knowledge to manipulate and calculate data and to format, analyse and present it - without realising that essentially they were programming.

The dBase II software, with its simplicity of approach and ability to allow users to customise it extensively, rapidly became the first widely-used PC database management system.

Both Wayne Ratliff and Jeb Long, of JPLDIS, were recruited to join the Ashton-Tate company at its formation. By 1982 it had turned over just under $4 million, yet it managed to lose money that year through poor internal controls. But that same year it ported dBase II to MS-DOS and the new IBM PC; and this was when it really took off.

By 1983 Ashton-Tate had acquired all of the rights in the program and the copyright from Ratliff.

Sadly George Tate died of a heart attack in 1984 at just forty years of age. Ed Esber, who had worked with both TI and VisiCorp, was recruited to become the new CEO. He took the company from $40m turnover to over $300m, through maintaining its status as the databasing standard and through several judicious acquisitions.

In 1988 Ratliff left and developed Emerald Bay, a client/server database program.

California-based WordTech Systems Inc had created a database product back in 1988 called Arago Quicksilver; compatible with dBase IV it was advertised as the world's fastest database software. Naturally this operation would become Borland's next target.

Having acquired the company and the WordTech team in 1992, the product was used as the basis for dBase for Windows 5.0 released in August 1994. But by then Microsoft had also entered the fray.

Dave Fulton and Bill Ferguson founded Fox Software and in December 1984 created FoxBASE, a clone of dBase II; apparently the 'fox' was to imply the system ran much faster than dBase.

Fulton was an intriguing character. In his childhood he played the violin and at sixteen years of age arriving at the University of Chicago to study mathematics he was appointed concertmaster for the student orchestra.

At university he gained a master's and a PhD in statistics and subsequently for ten years presided over the computer science department of Bowling Green State University, located south of Toledo in Ohio. He started several businesses during this period.

Fox Software launched a multi-user version of FoxBASE in 1985. But the company really took off in 1986 when it launched FoxBASE+, an MS-DOS version directly competing with Ashton-Tate's dBase III.

In 1987 it went on to produce a Mac version, unsurprisingly called FoxBASE+/Mac. This rapidly consumed the lion's share of the Mac market. The product led on to the introduction in 1989 of FoxPro, an MS-DOS program.

Back in 1987 Fox had also taken a licence with Santa Cruz Operation (SCO) to launch FoxBASE+ for SCO UNIX. The Fox products had secured a strong second place in the database software market.

During 1986-7 Ashton-Tate discussed the possibility of acquiring Fox Software but discussions broke down. It was in November 1988 when Fox launched the dBase IV clone FoxPro that Ashton-Tate decided to take legal action claiming copyright infringement. The company also sued SCO for similar cause for the UNIX version.

It claimed that the dBase products,

'...reflect imaginative and original forms of expression which distinguish them from database management software offered by other companies and which have helped make the dBASE programs industry leaders.'

'Ashton-Tate developed the design of its dBASE software products through the expenditure of substantial time, effort, money and ingenuity.'

The early history of dBase did however come back and haunt it when the action was to prove both ineffectual and highly damaging. Software developers who had used the dBase language ran for cover, seeking alternative sources to avoid being dragged in to the action.

The judge decided in December 1990 that Ashton-Tate had 'unclean hands' in that it had wittingly withheld from the copyright authorities the fact that it fully understood the program had been originally based heavily upon JPLDIS. The judge also concluded that the company had repeatedly failed to reveal this fact when registering its various versions of the product.

In effect this meant it had no copyright and anyone would be permitted to use the content! Borland acquired Ashton-Tate in July 1991 for $440m and promptly withdrew all legal action and agreed not to file a similar suit for ten years.

FoxPro 2.0 was launched in 1991 incorporating SQL. It had a graphic-based Screen Builder and a user-friendly Report Builder, called Rushmore; Rushmore enabled a very fast query operation.

Fox Software had already been in discussions with Microsoft when Borland's court decision opened the door to what was described as a merger of Microsoft and Fox. It was more an acquisition that was agreed in March 1992 for $173m; at the time it was the largest software 'merger' in history. Fulton and others of the team joined Microsoft as part of the arrangement.

From his youth Fulton had derived great pleasure from classic violins; for example in 1981 he bought a 1698 violin created by Pietro Guarneri of Mantua. He commented that it cost him more than the house he was also buying at the time.

His success in software allowed him to become one of the world's top collectors. He was reported at one stage to have sixteen violins, mostly fashioned by Antonio Stradivari and Giuseppe Guarneri del Gesù, plus three cellos and four violas. He also established the David and Amy Fulton Foundation with his wife to support the concertmaster's chair at Seattle University.

Omega to Access

Naturally Microsoft wanted to have its own database product and made several internal efforts to do so. One early project was Omega, but it was not in fact to prove the last. Microsoft File was another entry but it was outsold by FileMaker and soon discontinued.

A more significant approach was the establishment of an internal project named Cirrus that Microsoft ran for around three years; this represented a significant investment in seeking a database solution. The project had a number of outcomes, the Jet database engine and the Ruby forms engine to name just two.

Alan Cooper at Tripod created a form generator that allowed a drag and drop design approach for GUI applications, Microsoft contracted with him to incorporate this into its Ruby. This effort would in fact prove to be the inspiration for Visual Basic.

Microsoft's timely acquisition of Fox Software allowed it to integrate its Rushmore technology with it to create Microsoft Access, the ultimate product was launched in November 1992. It was launched as a bundled part of the Microsoft Office Suite.

Microsoft already had the rights to the name Access from an earlier terminal emulator product.

'There's a rumour that Excel was going to be combined with Access, but the project was abandoned because the combined product would be called "Microsoft Excess". Perhaps a similar reason as to why Dire Straits never hooked up with Chris Rhea.' Amusing blog posting in 2006 by Alun Jones.

Access proved to be very user-friendly and 500,000 copies were sold in the first year. However early versions appeared to have a problem when the dBase was any larger than 10 Mbyte - it became very slow and often experienced data corruption and occasional data loss. Given the capacities of disk drives back then this did not initially prove to be that serious a concern. Upgrades both of the Jet database engine and of Windows itself removed this limitation.

Access 1.1 was released in 1993 addressing compatibility issues with other Office Suite applications. Access 95 was slow and unpopular, but Access 97 remedied this and Access 2000 later integrated the SQL features. With regular development it has become a leading PC sector product right up to current times.

Back in 1987 Microsoft had worked with Sybase to define a new database product. The original arrangement was that the Sybase plans for a DataServer program would be jointly developed. But later this was altered so Sybase would retain any interest in the UNIX and minicomputer markets and Microsoft's interest would be in the rights for IBM's forthcoming OS/2 operating system

Ashton-Tate too was enjoined in this effort with dBase IV envisaged as the front-end of the Microsoft SQL Server. Microsoft obviously saw the potential for leverage with all those dBase users and history. However Ashton-Tate's dBase IV problems saw this part of the arrangement terminated.

Microsoft SQL Server 1.0 was released in 1989.

By 1990 Sybase had developed the software to support Windows with SQL Server 1.1. This was based on Microsoft project managing and Sybase providing all the programming. During 1991 Microsoft was given access to the code and played a more proactive role with subsequent versions.

As OS/2 was on the wane and Windows NT was coming together the Sybase-Microsoft relationship became less useful to Microsoft. In 1994 the arrangement was formally ended with Microsoft retaining rights in SQL Server for all its operating systems.

Microsoft, with its control of the product now secured, radically expanded its team and later versions of SQL Server continued to add additional features and capabilities. It remains a key player.

RANDOM ACCESS MOMENT:
IBM's 2008 Smarter Planet advertising campaign estimated that there were 43,000 GBytes of data being generated per day around the world; how it set about calculating that would probably take us way off track. But 'giga' means 10-to the-power-of-9 – so it's saying 43,000,000,000,000 bytes are created every day. It added,

'The computing models and advanced analytics we have today actually allow us to use that information, not merely to sense and respond but to predict. So data isn't just telling us what's going on in the world – it's telling us where the world is going.'

Nice concept and perhaps just what Vannevar Bush had in mind for his Memex. But I know that I am well overdue to clean up the accumulated nonsense currently on my PC and laptop, by way of files, contacts and emails. I think I personally could easily lose at least 43k bytes every day if I put my mind to it. If all one billion PC users did the same we would be at stasis in terms of data generation in just one day; but I predict that none of us will get around to it!

That's it in a nutshell – the path to FileMaker

Nashoba Systems developed the program Nutshell in 1982 as an MS-DOS database. It was distributed through the Leading Edge mail order and electronics sales operation that diversified into IBM PC compatibles.

Inspired by the launch of the Apple Mac, Nashoba came up with a GUI version of its software but Leading Edge decided to focus on the IBM PC market so chose not to represent them; it did arrange to hold on to the original Nutshell product.

Nashoba therefore appointed a new distributor, Forethought Inc, for its other thrusts and renamed its product FileMaker. Microsoft had at the time its own 'File' database and was attracted to the FileMaker product, seeking the right to publish it, but Nashoba decided to press on alone.

Forethought was founded by Dennis Austin and Thomas Rudkin. It had its own software including one developed for the Apple Mac called 'Presenter'. Microsoft bought Forethought Inc for $14m in 1987 to acquire Presenter which they would enhance and release it as Microsoft PowerPoint.

Apple soon after formed its own software subsidiary Claris, which acquired Nashoba. Claris renamed Nutshell as FileMaker II so it was seen as part of the Mac software family, aligning it for example with MacWrite II.

FileMaker Pro v 1.0 followed in 1990 and in five years FileMaker had become the Claris cash cow. Apple decided to bring the other products back under its wings in 1998 and changed the Claris operation's name to FileMaker Inc.

By 1997 FileMaker had developed a plug-in approach that encouraged third party developers to work with the software. It continues as a strong player in the Mac community; including applications for both iPhone and iPad.

Bean counting – accounting by computer

Of course the fundamental application that computers and thus PCs were asked to address was managing the accounting tasks for an organisation, whether large or small.

In the mid to late 1950s IBM was slowly moving its approach from merely data processing towards providing more tailored business computer systems. But it had initially expected users to develop their own operating systems and software.

IBM made a move towards changing this when it created SHARE in 1955 so users might share commonly-used routines among themselves. For example IBM developed and distributed a software program it called a report program generator. It was for punched card systems, simply gathering data from the cards and providing a series of subtotals and totals of what it encountered.

The early problem facing both the businessman and the programmer was that neither really understood the other's business or needs. Colleges stepped up to tackle this by developing courses in management information systems seeking to bridge this gap in understanding.

Another program for IBM's 709/7090 computers was a report generator called 9PAC, a simple abbreviation of 709 Package. This software proved useful for those not skilled in programming, enabling them to obtain information such as sales analysed by department or by salesman; of course this was something that cash registers had done for years!

But these seemingly minor moves plus the definition of the COBOL language at around the same time were the first faltering steps towards providing sophisticated business applications. IBM then began to pursue the commercial sector with the progressive launches of its 702, 705, 7010, 7070 and 7080 computers, offering them with compilers for both COBOL and FORTRAN.

Specialist organisations for business accounting software emerged in the 1970s. For example SAP AG was founded in 1972. It was originally defined as meaning System Analysis and Program development, later this was updated to mean Systems, Applications and Products

SAP was founded by five ex-IBM employees, Hans-Werner Hector, Dietmar Hopp, Hasso Plattner, Klaus Tschira, and Claus Wellenreuther. There initial goal was to become a significant German software organisation, but by the late noughties it had become the world's largest business software company

Back in 1973 SAP released the SAP R/1, a financial accounting package for mainframes; the R stood for real-time data processing. By the late '70s, SAP R/2 used a time-share process that integrated accounting, manufacturing, supply chain and human resources within an enterprise.

Today the available packages usually include payroll, credit control, sales tax accounting, payment processing, cash flow management, purchasing and stock control and financial reporting and forecasting.

Business accounting

One of the earliest accounting packages for PCs was generated through a complex series of ownerships down the years.

Computer System Center was founded in 1976 as Atlanta Georgia's first computer store, formed originally to sell Altair kits. In 1977 the store's team developed an accounting program that was later called Peachtree Accounting, the name inspired by Atlanta's famous peaches.

Retail Sciences Inc then purchased rights in the software and founded Peachtree Software the following year; it was turning over $1.5m by 1980.

Peachtree then negotiated with IBM to provide a bundled accounting package for the IBM PC launch and publicity for this attracted more acquisitive attention.

Back in 1963 Management Science America Inc had been founded by five Georgia Tech alumni and it rapidly expanded outside its original aim to be a contract programming company. But this expansion ran it into difficulty by 1971 and it was rescued by its bank and John P Imlay Jr who became CEO.

Imlay directed MSA's attention to software products and turned the operation around, making a public offering in 1981 and using the benefits to acquire Peachtree Software for $5.7m that year. On the basis of this acquisition MSA became the world's largest application software company.

Under MSA's stewardship Peachtree expanded to a $22.5m turnover in 1983, but then it sold the company on to Intelligent Systems for a mere $1m in 1986. Clearly there were problems as MSA had ceased trading in 1990.

Intelligent Systems moved to reduce the software package price from c$5,000 to $200 and changed its direction to direct selling off-the-page in the Wall Street Journal. It clearly lost interest in this and in 1988 Peachtree Software was sold back to its management team for $20m.

The worm in the peach had clearly turned. Layered Inc, a company that had developed an accounting package for the Apple Mac with a market leadership position, was acquired by Peachtree in 1990.

Peachtree continued support for its own product launching the first accounting software available with Microsoft Windows in 1991.

As if this was not enough, Automatic Data Processing acquired Peachtree on 1994 and over the following years expanded its business vertically. First it acquired One-Write Plus that was a software package that automated the widespread manual paper-based accounting system. Second, it launched an early eCommerce solution for small businesses to use via the Internet.

By 1988 Peachtree launched Peachtree Office Accounting which used open architecture so it integrated readily with Microsoft's Word and Excel.

Peachtree was subsequently acquired by the Sage Group in 1998 for $145m, who continue its innovation.

A student at Newcastle University in the North East of England took a summer job with a small accountancy practice. The practice had received a government grant to develop software for use in its business and it fell to the student, Graham Wylie, to create a program for them.

After the success of his summer job, Wylie was commissioned by printing company Campbell Graphics to develop some estimating software for the business. Wylie combined this and his previous work to define and create Sage Accounts.

Campbell Graphics' principal, David Goldman, took the product seriously and hired both Wylie and Paul Muller, an academic, to found Sage in 1981. They started selling this as a vertical package to other printing companies but soon the company broadened its approach and sold it through a network of resellers.

In 1984 the company developed a CP/M version, authored originally for the Amstrad PCW platform; its sales volume grew ten-fold. Sage was listed on the London Stock Exchange in 1989 and continued massive growth to become one of the FTSE 100 by 1999.

Its acquisition of Tetra in 1999 gave it leverage into the mid-range business sector.

As the end of the millennium approached, fears of the Y2K bug (year 2000) presented new opportunities. Many enterprises were forced to review their, often mish-mash, software controls and move towards a more integrated approach using systems that linked manufacturing, inventory, logistics, invoicing and accounting. Sage through development and acquisition became a serious player in this broader market. Sage did not just rely upon back office solutions. Aided by its acquisition of Interact Commerce Inc it entered the front-end customer relationship management (CRM) sector and business intelligence too.

Today Sage operates globally in a broad range of vertical sectors including construction, distribution and transportation, healthcare, human resources, manufacturing and retail. It has over 6 million customers and revenues of almost £1,500m.

Gartner defines its global market share in enterprise resource planning (ERP) at 9%, and the International Date Corporation (IDC) shows it market leader in the small business market at 21% (with Microsoft at 12%, Oracle at 9%, Intuit at 6% and SAP at just 3%),

In just over twenty years Wylie would retire – at just forty-three years of age. He had shares in Sage worth £146m which placed him as the 109th richest person in the UK's *Sunday Times* annual listings.

Microsoft actively addressed this market sector with several acquisitions and the formation of a business solutions group in 1993.

Great Plains Software developed Great Plains Dynamics, one of the first accounting packages available in the USA. The name was derived from its location in North Dakota

It was written by Doug Burgum in a language developed internally called Great Plains Dexterity (just a tad overworking a theme?), which by being based on the 'C' language allowed a cross-platform GUI approach.

Great Plains Dynamics ran on Windows and was one of the first to use a macro approach so the user could save and re-use useful routines as .MAC files. Microsoft acquired Great Plains for $1.1 billion in April 2001; promptly renaming the software as Microsoft Dynamics GP.

Its next acquisition was the Danish operation Navision Software A/S, formed back in 1984 as PC&C A/S (personal computing and consulting). The company had developed a reputation in ERP software, merging with a second Danish company Damgaard A/S in 2000. Microsoft acquired it in 2002 and this software became known as Microsoft Dynamics NAV.

These two acquired programs were joined by a 2003 in-house development of Microsoft CRM to become the new business solutions group. Though it was not until version 3.0 was released late in 2005 that the package achieved much in the way of sales.

The group operates from a base outside of the main Microsoft HQ maintaining teams at the original base of Great Plains Software in North Dakota and Navision in Vedbæk, Denmark. Today the company offers Microsoft Dynamics ERM, Microsoft Dynamics CRM and two retail solutions, Microsoft Dynamics PoS released in 2009 and Microsoft Dynamics RMS (retail management system).

Distribution arrangements are established so that value added resellers are prompted to offer specialised support in vertical market applications.

Worldwide some 10,000 Microsoft Dynamics partners have been appointed, with 750 of these certified to offer Microsoft Dynamics solutions. Between them they serve over 300,000 business users.

Clouded thinking - SaaS

During the 1960s John McCarthy at MIT first proposed that perhaps,

'...computation may someday be organized as a public utility...'

This was the approach adopted by 'cloud computing'. Instead of the necessity to purchase software it offered an Internet-based utility for clients to remotely access programs on demand on a rental basis. The term 'cloud' derived from an earlier service offering the sharing of bandwidth in telephony.

An alternative approach was fully defined in an article published in February 2001 by the SIIA (Software & Information Industry Association). It outlined the current state of what was termed SaaS (software-as-a-service). Again this used the Internet to offer a licence-cum-subscription means of accessing software on demand.

SaaS became a popular means of acquiring CRM software particularly for sales force systems.

However Richard Stallman, champion of open software, was very mistrustful of both approaches. On cloud computing he is quoted as saying, *'It's stupidity. It's worse than stupidity: it's a marketing hype campaign. Somebody is saying this is inevitable – and whenever you hear somebody saying that, it's very likely to be a set of businesses campaigning to make it true.'*

On SaaS he was no more impressed, pointing out that users could not modify or personalise their SaaS software just as they could not modify proprietary software, something he advocated to be key to a proper usage of the product.

Of more pressing concern was of course that the organisation using the cloud or SaaS service was risking its company data being stored and processed by a third party software operation; this is perhaps an issue that has constrained this market.

NetSuite was an SaaS package that grew to dominate the mid-market and big corporate division sectors. While working at Oracle, Evan Goldberg helped develop NetLedger, subsequently renamed as the Oracle Small Business Solution.

With some venture capital, largely funded by Larry Ellison, this operation was spun off in 1998 as a separate operation, called NetSuite. Ellison controlled the majority of the company, though it went for a public listing in 2007; the relationship between Oracle and NetSuite remained close with both NetSuite's chairman and CEO hailing from Oracle.

NetSuite has a global network of partners supporting the ERP and CRM software for its 6,500 customers. Partners include solution providers who sell NetSuite licences and help with installation and support; systems integrators and SuiteCloud developers consult to provide customised vertical solutions based on the core software.

Intacct (Internet accounting) was another early service founded in 1999 by David Thomas. Along the way it attracted over $80m in venture capital, the most recent round in April 2008.

It offered financial management and accounting for small to medium enterprises and soon boasted over 30,000 users from some 3,000 organisations.

Progress was much assisted when Intacct was selected as the preferred approach by the American Institute of Certified Public Accountants; it urged its members to use the software.

Thomas produced an early accounting package while attending Arizona State University. He patented the software security dongle to copy-protect software. Today he is chief VP and general manager of the Software & Information Industry Association.

Other players in SaaS include SAP Business One and SAP Business by Design, also aimed at small to medium enterprises.

By 2006 Amazon had updated its data centres and realised it was on average using only 10% of its available capacity; it therefore developed Amazon Web Service (AWS) as an on-demand utility service for others.

The University of California Santa Barbara ran a research exercise on high performance computing that led to the development of an open-source cloud approach.

Eucalyptus Systems Inc founded in January 2009 provided IaaS (infrastructure as a service), offering a public cloud service compatible with Amazon's AWS. It is made available as open-source or as a chargeable enterprise solution.

In March 2010 Microsoft went on record suggesting it was espousing the cloud approach; it has also proposed the use of clouds for government establishments.

Home budgeting
Founded in 1982 Meca Software was the first to pursue the personal finance market with its personal finance management software 'Managing Your Money'. However its marketing approach left it vulnerable to those that followed and it fared poorly. H&R Block acquired Meca in October 1993 for $32.2m.

From 1993 to 1995 Meca, as a division of H&R Block, specialised in tax preparation and today has 22 million clients across 12,500 tax offices in the USA and another 1,400 overseas. The notion for Block was obvious - to provide software that would deliver new clients for its services.

But when Meca was overtaken by its competitors Block sold it off to the Bank of America and NationsBank its thinking was fairly obvious too, leveraging sales of software through their many clients.

By 1987 its updated program had gained some 350,000 users which sounds substantial until placed it alongside the then 10 million users of Quicken.

Meca's ownership was changed again when a further five banks bought in; between them the seven bankers managed the accounts of some 50% of US households.

Meca transformed its approach to that of providing customised packages for its owners and progressively moving into Internet banking packages, each branded to an individual bank.

In 1983 Scott Cook, while at Stanford, realised that personal computers could be applied to his personal financial accounting. He sought assistance from Tom Proulx who was studying computer science at the same university. The meeting led to the two of them founding an operation they named Intuit.

Proulx wrote Quicken, a program allowing individuals to manage budgets, balance bank accounts and keep on top of their finances. It was produced in BASIC for the IBM PC and Tandy TRS-80, and in UCSD Pascal for the Apple II.

The software was market tested by people recruited off the street who were challenged to use it; each such session prompted advances to make it simpler and quicker.

By good off-the-page marketing, an efficient retail distribution and a focus on providing strong customer support it became the market leader by 1988.

When Windows 3.0 arrived in the early '90s the company took off and expanded into tax accounting. This growth saw it go public in 1993 and resources were used to acquire Chipsoft, another tax software company

Chipsoft had been founded by Michael A Chipman with its major product named TurboTax. The acquisition saw Intuit move into tax software, selling TurboTax and its own QuickBooks business accounting program; this spread its base even more securely.

QuickBooks, launched in 1992, was a great success with small businesses where owners were not particularly accounting savvy. In no time it had an 80% share of the sector despite early concerns raised by accountants for its lack of an audit trail.

It was soon updated to include the missing audit trail and offered full double-entry. It was offered in a Basic and Pro version by 2000, as a medium-size enterprise solution by 2002 and went on to develop vertical market versions by 2003.

QuickBooks also created a network of 50,000 ProAdvisors to support its users. These moves secured its pre-eminent market share.

Microsoft came a-knocking but failed to acquire the business, and responded by aggressively marketing its own software, Microsoft Money.

Today Intuit is valued at $9.8 billion with an annual turnover of £3 billion. *Fortune* magazine ranks it 'America's most admired software company'.

As part of the GNU Project an open-source system was produced to emulate Quicken and offer a simple double-entry accounting program. It was written in the 'C' language and called GnuCash, able to run on UNIX, Linux and Mac OS X.

In 1991 Microsoft launched a personal finance product 'Money'.

Money became part of the Microsoft Home initiative with a range of some sixty multimedia products available on Windows and Macintosh by 1994. Microsoft Home offered solutions for entertainment, home productivity, reference...

Quicken's success had Microsoft's full attention and in 1995 it had made a $1.5 billion acquisition offer. Any such move by Microsoft always came under investigation by the US courts and this was no different. The court duly concluded that this move would give Microsoft far too dominant a position in the sector.

The court noted that H & R Block had exited the sector by selling off its Meca Software because of the combined strengths of Quicken and Money. Microsoft volunteered to sell off its own Money program to Novell but this did nothing to placate the court, and the acquisition fell through.

Microsoft responded by launching Money 95 as a free download throughout autumn 1995, or users could opt to pay $9.95 for a CD-ROM or floppy supplied with a manual.

Microsoft Money was routinely upgraded and re-issued from 1997 to 2007 but it discontinued the practice in 2008. It continued to offer online downloads of Money Plus for a year and then stopped all development in June 2009, stating,

'With banks, brokerage firms and websites now providing a range of options for managing personal finances, the consumer need for Microsoft Money Plus has changed.'

A no-activation Money Plus Sunset was released in June 2010.

22 - Publish and be damned – WP and DTP

'The typewriting machine, when played with expression, is no more annoying than the piano when played by a sister or near relation.' Oscar Wilde

Typewriting

The whole process of automating writing began with Henry Mill, an Englishman who patented the first typewriter way back in 1714. It was described as a machine for transcribing letters, though the patent expressed this in a more flowery form,

'...That he hath by his great study and pains and experience invented and brought to perfection an artificial machine or method for impressing or transcribing of letters, one after another, as in writing, whereby all writing whatsoever may be engrossed in paper or parchment so neat and exact as not to be distinguished from print; that the said machine or method may be of great use in settlements and public records, the impression being deeper and more lasting than any other writing, and not to be erased or counterfeited without manifest discovery.'

Boy, if he was that longwinded he really did need his new device to assist him. No example of this machine has survived however.

In 1829 William Burt from Detroit came up with the 'typographer', a rotating frame device but it was so cumbersome and unreliable that it was much quicker to write by hand.

Mightier than the sword - Remington

For some unknown reason, typewriting, word processing and electronic graphics do appear to routinely have connections with Utah and the Mormons.

Christopher Latham Sholes who worked for a newspaper had at some stage interviewed James J Strang, the Mormon who was one of many who sought to take over the church's reins from Joseph Smith Jr.

Smith said he had been given some 'golden plates' by an angel, these plates were translated by Smith to become the Book of Mormon, but they were not witnessed by others and were later given back to the angel. When Sholes met Strang he was shown three small inscribed brass plates that Strang suggested illustrated that he himself was a true prophet and the fitting successor.

The focus on transcribing vitally important material was perhaps the inspiration when Sholes in 1867 produced the first successful mechanical typewriter. It was manufactured for him by Remington, a gun manufacturer - mightier pens than swords come to mind.

This typewriter design was odd in that the 'business end' of the device was located on the underside of the roller - not terribly user-friendly. However it was Sholes who invented the QWERTY keyboard layout we still use today. His patent was much more straightforward in its description,

'... characters similar to those produced by printer's type by means of keyboard-operated types striking a ribbon to transfer ink or carbon impressions onto the paper.'

Thomas Edison later patented the electric typewriter in 1872 but the product soon took a separate course to turn into the ticker-tape printer.

Upgrades and development to the typewriter arrived pretty regularly thereafter. The shift key was introduced in 1878 permitting keys to deliver both upper and lower case letters. The typing being visible on the upper part of the roller was introduced by 1880. A tab key to set margins was added in 1897.

The French AZERTY system was launched in the 1890s as more appropriate for Latinate languages, though the Belgian and French systems do vary a tad in terms of the non-alpha keys. A new approach using ZHJAY in the early 20th century lost out to the momentum that typists had developed for the AZERTY approach.

The launch of the first portable typewriter happened in 1900.

Dr August Dvorak, an educational psychologist in Seattle, concluded that the QWERTY system had some disadvantages and sought a better system that would reduce fatigue and errors. He developed and launched his simplified Dvorak keyboard in 1936. Apple offered a Dvorak keyboard option in its ROM and early Windows versions could recognise it too. Today Linux, Mac OS and Windows still permit its use but this remains limited.

IBM typewriters

During the 1920s James Smathers developed a typewriter powered by a continuous moving roller. In seeking to source an electric motor Smathers visited the North East Electric Company. He sold them his patent rights and it negotiated a contract to produce 2,500 units for Remington in 1925.

But things did not run smoothly as Remington was preoccupied with the merger that eventually saw it become Remington Rand. North East Electric became frustrated, broke off its relationship with Remington and went on to develop the Electromatic in 1929.

One of its merits was that, being electrically powered, the unit struck strongly enough to give good multiple carbon copies. It soon changed the company name to that of its product, The Electromatic Typewriter Company.

IBM purchased this company in 1933 and invested $1m to redevelop the product which was relaunched as the IBM 01 Electric Typewriter; it had a sustained and successful product life.

It is usually suggested that Ulrich Steinhilper, while working for the IBM Office Products Division in Germany during the 1950s, first coined the

German term *textverabeitung* that on translation into English became 'word processing'.

Steinhilper, through the late 1950s, promoted the notion internally at IBM. Just as IBM assisted its clients with processing data he suggested it could also help word processing. He developed an associated chart and submitted the notion to the organisation's suggestion system. He was paid 25 Deutschmarks for the idea but advised that his notion was much 'too complicated to explain'. IBM did not advance the approach.

He used the term again at a 1966 Miami 'Hundred Per Cent Club' for those who had hit their sales targets. This time the expression caught on and he later received an outstanding achievement award and a round-the-world trip for his persistence.

In the late 1960s companies tended to have a range of capabilities in office equipment and also a breadth of individual skill levels in its personnel. They could not afford to have all typists kitted out with the latest equipment.

The term originally implied the process by which work was put through a form of text 'triage' so the more demanding tasks were allocated to the more experienced individuals and the best equipment.

Perhaps the first step towards what we consider to be word processing today was made back in the 1930s when the M Shultz Company introduced the automatic repetitive typewriter that would take what was entered and output it as punched paper tape. In this manner a standard letter could be prepared and reliably reproduced. The name and address would be manually typed and then the tape fed through a reader to repeat the standard text for each proposed recipient.

In 1961 IBM introduced the Selectric which replaced the typewriter's moving carriage with a golfball device that was faster and more reliable than the old electromechanical typewriters.

The young industry was keen to promote the fact that while companies thought nothing of providing the average factory worker with $25,000 worth of equipment to perform tasks, they gave only $2,000 in kit to a clerical worker. Nice try!

The next step in word processing development was to find ways to integrate new technologies, for example linking dictation equipment through an internal telephone system and working with automated typewriters, often expanded to include the copier and duplicator; rather like Xerox's office of the future.

By 1964 the MT/ST (magnetic tape Selectric typewriter) was launched with a reusable storage medium for text that was prepared on the unit; this led to more automation of output. In its promotion the MT/ST was the first product to use the term 'word processing machine', and it became the basic equipment for many early word processing centres.

In 1969 IBM introduced the MC/ST (magnetic card Selectric typewriter). This had a magnetic card which was useful to improve the output of for organisations using standard form letters, standard forms, standard paragraphs.

The use of more convenient and larger capacity floppy disks followed in the 1970s; the cards had a capacity of one or two pages of text, the floppy disk some 80 to 100 pages. It did not take too long to realise that the floppy disk could be used to load programs too.

RANDOM ACCESS MOMENT:
The floppy disk is one of the few products that just about spanned much of our PC story, albeit in different sizes and with ever increasing capacities. The technology was first released commercially by IBM in 1971 and by 1996 in its heyday some five billion of them were in use.

But the ceiling of 2 MBytes in memory was soon surpassed with the advent of CD and DVD drives and later USB pens would prove even more convenient; today's eight gigabyte USB pens are more resilient and have 4,000 times the capacity.

By the late noughties fewer than 2% of PCs were supplied with a floppy drive, though they remain popular in Asia. By 2009 Sony was the last remaining large scale maker of floppy disks, selling 12 million in Japan alone. In 2010 it announced that it too would be discontinuing production.

In 1970 *Administrative Management* magazine carried a report headed,
'*Auburn U[niversity] Learns about Word Processing*'

This described how, assisted by IBM, the university had centralised dictation and typing. This was claimed to be the first mention of the term in print.

'*"Word processing," a concept that combines the dictating and typing functions into a centralized system, is replacing the one-man, one-secretary, one-typewriter idea in a growing number of firms.*'

The magazine spun the feature into a supplement and then a bi-monthly newsletter *Word Processing Reports*. A book was released and inevitably conferences and consultancies soon followed.

The editor claimed a 500% or more increase in speed using the new word processing approach. However I recall a debate at the time about whether word processing could save an organisation any money. Most concluded that while it would make the output from the company significantly more professional and accurate it seldom did much in the way of cost savings.

Meanwhile at National Physical Laboratory in the UK, David Yates independently developed the program Scrapbook that went live in 1971. It was a word processor that used hypertext and email; it outlined and presaged some of the features that would become standard on the World Wide Web.

WP machines

The next developments shifted the term word processor more securely to be considered as a device, rather than a series of procedures.

Dr An Wang, a Chinese-American, worked with Howard Aiken on the Mark IV development at Harvard and co-invented a pulse transfer controller that would write-after-read to make magnetic core memory practical. He sold the benefits of this invention on to IBM in 1955 for $500,000 and founded Wang Laboratories on the proceeds. Perhaps showing his oriental roots, he once said,

'Success is more a function of consistent common sense than it is of genius.'

The Wang company grew through selling scientific electronic calculators, including one with a central calculator serving a series of remote terminals. By 1970 it had 1,400 employees and $27 million in turnover; it began to diversify into mini-computers.

In 1971 Wang launched the model 1200 dedicated WP system. In 1975 the Xerox 800 was introduced with a Diablo printer. Using a daisy wheel approach this system had twice the speed of the Wang 1200. Wang countered in 1976 with the Wang Computer System (WCS) that was an early product to offer on-screen editing of text.

Word Processing Software

Apple, Commodore and Radio Shack had ignited the market with their computers – still largely a hobbyist phenomenon. But VisiCalc took them into the small businesses and executive sector.

VisiCalc had been the killer-app that made the Apple II take off, but there were soon two other significant legs to the software 'milking stool' of the time – word processing and databasing.

The early '70s was the era of specialist word processing devices from IBM, Lanier, Lexitron, Vydec, Wang, Xerox and others. By the mid-'70s WP machines had moved on from being electromechanical systems to having microprocessors at their heart. But at a price tag of $30,000 these were not going to create a mass market for WP.

The floppy disk was a boon for word processing. Initially used simply for storing a typist's output but later for loading data and programs onto the device, the word processor began to look and act more and more like a PC.

IBM introduced the DisplayWriter System in 1980, a dedicated word processor that looked just like a PC. It had a desktop CPU cabinet sitting beneath a mono screen, a detached keyboard, a single-sided floppy drive and software that would store and retrieve prepared material, allow manipulation of the text, mail merge and even provided a spellchecker with a vocabulary of 50k words.

The basic system sold for just $7,985 as a stand-alone but it was also available with a central storage system sharing printers; the software developed for this system would later be made available on the IBM PC as the DisplayWrite program.

In the early 1980s programmer Wilton H Jones landed a contract from the Connecticut Mutual Life Insurance company to create a WP system. He hired in a group of young programmers and developed the MultiMate.

Its benefit was that it was a general PC and not simply a dedicated WP machine like the Wang. It achieved strong sales in insurance and professional offices.

With over 150 staff and a vibrant order book, MultiMate was acquired by Ashton-Tate for $20m in 1985; this was described then as one of the largest IT business deals.

Thereafter this sector became a natural target for the new PC makers. Surely they could deliver the hardware and software for a tenth of the price?

In 1976 Michael Shrayer created the first PC word processing approach for the 8080, and later the Z80. It required the user to invest in an add-on card to provide a 16 line by 64 character display. He wrote it in assembler and it was originally his way of keeping a record of his own programming documentation as he went. He had no original intentions for it as a product, but Electric Pencil was soon to be distributed with the Altair, Sol-20 and even the IBM PC.

While IMSAI's director of marketing, Seymour Rubinstein met up with Rob Barnaby. When he left in 1978 to form his own operation MicroPro International Inc, he asked Barnaby, a programmer, to join him to look at word processing opportunities.

Barnaby had become frustrated by the line editor built into the CP/M operating system. Called ED, it was a residual component of Kildall's original PL/M package inherited by CP/M. Barnaby came up with his own updated version and called it NED (new editor). NED added further features including a video mode.

At MicroPro Barnaby worked on several packages that operated within CP/M. The first was WordMaster an enhanced version of NED, a simple text editing system. It required the subsequent addition of a TeX program that delivered formatting for it to become a rounded word processing package. He also developed SuperSort to manipulate data.

Subsequently Barnaby added print functions to his thinking and developed WordStar, a full WP package. It was designed to work with early terminals and PCs which did not have the function keys and keyboards that we expect today; these had to be replicated instead by the use of a sequence of codes. Its command functions used the Control key and video functions used the Edit key.

It was WordStar that first introduced the routines using CTRL-C to copy blocks of text, CTRL-X to cut them, and CTRL-V to paste them. Given the frequency that we all use these, just imagine if they had patented this?

WordStar still had its history set in its genes. The process it used was for software to capture all entered material first, à la NED, and the formatting and layout was then applied subsequently with Tex. It was launched in September 1978 and first shown at the West Coast Computer Faire.

The IMSAI founder, William 'Bill' Millard, had found the going tough as a plethora of products and expansion boards emerged to overwhelm his products and it was the lack of any real distribution channel that caught his eye.

With IMSAI Sales Manager Ed Faber, he opened ComputerLand as a full-service retail outlet to support the growing number of products professionally. The first store was opened in 1976 and through franchising by 1985 had grown to around 800 stores, a quarter of these outside the USA.

ComputerLand became a prime outlet for WordStar. WordStar was compact and able to fit onto a single-sided 5.25" floppy. This and its availability rapidly made it the most popular WP system available for the CP/M operating system.

Barnaby had been operating flat out on this and eventually 'hit the wall', he left MicroPro. Jim Fox who had worked with him through the final phases took up the mantle and ported WordStar to other platforms. He developed it to work on the Apple II with its Microsoft CP/M plug-in board, on the Radio Shack TRS-80, the Osborne 1 and on other PCs.

WordPerfect

In a similar way to the spreadsheets VisiCalc and Context MBA, WordStar had been merely ported across to the IBM PC and this work-around soon opened the door for someone else to come along and unseat it by developing a WP package tailor-made to the IBM product.

This was achieved by Satellite Systems International and its WordPerfect software. Its origin was based upon a desire to develop software for a Data General minicomputer, in this case for the minicomputer owned by the city of Orem in Utah, near Salt Lake City. The originators were a student, Bruce Bastian, and a computer science professor, Dr Alan Ashton, at Brigham Young University (BYU).

Brigham Young, known as the 'American Moses', was a president of the Church of Latter-day Saints, more commonly referred to as the Mormons; he founded Salt Lake City and was the first governor of Utah.

Ashton was a committed member of the Mormon Church and the grandson of one of its presidents. For clarity, he was nothing to do with the Ashton of

Ashton-Tate; there never was an Ashton in that organisation (provided we discount Tate's parrot).

Somewhat mirroring the approach of Kapor and Sachs, Ashton defined the requirements for an improved word processing program. He came up with some interesting enhancements including editing innovations, function key shortcuts and WYSIWYG (what you see is what you get) formatting.

Bastian was at the college studying music and director of BYU's marching band. He initially became interested in computing to help with choreography for the band, and it was Ashton who assisted him. Bastian later switched to a computer science course and while studying he helped Ashton with the word processing project.

After graduation he joined Eyring Research Institute (ERI) where he worked on a language translation project. When the company was contracted to resolve a WP program for the city of Orem's PDP-11 it naturally looked to Bastian given his past WP experience. Ashton and Bastian developed it in DEC Assembler.

In September 1979 they founded WordPerfect Corporation with equity arranged as 49.5% each to Ashton and Bastian and 1% to the guy hired to run the administration.

In 1982 WordPerfect was ported to the IBM PC, but when it was subsequently rewritten directly for the IBM PC it started to take over the WordStar mantle.

WordPerfect had some important benefits in its approach. For example it had streaming code architecture that overcame the two-step approach of WordStar.

WordPerfect inserted codes within the text of the document as it was prepared to define its formatting and style. The codes would show the start and end point of a particular style or format and they could be nested within each other, rather like today's HTML (hypertext markup language). It also used a 'reveal codes' feature where the user could see the text with the interspersed codes; this offered more clarity than style-based predecessors.

It proved to be a step-function on from WordStar in using a whole series of sequences of function keys using Ctrl, Alt and Shift, rather than just the Alt functions of its predecessor. The Alt key was also used to create and access a macro library; this would save any series of keystrokes and functions as a subroutine that could be recalled and reused as required.

One thing WordPerfect did that was very different from most PC start-ups was not to give its team members stock options; this meant it was under no pressure to list its shares publicly. It maintained just three shareholders and held on to its cash and its control.

By 1990 Ashton was listed by *Forbes* magazine in the top 500 high-net-worth individuals, valued at over $1.1bn. He had not abandoned his Mormon principles and he and his wife put some of this wealth into giving something back. They founded Thanksgiving Point in Utah which among other things teaches children and adults about farming, gardening and cooking. It also has a Museum of Ancient Life.

WordPerfect ran in to some difficulties as it sought to espouse Windows and worked with Borland to integrate the WP software into an Office suite to sit alongside Quattro Pro and Paradox. Called Borland Office for Windows it did not stand up well against Microsoft Office. Novell, another Mormon-managed, Utah-based organisation, acquired WordPerfect in 1993 for $850m. T the same time Borland sold Novell its Quattro Pro and Paradox for $140m.

The suite was sold on to Corel in 1996 though Novell retained rights in the technology and included this in GroupWise, a collaborative software package with email and instant messaging, document management, personal information and time management.

Ashton was in the limelight again when in October 2008 he donated $1m to the California Proposition 8 Campaign. The proposition sought to establish that only marriage between a man and a woman should be valid and/or recognised in California.

Graphics

It was MIT and its Tech Model Railroad Club that were the first to stretch the features of the early mainframe computers.

Vannevar Bush established the basic theories of a man-machine symbiosis; the thoughts of artificial intelligence were born in MIT. Whirlwind and SAGE pushed the hardware forward, prompting the first mass-produced computer the IBM 704 and a little later the DEC PDP range.

The MIT team applied the capabilities of its TX-O with games like the Mouse in the Maze and Tic-Tac-Toe. MIT's TX-2 was the first computer with a graphics capability. Slug Russell developed Spacewar! for use on its PDP-1 and others evolved the graphics to handle star charts and sprites. It also created the first computer chess game.

Peter Samson, Alan Kotok and others also produced a technical drafting program on MIT's PDP-1 in 1962. Called T-Square, it was later used and developed by Bolt, Beranek & Newman.

The next year another MIT student of note was Ivan Sutherland who produced a more expansive drawing program he called Sketchpad; he indicated this work was inspired by Vannevar Bush's Memex and *As We May Think*.

Sutherland developed Sketchpad on the TX-2 enabling its light pen to create both technical drawings and artistic sketches. As part of the program Sutherland established many techniques still in use today. For example instead of making the user have the hassle of drawing all four sides of a square, one need only specify that the requirement is a square, define the length of each side and one corner location and the computer draws it automatically.

In 1968, while an associate professor at Harvard, Sutherland worked with student Bob Sproull on virtual reality and augmented reality systems, developing what they called The Sword of Damocles.

In 1966 ARPA provided Utah with $5m in pure research funding across three years, for Dr David Evans to create a computer science department to look at the man-machine interface. Over sixty companies were formed to exploit technologies developed there. Sutherland moved to the University of Utah.

The influence of Dr David Evans and Dr Ivan Sutherland cannot be understated as they inspired many and also formed the first computer graphics company, Evans & Sutherland.

Sutherland played a significant role with ARPA's IPTO and operated from the University of Utah as it was awarded the fourth ARPANET connection.

Alan Kay earned his PhD at Utah in 1969 and developed SmallTalk which later came alive in the Apple Lisa and Macintosh products. Kay was a key player at PARC where he developed the overlapping windowing approach, and his Dynabook concept was credited with inspiring laptops and eBooks. Kay became a Fellow at Apple, and worked with both Walt Disney Imagineering and Hewlett-Packard.

While at the University of Utah, Henri Gouraud devised the Gouraud shading technique, a method of smoothing the light and colour of a surface in a computer 3D graphic.

Frank Crow developed anti-aliasing techniques that controlled the tendency for distortion when sending a hi-res file over low-res transmissions by smoothing the graphic edges.

Evans & Sutherland employed some subsequent big-hitters too. Jim Clark the founder of Silicon Graphics Inc and Netscape Communications Corporation earned his PhD there in 1974.

John Warnock also completed his PhD at Utah in 1969 and went on to work at PARC and later co-found Adobe and developed the Postscript language, essential for desktop publishing.

Chuck Seitz, designer of graphics machines, and Ronald Resch, a pioneer in computer art, were both on the Computer Science faculty. Duane Call went on to found Computer Systems Architects and design a supercomputer for vector calculations.

Atari's Nolan Bushnell had also graduated from there in 1968. Bui Tuong-Phong developed the Phong shading and Phong reflection models for highlighting graphics images. Ed Catmull went on to co-found Pixar and was involved with Toy Story later working with The Walt Disney Company. Henry Fuchs was significant in 3D medical imaging.

It wasn't just graphics, another member of the faculty Robert Barton was the principal architect of many Burroughs computers. Also on the faculty there was Tom Stockham who created the field of digital recording, formed Soundstream Inc and was one of the panel at BBN to investigate the gaps in Nixon's Watergate tapes. Tony Hearn was to develop the REDUCE algebraic mathematics package at Utah.

Warnock and his wife later bestowed $6m to the college and the John and Marva Warnock Engineering Building is now the College of Engineering office.

RANDOM ACCESS MOMENT:
One of the very few graphics innovations that did not occur at Utah was when morphing was developed at the New York Institute of Technology - but to keep a Utah connection intact the developer was Tom Brigham!

But with absolutely no connection to Utah, Tom DeFanti developed the GRASS language for 3D animation *between 1974 and 1978 at Ohio State University; it was used for the Star Wars Death Star sequence.*

Going in to print - TeX

It was the Apple Mac's WYSIWYG capabilities that opened up a whole new business opportunity and provided its killer application, desktop publishing.

It was a business opportunity that, like many key steps in the PC journey, started in a serendipitous manner. However unlike previous applications in this sector the PC was seeking to enter a pre-existing and long established market.

Donald Knuth earned his PhD in mathematics at CalTech and then took a professorship there. He wrote a book entitled *The Art of Computer Programming,* which grew like Topsy and ended up as a seven-volume series first published in 1968. This rapidly became the seminal text on the subject.

In the process of publishing his books Knuth was made painfully aware of progress in typesetting technology. His first edition was produced and typeset using the traditional 'hot metal'; Knuth found the finished product using this process to be 'classically pleasing'.

When the second edition was being prepared in 1976, many original fonts were unavailable with the then current approach that utilised a technique of photographic typesetting. The galleys, or proofs, that were supplied to Knuth for approval were unacceptable; this led him to investigate the whole subject of digital typesetting.

In 1977 Knuth produced an internal memo at CalTech to describe a system that he called TeX, a typesetting software program to be used together with a Metafont language that he also defined. This would describe the required fonts by means of a series of vectored lines and curves to create the font outline, or glyph.

Knuth had an interesting sense of humour and as a result both pieces of his software did not follow the normal approach for software-update version-numbering. Most initially launch a package as version 1.0 with any regular small updates incrementing this in tenths, so 1.1 and 1.2; then any major updates jump by a whole unit, so 2.0, 3.0 and so on.

TeX however started at version 3.0 and advanced towards an ever more accurate definition of 'pi' so 3.1, 3.14, 3.141; by the noughties it had reached 3.1415926 and it proceeds. Metafont started at 2.0 and approaches a more accurate definition of 'e', or Euler's constant, the base of the natural algorithm, so 2.7, 2.71, 2.718 and so on.

Founding Adobe and developing Postscript

We saw earlier how Xerox PARC was responsible for two major steps in the process towards desktop publishing; first the development of the laser printer, then its creation of Interpress to define the pages to be printed by laser.

But as the manager of the team Chuck Geschke failed to get the Xerox senior management buy-in to launching Interpress; not much of a surprise for the PARC team. John Warnock and Geschke left and founded Adobe Systems Inc and soon created Postscript, based on their experience of Interpress.

Postscript is a language completely independent of the printer in use, so with early laser printers it could operate at their 300 dpi, dots per inch, but work just as well with a 2,400 dpi image-setting device.

Adobe then offered Postscript licences to any manufacturer and made the rules for the syntax of Postscript freely available so software authors could and would use it without any hindrance.

Steve Jobs attention was captured and he arranged for Apple to buy 15% or 3.4 million shares in Adobe, investing some $2.5m on the basis that Warnock would develop a PostScript controller for his new Apple laser printer. The Apple LaserWriter when launched in 1985 was thus the first with built-in Postscript.

This development gave it the unique ability to print with the quality of a typesetting machine and opened the door for Mac's killer application to emerge.

But one further component still needed to emerge.

15th century printer to PageMaker - Aldus

Paul Brainerd earned his publishing spurs as the editor of the University of Oregon's newspaper. He then co-founded Aldus Corporation to create what he became the first to call desktop publishing (DTP).

The company name was taken from a 15th century printer based in Venice - Aldus Pius Manutius the Elder. He introduced inexpensive books that were a precursor of today's paperbacks. He also developed italic type and established the modern usage of the semicolon; good choice of name then for floating a DTP business.

Aldus Corporation launched its DTP package PageMaker in July 1985. It did not have the field to itself however; it was been beaten to the market by Boston Software releasing MacPublisher during 1984. The latter therefore can lay claim to being the first available DTP package. Manhattan Graphics too launched a DTP package called Ready, Set, Go! Each of these allowed users to design, review and print page layouts using both text and graphics.

But when Apple LaserWriter, Adobe Postscript and Aldus PageMaker were combined, desktop publishing became the killer application that saved the Macintosh - and Apple; initially only Apple could offer this full DTP solution.

RANDOM ACCESS MOMENT:
Adobe, Aldus and Apple – all short names beginning with A. This was an extremely popular approach in the PC market - Acorn, Amiga, Atari, plus all those Atari émigrés beginning with A.

A five letter length proved popular too - Canon, Cisco, Corel, Eidos, Epson, Intel, Lycos, Quark, Psion, Sharp, Skype, Xerox, Yahoo!...

By 1986 desktop publishing was available as a home computer application with packages released for all the home computer platforms. Suddenly members of clubs and associations had the means to prepare professional bulletins, press releases, newsletters and brochures.

The first IBM PC package for DTP was Ventura Publisher, not released until 1986; it was later acquired by Corel in 1993.

RANDOM ACCESS MOMENT:
One of my early DTP experiences was when I had prepared a 4-page newsletter in which I had some pride; I thought it looked pretty darned good. But when I showed it to a magazine designer he made just a few tweaks, each of which were techniques that I fully appreciated how to use, but these changes radically altered the look and appeal of my document. That was the moment I realised that while I had DTP technology at my fingertips, I was no designer - art and skill still held sway.

Quark was a relative latecomer to the DTP scene, launching its package in 1987. But just as those coming late to the industrial revolution took advantage of latest developments, so too could QuarkXPress. It rapidly became the DTP package of choice for professional designers.

The whole DTP revolution was so powerful that the pre-press market inevitably had to bend and accommodate it. Linotype was the first professional organisation to offer Postscript with its typesetting equipment, the others followed.

Juggling the catalyst for Quark

Word processing moved on too. It was not used simply to prepare letters and memos more accurately, now this was an integral part of a package to deliver material as newsletters, brochures, advertisements, magazines and books.

Quark, a major business software player that emerged in this sector was founded by Tim Gill and Mark Pope in 1981.

Born in Indiana, Gill studied computer science at the University of Colorado. He worked with HP and other companies before being made redundant. He borrowed $2,000 from his parents to found Quark Engineering, named for the sub-atomic particle.

Quark had some early success with the Apple platform. It developed Word Juggler, the first word processor for the Apple III. It also created Catalyst for the Apple IIe which allowed earlier floppy disk-based applications to be run with a hard drive.

But its subsequent move into Quark Peripherals, data storage products, could well have brought about its demise; it certainly led to a considerable loss.

Gill met Farhad 'Fred' Ebrahimi, an Iranian-born realtor, sold him a share in the company and appointed him Quark's CEO in 1986; Gill was chairman. Ebrahimi and Gill later bought Pope out in 1990 and later still in 2000 Gill sold his shares on to Ebrahimi. Quark never went public at any stage of its life.

So in 1987 it was Ebrahimi who presided over the development and launch of its salvation, QuarkXPress for the Macintosh.

The program offered a new level of precision in defining typography and layout and handling colour management. It was well received by an industry eager to move away from mechanically laying out pages. The QuarkXPress version 1.0 at $695 rapidly became the standard for desktop publishing for professional designers in the magazine and general print profession.

In 1988 Quark expanded into Europe and the Far East. Version 2.0 was priced at $795 and aimed directly at newspaper and magazine publishers.

The next year Quark introduced two enhancements. QuarkStyle was a detuned QuarkXPress aimed at business users. XTensions was a process that encouraged third party developers to offer custom-designed add-ons to create vertical applications and utilities. This opened the door to a whole raft of vertical applications.

PageMaker was priced at just $495 and achieved a 61% share of the business. Ventura, a Xerox subsidiary, was securely in second place. A much improved QuarkXPress 3.0 launched in 1990 in competition with them.

The DTP market had moved away from Apple by1992 with just 5 million users on the Mac platform and a massive 70 million on the Windows platform. A much delayed Windows 3.1 was seized upon by DTP developers to expand ideas further.

Quark rapidly overtook the lower-cost PageMaker when it had launched a rather shaky version 4.0 that just did not match up with the Quark features.

In 1992 the company also launched the Quark Publishing System (QPS) as a networked package for work groups from $100,000. Sales were taking on a hockey-stick look with $60m in 1991 and $120m in 1992; staff numbers reached four hundred.

By the end of the '90s Quark commanded a 90% worldwide DTP share.

However the particle quarks come in three varieties - up, down and strange. The early history of Quark had its ups and downs, but its customer relationships started to exhibit the 'strange' variety.

First Quark maintained rather high prices for its software; no Moore's Law reductions were being applied. Then its development rather stagnated; it appeared not to respond satisfactorily to client concerns and requirements. Its product evolution began to look tardy.

This opened the door to a competitor and Adobe stepped right up with the InDesign product. Although Quark compared well against it, it was its own inaction that had let Adobe into the broader DTP sector.

In 1998 Quark launched an unlikely takeover of Adobe which was taken seriously by few - certainly not Adobe itself!

In fact the first real promotion of QuarkXPress since its launch came much later in 2006 with the launch of version 7. This took place in New York and my company, subsequently organised seven major launch events for v7 in London, Paris, Frankfurt, Stockholm, Utrecht, Milan and Madrid.

Today QuarkXPress is claimed to have had some three million users and it is suggested that over five billion pages have been designed using the program.

Adobe's rapid progress

Geschke and Warnock had met at Xerox PARC and developed Interpress, subsequently leaving to establish Adobe.

Dr David Evans of Evans & Sutherland introduced them to a venture capitalist, William Hambrecht, who on a handshake gave them a personal cheque for $50,000 to help the start-up, and later went on to procure a further $2.5m in venture capital.

Adobe Postscript, a universal print language, enabled the DTP application to take off. This and its related licensing of a series of fonts was the foundation of the business.

In 1983 Steve Jobs arranged for Apple to acquire 20% of Adobe for $2.5m, a shrewd investment as Postscript and DTP would directly deliver $10m in sales for Apple as an OEM provider of Postscript.

Adobe turnover grew from $2.5m in 1984 to $4.4m by 1985. Subsequently the first Postscript LaserWriter was launched and sales then really took off to reach $16m by 1986. Also in 1986, Adobe issued 10% or 550,000 shares on NASDAQ at a par value of $11; they rose to $14 on the day.

Having delivered the killer-app for desk top publishing, Adobe was not finished. It continued to innovate and revolutionise a whole series of industries and applications.

Adobe moved into application software in 1986, combining its two skill sets to produce Adobe Illustrator, a vector graphics system using 'primitives' to create images. The primitives were points, lines, polygons and Bezier curves that could be combined to build any graphic image. Its predecessor of course was raster graphics which need to be painstakingly defined pixel by pixel.

This decision was probably prompted by the Apple involvement in Adobe as the Illustrator was initially only available on the Mac with its 9" (23cm) black & white screen. It would only work with a LaserWriter, thus giving it a limited niche appeal.

It was however a step-function on from MacDraw and a user-friendly stepping stone towards a full CAD package. It was reliable and intuitive to use. By interweaving the Postscript features, software developers were able to work in Illustrator very easily too.

RANDOM ACCESS MOMENT:
Under licence Adobe uses the face of Venus from Botticelli's 'The Birth of Venus' as the 'branded' image of Illustrator. It is assumed this indicates Illustrator is not just for the technical but also for the artistic user.

Illustrator 1.1, code name Inca, sold well but the first truly marketable package was version 1.6 released in 1988 as Adobe Illustrator 88, code name Picasso. It too was initially focused on the Apple Mac; later versions were for other platforms.

Adobe was slow in creating a real equivalent for Windows. In 1989 version 3.0 for Windows, code name Desert Moose, was seen as underspecified compared to the current Mac version. As a result, in the Windows' market, Illustrator allowed itself to be overtaken by CorelDraw.

Adobe sales still grew to $121m and Apple was able to sell off its 20% holding, purchased for $2.5m six years earlier, realising a 34-times return at $85m – that is on top of the increased Apple product sales due to the PostScript arrangement.

In 1996 the Illustrator 6, code name Popeye, made a number of significant changes. It had the same user interface as Photoshop and plug-ins too. In 1997 Windows version 7, code name Simba, finally caught up with the Mac versions.

RANDOM ACCESS MOMENT:
I mention the Illustrator code names of the versions only because they are so delightfully eclectic and apparently random with no obvious theme. Other code names used included Pinnacle, Saturn, Janus, Pangea, Paloma (pigeon in Spanish!) - even Elvis lived on as v8.0 released 21 years after his death.

Make it snappy - Photoshop
Adobe's next major launch was Photoshop, but this was not developed internally.

Photoshop started life as a program written by a PhD student at the University of Michigan in 1987. The student was Thomas Knoll, the son of a photographer who had been an early Apple II and later a Mac user. He and his brother cut their technological teeth on these early products.

At Michigan, for his PhD on image processing, he purchased an Apple Mac Plus and was disappointed that it could not display simple black & white images on its monochrome monitor. He set out to create something he called simply Display.

His brother John was working at the special effects company Industrial Light and Magic, founded for the work needed for Star Wars - that recurring space theme again! He realised that Display mirrored a number of developments within the Lucasfilm subsidiary and so was in a strong position to suggest additional features, to develop it into a full image editing package.

When John later bought a colour Macintosh II he encouraged Thomas to develop a colour capability too. Thomas rose to the challenge adding features to control colour balance, hue and saturation. He also added various processes for image processing in the whole image or just for a selected area.

Display became ImagePro when John travelled to the West Coast and hawked it around to the leading players. Apparently in one of these demonstrations someone used a term soon to become adopted as its final name - Photoshop. This was originally written as PhotoShop but the capital S was dropped before it reached the market.

At Adobe John received some interest and a deal was proposed. This was slow and protracted so for a short time the software was sold by Thomas via a scanner company called Barneyscan; Photoshop was offered as Barneyscan XP.

John went back to Adobe and met with its art director, Russell Brown. While they could easily have proposed some other style of deal, in September 1988 Adobe took a licence for the product. Thomas and John were charged with evolving the package that was eventually launched as Photoshop 1.0 in 1990; again this was initially for the Mac only.

Russell Brown was a Photoshop Evangelist for many years. For example he was quite a character when he spoke at one of the Adobe Live events that my company organised in the UK in the early noughties.

Today Photoshop is a pixel-based image editor works with images in greyscale, RGB (red, green, blue), CMYK (cyan, magenta, yellow, and key black), bitmap and other formats. It can also work with vector image formats such as GIF (graphics interchange format), EPS (encapsulated PostScript), JPEG (Joint Photographic Experts' Group) and PNG (portable network graphics).

Photoshop propelled Adobe into becoming a globally-known brand; by 1991 the company had over 700 employees.

Photoshop was sold for under $1,000 against its closest competitor, Letraset's ColorStudio, which was priced at $1,995. It rapidly became the industry standard, and also perhaps one of the most pirated packages.

One late noughties survey of photographers estimated that some 60% of Photoshop users had a pirated copy, compared with 38% of other software being pirated. Naturally Adobe is prominent in anti-piracy but perhaps the inclusion of Photoshop at the heart of the Creative Suite series has had the most positive impact.

Who says they're not out to get me? Geschke's kidnapping

Success brings with it the attention of others and not always in a positive manner. By the early '90s Adobe was making strong profits and its founders were still driving the company forward despite their developing wealth. Heads down, working hard, right at the heart of the business they suddenly had a wake-up call.

In May 1992 Chuck Geschke arrived at the offices just before 9am, parked up his Mercedes 500 SL and was not initially surprised when a car pulled up next to him and a young guy approached him carrying a map; after all Mountain View was a maze of similar looking buildings.

He was asked if he worked at Adobe and he happily offered his assistance with directions, but the guy lifted the map to reveal a gun. Mouhannad Albukhari, a twenty-six-year-old Syrian, then gaffer-taped Geschke's eyes and bustled him back to the other car, threatening to kill him and suggesting he knew where his family was and would kill them too.

The kidnap driver was a Jordanian, Ahmad Mohammad Sayeh, twenty-four years old. The two suggested they were part of a Middle-East organisation with the technology to blow up his home and those of his neighbours too.

Arriving at a motel they questioned him on what liquid funds he could access. They called his wife, Nancy, instructing her to assemble $650,000 in ransom money and await instructions, warning that she was being watched and she should not contact the authorities.

On the way to collecting Geschke's car, as instructed, she phoned some brokers to acquire the cash and also called to warn John Warnock at Adobe as to what was happening.

Warnock's wife, Marva, believed they should involve the FBI and Geschke's children concurred. Nancy reluctantly agreed and the FBI was brought in.

Coached by an FBI agent, Geschke's daughter, Kathy took the kidnappers' calls. They initially offered a seven-day period for funds to be assembled but Kathy advised she could get the cash more speedily than that. The FBI mobilised two hundred agents on the case; this was the biggest task force in the region since the high profile Patti Hearst kidnapping in 1974.

It all read like a movie script. Kathy drove to the rendezvous with an FBI agent concealed in the rear passenger-well; she was wired for sound and wore a bulletproof vest. She was instructed by the kidnappers to go to the end of a cul-de-sac and leave the ransom money. She was advised by the FBI to put it under a light so the kidnapper could be seen when it was collected.

Albukhari fetched it; he quickly discarded the bugged bag that held it and initially was successful in escaping across some nearby dunes. But apparently he had arranged no escape vehicle and was eventually captured. He then guided the FBI to where Geschke was being held. He was released and the kidnappers received life sentences for the crime.

This was the highest profile such event in the burgeoning PC business, but not the first. James Hewlett, son of the cofounder of HP, was a kidnap target in 1976 but he had managed to escape.

John Sculley too, while head of Apple, was the subject of an attempted kidnapping while he was out jogging in 1984. Thereafter he jogged with an armed bodyguard at all times.

As a result of paranoia many PC companies would fund security for their CEOs. As Andy Grove of Intel would regularly state,

'Only the paranoid survive.'

Steve Jobs attended the 1985 Super Bowl with five armed bodyguards. I was advised that visiting the Paris Apple Expo in 1998 he would routinely book six restaurants for dinner and leave his decision as to which to use until the last minute.

Oracle paid out $1.8m in 2006 to secure Larry Ellison, Google provided over $500k to avoid any 'evil' being done to Eric Schmidt, others gave hefty allowances to key men to secure their homes.

The effect on Geschke and Warnock was to advance their philanthropic tendencies; for many years Adobe set aside 1% of annual net income. In the noughties this was formalised into the Adobe Foundation; the foundation has distributed well over $40m in cash and in kind.

Moving it around – Acrobat and PDF
In June 1993 Adobe created yet another industry standard when it addressed the matter of exchanging documents between computer users. It wanted a package that could send a document from user to user totally independent of the PC platform or the application software.

John Warnock code-named the project as Camelot and he outlined the requirement as being as much for internal use to eliminate paper around the Adobe offices. This was perhaps the first product truly seeking to create a paperless world; but just what happened to that?

Adobe first mentioned its plans at the Seybold event for 1991 in San Francisco. It was described as IPS (Interchange PostScript). By Comdex 1992 it had become PDF (portable document format) and there was also a project to create a package to write and read these PDFs.

In 1993 the tool for using PDFs was announced as Adobe Acrobat; it could both create and read PDFs. Acrobat 1.0 included the first version PDF v1.0, with Acrobat Distiller to create PDFs, plus Acrobat Exchange for printing and Acrobat Reader to read and review PDFs. It was available for Mac, DOS and Windows 3.1.

Addison Wesley published a book in 1993 detailing PDF standards and its potential; this publication assisted with a rapid adoption of the approach.

Adobe marketed PDFs permitting anyone to create applications using PDFs without a licence fee and promoting the development of plug-ins to enhance the application. Its v2.0 in 1994 allowed multimedia files to be attached to a PDF.

Yet initially Acrobat was slow to take off, in part because the production of a PDF file was very slow with the low-powered early PCs and even slower when sent across the early 28k/56k modems. It was also not without competitors.

The US Internal Revenue Service (IRS) purchased the right to use and distribute Reader 1.0 and this prompted Adobe to split this part off to become a stand-alone Adobe Reader. Better still it was available free of charge; it had originally sold this at $50 a copy. This move rapidly saw off the competition and made it the industry standard.

RANDOM ACCESS MOMENT:
I first met a PDF in 1995. Being in sales and marketing I had spent years marking up galley proofs and checking bromides and chromalins. Galley proofs were named for the metal trays into which printers would fix the type and run a preliminary copy for author correction. Bromides were high-contrast black and white images on photographic paper also used for checking printwork. Chromalins were high quality colour printing proofs to not only check spelling and layout but also colour integrity.

Then one morning a young guy working in my team showed me a PDF sent from a printing company. It came as a complete surprise to me (annoying how the young always get to these things before you!) and changed absolutely everything. This first one we could only examine and make our comments back to the printer, but pretty soon we had a full copy of Acrobat and could make changes directly - I'm not sure the printers really appreciated this latter facility as much as we did.

PDF has become a standard used by the vast majority of PC users and was adopted by the International Organization for Standardisation (ISO) as the standard for electronic document archives.

Today over 1,500 organisations have created solutions based around the PDF. Perhaps the ultimate accolade is that there are estimated to be over 200 million PDF documents on the Web.

By 1994 Adobe sales had grown to over $500m.

The DTP market was founded on the three building blocks of the Apple LaserWriter, Adobe's Postscript and the Aldus PageMaker software. In 1994 two of these elements came together when Aldus PageMaker was acquired by Adobe and it soon added PDF capabilities into the Aldus package.

Adobe added the capacity to work with external hyperlinks and the facility to form fill to Acrobat v3.0. From 1995 its Reader was integrated into websites to extend its usefulness ever more significantly. By the noughties Adobe Reader was available in some forty languages and on 85% of all PCs.

RANDOM ACCESS MOMENT:
While working with Adobe organising its Adobe Live! events I became familiar with an internal acronym of its. This was DACI (driver approver contributor informer). Everyone involved internally in an Adobe project was designated as having one of these four roles. It seemed to work well and was a very straightforward communication device that made one's status clear within the task. However if you were merely an 'I' then you really had no status at all, you were simply the organic material used to mix with the sand, clay and water to create the adobe building material.

Adobe was clearly losing to QuarkXPress in the printing business and had yet to truly espouse the potential of the Internet, leaving that field wide open to others.

Laying it out – Adobe InDesign

To address the printing market Adobe decided to update the aging PageMaker program acquired from Aldus in 1994.

By 1998 QuarkXPress was the clear choice of the professional printing market, largely because PageMaker had not kept current with features as Quark's 3.3 and 4.0 stepped away from it in utility terms. PageMaker still enjoyed business in the SoHo market (small-office home-office) but Quark controlled the more valuable professional sector.

An Adobe SWOT analysis of the time might have looked like this:
- although Postscript was a key technology in the DTP business it had the disadvantage of being transparent to users. Postscript was there doing its job in perhaps 90%+ of the DTP market but users did not know it was there; it just did its stuff uneventfully and efficiently doing nothing to promote the Adobe brand;
- Adobe was too heavily identified with the Apple Mac which was by then achieving only a small percentage of the overall market;
- the Postscript royalty was of course paid by the DTP application developers; this was a one-off charge down at the cost of sale or wholesale levels. While Quark was taking its income from the higher finished product revenues;
- the Web's HTML format was taking off and Acrobat and PDF had not yet achieved supremacy there.

The market saw this and Adobe's share price dropped by half to a five-year low and this was when Quark rather ambitiously offered to buy Adobe. As part of the deal it offered to terminate the PageMaker solution so as not to face any anti-trust problems. The print and design industry was quick to show its antagonism to the idea of the two key players becoming one.

Adobe countered this with plans for a Quark-killer. It derived from a project started by Aldus that it had called Shuksan.

Adobe introduced InDesign 1.0 in 1999. This version 1 had a mixed response since it overlooked certain features that were standard on PageMaker. But it beneficially had the look and feel of Illustrator and Photoshop and there were new features such as using frames in the page-layout process; it also offered a number of 'missing' Quark features.

By the next release, version 1.5, InDesign had its own market presence and the interaction with the other Adobe products proved highly attractive. In 2002 it was the first DTP package designed directly and available for the Mac OS X.

With InDesign, Adobe put the Quark bid successfully behind it. Adobe sales were approaching $1bn and its staffing level had grown to almost 3,000.

On 1st September 2003 Adobe began to gather its various stand-alone software packages and assembled these into what it called Creative Suite.

Today this package includes Acrobat (Reader Writer and Distiller), After Effects, Bridge, Dreamweaver, Encore, Fireworks, Flash, Illustrator InDesign, Live, Photoshop...

Corel

Corel was originally founded by Michael Cowpland as a research lab in 1985, its name standing for Cowpland Research Laboratory. It was based in Ottawa, Canada and much of its success was due to CorelDraw.

Cowpland hired Michel Bouillon and Pat Beirne to develop a vector-driven illustration programme, which they first released in January 1989. It was a significant app for both OS/2 and Windows 3.1; for the latter it included TrueType.

Version 3 included the photo-editing software called PhotoPaint, CorelShow, CorelChart and Corel Trace to create an integrated graphics package.

In 1996 Corel acquired WordPerfect from Novell, at the time the market leader in word processing software; though Microsoft soon challenged this by bundling Word with many new PCs.

Cowpland left following insider trading allegations and the new management soon formed an alliance with Microsoft, MS investing $135m in Corel. Buoyed by this Corel acquired Micrografx for its Picture Publisher and Designer graphics packages. The Micrografx ABC Graphics Suite seemed to be more accepted in the small business sector rather than Corel's pro-graphics target market.

But in 2003 Corel was acquired by Vector Capital, a private equity operation, and delisted from the NASDAQ and Toronto exchanges.

By 2005 it claimed that some 20 million WordPerfect licences were issued and that this was growing by 4 million each year by virtue of a bundle deal with Dell. Based on this Corel was re-quoted on the NASDAQ in 2006 and promptly gobbled up WinZip with the proceeds.

RANDOM ACCESS MOMENT:
One of the most useful CD software items I ever acquired was the Corel Gallery boasting over 1,000,000 royalty-free useable images. It consisted of 14 packed CDs with all sorts of clipart and photos that I used mercilessly in various consultancy tasks.

Macromedia coalesces

Another major player emerged in 1992 when several organisations came together to create a business that would respond to the needs of the Web sector more directly than either Quark or Adobe.

MacroMind was a third party Apple Macintosh software developer based in Chicago. It was formed in 1984 by Marc Canter (ex-Bally-Midway), Mark Pierce (ex-Atari) and Jamie Fenton who had written the Gorf arcade game (later trans-gendering from male to female, becoming Jay Fenton).

Its first product was SoundVision planned as a combined music and graphics editor, but the graphics element was later removed to become

MusicWorks. The graphics application emerged later as VideoWorks which would become better know when renamed Director in 1988.

Director was launched initially for the Mac and only later in 1990 for Windows. It allowed the user to become a virtual movie director able to cut and paste source material, add a script using its Lingo language and author CDs and DVDs.

A key player in the Director team and the inventor of Lingo was John Thompson who was later chief scientist at Macromedia for many years and a new media professor at New York University.

MacroMind moved its operation to San Francisco where it merged with Paracomp in 1991. Paracomp specialised in Macintosh 3D software with Swivel 3D, a modeling program, and ModelShop, aimed at the architects' market.

The organisation gained a great deal of publicity from production of a 3D representation of San Francisco using ModelShop following the Loma Prieta earthquake in 1989. The mayor of SF used the software to present his ideas for redeveloping the damaged Embarcadero Highway; it was cleared to make way for today's Pacific Bell baseball stadium.

Another organisation, Authorware Inc, was created in 1987 by Dr Michael Allen. Allen was involved with Plato (programmed logic for automated teaching operations), an online computer-based instruction system.

Plato was built initially at the University of Illinois on an ILLIAC 1 and later ported to CDC equipment; it spread to several thousand terminals across a number of networked mainframes.

Allen was a director of R&D at CDC working with Plato and its programming language Tutor. Authorware was created as a Microsoft Windows version of Tutor, using an icon-driven visual interface able to work with multimedia material; it became a valuable e-learning package. Authorware developed an 80% share of this market by 1992.

Authorware then merged with MacroMind/Paracomp and these various businesses combined to form Macromedia.

In 1995 Macromedia acquired Altsys. Founded by James R Von Ehr II, Altsys was Texas-based and created a series of programs suitable for print and graphics – Fontographer, a font editor for Mac and Windows; Font-O-Matic, a font transformer for Windows; Metamorphosis, a font utility for the Mac.

Most importantly it developed Virtuoso, a program for Windows NT and NeXT. This was similar to Adobe Illustrator offering vector-drawing and page creation routines; it had been licensed to Aldus and soon became Freehand.

When Aldus was purchased by Adobe, Altsys contractually ensured that the Freehand product was not part of the deal. So when Altsys was later acquired by Macromedia the rights in Freehand finally came with it.

This took Macromedia nose-to-nose with Adobe in the image/illustration sectors when prior to this it was aligned much more towards multimedia.

Multimedia waves

Like Adobe, Microsoft too came to the Internet somewhat late; its first proposed launch into the sector was code-named Blackbird. It was a move to create its own Internet publishing suite for Windows and early on it was decided not to use http (hypertext transfer protocol).

Macromedia was involved in developing a multimedia plug-in for Blackbird, but the Microsoft approach proved far too complex and it was dropped. Microsoft soon changed its thinking too and moved to espouse http.

However, based upon this plug-in effort, in 1995 Macromedia developed Shockwave, a multimedia package. Shockwave operated as a plug-in to Macromedia Director to produce animations and movies for websites, just as the demand for these enhancements was beginning to come about. It was designed originally for use with the Netscape Navigator 2.0 browser but its versatility created a great deal of success in games development too.

Shockwave's key attraction was the way it compressed multimedia routines so they could be readily used on the Web. It could be expanded by the use of Xtras; these were usually third-party developed routines and specialist web development tools.

Strategic relationships with both CompuServe and Sun gave Macromedia ever more credibility for its products. CompuServe integrated Macromedia software into its software, Sun worked with Macromedia on the Java language and tools. Netscape also agreed to integrate Macromedia Shockwave into its browsers.

Shockwave's penetration with Web users today is still a remarkable 60%.

It came to me in a flash

Macromedia was offering two different multimedia plug-in solutions, Authorware and Shockwave, when it promptly added a third - Flash.

Macromedia was by then repositioning itself to become the software of choice for the Web. Flash was designed from the outset for Web use; today it has a 90% penetration of all users.

Charlie Jackson was born in California and had an unusual early education, spending three years at a French school in Istanbul. He returned to the United States, earned a BA in Near Eastern Studies from UCLA, then joined the US Marines from 1972 through 1976; he gained his master's at San Diego State in 1978.

To say he was involved in sports would be an understatement. He won prizes for pole vault in Istanbul, track and field at school, soccer and rowing at UCLA, and he competed in rifle and pistol shooting in the marines. He was on the US National Team for pistol shooting. As a senior he gained gold medals at the World Masters' Games in pistol shooting and volleyball. He went on to chair USA Volleyball and later owned a US professional beach volley tour - exhausting just to list these!

Jackson created the San Diego Macintosh User Group and founded Silicon Beach Software in 1984 specialising in Mac software. The company produced Digital Darkroom, the first software program to use plug-in architecture, and it created the Magic Wand tool; both were taken up as an approach by Photoshop.

Other products included SuperPaint and SuperCard. The operation was sold to Aldus Corporation in 1990.

In 1993 he co-founded FutureWave Software with Jonathan Gay. Operating from San Diego it developed software for pen-based systems. SmartSketch was, as its name suggests, a vector drawing program written for the GO Corporation's EO Communicator, a tablet computer, and utilising its PenPointOS.

Pen computing however failed to take off and the work on SmartSketch was ported to the Mac and Windows platforms. Later animation was added and it was renamed as Future Splash Animator in May 1996. This was a compact program and therefore readily adopted by the evolving World Wide Web. Microsoft used it on MSN, Disney used it for Disney Daily Blast and Fox Television used it for the Simpsons' site.

It is suggested that it was probably through its use by Disney, where Macromedia's Shockwave was also applied, that Macromedia came across it and was prompted to buy FutureWave Software late in 1996. Future Splash Animator was renamed Macromedia Flash 1.0; later of course it was to become Adobe Flash when Adobe acquired Macromedia.

Flash was made available as an open-source program and its success was also based upon it loading much more speedily than Shockwave files.

Weaving dreams

Macromedia's next acquisition provided the final link for the company to take a significant lead in the rapidly expanding dub-dub-dub, or World Wide Web, market. This was the purchase of iBand Software and its Backstage program, an html authoring and application server.

Acquired in 1996, the routines in Backstage were the foundation of what became Macromedia Dreamweaver, developed for both Windows and Mac.

Dreamweaver 1.0, released in 1997, allowed web authors to work at the html code level where they were most comfortable. But for those less technical it permitted working within a WYSIWYG presentation of the web page itself. It also allowed websites to be previewed offline in a local browser before publication to the Net using ftp (file transfer protocol), SFTP (secure file transfer protocol) and later WebDAV (web-based distributed authoring and versioning).

Dreamweaver also allowed the use of third party extensions for ever more sophisticated website development.

Look out for the fireworks

Yet another acquisition, Fauve Software Inc, brought Matisse, an image creation program and XRes, a high-end image manipulation program, to Macromedia,

Matisse introduced the notion of layers, virtual transparencies laid on or behind others to develop a more sophisticated integrated image; XRes had layers too. Adobe's Photoshop followed the example in 1994 with its version 3.0 using the same approach; all image editors today have layers.

Macromedia took a cut-down version of XRes and developed Fireworks for web graphic design using bitmaps or vector graphics. Fireworks could be used in conjunction with other Macromedia products like Flash and Dreamweaver.

By 1995 Macromedia was at its peak, shares trading at $63, but towards the end of the millennium it was experiencing difficulties. By 1997 shares had dropped to just $8 and in the year's fourth quarter they showed a loss of $15.3m. The company rallied with the Universal Media Initiative in late 1998, driving its software even more towards the Web market. Flash and Shockwave were adapted to work with Java and Dynamic HTML.

With these moves Macromedia had reversed its situation and achieved $114m in revenues in 1998. As part of this renaissance it launched www.shockwave.com, a site that quickly attracted 60,000 visitors every day and generated $3.3m in advertising revenue during 1999.

A further setback came when Macromedia shareholders accused five executives of insider trading; they finally settled this in 2001 by paying $48m back into the company.

In April 2005 Macromedia was acquired by Adobe for $3.4bn and the teams merged; many Macromedia products were soon renamed as Adobe.

23 - Read all about it – the PC and books

'The saddest aspect of life right now is that science gathers knowledge faster than society gathers wisdom.' Isaac Asimov

Early digitisation

It was a given that computers should be applied to the task of cataloguing of books and other publications.

The OCLC (online computer library center) was established in 1967 as a global cooperative, non-profit organisation. It was created as a membership of libraries. Its aim was to reduce the costs to libraries for cataloguing and accessing information about publications.

Fred Kilgour graduated in chemistry at Harvard before taking a position in the Harvard University Library. During WWII he was acting chairman of the Interdepartmental Committee for the Acquisition of Foreign Publications (IDC) a committee that acquired publications from enemy territories and occupied countries to be used as a valuable intelligence source.

After the war he became librarian at Yale where he published papers on the value of libraries. Heavily involved in early automation efforts, he experimented with punched cards, microfilm and other early technologies. He founded OCLC as a network of libraries.

In 1974 a degree of friction resulted from the formation of another non-profit operation, the Research Libraries Group (RLG). This was founded by a group of research libraries at Columbia, Harvard and Yale.

In 2003 RLG set up its own RedLightGreen bibliographic databases and by 2006 upgraded this to ArchiveGrid. It developed its own search engines the Research Libraries Information Network (RLIN) in 1978 and later Eureka in 1993. However in 2006 the two were finally united under OCLC.

Today OCLC has an online union catalog called WorldCat.org that assembles data from over 72,000 libraries operating in 171 countries. These libraries include the British Library, the Library of Congress, the Russian State Library...

Almost 213 million bibliographic records are held and these are categorised by 1.6 billion physical and digital assets. They are recorded in 470 languages and dialects; a new item is added every ten seconds.

This is the world's largest bibliographic database with over 1,000 employees located in seven countries to sustain it.

OCLC membership and access for libraries and universities is provided free. Students, scholars, researchers, librarians and other information seekers can find bibliographic details, abstracts and in many cases the full texts of items that are catalogued.

Project Gutenburg

Vannevar Bush's Memex was defined as a device holding the sum total of the world's books with a ready access for all. Others recognised this goal was becoming a reality as the capability of computers expanded.

The parents of Michael Stern Hart were professors, his father in Shakespearean studies and his mother in mathematics. Hart graduated in just two years from the University of Illinois. While there he was given valuable free access to the mainframe computer, which at the time was one of just fifteen nodes of what would become the Internet.

Hart was motivated to type in the full text of the US Declaration of Independence and published it digitally to the university network.

In December 1971 Hart founded Project Gutenberg in which he set the task of doing the same for the most referenced 10,000 public-domain books by the end of the 20th century.

He personally started the process by typing in the complete works of Shakespeare and Mark Twain. By 1987 he had typed in over 300 books for the project. This was further advanced by the assistance of a growing number of volunteers.

Michael Stern Hart the project's CEO, stated its aim as,
'to provide as many eBooks in as many formats as possible for the entire world to read in as many languages as possible.'

In 2000 the project became formalised into a non-profit organisation, the Project Gutenburg Library Archive Foundation Inc.

An Italian volunteer, Pietro Dim Miceli, created the project's website and catalogued the eBook texts through the nineties and early noughties. The catalogue was upgraded and improved in 2004.

It is hosted by ibiblio, the US public library digital archive, operating from the University of North Carolina. Ibiblio itself derived from the Sun Microsystems' funding of the site originally named SUNsite.unc.edu

A distributed computing exercise called Distributed Proofreaders, founded in 2002 by Charles Franks really gave the project some oomph. Via a separate website he prompted volunteers to proofread submitted texts; by now these were mostly being OCR-scanned (optical character recognition) rather than being manually typed; and OCR left many misreads in the text.

By late 2004 this service had submitted 5,000 eBook texts to the Gutenberg project, within three years there were a further 5,000 - by then the project had amassed 34,000 books in total. This editing service was formalised as the Distributed Proofreaders Foundation in July 2006. By mid-2010 Distributed Proofreaders had submitted 18,000 eBooks.

Project Gutenburg stated at the end of 2009 that it was adding some fifty books every week. Most are in English and usually in plain text to make their application more flexible.

Each eBook is first checked against US copyright law and only when cleared is it offered copyright-free; the Project's eBooks are not allowed to be used commercially.

During 2003 the project launched a CD of the top 600 eBooks from the catalogue and in the December released a DVD of 10,000 eBooks. By July 2007 the DVD had 17,000 eBooks and in April 2010 a dual-layer DVD offered 30,000 eBooks. Some 40,000 disks had been issued by late 2010.

Floppy books

Another player in the theory and practice of eBooks emerged in 1985. The Voyager Company was founded by Bob Stein and his wife Aleen in association with Bill Becker and Jon Turell of Janus Films. It was an early pioneer in CD-ROMS, DVDs and eBooks.

Bob Stein majored in psychology and education and set up several radical bookshops and some publishing operations. Stein was a self-declared Maoist. He was employed in the early '80s by Encyclopaedia Britannica to investigate the possibilities for an electronic encyclopaedia. He was soon attracted towards CD-ROM and laserdisc technologies to achieve this.

Becoming aware of Alan Kay's work on Dynabook, Stein approached him with the material he had prepared for Britannica and on the basis of this Kay employed him at the Atari Research Group.

He studied how CD-ROMs might be used at Warner Bros, the Atari owners. As part of this effort Stein worked with children at the MIT Media Lab and was able to refine the definition of how to develop his future encyclopaedia.

In 1984 he was somewhat sidetracked when he met with RKO Home Video and realised that for just $10,000 he could acquire the rights for laserdisc for two famous movies - Citizen Kane and King Kong. This led him to create what became Criterion Collection, a published series of classic movies released on laserdisc.

In mastering the King Kong material, Stein asked the curator of films for the LA County Museum of Art to record a piece on the making of the movie. He assigned this to the second audio track on the laserdisc; this approach was to inspire the 'extras' material included with DVDs today.

King Kong was offered as a three-laserdisc set for $125. However the biggest seller was Blade Runner which achieved over 20,000 unit sales.

In 1985 the four partners founded Voyager, named for the famous space craft of the time, and they acquired the rights in the Criterion Collection business. By 1988 the operation had sales of $3m.

A similar approach was taken by the Voyager team when it acquired an early Apple CD-ROM drive and decided to create a tool to record music on to CD-ROMs. Its Companion to Beethoven's Symphony No 9 sold over

130,000 units, though 100,000 of these were purchased by Microsoft to bundle with Windows.

But Stein still routinely harked back to his earlier thoughts of producing a digital book. In 1990 a visiting friend from the National Library of Austria grabbed an early prototype Apple PowerBook that Stein had received. He typed in the first ten pages of *The Sheltering Sky* by Paul Bowles into a HyperCard stack so it could be scrolled through a page at a time.

They raised cash in the form of a loan for $480k from the Markle Foundation and a cheque from John Sculley at Apple for $500k. These funds were used to acquire the rights to the *Hitchhiker's Guide to the Galaxy*, *Jurassic Park* and *Alice in Wonderland* for release on floppy disk for the Apple Mac.

They grew this library up to 70+ titles. They also launched the Expanded Books Tool Kit allowing educators to create their own eBooks with HyperCard. But sales were not great; Jurassic Park achieved fewer than 10,000 units.

The partners had an informal relationship but in 1994 they took in a fifth player, the Georg von Holtzbrink Publishing Group. This German group had already acquired Scientific American Inc and was later to acquire Macmillan Publishing.

It paid $6.7m for a 20% share in Voyager, yet in 1995 it achieved sales of only $5m with a loss of $1.7m. Much of the injection of money had been spent on clearing past debts.

The divorce of Bob and Aleen did not improve the operation's atmosphere.

While this internal strife was being experienced the DVD was emerging and appeared to be set to overtake the CD-ROM business but the team could not agree to espouse it. The discord led to the relationship being dissolved in 1997.

At one stage during the decline Paul Allen, co-founder of Microsoft, had offered them $35m but the partners could not reach agreement.

Undaunted, Stein went on to found Night Kitchen that produced the TK3 software in 2000. This enabled individuals to produce their own multimedia books. Microsoft again came calling wanting to use TK3 as a killer-app for a tablet computer it proposed to launch; but once again Stein walked away from them.

With funds subsequently supplied by the MacArthur Foundation Stein next founded The Institute for the Future of the Book. The institute produced Sophie software to allow programmers to prepare much more complex multimedia material. This operation concentrated on the production of tools for creating electronic documents and considered how to add value to the digitisation of books and other documents.

Subsequently Stein launched Media Commons on the Internet in November 2006 as a partnership of The Institute for the Future of the Book with New York University and the US National Endowment for the Humanities.

Media Commons aimed to transform scholarly publishing, not just in the move from print to screen but with whole new approaches, mixing the text with film and so on. For example, one of its goals was to speed up the process of publishing using web-based peer reviews.

This should not to be confused with the Open Media Commons Initiative, a computer industry group largely funded by Sun Microsystems concerned with the royalty-free management of digital intellectual property.

Books on CD-ROM

The CD-ROM had inspired others to look at multimedia eBooks.

Gary Kildall of DRI founded Activenture Corporation in 1984, later renamed KnowledgeSet. It created a CD-ROM version of the *Academic American Encyclopaedia*. This had 30,000 entries and contained nine million words; it was published by Grolier Inc, a major US educational publisher.

RANDOM ACCESS MEMORY:
Gary Kildall reputedly had some problems with alcohol and it is not known if this contributed to his death when on 8th July 1994 he somehow sustained a blow to his head in a bikers' bar in Monterey. He visited hospital several times but died three days later; the autopsy said his death was due to trauma from a blunt impact to his head. He was fifty-two years old.

In 1990 photos were added and released as *The New Grolier Electronic Encyclopedia*, and multimedia was added two years later in *The New Grolier Multimedia Encyclopedia*. In 1998 the French group Hachette acquired Grolier, selling it on to Scholastic in 2000.

Tom Lopez founded the Cytation company in 1984 and produced a CD-ROM called CD-Write that used a Hypertext engine able to call up a whole stack of subdocuments. Each sub file was compiled and mark-up codes made it tough to pirate any data, which was clearly a concern for IP owners.

Cytation was acquired by Microsoft in January 1986. Lopez joined as head of the new CD-ROM division and this was the basis for its multimedia plans.

CD-Write was renamed Microsoft Bookshelf and launched in 1987. It was almost an overkill in that it contained The American Heritage Dictionary, Roget's Thesaurus, The Chicago Manual of Style, the Houghton Mifflin Spelling Verifier and Corrector, Houghton Mifflin Usage Alert, Bartlett's

Familiar Quotations, World Almanac, Business Information Sources, Forms and Letters and The US Zip Code Directory.

UK editions were supplied with several different local publications – *Chambers Dictionary*, *The Hutchinson Concise Dictionary*, *The Bloomsbury Treasury of Quotations*. Later editions added further reference works.

By 1992 an upgraded version of Bookshelf software took on a new life as the development engine Microsoft Multimedia Viewer. Microsoft used it to develop the Gandalf project.

Gandalf planned a multimedia encyclopaedia and initially Microsoft approached the Encyclopaedia Britannica but was turned down as the owners feared the impact on print sales. The project therefore purchased non-exclusive rights to the material within the *Funk & Wagnalls Encyclopedia* and the Microsoft project was renamed Encarta.

The Encarta digital multimedia encyclopaedia was launched in 1993 with around 50,000 articles, 25,000 pictures and illustrations and 300 videos and animations. Encyclopaedia Britannica's fears were realised when it fared poorly against Encarta; as a result the organisation was later sold off for less than its assumed value.

Microsoft went on to acquire *Collier's* Encyclopaedia and *New Merit Scholar's Encyclopaedia*, and inserted their content into Encarta. None of the three original sources survives in normal print.

Encarta and Bookshelf were bundled together in 1998; Bookshelf was discontinued in 2000 with any useful parts of it subsumed into Encarta.

First digital book?

But floppies and CD-ROMs did not have the vital look-and-feel of books, and other development approaches followed.

A Colombian poet and philosopher, Zahur Klemath Zapata, in the late '80s conceived of a book displayed upon a computer screen. By 1993 he had developed the software to enable the eReading of a digital book which he very logically called Digital Book v1.

He also published the first digital book, Thomas de Quincey's *On Murder Considered as one of the Fine Arts*. He followed with other public-domain books by classic authors including Kafka and Cervantes.

Later that same year Digital Book Inc offered fifty eBooks on floppy disk using its own DBF (digital book file) software. Today this organisation is owned by ZahurK Technologies Corp with offices in New York, Colombia and Pakistan.

Zapata did try to patent the Digital Book in the USA but the filing is shown as 'abandoned – failure to respond or late filing'.

BiblioBytes

Glen Haumann, an American writer, columnist, editor and publisher, was a consultant to Simon & Schuster Interactive. He assisted them in publishing CD-ROMs such as the *Star Trek Encyclopaedia* and many other Trekkie publications.

He founded Hell's Kitchen Systems Inc with L Todd Masco in 1994 and using the Linux kernel developed CCVS (credit card verification system) software. For the USA and Canada, CCVS emulated a retail swipe machine on the Internet; it was sold in 2000 to Red Hat for 400,000 shares in the Linux-sector company, then worth c$85m.

In 1993 Haumann went on to launch BiblioBytes, one of the first websites for downloadable eBooks; he contributed several eBooks of his own. This was two years before Amazon started selling physical books!

Downloading books

US Libraries was one of the innovators in terms of offering books in electronic form. In 1998 it began offering the US public the facility to consult reference books electronically via its website; this allowed access to the text but without the facility to download it.

US Libraries was early in experimenting with downloadable fiction-based eBooks from 2003. By 2010 a study showed that two-thirds of public libraries in the US were offering to lend e-books,

eBooks and ISBN

The first ISBN issued to an eBook was acquired by Kim Blagg in 1998 for what was in fact a CD-ROM multimedia publication.

She later launched Books OnScreen in time to show eBooks at the Chicago-based Books Expo America to an uninterested audience of booksellers.

The ePub format

SoftBook was one of the earliest eReaders and it originated many features used today including bookmarks, searches, hyperlinks, highlighting…

Its design also heavily influenced the Open eBook Forum when in 1999 it published its OEB (open eBook format); more completely termed the OEBPS (open eBook publication structure).

The OEBPS consisted of a series of compressed text files and its software was based around HTML to define a series of three standards for ePublishing - the OCF (open container format), OPF (open packaging format) and OPS (open publication structure).

Subsequently the International Digital Publishing Forum (IPDB) was established to manage standards as the sector moved ever forward. It moved away from HTML to XML, and this is the basis for the Mobipocket and ePub file formats.

The IDPB continues to control the ePub standard.

Early eReaders

One of the first eBook readers released was the SoftBook in 1998. It was produced by a Menlo Park operation called SoftBook Press Inc; this was founded by Tom Pomeroy and James D Sachs in 1996.

Sachs is perhaps more famous for creating the popular aquarium screen-saver SereneScreen Aquarium. He also wrote a series of games for the Commodore and Amiga platforms; but seemed to be quite an unlucky guy. One of his titles was heavily pirated; another that he was developing was lost when a virus hit his computer.

SoftPress set out to publish eBooks and contracted with a Canadian operation, The Lowe-Martin Group, to capture the book contents. IDEO and Lunar Design were commissioned to produce the reader which was named SoftBook.

The SoftBook approach was adopted by the OEBPS standard, so it is unsurprising that it was the first to meet the standard. The use of a leather case with a front cover to the device made it look and feel quite book-like; however it was not particularly light at 1.3 kilos (2.9 lbs).

A 24 cm (9.5") diagonal touch screen allowed the user to flip through HTML pages; it had a capacity of 1500 pages. There was a five-hour reading time between charges.

SoftPress had deals with major book and magazine publishers; its material was distributed down a phone line using of a 36K modem on the device; download rates were around 100 pages a minute.

It had some 1,700 publications from HarperCollins, McGraw-Hill, Newsweek, Time, Simon & Schuster, the Wall Street Journal...

In the US in March 2000 SoftBook was acquired by Gemstar-TV Guide, a company perhaps more memorable as the licensor of the bar codes used by consumer electronic and broadcasting companies to provide easy video recordings for users; this was called VCR Plus in the USA and Video Plus in the UK.

The Rocket eBook was also launched in 1998 with a 4 MByte flash memory that gave it the capacity of 4,000 pages, or approximately ten books. A Pro version was available to quadruple the capacity up to forty books.

It used a serial port to download books that were acquired online by a PC. It had an LCD touchscreen and a system called Allegra, a Palm Graffiti-like method, for recognising finger-scribbled letters on its screen. The screen was black and white, ie not grayscale.

It was much lighter at just 22 ounces (0.6kg) and claimed to have 3,000 titles downloadable from the Internet.

Its backlight and choice of fonts and font sizes (from 10 to 28 point) helped make it very flexible. It also had a battery life that allowing from 15 hours of reading with the backlight on and up to 35 hours without it.

Gemstar-TV Guide acquired the parent company, NuvoMedia Inc, in March 2000 and combined it with the SoftBook acquisition to relaunch these as the Gemstar eBook Group.

From 2000 onwards the Rocket eBook was manufactured by RCA for Gemstar and renamed the REB 1100.

A third eReader player emerged in 1998 in Europe. It was Cybook Gen1; created by Cytale in France; but it had failed as a company by 2003.

Two ex-Cytale engineers, Michael Dahan and Laurent Picard, bought the rights and redesigned and relaunched it for their own operation, called Bookeen.

The Cybook Gen1 had a 10" LCD screen with 256 colours and a battery life of 3 to 5 hours; it had 16 MBytes of Flash Memory.

Online eReading
A series of initiatives sought to preempt the portable eReaders by offering access to digitised books on the Internet that could be viewed on laptops, tablets and PDAs. Unsurprisingly these initiatives were led by those who already had a dominant Internet presence.

Amazon launched Search Inside This Book in October 2003. It offered the facility to access some 120,000 books and thus some 30+ million pages of text.

This was not a substitute for an eReader however. As it provided a picture of the page/s, these could not be downloaded or printed and the service was limited in terms of the number of pages a single user could access.

Today some 130 publishers and 250,000 books are offered with this simple feature.

In October 2004 Google launched its plans in this sector at the Frankfurt Book Fair; it was announced as Google Print. The notion was to make books more accessible by having Google provide searches from within the entire text of the publications.

However Google was proposing to offer this access free and derive benefits from advertising links. Of course publishers were nervous as their interest was not the free dissemination of books, but rather the sale of the books.

Google proposed that they would bear all the costs of scanning and, like Amazon, it would reveal only a sample of the book that came up in response to the user's search; the suggestion was that this would prompt a subsequent purchase from the publisher.

Google would link users to publishers to make the purchase more likely. To clinch the deal it would share its derived advertising revenue with the publisher. As a result many publishers did sign up.

Google Print was later renamed Google Book Search and the Google Books Partner Program was launched so publishers and authors could choose to opt in to the service.

Full text – Google Library Project

However in the background to Google Print another project was under way at Google. This would scan in the full text of books using OCR (optical character recognition).

It was formally announced in December 2004 as an extension of Google Print, named the Google Library Project.

In most cases Elphel 323 cameras were used. This could scan 1,000 pages per hour. It was a 35mm format with 11 megapixels and used a Kodak CCD (charge couple diode). Elphel was founded in 2001 and had the benefit that it operated an open software policy under a GNU (general public licence).

Google announced that it would start with some seven million books held at the University of Michigan, 40,000 books in the Harvard University Library, 12,000 from the New York Public Library, all the books held at the Stanford University Libraries and a million plus books held in the UK's Bodleian Library at Oxford.

The announcement suggested that they planned to scan some fifteen million books over just a few years. As many would still be in copyright there was a fairly speedy backlash from publishers and authors.

In September 2005 the Authors Guild launched a legal challenge and the next month the Association of American Publishers followed suit (pun intended). Other actions were to follow.

None of this legal furore appeared to stop many more libraries announcing that they would join the scheme. The University of California System decided to have its 34 million books digitised in August 2006 and the University of Virginia added its 5 million books and 17 million manuscripts in November 2006.

In September 2006 the Complutense University of Madrid was the first Spanish-language library to sign up. By March 2007 the Bavarian State Library included its one million books, and the Boekentoren Library of Ghent University added its 19th century books too.

In September 2007 yet another Google service called My Library prompted users to customise their own libraries from a store of digitised books.

Open Content Alliance and MSN Book Search
As a reaction to Google's plans, Brewster Kahle was prompted in October 2005 to found the OCA (open content alliance). This was to some extent prompted by the books that were in limbo, not yet public domain but with no clarity as to copyright. He feared that Google's initiative would seize the rights in these books.

The OCA was launched with the backing of a number of universities and Yahoo!, who of course had their own issues with Google.

It sought to create a permanent public archive of digital material. Significantly it planned to do this with the prior approval of copyright owners and with careful investigation of any in limbo in an effort to resolve their status.

Microsoft entered the market sector with an announcement in October 2005 that it would commit $5m to digitizing some 150,000 books. It announced its intention to work together with the Open Content Alliance to develop MSN Book Search, later renamed Live Book Search.

The Microsoft search engine MSN at that time had some 400+ million unique users globally each month and was operating in 41 markets with over twenty different languages.

Microsoft suggested that 50% of Internet searches did not get an adequate response and only by this effort to digitise books, magazines and journals could it satisfy this shortfall.

However it fully understood the size of the task, citing a UCB research that had calculated that books, radio and television in the USA were producing 800 MBytes of information per head of population each day.

Microsoft worked with the Internet Archive; its founder, Brewster Kahle, had high ambitions too,

'...to digitize and make available globally sourced digital collections, including multimedia content, representing the creative output of humankind.'

Their effort opted to use a Kirtas APT Book Scan 2400 Gold robotic scanner that could read and digitise some 2,400 pages every hour.

However in May 2008 Microsoft announced it would stop its digitization project, after it had impressively digitised some 750,000 books and 80 million journal articles.

Some 300,000 of these books are now a part of the Internet Archive collection. The Open Library, a project of the Internet Archive, today has over one million eBooks, almost 700,000 different works - all available to download free of charge.

Books can be obtained in an audio version using LibriVox software and Lulu.com will even supply a bound copy on demand at around $8 for a full book and $1 for a short mono book.

Pulp fiction – backlash against Google plans

By this time Google was adding 3,000 books per day and in November 2008 Google Books announced that it had reached seven million books digitised. The next month Google announced it would also be adding magazines to the service.

It took until October 2008 for a legal compromise to be reached by Google with its first two complainants; it would compensate authors and publishers in return for the right to digitise millions of books.

This included the payment of $125m to the copyright owners of books already scanned; Google agreed to meet the legal costs of the claimants too. The deal pledged 63% of all advertising and e-commerce revenues to be payable to the author and publisher.

Harvard withdrew from the Google project believing the deal to be inadequate and many others, not party to the action, have also been critical.

In France the Bibliothèque Nationale de France was even more voluble, believing this to be yet another American plan for global domination of ideas and technologies. In 2009 a French court agreed and upheld that digitising copyright books was illegal in France.

Google France was fined and had a daily penalty imposed until it removed books from its database. At the time there were around 100,000 copyrighted books in the database.

Sergey Brin pointed out that Google's objective was to preserve the world's cultural heritage, remarking that,

'The famous Library of Alexandria burned three times, in 48 BC, AD 273 and AD 640, as did the Library of Congress, where a fire in 1851 destroyed two-thirds of the collection. I hope such destruction never happens again, but history would suggest otherwise.'

Books out of copyright or in copyright with the prior author-publisher agreement were to be shown in full. Those still in copyright but without agreement offer just a limited number of pages.

From August 2006 Google began to offer PDF downloads of parts or the whole of a book.

Bookselling – Google Editions

In May 2010 Google announced the Google Editions service whereby it would sell e-books online. By December this was renamed Google eBookstore and launched with its own Android eBook Reader App. The service is compatible with Apple iOS so it can also be used with iPod, iPhone and iPad.

At launch some three million books were available for eReading and hundreds of thousands for purchase.

In August 2010 Google announced its plans to scan all known and existing books. It looked at the ISBN numbers, but these have been applied only to books since the 1960s. It calculated books with ISBN numbers and then scanned catalogues of pre-1960 listings to come to an estimate. It suggested there were 129,864,880 books.

In its announcement it stated that,

'About 20 percent of the world's books are in the public domain. About 10 to 15 percent of these books are in print. The remaining books, the vast majority of all titles, are still under copyright but out of print. Google is in the process of borrowing copies of these books in order to digitize them, from about 40 large libraries worldwide. It's this act of scanning in books that are out-of-print but still covered by copyright that has been met with some resistance by the publishing industry.'

At the time it had scanned some twelve million books and claimed it was capable of scanning all known books within a decade. This would amount to 4 billion digital pages and some two trillion words! Its search facilities among all this material could prompt new insights and juxtapose ideas in new and exciting ways.

Yet still there are those in Europe who are concerned that the vast majority of books scanned will be only available in English; this could marginalise other languages and also the works of non-English authors.

Digital rights – Adobe and Microsoft

Once it was clear that photographs, music and books were to become a digital medium, the intellectual property owners, publishers and distributors needed some form of management to protect their interests.

For example, digital watermarks were added to data, pictures, audio and video. This was done both openly and invisibly to allow the IP owner a means of tracing an illicit release back to the original user.

Back in 1991 John Warnock, co-founder of Adobe Systems, had defined what he called Camelot. This became the PDF (portable document format) which defined an open format for the exchange of documents; it delivered a standard form to all manner of original source file formats. Adobe soon became part of the process to make the content of eBooks secure.

Adobe cooperated with a number of eReader makers to develop a series of eBook and eReader applications to secure the digital rights management (DRM) for the property owner.

Adobe Content Server is used to digitally protect a PDF or ePub file so it can be safely distributed using Adobe Digital Editions. Adobe Content Server is added to the intellectual property owner's content management system. It can control the supply of an eBook as read-only, or issue a book for just a specified time, or manage a pay per transaction approach and so on…

Adobe Digital Editions uses Adobe Flash software to provide the software to then download, manage and read the protected eBooks in PDF, XHTML or ePub formats.

The system uses ADEPT (Adobe digital experience protection technology) to secure the digital rights of the intellectual property owner. For example it locks the software to no more than six machines. The system is used by the Sony Reader; a variant is used by the Nook from Barnes & Noble.

However in March 2009 a reverse engineering blog site announced it had breached the security and software began to appear on the Internet. This was Inept for the Sony, Ignoble for the Nook; a program called Digital Editions Converter converted encrypted formats into a readable PDF.

Microsoft Reader is an alternative approach to eBook DRM. It operates with .lit files and offers various levels of control. It will digitally 'engrave' the user's name into the file so if it is illicitly distributed the fact of the piracy is quite clear.

At the highest level of control the user must open Microsoft Reader to download the eBook; a Microsoft Passport account is added to the file so it can only be used on that specific PC or eReader.

When Amazon lost a legal case against the George Orwell estate it used its DRM software to remotely delete copies of *1984* and *Animal Farm* supplied prior to the legal decision. Many considered this remote deletion to be a 'Big Brother' Orwellian action!

The British Library operates a form of DRM to offer remote access to scholars and researchers wishing to study extremely rare books and manuscripts.

E-DRM (enterprise DRM) is a similar approach used to secure an organisation's proprietary Intranet, Word, CAD or PDF material.

Second generation eReaders

The early eReaders used conventional screen technology and most PDAs or tablets also had the capacity to display an eBook. It was the introduction of a specialist screen that made eReading more attractive.

E-Ink Corporation was founded in 1997 to follow up on work in developing EPDs (electrophoretic displays) at the MIT Media Lab.

Joseph Jacobson, an MIT professor in charge of the Media Lab's Molecular Machines research group, co-founded the organisation which later partnered with Philips to develop the technology.

Initially this worked only for grayscale images. The technology has very low power consumption and consists of millions of microcapsules, each the diameter of a human hair. These microcapsules contain positively-charged white capsules and negatively-charged black capsules suspended in a clear fluid.

When a charge is applied at the surface of the screen it attracts its opposite charge to create a point of white or black. The technology reinforces the image by simultaneously applying the opposite charge to the rear of the screen to attract away the other colour.

e-Ink then partnered with Amazon, Barnes & Noble, Motorola and Sony to develop a series of products. In 2005 Philips sold its interests in the technology to a Taiwan-based company Prime View International (PVI) on the basis that it was better able to pursue the search for a colour version.

In June 2009 PVI secured its position by purchasing e Ink Corporation for $215m; it was then renamed e-Ink Holdings Inc.

By July 2010 a second-generation of a higher contrast e-ink system called e-Ink Pearl Imaging was available. Using this improved system, in November 2010 the e-Ink Triton was announced with the ability to display sixteen shades of grey and thousands of colours. These displays were to have a profound effect on eReaders.

A Dutch company, a Philips spin-off called iRex Technologies announced the iLiad eReader in December 2005.

It was actually launched in July 2006 with a large e-Ink screen (124mm (4.9") x 152mm (6")) beneath which was a stylus-driven Wacom tablet so users could add notes to eBooks as they read them. It was quite expensive at €649 in Europe and $699 in the USA.

An upgraded iLiad 2nd Edition released in September 2007 was then followed in May 2008 by the iLiad Book Edition that stripped off some of the 2nd Edition features to get the price down to €499/$599.

The subsequent Book Edition included fifty free classic books including those by authors Lewis Carroll, Charles Dickens, Leo Tolstoy and Jules Verne.

However iLiad failed to meet the FCC regulations and was withdrawn in the United States. By June 2010 the company had filed for bankruptcy.

Tianjin Jinke Electronics Co Ltd, a Chinese company, was founded in 1985 as a joint venture between the Nankai University and the Hong Kong Proud Growth Group. It had a high staff count of graduates, 20% with a master's or doctorate.

With the shortened name of Jinke Electronics it developed a series of Hanlin eReaders. The Hanlin eReader V2 was also branded as Readman and launched in April 2006 with a 152mm (or 6") diagonal e-Ink display.

The broad range included the Hamlin eReader V3; its V5 with a number of languages retailing at just $169; the V3+ at $199; the A9 with a 9" display at $349; the A6; the V60 with a 6" display at just $249.

Endless Ideas BV launched its brand of BeBook eReaders using Hanlin products. BeBook boasted that it supported over twenty file formats and that it had a 7,000 page-turning battery life.

The BeBook Club sells at €189 with support for PDF and ePub, with or without Adobe DRM, and an array of text, photo and music formats.

Its BeBook Neo at €269 is supported by the Neo eBook portal enabling users by Wi-Fi to click on a map of the world, show their location and receive a list of local eBook sources. It has a Wacom touch panel for notes and annotations.

Sony entered the eBook market in October 2006 with the Sony Reader, initially only able to read in the ePub format. It too used an e-Ink display with an 8-level grayscale to be used in portrait or landscape mode.

The Sony eBook Library, originally named Sony Connect, offers eBooks, music and images for use with the eReader. The material works with the Adobe DRM software and will handle PDFs, JPEGs, RSS feeds and ePub, plus the Sony proprietary BBeB (broadband eBook) format.

A series of nine eReaders have been released to date.

The first of these was the PRS-500 (portable reader system) supplied exclusively through Borders bookstores in the USA during 2006. By April 2007 other multiple retailers were added to its distribution.

On 3 September 2008 the PRS-505 reader was released in the UK through a special relationship with Waterstones bookstores, and via Argos, Dixons, John Lewis and Sony Centres.

By the end of 2008 Sony had sold over 300,000 Sony Readers. With its early readers Sony used a proprietary DRM system to control issue of the eBooks.

In August 2009 Sony released the Pocket Edition PRS-300 at $150 and the Touch Edition PRS-600 at $170. The Touch allowed users to highlight and underline text. The 600 had casings available in three colours, more font options and a jack for audio. These editions used ePub files and the DRM was not included.

Twenty days later Sony launched the Daily Edition PRS-900 as a direct competitor to the Kindle DX. The PRS-900 also introduced 16-level grayscale and a 3G wireless system allowing books to be acquired without the use of a computer.

In September 2010 the upgraded PRS-350 and PRS-650 had 16-level grayscale and were launched in to Australasia.

The Sony LIBRIé EBR-1000EP is another eBook reader, launched for the Japanese market using Japanese language and BBeB format. The BBeB content is provided by a number of Japanese publishers via the Publishing Link service; this delivers the eBook with a 60-day time-bomb so it becomes unreadable after those days have elapsed.

Bookeen upgraded its inherited system to a 6" e-Ink screen in October 2007 and launched it as the Cybook Gen3. It had 16 or 32 MByte of memory and intriguingly expressed its battery life as 8,000 page flips.

Cybook Opus followed in 2009; it was a much smaller and lighter device with 1 GByte of memory. The 5" screen had only four shades of grey but supported twelve font sizes and twenty-three languages.

Amazon Kindle

Amazon's Kindle 1 eReader was launched on 19 November 2007 in the USA. It used Linux software and the US-only Sprint network to download e-books, magazines, newspapers and blogs; it developed a whole new market in eBooks.

It had a 6-inch diagonal screen, 91mm (3.6") x 122mm (4.8") to display 600 x 800 pixels on what was termed 'e-ink electronic paper', offering four shades of grey. It had the capacity to hold 200 books, without illustrations, in its 250 MByte memory. It had a strange split keyboard with QWERTY keys placed at various angles branching away from the gap in the middle.

88,000 books were offered at the Kindle 1 launch. Initially 65% of revenues went to Amazon with the remaining 35% split between author and publisher.

The eBooks were supplied either as unprotected files such as MOBI (Mobipocket), TXT (simple text files) or TPZ (topaz format) or as files encoded in the Amazon Kindle proprietary format, AZW. Other formats (BMP, GIF, HTML, JPG, PNG, Word...) could be submitted to Amazon by email for preparation to the AZW format for the user.

Users were able to look-up items, highlight them, make notes and bookmark them. The Kindle retained a record of the last page read so on return the user could quickly and simply carry on reading.

Kindle 2 was released in February 2009 with many improvements including a screen presenting sixteen shades of grey and a 2 GByte memory; 1.4 GB available to the user. Amazon negotiated for Stephen King to distribute his new novella *Ur* exclusively via the Kindle Store. Kindle 2 had an upgrade that allowed PDF files to be used too.

The 3G mobile network standard was introduced on a new international version. It added a higher contrast screen and superseded the US Kindle 2 from October 2009; it was launched in one hundred countries.

Wi-Fi was still available as an option but Amazon's own Whispernet became an option via the 3G mobile circuits. This product added a service to synchronise the user's e-Reading across different readers.

In June 2009 the Kindle DX was the first eReader launched with e-Ink Pearl Imaging technology, and the larger screen was promoted as better for reading newspapers and magazines.

By July 2010 Amazon announced that sales of eBooks on Kindle had exceeded its sales of hardcover printed books; 140 eBooks for every hundred hardbacks. But paperbacks still dominated with the American Publishing Association giving eBooks' overall market share at just over 8% at that time.

Kindle 3 became the fastest selling model when it was released in August 2010 in a slightly smaller case, with keener pricing and 4 GByte total memory - 3 GB available to the user. This also had the e-Ink Pearl Imaging technology screen. The Wi-Fi only version was priced at just $139 in the USA, £109 in the UK. The 3G/Wi-Fi version was $189/£149. This also came in two different colour schemes for the casing.

Some 650,000 eBooks were available at the time of the Kindle 3 launch. Early chapters were offered free of charge as a promotional tool, with a best-seller available made available in the USA at just $11. Subscription arrangements for magazines and newspapers were offered too.

As soon as Apple launched its iPad, Amazon had to change its profit-sharing model to match that of Apple Apps Store where some 70% of the revenue goes to the author/publisher.

A Kindle for PC software application was released late in 2009 as a free download working within Windows XP, 7 and Vista. An Apple Mac version followed early in 2010 and there was a Kindle for Android version in June that year. There were also versions for Blackberry, iPhone and iPad.

Amazon operated its Digital Text Platform prompting authors to self-publish and price their material from 99 cents upwards per download. A percentage share of net revenue, after any Amazon discounts, was then paid to the author.

Stieg Larsson was the first author, albeit posthumously, to sell a million books on Kindle and he was joined in the Kindle Million Club in October 2010 when James Patterson (Alex Cross, Women's Murder Club…) became the second author to reach a million Kindle eBook sales.

Even more eBooks
ECTACO (East-Coast Trading American Company Incorporated) was founded in New York by Russian-born David Lubaynitsky in 1989.

It started as a reseller of electronic dictionaries but moved into manufacturing its own products for Russian-English and Polish-English...

In October 2008 it launched the jetBook using Linux software with a 13 cm diagonal (5") screen and a 16 greyscale capability.

In January 2010 it upgraded this with the ECTACO jetBook Lite. Bizarrely it came preloaded with both the *Bible* and the *CIA World Factbook*.

In September 2010 the ECTACO jetBook mini was launched with a price point of just $99.

The US multiple bookshop retailer Barnes & Noble introduced the Nook in November 2009. It was based on the Android OS and used an e-Ink display.

The full-blown Nook offered Wi-Fi and 3G at $259 but this was quickly reduced to $199; a Wi-Fi only version was available at $149. Delays in delivery led to a $100 gift voucher being issued to those who failed to receive their Nook in time for Christmas.

A year later in November 2010 a colour Nook was released with an LCD screen. Some reports suggested that Nook sales exceeded those of the Kindle at launch.

The Canadian Kobo eReader was launched in July 2010.

Kobo Inc is 58% owned by Indigo Music Books & Music, the Canadian multiple retailer. It sold the Kobo locally for CAD$149 or in Australia at A$199 and delivered it with a hundred public-domain classic books. It had the capacity to hold 10,000 books.

Initially it worked only via a Blackberry, but Wi-Fi and 3G versions were added in October 2010.

Apple iPad
Apple learned a hard lesson back in 1993 when it launched the Newton, a tablet computer-cum-PDA. It had limited success and was discontinued by 1998.

But the launch of the iPod in 2001 and then the iPhone in 2007 brought Apple securely back into the mobile computing sector.

It has been said that the iPad was in fact defined and ready before the iPhone but Apple chose to hold back its launch until April 2010 in the USA and late May in Australia, Canada, Japan, the UK and the other major European markets.

What a launch! 300,000 units were purchased on the first day and a million units sold in half the time that the iPhone had taken to achieve the same figure. Over three million iPads were sold within three months of launch, capturing a 95% share of the tablet market. Some 7.5 million of the Chinese-built iPads were sold within six months.

The iPad proved very stable; it used the Apple iOS operating system refined by use with the iPod Touch and iPhone. Its 25cms display (9.7"), half-inch depth (13mm) and low weight of 680 grams (1.5 lbs) added much to its allure.

iPad had two formats, Wi-Fi-only to download books and other material from the Internet via the iTunes Store and Apps Store, and a 3G/Wi-Fi version working additionally across GSM mobile circuits. It was supplied with 16, 32 or 64 GByte flash memory. The iTunes software allowed the iPad to be synched with another device.

One downloadable app at launch was iBook which displayed ePub files; HarperCollins, Macmillan, Penguin Books and Simon & Schuster were on board at launch. The iPad's hardware sales success soon had other book publishers plus magazine and newspaper publishers supporting the platform.

This was unsurprising in that Apple offered 70% of the revenue to the IP owner, compared with 30% from Amazon's Kindle for example; but Kindle promptly changed to offer its IP owners 70% a week before the iPad launch!

The multi-touch touchscreen allowed rapid searching, expanding and shrinking of screen images. It had a light sensor to adjust screen brightness to match the ambient light. Its 3-axis accelerometer sensed its real-world orientation and switched the image between portrait and landscape views as appropriate.

The iPad Wi-Fi could triangulate using Wi-Fi to give the user a current global location which assists with the use of software like Google Maps. The 3G version of course obtained its location awareness from 3G's GPS service.

The iPad used Digital Rights Management software to restrict the use of software apps and other downloadable material to the platform. It could delete or disable material remotely. This led to the suggestion that this might stifle software development for it, but little sign of that so far!

iPad was also criticised as seeking to create an enclosed community away from the Internet where IP owners could control usage and access more profitably. Others saw a more secure environment as a benefit.

While some questioned whether it was actually a PC, most saw it as entering the market between PDAs, smartphones and laptops; many viewing it as a 'lite' replacement for the laptop.

24 - Dub dub dub

'Anyone who has lost track of time when using a computer knows the propensity to dream, the urge to make dreams come true and the tendency to miss lunch.' Tim Berners-Lee

Early search engines

A huge amount of information was accumulating and accessible via the various computer networks, but users needed to find a simple means of reviewing it and searching it an organised manner.

A number of people and services sought to catalogue the Internet content. However they soon found it was growing to be so large, and at such a rate, that this proved to be an impossible dream.

Archie, the first search engine was released in 1990. It was software that indexed FTP services from around the various networks that were springing up.

Alan Emtage from Barbados had been the proud owner of a Sinclair ZX81 and won a scholarship to McGill University in Montreal Canada for a course in computer science.

He became involved in managing the university's computers and ended up in control of the first eastern Canada Internet link too. He was frustrated by the amount of time it took him searching for free software and he wrote a small UNIX routine that each night would call up any interesting ftp sites he had discovered and list all their contents.

This was far from the end of the matter. Of course not all file names were meaningful back then so poring over his captured lists was still time-consuming. The manager of the university team was Peter J Deutsch (not the L Peter Deutsch we met at MIT, TMRC, Xerox PARC, Sun...), who seeing a query on a newsgroup about accessing information, mentioned Emtage's Archie routine; this led to many requests for more information.

Emtage decided to solve the issue by making the software available to all; this involved him working with Bill Helan to develop something reliable enough to be released. It was named Archie from the word Archive but without the 'v'.

A server was provided by Deutsch and the software was issued to enquirers; the subsequent volume of traffic took them completely by surprise; it soon exhausted the total bandwidth of eastern Canada.

But that was not the only problem. Inadvertently they had brushed up against the copyright of the comic character Archie, and this caused them grief too.

Far to the west in December 1994 at the University of Washington Clifford Neuman ambitiously set out to catalogue the whole Internet. His approach was planned to make it look to the user as if it everything he could find was resident on the local computer.

He called his software Prospero; it was a directory that would index what was found and allocate attributes to the file names. But to succeed he needed to arrange that the Prospero Directory Service was resident on all the host computers - a big ask.

Neuman was aware of Archie and realised that its method of gathering indexes of files and directories perhaps offered him a two-step approach to create his own catalogue.

Not everyone was quite so altruistic. Some sought ways of making money from the new capabilities presented by the Internet. Back on the East Coast Brewster Kahle was inspired by the way in which Minitel and Prestel had been able to charge for access.

He graduated from MIT where he had studied under Marvin Minsky in artificial intelligence.

Working at Thinking Machines, a supercomputer company, Kahle was the manager of the project that in 1992 created WAIS (wide area information servers) based on its parallel computers. The project was managed by Thinking Machines but also involved Apple, Dow Jones and KPMG Peat Marwick.

WAIS was developed for Windows, Mac, NeXT and UNIX. Thinking Machines then created the Directory of Servers, a central service. Whenever a new WAIS was established the software generated metadata that would describe the content of the site and to assist other users this was filed at the central directory.

Ross Perot used WAIS in the 1992 presidential campaign to link all his field offices. WAIS was eventually acquired by AOL in 1995 for $15m. Kahle went on to found a number of operations, including Alexa Internet, the Internet Archive and the Open Content Alliance.

CWIS and Gopher

Yet another approach was initially free and became chargeable later. The original aim was to create a CWIS (campus-wide information system) which had become a well-publicised ambition for many US universities in the early 1990s.

A large committee was formed to pursue the goal for the Michigan University CWIS. This included Bob Alberti, Farhad Anklesaria, Adam Huminsky, Paul Lindner, Mark McCahill, Daniel Torrey and others; but it experienced the problems of all committees with its over-complicated brief and constantly changing requirements.

Anklesaria, from India, had worked with McCahill on producing the Popmail program and they set about using this as their approach. Popmail was a user-friendly UNIX mailer for Macs. They worked outside the committee to develop the new protocol for PC, Mac and UNIX. This was a TCP/IP layer protocol to distribute, full-text search and receive documents across the Internet.

It was called Gopher, a name drawn from the university mascot, the golden gopher, and of course the implication of 'go-for'. It worked with FTP sites, Usenet, Archie and WAIS.

At the University of Nevada in 1992, Steven Foster and Fred Barrie subsequently developed a search engine for the Gopher protocol which they called Veronica - described as meaning 'very easy rodent-oriented net-wide index to computer archives', but also apparently a sideswipe reference to Veronica Lodge from the Archie comics.

Gopher was so simple to set up and use that it became the basis of many a CWIS. It was written up as RFC #1436 in 1993 and grew in nine months from under 500 gopher servers to almost 5,000.

But in 1993 the university managed to snatch success from the jaws of victory by deciding to charge a licence fee. As a result users sought and found alternatives in their droves. As the World Wide Web started to take off, Gopher was digging itself a very large hole.

Gopher does live on within a number of modern search engines including Mozilla Firefox.

CERN

CERN is a government-funded European operation located on the French-Swiss border; it stands for the *Conseil Européen pour la Recherche Nucléaire*, the European Organisation for Nuclear Research.

It was an assembly of many nationalities, each with differing hopes and aspirations and each country bringing its own preferred computer processes and suppliers. It was something of a modern Tower of Babel, seeking to get closer to the creator by understanding the minutiae of matter – some spark just had to fly out of there!

Initially it operated the Super Proton Synchrotron (SPS), a cyclotron used to accelerate and crash matter together and see what might fly off. It was used initially to search for bozon particles and it was theorised that eventually it would manage to experimentally show other particles called quarks; this was achieved in the year 2000. The software company Quark was formed in 1981, well before CERN managed to exhibit them experimentally.

By the end of the noughties the SPS had become just a sideshow to the Large Hadron Collider that continued to crunch matter ever smaller in the search for knowledge.

In the 1970s CERN used a computer system they called Index. It connected hundreds of dumb terminals using RS232 connections. By 1976 this was upgraded to CERNET, created to facilitate a much faster exchange of large files. CERNET was similar in approach to the USA's ARPANET system but it was developed independently and thus it had no compatibility with it. Eventually it was to be superseded and stifled by its 'rival'.

Various computer networks and processes were tested and evolved at CERN throughout the 1970s. CERN also became a centre for 'grid computing', the technique of using many computers to share resources and tackle a common task.

Nuclear research at CERN had started just as mainframe computing was taking off in 1954. Down the years it developed a complete mishmash of computers and systems, each applied to the very different and highly specialised requirements of the many research groups working at CERN.

Tim Berners-Lee joined CERN and after some early exercises he wrote a proposal to create an improved information system for the research facility. This would change the world.

Berners-Lee was a Londoner whose parents were mathematicians who met while working on the Ferranti Mark 1, an early computer that promoted itself thus,

'In a day it could do more arithmetic than the average man could do in many years ... and will make fewer mistakes.'

Berners-Lee had graduated in physics at Oxford and had a strong interest in electronics; he even designed and built his own PC from components. After qualification he took jobs with Plessey and a printer manufacturer, both located on the UK's south coast.

Berners-Lee first worked as an independent contractor at CERN for six months in 1980. At that time he developed a point-and-click approach allowing users of a video console to call up specific areas of a schematic.

He also sought a way to organise often diverse thoughts and connections while he was programming into a brain-like, rather than computer-like, approach. In doing so he inevitably studied hypertext.

For CERN's Norsk Data computers he proposed a hypertext-based facility to allow sharing and collaborative updating of information between the CERN researchers using its many computers. He developed a prototype of this software project named Enquire, after the reference book *Enquire Within*.

It was written in Pascal using a database that was accessed using hypertext. He built this upon Ted Nelson's work in Project Xanadu to define hypertext and Doug Engelbart's innovations with the NLS system. It was not written for general use.

Returning to the south coast of England he joined John Poole who had founded Image Computer Systems Ltd, a company focusing on label printing and bar code reader systems. But he soon applied to return to CERN.

Initially CERN offered him the role of developing databases for the civil engineering project that was underway to build its bigger collider, but he managed to convince it to give him a role in the Online Computing Group.

He became involved in distributed computing and was drawn to the idea of remote procedure call (RPC), a means of distributing a program across several PCs. He saw this as a way to link the many stand-alone computers in use at CERN. This was adopted as a standard approach.

CERN was one of the biggest Internet nodes in Europe when Berners-Lee was considering adding his hypertext Enquire notion to the Internet's TCP and domain name approach. But he soon realised that Enquire could not be expanded to achieve what he now had in mind.

Robert Cailliau, a Belgian, was working independently on computer applications that could be used by CERN administrators and secretaries who were not computer literate. Using Apple's HyperCard he developed something not dissimilar to that which Microsoft PowerPoint would later offer. It allowed presentations to be simply prepared and displayed.

He presented his thinking to Mike Sendall who, being fully aware of Berners-Lee's project, arranged for the two of them to get together to take a joint project forward.

World Wide Web

In 1989 Berners-Lee and Cailliau jointly published an internal paper entitled *Information Management: A Proposal*; this paper first introduced the term for their concept of the 'World Wide Web'.

Mike Sendall, was impressed by the thinking but somewhat confused and described the paper as,

'Vague but exciting...'

With this doubtful accolade ringing in his ears Berners-Lee set about developing it on a NeXT workstation that had been purchased for him at CERN. It was the object-oriented programming system of the NeXT that attracted his attention; he saw its object library as invaluable for developing his ideas.

This was all happening as the Large Hadron Collider project was getting underway; it was clear that the exploding matter that would be flying around inside the Collider needed something that would control the mass of information that would be flying around the site.

Berners-Lee developed a server and a browser; the Nexus browser was written for use with the NeXTSTEP OS. It had an edge on most browsers that followed, in that it was capable of writing web pages as well as reading them.

This was due to the editable text object routine in the NeXT software. This read-and-write was something that subsequent browsers left out!

In the 1960s IBM developed its GML (generalised markup language) that used macros and tags to define a document's elements, such as establishing the page set up, line spacing, font and so on and whether the item was a paragraph, a header, a list, a table... GML was also claimed by some to come from the surnames of the team that created it - Goldfarb, Mosher and Lorie.

GML was influential in the eventual industry standard SGML (standard generalised markup language) in 1986 and in the much later streamlined version XML (extensible markup language).

Berners-Lee simply took a version of SGML in use at CERN for the basis of his development of HTML (hypertext markup language) which he saw merely as an application of SGML.

Berners-Lee and Cailliau took their developments and presented them as the *World Wide Web: Proposal for Hyper Text Project* in 1990,

'... *describes in more detail a Hypertext project. HyperText is a way to link and access information of various kinds as a web of nodes in which the user can browse at will. It provides a single user-interface to large classes of information (reports, notes, data-bases, computer documentation and on-line help). We propose a simple scheme incorporating servers already available at CERN.*'

The report was forward-thinking too,

'*Future developments which would further enhance the project could include:*

Daemon programs which run overnight and build indexes of available information.

A server automatically providing a hypertext view of a ... database, from a description of the database and a description ... of the view required.

Work on efficient networking over wide areas, negotiation with other sites to provide compatible online information.'

Daemons have nothing to do with demons; they are routines that run in the background of an application. In Greek mythology daemons did the bidding of the gods, a little like guardian angels.

In 1867 James Clerk Maxwell postulated a similar imaginary being that sorted molecules to formulate his second law of thermodynamics function. Modern usage originated at MIT with Project MAC and subsequently BSD UNIX created its own BSD daemon known as Beastie. Most of us encounter one most frequently with a bounced email message; the automated daemon alerts us of the bounce.

From January 1991 Berners-Lee's browser was available on the CERN site and users with FTP software could download the code to their own systems. But of course it was a NeXT-based browser and had limited potential users. However this is usually cited as the time when the World Wide Web went public.

On 6 August 1991, Berners-Lee published outline details of the World Wide Web project on the alt.hypertext newsgroup - the public announcement of the Web as a service on the Internet,

'The World Wide Web (WWW) project aims to allow all links to be made to any information anywhere. ... The WWW project was started to allow high energy physicists to share data, news, and documentation. We are very interested in spreading the web to other areas, and having gateway servers for other data. Collaborators welcome!'

www.info.cern.ch was also opened on that date as the world's first-ever website. It ran on a NeXT computer and its major purpose was to describe the World Wide Web and advise how users might develop their own websites. It also included a CERN telephone directory for the site.

The web spreads
One of the first to adopt the approach was Paul Kunz of the Stanford Linear Accelerator Center who during a visit to CERN sent the NeXT software to his NeXT computer and watched with interest as he were able to request and display material from his remote California-based computer.

Kunz and his team were using an IBM computer for an intriguing application. Whenever a scientist published a paper, any journal required a review by his peers and this often delayed publication. It had become the practice for scientists to pre-publish papers as 'preprints' so colleagues and peers could have early access, with the proviso of course that reviews were still pending.

In the early '80s managing these preprints at Stanford had become something of a nightmare with a hundred new preprints received every week. Stanford had handled this from the '70s with the SPIRES database (Stanford public information retrieval system) but this was showing signs of strain.

Kunz saw the CERN approach as a solution to providing rapid access to these preprints. He and his team ported the WWW software to an IBM and in December 1991 launched the first US web server at www.slavcm.slac.stanford.edu

Berners-Lee and Cailliau wanted to use this timely new US facility at the ACM's Hypertext 91 Conference held in mid-December 1991 in San Antonio Texas. But the conference committee rejected their paper; they were however allowed to demonstrate the WWW at the event.

Published in 1993, Berners-Lee's definition of HTML would become the lingua franca of the World Wide Web, defining the text and image formatting of web pages. It initially had twenty elements; thirteen of these are still in use and unchanged.

In 1994 Berners-Lee went on to establish the W3C World Wide Web Consortium at MIT. Its purpose was to create standards and improve the quality of the Web. Most importantly, any standards produced by W3C were to be released royalty-free.

Also in 1994 an HTML working group was formed to maintain standards; this group published HTML 2.0 in 1995 as RFC #1866. From 1996 onwards the views of the W3C and of commercial software vendors was also included in the group's deliberations.

Early information providers

Remote access to information was not just a feature of the Internet and the World Wide Web. It had previously been attempted through a number of technologies.

One of these was videotext. The European Prestel and Minitel services had offered this and there were several US services too.

The Dow Jones News/Retrieval financial information service was videotext-based and launched back in 1973. It offered a fully indexed quotation service on stocks and bonds, punctuated by new, sports, electronic shopping and email.

It cost $30 to join, $12 per annum thereafter and usage was $2.30 per minute at peak times and 44 cents off-peak; though some information carried a premium. It achieved a peak of just over 300,000 subscribers, before the market moved towards the Internet.

Another early player was The Source, from Source Telecomputing Corporation. This was founded by Bill von Meister and Jack R Taub in 1978. The original notion was to use a subcarrier frequency within FM radio broadcasts to send and receive emails; similar to the Paul Baran idea at RAND. But they changed their approach and launched a videotext service instead, describing it thus,

'It's not hardware. It's not software. But it can take your personal computer anywhere in the world.'

The Source was announced at the summer Comdex in 1979 and the next month there was a high profile launch in New York with sci-fi author Isaac Asimov as the guest of honour. Asimov hailed it as,

'the start of the information age.'

It offered text-based news, information, stock quotations, airline schedules, email and newsgroups.

The Source achieved at its peak some 80,000 users for its $100 subscription and $2.75/hour off-peak access. It soon ran in to debt; *Reader's Digest* bought an 80% control but this added to the overhead, making the break-even point recede further.

CompuServe was founded in 1969 as a subsidiary of Golden United Life Insurance; its task was to develop internal computer support for the organisation but also to develop a time-share business around its PDP-10.

John R Goltz and Jeffrey Wilkins, son-in-law to the insurance company founder, ran the business. It acquired a NASDAQ listing in 1975 and was sold to H & R Block in 1980. CompuServe went on to develop its own packet-switching service based on a network of PDP-11s.

It evolved some interesting commercial applications that collected and presented financial data from a plethora of sources and included a price quotation service. These were used by most US Wall Street investment banks and the company also sold network services into major corporations.

But it was its consumer business that is of most interest. It expanded by selling access to the service during evenings and this rapidly made up 50% of its business by 1979. By 1989 it was able to buy The Source, its main competitor - and junk it.

In 1981 CompuServe added the facility for users to transfer files; in 1982 it created the CompuServe Networks Services department. This sold connection services; for example it gained a major deal with the Visa credit card company for online authorisations.

Back in the consumer team, Sandy Trevor came up with what he called the CB Simulator to emulate citizen band chatter. This developed the notion of chat forums which soon proved extremely popular. Each forum had a distinct subject area and was run by a 'sysop', an independent mediator who received payment based upon the success of the forum's activity levels.

Given this history CompuServe was particularly well placed to meet the Internet and was one of the first online services to offer interconnections with the Net in 1989; its broad range of forums was one of the hits of the early Internet. PC companies also used them for customer support and this brought even more users to the CompuServe 'party'.

By 1992 it was the first to introduce a full graphic service on the Net. Its growth allowed it to drop its hourly rates from $10 to just $1.95. By spring 1995 it had three million users, each using a Mosaic-cloned browser for access through to the WWW.

But as the WWW grew more popular many companies using CompuServe as the medium to communicate their aims and support services were to leave the service as they gained the confidence to set up their own websites.

GEnie and Prodigy

The General Electric Network for Information Exchange (GEnie) was a somewhat late arrival launching only in 1985.

Bill Louden was the product manager for CompuServe's forums before he left to found GEnie which was backed by GE's network of electronic services.

The aim was for GE's computers to be used at off-peak times. It initially charged $5 per off-peak hour and $36 at peak times.

It was launched with a similar line-up of text-only services. Its forums were called RoundTables that provided a bulletin board, a chat room and a library archive service.

But Louden also gave the service a particular focus for online games and had MegaWars (based on DECWAR) as a multi-player game for the service.

GEnie did build up a 350,000 user base, but GE only wanted it to use up spare off-peak capacity and was not interested in growing it beyond that goal. When Prodigy and other online services introduced graphics, it failed to match them. It was also rather late in interconnecting with the Internet.

GE sold GEnie to an organisation with plans to turn it in to an ISP (internet service provider) with a GUI but by 1999 it closed, citing Y2K problems.

Prodigy started out as a videotext service in the 1980s when AT&T and CBS formed Venture One. The operation carried out market tests of news, weather, sports and shopping services that led to the involvement of IBM and Sears Roebuck in launching Prodigy in 1984. It was managed by Theodore Papes, a long-term IBM employee.

The expansion of Prodigy followed the IBM expansion of its Systems Network Architecture (SNA) and rolled out region by region. It created a network of local telephone numbers and charged a low flat rate monthly subscription for limited access, relying on advertising and online shopping for its revenues. Supported by J Walter Thompson it launched a high-profile campaign in 1990 and rapidly attracted a million users.

It developed online communities with tailored content for different interest groups and was the first with what could be described as a GUI while CompuServe and GEnie were still text-based. However its NAPLPS (North American presentation level protocol syntax) graphics were not able to show product images.

Perversely the user paid a premium for online shopping rather than getting a discount, but for this they would have ready access to better information.

The email and message boards took an unexpectedly high percentage of the access time and Prodigy responded to this by raising the price for both. The flat fee allowed just thirty email messages a month with a 10 cent charge per message thereafter; an hourly rate was introduced for the message board.

To counter what might have been an early demise, in 1994 Prodigy linked to the WWW and over the next few years transformed itself into a full ISP. It also offered a connection to USENET, introduced a news and information service called Astranet and market-trialled an ISP service; in 1996 it was ready with Prodigy Internet.

The business was sold for $200m in 1996, though it is suggested that IBM and Sears had expended over $1bn on its creation and management. In late 1999 it closed down its original videotext service which still had some 200,000+ users.

Prodigy entered a strategic arrangement with SBC Communications and promoted its broadband services from 1999. SBC progressively bought Prodigy, getting control for $465m. Prodigy was by then the fourth largest ISP (behind AOL, MSN and EarthLink) with over 3 million subscribers, of these 1.3 million also had broadband.

Completing an intriguing circular path, SBC bought AT&T in 2006.

Browsers

The first browser was developed on a NeXT computer at CERN by Tim Berners-Lee over Christmas 1990. It was released in March 1991 and spread through the research physics community. He called it the World Wide Web.

During 1991 and 1992, Jean-Francois Groff and Berners-Lee ported the browser to the 'C' language which gave it more currency. Groff went on to launch InfoDesign.ch, one of the first web design companies.

Nicola Pellow, an intern at CERN, developed a browser able to work line-by-line on devices such as teletype terminals. In 1991 this version was ported to DOS and to UNIX.

A host of browsers followed, though most achieved a limited circulation.

At the Stanford Linear Accelerator Center, Tony Johnson created Midas which was written in UNIX. His intention was largely to distribute his research to colleagues.

Robert Cailliau created Samba, the first browser for the Apple Macintosh. Nicola Pellow assisted in this effort and it was launched in 1992.

In 1993 the Arena browser was developed in Bristol UK by Dave Raggett who was based at Hewlett-Packard. It added new graphic facilities and tables for positioning text and images.

Lynx was a service developed by the University of Kansas for internal distribution of information. Lou Montulli, a student at the university, created an interface for Lynx to the Internet in 1993. It was popular where graphics were not required.

O'Reilly & Associates collated all the necessary software and launched 'Internet in a Box' in January 1994. This user-friendly approach made the Internet more approachable for the less-informed user.

In February 1994 Navisoft released Navipress for the PC and Mac. It included an editor, as had Berners-Lee's World Wide Web browser, but this was not the case with subsequent browsers. Navipress later became

AOLPress but it was not upgraded to include html updates and had fallen out of service by 2000.

CERN was quick to realise that internally it could not handle all that was required for the WWW and so was keen to find others to develop the required approaches for the service to take off.

The first new browser came from a group of Finnish students at the Helsinki University of Technology. The early Norwegian ARPANET node in 1973 gave Scandinavian computer scientists an early role in networking.

The Finns had developed an early network called 'funet' (Finnish university and research network) and of course Linus Torvalds later developed the Linux operating system.

Robert Cailliau visited the students and prompted them to design a web browser as a final year project; they formed a programme working group, called OHT.

The team - Kim Nyberg, Teemu Rantanen, Kati Suominen and Kari Sydänmaanlakka - came up with the Erwise browser in April 1992. The name came from the word 'otherwise' minus the letters in their group name – OHT.

Erwise was written in UNIX and thus had broad appeal. However when the developers graduated, the project simply halted, despite Berners-Lee visiting and encouraging them to continue.

Music to our eyes – Viola, Cello and Opera

Pei-Yuan Wei, a student at the University of California, Berkeley, met graphic software through Apple's HyperCard. He was working with an X-Window system with UNIX and TCP/IP built in, so it was perhaps inevitable that he would apply his interest to the WWW.

He ported HyperCard to his X-Window system and from this developed an early version of Viola 0.8 in 1991. After qualification he found work at the Berkeley Experimental Computing Facility and was able to continue his work.

He was a recipient of Tim Berners-Lee's 'collaborators welcome' email and replied that he would look at developing a browser. This received enthusiastic and positive feedback from Berners-Lee.

Four days later Wei announced ViolaWWW which then evolved through 1992. It had a bookmark feature, could navigate back and forward through pages and maintained a history of those visited. By 1993 it had tables and graphics.

Viola stood for visually interactive object-oriented language and applications. The software was very fast but it was limited to X-Window and therefore soon surpassed.

Pei-Yuan Wei routinely enhanced the browser with features including a graphical network traffic monitor, chat applications and so on. These mini applications were shown to Sun Microsystems and became part of the inspiration for the Java language launched by Sun several years later. Developed by James Gosling, Patrick Naughton and Mike Sheridan, this was launched in June 1991.

Lawyers in the USA were mainly using Microsoft Windows for their legal work and when services for lawyers appeared on the Internet and World Wide Web it was none too helpful that most web browsers were using UNIX.

The Legal Information Institute at Cornell Law School created the first website for lawyers in 1992 and, to be assured of traffic, developed the very first browser for Windows. Tom Bruce the co-founder of the institute wrote it and named it Cello.

It was not particularly satisfactory with relatively poor graphics, but then lawyers tended not to need graphics. It delivered a dubious presentation of web pages and documents, and was not very stable. Yet on its launch in 1993 some 500 copies per day were downloaded and it grew a user base approaching 200,000.

Its basic failings and the lack of upgrades and support, worsened by the changes inherent in Windows 95 and the advent of new browsers, effectively meant Cello played out of tune and fell by the wayside.

In 1994 a team led by Telenor, the Norwegian telecommunications company, started work on the Opera browser. It seems sensible to assume that the use of musical terms like viola, cello and opera were sequential inspirations.

Jon Stephenson von Tetzchner and Geir Ivarsøy left Telenor to form Opera Software ASA in 1995. They launched Opera v2.0 in 1996 to work with Windows PCs.

This browser really took off when version 4.0 was released in 2000, designed to work with mobile devices. Later that year the V 5.0 moved the browser from being a trial product which users could try and buy after a time period to being free; the cost was supported by advertising. By 2006 a version to work with Nintendo DS and Wii games was available.

Opera V10 released in 2009 recorded 10 million downloads in its first week, but by 2010 Opera was rated as having a worldwide browser share of only 2.4%. But this statistic somewhat concealed its 43% share in the Ukraine, 36% share in Russia and circa 10% shares of the Czech, Latvian, Lithuanian and Polish markets.

Opera technology is also included within a number of elements of the Adobe Creative Suite.

The next medley – Mosaic, Spyglass, Microsoft and Netscape

Among the first twenty or so World Wide Web servers established was one at the NCSA (National Center for Supercomputing Applications). But it was a subsequent NCSA development that was the to become the www killer-app; it set the World Wide Web on track to justify the word 'world' in its title and achieve its global acceptance. Most significantly this development was the catalyst to create most of the browsers used today.

The NCSA was based at the University of Illinois Urbana-Champaign and benefited from funding by the 'high-performance computing and communications initiative', instigated as part of the 'Gore Bill'. This bill sought to build on the success of the ARPANET and NSFNet to create what Al Gore popularised (or did he just hi-jack?) as the 'information superhighway'.

Mark Andreessen and Eric Bina started work in late 1992 using an X-Window System. Given their funding they were able to apply a full-time team of programmers. They came up with the first version of NCSA Mosaic in 1993; it worked with FTP, Usenet and Gopher.

But they went further to make it user-friendly and easy to install; it also had a GUI (graphics user interface). A further innovation enabled it to display images in the same window as text rather than in a separate one. The other benefit was that while earlier search engines and browsers tended towards being based on UNIX, Mosaic was ported to Windows and Macintosh and others including the Commodore Amiga, Acorn Archimedes...

Wired magazine commented in 1984,
'Don't look now, but Prodigy, AOL, and CompuServe are all suddenly obsolete - and Mosaic is well on its way to becoming the world's standard interface.'

The program's source code in its X-Window format was freely available to all; its other formats were also available following the signing of a simple licence.

In this way Mosaic made the Internet and World Wide Web readily accessible to the non-computer-user and this led to the service flourishing.

The first move that led to a browser war was struck when the University of Illinois at Urbana-Champaign established the company Spyglass Inc in 1990. Spyglass was created to commercialise the university's inventions.

In August 1994 Tim Krauskopf of Spyglass obtained exclusive rights to license Mosaic software; as part of the deal it obtained the name and the technology but not the source code. It was launched as Spyglass Mosaic.

Spyglass went on to develop the first commercially maintained and supported web server, the Spyglass Server and Server SDK first released in 1995.

Open TV, an interactive television company bought Spyglass in 2000 for a $2.5bn stock swap, but not before Spyglass made a deal that would change the future of browsers.

In April 1994 Jim Clark, co-founder of Silicon Graphics Inc, raised the necessary funding from Kleiner Perkins Caulfield & Byers to establish Andreessen and others from the NCSA Mosaic team in the newly founded Mosaic Communications Corporation.

By October it had released Mosaic Netscape 0.9 as a downloadable file via the Internet. It was available in X-Window, Microsoft Windows and Apple Macintosh versions. The arrangement was that it was free for personal use or $99 for commercial use. The product was a great success.

During development it was referred to as Mozilla, derived from 'Mosaic killer' with the obvious sideways reference to Godzilla. A mascot was designed which appeared on the company website but dropped away somewhat as the company 'grew up'.

Microsoft rather belatedly realised it needed to address the Internet market. In May 1995 Bill Gates issued an internal memo entitled *The Internet Tidal Wave* stressing that the Internet was 'critical to every part of our business'. He assessed it as the most important computer industry event since the IBM PC.

Back in 1994 Microsoft first approached Mosaic Communications Corporation and offered $1m to license its browser code; Jim Clark chose not to accept the deal.

Soon after the product was renamed Netscape Navigator and by November 1994 its company name was changed to Netscape too; this was to avoid any ownership issues with the NCSA.

Also that month the company took legal action against the University of Illinois and Spyglass to obtain a ruling on whether there was any infringement between the three products. By December 1994 the issue was settled out of court by Netscape handing over $2.2m in damages and $1.4m from licensing deals it had in place with other companies.

That same month Microsoft reached a direct agreement with Spyglass to license the Spyglass Mosaic browser and this was the basis for developing its own approach that would be named Internet Explorer. They agreed royalties of around $1 for each web browser shipped for Windows 3.1 and the Mac OS.

The relationship was by no means smooth with Spyglass deciding to take action in January 1997 complaining that Microsoft paid only the minimum quarterly royalty envisaged in the agreement. A revised agreement with a circa $8m payment resolved the matter.

By June 1995 Microsoft was back talking with Netscape and asking that it agree not to compete with Microsoft in browsers for Windows 95 and any subsequent versions. Jim Clark not only refused but referred the conversation to the antitrust division of the US Department of Justice.

Within a month the department filed in the federal court in New York that it believed Microsoft was breaching the Sherman Antitrust Act.

In the meantime version 1.1 and 1.2 of Netscape Navigator were released and by March 1995 six million copies had been downloaded.

In August 1995, Netscape Communications was launched on NASDAQ. Shares were priced at $28 but they opened at $71 and peaked at $74.75. This was the best opening day performance for an issue of its size and valued the company at $2.2bn.

Version 2.0 of Netscape Navigator was released in September 1995 and AOL agreed to bundle the software so its users could access the Internet.

In June 1996 things notched up again when Microsoft threatened to cancel Compaq's licence for Windows when it announced plans to bundle Netscape Navigator. Netscape was once again talking with the US Department of Justice as a result, highlighting this anti-competitive activity.

August 1996 saw Netscape v3.0, and by the end of 1996 the browser market was recording the market shares as 55% to Netscape and 30% to Internet Explorer.

At a senatorial meeting in March 1997 Bill Gates admitted that Microsoft contracts with Internet content companies did restrict them from working with Netscape.

V4.0 was released in June 1997. When v5.0 arrived in Feb 1998 the writing was on the wall - Internet Explorer 4 was taking market share from Netscape despite the hotting up of the legal action.

The US Department of Justice filed a lawsuit against Microsoft in May 1998, charging the company with violation of the Sherman Act in attempting to achieve a monopoly of the browser market. An injunction required Microsoft to either offer Windows 98 without Internet Explorer bundled in, or it should bundle Netscape Navigator too. Despite all this, by September 1998 Internet Explorer was the market leader, and it has never really looked back.

In November 1998 AOL was ready to acquire Netscape for $4.2bn in stock, which it completed by February 1999. By the end of 1999 the browser market shares were 75% to Internet Explorer and just 23% to Netscape.

But Netscape would be back – as Mozilla!

Colonisation – navigators, explorers and safaris

Microsoft came late to espousing the Internet and achieved its entry by acquiring the licence to Spyglass Mosaic which it modified to launch as Internet Explorer 1.0 in August 1995. So there was now a Navigator and an Explorer!

Controversially the IE browser was included with copies of Windows 95 that were supplied under all OEM agreements through PC manufacturers; v1.5 was released a few months later to work with Windows NT Server.

V2.0 had additional features and was launched in late 1995, rolling out for Windows 3.1, Windows 95, Windows NT; a Mac version followed in April 1996.

IE v3.0 arrived in 1996. It was bundled free of charge with Windows 95 which led to Microsoft only paying the minimum royalty to Spyglass and this generated the legal action from its licensor.

V3.0 also included Internet Mail and News 1.0 and this brought Microsoft much closer to Netscape in its competition for the market. But it was v4.0, released in September 1997, bundled with both Windows 95 and the beta version of Windows 98, that worked best within the Windows services and allowed Microsoft to prevail in the 'browser wars'.

It also came with Outlook Express as a necessary update to Internet Mail and included DHTML (Dynamic HTML).

The legal wrangles cascaded around these developments, Microsoft insisting that Windows 98 could not function without IE - though an Australian computer scientist was able to demonstrate that it could.

The proposed resolution at one stage was for Microsoft to be split into two parts but this was eventually defeated. In the end, despite the painful arduous process, it was all just too late for Netscape. Internet Explorer was the market leader by 1998 and grew at its peak to control some 95% of the business.

By August 2010 the IE market share had slipped back to just over 60% - yet it still held a majority!

Initially Apple offered Netscape for the Mac and at one stage tried internally to create its own browser Cyberdog, a name inspired by a character in Aardman Animations' *A Close Shave* starring Wallace & Gromit.

Cyberdog was released in 1997 but 'kenneled' soon after when Apple and Microsoft entered into a five-year agreement that saw Mac versions of Internet Explorer being bundled with OS8, OS9 and OS10.1/10.2. Apple decided to hedge its bets given all the browser legal hassle and offered Netscape too.

In the meantime another course in the browser development path was opening up in one of Germany's oldest institutions, the Eberhard Karls University of Tübingen.

Matthias Ettrich created the KDE project; the name was a sideways reference to the Common Desktop Environment, the 1993 agreement made by most UNIX proponents. Originally KDE was defined as the Kool Desktop Environment; but as the operation became serious the 'K' was said not to stand for anything.

Ettrich believed the UNIX desktop applications were too dissimilar in look and feel and KDE was intended to create a truly common desktop environment. He explained his objectives on USENET in 1996 and stirred up a great deal of interest.

He set out to achieve his objectives by using the 1994-issued Norwegian Trolltech or QT Software. This supplied a development framework operating in C++ with a built-in cross-platform GUI. The software was open-source. Trolltech was acquired by Nokia in June 2008.

Within the KDE project the university produced Konqueror in 1996, a web browser and file manager. Konqueror ran on most UNIX platforms and on Windows. The name was to suggest that after the Navigator and the Explorer, the next to arrive would be the Konqueror!

Konqueror initially used the KDE HTML Widget, but by 1998 it launched the KTHML layout engine, a program that displayed HTML, XML and images based on CSS, XSL and other formats. In other words it was the program that allowed the browser to display WWW pages.

KHTML had the supreme benefit of being small with just 140,000 lines of code; it was well conceived and worked with all standards of the time. KHTML was also designed to handle right-to-left languages like Hebrew and Arabic.

So in 2002 perhaps not surprisingly Apple, seeking a browser for the OS X, chose KHTML to develop WebKit which it embedded in its own internal web browser development. We already had the Navigator, Explorer and the Konqueror; Apple perhaps decided to name it for the fun that is available after the navigation, exploration and conquest, it became Safari.

Safari was announced in January 2003 as part of Mac OS X and became its browser of choice from Panther or OS 10.3 onwards. Version 1.0 of Safari was completed by June 2003, v2.0 arrived in April 2005 but it was not until October and v2.0.2 that it was able to show it could meet the WaSp (Web standards project) Acid2 test.

RANDOM ACCESS MOMENT:
Acid1 confirmed compliance with the HTML4 standard and CSS1, Acid2 with CSS1 and CSS2. CSS stands for 'cascading style sheets', a language to control the display of a web page, its look-and-feel. CSS2 was published in May 1988 with new positioning techniques, bidirectional text and new fonts and features.

But Apple soon alienated the KDE developers when it did not readily document upgrades to their source code. In 2005 Apple made the core of Safari open-source though it retained proprietary control of its GUI and other features. This removed the issue and the KDE and Apple relationship quickly improved.

Safari was also the default browser on iOS, announced in 2007 as the Apple operating system for the iPhone and subsequently on the iPod Touch and iPad products.

The return of Mozilla

The Netscape team used the Mozilla name and mascot in its early days and it took on more meaning in 1998 when the Mozilla Organization was formed.

This was set up as a separate entity, staffed by Netscape personnel. The intention was to use the release of the Netscape browser source code to annexe the enthusiasms and ideas of thousands of programmers from around the world. It also established mozilla.org as the host of the open-source version of Netscape Communicator.

In 2003 AOL started to reduce its commitment to Netscape and the Mozilla Organisation. They responded by founding the not-for-profit Mozilla Foundation in July 2003. Its intellectual property, some hardware and seedcorn capital was invested in the new operation; AOL donated $2m over the first two years and Mitch Kapor gave $300k.

The free-booting and loose team worked for several years as Internet Explorer continued to dominate, at one point taking a 95% share of the browser market.

In 2002 as a result of this collaboration it developed what was originally named Phoenix but renamed the Firefox browser and Thunderbird email services.

In August 2005 the Mozilla Foundation created a wholly-owned subsidiary called the Mozilla Corporation and passed all development and commercial activities across to this new trading entity.

Within six months of the launch of Firefox 1.0 in November 2004, its anti-spyware and anti-pop-up features led to it being downloaded 40 million times. Within a year it had recorded 100 million downloads; many were keen to find an alternative to the monopolistic Internet Explorer. In July 2009 the billionth download of Firefox was achieved.

The Firefox browser operated a close contractual relationship with Google and by 2006 some 85% of its revenue, about $57m, was achieved through Google being its default search engine.

In July 2010 IE was shown as having 52.5% of the market, Firefox at 30.5%, Google Chrome at 10%, Safari at 5%, and Opera still there at 2%.

We cannot leave Mozilla without talking of the 'Chief Lizard Wrangler', Winifred Mitchell Baker, usually referred to as simply Mitchell Baker. In 2005 she was included in the list of *Time* magazine's '100 most influential people in the world'.

A lawyer, she achieved her BA and JD at University of California, Berkeley. Having worked in corporate and intellectual property for a high-tech practice, she joined Sun Microsystems and then moved to Netscape in 1994.

At Netscape, reporting directly to the CEO Jim Barksdale, she set up the busy legal department and was involved at the start of the Mozilla project.

She took the title Chief Lizard Wrangler when she became general manager of Mozilla.org in 1999.

When AOL's interest waned she became CEO of the Mozilla Corporation. In 2008 she relinquished the role but remained chairperson.

Another open-source cross-platform browser emerged from the Mozilla camp. In March 2005 the Mozilla Foundation concluded not to continue developing the Mozilla Application Suite but to concentrate on Firefox and Thunderbird.

But it confirmed it would provide support for those wanting to go forward with the open-source suite. A team stepped up to do this and called itself The SeaMonkey Council; its program was SeaMonkey v1.0 released in Sep 2005 with v2.0 passing the Acid3 test by Dec 2008.

Shiny new approach - Google Chrome

Google had always been a search engine and maintained that it would not have a web browser of its own. Its simple home page was an absolute joy for browsers to access speedily, its high traffic made deals with the many browser teams easy to achieve.

Google hired two Firefox developers to establish a browser approach and this changed the view internally. They used the Apple-developed WebKit layout engine to launch Google Chrome in September 2008. It was a beta version released in forty-three languages; initially it was for Windows-only yet it quickly gained a 1% share of the browser market.

Google Chrome followed the Google concept of clean and simple pages and its use of JavaScript made it fast. It maintained blacklists for phishing and malware, had an incognito mode so sites could not garner who you were - all in pursuit of its 'Don't be evil' corporate slogan.

In December 2009 Mac OS X and Linux versions were available. By August 2010, according to Net Applications, Chrome was the third most used browser with a 7.5% share.

Web services

Bill von Meister (co-founder of The Source) set up an organisation named CVC (Control Video Corporation) to offer a Gameline cartridge, compatible with the Atari VCS/2600 games console. He used modem technology that he had developed for an earlier cable TV business.

The Gameline cartridge was larger than the usual VCS cart with a phone connection; it sold for $49.95 and a set-up fee of $15. It allowed users to call up a central server and download a game for a $1 fee; the game could be played, usually five times, before it expired. Some of the selected games had the facility for a user to upload a top score to match against other players for regional and national prizes. One of the prizes was far from subtle – a Gameline anorak!

Von Meister had success with the third party software houses but console manufacturers shunned the idea. There had been plans for other services - news, sport, travel, financial, banking, email - but the notion was caught up in the 1983 video console crash and faded away.

Von Meister moved on, but from the ashes of CVC a new organisation called Quantum Computer Services was formed in 1985. It developed Quantum Link, or Q-Link, for use with the Commodore 64 and 128 PCs. It offered a mix of email, file sharing, chat rooms and multi-player games. It went on to launch Apple-Link and PC-Link in 1988.

In 1989 the name was changed to America Online, or AOL.

Stephen McConnell Case had a degree in political science, and worked in marketing at Proctor & Gamble and Pizza Hut before joining CVC. He was key in the transition to Quantum Link and in 1991 became CEO at AOL.

He decided AOL needed a user-friendly GUI and marketed it to those who were not computer-literate; CompuServe tended towards the technical sector.

Given the organisation's history, games featured strongly and AOL was a pioneer in graphic-based MMORPGs (massively multiplayer online role playing games). Neverwinter Nights, a Dungeons & Dragons game, was the first graphic MMORPG and ran on AOL from 1991 to 1997.

Case moved the chat room away from the CB-style and instead went for larger groups. There were private rooms for twenty individuals, conference rooms with a moderator and up to forty-eight contributors, and auditoriums for larger audiences. Even the chat room had text based role-playing games like Black Bayou, a horror game that ran from 1996-2004.

AOL started as a Mac-only service in 1989 but two years later it was DOS-compatible and by 1993 there was a Windows 3 version. AOL interconnected with USENET in 1993.

It quickly overtook GEnie and through the mid-90s surpassed Prodigy and CompuServe. In 1996 it changed from hourly charges to a flat-rate fee and within three years had over ten million users.

AOL was one of the first to market itself with giveaway disks to guide the technophobes through the enrolment process. A five-year deal for AOL to be bundled with Windows saw it grow to a peak of over 30 million users worldwide. At this time it was estimated to be worth $240bn.

In the year 2000 Case parlayed this power into a merger with Time Warner; AOL Inc ended up with 55% of Time Warner and Case became chairman of the overall group. In 2011 the new merged entity was the world's second largest entertainment conglomerate by revenue, second only to Disney and with News Corporation and Viacom in its wake.

The v5.0 software came under a great deal of legal attention when it appeared to block other ISPs; this resulted in a $15m out-of-court settlement by AOL. The v9.0 seemed to download software without the user being aware. And having once been an AOL user myself I must mention that its retention policy was rigorous; trying to extricate oneself from it took an age and left a sour taste.

Architext to Excite

A group of six Stanford political science students dined at Rosita's Taqueria in Redwood City, California in February 1993.

The students were computer hackers who came up with the idea of developing their own search engine using the statistical occurrence of the structures of words within phrases. They concluded this would be a more effective way of accessing Internet information.

Joe Kraus, Ben Lutch, Ryan McIntyre, Martin Reinfried, Graham Spencer and Mark Van Haren gathered the funding to develop and launch the Architext search engine. In July 1994 the publishing group IDG (International Data Group) also paid them $100k to develop an online service for it.

By December 1995 they had attracted venture capital to formally launch what they named Excite. There was an initial public offering in April 1996 and they signed distribution deals with Apple, Microsoft and Netscape; they also attracted investment from Intuit, the Quicken organisation.

Acquisitions and growth led to it recording losses in 1998 and Yahoo! seeing an opportunity offered between $5-6bn for Excite. This was rejected and instead it was acquired and merged for $6.7bn with William Randolph Hearst III's @Home Network in January 1999 to become Excite@Home.

RANDOM ACCESS MOMENT:
George Bell, CEO of Excite@Home, is credited with one of the worst PC decisions of all time when two young Stanford students approached him to buy their search engine development as it was interfering with their studies. They wanted $1m but Bell refused. When one of the Excite venture capitalists persevered and negotiated it down to $750k, Bell still rejected his chance to acquire Google from Sergey Brin and Larry Page. Today Google is valued c $200bn.

The merged organisation failed to hit its targets, frightened investors by changing auditors and by October 2001 had filed for Chapter 11 protection from bankruptcy. Its 1,000+ workforce was laid off and the assets were picked over.

iWon.com was hopeful of acquiring the Excite.com brand and domain and developed a new portal approach for it. In December 2001 Excite Network launched and transferred most Excite users in the USA to the new service; Excite Italia took over most of the European business. However it was InfoSpace that owned and operated the web search function.

Ask Jeeves, aka Ask.com, acquired the Excite Network in March 2004 and Excite Italia in 2005. It also came to a revenue-share deal with InfoSpace on the web search operations.

Filo and Yang's Yahoo!

David Filo and Jerry Yang were pursuing doctorates in Electrical Engineering at Stanford when they decided to try to keep track of interesting stuff they found on the Internet. Not for them the ubiquitous PC garage, they started in a trailer.

In February 1994 they maintained a catalogue on their student workstations that they had named after Sumo wrestlers, Akebono and Konishiki. Like the wrestlers the catalogue grew to an enormous size, forcing them to group material under categories and subcategories.

This was launched as *Jerry and David's Guide to the World Wide Web* while they looked around for a snappier title. They liked the dictionary definition of 'yahoo', a word created by Jonathan Swift in *Gulliver's Travels*; meaning rude, uncouth and unsophisticated - Yahoo! was born. Its original url was akebono.stanford.edu /yahoo. Its name was retrospectively justified as meaning 'yet another hierarchical officious oracle'.

The idea attracted others at such a pace that by autumn that year they were already achieving a daily rate of one million hits, some one hundred thousand unique visits. This attracted the attention of Sequoia Capital, venture capitalist to Atari, Apple, Oracle and Cisco. One month after incorporation it concluded two rounds of investment of more than $2m.

The duo hired Tim Koogle from Motorola as CEO, and Jeffrey Mallett from Novell-WordPerfect as COO. The team grew to almost fifty employees and this led to a second round of funding in autumn 1995, from Reuters and Softbank.

An IPO followed swiftly in April 199 raising $33.8m by selling some 2.6 million shares at $13; by the end of 1999 shares were valued at $118.75.

Yahoo! grew both organically and by acquisition. For example the organisation acquired Four11 Corporation in 1997 for $92m as the basis for one of the leading free email services called RocketMail which they turned in to Yahoo Mail.

The leading competitor of the time was Hotmail (a reference to the web software html, ho<u>tma</u>il); Hotmail was acquired in 1997 by Microsoft for $400m.

In October 2008 Yahoo! launched Content Match, a paid for service allowing advertisers to ensure their messages were attached to appropriate searches and articles.

By the end of the noughties Yahoo! had offices around the world and its search engine and directory had grown into a web portal used by over 1.6

billion individuals, recording over 3 billion hits per day and with the largest share in online display advertising.

DEC's AltaVista

Researchers at the DEC Western Research Labs in Palo Alto set out to create a means to assist general users to find information more readily on the Web. Among the team were Louis Monier who developed the crawler, Michael Burrows who wrote the indexing system, Joella Paquette, a marketeer, and Paul Flaherty a researcher with DEC.

The outcome was Alta Vista; the name literally means view from on high or from above. Its speedy crawler trawled much of the Net and the serious hardware support that DEC was able to throw at it gave it an edge over other systems.

DEC's new 64-bit Alpha 8400 TurboLaser computer was particularly speedy with database software. The service was able to crawl, capture and index the whole content of some ten million pages on its first foray; from this database it provided the user with a rapid list of items matching an enquiry.

Initially users were its 10,000 employees, but in December 1995 it was released for general use; by then it was indexing some 16 million pages.

On launch day it handled 300,000 hits, in two weeks this had grown to 2 million enquiries per day. By the end of 1996 it was handling 19 million requests each day and within two years AltaVista routinely recorded 80 million hits per day - all without any drop-off in service levels.

It also introduced searching with a more natural language approach so a question could be phrased without providing spurious hits for minor words.

Yahoo! was quick to contract with AltaVista to provide its searches. Its volume attracted heavy sponsorship and by 1997 it was recording over $50m income.

DEC was acquired by Compaq in 1998 for $9bn and it ensured it acquired the altavista.com domain by paying a further $3m. Compaq decided to change the AltaVista approach to that of a portal, at a stroke eliminating its raison d'être by losing the search page approach.

The failed portal strategy was followed by a disposal of 83% of AltaVista by Compaq to the Internet investment organisation CMGI for $2.3bn. But this was just as the dot.com bubble burst and halted its planned IPO.

In 2002 the service had a facelift to add images and multimedia and it launched Babel Fish, a service that would translate whole pages, phrases or individual words between English, French, German, Italian, Portuguese, Russian and Spanish. AltaVista was also the first search engine to offer a service in Chinese, Japanese and Korean.

But the success of Google was the final nail for AltaVista which was sold on to Overture in February 2003 for just $140m. Overture, including AltaVista, was later acquired by Yahoo! in July 2003.

In 2011 AltaVista remained as a small search engine, in a bizarre reversal of fate using the Yahoo! search index.

Microsoft MSN

To coincide with the launch of Windows 95, Microsoft gathered all its Internet services within an integrated service initially known as The Microsoft Network, but this soon became MSN; it was launched in August 1995.

This was first conceived by Nathan Myhrvold of Microsoft's Advanced Technology Group as a riposte to AOL, a dial-up service offering online content and services.

Myhrvold was an interesting character whom we should not pass over too quickly. He went to college at the age of fourteen and had achieved his PhD in mathematics, geophysics and space physics from Princeton at twenty-three. He spent a post-doctoral year working on cosmology and quantum theory in Stephen Hawking's team at Cambridge University, but then returned to the United States.

He helped his brother on a software project leading to a start-up IT company, Dynamical Systems Research Inc; DSR sought to clone a multitasking environment operating within DOS; it was purchased for $1.5m by Microsoft in 1986.

Myhrvold joined Microsoft as a director of special projects at a time when it held only two patents. He was heavily involved in Windows and helped create Microsoft Research, becoming its chief technology officer presiding over a 700-strong research team. He was also VP of the Microsoft Applications and Content Group. When he left thirteen years later it held some 5,000 patents.

He worked with Bill Gates and Peter Rinearson to prepare *The Road Ahead* book which was a New York Times bestseller for Bill Gates in 1995 and 1996. Myhrvold maintained a broad interest in many sciences and he partnered Paul Allen in donating $1m for a powerful telescope to assist the SETI project (search for extra-terrestrial intelligence).

He left Microsoft to form Intellectual Ventures, a company that hoovered up patents. It was cofounded with Chuck Witmer, and they were later joined by two more managing directors, Edward Jung from Microsoft and Peter Detkin; the team became an interesting blend of thinkers and patent holders supported by high achieving intellectual property lawyers.

Intellectual Ventures acquired patents from colleges, companies and individuals that did not have the financial wherewithal to exercise their ownership.

The original MSN, which was renamed MSN Classic, operated within Windows Explorer and appeared as a virtual series of Explorer files. It offered the usual fare of news, weather, message boards and chat rooms and had a rudimentary email facility. It did not initially offer www services but this was remedied by the Microsoft IE browser, available via MSN.

MSN v2.0 was released in 1996 to offer full Internet access, distributed as a glitzy CD-ROM with the strapline 'every new universe begins with a big bang'. The MSN Program Viewer was essentially IE v3.0 and it was one of the first programs to feature strongly both interactivity and multimedia capabilities. Perhaps as a result, the software was none too reliable and often quite slow.

MSN evolved with less of a multimedia approach, a partnership with the broadcaster NBC giving it additional appeal. By 1997 it was much more conventional but in 1998 its Program Viewer was superseded by the Internet Explorer format.

One component of MSN, MSN Search, was launched at the end of 1998 using Inktomi as its search mechanism.

The name Inktomi derived from a Sioux tribe legend of *Iktomi*, a spider able to overcome larger enemies by applying its cunning. The name was however modified to sound like 'INK-to-me'.

Founded by University of California Berkeley professor, Eric Brewer, and Paul Gauthier, a graduate student, the search engine supplanted Alta Vista, only to be overcome by Google. It was acquired by Yahoo! in 2002 for $235m.

MSN successfully switched its approach to that of a portal, MSN.com, and its email service evolved with the acquisition of Hotmail in 1997 and the subsequent launch of MSN Messenger in 1999.

A number of the MSN services were renamed Windows Live in 2005, to give Windows Live Hotmail and Windows Live Messenger…

In June 2009 the MSN service was renamed as Bing, a decision engine using the promotional message 'bing and decide'.

This regular series of initiatives and the security features, anti-virus and firewalls, maintained MSN as the second largest Internet service provider in the USA with some 100 million users in 2010.

Hotmail

Hotmail was launched by Sabeer Bhatia and Jack Smith as HoTMaiL in July 1996.

Bhatia, born and bred in India, moved at college age to attend Caltech and later went on to Stanford. After his master's he joined Apple, but left to form Firepower Systems Inc innovating ICs for use with PowerPC workstations. Jack Smith, also an ex-Apple employee, joined him with the notion of a web-based email service.

The duo first created a system called Javasoft and, gaining funding for their webmail idea, they launched HoTMaiL as an advertising-funded service free to the user.

HoTMaiL was one of the first webmail services, that is a service that provides email services via a browser. It was written in FreeBSD and Solaris; within just six months it had attracted over a million users.

Eighteen months later in December 1997, it had grown to 8.5 million users; Microsoft then moved to acquire Hotmail. Bhatia was obviously a tough negotiator, rejecting an initial offer of $150m and also a subsequent offer of $350m; he held out to achieve an impressive $400m.

Under Microsoft's wing the service was quickly customised for each local country to operate in over thirty languages. By 1999 it had grown to some 30 million users. Successfully negotiating some security breaches, adding support for Mozilla and other services and weathering the launch of Google's Gmail, in 2011 it had approaching 400 million users worldwide.

Bhatia went on to develop other ideas; including a teleconferencing web service called SabSeBolo.com, which in Hindi means 'talk to everyone'. Smith too was CEO of a number of ventures.

Messenger

MSN Messenger was an in-house Microsoft development launched in July 1999. It was initially a simple instant message service using text-only and with quite a rudimentary contact list service. Version 2.0 followed in November 1999; this bore a banner that could rotate advertising and offered some additional though limited customisation options.

Its v3.0 released in May 2000 offered one of the earliest VOIP services (voice over internet protocol) and the facility to both attach and send files. To coincide with the launch of Windows XP in October 2001, v4.6 of Messenger expanded the features to allow both contact groups and voice conversations.

Constant evolution since then saw, for example, v7.0 introduce emoticons and animated pictures, something that rather overwhelms messages I receive from my grandchildren! This version also permitted integration with Xbox Live.

To date Messenger is integrated with Facebook, Apple Mac and the Apps Store, and has gone mobile given its compatibility with Windows Phone, Blackberry, Symbian, Zune… In 2011 it attracted over 300 million active members a month.

Jeeves and Ask.com

Garrett Greuner, a UCSD graduate, and David Warthen, from Stanford Law School, founded the service Ask Jeeves in 1996.

The search engine software was designed by Gary Chevsky, a Russian who had moved to San Francisco. Three venture capitalists provided the initial funding and Ask.com was listed on NASDAQ from 1999 until it was acquired by InterActiveCorp in July 2005.

Its prospectus in 1999 explained that it drew upon the image of Bertie Wooster's valet as a metaphor for the search engine fetching and carrying for the user. But by 2005 they chose to phase out the valet and present themselves as Ask.com; though in the UK the name Ask Jeeves was resurrected in 2009.

The service used natural language to allow users to phrase a conventional question rather than simple text queries.

'The Ask Jeeves question answering services allow users [to] ask a question in plain English and receive a response pointing the user to relevant Internet destinations that provide the answers. We believe that our question answering services make interaction with the Internet more intuitive, less frustrating and significantly more productive.'

It progressively found the going tough against Google and switched to promoting its service as more of a Q&A site than a full-blooded search engine.

Greuner stood for the California gubernatorial election in 2003, investing much of the $1m fighting-fund himself. He garnered just over 2,500 votes, at a cost therefore of c$400 per vote; Arnold Schwarzenegger was the winner.

As an interesting piece of vertical marketing, in 2009 Ask.com sponsored a NASCAR entrant, the #96 car driven by Bobby Labonte in the Sprint Cup Series. This was part of an overall deal that saw it appointed the official search engine for NASCAR, as Nascar.com, and its Hall of Fame Racing. NASCAR dominated the USA's top 20 sporting event attendance charts each year and rated second in TV ratings for USA regular-season sports.

25 - Creating Google

'Getting information off the Internet is like taking a drink from a fire hydrant.'
Mitch Kapor

Larry Page used a computer at home from the age of six. His father was one of the first to achieve a computer science degree and later a PhD at the University of Michigan. His mother was a database consultant and both parents taught computer programming. Page himself graduated in computer engineering but also took a series of business courses to broaden his experience.

Sergey Brin attended a Montessori school (as did Page). His father was a professor at a nearby university in mathematics. His mother worked at the NASA Goddard Space Flight Center simulating how weather might affect space travel. Brin had moved to America from Russia with his parents at the age of six. By the age of nineteen he had graduated with honours in mathematics and computer science.

The two met at Stanford where Brin was assigned to give Page an introductory tour of the college. Page and Brin suggested later that they were keenly pursuing PhDs to follow in their father's footsteps and had absolutely no plans to enter the commercial world.

In 1996 the computer science department moved into the William Gates Computer Science building, heavily funded by the Microsoft chairman. Brin worked there on data mining and co-founded the MIDAS group (mining data at Stanford). This naturally applied much attention to the somewhat disorganised Internet.

Early services had attempted to 'mine' the information on the Net by matching text or answering questions. Yahoo!, another Stanford innovation, had come up with an alphabetic guide. What they shared was the lack of capability to keep up with the Net's growth and the delivered results were none too comprehensive and in many cases not that helpful.

Page meanwhile was working on the Stanford Digital Library Project which was attempting to define a universal integrated digital library.

RANDOM ACCESS MOMENT:
The National Science Foundation provided funding from its Digital Library Initiative fund for Stanford to investigate search engines. This was managed by Mike Lesk, who while at Bell Labs had developed the UUCP networking tool. Page later sought seedcorn from this fund and so in a sense Lesk was one of the earliest investors in what would become Google.

In this work Page routinely used AltaVista to research the Net. He found that not only did it return the urls of discovered sites but also showed the links from pages to other sites.

Page realised there was mileage in these links and to investigate this he decided he needed to download the whole of the World Wide Web onto his computer!

Page and Brin cooperated in dispatching spiders to crawl around the Net to gather the data needed. Page concluded that counting the number of links to a web page would be a smart way of establishing its popularity and relevance. By ranking where the links came from, their importance and significance, he realised that even more of a measure would be achieved.

Page called this system PageRank and it was the basis of his PhD dissertation in 1996. Supported by Brin's professor, Rajeev Motwani, the three realised they had something more than the basis for a thesis. They had soon created BackRub, a search engine that looked back at a web page's incoming links.

When it came to a proper name for their search engine they brainstormed a whole series of names with others until Sean Anderson wrote on a board the word Googleplex on a board. This was shortened to Google and Google.com was registered in September 1997. Overnight a colleague saw the name and indicated that it was misspelled and should have been Googol, which was the correct spelling of the term for 10 to the power 100. But Googol.com had already been taken!

RANDOM ACCESS MOMENT:
The definition and naming of large numbers is something of a quagmire. The American billion is 10 to the power of 9 or a thousand millions, while the European billion was originally 10 to the power 12, a million millions; the French call the American billion a 'milliard'. Harold Wilson in 1974 confirmed that the UK government would move over to using the American billion.

The original mathematical term for 10 to the power of 100 was 10 duotrigintillion or ten thousand sexdecillion. So it was not surprising that Edward Kasner, a US mathematician, challenged his young nephews to come up with an improved name for the large number. Nine-year-old Milton Sirotta proposed the term 'googol'. Kasner popularised the usage in his 1940 book 'Mathematics and the Imagination'. It has little value in pure mathematics but is useful when trying to express the number of subatomic particles in the universe.

In 1997 the Google service was released internally to Stanford personnel on the college url as google.stanford.edu. It received an amazing response, rapidly supplanting all other search engines in use.

Stanford's Office of Technology Licensing promoted the idea of PhD students being entrepreneurial and worked with them to patent their ideas and to find commercial partnerships. This was no surprise in that Stanford was at the heart of Silicon Valley and close to many leading venture capitalists.

But Google soon reached the point when the bandwidth it used was far too heavy for the college. Increasing numbers of users and searches necessitated more computers and it gratefully received $10,000 from the Stanford Digital Libraries Project on which they were working, but this clearly was not enough.

A professor suggested a meeting with his friend, Andy Bechtolsheim. Bechtolsheim was born in Germany, from where a Fulbright Award took him to the United States, he had developed a 3M UNIX workstation that was the basis of Sun Microsystems.

Bechtolsheim left Sun in 1995 to co-found Granite Systems, with David Cheriton, a computer science professor at Stanford; it specialised in Ethernet networking devices. Granite was acquired by Cisco Systems for $220m in 1996. He still owned 60% at the time and was appointed a VP at Cisco Systems.

He and Cheriton with other colleagues from Sun developed a business as 'angel' investors, providing the earliest capital for start-ups at a stage where venture capitalists feared to tread. Bechtolsheim always recalled someone having provided early funding for himself and he found Page and Brin's proposition compelling.

This was at a time when most in the early Net business felt that 'search' was a minor and insignificant tool and not really worthy of much time or effort. In August 1998 Bechtolsheim wrote a cheque to Google Inc for $100,000 seedcorn so it could acquire the hardware it needed.

Google as a company did not exist at the time, and was incorporated subsequent to the meeting on 4 September 1998 - they needed a bank account to pay in the cheque! With the help of family and friends their seedcorn was increased to $1m.

Google was underway; it managed to fulfil two of the PC folklore requirements by starting business in a garage (of a fellow PhD student) and in Menlo Park!

From an early stage the operation was very successful in getting word-of-mouth promotion of its aims and capabilities. It maintained an attractive and 'clean' home page that assisted in achieving a quick response to searches.

Significantly in December 1998 *PC magazine* announced Google as the search engine of choice for

'Its uncanny knack for returning extremely relevant results.'

This was not happenstance but achieved by the ranking of links and by organising pages according to the selected font size, style and relative position of terms used. It was also greatly assisted by a careful blending of its DiY hardware and software.

By 1999 the two felt the development of Google was interfering too greatly with the work for their PhDs; the service was handling over 500,000 searches a day. They set about trying to sell it off to someone else.

They approached AltaVista, a company that was then maintaining a greater than 50% share of the search business. They hoped AltaVista might be well placed to appreciate the benefits of PageRank for its business and proposed a $1m price tag for it. But DEC, the owners of AltaVista, were strong believers in supporting only in-house development and politely refused the offer.

They then offered George Bell of Excite the opportunity to buy the business for the $1m sum and even agreed with one of his advisors, Vinod Khosla, that this asking price might be reduced to $750k. Bell could not see the potential and thus lost out on a major coup.

Failing a disposal the two's attention turned to licensing the Google service to others. Yahoo! had the declared mission of attracting users to its site and keeping them there to review information, to see advertisements and to buy. Google's approach of a quick in-and-out to search and leave the site was not of appeal; they also passed.

They achieved a little progress when Red Hat licensed their search software.

The Google founders worked hard from the outset on the company's internal morale and well-being; for example team members were allowed 'time off' - 20% of the working week could be used to pursue personal projects.

Paul Buchheit, a Google engineer, came up with its unofficial watchword, *'Don't be evil.'*

Attracting income - advertising on Google

The early success of Google provided it with the momentum to acquire a series of other operations to sustain a massive expansion.

In March 1999 the founders finally relented and began to sell advertisements on Google, but these were only text adverts so the clean look and feel of the site would not be lost.

Having failed to acquire or license the Goto.com/Overture pay-per-click software, Google produced its own called Google AdWords, launched in October 2000. This was very lucrative; research showed that a Google sponsored link, which appeared beside or above a search, had an 8% click-through for the first advert, 5% for the second and 2.5% for the third.

Google's service ranked the advertisements by past click-through data, the relevance of the advertising text and the advertiser's account history. Google suggested that this made for a quality performance. Some advertisers suggest that, as with its general searches, it does tend to give priority to past performers at the cost of newer organisations.

By 2003 advertisers could use a control panel to define target demographics, topics, keywords and domain names which were then paid for as a cost-per-impression (or appearances on websites, often referred to as cost per thousand impressions) or cost-per-click (the advertiser only paid if the advert was actually clicked). By then adverts were placed not just on Google searches but with AOL, Ask and Netscape too.

Oingo Inc was founded in 1998 by Gilad Elbaz and Adam Weissman. It developed a search algorithm, WordNet, based upon a Princeton University project for a lexicon. This grouped English words into synsets (or synonyms) with their semantic relations in order to become a combined dictionary and thesaurus. Oingo became Applied Semantics Corporation in 2001 and was acquired for $102m by Google in April 2003.

This acquisition formed the basis of Google AdSense launched in June 2003. It allowed website owners to enrol into the service, and relevant Google adverts would appear on the site in return for a share of revenue per-click or per-impression. The AdSense service also extended to search. Where a website owner placed a Google search box on its site, it was offered 51% of revenues generated from any search resulting in an advert click-through.

Double-Click derived from the Internet Advertising Network that had been founded by Kevin O'Connor and Dwight Merriman in 1995. Double-Click went through a number of ownerships but was always an online marketing operation selling web advertising space via marketing companies and agencies.

In April 2007 it was acquired by Google for $3.1bn in cash. Microsoft (rather amusingly?) warned of the monopoly and antitrust possibilities of this takeover. Nonetheless it was approved in December 2007 by the USA and by the EU in March 2008.

These various Google services have been criticised. For example, Double-Click uses cookies to track a user's progress around the Net; this is not dissimilar to spyware. AdSense also uses cookies and has been used by unscrupulous advertisers to take a user to a completely irrelevant site simply to earn click-through benefits. For its AdWords service Google paid out $90 million to settle an action generated after a click fraud breached a trademark.

Advertising still provides almost all its revenue stream; in 2010 advertising revenues were $28bn.

RANDOM ACCESS MOMENT:

One serious challenge to the Google and Yahoo! control of the contextual online advertising business was by Quigo, an *Israeli company that opened its HQ in New York. Quigo was founded in 2000 by Yaron Galai and Oded Itzhak who also developed AdSonar and FeedPoint. Like Google's AdSense and Yahoo's Content Match, these could target appropriate advertising to match the content of web pages. Quigo grew successfully against its better-known adversaries until AOL acquired it for $363m in December 2007.*

Lift off – Google attracts investment

In June 1999 Google achieved an unlikely funding deal that ensured the two founders would retain control. Michael Moritz at Sequoia Capital and L John Doerr at Kleiner Perkins Caulfield & Byers were both ready to invest but each made clear that he wanted his to be a solus deal.

Moritz was born in Cardiff, Wales and studied at Oxford and the University of Pennsylvania. He worked for a period at *Time* magazine where he wrote *The Little Kingdom: the Private Story of Apple Computer*, and co-wrote *Going for Broke: The Chrysler Story*. Working at Sequoia his investments included Apple, Cisco, Google, PayPal, Yahoo! and YouTube.

Doerr, with a Harvard MBA, had been with Intel as the 8080 was being developed. Joining Kleiner Perkins Caulfield & Byers in 1980, his investments included Amazon, Compaq, GO Corp, Google, Intuit, Netscape, Sun and Symantec.

Neither was easily turned, but the Google founders and its advisors worked on them and they agreed to each provide 50% of the funding. The two combined in June to provide $25m and there were to be no regrets.

Five years later in August 2004 the Google IPO raised $1.7bn, selling 19.6 million shares at $85 per share, valuing the organisation at $23bn. By October 2007 the shares reached $700 each.

Foundation – Google's early commitment to philanthropy

The founders ring fenced three million IPO shares to establish an untaxed operation called Google Foundation; it is managed by Google.org. This was their vehicle for philanthropic initiatives, centred on reducing global poverty, improving international health and countering climate change – established with a $1bn fund.

By 2004 this operation was headed by Larry Brilliant. He came to public attention when a group of Native Americans, called United Indians of All Tribes, occupied the island of Alcatraz and Brilliant was the doctor present when a pregnant woman gave birth.

Brilliant later spent time at an ashram in the Himalayas and then worked with his wife at the World Health Organisation helping to stamp out smallpox; the WHO announced that this had been achieved by 1980. By 1985 he had co-founded the WELL with Stewart Brand.

One of the first projects of the Google Foundation was working to develop hybrid electric vehicles with low fuel consumption.

Brilliant served as executive director of Google.org until 2009 when he moved to look after the Skoll Urgent Threats Fund established by the eBay co-founder Jeff Skoll.

Culture of non-compliance with the norms

On 1st April 2000 a regular Google feature was originated with the announcement of MentalPlex that could read the mind to reach the desired search results.

By March 2001 Google operated in twenty-six languages and on All Fools' Day the organisation added 'Swedish Chef' as a language option; 'Klingon' would be added later.

Subsequent years saw spoofs on the significance of pigeons in the delivery of searches, the announcement of the Googlunaplex research base on the Moon and a drink that would make imbibers more intelligent. By 2008 Google's various international bases had sprung no fewer than sixteen April Fool jokes.

Other early traditions to stand the test of time were the regular 'doodles' on the home page to commemorate major events and people.

This quirky culture was also exhibited at the Google IPO when the initial filing to the SEC suggested they wished to raise \$2,718,281,828, this number being the mathematical constant 'e' or Euler's number (2.718281828). The number of shares to be Google's proportion of the 19+m floated was set at 14,142,135 a clear reference to the square root of two (1.4142135).

Google growing up – attracting professional management

In June 2000 a strategic relationship was agreed with Yahoo! to make Google its default search provider. A month later Google was able to announce that it was the first search engine to index a billion urls.

In Dec 2000 Google made the 'Google Toolbar' available. It would insert itself on a browser page below the current tab bar and offer a quick Google search. Today this also provides a quick access route to Gmail accounts. It was initially only on Internet Explorer v5.0 or later, but by 2005 it was also available with Mozilla Firefox.

The two venture capitalists, both now on the Google board, were eager that the founders should recruit a professional manager for the business.

Eric Emerson Schmidt earned his degree at Princeton and his master's and PhD in electrical engineering and computer science at the University of California Berkeley. He then spent time at Bell Labs and at Xerox PARC, before leading the Java development at Sun Microsystems, becoming chief technology officer. From 1997 he was CEO at Novell.

The Google founders and Schmidt were rather forced into a meeting by the venture capitalists but they hit it off and Schmidt joined the Google board as chairman in March 2001.

He agreed to invest $1m of his own funds to buy preference shares. The voracious appetite of the organisation for ever-more computer power found this a timely injection of funds and helped make the appointment an easy decision.

The value of his appointment was underlined when Schmidt asked several simple yet pertinent questions that had not been addressed before. Who was initiating the searches? Who was advertising? This helped the expanded team to define future strategy. Yet it was not without friction. Schmidt was keen to have a proper financial accounting system in place - unsurprising when they were turning over $200m and had 200+ employees. Conflict ensued when the founders were content to bounce along using Quicken, while Schmidt wanted an Oracle system installed. But the relationship sustained and flourished.

Google constant innovation

The team constantly managed to originate and launch additional services. In July 2001 Google Image Search provided users with access to some 250 million images. By 2005 this was one billion and today, renamed Google Images, it has over 10 billion images indexed.

By the end of 2001 Google had indexed three billion websites globally. But not resting on its laurels in February 2002 it launched the Google Search Appliance, a piece of hardware that could be 'bolted on' to organisations' own networks to provide a Google search facility internally.

During 2003 Stanford was finally granted a patent in PageRank with Larry Page listed as its inventor. By February 2004 Google was able to announce that its index had reached 6 billion items, which included over 4 billion web pages and almost 900 million images...

In October 2004 Google Desktop Search was released allowing its technology to be applied to searching personal hard disk files and documents.

The pace never slowed. In October 2004 it launched Google Print which later became Google Book Search.

In September 2005 came Google Blog Search, a service that aimed to search across all blog sites having a site feed, either RSS (really simple syndication) or the Atom syndication format. It was assisted by the February 2003 acquisition of Blogger. This service ranked the popularity of blogs within the blogging community and displayed a home page of the most popular items, both overall and within a series of categories.

In November 2005 Google Analytics provided marketeers with a means of assessing the visitors to a particular website. In 2011 it analysed around a third of the top million websites (based on Alexa rankings).

Alexa Internet was founded in 1996 by Brewster Kahle and Bruce Gilliat; named apparently as a reference to the Library of Alexandria. Alexa was sold to Amazon.com in 1999.

Kahle received a degree at MIT where he studied artificial intelligence under Marvin Minsky. With Gilliat he developed WAIS (wide area information service) and founded WAIS Inc which was sold on to AOL in 1995.

Kahle's subsequent focus was to create a permanent and accessible archive of digitised records. Alexa's prime purpose was the ranking of website traffic. In part this was done by a website using an Alexa toolbar to capture its data; this did of course mean its effectiveness was limited by those who chose not to use the toolbar.

However in crawling around the Net it assembled an archive of the website as it was scanned. This database was used in two ways. A copy, some two terabytes of data, were supplied the US Library of Congress in 1998.

The Internet Archive, also founded in 1996 by Kahle, was a non-profit operation. The Wayback Machine maintained a record of each crawl through the Net. The intention was that researchers (and litigators) could go back to see how the Internet looked at a specified moment in time. However the Wayback Machine was no longer updated after August 2008.

In December 2006 Google launched the Patent Search offering access and search of some seven million US patents. It had an agreement with the USPTO (US Patent and Trademark Office) to provide detailed data on both patents and trademarks at no charge to the general public.

In June 2008 Google Finance began to provide real time stock quotes, currency rates and financial news.

Google Translate routinely added languages such that to date it offers translation within fifty-nine languages, virtually covering every language in use on the Internet.

Google and AOL

In May 2002 AOL decided to drop the use of Overture search and to partner instead with Google; the 34 million users of AOL, Compuserve and Netscape would be offered 'search powered by Google'. Overture's stock price lost a third on the news.

Google negotiated not just to provide searches but also all the search-related advertising for AOL clients. This would of course prove to be a significant deal that contributed strongly to its buoyant IPO two years later.

In return AOL required stock options but also revenue guarantees of several million dollars; at the time the deal was expressed as being worth $1bn.

In 2005 the deal was up for review and once again it was awarded to Google; AOL also sold a 5% holding of itself to Google. Google agreed to break one of its traditions and show an AOL logo on the search result's page.

Both deals effectively delivered body blows to Microsoft. In 2010 the AOL deal was extended another five years; that year Google's contribution to AOL was $209m.

Google Compute

Google Compute ran from March 2002 to October 2005 as an add-on to the Google Toolbar. Its intention was for users to volunteer to share unused computer time in a distributed computing project aimed at assisting with scientific research.

It appeared to only have been used with Folding@home, a modeling exercise looking at why and how proteins mis-fold in order to provide a better understanding of some diseases. Folding@home continued away from Google and had reached 5,000 teraflops in 2009 and became the largest distributed computing project.

Gmail

Paul Buchheit, the engineer who initiated the 'Don't be evil' motto at Google, worked on an internal email service announced by invitation only on 1 April 2004 as 'Gmail'. Choosing that date was clearly running the risk, given Google's culture, that this would be dismissed as an April Fools' joke; it did in fact become the basis of hoaxes in 2007, 2008 and 2009.

The service was offered generally from February 2007 and was fully released in July 2007. Google had to buy the preexisting gmail.com domain from a free email service run by Garfield.com.

This quickly unsettled other webmail services by offering users 1 GByte of storage per user; the norm had been 2 to 4 MByte. In 2011 it recorded 193 million users each month; users can pay to have more capacity, up to 16 terabytes. Other webmail services had to quickly raise their storage offerings to compete.

Gmail was not without controversy. A Gmail user had to provide details of a mobile with SMS text facility. If Google believed that the email had abnormal usage it was locked down for 24 hours. Google also scanned emails to provide 'relevant' advertising which brought privacy into question. It frustrated users by not allowing the attachment of executable files. It also had some outages leaving users without access for up to several hours; business users were particularly incensed by this. Yet it continued to grow.

Picasa

Lars Perkins worked at Idealab, founded by Bill Gross, where in 2002 he developed Picasa, a photo-sharing website.

The name was described as a deliberate contraction using part of Picasso's name and the Spanish word for house *casa*. Software was sold at $29 per copy.

In February 2004 the Flickr site was launched by Ludicorp of Vancouver. It set out with a number of similarities to Picasa but focused more on MMOGs (massively multiplayer online games). Yahoo! acquired Flickr in March 2005 and the battle was on.

Picasa was acquired by Google in July 2004 and offered its software free of charge. Google Picasa allowed users to store photo libraries, to be indexed and searched using keywords. By August 2006 the search could be performed using facial recognition, courtesy of another Google acquisition - Neven Vision.

In June 2007, provided the user had Google Earth an image could be given its geographic coordinates to be included as a search parameter.

Google Web Albums allowed a user a GByte of photo storage that could be reviewed by family and friends free of charge.

Google v Overture

Idealab was founded by Bill Gross, a Caltech mechanical engineer. He used Idealab as an incubator to launch a large number of Internet businesses. Notably this included an audio equipment company bought by Lotus Software and an educational software operation sold to Cedant. Idealab's eToys flourished before crashing and being sold on to KB Toys.

In 2000 Idealab was valued at $8bn and raised a further $1bn in venture capital.

With this funding it negotiated the rights in the Tuvalu Island's allocated web domain of .tv and launched an operation called dotTV. He sold enough urls with this valuable suffix to enable the island nation to afford to join the UN! VeriSign acquired dotTV in 2001.

But this was not the only time Bill Gross and Google crossed paths. He was also the founder of Goto.com and is thus credited with developing the first pay-per-click search engine.

In February 1998 Goto.com offered advertisers the opportunity to bid against each other to 'own' specific search requests and by July some words and phrases were fetching a dollar per click. The rather simplistic and opportunistic theory in this was that the site willing to pay most was probably the most relevant. Google did make an approach to buy a licence for the software but was unsuccessful.

In 2001 Goto.com became Overture Services Inc and was highly successfully providing MSN and Yahoo! with strong revenue streams. It applied for and received a patent in 2001. It used this strength to buy AltaVista and AlltheWeb before being itself acquired by Yahoo! for $1.6bn in 2003.

In January 2002, smarting from losing out to Google at AOL, EarthLink and Ask Jeeves, Goto.com launched litigation against Google AdWords for infringement of its patent. However when Yahoo! acquired Overture the action was settled when Google gave Yahoo! 2.7 million shares in return for a perpetual licence.

RANDOM ACCESS MOMENT:
There are a number of games that users can play with Google, for example seeking a Googlewhack. This is a two-word search term that will return a single Google result. Inverted commas cannot be used because that tells Google to return only those instances where the two words appear side-by-side. The words must also be 'legitimate'. Recent examples include 'Italianate tablesides', 'storywriters microculture, 'insomniacs speedwriter'...

Just as experimentation is affected by the observer, so too are Googlewhacks. Publish the fact that you have found one and you have created a second link for it, so it is no longer valid.

Gary Stock coined the term and established The Whack Stack at googlewhack.com allowing users to make their claims for a discovery.

A Googlewhackblatt is a version where one word searches are allowed to achieve the same singular result. It too has the Googlewhackblatt paradox that its very discovery is also its demise. Some have claimed a discovery by expressing the search back-to-front to avoid this paradox.

An Antegooglewhackblatt is where a search returns no results.

Planet Google

The next Google application came from outside the business and it too was rocket science! From 1976 to 1990 Lockheed manufactured a series of reconnaissance satellites originally called KH-11 Kenna, later renamed Crystal but for some reason usually referred to as KeyHole. These were US military spy satellites that used electro-optical digital imagery to give a real time view.

Brian McClendon received a patent for the KML (keyhole markup language), its name a direct homage to these satellites,

KML was an XML derivative designed to define a geographic visualisation upon the Internet for both two-dimensional maps and for three-dimensional earth browsers. KML allowed the definition of a longitude and latitude, and altitude for place marks and images; it also offered tilt and heading values to set a point of view.

In effect it brought video-game-like 3D graphics to satellite images and aerial photographs; by refreshing the screen 60 times per second the movement came to life.

McClendon worked on this software at his company Intrinsic Graphics, but in 2001 he met John Hanke and they co-founded Keyhole Inc.

Hanke graduated from the University of Texas, added an MBA from the University of California, Berkeley. Though he had developed two software operations in the entertainment market following his graduation, he initially eschewed the IT world and took up an unspecified role in foreign affairs for the US government based in Myanmar (Burma) and Indonesia.

Intriguingly Keyhole Inc was part funded by In-Q-Tel, a CIA operation, and by a Sony venture capital fund. Subsequently nVidia partnered Keyhole in a project to develop a consumer version of the software.

They developed KML into the 'Earth Viewer' program and gained contracts from governmental operations including the US Department of Defense, US Army CERDEC (Communications-Electronics Research, Development and Engineering Center) and the National Imagery and Mapping Agency.

Earth Viewer's real virtue was the way in which it speedily accessed huge amounts of data and presented it in a real time simulation. It was quoted as having a seven terabyte capability; 8,000 times more data than the human brain retains across its lifetime.

During the 2003 Iraq invasion a number of the major broadcasters, including ABC, CBS and CNN, used Earth Viewer images to broadcast 3D fly-bys. For example CNN showed a simulation of flying over Baghdad and sweeping in at street level to highlight bombing targets – and each time credited this to EarthViewer.com.

This high profile attention paid off when Google acquired the software in 2004 - to launch it in 2005 as Google Earth. Hanke became director of Google Earth and Google Maps and Brian McClendon the vice president of engineering at Google.

The software provided a varying resolution depending on the location. A remote island had 15 metres of resolution, while a major city was often offered at 15 cms of resolution. But it was the linkage of Google Search with Google Earth that added a whole other dimension, offering the user the means to find local businesses and data on tourist locations according to location.

Its effortless display of what represented a huge amount of data so speedily made it compulsive.

The images themselves came from services like TeleAtlas and EarthSat. Some areas covered had just a look-down 2D version while others allowed 3D by accessing data collected by NASA's SRTM (shuttle radar topography mission) and by DEM (digital elevation models) provided by radar satellites.

Google's acquisition of SketchUp in 2006 provided 3D tools to add buildings and structures to Google Earth images.

In February 2005 Google launched Google Maps. This too was developed elsewhere. Lars and Jens Rasmussen had founded Where 2 Technologies in Sydney, Australia and developed a downloadable C++ program. In meeting with Google they proposed instead that they develop a web-based-only version and this become the basis of Google Maps.

As this used the Mercator projection it could not display the polar areas. Images were mostly sourced from aerial photography but its high-res satellite-derived images were used for the whole of the USA, Canada and the UK, plus a series of special areas like the Nile Valley, Turin (for the Winter Olympics),,, Some military areas of the USA were deliberately 'smudged' to avoid terrorism concerns.

Later in 2005 an API was issued to allow developers to add Google Maps to their own sites. In 2006 a version was available for use with mobiles, PDAs, tablets...

Google Maps Navigation was launched free of charge and this directly adversely affected the share prices of satnav makers Garmin and TomTom.

On 20 July 2005 to mark the 36th anniversary of the Apollo 11 moon landing Google Moon included public domain images of the Moon within Google Maps. In March 2006 the first planet was included as Google Mars.

In January 2006 Google Maps and Google Earth were integrated to use the same database of satellite images. In December 2006 a new layer was added to Google Earth called Geographic Web. This interacted with Wikipedia and Panoramio to provide location specific information and photographs. By May 2007 Panoramio had been acquired by Google and in 2010 the Geographic Web layer was removed with Panoramio becoming part of the main layers. Wikipedia is still available through the 'More' layer.

David McCutchen founded Immersive Media Company (IMC), a Calgary based operation, basing it upon work capturing wraparound images in the 1980s. He received a patent in 1991 and founded the organisation in 1994.

He went on to develop the Dodeca System in 2004. This was a digital camera that took a spherical photograph; to date the current offering is its fourth generation.

By 2006 VW Beetles equipped with these cameras were despatched in an exercise known as the Geoimmersive City Collect Project. It recorded major streets in cities across Canada and the USA, not only as stills but also as full-frame video.

IMC introduced the concept to Google and provided the images of the first thirty-five cities for Google Streetview in May 2007.

Google later cancelled the arrangement with IMC and developed its own approach. IMC was still active with Patrol View, a service for the military providing mapping of Iraq and other war-torn locations. MapQuest is using IMC for its 360 View service and has been active with 360-degree images at sporting venues, including the Vancouver Winter Olympics.

Google Streetview displayed panoramic images taken by a fleet of specially adapted cars, trikes or snowmobiles. The vehicles had nine cameras, usually Elphel open-source cameras, to capture a full 360-degree view with a viewpoint set at 2.5 metres above the ground.

There was a degree of kismet about what was captured in the way of individuals' comings and goings as the vehicles happened to pass by. Examples cited were men leaving a strip club, people clad in revealing swimming costumes...

The concerns raised led to Google blurring any faces to protect privacy. In some markets it was also agreed to blur vehicle registration numbers. Austria operated a ban on the service and the Czech Republic stopped any new images being taken.

Streetview was added to Google Earth in April 2008 and Smart Navigation was included in 2009. Its European service started in July 2008 with the Tour de France route which rolled out through France in October 2008. This was rapidly followed by major Spanish and Italian cities in the same month.

Most major cities in the UK and the Netherlands went live in March 2009 and the bandwagon rolled on through Germany, Switzerland, Portugal... By the end of 2009 further French cities and UK tourist sites were also added. Scandinavia was completed during January/February 2010.

Google stated that it would provide street views of the entire world, and that it planned to return to reshoot some of the cities photographed with early cameras, as the quality was not as good as that achieved by its later equipment.

Controversially it also had antenna to scan for 3G, GSM and Wi-Fi broadcasts. This was established when a German regulator complained that between 2006 and 2010 Google had amassed some 600 GBytes of data about the networks encountered in more than thirty countries.

The suggestion was that no privacy policy was agreed and although Google insisted they had not used the data for its search engine or other services, the fear was that they might well have done so if there had been no complaint. As I write this they still have that data and wait on the regulators telling them they should delete it.

Others proposed that we should not look so introspectively but should recapture the ancient interest in the skies above us. Slooh.com founded in 2002 used the subtitle Space Camera and provided a web telescope controllable by users.

The original telescopes were on Mount Teide in the Canary Islands, one was optimised for planetary views and the other for deep space. In Chile a telescope for the southern hemisphere had been added, and a third location in Australia was being finalised.

Slooh.com had collected together volunteers who had supplied well over a million new images since its launch on Christmas Day in 2003.

In August 2007 Google Earth too flipped its point-of-view to launch Google Sky. Using NASA and Hubble Telescope imagery and the radio telescopes of the NRAO (National Radio Astronomy Observatory) this service within Google Earth provided a view of the sky as if looking from the centre of the earth.

It could display the motions of the Moon and planets as viewed from the user's specific location on Earth. The user could fly from Earth to any other point and look at specific galaxies and star clusters or take several predefined tours such as the 'life of a star'. It even offered the background mythology of the stars.

Microsoft entered the fray six months later in February 2008 with the WWT (worldwide telescope). A cooperative effort with Johns Hopkins University, it added the views of ten earth-bound telescopes as well as that of the Hubble. It had narrated tours, good zoom features and could show the sky at various wavelengths. By October 2008 Microsoft was attracting 1.5m regular users to this service.

In February 2009 Google turned its perspective again to launch Google Ocean which allowed the user to explore the depths. It developed the service after gathering an august advisory group, with inputs from National Geographic and the BBC. By April that year it had added the Great Lakes.

RANDOM ACCESS MOMENT:
Googling - by 2006 'to google' was an accepted verb listed in Webster's as, 'to use the Google search engine to obtain information ... on the World Wide Web.' That year the Oxford English Dictionary followed suit and also listed it.

Google communication

Not content to offer Gmail, Google developed a number of other offerings to its committed and loyal user base. In August 2005 it launched Google Talk allowing instant text messages and file transfers. Voice chat allowed free VOIP and audio conferencing services and later a free video-chat plug-in.

By December 2005 Gmail was available for mobile use and in November 2007 this was joined by Android, a mobile operating system.

Rebuffed by its approach to acquire Friendster, in January 2004 Google decided to annexe the current interest in social networking by launching a service developed internally by one of its employees, Orkut Büyükkökten; this service was Orkut.

It held similar objectives to other networks in seeking to help users maintain contact with their friends and through these meet new people.

Its initial success was in the USA but this rapidly shifted to overseas markets; in 2011 only around 2% of the 100 million users came from the USA. Brazil and India made up the bulk of them.

In November 2007 the Google OpenSocial initiative sought a coordinated effort with other networks to agree a series of standard APIs for social networking - APIs to work cross-platform and across all networks.

It received the support of MySpace, Friendster, Yahoo! and others, but notably Facebook did not participate. These APIs were prepared in HTML, JavaScript and within Google Gadgets, but the code proved easy to crack and the number of gadgets was limited; it did not take off in the social networking space.

By 2011 Google indexed trillions of web pages on more than a million servers located in centres around the world. Globally it dealt with over a billion requests each day and has over 700,000 linked sites.

It was ranked by Alexa as the world's top site and of course had that rank for the US too, where it maintained a two-thirds market share for USA searches. Its subsidiaries YouTube and Blogger also featured in the list of the top ten sites.

China and Baidu

Larry Page was not the only one to see the potential for web page ranking.

Robin Li was raised in Yangquan in China, a province directly to the west of Beijing and the first city created by the Chinese Communist Party. His parents were factory workers but his success at school enabled him to qualify for high school and Beijing University.

Through school he had success in a number of programming competitions and opted to study information management for his degree. He subsequently moved to the United States to attend the University of Buffalo where he pursued an MSc in computer science.

After qualifying he worked with IDD Information Services cooperating in producing software for *The Wall Street Journal* web edition. He also worked on picture search software for Go.com.

Li developed RankDex, a ranking system for which he received a US patent. In January 2000 RankDex was applied to develop a search engine with Eric Xu. They named it Baidu, a character from an 800 year-old poem; an allegory about perseverance in pursuit of the ideal.

Baidu did not have the indexing breadth of Google and yet it developed a 70% share of the Chinese market, with Google China running a very poor second. Its major penetration of the vast market meant it ranked seventh on the global website league. But the reason for its Chinese dominance was none too subtle.

Google launched its China operation in 2005 with a Chinese-language version. Kai-Fu Lee, the founder of Microsoft Research Asia, was appointed to manage the operation. Microsoft was none too pleased by this 'abduction' and took action against Google and Lee; a confidential deal was struck.

But by 2009 Google China was in trouble with the authorities. This was more to do with its YouTube ownership than its search services, but the censorship sporadically interrupted its other services. Google countered by moving the operation to Hong Kong and redirecting all search requests from China to the new base; Hong Kong's special enterprise status allowed more freedom than its parent.

It was because Baidu better understood and respected the Chinese government regulations and censorship that it gained market leadership. Baidu was registered in the Cayman Islands and was the first Chinese company to be listed on NASDAQ.

Freenet

There are many who baulked at the notion of monitoring and censorship of the Internet and inevitably this led to organisations and services arising to counter attempts at such management.

One high profile case was of course WikiLeaks which published US diplomatic documents and other whistleblower-sourced material to the Internet. It described itself as being,

'...founded by Chinese dissidents, journalists, mathematicians and start-up company technologists, from the US, Taiwan, Europe, Australia and South Africa.'

The US government appeared powerless to stop the releases; however its spokesperson Julian Assange was arrested in the UK for extradition to face alleged sexual crimes in Scandinavia. I cannot help but think that if you want to discredit someone then an alleged sexual crime is a pretty useful approach. However Amazon and others have decided to stop listing and linking to WikiLeaks.

The Electronic Frontier Foundation (EFF) was founded back in July 1990 to fight for individuals to have freedom of speech and privacy. Its formation was prompted by the actions of the US Secret Service when they responded to distribution of the E911 document, an internal Bell company document describing how the emergency 9-1-1 service operated.

The Secret Service descended on the small publisher, Steve Jackson Games, which as its name suggested specialised in games books. It was alleged that the publisher had received a copy of the E911 document.

The Secret Service confiscated the company computers and interfered with the progress of the business only to fail to find the document. While it had the computers it viewed all communications on the company's bulletin board and deleted them. The publisher sought an organisation to assist his subsequent claims against the Secret Service but found no group that understood the technology well enough.

Those at WELL.com (whole earth 'lectronic link) did understand the issue and three people emerged to create the EFF - the Lotus founder Mitch Kapor, John Perry Barlow of the Grateful Dead and John Gilmore of Sun Microsystems.

They first took on the Steve Jackson Games matter and a court concluded that the privacy of email should be afforded the same legal basis as a phone call.

EFF next tackled the US government over an archaic law that held that any form of encryption was a national security matter. When in 1995 Daniel J Bernstein, a UCB student, wanted to publish and export an encryption program he had written, he was told he had to register as an arms dealer to do this!

EFF sought and received judgement that software code was protected by the US First Amendment which, among other things, guarantees the freedom of speech, the freedom of the press and the freedom of religious pursuit.

The US government subsequently sought to water down the decision and Bernstein, by now a professor at the University of Illinois, once again took action. But this time the court took nine years to reach no decision; instead it advised Bernstein to come back if and when he could show that the government had breached the spirit of the First Amendment.

Ian Clarke, a bright Irishman, showed early promise when he twice won the Young Scientist Exhibition's senior chemical, physical and mathematical prize at the age of sixteen and seventeen. At Edinburgh University he helped resurrect the Artificial Intelligence Society as its president.

In his final year he published *A Distributed, Decentralised Information Storage and Retrieval System*, a blueprint for using the Internet without being detected or censored. His stated fear was that authority would be able to monitor Internet traffic rather more readily than the pre-existing snail mail and phone services. Clarke published this notion on the Internet, seeking volunteers to help him in building it. The project became known as Freenet.

When Clarke moved to California and co-founded Uprizer Inc he started to commercialise the Freenet notion, successfully raising $4m seedcorn in 2001. Clarke moved away but continued to work in web innovations and distributed computing.

Freenet was the first service to offer an anonymous peer-to-peer network to ensure freedom of communication. Some two million copies of the software have been downloaded, despite being blocked by some countries, including China. These copies can be freely transmitted between friends and other contacts so the user base is impossible to define.

Subsequent versions ensured that not only were users impossible to identify, but the fact that they were using Freenet was not discernible either.

But it was not without detractors, often being termed as the 'dark side' of the Net. This was because its anonymity was suggested to be being used by criminal syndicates. It is accused by some of being a refuge for paedophiles and pornographers, a location for hackers to distribute access codes, stolen identities, viruses… A list of Freenet freesites does include, perhaps tongue-in-cheek, *The Terrorist's Handbook: A practical guide to explosives and other things of interests to terrorists.*

Because of its confidentiality the size of what is in the 'deep web' or 'darknet' is difficult to assess; estimates published at one stage suggested it was anything from 400 to 500 times the size of the overt Net. Since Google and other search engines do not dredge these sites they cannot provide any form of measurement.

A similar approach is used by the Tor network (the onion routing) developed by Roger Dingledine, Nick Mathewson and Paul Syverson to ensure anonymity for its users - WikiLeaks among them. Funded by the US Naval Research Laboratory it appeared in 2004 as a C programming language consisting of just under 150,000 lines of code.

For a year it was supported by the EFF; it is now run by a non-profit organisation project. Law enforcement agencies however insisted that they have ways to get around these systems, and there was always a record held somewhere…

Amazon – online bookseller

The World Wide Web was open for business in 1991 but it was in 1994 that it began to pick up momentum with the advent of online banking.

In the same year a German company, Intershop Communications, launched an e-commerce solution enabling website owners to retail on the Net.

It was not until 1995 that Netscape introduced SSL encryption to make online shopping and payments more secure and therefore more likely. SSL (secure sockets layer) and its successor TLS (transport layer security) were protocols that encrypted the process of an Internet transaction. Netscape developed SSL but never released version 1.0; its v2.0 was published in February 1995, and v3.0 resolved some early glitches.

Its application changed http pages into https (hypertext transfer protocol secure) and ensured secure identification of the web server being used to create a safe channel across what was otherwise an insecure network.

It was also used to secure emails and enable VPNs (virtual private networks) which previously required the use of expensive leased lines. SSL/TLS allowed businesses to espouse the Internet enthusiastically.

One of the earliest players was Amazon.com founded originally as Cadabra Inc in 1994 and launched in 1995. It realised that many heard the name as 'cadaver' and so it was changed. The word Amazon was later explained as indicating that it offered an A to Z service.

Jeff Bezos was the founder, Bezos being the surname of his stepfather following his teenage mother's short term relationship with his biological father. Bezos was educated at the University of Princeton where he earned a BSc in computer science and electrical engineering.

His early work experience was with various financial and trading services in New York. But at the age of thirty he travelled to Seattle with his plan for Amazon 'in development'.

It was launched as a book-selling site on the basis that traditional booksellers would never be able to equal the range that Amazon could achieve online. Bezos made it clear that he did not expect to show profits for the first four years and perhaps this allowed the organisation to weather the dot.com bubble when it burst. In 1997 it acquired the UK online bookseller Bookpages.co.uk and renamed this Amazon UK in October 1998.

From 2007 Amazon became the leading supplier of eBooks with its series of eReaders, the Kindle.

Through acquisition and organic development it added a broader electronic range of music CDs, video DVDs, video games and computer software and later still added toys, clothing, furniture and even food.

It evolved a broad series of services to maintain customers' attention - gift certificates and wish lists, product reviews and listings, travel and photo processing…

Amazon became the USA's top online retailer, leaving Staples way behind in second place. According to Alexa it is the 5th ranked website in the USA and in the top fifteen globally.

Napster – music sharing

Sean Parker and Shawn Fanning launched Napster in June 1999. The site was designed for music lovers to find and download MP3 tracks easily.

By February 2001 it had attracted some 25m users and they were exchanging 80 million music files between themselves at no charge.

The Recording Industry Association of America (RIAA) was quick to take legal action and it was soon followed by big hitters like Madonna and Metallica when they found their music was being distributed through Napster.

Counter-arguments by Napster suggested that it provided a valuable promotional service for artists and bands, but the courts were unimpressed.

Napster paid over $26m to intellectual property owners and tried to switch to a chargeable service but the attempt was not well received.

In July 2001 Napster closed down its site. It tried to sell its assets to Bertelsmann of Germany but a judge blocked this and so the operation went through Chapter 11 to Chapter 7 in September 2002.

Wikipedia reference source extraordinaire
In 1996 Jimmy Donal Wales and Tim Shell launched Bomis, a website that offered adult material, glamour to pornographic. It included a Babe Report that tracked celebs and models in the adult entertainment business. It also operated nekkid.info, a free site offering erotic photos.

Wales had another concept in mind when he later hired Larry Sanger. Sanger graduated in philosophy, but was perhaps wavering when he once stated in a journal he published,
'The history of philosophy is full of disagreement and confusion.'

He was appointed editor-in-chief to develop *Nupedia* a web-based encyclopaedia; the business was underwritten by Bomis. The notion was to acquire expert articles on all manner of subjects that would be reviewed and published free of charge to the user.

Wales and Sanger were introduced to the concept of a 'wiki' by Ben Kovitz in 2001; Kovitz was a contributor to the WikiWikiWeb.

In seeking a way to make progress with *Nupedia* more speedy, Sanger created a wiki site which would permit the creation and editing of interlinked articles online.

Wiki was first developed by Ward Cunningham in 1994 when he developed a wiki engine for what he called WikiWikiWeb. His concept was a web application that stored all entries in files or a database format so they could be accessed with a browser. It was inspired by Apple's HyperCard in that the entries were like a stack of cards. Sanger's innovation was that they could be edited collaboratively.

Wiki derived from a Hawaiian experience when Cunningham was advised to take the Wiki-Wiki Shuttle between airport terminals; the term *wiki* means quick – so wiki wiki must be very quick.

Sanger's Wiki was originally intended as a feeder site to *Nupedia*, giving a means for fast entries and updates. But the notion proved so compelling the whole project was changed to become Wikipedia in January 2001.

The name, its trademark and the operation are owned by the not-for-profit Wikimedia Corporation. Wales insisted the editorial effort should not be constrained to an expert panel à la *Nupedia*, but instead be thrown open to all Internet users. Wikipedia outgrew *Nupedia* within a few days of its launch.

But Sanger was quick to notice that it was being hijacked by those who were anti-authority and that his desire for expert articles was being overwhelmed.

In May 2001 a dozen and more non-English language Wikipedia were launched.

In February 2002 Bomis with troubles of its own withdrew its investment, and lacking funding himself Sanger stepped down as editor of Wikipedia in March 2002. Nupedia closed down in 2003.

After he left Sanger was critical of the accuracy of Wikipedia and suggested that there was,

'...a certain poisonous social or political atmosphere in the project.'

In September 2006 he launched the *Encyclopedia of Earth* encompassing his original notion of expert articles. He launched with fewer than four hundred articles but by late 2010 there were over 7,500. He then launched Citizendium in March 2007 to be 'all that Wikipedia was not' though it had just 15,000 articles, with only 10% of these editorially approved, by the end of 2010.

Compare this with the 3.5million articles on Wikipedia running to some 23 million pages of information being read by around 80 million monthly visitors and 'managed' by some 1,750 unpaid administrators.

In January 2011 Wikipedia stated that it had 91,000 active contributors developing some 17 million articles in 270 languages.

But of course all users could add and edit, provide references and images. The administrators had special powers to clear up and remove anything that breached the Wikipedia policies or infringed copyright.

The contributions remained the property of the contributor but Wikipedia operated two licences - Creative Commons Attribution-Sharealike 3.0 Unported License and the GNU Free Documentation License - to ensure the pages could be freely distributed and reproduced.

Contributors are requested to follow the Wikipedia Manual of Style and their contributions are recorded in the page history.

While one could not take it for granted that a Wikipedia article was accurate, the approach did air the issues surrounding a subject rather well, a little judicious second sourcing and background research soon provides any needed clarity.

26 - Online auctions - eBay

'We have technology, finally, that for the first time in human history allows people to really maintain rich connections with much larger numbers of people.' Pierre Omidyar, eBay founder

Born in France, Pierre Morad Omidyar, had Iranian parents, a surgeon father and a mother with a PhD in linguistics. When he was six years old his family moved to Maryland, USA where his father took up a residency at the John Hopkins University Medical Center. Omidyar grew up in Washington DC.

His interest in computing stemmed from learning to programme in BASIC on a Tandy TRS-80 and then later switching to Apple computers. His first serious program was produced at the age of fourteen when he developed software to catalogue his school's books. He attended Tufts University, near Boston, graduating in 1988 in computer science.

He joined Claris, an Apple subsidiary, where he was part of the team involved in the MacDraw product. In May 1991 with friends he co-founded the Ink Development Corp. It set out to develop software for GoCorporation's PenPoint operating system; but this high-profile project failed, in part as a result of the Apple Newton and Microsoft's entry into this space. 'Ink' switched camps to work on Windows for Pen Computing.

Rather more successfully it also came up with solutions for Internet shopping; the company was soon renamed eShop Inc. As eShop it developed eShop Technology, to satisfy the eCommerce requirements for a merchandising and shopping system, and eShop Plaza, a virtual mall.

Omidyar worked on eShop but later suggested he was more interested in the consumer-to-consumer market, rather than the business-to-consumer aspects. He moved in 1994 to work with General Magic and the Magic Cap (Magic communicating applications platform), a platform for mobiles.

eShop Inc was acquired by Microsoft in June 1996 for its patents in online sales technologies and was incorporated into Merchant Server.

While still working for General Magic, over the weekend of 3-4 September 1995 Omidyar launched a service that he hoped would create a perfect market between consumers. He had designed Auction Web in his spare time from home; it was an online auction site designed for individual consumers.

Person-to-person trading had in the past been via classified advertising, car boot sales, garage sales and hobbyist events. Omidyar saw a way to connect people in a new process via the Internet.

The early focus was aimed at the enthusiastic people involved in collectibles and computer parts. This was not, as some of the organisation's early PR suggested, designed for his girlfriend Pam's interest in Pez candy dispenser collectibles.

The seller would set a minimum price for an item on the site and buyers would compete to outbid each other; in this way the seller would get the maximum price for the item. Browsing and bidding on items was established as free of any charges; at first sellers had a free ride too.

But to meet the costs levied by the internet service provider Omidyar soon introduced charges for the seller. There was a basic listing fee (optional add-on charges to make the listing more noticeable) and a nominal percentage of the finally agreed selling price to be paid. The site would notify the buyer and seller of the agreed deal, presuming the auction reached a price in excess of the seller's minimum.

This notification made clear that the contract was between the seller and buyer (not the site) and the transaction was completed offline.

Early eBay progress

Omidyar was also selling his consulting services at the time through his company Echo Bay Technology Group. He decided to reuse this, and a pre-existing website, for this latest idea - his service became eBay.

As it was a part-time activity Omidyar tried to ensure there was only a need for a 'light hand on the tiller'. He kept the design and processes very simple.

The first auctioned item was a broken laser pointer, as much to test the service more than a serious attempt to sell it. But it went for $14.83, prompting Omidyar to call the buyer and ask why. The story was that the buyer was a collector of broken laser pointers! Revenues from the first month's business exceeded direct costs and the business was immediately self-funding.

At first he personally adjudicated by email in any disputes, but in February 1996 he streamlined this by creating the 'feedback forum'. In this way the site would become self-regulating by inviting users to rank and report on deals; not just whinges and complaints but also thanks and praise.

By overlaying this feedback with his own image of a set of community values he ensured that users would be prepared to send money sight-unseen to sellers, who were of course strangers.

If you have never bought or sold something on eBay then it is difficult to imagine the buzz in the last few moments of an auction. Although the site set out to be the perfect market it did also inspire bidders to place that extra bid to secure the item and perhaps pay a tad more than planned.

The site took off so quickly that his first recruitment was for someone to open all the envelopes that were being received from sellers and to pay them in to a bank. This individual was Chris Agarpao. Once all the envelopes were opened the revenues had hit $10,000.

But Omidyar soon realised he needed management assistance too and in 1996 Canadian Jeff Skoll was appointed the organisation's first president; Omidyar was its chairman.

Skoll graduated from the University of Toronto, and had founded two Canadian companies, in IT consulting and computer rentals, before going on to achieve a Stanford MBA in 1995.

The first partnership deal struck was in November 1996 with Electronic Travel Auction which used eBay to sell travel products, including air tickets.

During the year of 1996 the site handled 250,000 auctions but things changed in 1997 when in January alone it handled 2,000,000 auctions; by mid-1997 it was hosting 800,000 auctions a day.

In September1997 Omidyar travelled to Sacramento and tried to register the domain echobay.com for the growing service. When he found it was already in use, by Echo Bay Mines, and not wanting to make the trip twice, he shortened the name to eBay and registered the domain as eBay.com.

During 1997 the millionth item was sold - a Sesame Street Big Bird toy – and the team started spending marketing money on logos and advertising. It needed the funds to manage the phenomenal growth and increased marketing costs. Benchmark Capital stepped up to invest $6.7m in eBay.

From the outset there had been a bulletin board service for questions from users but the eBay Café span off from this when it was realised that many users enjoyed the community aspect of the site.

eBay management team

In January 1998 Meg Whitman, from Princeton and Harvard Business School, became eBay president. She had previously worked as a brand manager with Procter & Gamble, as a VP for strategic planning at The Walt Disney Company, as CEO at Florists' Transworld Delivery and as divisional general manager for Hasbro's Playskool Division (while there she imported the UK Teletubbies show into the USA).

Skoll stepped down to become VP for strategic planning and analysis until ill health forced him to relinquish the post. He was later involved in the eBay Foundation that was granted almost a billion dollars worth of eBay stock, as well as his own Skoll Foundation.

Whitman served as president and CEO for ten years. She fundamentally reorganised the business, appointing a large and experienced team, many from Disney and Pepsico. She organised the company to operate more divisionally, supervised its international growth, its initial public offering and its many acquisitions. Most importantly she stewarded it safely through the bursting of the dot.com bubble.

Her theme was that the organisation was about connecting people, not selling them stuff. Her direction was to raise the average sales price of the items, in part by creating partnerships with key brands. Companies like IBM and Sun subsequently offered products through eBay.

On her watch eBay grew from thirty employees, 500,000 users and $4.7m in US revenues to a staff of 15,000, hundreds of millions of users worldwide and revenues of $7.7bn.

In Feb 2009 Whitman stood for governor of California. She gained the republican candidacy and spent some $160m on her election, but in the event lost out to Jerry Brown.

In September 1998 eBay's IPO had a target share price of $18 but it hit $53.50 per share on its first day, valuing it at $2bn - just three years from launch! By the end of 1998 it had 2.1 million members and $750m in revenues. Its success bred interest elsewhere and Amazon, for example, started its own auctions in 1999.

In 1999 Omidyar married his girlfriend Pamela, who had by then taken advantage of eBay to amass some 400 Pez dispensers.

eBay encountered some problems in its early days. In 1999 eBay experienced one of its worst crashes when it was offline for a full twenty-two hours. Omidyar and Whitman directed its team to make around 10,000 phone calls to the most active users and apologise personally one-on-one. It was surely this strength of company ethos and its critical mass of buyers and sellers that enabled it to see off all the copycat sites that emerged along the way.

eBay Motors

In 1999, Simon Rothman was working as a business development strategist at eBay and looking for a die-cast model of a Ferrari. He was surprised to find a full-size one being offered through its service.

This led to a review that gathered vehicles together into a separate category; this was then spun off as ebaymotors.com in April 2000. The new sub-site researched the barriers to buying and introduced independent vehicle inspections and vehicle history reports. From May 2003 it offered financing through the eBay Financing Center.

By April 2004 it had sold over one million vehicles through the site. The purchaser of a Honda Odyssey was refunded his purchase price by eBay to mark the occasion.

The service was expanded into Australia, Germany and the UK in 1999; by 2004 it was available in almost thirty different national markets. In 2000 services like the site's 'buy it now' offers moved it away from its auction roots to become a straightforward retail site as well.

The site offered collectibles, home decoration and electrical appliances, computers, and other equipment, but perhaps the strangest was in late 1999 when one user offered to sell his kidney on eBay - but the sale of organs in the USA is illegal.

If eBay sees something is illegal or outside its terms, it reserves the right to take the auction or advertisement down from the site. Across the years of eBay this list has of necessity grown. It does not permit - drugs, firearms and military equipment; live animals, ivory and human parts; bootleg audio and video material; offensive material like pornography and Nazi accoutrements; plus things that are banned in certain local markets like alcohol and tobacco.

Remarkable eBay transactions

Some remarkable sales have been achieved through eBay.

In May 2005 a Volkswagen Golf that belonged to today's Pope Benedict XVI while he was still a mere cardinal sold for over $277,000. The buyer was an online casino - perhaps a classic case of going from the sublime to the ridiculous?

The original Hollywood hillside sign was sold in November 2005 for $450,000...

RANDOM ACCESS MOMENT:
The UK would seem to be involved disproportionately in the oddest auctions on eBay. Brit Leigh Knight sold an unwanted brussel sprout from his Christmas dinner for £1,550 in aid of cancer research.

Hearing a British DJ hard flirting with model Jodie Marsh on air, his wife was prompted to sell his Lotus Esprit sports car for £0.50 - of course it sold within five minutes.

Paul Osborn in the UK offered his wife Sharon for sale when he believed her to be having an affair with a colleague. Briefly Tranmere Rovers FC was offered for sale by one of its investors, but without the approval of the chairman, so it was removed.

Richard Harrington, VP of the Royal Entomological Society, bought an aphid in amber from a Lithuanian seller for just £20 to find the 45 million year old insect was a new species, he tried to name it 'Mindarus ebayi' but this was dismissed as too flippant, so he named it after himself, 'Mindarus harringtoni';

Michael Fawcett from the north-east tried to sell a ghost, but eBay removed it as they do not sell 'intangible items'.

eBay Traders

eBay became the vehicle for many individuals to create businesses operating solely within the site. Many are sole traders working from home; in 2002 the New York Times reported that some 75,000 people in the USA were solely deriving incomes from selling through eBay. By 2005 A C Nielsen placed this number at 724,000 people in the USA with their livelihood depending on eBay trading.

Many have established global businesses, shifting significant amounts of merchandise. Traders can opt to establish an eBay store which gives them more flexibility in presenting their wares at two levels of investment, a basic store or a featured store. But most still list their items for auction and as 'buy now' items in the general site.

eBay Express was launched in 2006 in the USA, UK and Germany to create more of a standard Internet shopping experience with a shopping cart and checkout approach. This service lasted only until 2008 before it was withdrawn.

In part the success for eBay traders was due to the online payment schemes that permitted businesses to have confidence that they would receive payment for their shipments, usually instantly.

eBay acquired Billpoint, one such early payment system in May 1999. It was taken out of service when eBay developed its own version, eBay Payments, in spring 2000. It was launched as a joint venture with the Wells Fargo bank. But it had a flaw as it was only valid for eBay auctions and it lost money.

While all this was going on PayPal was launched and it had achieved a strong popularity among the eBay community. There was little surprise when eBay later acquired PayPal in October 2002 for $1.5bn.

PayPal

PayPal was born from two operations that both launched websites in 1999.

Confinity was founded by Peter Thiel, Max Levchin, Luke Nosek and Ken Howery to securely process payments through Palm Pilots. They developed a means of sending money tokens between Palm Pilots which could be cashed in or reconciled through a website established later in November 1999. This website was named paypal.com. Confinity received its first round of funding, $4.5m from Nokia Ventures and Deutsche Bank, by having it beamed to a Palm Pilot.

The second organisation was X.com, a close Palo Alto neighbour founded by Elon Musk, a South African. It was an Internet financial services company backed by Barclays Global and First Western National to give it a banking status. It had much broader ambitions although it enjoyed success in email payments.

The two organisations got together to compare notes in late 1999 and merged in February 2000, still retaining the X name. Supported by funding from Michael Moritz at Sequoia and others, it became PayPal in 2001.

Max R Levchin, a Ukrainian educated in the USA, helped develop the Gausebeck-Levchin, a cryptographic routine that displayed a blurry picture that a user had to read and enter; this eliminated any access by computer. The system was later in general use under the name Captcha which did have an artificially applied acronym - completely automated public Turing test to tell computers and humans apart - but it is of course simply a stylised version of the word capture.

PayPal saw eBay as a major target for its services and went after the USA business aggressively. It offered new users a free $10 balance and $10 for anyone they introduced to the service. PayPal also assisted smaller eBay traders who were not significant enough to obtain merchant status with credit card companies. Card companies did not like to issue an Internet merchant account when the trader was working without the buyer present.

For buyers the really valuable feature was that PayPal accounts could be fed from various sources and there was no need to give credit or debit card numbers to third parties such as websites or eBay sellers and traders.

But PayPal had a problem. It assumed it would earn interest on the balances held on PayPal accounts but it found that users kept these to an absolute minimum. Worse, the users often paid in the funds using credit cards which meant PayPal had to carry the card companies' fees while still allowing the users full value on their accounts. Add to this the insurances PayPal needed to cover its exposure to non-payment, its technical and physical overheads and it realised that it would not run profitably without other revenue sources.

It had to move away from offering its service free and introduce a transaction fee; fortunately by then its penetration into the eBay space was relatively secure.

One of PayPal's innovations was the way in which it would authenticate a user's bank account. It made two very low deposits into an account and this created a four digit password for the user. This not only gave positive feedback that the user and account were genuine but also made the user predisposed towards paying into PayPal from this account and not a transaction-fee-bearing credit card.

PayPal bucked a trend in February 2002 when it was one of the first IPOs to be mounted after the 9/11 attacks dampened the US enthusiasm for the market.

At the time it had 10 million registered users inclusive of 2 million business accounts. It processed transactions for $747m in the quarter prior to its IPO. But it had accumulated losses of $231m between start-up in March 1999 until June 2001. It sought to counter this by suggesting it had only spent $48,000 on marketing to record this impressive growth. It was rather proud that it had made only $56.9m loss on its revenues of $34.2m in the first six months of 2001. Compared with the first-half 2000 performance of $70.6m loss against a $3.3m revenue you can see what they mean.

It also revealed that 63% of its business came from eBay which had a competing service; PayPal handled one in four of eBay's transactions.

Despite this it launched its IPO in February 2002. It was delayed for a week or so by a lawsuit placed against it for patent infringement. All this did reduce its expectations somewhat and yet the offered 5.4 million shares were released at $13 each and closed that day up almost 55% at $20.09. This valued PayPal at $1.2bn and after expenses the operation received $61m from the exercise.

But during the following week shares dropped back to $12.86, when eBay announced it had bought Wells Fargo's 35% share in Billpoint; it was also a poor week generally on the NASDAQ.

In July 2002 eBay announced it would acquire PayPal later that year and phase out its own service; this was with some sense of relief as it had been losing $10-15m per year. At the time eBay revealed that 40% of its transactions were settled electronically; they expected to increase this with the acquisition to nearer 60-70%.

Subsequently eBay became quite heavy-handed and used various exercises and exclusive schemes to drive users towards using PayPal. For example, in August 2007 both its Health & Beauty and Video Games listings made it obligatory to accept only PayPal payments.

By early 2008 the list of PayPal exclusive categories was expanded further. Then it announced that any seller with fewer than a hundred feedbacks had to use PayPal. Certain geographic areas were designated as PayPal only, the UK being one of these.

eBay acquired Fraud Sciences, an Israel and Palo Alto based operation, for $169m in January 2008. It offered new merchant solutions and was integrated into PayPal. By mid-2008 PayPal was said to be handling 9% of all eCommerce global payments, turning over some $14.4bn.

In 2010 PayPal signed a deal with CUP (China UnionPay), the association of banking card companies in China; this provided it with access to fourteen of the major Chinese banks, and a number of the smaller ones.

In 2011 PayPal had around 90 million active registered users, operating some 230 million accounts. It has localised its websites for twenty markets and operates in a total of 190 markets, in twenty-four different currencies. It works with millions of merchants worldwide, both via eBay and outside the site.

It represents over a third of eBay revenues, transacting some $2,700 every second, 47% from outside the USA.

The careers of the innovators involved in the creation of PayPal were certainly worthy of inspection post-PayPal. Musk founded SpaceX and developed rockets and his Tesla Motors electric sports car.

Max Levchin left PayPal to found Slide.com in 2004, providing services for social networking sites. It started with photo-sharing software for MySpace and went on to be the largest third party provider of applications for

Facebook. Slide was gobbled up by Google in August 2010 for $182m; Levchin then joined Google as a VP of Engineering.

Peter Thiel, born in Frankfurt-an-Main Germany, launched Clarium as a hedge fund business soon after the sale. As an angel investor he placed $500,000 in Facebook for 5.2% of the company which is today worth $1.7bn. He also invested in Friendster, LinkedIn and others.

Later he and Ken Howery, the CFO at PayPal, went on to found the Founders Fund in 2005, starting it with $50m assembled from angels and entrepreneurs. Luke Nosek and Sean Parker of Napster joined in 2006. The fund in 2011 handled $275m and invested in SpaceX, slide.com and many other ventures. Noske sat on the board of a number of the invested companies.

Giving Works

Back in 1998 the eBay Foundation was established and allocated pre-IPO stocks which became worth $32m.

In 2003 eBay launched the 'eBay Giving Works' scheme in the USA, a similar 'eBay for Charity' was established in the UK. These encouraged using eBay to sell items with all or part of the proceeds going to a charity. This was handled through an operation called MissionFish, a non-profit organisation that checked out the charity, took the money from the sale and passed it on, maximising any tax benefits for the donation. The 'Fish' in the title is taken from the sentiment of the leading non-profit prophet Bill Shore who said,

'Rather than "giving fish" to keep a non-profit running, or even "teaching them to fish," we're trying to "build fisheries" that sustain good causes over the long-term.'

Over $150m has been raised in the USA using this scheme. eBay would often refund part of the fees where an item was sold for charity. Notably, one charity auction achieved $2.63m for the bidder to have lunch with Warren Buffett at the Smith & Wollensky Steakhouse in New York.

Quite separately Omidyar and his wife became major philanthropists, founding the Omidyar Network in 2004, dedicated to helping people improve their lives. It invested almost $300m in this manner. They also established the Omidyar-Tufts Microfinance Fund, endowing it with $100m for the Tufts University board of trustees to invest on initiatives in developing countries.

In 2009 eBay had revenues of almost $9bn and Omidyar's worth was estimated at $3.6 bn. In 2010 Omidyar joined Bill Gates and Warren Buffett as one of forty billionaires who pledged to donate at least half of their wealth to charity; Omidyar went further and pledged to give all but 1% away!

eBay pushing the fabric

eBay had unleashed a whole new world of person-to-person trading - individuals disposing of accumulated stuff for which they had no further use, those pursuing collections of almost anything and everything, those forming new business opportunities, and established concerns espousing a new trading platform.

Of course this meant that eBay traders had to become mindful of trade descriptions issues and trading standards within national markets. eBay traders also had to recognise when they should register as a business, and what permits and insurances were required to trade in their local market. For example, in UK the registration as a business automatically propelled the trader into the administration of income tax, National Insurance and value added tax.

But much of the activity engendered sat slightly outside the normal governmental controls, off to one side of sales tax. Did value added tax apply? Should income tax returns be made? Should corporation tax be calculated and paid?

Commentators were highlighting that the business eBay was doing made it equivalent to a top-sixty nation state - and the tax collectors were coming!

In the USA cross-state business brushed up against the varying sales taxes levied in each state. eBay solved this by insisting sellers included the applicable sales tax and any packing and despatch costs in their posting of an item for sale; the tax was added automatically when the buyer went through the checkout process.

In the UK the HM Revenues & Customs indicated that an individual selling a personal possession through a newspaper classified section or via eBay was not trading. But at the same time it scoured eBay to identify those who received a large number of feedbacks. It was presumed that these were traders rather than individuals and set about investigation.

But eBay has seldom stayed still. It constantly innovates through the tools it uses, through its look and feel, and through a whole string of acquisitions.

Half.com

Josh Kopelman cofounded Infonautics Corporation with Sunny Balijepalli while at the University of Pennsylvania in 1992. They took the company public in 1996 but Kopelman left in July 1999 to found Half.com.

Half.com focused very successfully on attracting those selling second-hand books, music and movies. A year later in July 2000 eBay acquired the operation for $350m. Kopelman stayed with eBay for three years managing the Half.com activity.

Half.com also specialised in those who offer a low fixed price sale for items that have an ISBN (international standard book number), a UPC (universal product code) or any other SKU (stock-keeping unit) reference number. In this way buyers could review offers using the required code and sellers would compete for attention - thus reversing the eBay model where it was the buyers who competed.

There were no fees; instead Half.com charged a percentage of every sale - 15% for items under $50 and above this figure the rate decreased as the sale value increased. The trader agreed to ship within three days and to meet all despatch costs. Half.com insisted upon a credit card payment and did not accept PayPal; but then its percentages allowed it the luxury of accommodating the credit card company charges from its take.

In January 2004 Kopelman left to launch TurnTide, an anti-spam company. Known as SpamSquelcher, the TurnTide ASR (anti-spam router) did not filter spam but instead looked at a message's path and dealt with suspicious traffic directly. TurnTide was acquired six months later by Symantec for $28m.

Kopelman went on to advise venture capital companies and with the non-profit Kopelman Foundation made angel investments with social entrepreneurs.

Craigslist

In 1995 Craig Newmark began issuing emails detailing events in the San Francisco Bay Area. In 1996 he developed a website for the same purpose. By 1999 Craigslist was incorporated and it was running the service across nine US cities the following year.

Craigslist's approach was to bring classified adverts to the Internet. Its prime income came from paid-for job advertisements, cars, apartments...

By 2011 it served some 700 cities in fifty countries and achieved twenty billion page viewings per month. It was ranked as the seventh busiest site in the USA and was in the top forty globally.

In August 2004 eBay acquired 25% of Craigslist from a departed founder but did nothing to use this ownership to change the operation's approach; though it did take legal action in 2008 when the Craigslist board took actions that would dilute the eBay holding. In September 2010 eBay's complaint was upheld and its holding reinstated to 28.4% from its reduced holding.

The relationship between the two organisations was understandably strained. In 2004 eBay acquired Marktplaats.nl, the leading Dutch classified site and a competitor to Craigslist. eBay became a direct threat when it launched Kijiji.com, its own classifieds site in March 2005. By March 2010 this was relaunched as eBay Classifieds. How much eBay learned from its ownership in Craigslist can only be surmised.

Adding eBay categories

In February 2005 eBay acquired Rent.com, an online apartment listing service, for $415m. The site provided rental rates and availability, gave virtual tours of the apartment, searched on roommates and supplied lists of moving services.

In the same year it launched a Business & Industrial sector for buying and selling surplus business and industrial equipment.

The eBay Pulse site tracked popular search items to provide users with trends. Reviews & Guides provided more insight. Best of eBay highlighted the more unusual auction items.

Drop shipping

In 2007 a phenomenon known as 'drop shipping' emerged on eBay. It promised individuals a business model to start making money immediately without the need to buy or hold stocks; they could concentrate solely on marketing and promotion aspects.

Individuals were offered this business opportunity by making a monthly or annual fee to the 'drop shipper'. In some cases these were manufacturers or wholesalers, but just as often were middlemen taking their own margin, who sat between the suppliers and the eBay traders. A large number of China-based drop shippers emerged.

The business case was that eBay traders were able to trade from a catalogue of suitable products that they did not have to hold or own. They would merely advertise them on eBay and only when they made a sale would they arrange for the drop shipper to despatch the item for the cost price and the despatch costs. Of course an eBay sale meant the trader had already been paid the sale price so cashflow was instantly positive.

The drop shippers set out how a turn could be made on each item and highlighted the potential high numbers of sales that could be achieved globally. Clearly some traders used this route successfully because the phenomenon continued.

But of course hundreds or thousands of other eBay traders were drawn into the same scheme and items were undercut from the recommended sales price by those seeking an edge. Margins were severely eroded and the trader still had to meet the costs of eBay, PayPal and others from this diminishing return.

Further, the risk the trader faced was whether the drop shipper would reliably and speedily make the deliveries; if not then the trader's reputation and feedbacks would be negative.

That is not to mention those drop shippers who were just a scam from start to finish. It was all a case of *caveat venditor* - 'let the seller beware'.

Skype

BlueMoon Interactive, an Estonian company founded by Ahti Heinla, Priit Kasesalu and Jaan Tallinn, created two software products Kazaa and FastTrack.

These were sold on to Janus Friis, a Dane, and Niklas Zennström, a Swede, who marketed them from March 2001 through Consumer Empowerment, a Dutch company that they jointly owned.

FastTrack was the protocol and Kazaa was the file-sharing service that was heavily used in distributing music tracks. But this was discredited, by being accused of distribution malware and by being routinely sued by record companies for copyright infringement. FastTrack was also utilised by Grokster and iMesh. However the demise of Napster in July 2001 rather took the wind from its sails.

The same Estonian team developed Skype and sold it through the same Scandinavian partners, releasing it in August 2003. The name was a contraction of 'Sky peer-to-peer'.

Skype asked users to define unique Skype identities and using these they could talk to others by text or chat. Video was soon added and users were able to make unlimited text, chat and video calls at no charge.

For a fee users could use the service to make and receive phone calls to and from phone subscribers, though there was no connection to emergency services.

In October 2005 eBay acquired Skype for $2.6bn. New features were regularly added, for example from January 2006 video conferencing was available. By April that year Skype had 100 million users.

During 2008 the relationship between eBay and the Skype founders was fraught.

eBay sold off 65% of Skype in November 2009 for $2bn to the founders' company and a series of investing organisations. By then Skype had around 500 million registered users spread across the globe; the sale valued it at $2.75bn.

By the end of 2010 Skype had 663 million registered users and in May 2011 Microsoft acquired it for $8.5bn – some thirty-two times its operating profit!

It was to be operated by the Microsoft Skype Division, based in Luxembourg with most of its executive team in Estonia.

Ranking sellers

From 2007 eBay allowed buyers to rate sellers within four categories, each with up to a five star rating. The ratings were submitted anonymously and provided buyers with some confidence as to those with whom they were dealing.

27 - It's a date – social networking

'The value of a social network is defined not only by who's on it, but by who's excluded.' Paul Saffo

Texting or SMS (short message service) on mobile phones was a rather unexpected success. It was a service that came about almost as an afterthought but was thoroughly espoused by users, particularly the young.

In 1984 a Frenchman, Bernard Ghillebaert, and a German, Friedheim Hillebrand, developed SMS which was adopted by all mobile networks. It was estimated that in 2011 some 2.4 billion users, 74% of all mobile users, regularly used the text service. As I wrote this my dentist sent a text reminder for an appointment.

In much the same way, despite never being on its originators' list of benefits of the Internet, once the notion of a web-based social network was conceived the idea just took off. There were hundreds of such networks and millions of regular users who made social networking central to their lives.

Most services shared the notion of a user establishing a profile before creating and approving a list of friends, family and colleagues able to view it. The behaviour of the many interconnections on these networks was of itself interesting.

Six Degrees of separation

The idea of 'six degrees of separation' was expounded by Hungarian author Frigyes Karinthy in his 1929 short story *Chains*. His notion was that no two individuals were ever more than six links away. It suggested that by routing via friends of friends one could plot a course to any other human on the planet using fewer than five links.

John Guare, an American playwright, gave the term 'wings' by featuring it in his play in 1990 and the subsequent film of it in 1993.

Established wisdom is not convinced that this can be shown to be true; killjoys cite remote communities in several parts of the world that would not suggest this to be a universal rule.

Duncan Watts, a Columbia University professor, used some 48,000 emails to try to reach nineteen targeted individuals and test the theory. He concluded that six was about the correct number.

Jure Leskovec and Eric Horvitz in 2007 used instant messaging services and analysed 30 billion of these between 240 million people. They came back with 6.6 as the result.

A Facebook application developed by Karl Bunyan calculated the 'separation'; this considered almost 6 million users. While it showed that in some instances there was as much as twelve degrees of separation, the average did prove to be 5.73!

The early social network Digrii.com, launched in 2008, took the approach that any user accessing a profile on the site was provided with a report of the degrees of separation between himself and the profile clicked.

The game Six Degrees of Kevin Bacon was to become very popular. The challenge was to link Kevin Bacon the actor to any other actor - costarring in a movie or an advertisement was considered a suitable connection.

This led to the actor in January 2007 launching a website called SixDegrees.org together with AOL, Entertainment Weekly and the Network for Good. It was used to interconnect celebrities and the charities they supported, seeking contributions to a favourite celebrity's cause from those who accessed the site.

Ten years earlier a site called SixDegrees.com is usually credited as being the first social networking site, though many features of the social network existed before it, particularly on dating sites.

Its founder Andrew Weinreich set its goal as meeting people you did not know, through those that you did. At its peak it had around a million users. Running from 1997 to 2001 it dropped out before the notion really took off - the fate of many pioneers.

Keeping in touch with old friends
After graduating from Oregon State University, Randy Conrads worked for Boeing for over twenty years. He left to launch classmates.com in 1995.

This was a website that facilitated the process for individuals who wished to find friends and classmates from their school or college days; it also included military service contacts. It prompted the creation of reunions and detailed a process for doing so. It was keen to stress that users used their real names with the service.

By 2004 it had 38 million registered users and 1.4 million paying subscribers, giving it a turnover of $54m for nine months of that year. When its plans for going public came to naught it was acquired for £100m in cash by United Online Inc and formed as a subsidiary called Classmates Media Corporation.

United was a low-cost Internet service provider that had unified the brands NetZero and Juno Internet in 2001. Clearly United saw the opportunity to sell its services to the classmates.com users and to promote itself from second place and overtake AOL.

In March 2006 Classmates acquired the Names Database for $10m, which as it had twenty million users represented an investment of just 50 cents per contact. It permitted a user to join on supplying five email addresses and then they were able to search the whole database. However it only opened the site fully for the user to contact any of the other users after they had supplied twenty-five email addresses.

By 2011 it had some 33 million users, though it had data on over 50 million people via its email supply policy; removal from the site was sometimes claimed to be difficult to achieve. Its policy did not forbid the use of the service for spamming!

It also operated the StayFriends services in Austria, Germany, Sweden and Switzerland and Trombi in France.

In 1999 Julie and Stephen Pankhurst were a married British couple of thirty-somethings. When Julie became pregnant she started to wonder what her old school friends might be doing. They realised that Classmates.com had done nothing to annexe the UK market and so decided to fill the void.

With a friend, Jason Porter, they founded HappyGroup and launched Friends Reunited in July 2000; within eighteen months it had 2.5 million users. In 2002 it went international with sites in Australia, New Zealand and South Africa.

In 2005 they appointed Michael Murphy, ex-Financial Times, as CEO and by the end of the year it was sold to the UK's ITV television company for £120m.

The approach was that registration was free but if someone wished to contact you there was a fee of £5. This fee was dropped in 2008 when the website appeared to be in decline, not faring well against other social networking sites.

The site had chequered press when it emerged that some employers had used it to screen staff applications. Also some individuals had used the service to meet up with old flames and walked away from current relationships. Further, comments about teachers made on the site became the basis for a series of legal actions. These issues would later inspire several plays and books.

Friends Reunited seemed to lose its way as the whole social networking scene was taking off. The site was sold in August 2009 for just £25m to a Scottish company, the DC Thomson subsidiary BrightSolid Limited.

In March 2002 Friendster.com was launched by programmers Jonathan Abrams, Peter Chin, and Dave Lee. It had similar objectives in that users could contact each other to share messages, photos and videos, dating was also a theme.

Abrams is credited as being the driving force. He worked with Nortel and then joined Netscape, working on the Navigator browser software. In 1998 he founded HotLinks that ranked sites by its users' preferences. It grew to 500,000 users but ran out of cash when the dotcom bubble burst. The operation merged with a British software operation and he left.

He studied the dating system Match.com, and was concerned about the notion of linking an online profile with an individual's off-line real life. He came up with an approach where the user would publish a profile and then create a network of friends who could intercommunicate. He foresaw that having mutual friends might make dating approaches easier.

He produced a system to test the idea with his own circle of friends and went on to patent it. It included a routine that calculated networking connections between users to four degrees of separation.

Friendster was formed in his San Francisco apartment and he raised around $400,000 from his contacts to set it in motion. It launched in March 2003 and by June there were over 800,000 users. By autumn that year it had grown two million users and some 10 million page-views each day.

Its calculation of connections became an issue as the sheer scope of the arithmetic expanded exponentially and the service proved slow as a result. The approach adopted was to throw expensive hardware and software at it rather than modify the general process. Abrams appeared to be more engrossed in the publicity the operation was generating than resolving its internal issues.

He turned down a $30m offer from Google to buy Friendster and instead went through Kleiner Perkins Caufield & Byers and others to receive funding of $13m in 2003. But this diluted him to a one-third ownership and he no longer exercised control of the operation.

The new organisation added a whole layer of august individuals to run the day-to-day business. But these egos failed to agree on an approach and became more involved in internal politics than addressing their users' needs.

In 2006 there were two more rounds of funding, making it essentially a subsidiary of the venture capital company; it needed yet more funding in 2008.

When they did research the users they found the peak access time was at 2.00am. Further investigation revealed that most were located in Asia, yet the company was spending its marketing budget in the USA. More research showed that dating was not the main application; merely looking at each others' interests was more of a draw.

By 2009 there were 75 million registered users with 90% of the traffic in Asia. Little surprise then that it was acquired in December 2009 by Tan Sri Vincent Tan's MOL Global (money online) operation in Malaysia; the site was relaunched as part of the takeover. MOL described itself thus,

MOL uses the leverage of a network of over 500,000 physical and virtual payment channels across 75 countries worldwide and linked to 65 banks in 15 countries worldwide to collect payments for content and services. Its core markets are Malaysia, Singapore, Indonesia, Philippines, Thailand and India. MOL has relationships with over 70 online game publishers that have a suite of over 200 online game titles. It also has partnerships with music, movie and video content owners and distributors across the region.

By 2011 Friendster had 115 million registered users and recorded 19 million page views per month; it offered a range of Asian languages in addition to English and Spanish.

Because Friendster had predated MySpace, Facebook and others, that each proved to be so successful, its failings in the USA became much-discussed and it earned the unwanted accolade of featuring as a Harvard Business School case study.

Video file sharing - YouTube

In February 2005 a group of PayPal employees got together and came up with the idea of establishing a video-sharing site with a simple system for users to upload videos. The users could then watch the videos using Adobe Flash Player.

Chad Hurley studied design at Indiana University. He joined PayPal and his first challenge was to design a logo for the operation; this remained its logo for a number of years.

While at PayPal Hurley met with its CFO, Roelof Botha, the South African son of Pik Botha, the country's liberal foreign minister during apartheid. Roelof subsequently joined the YouTube board. He would subsequently become a venture capitalist, working with Sequoia Capital.

Steve Shih Chen and Jawed Karim studied computer science at the University of Illinois at Urbana-Champaign; both were engineers at PayPal.

Chen moved from his birthplace of Taipei, Taiwan to America at the age of eight. He met the other cofounders at PayPal and was also briefly at Facebook.

Karim had Bangladeshi roots; he was born in what was then East Germany before moving to the United States at thirteen years old. Working at PayPal he was responsible for developing many real-time anti-fraud processes.

It was the bonus they each earned in 2002 when eBay bought out PayPal that provided them with the seedcorn for launching what would become YouTube.

But the three set out to develop 'Tune In Hook Up', a dating site which soon crashed and burned. They are said to have come up with the notion for YouTube over a dinner party. Apparently influential in their thinking were two major yet very different events in the previous year,

These were Janet Jackson's 'wardrobe malfunction' or 'Nipplegate' during the February 2004 SuperBowl and the images of the Asian tsunami on Boxing Day. They found that accessing videos of these on the Internet was not easy; they resolved to change that.

Hurley designed the site's interface and logo, Chen and Karim developed the approach. Hurley became CEO, Chen its chief technology officer while

Karim wanted to continue his education and took more of a consultative role. The shareholdings reflected these levels of commitment.

It was Karim's video 'Me at the zoo', based on a trip to San Diego Zoo, that was to be the first uploaded onto YouTube in April 2005.

The YouTube launch proved timely; it was just as the proliferation of camera-phones, web cameras and digital cameras took off globally. The really clever bit was that of course that the users became the content providers and YouTube merely facilitated the site.

At the end of 2005 they received an $11.5m investment from Sequoia Capital and the site went fully live in November 2005. By the middle of 2006 there were more than 60,000 videos being uploaded each day and it achieved over 100 million daily viewings.

One feature that gave the site such appeal was that its clips could be downloaded and embedded into other sites, blogs and social networking sites to give the video even more currency; though this could be blocked by the video uploader if requested.

Advertising was introduced to the site in March 2006 and YouTube soon recorded $15m per month in revenues. Warner Music Group provided its full music video library to YouTube for free download in return for an advertising revenue share.

In November 2006 Google acquired YouTube for $1.65bn in stock. The move by Google was said to be a reaction to rumours that Yahoo! was in talks with Facebook. The founders themselves received shares worth $346m to Hurley, $326m to Chen and $65m to Karim.

In recent years YouTube has been 'infected' by Google's culture of playing April Fools' Jokes on its users.

RANDOM ACCESS MOMENT:
In May 2007 the British father of three-year old Harry and one-year old Charlie Davies-Carr uploaded a 58-second video so their godfather, living in the States, could see the clip. By the autumn of 2010 this video had recorded 228 million viewings, a record only surpassed by Justin Bieber and Lady Gaga!

YouTube Mobile was launched in June 2007, enabling videos to be viewed on smartphones and tablets.

YouTube did have issues with copyright material being uploaded, though it did state clearly, if rather ineffectively, that this should not be done. It relied instead on copyright owners instructing it to remove any infringing material.

Initially the length of videos was unlimited and one way YouTube tried to combat the copyright issue was by reducing the time limit to ten minutes in 2006, on the basis that longer videos were often pirated TV shows or movies.

It raised this to fifteen minutes in July 2010 for standard users, while partner account holders could upload longer videos. In December 2010 standard account holders, with a good record of past uploads, were once again offered the facility of unlimited video lengths.

It has faced regular legal action from England football's Premier League among others. Viacom established that some 150,000 clips of its material were on the service and won the right to usage data from YouTube. It found these had been viewed 1.5 million times and sued for $1.5 billion; though the action was unsuccessful.

YouTube does now run a check against a database of copyright material to try to minimise its exposure.

Music videos have also caused grief with both UK and German royalty-collection operators taking action, though this too has had some degree of resolution.

The offensive content of some of the videos also raised regular concerns with calls for YouTube to be more proactive and to censor extreme material. YouTube did delete a number of videos calling for *jihad* for breaching the site's guidelines.

Users can comment on the videos and these comments also come under attack. The UK's Guardian newspaper for example described these as,

'Juvenile, aggressive, misspelled, sexist, homophobic, swinging from raging at the contents of a video to providing a pointlessly detailed description followed by a LOL, YouTube comments are a hotbed of infantile debate and unashamed ignorance – with the occasional burst of wit shining through.'

Various countries have reacted rather more strongly with China, Iran, Libya, Morocco, Pakistan, Thailand and Turkey all blocking the site for periods of time.

In November 2008 deals were agreed for full-length television programmes and films to be uploaded from companies including CBS and MGM; this was to combat competition from other broadcasters.

Various formats, qualities and now even 3D video facilities were offered.

In January 2010 YouTube presented a film rental service in the USA. It also previewed a service using HTML5 which would invalidate the need for Adobe Flash Player, though this was already installed on more than 80% of PCs.

In spring 2010 YouTube streamed sixty matches of live cricket from the Indian Premier League free of charge. This was a first and may have indicated a new direction, though sporting bodies usually jealously guard their chargeable rights.

In 2011 YouTube was available in around thirty languages and could be viewed on a worldwide basis or in one of twenty-four local versions; it is the IP owner that decides which to offer.

By the middle of 2010 YouTube suggested that thirty-five hours of video was being uploaded every minute of the day and it was receiving 2 billion viewings a day. However after Google's acquisition it chose not to separately define YouTube accounts within its annual report.

Hurley married Kathy, the daughter of Jim Clark of Silicon Graphics and Netscape. He relinquished the CEO role in October 2010. Earlier he tried to fund a Formula One team called Team US F1 for the 2010 season but this failed to materialise; he is apparently still keen to become involved.

Business Networking - LinkedIn

Also launched in a living room – were their garages full? – was LinkedIn. It was at the home of Reid Hoffman and was co-founded with others including Allen Blue, Konstantin Guericke, Eric Ly and Jean-Luc Vaillant,

Hoffman was a Stanford graduate, before working at Apple, Fujitsu and SocialNet. He had also been an executive VP at PayPal, responsible for its business relationships.

Allen Blue was also at Stanford and became director of product design at SocialNet before working as consultant web designer at PayPal.

Konstantin Guericke, a Stanford engineering graduate, was the marketing specialist among the founders. He suggested that LinkedIn was a sensible next stage in social networks. Initially someone under twenty-five wants a network to serve a social life, but on having a family and responsibilities the need for a social life declines, and a professional network becomes more relevant.

Eric Ly qualified at Stanford and MIT. He had roles and consultancies at a number of leading Silicon Valley companies. He was responsible for defining some core product features at LinkedIn.

Jean-Luc Vaillant, as French as his name suggests, qualified at the University of Marseille. He worked at Logitech and with SocialNet, and at MatchNet after it acquired SocialNet.

The concept was for a networking site for business users; this was developed in late 2002 and the site was launched in May 2003. The aim was for users to be able to freely network with those they could trust within a business sector; LinkedIn Groups provided a means for 'safe' introductions to business contacts of contacts.

Among its angel investors was Marc Andreessen of Netscape fame. The founders invited 350 of their own contacts to join; by the end of May they had 4,500 users. It later described itself as,

'...a referral-based professional networking tool... ...The premier provider of professional networking tools for hiring managers, job seekers and professional service providers... ... LinkedIn not only enables professionals to discover inside connections they never knew they had, but also allows them to

receive referrals to deal makers, hiring managers and other highly sought-after executives through the people they already know and trust'

New users created a professional profile and invited contacts to join and make enduring connections; through these contacts' contacts they were effectively connected to a vast network of specialists and professionals. One of the features was that LinkedIn enabled professional business people to exercise a degree of control of their own professional identities.

In October 2003 Sequoia invested $4.7m and by the end of the year there were over 80,000 users with some 50% of these outside the USA. By April 2004 they had over 500,000 users and by the December it and reached 1,600,000. A further funding round raised $10m in October 2004.

Although joining LinkedIn is free, in 2005 it offered five levels of premium services to generate revenue. The first level for $60 a year permitted a user to post information, at $200 per year they were allowed to contact three users a month, and so on, up to $2,000 for the top-tier service.

The LinkedIn Answers feature allowed users to place questions for the community to answer; the LinkedIn Polls service provided research feedback.

During 2008 LinkedIn introduced sponsored advertising but also sought business-to-business opportunities as other forms of revenue. In June 2008 Sequoia and the other venture capital companies bought 5% of LinkedIn for $53m, which valued the company at c $1bn.

By 2010 Tiger Global Management LLC, a New York based private investment company, lacking IPOs in which to invest, acquired a 1% stake for $20m valuing it at over $2 billion.

In November 2010 LinkedIn permitted users to list products and services, or to recommend products to other users.

In 2010 LinkedIn acquired Mspoke, the SaaS (Software as a Service) provider for $5m.

Dave S Mawhinney was one of the cofounders of Mspoke. He had quite a record of rapid start-ups and successful onward sales. Having earned a master's at Carnegie Mellon University, in 1990 he co-founded Industry.Net Corporation which merged in 1996 with AT&T Business Networks.

In 1997 he cofounded Hawk Medical Supply which was sold at a three times multiple within twelve months. Then in 1998 he set up Premier Health Exchange which merged with Medibuy.com in March 2000 in a deal worth $500m.

He co-founded Peak Strategy Inc that helped to optimise trading in stocks and shares and sold this on to a global financial services organisation. In 2002 Mspoke was co-founded with a similar approach.

Mspoke's specialty was browsing web content to make recommendations by constantly updating algorithms to identify relevant content and advertising.

It set out to correct wrong assumptions made by sites so they could improve their targeting. LinkedIn saw the team and its processes as a natural fit for use within its network of users.

By 2011 LinkedIn had grown to 85 million users in over two hundred countries, of these 11 million were in Europe and 3 million in India; it achieved almost 50 million unique visitors each month. Google employees were said to have 47 LinkedIn connections each, Harvard Business School graduates 58 each.

It offered a directory of some 250,000 service providers and supported over 1,000 membership organisations in LinkedIn for Groups.

LinkedIn Personal Plus Accounts offered services giving extra visibility for job seekers; LinkedIn suggested that a user with twenty connections was thirty-four times more likely to be offered a job opportunity than one with just five connections.

They claimed a new member joined every second and boasted that every one of the *Fortune 500* companies had executives or directors who were LinkedIn members.

Give me a Hi5

Ramu Yalamanchi, of Indian ethnicity, grew up in Chicago and qualified in computer science at the University of Illinois at Urbana-Champaign. While at college he was a partner in SponsorNet New Media that would auction off online advertising opportunities. He worked with several businesses, ClickOver and eGroups, and learned his trade.

In 2003 he saw the opportunity for web-based communication to improve upon instant messaging and email and formed Hi5 as a social networking site. His initial focus was on expat Indians in the USA; there was a matrimonial theme too.

He trawled around friends for start up money and by April 2004 had raised $50,000. He had set out to raise $250,000 but was assisted when the costs of web services, server hardware and memory all became less expensive.

Within six months of launch the service had grown organically to a million users. These users were first attracted to share photos with their networks of friends and 80% were from outside the USA; Hi5 had a very simple and speedy upload service for photos. At this time MySpace checked a user's IP address and would not allow non-USA based users!

Hi5 was initially only offered in English but an analysis of its users led them to introduce a Spanish version. When analysis also showed that Spanish-speaking markets appeared to be more similar than other cross-national boundaries they focused on these too.

By 2011 it was the number one social networking site in Spain, Mexico and Portugal. Hi5 was in the top ten sites in twenty countries, some as diverse as Mongolia, Romania, Thailand and Tunisia.

It used advertising sales organisations to drive advertising to the site. This and other exercises grew this business to some 30 billion advertisement viewings a month, compared with its twenty million page viewings per month.

Its growth was meteoric – 5 million users by the end of the first year. By the end of 2005 there were 20 million users and a year later, 40 million - all without any marketing costs!

In 2007 it raised $20m in equity from the venture capitalist Mohr Davidow Ventures to fund its continued growth.

In 2009 it needed more capital but failed to attract it. As a result some 40% of its staff was laid off and Bill Gossman, a past steady-hand for many IT ventures and once a partner in Mohr Davidow Ventures, was appointed as CEO;.

Hi5 encourages the user to develop a profile and upload photos, music and play games; thus users prove largely to be in the 15-24 age group. It recognised that it had to develop services to encourage users to remain with it as they grew older. Facebook's success at growing its base to five times that of Hi5 also brought pressure.

Virtual games and virtual goods became its chosen strategy. A new president, Alex St John, joined Hi5 from WildTangent and developed the plan for social gaming.

WildTangent was a game network operator for third-party PC manufacturers with some 20 million gamers every month playing some 1,000 different games from third-party developers. St John was in charge of the relationship with these developers.

In 2010 Hi5 acquired the games company Big 6 and moved its emphasis even more towards social gaming – it judged to be more interesting to its 'ageing' users.

Big 6 had been founded by three games specialists. Kevin Gliner had been involved in developing mobile phone games at Knockabout Games. Monty Kerr had done the rounds at Microprose, Maxis and Electronic Arts before founding Red 6 Games and Glass Eye Entertainment; he then co-founded Knockabout with Gliner. Chad Hansing had previously worked with the other two.

Hi5's games were supported by the Coins service; this provided virtual money for use in a range of Flash-based arcade, card, sports and strategy games. Initially this was free but to unlock higher levels and upgrades the user needed to use real money. Coins supported some sixty different payment methods and thirty currencies around the world.

In 2011 Hi5 had over 60 million active users recording a little under 3 million monthly visitors from the USA, but over 45 million from the rest of the world.

I need my space

Prompted by the launch of Friendster, a team within eUniverse decided to set up its own social networking site.

eUniverse was founded by Brad Greenspan in 1998 and taken public in 1999. The operation had developed a network of some thirty websites operating in the online entertainment space - gaming, humour, sharing of photos, music and videos. It had also developed analytical marketing tools to maximise its eCommerce potential.

So when it set out to create a social networking site there were none of the issues that normally face a new venture - it could get straight on with things.

The eUniverse founder Brad Greenspan supervised employees Tom Anderson, Josh Berman and Chris DeWolfe who were supported by a team of programmers and were able to utilise pre-existing eUniverse resources. Anderson was the president and De Wolfe the CEO of the new venture that they named MySpace.com.

Chris de Wolfe had previously acquired the url MySpace.com as a web hosting site but it had not yet been used. It was ready to go in August 2003 when it was tested by eUniverse employees who were challenged to see who could sign up the most users.

In 2004 Greenspan was forced out of the operation when an SEC (Securities & Exchange Commission) investigation insisted its earnings had to be restated and ordered a temporary suspension of its stocks.

Around this time the New York Attorney General, Eliot Spitzer, took action against the company for the use of spyware and pop-up adverts that drove users towards its search engines.

In February 2004 the group operation was renamed Intermix Media Inc and Richard Rosenblatt was recruited to become the CEO of Intermix and chairman of MySpace.

Later, as it was shaping up for a 2006 takeover by News Corp, Intermix agreed to pay $7.9m to make the law suit go away; although it was not prepared to admit that it was guilty of any wrongdoing.

Rosenblatt had graduated from UCLA and USC Law School. He founded iMALL in 1994, offering online tools for users to create their own eCommerce stores and do business on the Internet. He had sold this to Excite@Home for $565m.

Rosenblatt was credited with turning things around at Intermix; in just eighteen months its value grew from $70m to $650m.

He was also heralded as presiding over the success of MySpace which had just 100,000 unique visitors when he took over. The growth was stated to be through viral marketing; in a large part this was to Intermix's pre-existing 20 million users and email subscribers gleaned from its other activities.

By the end of 2004 MySpace had eclipsed Friendster and by autumn 2005 there were 22 million unique users in the USA compared with Friendster's 1.1 million.

This was achieved by integrating open user web profiles with emails, instant messages, blogs and user forums to make and retain contact with friends by exploring shared interests, networking and dating plus the sharing of photos, music and video.

Its growth attracted advertisers and by June 2006, with 17-18 million unique visitors, it could boast it carried 8% of all advertisements on the Net.

It also became the preferred site for music with some 350,000 bands and artists using it, most notably with REM and Black Eyed Peas launching albums on MySpace. It became the fifth most viewed internet site in the USA.

In July 2006, the publishing and TV giant News Corp concluded that it needed more presence on the Internet. It was seeing advertising dollars moving to online and away from its more traditional properties. Internet advertising had grown by 15% in the USA during 2005.

News Corp purchased Intermix, Alena Analytics and MySpace.com for $580m. At a stroke the News Corp USA web traffic was doubled to 45 million unique monthly visitors and this was seen as a means to drive users to Fox Television sites too.

According to comScore, on 9 August 2006 the 100 millionth MySpace account was opened in the Netherlands.

In April 2008 Facebook overtook MySpace in the measure of unique monthly visitors. In 2009 some 30% of the MySpace workforce was laid off, but little more is clear as News Corp do not analyse the contributions of MySpace separately.

Rosenblatt stayed on as a consultant to News Corp for a period. In May 2006 he had cofounded a new operation with Shawn Colo, an acquisitions specialist. The pair raised over $355m to launch Demand Media Inc.

It acquired a whole series of domain names and destination websites, which it refreshed with social networking features. It claimed $200m advertising revenue in 2009 from some 3 billion hits.

It was the largest contributor to YouTube, uploading over 10,000 to 20,000 videos every month which achieved 1.5m hits each day.

Yahoo! had been interested in acquiring it in July 2008 for around $2 billion but Rosenblatt stuck out for $3 billion - no deal! In mid 2010 it was reputed to be shaping up for an IPO, at a detuned $1.5 billion estimate.

Survival of the fittest - Facemash

Mark Elliot Zuckerberg, a psychology student at Harvard, also became a keen computer programmer. His dentist father taught him Atari Basic and then hired a private software tutor for him.

An early project saw him develop ZuckNet that allowed the home and dental practice computers to communicate with each other, a type of instant messaging forerunner.

He went on to develop games. With his school friend Adam D'Angelo he created the Synapse Media Player that used AI to learn the user's preferred listening. Both Microsoft and AOL wanted to buy it and hire him but he chose to go to Harvard. D'Angelo went to CalTech and would later return to become the CTO of Facebook.

At Harvard Zuckerberg studied psychology and computer science. In October 2003 he hacked in to the college computer system to acquire the college administration's photos of students. These files of photos were known as Face Books.

He used these garnered photos to develop Facemash; he placed two pictures on the site and asked students to decide which was the fitter and hotter. A friend's chess algorithm was used as the ranking software.

This type of thing had already been done by sites like *Hot or Not?* and *F*** it or Chuck it*, but with those the featured images were usually anonymous, not in a closed community. Within four hours of launch Facemash had 450 visitors and 22,000 viewings of the vying images; it spread quickly to other campuses. This high level of traffic soon interfered with the Harvard network.

Not only the selected students were annoyed, the college also took a dim view and took down the site, putting him 'on probation' for breaching security and invading privacy; the charges were ultimately dropped. The daily student paper *The Harvard Crimson* wrote up the Facemash event which gave Zuckerberg some notoriety.

He knuckled down and used his skills to upload material to a site where he prompted fellow students to comment so they could share study notes. But he was never to be far from controversy and legal action.

In April 2003 Zuckerberg spent some time working on the StreetFax project with Paul Ceglia. Ceglia would emerge again in 2010, claiming he had a signed contract with Zuckerberg from back then that gave him an 84% ownership of Facebook. This was based on an initial 50% holding in the website revenues plus a penalty 1% additional interest added each day from 1 January 2004 until the website was completed – thirty-four days later. Zuckerberg and Facebook suggested the claims were frivolous, however the court ordered no transfers of ownership could be executed while the claim was under investigation. This is still proceeding.

Rowing rows - Harvard Connection

Three Harvard seniors had been working on a social networking site since December 2002 to develop the HarvardConnection.com. Its aim was to interconnect students and alumni of Harvard and then roll it out to other universities and schools,

The founders were twins Cameron and Tyler Winklevoss, who competed for the USA at the Beijing Olympics in the men's pairs rowing, and Divya Narendra. They enlisted the help of a programmer, Sanjay Mavinkurve, who progressed the project but then left to join Google. A second programmer, Victor Gao, was brought in as a paid consultant but he also left the project in late 2003.

Perhaps prompted by the write-up on Facemash they approached Zuckerberg whom they met on 25 November 2003. They insisted on the secrecy of the project, stressing the significance of being the first out there. They showed him where they had reached with the project and how they intended to expand the service to include other universities later.

There appears to have been no contract signed between them but Zuckerberg became a partner and agreed to work on the project in return for equity; on 30 November he indicated that the task would not take him long to complete.

But through December he became unavailable and kept apologising that he was caught up in problems; at a meeting mid-December he indicated he was almost finished. In January he suggested all was still on track and that he would show them what he had achieved on 14 January.

In the meantime he was exchanging instant messages with his friend Eduardo Saverin while planning his own social networking site. Saverin provided cash to assist in funding the required servers, eventually supplying a total of $15,000 for a 30% share. On 11 January 2004 Zuckerberg registered the domain 'thefacebook.com'.

He did not mention any of this at the meeting with the HarvardConnection team, instead expressing doubts about their project and still pleading that he was too busy with college work. It did appear from later revelations that he was deliberately stalling their progress while getting his own site together.

Launching thefacebook

With Saverin's assistance, in February 2004 Zuckerberg launched the service 'thefacebook.com'. It was also a social networking site for Harvard students and it too planned to roll out to other universities.

Those who defended Zuckerberg suggested that he saw HarvardConnection.com as merely a dating facility, and that while both had Harvard students as users, there were different objectives.

At the launch of thefacebook.com the college indicated that it planned to have a universal face book itself, but users were attracted by Zuckerberg's non-passworded and more open approach with its extensive search and privacy options.

The HarvardConnection team was of course enraged by this turn of events. They instructed Gao look at the work Zuckerberg had completed for them and suggested that it was cursory; for example the registration he had worked upon was not connected to the back-end processes.

They proposed an investigation by *The Harvard Crimson* and took a legal 'cease and desist' action against him on 10 February. Some instant messages that Zuckerberg had sent at that time to 'friends' were later uncovered, and these served to inflame the situation - they made it seem that he had intentionally delayed the HarvardConnection's progress while planning his own launch.

Notwithstanding all of this legal background, limited to Harvard students, thefacebook.com spread to almost half the undergraduate body within a month of launch. Saverin focused on the business aspects of the operation and they were joined by other computer science students - Dustin Moskovitz and Chris Hughes as programmers. Moskovitz additionally worked on the graphics design.

Facebook insisted on users showing their true identity, unlike MySpace. The site allowed a user to set up a profile with photos and personal data, referencing personal interests and contact data. Users could communicate publicly, privately or through the chat function. They could join interest groups and 'like pages' (originally fan pages) and could set various privacy settings.

The Wall feature allowed users to post messages for friends to see. They could identify where they were with the 'status' feature. They could upload photo albums; unlike other sites, an unlimited number of photos was allowed. They could 'poke' or say hello to a user; the user would receive a message that the sender 'poked' them.

As proposed, 'thefacebook' expanded to other colleges - Columbia, Stanford and Yale in March 2004, then on to Boston, MIT and New York...

Further conflict - ConnectU
The Winklevoss twins and Narendra launched ConnectU in May 2004 and soon linked up with Wayne Chang and his i2hub which had been launched a few months earlier.

i2hub was a global network for universities and as it used Internet2 it provided a very speedy file-sharing service that soon had 400 universities and colleges using it. The two operations grouped together as the Winklevoss Chang Group.

Zuckerberg and others launched the Wirehog service to compete with i2hub but failed to unseat its progress; Wirehog was therefore shut down. But i2hub then ran into trouble with the RIAA (Recording Industry Association of America) who sued i2hub users who were distributing copyright material at high speeds. i2hub closed down and signed off with the message 'RIP 11/14/2005'.

ConnectU took legal action against Facebook early in 2004, Facebook reciprocated and the settlement in February 2008 saw Facebook acquire ConnectU for $65m – made up as $20m in cash plus 1,253,326 shares, said to be worth $45m.

In 2010 the valuation of this stock at $45m was queried through another legal case, the litigants suggesting that in fact at the time it was only worth $11m.

There was further legal action from Chang and i2hub against ConnectU to receive a share of the actual and any subsequent settlement that might be reached - yet another case of lawyers ending up as the big winners!

RANDOM ACCESS MOMENT:
The success of Facebook attracted unwelcome attention from 'cyberstalkers' who found the site a simple means of tracking individuals' photos, interests, work and contact details and then used this information to harass or threaten them.

A mild form of this is when someone checked a new friend's Facebook entries to gain insight into habits and interests. Prospective employers often look at applicants' Facebook pages to gauge their character and suitability for a new role.

Under the influence - Sean Parker

In the meantime Zuckerberg was introduced to Sean Parker who had co-founded Napster back in 1999 and Plaxo in 2002.

Parker advised the Facebook team and when it incorporated he helped supervise the move to Palo Alto (where else?) and served as its first president from 2004; he was granted a 7% equity holding in the operation.

In 2005 the company acquired the domain facebook.com for $200,000 and dropped the 'the' from its name.

Through his past experience Parker was able to introduce the team to various angels and venture capitalists. The first round of investment included $500,000 from Peter Thiel, the co-founder of PayPal. This investment valued the operation at $5m; Thiel was invited on to the Facebook board.

The second round in April 2005 was $12.7m from Accel Partners, the third round was for $27.5m, mainly from Greylock Partners but with Meritech Capital Partners joining them and Accel and Thiel increased their investments too. Accel placed Jim Breyer on to the board.

Saverin later learned that the agreements with Parker and the other investors included a clause that could dilute his 34% without reducing their own holdings; he took legal action. By 2011 his holding was diluted to 5%.

In late August 2005, following three nights of partying at a rented beach house in North Carolina, Parker was arrested for cocaine possession; his was the signature on the beach house rental agreement.

Though no charges were brought and Zuckerberg stated he was not particularly concerned by the event, the biggest Facebook investor forced Parker out. He of course retained his shareholding (4% in 2011) and unrepentantly in 2010 donated $100,000 to the Californian campaign to legalise marijuana.

Progress through new services
Joining the site was originally by invitation only but this was steadily expanded; for example employees at Apple and Microsoft were allowed to participate. In September 2005 a high school version of the site was launched, still by invitation only.

Like the term 'to Google', 'to facebook' became an accepted verb by 2005.

In August 2006 the blogging service Facebook Notes was introduced; this allowed blogs to be imported, tagged and images embedded.

In September 2006 Facebook was opened to anyone over thirteen years old and a News Feed feature (patented later) which presented profile changes, birthdays and events was introduced. But this led to security concerns and was abused by many to post fake information to drive traffic towards them.

Most Facebook income came from advertising. In October 2007 Microsoft acquired 1.6% of Facebook for $240m, valuing the company at £15bn. Subsequently Microsoft was allowed to run international advertisements on Facebook and was its exclusive partner for banner advertising.

Google stated that its users clicked on the first advertisement in a search result an average of 8% of the time, ie 80,000 clicks per million searches. Data leaked from Facebook suggested its level was just 400 clicks per million pages.

In 2007 it added two new features. Through Facebook Gifts users could send gifts to each other for a fee, and Marketplace allowed free classified advertisements.

May 2007 saw the advent of Facebook Platform, a development platform for programmers to produce applications within Facebook. Some 800,000 developers promptly took up the facility. By 2011 Facebook Platform had attracted 2.5m developers and partners from 190 countries.

Facebook Connect was released in July 2008 as a similar facility for users themselves.

Another service launched back in November 2007 was not so well received. Facebook Beacon enabled users to share information with friends on browsing and other Internet activity. But this caused renewed privacy concerns and was modified to allow users to opt out on request.

By 2008 Facebook had overtaken MySpace and started to experiment or upgrade its service with a simpler registration process and new user interface. On 26 August 2008 Zuckerberg announced,

'We hit a big milestone today - 100 million people around the world are now using Facebook. This is a really gratifying moment for us because it means a lot that you have decided that Facebook is a good, trusted place for you to share your lives with your friends. So we just wanted to take this moment to say, "thanks."'

This number would come back to haunt him in 2010 when 'security consultant' Ron Bowes downloaded and distributed the profiles of 100 million Facebook users. He stated that this was to highlight the lack of security. Facebook dissembled with,

'It is similar to the white pages of the phone book, this is the information available to enable people to find each other, which is the reason people join Facebook.'

This episode led to a series of apologies and much more concentration on privacy and security matters at Facebook. A number of countries have blocked Facebook based on the discussion content offending their local sensitivities.

Also in 2008 Facebook launched the US Politics service which one million users installed. This enabled them to give feedback on the democrat and republican debates.

As the business grew it attracted some big hitters to its board. Marc Andreessen, (Mosaic and Netscape) joined, as did Don E Graham who had held many senior roles with the *Washington Post*, including general manager, publisher and director.

Facebook set up its international headquarters in Dublin, Ireland in October 2008.

It was not until September 2009 that Facebook was able to announce its first cash flow positive period with revenues of over $800m, and in July 2010 it announced its 500 millionth user.

Fact being stranger than fiction, it is not surprising that the Facebook story inspired the 2009 book *The Accidental Billionaires: The Founding of Facebook, A Tale of Sex, Money, Genius, and Betrayal* by Ben Mezrich and that this in turn led to the October 2010 movie *The Social Network*, also based on the early years of Facebook. Eduardo Saverin consulted on both and maybe this is the reason Zuckerberg is not presented very favourably.

In November 2010 an internal project called Titan was revealed to be Facebook Messages, a service which gave users an @facebook.com email address, although the service was actually an amalgam of email, text and instant messaging.

At this point the organisation was said to be worth $41 billion, just a tad ahead of eBay, and was feted as the third largest US Internet company behind Google and Amazon.

Its advertising revenue in 2010 was estimated at $1.1 billion. More than two million websites had integrated with Facebook including eighty of comScore's top hundred USA sites and over fifty of its top hundred global sites. Some two hundred mobile operators in sixty countries also worked with Facebook's mobile products.

By 2011 Facebook had over 500 million active users with 50% logging on each day and amassing 700 billion online minutes each month. The average user had 130 'friends'. It was the leading social networking site in Canada, the UK and USA; in the USA it had over 135m unique monthly visitors. Some 70% of its activity was outside the USA and it was translated into seventy languages.

Facebook had a 69% penetration in the USA, 67% in the Middle East and Africa, 58% in South America, 57% in Europe yet only 17% in Asia and Australasia. But although Indonesia had just 10% penetration this still meant over 24 million users, making it Facebook's second largest market by finite number of users.

Happy Birthday Bebo

Michael Birch studied physics at Imperial College London but was a regular web innovator. With his brother Paul he launched BirthdayAlarm.com in September 2001 as an eCard reminder service. This was still being run profitably by the Birch brothers and Michael's wife a decade later.

The team plus another friend then founded Ringo.com, a Friendster-like service which, with 400,000 users, they sold on to tickle.com in 2003. Tickle.com was founded in 1999 and was itself acquired by Monster Worldwide in 2004 but was closed down by the end of 2008.

Moving to the United States, Michael Birch and his wife Xochi launched Bebo from their home in San Francisco. They bought the domain name and then retro-defined it as standing for 'blog early blog often'.

Bebo was soft-launched in January 2005 and relaunched in July 2005; it followed a tried and tested approach with users setting up a profile, adding friends, posting blogs, photos, music and videos. It also featured quizzes for users to post and/or answer. It did not display adverts on the user's home page but any other viewing came with advertising.

Its simplicity of use developed a loyal teenage and young adult market. There were some 25million users by the middle of 2006.

In January 2007 it added Bebo Authors where writers could publish chapters of books for comment and promotion. That year it became the sixth largest site in the UK, ahead of stalwarts such as bbc.co.uk, Amazon.co.uk and AOL.

To beef up its US performance Birch raised $15m in venture capital and by 2008 it was the third-largest social networking site in the USA, behind MySpace and Facebook. It had a worldwide 40 million membership looking at an average 78 pages per day.

Perhaps it was motivated by News Corp's purchase of MySpace for $580m in 2005 and Microsoft's acquisition of 1.6% of Facebook for $240m, Bebo sought a suitor and AOL acquired it in March 2008 for $850m.

The Birches pocketed over $595m from the deal; Michael would go on to invest in MyStore.com and Goodreads, a social networking site for book lovers. Most recently he invested in Punktilo, a social media start-up operator with Arsenal FC, Phones 4U and Simon Cowell's SyCo music label among its clients.

He has also joined up with Brent Hoberman of LastMinute.com to create European Founders Capital, a start-up funding operation.

By April 2010 AOL found Bebo had declined to under 13 million unique visitors; by then MySpace had 111 million and Facebook 519 million. In June 2010 it was sold off to the LA-based investment firm Criterion Capital Partners, reputedly for c$10m which was less than 2% of AOL's purchase price. Criterion Capital's managing partner Adam Levin believed that its ability in managing turnarounds and the strength of the Bebo user base would show returns.

Russian socialising - Badoo

The social networking site Badoo was developed by Andrey Andreev and is based out of Cyprus, with offices in London; it was launched in May 2006. It is most successful in France, Italy, Spain and South America.

The Russian investment organisation Finam Investment Company paid $30m to acquire 10% of Badoo in January 2008 with plans to expand it into Russia where social networking was beginning to take off with around 10 million users.

Finam, the largest Russian brokerage operation, also purchased Mamba back in 2005; this was the number one Russian online dating community with some 11 million users by 2011; 40% of these were active. Finam sold 31.5% on to mail.ru, the leading Russian Internet and email operator.

At the time of Finam's investment, Badoo had some 12.7 million users and made a virtue of having no advertising; instead it made money from a feature called Rise Up. (I can't help wondering what the Russian government thinks of that name.) It allowed users to pay for their profiles being highlighted for a limited time to attract more attention, most take this opportunity every month.

Badoo had grown to 83 million users by November 2010.

From despatches to Twitter

Jack Dorsey was raised in St Louis Missouri and took to programming from a young age. At just fourteen he developed software for despatchers to route taxis, couriers, cycle and motorcycle messengers, pizza delivery teams and emergency services.

He qualified at Missouri University of Science and Technology and subsequently at New York University. He then worked at DMS, a significant courier service, once again working with despatch software.

He moved to Oakland California and at the age of twenty-four formed a company to develop his own despatch software ideas. Despatchers have to regularly ask their team 'Where are you?', 'What are you doing?' and this constant enquiring needed to be achieved by a mixture of radio or phones, and later emails or mobile texting. He sought a way to combine texts, emails and web instant messaging to create a broad mobile and Internet-based real-time communication service.

He experimented with the RIM 850 (Research in Motion) the forerunner of the Blackberry. But the problem was that it depended on everyone having one and at $400 a pop this was too expensive. It was the mobile SMS (short messaging service) that took him forward when he saw that the service transcended many services and devices.

Dorsey later approached Evan Williams at Odeo.

Evan Williams and Blogger.com

In January 1999 Williams and Meg Hourihan had co-founded Pyra Labs. Its first product was also called Pyra and offered tools for web project management and contact management.

Pyra was the operation that first coined the term 'blog', a shortening of web-log, and subsequently in August 1999 it renamed its product Blogger.com, a blog publishing tool.

Blogger developed into having over a million registered bloggers, with 200 thousand of these active, but at first it had no revenue plan and the seedcorn soon ran out. Williams negotiated an investment from Trellix and its founder Dan Bricklin, the co-creator of VisiCalc. With this new capital he set about encompassing advertising within Blogspot and Blogger Pro, attracting an annual $35 fee in return for advanced features.

In February 2003 Blogger was sold on to Google for an undisclosed sum. Google quickly integrated it with its other services, Picasa and Hello, to raise the bar even further with its search reach and other capabilities.

In October 2004 Williams left Google and co-founded Odeo, a new operation that developed tools for users to develop and distribute podcasts. It drew upon capital from Charles River Ventures and others. But Williams himself was not committed to the notion of podcasting and as a result the business was wavering.

It was Dorsey, Williams and Biz Stone, who had worked with Williams at both Blogger and Odeo, who took Dorsey's notions forward to develop Twitter.

A brainstorming session was held in 2006 to see where they might take Odeo next and Williams urged Dorsey to describe his thoughts for a cross-system short messaging approach to satisfy not just the courier business but the general public too. Initially the service was called 'status' or 'stat.us' on the basis that it told others of your current status - where you were, what you were doing.

But it was Williams who came up with the eventual name of the service by comparing the proposed traffic to the chatter between birds, short bursts of seemingly random information - hence Twitter. Definitions vary but my preferred one is the rather English and thus suitably pompous 'drawing room chatter'.

They realised that the word could be used as a noun or a verb and suffixes could be added. The action would be 'twittering'; if you were getting too many messages you would be 'twitterpated' and so on.

Dorsey (@jack), Stone (@biz) and others took just two weeks to come up with version 0.1.

For the messaging service they came to the conclusion that use of mobile SMS was compelling as it could bridge the gap between PCs and mobiles. SMS allowed the user 160 characters per message before it broke it into packages.

They needed therefore to have a five letter SMS code and selected 'twttr', apparently inspired by Flickr - though that's six letters! 'twttr' was unavailable and they soon switched from their first used code of '10958' to the more memorable '40404' as its US SMS short code and reinstated the vowels to make the service Twitter.

Dorsey sent the first ever web-based twitter at 9:50am on 21 March 2006. *'just setting up my twttr'*

RANDOM ACCESS MOMENT:
Many have suggested that Twitter is similar to the IRC (internet relay chat) service launched back in August 1988 by Jarkko Oikarinen; IRC is often used for chat forums but can be used one-on-one and privately. It proved very useful during the 1991 Soviet coup attempt against Gorbachev and also during the first Gulf War that same year.

All of a twitter

At first the Twitter service was used only internally by some fifty people at Odeo. The service was monitored from an admin page and concerns over the security of this, even at that early stage, led to the idea of private accounts on the service.

The social networking service registered users on the site at no charge after which they could send and receive short, 140 character, text-only messages. This short message was known as a 'tweet'.

A tweet was 140 characters, unlike the 160 of SMS; in this way twenty characters remained for the Twitter username and a colon.

Users controlled their own network of 'friends' and the prime intention was to keep friends up to date with what they were doing, where they were and of course it was possible to arrange meetings or simply carry on group conversations. Instead of sending a series of texts, instant messages or email messages to individuals, the service automatically delivered a message to all your friends and contacts for you.

The 'lists' service allowed users to create schedules of those whom they wished to follow constantly, those they wished to dip in to occasionally, and those they wanted to veto.

And here was the clever bit - delivery could be to a PC, a laptop or via SMS to a mobile device. In the United States a mobile user texting 40404 could send a Twitter whether on PC or mobile. The mobile operator's SMSC (short messaging service centre), received the message and passed it on to Twitter.

If the user wanted to add attachments such as photos, music, or video then the tweet could send a web address showing where these were to be found. To facilitate this Twitter reduced any lengthy urls into usable 'tiny urls' using an acquired domain called 't.co'.

Prefixing a tweet with 'DM' made it a direct message delivered only to a specified recipient. If you received a tweet that you wanted to share, you prefixed it with 'retweet' to send it on to others.

Users could also 'follow' the tweets of others. It was not possible to see the full conversations if you did not belong to that network, but you could see the outward tweets. The original term considered for this was 'watch', rather than follow, but perhaps this would have been altogether too sinister.

By texting 40404 and stating 'follow twitter' the user received a stream of texts that kept them advised of current themes and activity.

Many used the 'follow' feature to espouse Twitter as a new and abbreviated form of blogging, known as 'micro-blogging'. A widget could be used to quickly identify your current status to others.

User-power was exhibited when it was realised that there was no easy way within Twitter to group tweets for those seeking specific information. Users decided to introduce a 'hashtag', placing the # (hash) symbol before a word, for example '#haiku'. Twitter Search would then find all mentions of haiku in the Twittersphere. Twitter responded favourably by frequently displaying hashtags in 'Trending topics' links on the search page.

Of course micro-bloggers loved the almost haiku-like discipline of expressing themselves in just 140 characters; though of course the Japanese haiku is much shorter at just seventeen syllables.

Users wishing to receive a member's tweets would simply send a message to Twitter saying 'follow' plus the username. If they became bored or overwhelmed by the material, they texted 'off' and the username! Don't you sometimes wish for that feature in a real conversation!

Of course many mobile users had to pay for these texts and Twitter was not an overnight success when the service was launched publicly in July 2006.

But the situation within Odeo was not getting any better and there were soon layoffs. The relevance of Twitter to Odeo was being questioned, and in October 2006 a new company was formed.

Obvious Corp paid off the other investors and shareholders so that they would own Twitter and some other assets. Shortly after launch twttr.com was replaced by Twitter.com. By February 2007 the team was seeking to sell off Odeo and its monthly unique visitor rate of around 685,000 with 3 million page views and 1.5 million Flash plays.

During March 2007 at the SXSW (South by Southwest festival) Twitter was used with a 'vizualiser' to display seminar attendees' comments and messages on several large plasma screens as they left the sessions. Twitter became the talk of the show and won an award.

The Twitter team responded by tweeting,

'We'd like to thank you in 140 characters or less. And we just did!'

This exposure at the SXSW event saw the numbers of tweets accelerate radically, trebling from 20,000 to 60,000 a day. A similar process was adopted at the MTV Awards and at Apple's WWDC (worldwide developers' conference).

Obvious Corp then spun off Twitter Inc as a stand-alone operation with Dorsey as its CEO in April 2007.

Twitter achieved its broad reach through the launch of its API (application programming interface). This smoothed its passage across networks and services. In part success was based on its compatibility with the major syndication formats operating in XML (extensible markup language); these were RSS (really simple syndication) and Atom Syndication Format.

As the service took off it was soon necessary for recommendations known as 'Tweetiquette'. Suggestions included not overwhelming the network with too much traffic, not impersonating others, taking anything sensitive off Twitter and discussing it elsewhere, not wasting space on profanity…

A number of services provided an easier means of adding content and monitoring the tweet traffic. For example OutTwit enabled access to Twitter through the email software Outlook.

Pear Analytics analysed a sample of traffic in August 2009 and suggested that 40% of it was 'pointless babble', 6% was self-promotion, 4% was spam and 4% was news; this left 38% as conversational and 9% with pass-along value.

Twitaholic.com tracked those with the most followers. Late in 2010 the number one was Lady Gaga with almost 7.5 million; others in the top ten included Barack Obama and Oprah Winfrey. CNN Breaking News was only at #17, yet CNN ranks as the longest to remain in the top 100 – for more than four years.

RANDOM ACCESS MOMENT:
a Dutch team evidently found the constant bombardment from social networks was becoming too much. They created the Web 2.0 Suicide Machine that would remove all your private content and 'relationships' on Facebook, LinkedIn, MySpace and Twitter. It did not close down accounts but effectively committed social networking suicide – sorry but I can't help saying it pops your clogs from microblogs.

It described it as, 'delete all your energy sucking social-networking profiles, kill your fake virtual friends, and completely do away with your Web2.0 alter ego.'

The 40404 SMS service was for USA mobile users. Elsewhere in the world other gateway numbers were used and in several markets this meant it was limited to one local mobile service.

During 2007 the quarterly average of tweets was 400,000, but by 2008 this had grown exponentially to 100 million tweets a quarter.

In October 2008 Williams (@ev) took over as CEO and Dorsey took the role of chairman. Intriguingly Marc Andreessen was on both the Facebook and the Twitter boards. Twitter received an approach from Facebook offering to acquire it for 3% of its own stock, which valued Twitter at $500m.

Williams dismissed it pointing out that this value was true only if you accepted that Facebook was worth $15 billion, this was based upon its Microsoft deal in October 2007. But other commentators placed this more realistically at $5 billion, which would make the equity offer worth more like $150m.

Having no major revenue stream Twitter needed to go for its second round of fund-raising in 2008; it achieved $22m, which valued it at only $98m. However the founders did not feel that the Facebook deal came at the right time to sell, and payment in Facebook stock was not the right approach.

Twitter's benefits were underlined when its use was significant in the run up to the November 2008 presidential election and also in the Mumbai attacks that same month. Twitter was feeding the news ahead of CNN in January 2009 when the US Airways flight 1549 ditched in the Hudson River.

750 tweets a second

Entering 2009 Twitter became the third largest social networking site as it hit two billion tweets per quarter. In 2009 it attracted a further $35m in funding from Benchmark Capital, Bezos Expeditions, Digital Garage, Insight Venture Partners, Spark Capital, Union Square Ventures and others.

When Michael Jackson died in June 2009 the servers crashed as users were tweeting their status at the rate of 100,000 per hour for tweets including the words 'Michael Jackson'.

By the middle of 2010 traffic had increased to 65 million tweets per day - that's 750 every second!

A number of issues later emerged regarding the strength of Twitter's security. In January 2009 more than twenty high-profile Twitter accounts were compromised and sent pornographic and drug-related messages.

On 11 June 2009 Twitter introduced Verified Accounts so home pages could display a badge to confirm their authenticity. But this did not stop the Federal Trade Commission charging Twitter to beef up its privacy and security measures and insisting these be independently checked every six months. This was the first such government action against a social network.

On 22 January 2010 Twitter became other-worldly when astronaut Thomas J Creamer sent tweets from the International Space Station with the username @NASA_Astronauts.

In April 2010 Twitter acquired Atebits for an undisclosed sum. Loren Brichter had worked at Apple on the iPhone but left to found Atebits. The operation created Tweetie, an app for using Twitter on the Apple iPhone. It originally sold for $2.99 but after the acquisition Twitter renamed is as 'Twitter for iPhone' and issued it free of charge. Tweetie also had an Apple Mac version that ran advertisements from Fusion Ads, something Twitter was clearly going to have to consider.

So in April 2010 Twitter announced it would permit paid-for advertising tweets and that Red Bull, Starbucks and others were already signed up for the service.

During the World Cup in June 2010 the Twitter record of 2,940 tweets per second was reached in the half-minute after Japan scored against Cameroon on June 14. This record lasted just three days, beaten when 3,085 tweets per second was measured following the LA Lakers win at the 2010 NBA finals on June 17.

By autumn 2010 Twitter had 175 million registered users with more than a third of a million joining every day and it carried 95 million tweets daily.

Twitter allowed language preferences in English, French, German, Italian, Japanese, and Spanish. It is banned in China though still widely used - one sarcastic tweet earned a Chinese user a year in a labour camp! Twitter does seem to attract an older audience than the other social networks, and surprisingly for an IT phenomenon women users in fact outnumber men.

During September and October 2010 Twitter was heavily redesigned as New Twitter which allowed users to stay within Twitter.com to see tweet-referenced photos and videos, provided these were on supported websites like Flickr, Twitpic, YouTube...

Twitter came under attack in September 2010. A Japanese developer, Masato Kinugawa, found a way of making coloured tweets using XSS (cross-site scripting); he called it Rainbow Twtr. XSS uncovered a vulnerability of many web applications because it allowed a user to inject a modifying script. Kinugawa's application was innocent and to some extent he suggested its purpose was to alert Twitter of its vulnerability. Others launched an XSS worm which gave the user pop-up ads and links to porno sites. Twitter claimed the hole was subsequently fully patched over.

In October 2010 Evan Williams stepped down as CEO to focus on product strategy; he was replaced by Dick Costolo, the former COO at Twitter.

While many criticised tweets as being inane, the ease and freedom of tweeting became a cause for concern in some areas. One notable case was a confidential trade union negotiation with British Airways, the content of which was being tweeted real-time to the outside world by an attending trade union official. When the WikiLeaks founder was in court seeking bail while fighting extradition to Sweden, the court ordered that journalists were not permitted to tweet from the proceedings.

In November 2010 Biz Stone suggested that he was working on a news service that he called the Twitter News Network.

It was rumoured that Twitter planned an IPO in 2013, by which time one commentator suggested they would have a billion users, $1.5 billion in revenue and over $100 million profit. Twitter promptly denied these figures and threatened legal action.

RANDOM ACCESS MOMENT:
a resident of Bradford in West Yorkshire, England shamed all of us who are stuck in our ways and resistant to change as we get older. Ivy Bean, clearly an indomitable lady, joined Facebook in 2008 and then in 2010 joined Twitter - at the grand old age of 102 and 104 respectively!

An inspiration, she met the British prime minister in Downing Street and she had a number of fan pages. She had around 5,000 Facebook friends and almost 60,000 Twitter followers when she died in July 2010.

28 - On the move – PC progress

'...it used to be that if you wanted to make a record of a song, you needed a studio and a producer. Now, you need a laptop.' Bono

A PC exit for IBM

IBM was scourged through the 1970s with anti-trust actions, but following its entry to the PC business the US Department of Justice withdrew its action in 1982. By then the company had propelled itself into a hasty solution for the IBM PC and this allowed clones and other developments to erode its position.

It was Microsoft Windows and Intel that spawned the Wintel products that took valuable market share at a time when IBM should have been dominant. Yet perhaps IBM's attention on the volatile PC market caused it to take its eye of the mainframe business where there were also problems. As servers with PCs became the preferred business solution, mainframes were somewhat left in limbo.

Perhaps following too closely the Thomas Watson philosophy of following the herd, it found itself lurking at the back of every technology for a decade or so.

IBM eventually ran into difficulties in 1993 when its mainframe business imploded, dropping by 42%; it showed losses of $800m.

It hired Louis Gerstner, ex American Express and Nabisco, to steady the ship. In Gerstner's book *Who says elephants can't dance?* he commented,

'The single most important factor in our overall performance was that Intel and Microsoft controlled the key hardware and software architectures and were able to price accordingly.'

It was Gerstner who presided over the acquisition of Lotus.

In October 1999 the IBM PC was withdrawn as a retail proposition and sold thereafter only directly or via the Internet. IBM started to close its own factories, the last in 2003.

The ThinkPad brand was for example manufactured for it by the The Great Wall Technology company in China and the US Sanmina company.

According to Gartner, by 2004 IBM had just a 5.6% share of the desktop, laptop and notebook business. The PC had become a commodity product offering low margins and this had always been at odds with the IBM philosophy.

It looked around for a buyer, Toshiba being one early prospect. Toshiba was the sixth largest PC maker at the time and the third largest laptop manufacturer. It reportedly turned down the chance to acquire IBM and in the aftermath of the IBM sale it suffered the consequences when the market saw IBM quality combined with a low-overhead manufacturer as compelling.

In December 2004 IBM finally decided to call it a day in the PC space. It sold its PC division in a deal that saw all its global desktop and notebook computer business, including research and development and manufacturing, transfer to the Lenovo Group of China for $1.75bn. The deal was for $650m in cash and the balance gave IBM an 18.9% share in Lenovo; making IBM the second largest stakeholder in the company.

IBM was turning over $9bn in PCs so the deal did not sound that great given that the PC market at the time was valued at over $180bn a year. Gartner was projecting annual growth of 5.7% pa for the next three years and IDC was more optimistically talking of 10% growth.

But it was IBM's low profitability of course that dragged the valuation down, plus the $500m in liabilities that Lenovo had to assume. Even so this deal represented the largest overseas acquisition by a Chinese technology company.

Sam Palmisano, then IBM head, commented on the deal,

'...the PC segment of the industry continues to take on characteristics of the home and consumer electronics industry which favours enormous economies of scale and a focus on individual users and buyers. Today's announcement further strengthens IBM's focus on enterprise...'

The momentous deal was completed on 1st May 2005, so IBM, an organisation that was octogenarian, exited the PC business that it had been in for under twenty-four years.

The expanded Lenovo turnover quadrupled to $12bn with sales of 11.9 million units. This deal propelled it to become the third largest PC maker; behind Dell and HP. Lenovo's perspective was completely opposite to that of IBM; the US giant saw 20% margins as dire. Lenovo was operating at 15% under fierce home and Asia-Pacific competition.

The new operation was still managed by an American, Stephen M Ward Jr, and was based in New York. Yang Yuanqing became chairman.

PCs sold on-line – Dell and Gateway

While the large established makers were experiencing problems, the more flexible and responsive operations were able to take market share. PCs and other IT equipment were becoming commodity products and this inspired a new generation of businesses.

Patricia Gallup and Jack Ferguson set up PC Connection in July 1982 to sell computer technology with direct marketing techniques. Gateway 2000 was founded by Ted Waitt and Mike Hammond in September 1985 to do the same thing, but with spots on – they used spotted boxes and other cow imagery to highlight its rural Iowa base.

Michael S Dell was another child entrepreneur who earned money early and invested it in stocks and commodities. He encountered computers at a local Radio Shack and first bought an Apple II. Through high school he sold *Houston Post* newspaper subscriptions making $18k in a year.

Dell was nineteen years old and studying medicine at the University of Texas in Austin when he began to assemble PC-compatible computers from off-the-shelf components and to sell these and disk drives on the campus.

He called his business PCs Limited in November 1984 and discovered that this direct relationship gave him a real understanding of the end-user requirements; this was invaluable in terms of planning his production. Dell acquired a vendor licence so he could bid to supply State of Texas requirements and he scored well, given his lack of any overheads and his flexible approach to production.

In 1985, armed with $300k seedcorn from his family, he launched his own PC, the Turbo PC that retailed for $795. He operated on the 'just in time' principle and only acquired components against orders and only assembled for immediate delivery. Having no parts stock or finished product inventory kept him lean and mean.

He advertised it in national computer magazines offering to custom assemble the PC within certain parameters. PCs Limited turned over $73m that year! It soon went international. Still keeping close to his market, in 1986 Dell had the first toll-free technical support line - something the rest of the industry had to follow.

In July 1988 and renamed Dell Computer Corporation, the company had its IPO selling 3.5 million shares at $8.50, valuing it at $80m. By 1992 Dell was the youngest CEO of a *Fortune 500* company.

In 1996 the operation added servers and sold its equipment primarily through its own website, dell.com. At the time many were skeptical about the willingness of buyers to buy something so technical online, but through this vehicle he was soon achieving $1m in sales daily. By 2000 daily online sales were $18m.

According to IDC, by 2001 Dell was the world's largest PC maker as it surpassed Compaq and took a 12.8% share; Compaq had been the #1 from 1994 to 2000 but in 2001 achieved just 12.1%, HP was at 7.3% and IBM at 6.2%.

The Dell product range expanded into televisions, printers and digital audio players and the name was changed to Dell Inc in 2003.

In 2004 Dell stepped aside to become the chairman. The business was managed by Kevin B Rollins, another Utah man who had studied at Brigham Young University. Dell was valued at $20bn and in 2005 ranked as the fifth richest organisation in the USA.

But in 2007 Dell had slipped to be the second largest PC maker and Dell stepped in to reassume the helm. He presided over the introduction of the Inspiron 8000 which at the time was the most powerful laptop. He was there as the Dell range espoused Linux and other OSs.

In 2011 Dell was the third largest PC maker but with over $50bn in sales and over 100,000 employees.

Dell himself was valued at around $14bn. He and his wife Susan have a foundation that has already given over $500m to assist those actively helping urban communities in the USA and India. They also funded local Texas health organisations. Of course, being confirmed Texans, they were among the 50+ people who gave the maximum $250k contribution to the campaign for President George W Bush in 2004.

Into the new millennium with Apple

We last seriously looked at Apple when it acquired the NeXT OS to make it its own in December 1996. Apple tried in the interim to come up with a significant OS through projects named Taligent, Copland and Gershwin but with no major success. The NeXT OPENSTEP OS was used to create Mac OS X, this was properly released in March 2001.

During 1996 and 1997 the media had been writing 'obituaries' for Apple which had lost money for three straight years and in 1997 peaked at a loss of $878m.

However in February 1997 the founders were back. The then CEO Gil Amelio appointed Steve Jobs and Steve Wozniak to the executive committee. Amelio had at this point managed Apple for just seventeen months and had presided over losses of $1.6bn.

In June that year Jobs did not help the company's cause when he sold 1.5 million of his Apple shares and the share price took a tumble. Notwithstanding this he was offered the role of CEO and chairman in July 1997 but turned it down preferring to concentrate on his Pixar business.

A milestone deal was signed between Microsoft and Apple in August 1997 when Microsoft invested $150m in Apple stock and pledged to deliver Internet Explorer and Office for the Mac range.

However by August 1997 Jobs had become engaged in the development of what would become the iMac. By September he had relented and took on the role of interim CEO; on 5 January 2000 he formally took the role full-time.

The iMac G3 was launched in August 1998. It had a 233 MHz G3 processor, 32 Mbyte of RAM, a 4 GByte hard drive, a 15" colour screen and stereo speakers.

It was also the computer that introduced most of us to the USB (universal serial bus) so that keyboard, mouse and other peripherals were simple plug and play devices. This was developed at Intel by a team led by Ajay V Bhatt who was later promoted by his company as a sort of technology rock star.

It was also one of the first PCs to dispense with the floppy drive.

But these features were not really the point; it was the styling of the iMac that was almost visceral. Colourful cabinets were suddenly in! Jonathan Ive, a Brit, was chief designer at Apple and he is credited with the iMac approach.

The 'i' in iMac stood for Internet and Apple explained to log on required just two steps - open the box and plug it in. This featured in an advertisement with Jeff Goldblum.

In 1998 Apple was turned around and achieved a $414m profit through both the reduction of overhead and the success of the iMac.

Steve Jobs' four-cell plan

But this was just one of the four cells in a two-by-two block that Jobs regularly presented as his corporate mission for Apple. Jobs planned a desktop and laptop version for both the consumer and professional sectors.

The iBook followed in 1999. Securely targeted at consumers and education, it was advertised as the 'iMac to go'. It was the first mainstream PC offering wireless.

The colourful iBooks came in blueberry, tangerine, graphite, indigo and key lime. It was a great success, apparently somewhat disproportionately with Japanese female students. It was regularly upgraded until 2006 when replaced by the MacBook.

Buying an Apple product was truly a lifestyle statement. Who wanted to buy a boring old commodity PC?

John Sculley, once the CEO at Apple, was full of admiration for the man he had forced out of Apple, saying of Jobs,

'No one else on the planet could have done it. He has implemented the same simple strategy that made Apple so successful 15 years ago: Make hit products and promote them with terrific marketing.'

We should just pause and look at the launch of the PowerBook series back in October 1991. The use of a trackball and the deliberate location of the keyboard so there was room to rest the hands was very attractive. But strangely Apple had moved away from the 'Snow White' philosophy and the early PowerBooks were grey to look more 'corporate'.

In 1998 Jobs filled his third cell (professional laptop) with a redesigned PowerBook G3; this was jet black with attractive curves in the shape of the case. But the cell was only really fulfilled with the launch in January 2001 of the PowerBook G4. Its lightweight stylish titanium case and wide-aspect screen made it attractive for watching widescreen movies.

Though its battery life was superb there was an overheating problem leading to the initial recall of 128,000 faulty units. In August 2006 a further 1.1 million units were recalled when one battery had apparently exploded.

The fourth cell (professional/desktop) was filled in January 1999 with the launch of the Power Macintosh G3, aka the 'blue & white G3'. It superseded the beige G3, taking inspiration from the iMac and iBook in terms of look and feel. The PowerMac G4 with a graphite case was released in August 1999

Jobs had his four cells, Apple was back to profitability, and the future looked sound. Along the way it relaunched Apple.com that was attracting 10 million visitors a week and annual sales in excess of $1bn.

Jobs' Digital Hub

Jobs set about establishing the next corporate mission - for Apple computers to become what he termed the Digital Hub.

Most stand-alone electronic products like camcorders, MP3 players and digital cameras were manufactured to a price and thus had to constrain memory and could not afford to much user-friendliness. Jobs set out for the Apple to be the base to which these devices would be routinely attached. The memory of a Mac would archive all content and software packages would manipulate, edit and publish the finished material.

Randy Ubillos was working at Adobe to develop Adobe Premiere for the Mac. This was an early digital video editing tool. He left Adobe and was hired by Macromedia to work on KeyGrip which they defined as a more professional video-editing program operating with Apple QuickTime.

There was some hassle with sub-licensing rights that delayed its release. By 1998 it was being shown as a Windows or Mac programme, but only privately to interested parties. It had been renamed Final Cut.

Apple acquired the software and the team, including Ubillos, as much as a defensive move. From inside Apple the team continued work and launched Final Cut Pro in April 1999.

The program offered the facility to edit any QuickTime compatible format (2K, DV, HDV, P2 MXF and XDCAM). It could colour correct, filter audio and video, work with up to 99 audio tracks, add preset transitions, plus a whole raft of editing features. In 2003 an entry-level version called Final Cut Express was released.

iMovie was available in October 1999 as a consumer-level editing system for camcorders and home video.

This was the sort of application that Jobs envisaged as part of the Digital Hub. The home user could use an iMac to store all the camcorder material and iMovie, soon released free of charge, was able to provide the user-friendliness for editing.

iMovie liberated the camcorder material that would otherwise be lurking on tapes and disks in a drawer. Versions of iMovie would later be released for iPod Touch and iPhone.

iPhoto was another such application, It took all the photos taken on the users digital camera, or those scanned or downloaded, and archived them in an easy-to-find series of 'events' or groups. It worked with most cameras and most photo file formats.

Editing facilities then allowed filtering, cropping and resizing. The software offered a series of forms of photo sharing and could be used to create movie slide shows in QuickTime, to burn DVDs. The used could prepare the photos and order them in a book form or as individual prints via the Internet.

The professional version of this, Aperture, followed in November 2005.

At the Macworld event in January 2001 iTunes was launched as a digital media player but also as a package to manage a music collection and organise it for use with their iPod. iDVD was also launched at the event enabling Mac users to publish video material, music and photos by burning them on to a DVD. Burning DVDs had been a specialist and complex process prior to iDVD.

In January 2003 these various Digital Hub packages were integrated into the Apple iLife suite. These included iMovie, iPhoto and iDVD.

In Germany in the late '80s Gerhard Lengeling and Chris Adam at C-Lab developed Creator, a MIDI audio program for the Atari ST. They soon added music notation and this became Notator. The software allowed musicians to mix and edit material.

In 1993 the designers left to found Emagic and launched Notator Logic. As its Atari prospects faded the software was redeveloped from scratch with a GUI so it could be ported to various OSs. They shortened the name to Logic.

Apple acquired Emagic in July 2002 and quickly halted plans for a Windows version of its latest software; this caused some grief with those already committed to Windows equipment. But this was soon overcome by the integration of more features into Logic.

Lengeling worked with the Apple team to produce a consumer version, launched as GarageBand in January 2004.

iWeb was added to the iLife 06 version to enable users to create websites and blogs speedily and simply.

Revolutionising music - iPod

iPod was one of the digital hub initiatives . Jonathan Ive was once again the designer, working with Jon Rubinstein as the hardware engineer. The software was developed out-house with Portal Player's platform and Pixo writing the interface under the personal instruction of Jobs. It was launched as,

'1000 songs in your pocket.'

The name iPod appears to have been originated by freelance copywriter Vinnie Chieco who said he was inspired by the movie *2001: A Space Odyssey* and the 'Open the pod bay door, Hal' line. However the name iPod had been trademarked by a New Jersey company for its Internet kiosks. Other legal actions ensued though the trademark was fully transferred to Apple in 2005.

As one of iPod's main competitors, Creative Technology, sued on the basis that it held a patent for elements of the iPod interface. Apple settled for $100m, though this would be mitigated if Creative was able to sub-license its patented elements elsewhere.

But of course waiting in the sidelines was the Beatles record label Apple Corps that had been placated by Apple computers pledging not to enter the music business. Yet here it was throwing a huge rock right in to the centre of the music 'pool'. The record company sued in September 2003 for breach of contract.

The case opened in the UK in March 2006 and was decided in the musicians' favour, ordering Apple Corps to pay £2m in legal costs; they appealed.

RANDOM ACCESS MOMENT:
Briefly I shared an office with a prominent computer industry journalist back in the '80s. He was Guy Kewney, with whom I recall having one drunken evening where we proposed his new column in one of the industry magazines should be called 'Kewney Lingo'; but we all sobered up in the morning.

Guy Kewney was invited to appear live on BBC News 24 to discuss the Apple v Apple court case. Unfortunately Guy Goma, a business studies graduate, was waiting in the reception area applying for a job in the BBC's IT department. Ushered straight into a live studio, Guy Coma manfully tried to answer the interviewer's questions in his heavy French-accent; he was from the Republic of Congo. Guy Kewney was gaunt, bearded and gingerish, not a bit like the African who had been wheeled into the studio. As I recalled this incident I was made aware that Guy had recently (April 2010) been taken by cancer at the age of sixty-three. Thanks for the memories, Guy!

In February 2007 a final arrangement was agreed between the companies; this was confidential although several media reports suggested that Apple Computer paid Apple Corps $500m. As if to underline that all was now right between them, in November 2010 Beatles albums appeared on the iTunes Store.

Many saw the iPod as the first life-changing piece of technology for years. A great number of new products were merely enhancements of existing technology, but the iPod re-energised music collections. Users spent hours placing CDs into iTunes and the iPod. Personally I regularly use random-play; it's amazing what lurks there that would never have got an airing before iPod.

iPod quickly established a market leadership position, both in the hard-drive based sector and the overall music player market. Constant innovation has kept it there.

Late in 2009 Apple reported that it had sold over 220 million iPods. The appeal of the iPod also ensured the market took a fresh look at the Apple computer; Apple's fortunes and market shares in computing grew too.

Jobs went from strength to strength following his turnaround of Apple. Disney acquired his Pixar in 2006 for $7.4bn and Jobs joined the Disney board. However his health was another matter; there were a number of scare stories including a mistaken Bloomberg obituary issued in August 2008.

In April 2009 Jobs did have a liver transplant and he is reported as having pancreatic cancer.

He had been back at work for a year when the Apple market capitalisation reached $222bn in May 2010 following the iPad launch. This meant that it was greater than that of Microsoft, at a mere $219bn. The last time that had been the case had been twenty-one years earlier in December 1989.

Acquisitive Microsoft

Microsoft went public in February 1986. This placement created four billionaires and 12,000 millionaires from among its employees.

Its relationship with IBM seemed to flip-flop, perhaps best categorised by the OS/2 project. This began with the signing of a joint development agreement between the organisations in August 1985. But the project was overtaken somewhat by the move towards GUIs.

Microsoft routinely presented its approach for a GUI to IBM from November 1983 onwards, but by then IBM was already in development of its own TopView GUI as an IBM proprietary solution. The first version of OS/2 was issued in April 1987 and this was a text-mode system without a GUI. Presentation Manager was not available until October 1988.

Microsoft had been working on the Interface Manager GUI from 1982. C Rowland Hanson, head of marketing, suggested the name should be more user friendly and it was renamed Windows as early as 1983. It was dismissed by many as 'vaporware' because it took until 20 November 1985 to materialise.

But the first version Windows 1.0 was not really a stand-alone OS, it still required MS-DOS at its core. It drew heavily upon the Xerox PARC notions and also upon a Microsoft licence with Apple. This first version provided a simple graphics program, a simple word processor, a clock, a calendar, a clipboard, a notepad, a card file, a terminal mode...

When Lotus confirmed it would support Windows in 1986 this was something of a turning point for the OS, this was its first serious software application.

Windows 2.0 was released in December 1987 and benefited from working integrally with Excel and Word. When Aldus ported PageMaker to Windows this also helped the second version to develop some momentum.

Initially IBM asked that the APIs in Windows 2.0 be changed to fit OS/2 better. They also had wanted access to the code so Windows could be subsequently integrated into OS/2.

In November 1989 IBM requested Microsoft to agree that it would not push Windows against OS/2. This was the key difference between them, because IBM certainly needed OS/2 to drive sales of its 80286 hardware, while Microsoft's goal was fully cross-platform and cross-processor.

Squabbling ensued. IBM believed that Microsoft was diverting OS/2 resources and funding to its Windows effort. Progressively it took on the OS/2 development itself and Microsoft agreed to direct its attention to Windows NT (new technology) or OS/2 3.0 as a high-level, cross-processor, multi-user, server-based OS to incorporate many of the UNIX benefits.

However Microsoft maintained its development of Windows as it saw this as a lower-end less-resource-demanding OS that would have more general appeal.

The final nail in the relationship was when in May 1990 Microsoft launched Windows 3.0 and sold a million copies inside four months; a total of 2.7 million copies of Windows 3.0 were shipped by the end of 1990.

This success encouraged Microsoft to change Windows NT from its OS/2 roots to more of a Windows basis, adding to further tension in the relationship. Windows NT 3.1 was first released in July 1993 and proved more successful than OS/2.

But it was not all about OSs; applications at Microsoft were advancing at a pace too.

At Forethought Inc, Dennis Austin and Bob Gaskins developed the Presenter program for Mac in 1984. It was renamed PowerPoint in 1987. The same operation, also in 1984, had acquired FileMaker, a DOS program and ported it to the Mac.

PowerPoint for the Mac was released in 1987 and Microsoft bought the operation and the program for $14m that year. A Windows version of Microsoft PowerPoint was released in May 1990.

Alan M Boyd, the Microsoft head of product development, proposed an internal tool to assist his work; he provided a specification to a local Seattle company to develop what he called Project. This was produced for DOS in 1984 and acquired by Microsoft in 1985. The Windows version of Microsoft Project was also released in May 1990.

In October 1990 Microsoft launched Office Suite, bundling Word, Excel and PowerPoint. These gained significant market shares to continue the growth of the organisation.

Microsoft Money followed in 1991 as part of the Microsoft Home series. Microsoft Bookshelf was launched in October 1991 and Encarta a year later.

Moves into databases were assisted by the acquisition of Access in December 1991 and FoxPro in May 1992.

Whether it was the result of this plethora of application developments is unclear but it is evident that Microsoft neglected the Internet in the early '90s. A whole series of internal meetings and initiatives were rather belatedly deployed and Bill Gates publication of *The Internet Tidal Wave* in May 1995, was the catalyst to make sure it was taken seriously.

In December 1994 Microsoft tried to acquire the Mosaic browser, but rebuffed by Jim Clark and Marc Andreessen as they created Netscape Navigator, it settled later that month for signing a licence with Spyglass to get at the code.

Thomas Reardon took the Spyglass source code and by August 1995 had developed Microsoft Internet Explorer and the battle between it and Netscape proved nasty. By September 1998 Internet Explorer had remorselessly overtaken Netscape's market share.

Microsoft Office Outlook was a personal information manager that allowed the user to access a number of emails and organise them; it also had a contact manager, a calendar and a task manager. It was first generally released as part of Office 97 in January 1997. Third party programmes allowed Outlook material to be integrated with a Blackberry, with Skype and other services. Outlook Mobile offered a version for mobiles and smartphones.

Some confusion reigned as many believed that Outlook Express was a simpler version of Microsoft Office Outlook, but this was not the case.

In 1996 Microsoft updated its earlier Internet Mail and News program to create Outlook Express as an email and newsgroup client used for contact management. It was launched alongside Internet Explorer 3 and integrated within Explorer versions 4 through 6. In October 2005 Windows Vista launched Windows Mail, an upgrade of Outlook Express; Microsoft Entourage was the update for Macs.

By August 1995 Windows 95 was released and this was its most successful version; with some ten million lines of code and having consumed 300 person-years of effort it was certainly the biggest too. By December 1995 it had sold 11.4 million copies, with 19 million PCs being supplied with Windows 95 as its OS. By the end of 1996 some 65 million copies had been sold. Of course the popular jibe of the time was 'Windows 95, Mac 85', but there was no denying that sales performance.

Another Internet initiative was Microsoft acquiring Vermeer Technologies of Cambridge, Massachusetts, in January 1996 for $133m. Charles Ferguson and Randy Forgaard had founded the operation in 1994 and the following year had launched FrontPage, a website and web page development package, and Personal Web Server that worked with FrontPage.

FrontPage was a WYSIWYG editing program that kept all the nasty html stuff well hidden though at something of a premium in terms of lines of code.

This in essence allowed a novice to develop a website, but the user-friendliness made it code heavy and so it tended to run slowly.

It was launched as Microsoft FrontPage 1.1 in 1996 and bundled within the Microsoft Office Suite from 1997 to 2003. In 2006 it was replaced by Microsoft Expression Web and Sharepoint Designer.

Steve Ballmer took over the reins as the CEO in July 1998, and it was on his watch in September 1998 that Microsoft was valued at $261bn and therefore ranked as the most valuable company in the USA.

Windows has consistently innovated with its 98, 2000, XP, Vista and 7 versions; each had issues and complainants but this forward thrust has certainly maintained a strong market share.

Windows CE was launched in September 1996 for handheld computers and PDAs, CE standing for consumer electronics. In January 2000 Windows Mobile was launched, based upon the kernel of CE. It was for smartphones and mobile devices and was upgraded to Windows Phone 7 in February 2010.

Unusually for Microsoft it held just fifth place in the smartphone OS business behind Android, Blackberry OS, iPhone and Symbian.

On the 27th June 2008 Bill Gates spent his last day formally working at Microsoft, and left to concentrate on his philanthropic activities, channelled through the Bill & Melinda Gates Foundation. Their work on getting vaccinations to some 250 million children around the world is estimated to have avoided five million deaths!

Of this work he said,

'In the 1960s over 20 million children died a year. Now that number is down to somewhere between eight and nine million. Clearly that's incredible progress.'

In June 2010 Gates and Warren Buffet shared a stage to announce their 'Giving Pledge' and called upon other billionaires to make a moral commitment to give away at least 50% of their fortunes to charity. Some forty or so have joined them.

He has gone on record saying that he will pass some of his money to his three children but that this will not be a meaningful percentage.

Acquiring strength - HP

In reviewing the material in this book I realised that I have not paid enough attention to Hewlett Packard or HP. It has always been there and has always been prominent, it was not a 'flash' company claiming development firsts, mounting major marketing launches, shouting its own praises; but perhaps it might just have done so.

It deserves admiration for its acquisitions of Apollo graphical workstations in April 1989, of Texas Instruments computer systems in October 1992 and of the Convex Computers mini-supercomputers.

Then of course its takeover/merger with Compaq in May 2002 was massive. Compaq had itself acquired Tandem Computers in June 1997 and DEC in January 1998. Still not assuaged, Hewlett Packard acquired Ross Perot's EDS in August 2008, followed by 3Com in April 2010, and Palm in July 2010. Along the way in 2007 it was the first IT company to report sales of over $100bn.

It has been a global market leader in IT hardware and also leads in inkjet, laser and large format printers. It employed over 300,000, and in 2010 turned over $126bn with almost $9bn in profit.

HP was not omnipotent of course; it rejected the Apple I when it was offered by its employee Steve Wozniak. But it also had some firsts with the HP-35 first handheld scientific electronic calculator in 1972, the HP-65 first handheld programmable in 1974, plus the HP-41C and HP-28C. It was early to the Internet, registering HP.com in March 1986 - the ninth ever .com domain to be registered.

In 1999 it spun off all its non PC, storage and imaging products into Agilent Technologies. The Agilent IPO was Silicon Valley's largest IPO, creating a company valued at $8bn.

It achieved another first by having the first female CEO of a company listed within the Dow Jones Industrial Average. Carly Fiorina joined in July 1999, but her time at the helm was tough. During a general technology-sector downturn she presided over HP halving in value and a resulting massive series of job losses; she resigned in February 2005.

So HP was always significant for being technically up there, and for being corporately moral. It was prominent in open software, in recent years it has been a champion of green issues too.

But perhaps the overall impression is that it has been something of a steady eddie in the PC business, rather than being trend-setting, brash and sparkly - but it was certainly no also-ran!

PCs on the move
True mobile computing had a long gestation period and there was not much of a following for early products.

One of the first requirements was for the PC itself to be transportable. I do recall humping the quite compact Apple II with two disk drives and a small mono monitor around from place to place - but this was not that easy.

The early products designed specifically for transportability were still bulky, heavy and awkward. This led to the use of the term 'luggable' by magazines and others to imply to potential users that portability still required some physical skills.

Plans for portable computers, laptops and handhelds abounded in the late '70s and early '80s. In 1976 Xerox PARC was in the vanguard with the

NoteTaker, the first portable computer; but this followed its standard approach and was merely a prototype that was never brought to market.

A small company with a big-sounding name was GM Research; its James Murez developed Micro Star, aka The Small One, in 1979. It was taken up by the US government and others and was demonstrated at a computer show that year where it was certainly seen by Adam Osborne.

Osborne was born of English parents in Thailand; he was an author in the early days of PC development. Working with Lee Felsenstein and Al Alcorn he developed and launched the Osborne 1 in March 1981. Importantly they created an all-in-one hardware and software package to move the genre forward.

Priced at $1,795, it was a Z80 CP/M device designed as a 12kg [26.5lb] luggable; it certainly captured the imagination. They had revenues of $6m in 1981 and after launching the Executive version in 1982 the sales reached $68m. At peak 10,000 units a month were being shipped.

However the Executive failed to materialise until April 1983 and the delays, added to a competitive market, led to the company crashing in September 1983. Osborne was asked what happened and replied with a quotation that I thought brilliant at the time and have shamelessly plagiarised down the years, he said,

'Briefly I doubted my own infallibility.'

The Osborne success and its design would however serve to inspire Compaq.

Others had studied the Osborne story too. Andrew Kay graduated in 1940 from MIT. After a stint at the Jet Propulsion Laboratory he founded NLS (Non-Linear Systems) in 1952 where he designed a successful digital voltmeter.

In 1981 NLS released a PC, based on the Osborne 1. It was launched as the Kaypro II in March 1982; there had been no manufactured Kaypro I, just a prototype. Kaypro Corporation was formed as a subsidiary of NLS in 1982.

The Kaypro II weighed 13kg (29 lbs) had a larger 9" screen than the Osborne but it was also based on the Z80 and CP/M based, offering the Perfect suite of WP and spreadsheet; it was launched at $1,795.

Kaypro trained a strong dealer network and by1983 it too was selling 10,000 units per month. A dynasty of Kaypro computers followed. Its very success contributed to the Osborne demise of course. But it clung to CP/M as its OS far too long, only succumbing to MS-DOS quite late in 1985 with the Kaypro 16.

Its late adoption of MS-DOS marked the beginning of its end and in March 1990 it went into Chapter 11, by June 1992 it was liquidated and its assets were sold for $2.7m in 1995. The brand Kaypro was resurrected briefly from 1999 to 2001. Kay himself launched another operation, Kay Computers.

The Epson HX-20 was launched in November 1981, though it was not really available in quantity until 1983. It was claimed by some to be the first laptop though it was really more of a handheld device. Its display was a simple 4 line x 20 character LCD screen.

The Epson HX-20 was the inspiration for Kyocera to develop the Kyotronic 85 computer in 1983. This was successfully marketed by others as the TRS-80 Model 100, the Olivetti M-10 and NEC PC-8201.

However the GRiD Compass launched in April 1982 is more usually referred to as the first laptop. The company was founded by John Ellenby who had worked at PARC on the Alto II project. Ellenby was a Brit, educated at University College London, who worked at Ferranti before joining PARC.

The Compass drew on the Dynabook work at PARC, but was designed by another Brit, Bill Moggridge. He created it back in 1979 but it was not released for three years. GRiD patented the clamshell approach and was recompensed by a licence from others who took the same approach.

It weighed just under 11lbs [5kg]. The lower case 'i' in its name was a thank you to Intel who had assisted in the development phase. It used an Intel 8086 and its own operating system, GRiD-OS. It sold for $8,150.

GRiD also put the first laptop into space in a late 1983 Shuttle flight.

The design set the parameters for the laptops that followed. GRiD was acquired by Radio Shack/Tandy in 1988. In September 1989 GRiD released the GRiDPad - a touch screen computer using MS-DOS.

Dynalogic's Hyperion was announced in June 1982 but was not shipped until January 1983; the controlling company was Infotech Cie of Canada, it had acquired Dynalogic in the month that it commenced shipping. It was launched as
'A Star is Borne' And 'The World's most powerful portable computer'.

It was a chunky portable at 21lbs (9.5kg) with an 8088 at its heart, twin floppy drives and an amber 7" screen with 80 characters by 25 rows of text. It had an on-board 300-baud modem. But it was only 95% compatible with the IBM PC, failing to run a number of software programs and worse it had reliability problems. It was released on to the market two months before Compaq.

The Gavilan SC was available in May 1983, the product of another industrial designer, Jack Hall. It had the distinction of being the first to describe itself formally as a 'laptop'. Founded by Manny Martinez, the Gavilan organisation lasted only until 1985.

The Compaq Portable was announced in November 1982 and shipped in January 1983; it was the first cloned IBM PC with all its features packaged in a portable format. It sold 53,000 units in the first year and set all sorts of USA corporate revenue records in its first three years of operation.

The Commodore SX-64, aka the Executive 64, was announced in January 1983 and launched in January 1984 as the first full-colour portable computer. It had a small 5" composite monitor and sold at $995.
There were some limitations in terms of its power supply and software library, and attention was distracted by the announcement of plans for the DX-64. These facts all led to it not selling particularly well.

IBM had its own Portable PC 5155 launched in February 1984. Prism launched its Wren luggable in 1984. Apple's first portable was the Apple IIc in April 1984; the first Mac portable was in September 1989, followed by the PowerBook in October 1991 with iBook and MacBook much later.
Toshiba rather implausibly claimed the T1100, launched in 1985, to be 'the world's first mass-market laptop computer'; its claim all about that 'mass-market' phrase.
After his company's disposal to Amstrad, Sinclair came back with the Cambridge Computer Z88 in 1988. This had a limited appeal for Sinclair aficionados.

Wireless connectivity
What may have appeared as something of an aside later came back to make a major contribution to this market. Vic Hayes was born in Indonesia and lived in the Netherlands. He qualified in electrical engineering in 1961 and at first worked at Friden.
He joined NCR Systems Laboratory in 1974 to investigate standards for connecting stockbroker users of NCR terminals. Hayes established a series of protocols for a wireless system for cashiers, one of these being how an email might be handled wirelessly. This early work resulted in WaveLAN, a wireless alternative to Ethernet.
Hayes then turned his attention fully to WLANs (wireless local area networks). But standardisation was elusive. Progress was only achieved after Hayes was appointed in 1990 to chair the IEEE (Institute of Electrical & Electronics Engineers) standards committee.
Hayes gathered experts from around the industry and they thrashed out the WLAN standard by 1996. Formally known as 802.11 it was popularised as Wi-Fi, and Hayes is considered to be the 'father of Wi-Fi'. Wi-Fi itself stood for wireless fidelity.
Wi-Fi hotspots sprung up everywhere offering users with a Wi-Fi card or facility the opportunity to piggyback the system to reach remote servers and email services. The service is also defined to allow phone calls though this has not been broadly implemented.

Hayes went on to become a senior research fellow at the Delft University of Technology.

Personal Digital Assistance
The next major step in mobile computing was the PDA or personal digital assistant.

In January 1992 John Sculley was credited as the first to use the term PDA. He was talking fairly late in the development of the Apple Newton, his pet project. This was Apple's first PDA/Tablet computer, discussed as early as 1987 but first released in August 1993. Sculley had in fact left Apple by June 1993.

The software was developed on a LISP-derivative called Dylan, but this was replaced by NewtonScript, designed by Walter Smith. LISP, NewtonScript, Self and SmallTalk were later the inspiration for the 'Io' language in March 2002 – developed by Steve Dekorte.

The Newton look-and-feel was designed by (who else?) Jonathan Ive, and some of the construction was by Sharp. Apple sold 100,000 units in its first year and continued to develop new Newton MessagePads, the last being the 2100 released in 1998.

But problems meant that the Newton did not live up to Apple's expectations. It was talked up for rather too long before it became available and it had a whole raft of competitors against which it proved somewhat large and lumpy and, worse, quite slow.

Newton's handwriting software had several shortfalls as it was predicated on reading full words rather than characters. Finally it did not have a good synchronising solution.

Jeff Hawkins, Ed Colligan and Donna Dubinsky founded Palm Inc in 1992 to participate in the development of the Zoomer consumer-market PDA. This was manufactured by Tandy, with software from Geoworks, and it was distributed by Casio. It reached the market before the Apple Newton in 1993 but it failed to impress, selling only 10,000 units.

Palm survived in part because of its Graffiti software that recognised handwriting for the Zoomer and other GEOS-based devices.

Hawkins was inspired by the GRiDPad to create a dynasty of personal digital assistants starting with the Palm Pilot 1000 and 5000 in March 1996. Palm was acquired by US Robotics in 1995, and in June 1997 both were subsequently taken over by 3Com.

Pilot Pen, the largest Japanese and third largest US pen manufacturer objected to Palm's use of the word Pilot and subsequent products after 1998 dropped it.

Unhappy with the direction 3Com was adopting for its invention, in June 1998 the three founders left and formed Handspring. They developed the

Handspring Visor and Treo series of handheld computers; in 2003 the company was taken back into the Palm Inc stable.

Hawkins and Dubinsky went on to form Numenta in March 2005; it expounded theories about the neocortex of the human brain. Hawkins and Dileep George evolved some algorithms that they said defined the neocortex functions; this was termed HTM (hierarchical temporal memory). The NuPIC (Numenta platform for intelligent computing) launched in March 2007 providing a series of tools for PCs; a Windows version was released in August 2007.

DEC's Western Research Lab developed its Itsy Pocket Computer in 1999 which was taken to market by Compaq as the iPAQ in April 2000. In September 2001 HP took over Compaq and continued the line of iPAQs.

By 2003 Microsoft had launched the Windows Mobile 2003 OS and by 2007 the Windows Mobile 5 OS.

Phones get smarter

The market was moving towards a new theme - convergence. All the progress in PCs and the various portable versions of that technology were converging with developments in mobile phones and PDAs.

IBM developed a smarter phone called the Simon Personal Communicator, launched at COMDEX in 1992. It was sold jointly by IBM and BellSouth Cellular Corp from 1993.

Simon was a touch screen mobile with an address book, calculator, calendar and clock. It would send and receive emails, faxes and pages; it even had games and predictive text. It used the Zaurus OS but at $899 it was hardly inexpensive.

In August 1996 Nokia introduced its first contender, the 9000 Communicator, which was its first combined phone and PDA. This rapidly became the world's top selling PDA. It had a GEOS OS but was quite heavy at 14ozs (397g).

The third generation of Nokia Communicators, the 9210 launched in 2002, was the first to offer a colour screen. It was considered the first true smartphone in part because it came with the Symbian OS, developed and maintained by Nokia but released as an open-source programme. The OS originator, Symbian Ltd, to some extent derived its system from Psion's EPOC OS. Symbian was acquired by Nokia in December 2008.

The Nokia 9500 in 2004 worked with Wi-Fi; the Nokia 9300 in 2005 added GPS. The Nokia N800 was introduced as an Internet tablet in January 2007. It worked by connecting to a Wi-Fi network or via Bluetooth to mobile networks.

However the Ericsson GS88 released in 1997 was the first actually to call itself a smartphone. Ericsson launched the R380, its first touch screen smartphone, in 2000; it also offered the Symbian OS. The Ericsson P800 released in 2002 was the first camera smartphone.

Mike Lazardis, ethnically Greek though born in Istanbul, moved to Canada in 1966 at the age of five. In 1984, having not yet qualified in computer science, he won a tender for $500,000 with General Motors to develop a network computer control display system.

On leaving college, with the GM contract, some seedcorn supplied by his parents and a government grant, he founded RiM (Research in Motion) with Mike Barnstijn and Douglas Fregin.

It attracted venture capital and completed its IPO in January 1998 on the Toronto Stock Exchange.

Its first activity was to develop a two-way paging and emailing device, launched in August 1998. Initially called the Inter@ctive Pager it was renamed the BlackBerry 850. It was developed for the Ericsson Mobitex network as a competitor to Motorola's SkyTel.

In 1999 the first BlackBerry as a two-way pager was released, but RiM really set the world alight when it launched the wireless Blackberry in 2002. This was essentially a smartphone that was able to receive emails through mobile networks or Wi-Fi connections.

It had its own OS and offered BlackBerry Connect for devices such as the Palm Treo to offer email services. The BlackBerry Enterprise Server software package relayed and synchronised a company's email system via enterprise email servers including Microsoft Exchange, Lotus Domino or Novell GroupWise. Individual users could also work with the Blackberry Internet Service in over ninety countries; it allowed a user to manage up to ten email accounts.

BlackBerry and RIM experienced a meteoric rise as the BlackBerry became the de rigueur corporate tool; even President Obama confessed to needing his BlackBerry. Launched in 2002, by 2004 it had two million users and by 2010 over 100 million units had been sold; it controlled 10% of the global smartphone OS market.

Like all massive growth operations RiM picked up problems along the way. It spent many years in litigation trying to see off those seeking to infringe on patents. It also ran into problems when it tried to backdate employee stock options.

RiM routed all the email traffic for its users through its own servers and this led to concerns about security. The United Arab Emirates insisted that the service be brought within its borders but when it failed to get agreement it suspended the BlackBerry service in its market in October 2010. Algeria, Bahrain, India, Indonesia, Pakistan and Saudi Arabia each threatened to follow suit; RiM moved to placate some of these markets.

Apple entered the fray, working with AT&T Mobility (originally Cingular) and the pair spent some $150m over two and a half years on development of the iPhone. Apple made some two hundred patent applications in relation to it.

At the end of all this AT&T allowed Apple to run the final development exercise in return for AT&T having exclusivity of sales in the USA market. Apple was granted $10 per month from each AT&T iPhone client.

Wayne Westerman, a PhD student at the University of Delaware, based his dissertation on multi-touch surfaces. With John Elias, a professor in the department, he founded FingerWorks in 1998. The operation launched its TouchStream multi-touch keyboard but it was not financially stable.

Apple acquired FingerWorks in early 2005 and halted production of the keyboards merging the technology into its own plans.

The iPhone was launched in January 2007 and released in June; it reached major European markets by November of the same year.

The iPhone was launched with iPhone OS 1.0, or iOS, with a 9 cm (3.5") LCD multi-touch screen. By January 2008 it was able to use tri-lateration with mobile network aerials and Wi-Fi points.

Apple introduced a restriction on software apps for the iPhone, insisting all software had to include an Apple-approved cryptographic signature. Of course it was not long before 'jailbreaking' software was available to circumvent this control.

By the end of October 2008 iPhone had surpassed the sales of Blackberry. In the previous quarter Apple sold 6.9 million units compared to BlackBerry at 6.1 million. By October 2010 some 73.5 million iPhones had been sold.

Android Inc was a Palo Alto start-up to develop mobile phone software founded in 2003 by Andy Rubin, Rich Miner, Nick Sears and Chris White. Its acquisition by Google in July 2005, followed by several patent applications in mobile telephony did fuel speculation that Google was entering the mobile phone business.

Google announced the Android OS in November 2007, together with the founding of the Open Handset Alliance with Intel, LG, Motorola, nVidia, Samsung, Sprint, T-Mobile, TI and others. Android was therefore established as an open mobile device platform based around the Linux kernel. Developers worked in Java to write applications.

In February 2008 Google experienced a moment of panic when its internal data showed it was receiving fifty times more search requests via Apple iPhones than any other mobile. This was barely months before the third party Android-based smartphones were due to be launched.

Google released the entire source code of Android under an Apache free licence on 21st October 2008. That same month on 22nd October 20008 T-

Mobile announced its G1 handset, aka HTC Dream, the first phone built using the Android OS; by April 2009 it had sold over one million units.

Android OS was developed to work with netbooks and tablets. In July 2009 Android had a 9% share of USA smartphone unit sales; by the end of 2010 it had grown to 21.4%.

In July 2010 the 'App Inventor for Android' provided developers tools and supports for those writing apps for the platform. By December 2010 there were some 200,000 games, applications and widgets available via the Android Market; by then there had been some 2.5 billion downloads.

In May 2010 Blackberry was recorded as having 35% of the market, iPhone 28% and Android 23%. Briefly the Android platform overtook the iPhone in terms of unit sales in the USA but this was soon reversed with the launch of iPhone 4. By the end of 2010 some 30,000 Android smartphones were being activated daily.

Motivated by its poor performance against iPhone and Android, in February 2011 Nokia announced that it would throw its lot in with Microsoft. It proposed to move away from its own Symbian OS and adopt Windows Phone 7.

Keep taking the tablets

One of the key issues for mobile computing was concluded quite early to be the requirement to recognise handwriting in order to make interaction simple and speedy for the user.

This then required some form of tablet that could be written upon to enable the system to capture handwriting. Early steps to achieve this facility were tiny and across a long period of time.

The first patent for a tablet dated way back to July 1888. The Teleautograph, designed by Elisha Gray, could capture handwriting, send it over the telegraph system and re-constitute it at the receiving station.

In November 1914 Hyman Eli Goldberg patented the Controller. This actually recognised handwritten numbers that were converted into electrical data to be used to execute orders that could control equipment.

In 1938 George Hansel patented machine recognition of handwriting.

In 1945 Vannevar Bush included handwritten input as a key element of his plans for the Memex in *As We May Think*.

In 1957 Tom L Dimond patented the Stylator as an electronic tablet with handwriting recognition.

In the late 1960s Alan Kay at Xerox PARC suggested that his Dynabook should have a pen input facility.

With ARPA funding, in September 1963 RAND developed the RAND Tablet. It had a 10" x 10" surface on which a grid of 100 lines by 100 lines recorded anything written upon it with a pen or stylus.

In 1982 and 1983 there were pen-based systems with handwriting recognition launched by Pencept, Cadre Systems and CIC. Pencept developed a stable handwriting recognition algorithm, yet still it was not successful.

In July 1983 Wacom of Japan entered the market; the name derived from the Japanese words *wa* for harmony and *komu* for computer. It used a different approach with its patented technology using a wireless pen and a graphics tablet as a peripheral to PCs from other manufacturers.

In 1989 the GRiDPad was the first available portable tablet; significantly it was offered with MS-DOS.

In 1987 GO Corporation developed a pen-based user interface that by 1991 worked with the PenPoint OS for laptops and handhelds. It had some success when AT&T acquired its hardware. This was then spun off as EO and the telecom company launched the EO Personal Communicator. But it seemed that tablet computers failed to charge the imaginations sufficiently.

The early '90s was a busy time for the mobile computer sector. Apple entered the fray with the Newton in 1991; though deliveries were not made until 1993. Microsoft aggressively attacked the sector with Windows for Pen Computing in April 1992; this resulted in legal action by GO that subsequently accused Microsoft of copying its technologies.

The IBM/AT&T Simon and ThinkPad 750P and 360P portable tablet computers arrived in 1993. During 1994 HP developed a PDA/palmtop computer called the HP 200LX; this was later discontinued in favour of a Windows CE range, starting with the HP 300LX.

Nokia entered the tablet market with the Nokia 770 Internet Tablet in May 2005. It used the Linux-based Maemo OS and bundled the Opera browser, Flash and Gizmo VoIP (Gizmo was acquired by Google in November 2009). At $359.99 the Nokia 770 was competitively priced.

It was used with Wi-Fi networks to browse and would handle emails. But it also featured an eBook reader, Internet radio, RSS feeds and a variety of players for image viewing and media presentation. But it proved to be slow with limited memory and poor battery life.

Apple updates the tablet

Early on in his second period at Apple, Steve Jobs asked his engineers to look at touch screens and it was clear that he had a tablet PC in mind. He was unhappy with the PDAs and tablet PCs available on the market at the time and he urged them to identify a new approach.

Of course the Apple Newton had been announced back in 1987 but it failed to ignite much enthusiasm for the genre when it was launched in the early '90s. Apple also developed the Penlite, a tablet version of the PowerBook Duo, but it feared it would impact on sales of the Newton MessagePad and did not release it

But with the launch of iPod in 2001 Apple was indomitable once again. Work on the iPad is said to have started before the iPhone, yet it was to be the launch of the iPhone in 2007 that first brought together a multi-touch screen and the Apple mobile operating system, iOS.

From there it was a short step to the Apple iPad, though speculation as to its name was rife for some time - iSlate and iTablet were the Apple-istas' favourites. The Apple iPad was launched on 27 January 2010.

The iPad had a 25 cm (9.7") scratch resistant screen and worked with bare fingers - no need for a stylus or special gloves. It came with just a few physical switches; most operations were accessed through the touch screen.

It had several sensors; one measured the ambient light conditions and set the brightness automatically and the other recognised the orientation of the iPad to set the screen to portrait or landscape. There was also a landscape-left or landscape-right option.

Two versions were supplied, one that was Wi-Fi only and one to work with both Wi-Fi and 3G mobile networks. Both had location-aware processes. The Wi-Fi versions used the Boston-based Skyhook Wireless system (launched in 2003) which provided a tri-lateration of Wi-Fi locations. With the 3G version GPS was used to achieve the same awareness. These enabled Google Maps and other services to be used while on the move.

RANDOM ACCESS MOMENT:
Thomas Cauldell while working at Boeing in 1990 coined the phrase 'augmented reality'. This was soon applied to various virtual reality applications as for example head-mounted displays. By 2011 the term was applied to a system where a smartphone or tablet could be pointed at an object or scene in the real world and it superimposes a virtual message, graphic or animation. The effects can be informative to surreal.

29 - Analysis - what has the PC done for us?

*We are not even close to finishing the basic dream of what the PC can be.'
Bill Gates. 'The Web as I envisaged it, we have not seen it yet. The future is still so much bigger than the past.' Tim Berners-Lee*

The serendipitous nature of computer development does not leave us with an original set of declared goals that we can go back to, dust off and see just how we did against our ambitions. So many individual dreams and aspirations, so often very short-term, so many unexpected side issues and discoveries along the way, there is no arbiter of success or achievement.

I am personally delighted to see the 'happenstance' moments along the path. The way in which teletext utilised those wasted scan lines in our televisions. How unplanned-for SMS texts would become such a key part of our mobile experience. How email and Skype superseded the information dissemination objectives for the Internet. How social networking and file sharing dominate the World Wide Web.

But casting our thoughts back to those early heady days there are several objectives that were key back then.

Certainly Vannevar Bush and his Memex concept has been realised in today's ready access to information and books through the World Wide Web. The Bush-surmised trail of links leading through the material is certainly achieved by hypertext and by bookmarking. But the tools to create new knowledge and cross-fertilise ideas are still wedged securely between our ears.

What happened to the paperless society?

One of the other early objectives was for computers to eliminate the need for paper, thus saving forests of trees. Surely this was the first green or environmental goal most of us encountered?

In the early years of mainframe computing it was untrue – computers produced even more paper. And this was mainly of the continuous, spooled and green-lined variety that playschools and junior schools gladly used in art sessions.

Developments today have certainly brought about a global reduction in the use of photographic paper. Most digital photos are held in a camera memory or on a PC and never to actually make it to print!

But paper seems to be proving resilient.

Email challenges

Email has supplanted snail mail and today most stuff that drops through the letter-box are bills or unsolicited promotional material. Some 9% of all

Internet traffic is in email and this is the reason PTTs are raising prices routinely and regularly; their infrastructure remains unchanged while traffic has declined.

Communicating with business contacts, colleagues, friends and family is easy today. In 1996 I was posted to manage an event in Kuala Lumpur for seven weeks and had to write letters to my wife, something I had not needed to do for more than thirty years of married life; it was an amusing relearning process. But within just a few years we would have emailed and Skyped each other – I might then have seemed to be just around the corner.

But emailing has its pitfalls too. Surely I am not just a 'grumpy old man' when I bemoan the use of text-speak and slang, the decline of the adverb (losing its 'ly'), the poor punctuation and the non-existent grammar in many emails I receive.

I am known for not reading an email to its end, often missing the later points in a missive. Further there can be many misunderstandings of tone and intention in rapidly sent emails.

Certainly the Internet and emails have had an impact upon the global political scene. No longer are national borders able to prevent information from entering or leaving a country's territory. However politics has a way of overcoming drawbacks such as this and some have become adept at using these resources for their purposes. How often have we seen narrow-angle shots of locals giving a dictator popular support when careful examination of the surrounding area shows just a small number of individuals merely performing for the camera?

But are countries that stop foreign TV broadcasts, block Internet sites and monitor emails sending a clear message that they have something to hide?

The Net - a perfect market?

In theory when we buy something today we have access to a perfect market; there is no lack of information to assess and compare the right product or service, no shortage of suppliers at competitive rates.

But I regret the disappearance of teams of professional salesmen on the road presenting their wares and living on their wits to outsell their competitors. Not to mention the vanishing specialist shops facing the double jeopardy of mass merchandisers and online retailers eroding their livelihoods.

PC Productivity

Of course the other implicit benefit of computers was that they would increase personal and corporate productivity –wouldn't they? All that effort applied by PARC and others to define The Office of the Future must have paid dividends – hadn't it?

Professor Gary Loveman at MIT was early to discover what became known as the 'productivity paradox'. He rather innocently looked at the benefits to US businesses that were derived from investment in computer equipment. He found no positive effect and felt that indeed there might have been a negative one.

The use of PCs in the office is now de rigueur but in the early noughties I was working with an operation that had equipped all its accounts and customer support personnel with a PC but had never tested their skills or supplied any form of on-the-job training in typing.

A situation arose in which we decided to test their typing skills, supplying each PC user with a letter to simply copy type. As a long-term and competent PC user (though never touch-typing trained), I took around six minutes; the average for the team was well over twelve minutes with several taking over twenty!

Even where general typing skills are high there are many other issues around supplying computers so generally. Back in 1995 I ran a small sales team selling exhibition space at a consumer electronics show. As a company we were sold by News International to a major exhibitions' company. On arrival we were each supplied with a PC that had access to a central customer and sales prospect database; theoretically this should have at-a-stroke improved our potential sales figures.

However within a month our productivity was completely shot. We had to ban PC use between 09:30 and 16:30 so the team could concentrate on making sales calls rather than playing with their computers! They would then download contacts for the day's calls before 09:30 and update the dbase after 16:30. Another decision made was to stop them all trying to send out sales letters and instead have just one skilled individual do the task – the sight of someone plucking away for an hour at a simple sales letter was painful!

Today an office PC user can be distracted not just by emails but by instant messaging, tweeting and social networking - making the whole productivity issue much worse. Where employers as a result decide to monitor staff activity through their PCs, they run the risk of being accused of invasion of privacy.

Maintaining your identity

There is however another downside to the Internet. To use significant services such as online banking and eCommerce there is a need to supply personal information.

Many spam emails are overt attempts to acquire your credit card or password details; this is termed as phishing. They masquerade as bank, government office or other services requesting confirmation of details; the gullible can be taken in by these demands. Fortunately the poor formatting, spelling and grammar of many of these messages are all too obvious.

But there are instances of spam mails coming apparently from a friend; in this case the spammers have managed to penetrate that friend's email contact list.

Symantec cited a more aggressive form of spamming when the offer of a low-cost product would prompt a response, enabling the spammer to download porn to the user's PC. The spammer would then blackmail the user, threatening to inform partners or employers unless a payment was made.

Social networks have had issues too. Interesting stuff you put up about your life can be read by those with evil intent. An obvious result might be a burglary while you are posting pictures of your great holiday. Or prospective employers might look at your sites to see your spare time activities and perhaps change their minds about that job offer!

And then along comes the hacker to abuse the systems by penetrating the social network's processes and acquire more than you were prepared to share.

Not all hacks are deliberately malicious. When Apple launched its iPhone it was locked in to the AT&T service. In July 2009 George Hotz achieved a hardware hack enabling the iPhone to be used with other services. He traded his invention for a car and three iPhones and went on to develop a number of software hacks for the system.

Hotz attended the Johns Hopkins Center for Talented Youth and had a list of early achievements in robotics. In 2008 PC World voted him one of the top ten over-achievers under twenty-one years of age.

RANDOM ACCESS MOMENT:
for consistency I have used the word 'hack' but today this is viewed as something from an earlier era; currently the act of opening up an OS is termed as a 'jailbreak'.

Hotz was back in January 2010 with a jailbreak of Sony's PlayStation 3 giving himself access to the console to carry out homebrew experimentation. It also allowed him to emulate PS2 games, something Sony had removed. He countered Sony's attempts to shut him out by announcing plans to develop firmware which allowed the use of other OSs such as Linux. All this was shown online by Hotz with video and other material to help others mimic his approach.

Sony took legal action against Hotz and the courts granted it strong recourse. Sony was provided with access to his PayPal account and also provided with the IP addresses of everyone who had visited his site, geohot.com.

There is no suggestion that Hotz was involved with the PlayStation Network April 2011 outage. He is quoted as saying,

'Running homebrew and exploring security on your devices is cool, hacking into someone else's server and stealing databases of user info is not cool.'

But illicit entry into the Sony PSN service did give some other hacker/s access to 77 million users' details. As I write this, as yet there appears to have been no reported abuse of that data.

A constant battle of minds will be maintained between the protection industry and the hackers, each pushing to countermand the other's actions.

Artificial intelligence

So let's look instead at macro issues rather than the mundanity of saving paper, improving productivity and countering phishing. Surely computing is part of a major movement with real benefits that we will soon realise?

Yet the massive energy and enthusiasm applied to the high ideals of artificial intelligence and robotics show only a disappointing amount of progress; the report card would say 'could try harder'.

Artificial intelligence as a concept is something of a moveable feast; what one generation considered to be AI is viewed as mere software by the next. Optical character recognition and speech recognition were once considered AI objectives, but today these are offered by relatively straightforward solutions.

True artificial intelligence would be the creation of a thinking machine able to reason, deduce and solve problems.

Japan's Ministry of Trade and Industry pursued this form of AI through the development of fifth-generation computers from 1982; its forecast that it would be completed in ten years whimpered out. But not before other nations had poured research monies in to their own competing projects.

Not that all the effort was wasted; for example the Xbox 360 game applied AI developments and algorithms to develop its three-dimensional Kinect interface launched in November 2010.

Japan's efforts certainly led to it becoming world leader in the field of humanoid robots acting as security guards, receptionists... They even have one that walks the catwalk as a fashion model. Some play games or act as companions or pets.

As impressive as their skills and movements are these are very limited devices and they merely follow instructions set for them. However this effort has spin-off benefits; for example some of these developments have been used to create exoskeleton suits and limbs to assist the disabled.

Of course the power of computers is exhibited by advances in the capabilities of microprocessors and supercomputers and by the annexation of the spare capacities available out there in distributed computing exercises.

In February 1996 IBM's Deep Blue defeated the reigning world chess champion, Garry Kasparov, in a game of chess under the normal timed basis.

But it went on to lose 4-2 in that series. It was subsequently upgraded and in May 1997 defeated Kasparov 3½ to 2½.

But it could evaluate 200 million positions per second. It had direct access to records of some 700,000 grand master games, with 4,000 opening games and a huge database of end games at its disposal. It routinely looked six to eight moves ahead and could peak on occasion to twenty moves ahead.

Kasparov suggested he detected moments when human intervention was applied and accused it of cheating, but the unit was dismantled and there was no rematch.

In November 2006 a PC with two Intel Core 2 Duo CPUs used the Deep Fritz software which was able to review 8 million positions and in the middle game, thanks to a heuristic approach, it could consider up to nine moves ahead.

But this is all about databases and processing likely outcomes quickly; this is not exhibiting artificial intelligence.

In 2005 the Stanley robot built at Stanford claimed the cash prize for achieving the DARPA Grand Challenge. This required a driverless vehicle to negotiate a 132 mile (212 km) course unseen and uncharted. It had to pass through tunnels, negotiate hundreds of turns and travel up a mountain track with a sheer drop to one side. Five vehicles completed the distance but Stanley was fastest in under seven hours and claimed the $2m prize.

In November 2007 an urban challenge was set within an air force base. Vehicles had to negotiate a 60 mile (96km) course, obeying all the urban driving rules and complete the task in under six hours. A further complication was that the contestants were required to recognise and avoid each other along the course. Carnegie-Mellon University's Tartan Racing took 4 hours and 10 minutes and also won $2m for its achievement.

Of course none of this was for the fun of it. DARPA's goal was for a third of the USA's military ground-forces to become autonomous driverless vehicles by 2015.

As the investment in AI continues to fall short of expectation one reassuring fact is that the popular science fiction notion of computers taking over mankind has yet to come about. But just as you thought it was safe...

In December 2010 China established a national artificial intelligence agency to pursue the development of thinking computers. It also separately awarded a $500k grant to Dr Hugo de Garis to develop the first artificial brain at Xiamen University in China.

De Garis, born in Australia, is a frim believer in John Good's technological singularity - the moment when machines will take over. de Garis suggests that 'artilects', derived from the words artificial intellects, will be more intelligent than us and will seek world domination, resulting in billions being killed.

'Humans should not stand in the way of a higher form of evolution. These machines are godlike. It is human destiny to create them.' de Garis in 1999.

To hasten this moment he has been working with programmable gate arrays that use three-dimensional cellular automata to create neural networks. He then applies genetic algorithms to these devices searching for a method to emulate the way our human brain operates.

'Twenty years from now, the author envisages the brain builder industry as being one of the world's top industries, comparable with oil, automobile, and construction.' de Garis writing in 1996.

Early claims that he would have built a billion-neuron artificial brain by 2001 are clearly embarrassing today, but perhaps with Chinese backing he can move the field forward?

He certainly does not lack ambition,

'In the coming few decades, the rise of artificial intelligence will be a veritable goldmine for humankind. I predict that by the year 2030, one of the world's biggest industries will be "artificial brains," used to control home robots that will be genuinely intelligent and useful. Millions, if not billions, of people will be prepared to spend more money on a household robot than on a car. It is my personal ambition in the next five to 10 years to persuade the federal government in China (where I'm directing the building of China's first artificial brain) to create a CABA (Chinese Artificial Brain Administration), similar in scope to America's NASA, consisting of thousands of scientists and engineers, to build artificial brains for the Chinese home robot industry and other applications.' Quoted on Forbes.com

Looking for a DETAILED INDEX?

Categorising the 600+ sub-headings, 1,200+ pioneers and their related 1,000+ organisations and the many more than 3,000 events referenced in this book would have run to perhaps 100 or more pages of indexes.

Instead we have ensured that the material is on a wiki site www.wikiPCpedia.com, where you are encouraged to make comments, add your own memories in text, audio or video. This does provide referencing for the 600+ sub-headings.

The featured 1,000+ individuals are shown in the index starting on the facing page and they are also listed in a handy reference source on the sister website www.thepcpioneers.com/quick-link-to-the-pioneers/ where you can readily research their companies, colleagues and contributions. Their 1,000+ organisations are contained in www.thePCstory.com. These are all cross-referenced.

The 3,000+ events are shown chronologically on www.thePCtimeline.com with useful links to the other parts of the material.

'The PC Pioneers' book will be updated routinely to reflect the progress and the comments of those who visit the sites – so do keep in touch with new issues and releases at www.thePCpioneers.com.

ENDS

www.ingramcontent.com/pod-product-compliance
Lightning Source LLC
Chambersburg PA
CBHW060102170426
43198CB00010B/734